Luxembourg Court Cultures
in the Long Fourteenth Century

LUXEMBOURG COURT CULTURES IN THE LONG FOURTEENTH CENTURY

PERFORMING EMPIRE, CELEBRATING KINGSHIP

Edited by Karl Kügle, Ingrid Ciulisová and Václav Žůrek

THE BOYDELL PRESS

© Contributors 2024

Some rights reserved. Without limiting the rights under copyright reserved above, any part of this book may be reproduced, stored in or introduced into a retrieval system, or transmitted, in any form or by any means (electronic, mechanical, photocopying, recording or otherwise)

First published 2024
The Boydell Press, Woodbridge

ISBN 978 1 83765 005 7

This title is available under the Creative Commons license CC BY-NC-ND

This publication has received funding from the European Research Council (ERC) under the European Union's Horizon 2020 research and innovation programme (grant agreement no. 669190). Additional support was provided by the Slovak Academy of Sciences under its Seal of Excellence programme (no. Soe/2017/72.C/MOCAHIC) and the Centre for Medieval Studies, Prague

The Boydell Press is an imprint of Boydell & Brewer Ltd
PO Box 9, Woodbridge, Suffolk IP12 3DF, UK
and of Boydell & Brewer Inc.
668 Mt Hope Avenue, Rochester, NY 14620-2731, USA
website: www.boydellandbrewer.com

A CIP catalogue record for this book is available
from the British Library

The publisher has no responsibility for the continued existence or accuracy of URLs for external or third-party internet websites referred to in this book, and does not guarantee that any content on such websites is, or will remain, accurate or appropriate

CONTENTS

List of Illustrations   vii
Preface and Acknowledgements   xiii
List of Contributors   xv

Introduction: The 'Long Luxembourg Century' (1308–1437): Courtly Networks, Cultural Politics, Dynastic Legacy   1
Karl Kügle, Ingrid Ciulisová, Václav Žůrek

PART I: John the Blind and his Progeny in France

1. The 'Luxembourgness' of Things: Machaut C, Glazier 52, and Dynastic Presence in Early Fourteenth-Century France   21
Uri Smilansky

2. Guillaume de Machaut at the Court of John of Luxembourg: Defining a Social Milieu   57
Jana Fantysová Matějková

3. The Vyšší Brod Cycle and its Anonymous Painter: French and Bohemian Court Circles in the 1340s   105
Lenka Panušková

PART II: Marvellous Objects and Culture at the Court of Charles IV

4. Charles of Luxembourg and his Reliquary Cross: The Significance of Precious Stones   137
Ingrid Ciulisová

5. Charles IV and the Patronage of Multilingual Literature at his Court and Beyond   174
Václav Žůrek

6   Miraculous Objects and Foundational Sins: Verbal and
    Material Reality in the *Dalimil Chronicle*, the Chronicle of
    Přibík Pulkava of Radenín, and Charles IV's Autobiography   203
    Matouš Jaluška

PART III: Wenceslas and Sigismund: Art, Politics, and Diplomacy

7   The Making of the Wenceslas Bible, with Special
    Consideration of the Theological Concept of its Genesis
    Initial   243
    Maria Theisen

8   The Naked King: Representing Wenceslas in his Illuminated
    Bible   282
    Gia Toussaint

9   Dealing with the Luxembourg Court: Ellwangen Abbey and
    their Imperial Overlord   321
    Mark Whelan

10 Assessing the Luxembourgs: The Image of Wenceslas and
    Sigismund in the Correspondence of Italian Ambassadors   343
    Ondřej Schmidt

PART IV: Studying the Luxembourgs: What has been Neglected

11 Heiresses, Regents, and Patrons: Female Rulers in the Age of
    the Luxembourgs   375
    Julia Burkhardt

12 Image-making, Image-breaking, and the Luxembourg
    Monarchy   404
    Len Scales

13 The Absent Present: Luxembourg Courts, their Sonic
    Cultures, and Music Histor(iograph)y   429
    Karl Kügle

Select Bibliography   466
Index   486

ILLUSTRATIONS

Maps

1. Luxembourg Domains in 1308	xviii
2. Luxembourg Domains in 1378	xix
3. Luxembourg Domains in 1435	xx

Genealogies

1. Henry VII: Ancestry and Progeny	xxi
2. John of Luxembourg, King of Bohemia, and his Progeny	xxii
3. Charles IV and his Progeny down the Male Line	xxiii
4. Counts of Artois and Burgundy (HRE). Dukes of Burgundy (F)	xxiv
5. Counts then Dukes of Bar	xxv
6. Dukes of Brabant	xxvi
7. Kings of France	xxvii

1. The 'Luxembourgness' of Things, *Uri Smilansky*

Fig. 1.1.   MS C, fol. 23r and G52, fol. 1r compared   26–7

2. Guillaume de Machaut at the Court of John of Luxembourg, *Jana Fantysová Matějková*

Table 2.1.   The policy of John the Blind towards Poland and Silesia. Comparison between Machaut's *CA* and the *ZC* by Peter of Zittau   66

3. The Vyšší Brod Cycle and its Anonymous Painter, *Lenka Panušková*

Fig. 3.1.	Vyšší Brod Cycle, National Gallery in Prague, inv. nos. O 6786–O 6794, c. 99 cm x 93 cm	106–10
Fig. 3.1a.	Annunciation	106
Fig. 3.1b.	Nativity	106
Fig. 3.1c.	Adoration of the Magi	107
Fig. 3.1d.	Christ on the Mount of Olives	107
Fig. 3.1e.	Crucifixion	108
Fig. 3.1f.	Lamentation	108
Fig. 3.1g.	Resurrection	109
Fig. 3.1h.	Ascension	109
Fig. 3.1i.	Descent of the Holy Spirit	110
Fig. 3.2.	Annunciation, Private Collection, c.1350, 91.8 cm x 79.5 cm	119
Fig. 3.3.	Madonna of Kłodzko, Berlin, Staatliche Museen, Gemäldegalerie, inv. no. 1624, 186 cm x 95 cm	122
Fig. 3.4.	Annunciation, Cleveland Museum of Art, Mr and Mrs William H. Marlatt Fund 1954.393, c. 1380, France or the Netherlands, 40.3 cm x 31 cm	123
Fig. 3.5.	Madonna of Strahov, Picture Gallery of the Premonstratensian Monastery in Strahov, inv. no. O 539, 94 cm x 84 cm	124
Fig. 3.6.	Diptych of Karlsruhe, Staatliche Kunsthalle, Karlsruhe, inv. no. 2431a-b, 20 cm x 14.5 cm	125
Fig. 3.7	Kaufmann Crucifixion, Berlin, Staatliche Museen, Gemäldegalerie, inv. no. 1833, 67 cm x 29.5 cm	128

4. Charles of Luxembourg and his Reliquary Cross, *Ingrid Ciulisová*

Fig. 4.1.	Ambo of Henry II, Treasury of Aachen Cathedral, c. 1024. Ivory, copper plate, gemstones, agate and rock crystal vessels, agate and chalcedony chess figures, oak parapet, height 146 cm. Photo © Archive of the author	139
Fig. 4.2.	Cross of Lothair, Treasury of Aachen Cathedral, c. 1000 (cross), fourteenth century (base). Oak core, gold, silver, gemstones, cameos, height 50 cm. Photo © Domkapitel, Aachen, Pit Siebigs, Aachen	140
Fig. 4.3.	Portrait of the Roman Emperor Augustus. Cameo at the centre of the Cross of Lothair, Treasury of Aachen	

ILLUSTRATIONS ix

	Cathedral, first century, sardonyx. Photo © Genevra Kornbluth	142
Fig. 4.4.	Coronation Cross, front side. Gold, pearls, gemstones, rock crystal, glass, relics, with a new base made of gilded copper added in the 1520s, 62.5 cm x 41.5 cm. Treasury of St Vitus Cathedral, Prague. Photo © Courtesy of Prague Castle Administration/Jan Gloc	144
Fig. 4.5.	Coronation Cross, back side. Gold, pearls, gemstones, rock crystal, glass, cameos, and relics. Base of gilded copper added in the 1520s; overall dimensions 62.5 cm x 41.5 cm. Treasury of St Vitus Cathedral, Prague. Photo © Courtesy of Prague Castle Administration/Jan Gloc	145
Fig. 4.6.	Reliquary called the Libretto, front side. Gold, enamel, pearls, rubies, parchment, c. 1370. Museo dell'Opera del Duomo, Florence. Photo © Age Fotostock/Nicolò Orsi Battaglini	151
Fig. 4.7.	Portrait of Julia, daughter of Emperor Titus, Italy, Rome, before 90 CE. Mount: France, ninth century. Aquamarine (intaglio); gold, sapphire, pearls (mount); 10.5 cm x 9.5 cm. Paris, Bibliothèque nationale de France, Département des Monnaies, Médailles et Antiques. Photo © BnF, Paris	158
Fig. 4.8.	Imperial portrait cameo of Antonia Minor, first century CE, sardonyx, height 3.7 cm. Incorporated into Coronation Cross, Treasury of St Vitus Cathedral, Prague. Photo © Courtesy of Prague Castle Administration/Jan Gloc	161
Fig. 4.9.	Christ blessing, thirteenth century, amethyst, height 3.2 cm. Incorporated into Coronation Cross, Treasury of St Vitus Cathedral, Prague. Photo © Courtesy of Prague Castle Administration/Jan Gloc	162
Fig. 4.10.	Frederick II of Hohenstaufen, Holy Roman Emperor, after 1220, sardonyx, height 3.8 cm. Incorporated into Coronation Cross, Treasury of St Vitus Cathedral, Prague. Photo © Courtesy of Prague Castle Administration/Jan Gloc	163
Fig. 4.11.	Charles raising his Reliquary Cross with his third wife, Anne of Schweidnitz (?), before 1360. Fresco, gold, gemstones. Chapel of St Catherine, Karlštejn Castle. Photo © The National Heritage Institute, Prague	167

Fig. 4.12. Reliquary bust of Charlemagne, second half of the fourteenth century, oak wood, silver, gilded silver, gemstones, cameos, and intaglios, Treasury of Aachen Cathedral. Photo © Bildarchiv Foto Marburg   169

6. Miraculous Objects and Foundational Sins, *Matouš Jaluška*

Fig. 6.1. Prague, Národní knihovna České republiky, ms. XIX B 5, fol. 164r. Beginning of the *Vita Caroli*.   210

Fig. 6.2. Vienna, Österreichische Nationalbibliothek, Cod. Series nova 44, fol. 1r. Beginning of the *Dalimil Chronicle*.   221

Fig. 6.3. Prague, Národní knihovna České republiky, ms. XIX B 5, fol. 116r. Beginning of the *Chronicon Bohemiae* by Přibík Pulkava of Radenín.   228

7. The Making of the Wenceslas Bible, with Special Consideration of the Theological Concept of its Genesis Initial, *Maria Theisen*

Fig. 7.1. Vienna, ÖNB, Cod. 2759, fol. 93r – Wenceslas watching the collection of donations for the Tent of Revelation   252

Fig. 7.2. Vienna, ÖNB, Cod. 2760, fol. 180r – faded seven-line painters' instruction in the right-hand margin   253

Fig. 7.3. Vienna, ÖNB, Cod. 2761, fol. 137r – non-executed miniature and painters' instruction in the lower margin   255

Fig. 7.4. Vienna, ÖNB, Cod. 2763, fol. 175r – Madonna and Child enthroned, surrounded by seven virgins   259

Fig. 7.5. Vienna, ÖNB, Cod. 2759, fol. 2v – Genesis initial depicting God's work of creation within an architecturally designed frame   260

8. The Naked King, *Gia Toussaint*

Fig. 8.1. King and Queen enthroned in royal majesty, Vienna, ÖNB, Cod. 2759, fol. 2r   288

Fig. 8.2a. The beginning of the Book of Genesis, Vienna, ÖNB, Cod. 2759, initial I, fol. 2v   290

Fig. 8.2b. The beginning of the Book of Genesis, Vienna, ÖNB, Cod. 2759, initial I, fol. 2v, detail   291

Fig. 8.3. Creation of Eve, Vienna, ÖNB, Cod. 2759, fol. 4r, detail   293

Fig. 8.4. Expulsion from Paradise, Vienna, ÖNB, Cod. 2759, fol. 5r   295

ILLUSTRATIONS   xi

Fig. 8.5a.   Tower of Babel, Vienna, ÖNB, Cod. 2759, fol. 10v   296
Fig. 8.5b.   Tower of Babel, Vienna, ÖNB, Cod. 2759, fol. 10v, detail   297
Fig. 8.6.   Beginning of the Book of Deuteronomy, Vienna,
             ÖNB, Cod. 2759, fol. 174v, D initial, detail   299
Fig. 8.7a.   Beginning of the Book of Joshua, Vienna, ÖNB, Cod.
             2759, fol. 214r   300
Fig. 8.7b.   Beginning of the Book of Joshua, Vienna, ÖNB, Cod.
             2759, fol. 214r, detail: Wenceslas with a bath maid   301
Fig. 8.8a.   Golden Bull, Prologue, Vienna, ÖNB, Cod. 338, fol. 1r   304
Fig. 8.8b.   Golden Bull, Prologue, Vienna, ÖNB, Cod. 338, fol.
             1r, detail: King Wenceslas and bath maidens   305
Fig. 8.9.   Codex Manesse, Jakob of Warte, Heidelberg
             University Library, Cod. Pal. germ. 848, fol. 46v   308
Fig. 8.10.   Lovers in the bath, British Library, London, Royal MS
             17 F. IV, fol. 297r   308
Fig. 8.11.   Circumcision of Abraham, Vienna, ÖNB, Cod. 2759,
             fol. 14v   310
Fig. 8.12.   Lot and his daughters, Vienna, ÖNB, Cod. 2759, fol. 17v   311
Fig. 8.13.   Rebekah at the well, Vienna, ÖNB, Cod. 2759, fol. 21r,
             detail: Wenceslas and a bath maiden   313
Fig. 8.14.   Jacob, Rachel, and Leah; at bas-de-page: Wenceslas
             and bath maiden, Vienna, ÖNB, Cod. 2759, fol. 29r   314
Fig. 8.15.   Birth of Esau and Jacob; at bas-de-page: Wild Men as
             heraldic supporters, Vienna, ÖNB, Cod. 2759, fol. 24r   316
Fig. 8.16.   Beginning of the Book of Paralipomenon, Vienna, ÖNB,
             Cod. 2761, fol. 2v, detail: Wenceslas as a Wild Man   318

The editors, contributors and publisher are grateful to all the institutions and persons listed for permission to reproduce the materials in which they hold copyright. Every effort has been made to trace the copyright holders; apologies are offered for any omission, and the publisher will be pleased to add any necessary acknowledgement in subsequent editions.

PREFACE AND ACKNOWLEDGEMENTS

The idea for this book grew out of a workshop on Luxembourg court culture which was to take place at the Centre for Medieval Studies in Prague in spring 2020. Developed collaboratively with Ingrid Ciulisová (Slovak Academy of Sciences, at the time a Marie Curie-Skłodowska Fellow at Corpus Christi College, Oxford) and Václav Žůrek, the Prague Centre's scientific secretary, and actively supported by Pavel Soukup, the Centre's director, it was intended to be part of a series of events organized between 2016 and 2022 by the research team of the ERC Advanced Grant-funded project Music and Late Medieval European Court Cultures (malmecc.music.ox.ac.uk) under the direction of Karl Kügle at the University of Oxford. Like many other scholarly endeavours at the time, the Prague workshop had to be cancelled at short notice due to the emergency measures imposed by governments worldwide on account of the Covid-19 virus. Sensing that an extraordinary opportunity for scholarship was about to be missed, the three organizers Ciulisová, Kügle, and Žůrek spontaneously decided to transform what might have been a relatively low-key, exploratory workshop into something much more visible and permanent – a high-profile essay collection. We were driven by the idea that Luxembourg studies needed – and deserved – a boost in the English-speaking world; we hope to accomplish this by providing an essay collection written by an international group of specialists who offer a link between arts-related and historical perspectives, with the objective of re-assessing the cultural impact of the Luxembourgs on late medieval Europe. Much to our delight and satisfaction, we found our project readily supported by medievalist colleagues across Europe when we approached them to contribute to such a book project. The result is in front of you.

As ever with a project of this scale, many debts of gratitude are accumulated as work progresses. To begin with, thanks are due the

European Research Council (ERC); its grant no. 669190 made possible not only the planning of the Prague workshop and its subsequent redevelopment into an essay collection, but also its publication in open access. The Slovak Academy of Sciences contributed a publication subsidy under its Seal of Excellence programme (no. SoE/2017/72.C/MOCAHIC) which is herewith gratefully acknowledged. Although we could not avail ourselves of it in the end due to the Covid-19 emergency measures, the hospitality extended by the Prague Centre for Medieval Studies during the early stages of the project, and the Centre's sustained commitment to the volume in the aftermath of the workshop's cancellation, must be mentioned with gratitude. Special thanks go to Frieda van der Heijden for editorial assistance during the preparation of the texts; to Uri Smilansky for preparing the genealogies at the front of this book; to Jaroslav Synek for preparing the maps included in this volume; and to Michal Hokeš for help with the preparation of the index. For excellent support throughout the production process, our thanks go to Caroline Palmer and her team at Boydell & Brewer. Additional subsidies from a range of national funding agencies contributed to the genesis of many of the texts united in this book; they are acknowledged by the individuals concerned in their respective essays.

For their scholarly contributions, we cordially thank all authors present in this book. It was truly a pleasure collaborating with them.

Oxford, Bratislava, and Prague, October 2023

Karl Kügle
Ingrid Ciulisová
Václav Žůrek

CONTRIBUTORS

Julia Burkhardt holds the Chair in Medieval History at Ludwig-Maximilians-Universität (LMU) Munich. Her research interests cover political, cultural, and gender history in Central Europe, with a focus on dynastic history, history of representative assemblies, history of monastic communities, and monastic text production in Germany, Poland, Bohemia, and Hungary.

Ingrid Ciulisová is a Senior Research Fellow in Art History at the Art Research Centre of the Slovak Academy of Sciences in Bratislava and holds the title of *docent* at Charles University in Prague. Her research interests encompass late medieval and early modern art in Europe, the history of art collecting, and the historiography of art history. She was Marie Skłodowska-Curie Fellow in the Department of History of Art at the University of Oxford and a Research Associate at Corpus Christi College, Oxford (2019–20).

Jana Fantysová Matějková is a historian specializing in the political and cultural history of the Luxembourg period. She is a senior researcher at the Department of Medieval History of the Institute of History of the Czech Academy of Sciences in Prague. In her work, a focus on narrative and literary sources complements the traditional historical approach, thereby shedding new light on the social and historical context of literary works.

Matouš Jaluška received his PhD in comparative literature (2017) from the Institute of Czech Literature of the Czech Academy of Sciences in Prague, where he currently holds a research position. He also teaches in the Faculty of Arts at Charles University, Prague. His recent publications focus on religious motives in apparently secular texts, and the topic of human and non-human speech, with a focus on medieval Bohemia.

Karl Kügle is Director of Research in the Faculty of Music, University of Oxford, and a Senior Research Fellow of Wadham College. From 2016 to 2022, he was Principal Investigator of the ERC Advanced Grant-funded MALMECC project (malmecc.music.ox.ac.uk). His research interests focus on the history of European music cultures of the late medieval and early modern period (c. 1200–1600).

Lenka Panušková is a researcher at the Institute of Art History of the Czech Academy of Sciences in Prague. She works with medieval illuminated manuscripts with a focus on the function of the decoration, its iconography, and its reception by readers. Currently, she is preparing an essay collection with the title *Reflecting Jerusalem in Medieval Czech Lands*.

Len Scales is Professor of Late Medieval History at Durham University. He has published widely on medieval German history, the history of the Holy Roman Empire, and on medieval ideas about ethnicity and group identities. He has a particular interest in the political and cultural history of the Luxembourg era.

Ondřej Schmidt received his PhD (2020) in historical sciences at Masaryk University in Brno, where he currently holds a post as a research fellow in the Department of Auxiliary Historical Sciences and Archive Studies. His work focuses on relations between the Holy Roman Kings and Emperors and northern Italy at the turn of the fourteenth and fifteenth centuries.

Uri Smilansky specializes in the history, analysis, notation, reception, and performance of late medieval Francophone music, most notably Guillaume de Machaut and the so-called Ars Subtilior. Having studied at the University of Exeter under the supervision of Yolanda Plumley and Giuliano Di Bacco, he went on to hold postdoctoral positions at the Universities of Exeter and Oxford, and teaching positions at King's College London and Shakespeare's Globe. He is now Professor of Historical Notation at the Schola Cantorum Basiliensis.

Maria Theisen holds a doctorate in art history with a focus on book illumination and codicology of the Middle Ages and the early modern period in the countries of the Bohemian Crown. She has been working at the Austrian Academy of Sciences (Department of Palaeography and Codicology) since 2006 and teaches at universities in Austria and the Czech Republic.

Gia Toussaint studied art history, classical archaeology, and religion at the University of Hamburg, where she received an award-winning PhD in 2002. In 2009 she completed a Habilitation in art history at the University of Hamburg. From 2019 to 2022 she held a research appointment at the Herzog August Bibliothek in Wolfenbüttel.

Mark Whelan completed his doctoral thesis in 2014 on Emperor Sigismund of Luxembourg's efforts to combat the Ottoman Turkish threat. He has published widely on late medieval history in general, including studies on bees and beekeeping, the mead and wax trade, and ecclesiastical councils. He has held postdoctoral fellowships from the Stiftung Preussischer Kulturbesitz, the German Academic Exchange Service, and the Monumenta Germaniae Historica. He currently works at Queen Mary University of London.

Václav Žůrek completed his PhD in 2014 in co-tutelle at Charles University (Prague) and EHESS (Paris) on the instrumentalization of the past by the Luxembourg and Valois dynasties. He is a research fellow at the Centre for Medieval Studies Prague, which is part of the Institute of Philosophy of the Czech Academy of Sciences. His research interests encompass late medieval political and cultural history of Central Europe.

Map 1. Luxembourg Domains in 1308.

Map 2. Luxembourg Domains in 1378.

Map 3. Luxembourg Domains in 1435.

Henry VII: Ancestry and Progeny

HRE = Holy Roman Emperor

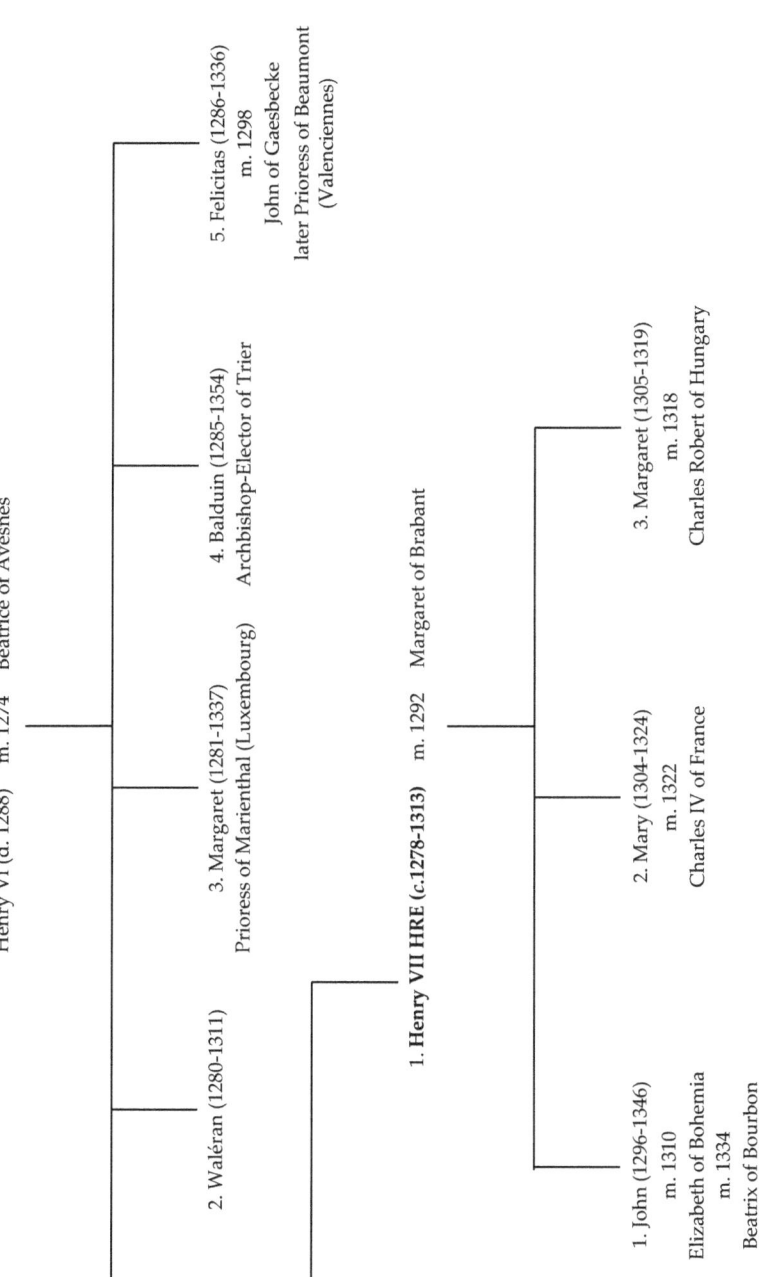

* Square brackets [ ] indicate dubious cases in which marriage is not clear

John of Luxembourg, King of Bohemia, and his Progeny

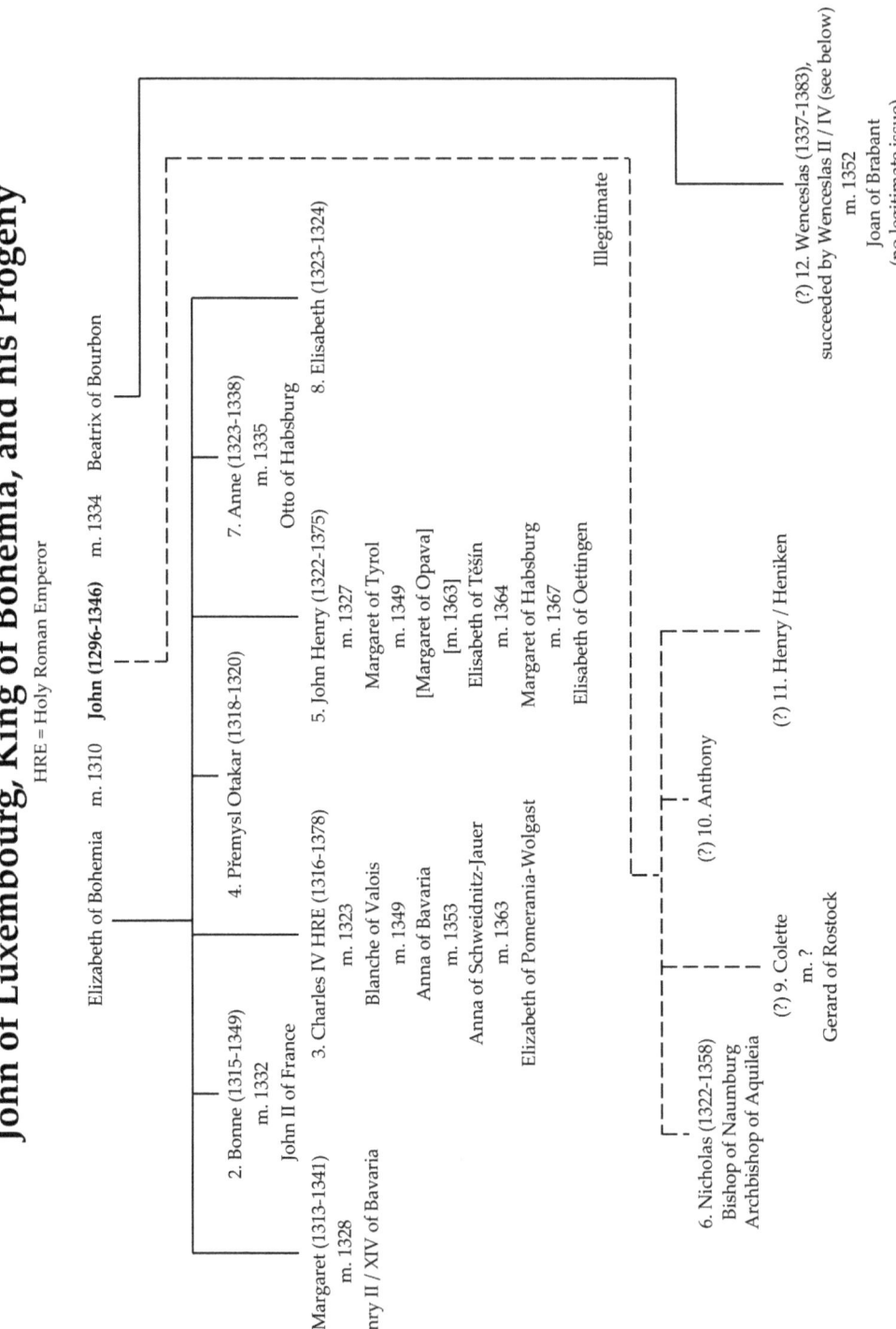

Charles IV and his Progeny down the Male Line

HRE = Holy Roman Emperor

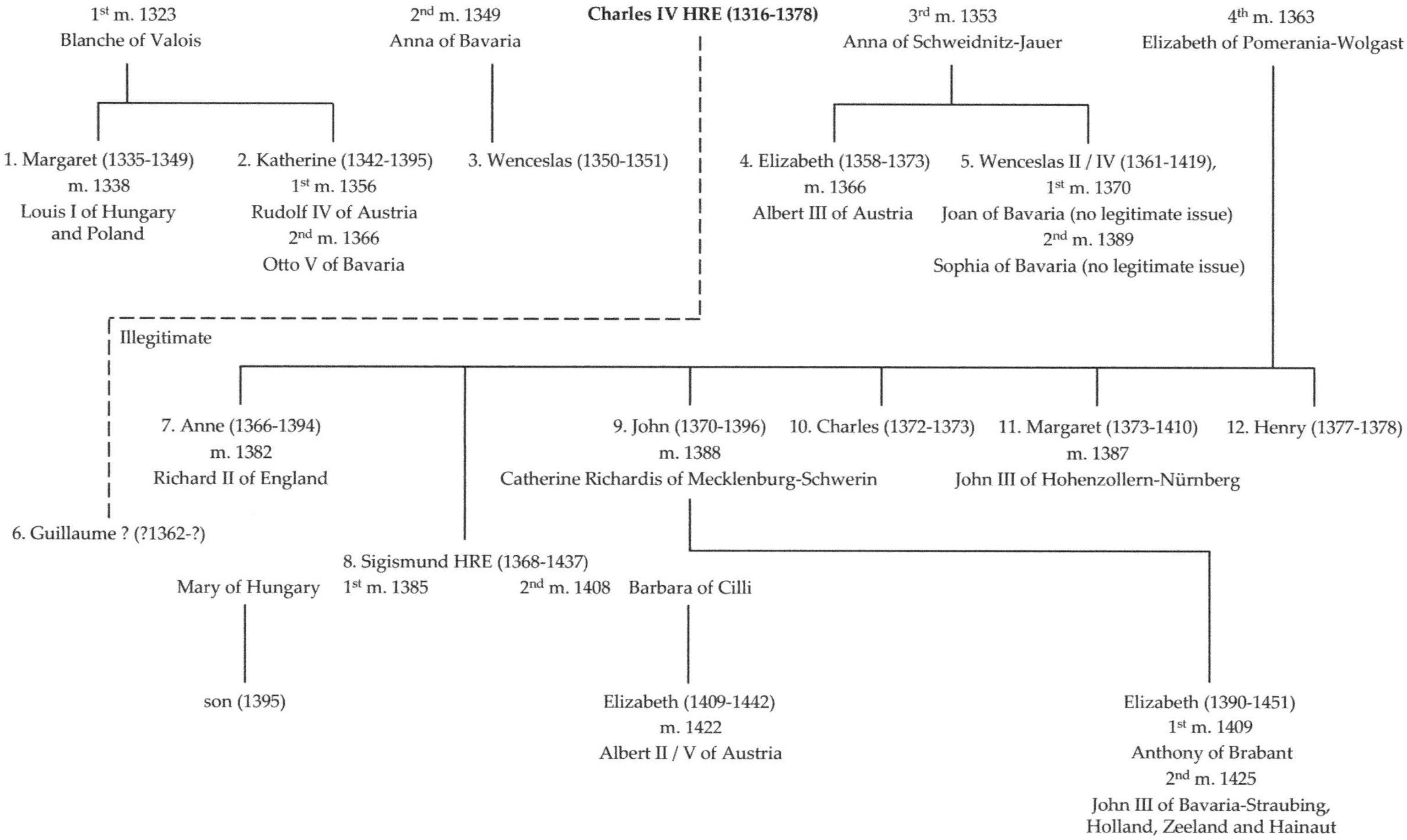

Charles IV HRE (1316-1378)

- 1st m. 1323 — Blanche of Valois
- 2nd m. 1349 — Anna of Bavaria
- 3rd m. 1353 — Anna of Schweidnitz-Jauer
- 4th m. 1363 — Elizabeth of Pomerania-Wolgast

Children of Charles IV

By Blanche of Valois
1. Margaret (1335-1349), m. 1338 Louis I of Hungary and Poland
2. Katherine (1342-1395), 1st m. 1356 Rudolf IV of Austria, 2nd m. 1366 Otto V of Bavaria

By Anna of Bavaria
3. Wenceslas (1350-1351)

By Anna of Schweidnitz-Jauer
4. Elizabeth (1358-1373), m. 1366 Albert III of Austria
5. Wenceslas II / IV (1361-1419), 1st m. 1370 Joan of Bavaria (no legitimate issue), 2nd m. 1389 Sophia of Bavaria (no legitimate issue)

Illegitimate
6. Guillaume ? (?1362-?)

By Elizabeth of Pomerania-Wolgast
7. Anne (1366-1394), m. 1382 Richard II of England
8. Sigismund HRE (1368-1437), 1st m. 1385 Mary of Hungary, 2nd m. 1408 Barbara of Cilli
9. John (1370-1396), m. 1388 Catherine Richardis of Mecklenburg-Schwerin
10. Charles (1372-1373)
11. Margaret (1373-1410), m. 1387 John III of Hohenzollern-Nürnberg
12. Henry (1377-1378)

Further descendants

From Sigismund & Mary of Hungary: son (1395)

From Sigismund & Barbara of Cilli:
- Elizabeth (1409-1442), m. 1422 Albert II / V of Austria

From John & Catherine Richardis:
- Elizabeth (1390-1451), 1st m. 1409 Anthony of Brabant, 2nd m. 1425 John III of Bavaria-Straubing, Holland, Zeeland and Hainaut

Counts of Artois and Burgundy (HRE)   Dukes of Burgundy (F)

During the late medieval period, the County of Burgundy was a fief of the Holy Roman Empire (HRE), while the adjacent Duchy of Burgundy was a fief of the Kingdom of France (F).

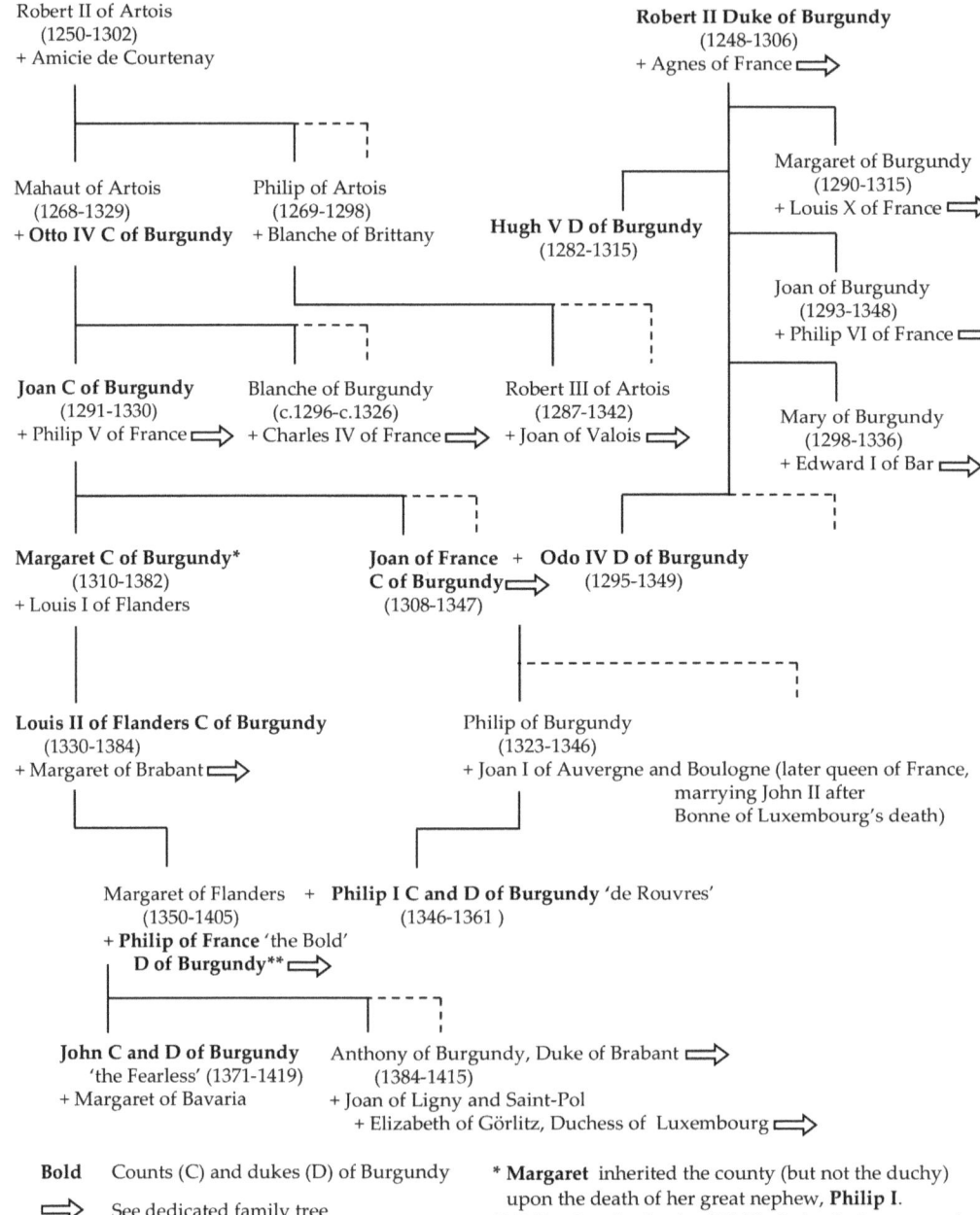

Bold Counts (C) and dukes (D) of Burgundy
⇒ See dedicated family tree
- - - Other children

* **Margaret** inherited the county (but not the duchy) upon the death of her great nephew, **Philip I**.
** Following the death of **Philip I**, the duchy reverted to the French crown, then re-established for **Philip II**.

Counts then Dukes of Bar

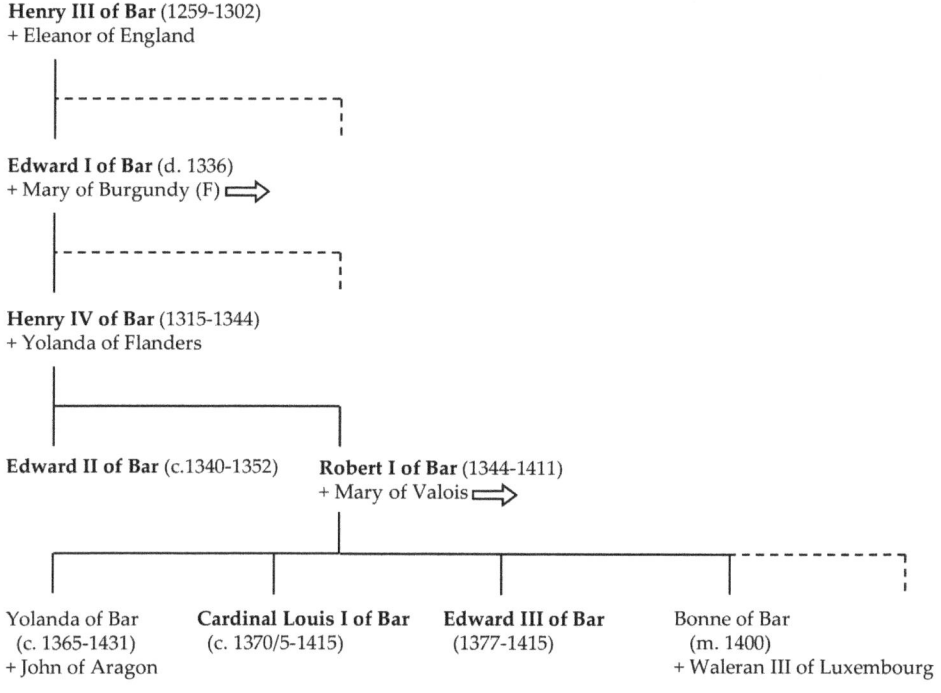

Bold — Counts, later dukes of Bar
⟹ — See dedicated family tree
--- — Other children

During the late medieval period, the County of Burgundy was a fief of the Holy Roman Empire, while the adjacent Duchy of Burgundy was a fief of the Kingdom of France. The tags (HRE) and (F) mark the affiliation of individuals with the sobriquet 'of Burgundy'.

Dukes of Brabant

Henry III of Brabant (1230-61)
+ Adelaide of Burgundy (F)

John I of Brabant (1252/3-1294)
+ Margaret of France ⇒
+ Margaret of Flanders

Mary of Brabant (1254/6-1321/2)
+ Philip III of France ⇒

John II of Brabant (1275-1312)
+ Margaret of England

Margaret of Brabant (1276-1311)
+ Henry VII of Luxembourg ⇒

John III of Brabant (1300-1355)
+ Mary of Évreux

Joan of Brabant (1322-1406) +
William II of Hainaut
+ Wenceslas of Luxembourg ⇒

Margaret of Brabant (1323-1380)
+ Louis II of Flanders ⇒

John of Brabant (1327-1335/6)
+ Mary of France ⇒

Margaret of Flanders (1323-1380)
+ Philip I of Burgundy (F & HRE) 'de Rouvres' ⇒
+ Philip of France 'the Bold' ⇒

Anthony of Burgundy, Duke of Brabant (1384-1415)
+ Joan of Ligny and Saint-Pol
+ Elizabeth of Görlitz, Duchess of Luxembourg ⇒

Bold   Dukes of Brabant
⇒   See dedicated family tree
- - -   Other children

During the late medieval period, the County of Burgundy was a fief of the Holy Roman Empire, while the adjacent Duchy of Burgundy was a fief of the Kingdom of France. The tags (HRE) and (F) mark the affiliation of individuals with the sobriquet 'of Burgundy'.

Kings of France

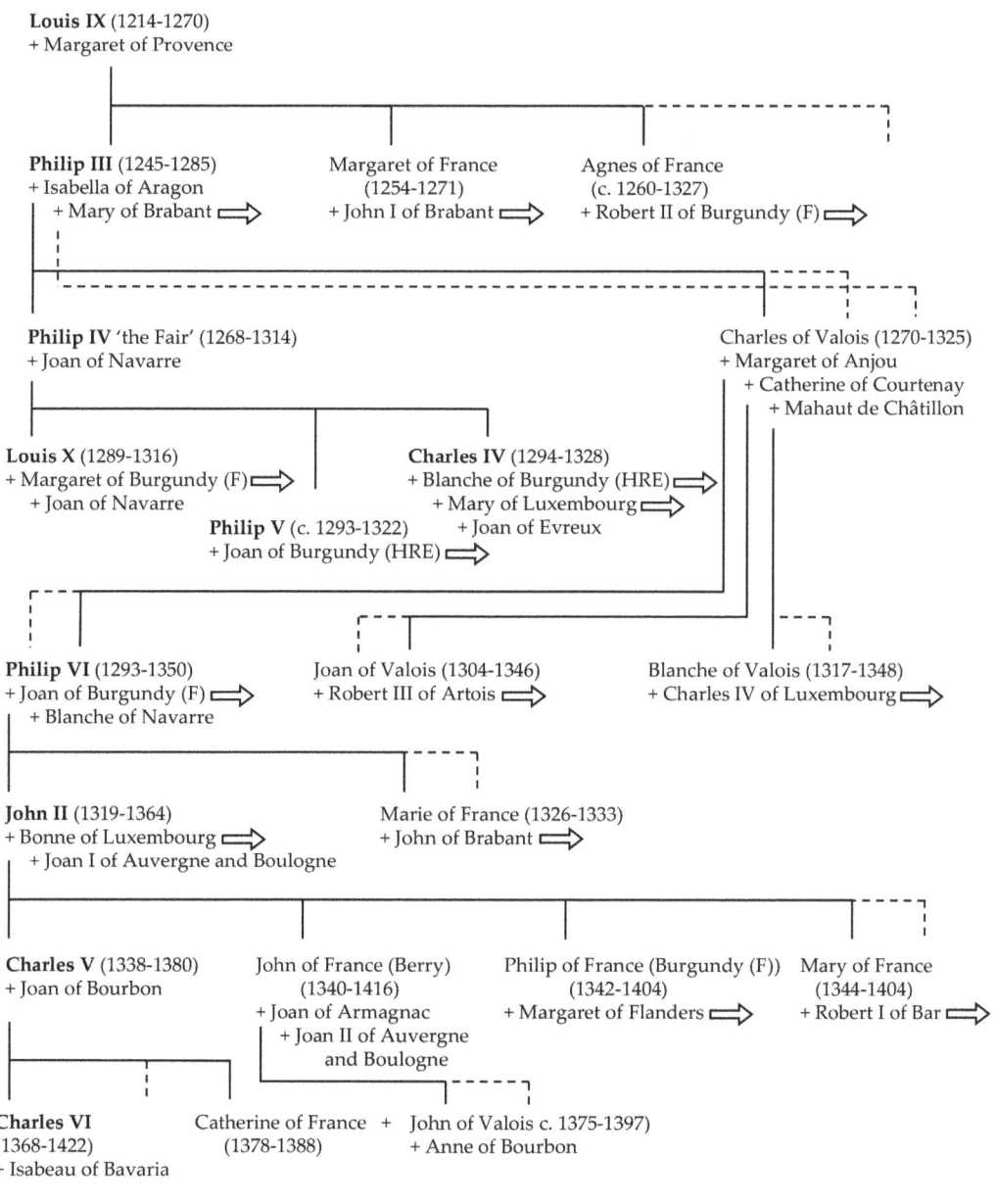

Bold — Kings of France
⟹ — See dedicated family tree
--- — Other children

During the late medieval period, the County of Burgundy was a fief of the Holy Roman Empire, while the adjacent Duchy of Burgundy was a fief of the Kingdom of France. The tags (HRE) and (F) mark the affiliation of individuals with the sobriquet 'of Burgundy'.

INTRODUCTION: THE 'LONG LUXEMBOURG CENTURY' (1308–1437): COURTLY NETWORKS, CULTURAL POLITICS, DYNASTIC LEGACY

KARL KÜGLE, INGRID CIULISOVÁ, VÁCLAV ŽŮREK

In the collective memory of most of today's Europeans, awareness of the house of Luxembourg is sketchy at best. This is astonishing as the Luxembourg dynasty arguably left an imprint on a larger geographical area of Europe than any other dynasty of the fourteenth and early fifteenth centuries. During the 'long Luxembourg century' (1308–1437), members of the dynasty held or aspired to the highest secular and ecclesiastic dignities of Latin Christendom. Three of them, Henry VII (1273–1313), Charles IV (1316–78), and Sigismund (1368–1437), were crowned Holy Roman Emperors (in 1312, 1355, and 1433, respectively); five (Henry VII, Charles IV, Wenceslas, Sigismund, and Jobst of Moravia) were elected King of the Romans (in 1308, 1346, 1376, and 1410 for both Sigismund and Jobst). Four Luxembourgs in succession (John of Bohemia from 1310 to 1346; Emperor Charles IV from 1346 to 1378; King Wenceslas from 1378 to 1419; and Emperor Sigismund from 1419 to 1437) held the title of King of Bohemia, inseparably intertwining the house of Luxembourg with the splendid heritage that to this day contributes to making Prague one of the most spectacular sites of late medieval art and architecture in Europe. Members of the house of Luxembourg, including John of Bohemia and Sigismund, also held, or at least entertained serious claims to, the crowns of Poland and Hungary. Luxembourg daughters and granddaughters were wives, mothers and grandmothers to four Kings of France (Charles IV, John II, Charles V, and Charles VI) as well as to the four successive Valois Dukes of Burgundy.¹ Seven Luxembourg women were queens of other realms: France (Marie of Luxembourg, 1323–4), Navarre (Marie of Luxembourg, 1323–4; Joan of France, 1343–73, regent 1369–72), England (Anne of Bohemia, 1366–94, r. 1382–94), Hungary (Beatrice, 1305–19, r. 1318–19; Margaret, 1335–49, r. 1342–9; and Elizabeth, 1409–42, r. 1438–42), and Poland (Elizabeth, 1436–1505, r. 1454–92). Balduin of Luxembourg (c. 1285–1354), archbishop and prince-elector of Trier from 1307 to 1354, ranks among the great ecclesiastical princes of the late-medieval Holy Roman Empire. All this puts the Luxembourg dynasty at the forefront of European cultural and political theatre during the fourteenth and early fifteenth centuries, not least when placed in the context of the undeniably impressive achievements of their main competitors on the continental stage, the Habsburgs and Wittelsbachs within the Holy Roman Empire, and the Valois, Plantagenet, and Anjou dynasties beyond the Empire's confines.

From the ancestral Luxembourg homelands on the western fringe of the Holy Roman Empire, the Luxembourg territories from the early 1310s onwards expanded eastwards, in due course forming a new centre of gravity in the heart of Europe. The keystone to this expansion was the acquisition of the crown of Bohemia (1310) by way of the marriage of Emperor Henry VII's only son, John of Luxembourg, and the Přemyslid heiress, Elizabeth of Bohemia. After the crown of Bohemia, the Luxembourgs acquired Silesia and the margravate of Brandenburg. Accordingly, the Luxembourg imprint on Central Europe remains strong to this day; it is probably strongest in the former Kingdom of Bohemia, which geographically, culturally, and historically is closely connected with the present-day Czech Republic and is where the Luxembourg period has acquired foundational character. But it is also clearly perceptible in present-day Germany, for example in the architecture and history of the imperial city of Nuremberg.² Further to the west, in their ancestral homeland, the Luxembourg name lives on in the

---

1   Marie of Luxembourg (c. 1305–24) was the second wife of King Charles IV of France (1294–1328, r. 1322–8); their marriage lasted from 1322 to 1324. Bonne of Luxembourg (1315–49) was the first wife of King John II of France (1319–64, r. 1350–64). She died before she could become Queen of France, but she was the mother of King Charles V (1338–80, r. 1364–80) and the grandmother of Charles VI of France (1368–1422, r. 1380–1422). Her three younger sons were Louis I, Duke of Anjou (1339–84); John, Duke of Berry (1340–1416); and Philip (the Bold, 1342–1404), Duke of Burgundy; through Philip's children, grandchildren, and great-grandchildren she became the ancestor of the three following Dukes of Burgundy. The two children of Marie of Luxembourg and Charles IV died in infancy.
2   See, for example, the discussion by Filip Srovnal, 'Der Trumphbogen für den kommenden Herrscher: Zur Ikonographie, Symbolik und Bedeutung der Skulpturenausstattung der Nürnberger Frauenkirche', *Umění* 67 (2019), 378–95.

independent nation state, the Grand Duchy of Luxembourg. It also lives on in the south-eastern Belgian province of the same name. Together, they cover a significant part of the late-medieval Luxembourg territories in the west, with the former County of Luxembourg – nowadays extending into parts of Belgium, France, and Germany as well as all of Luxembourg – at their core. Looking further westwards, the Luxembourgs also gave their name – through a cadet line – to the Palais and Jardin du Luxembourg in Paris, reflecting the traditionally bifocal nature of Luxembourg culture and politics. Owing to the geographical position of their homelands, the dynasty traditionally held significant stakes both in the Holy Roman Empire and in France and contributed to both the Francophone and Germanophone cultures of Europe. But, as the contributions to this book highlight, the bifocal – indeed, multifocal – nature of Luxembourg culture was also successfully transferred to Bohemia, where the Luxembourgs contributed significantly to Czech, German, and Latin literary cultures in the later decades of the fourteenth and the early fifteenth centuries. In fact, the pattern of multilingual courtly life that they were used to cultivating may even have been instrumental in the return (and ensuing revival) of English as a poetic medium to the English royal court during the late fourteenth century, a phenomenon associated with the poetic œuvre of Geoffrey Chaucer (c. 1340s–1400). On a more local level, the reign of Duke Wenceslas of Luxembourg (1337–83, r. 1354–83) in the Duchy of Brabant during the late fourteenth century may be eclipsed today by the Luxembourgs' Burgundian and Habsburg successors in the general public's perception of cultural history in the region; but the importance of Wenceslas' court as a node linking western and central Europe culturally and politically in the late Middle Ages becomes ever clearer the more closely it is reassessed.[3]

In short, during their late-medieval heyday, the Luxembourgs not only vied for supremacy with the Wittelsbachs, Habsburgs, and Valois in Europe, but were responsible for some long-lasting and highly impressive cultural and political achievements: in addition to what was already mentioned, their association with Francophone poet-musician Guillaume de Machaut (c. 1305–77), with historiographer and poet Jean Froissart (c. 1337–c. 1405) as well as with the South Tyrolean nobleman and Minnesinger Oswald von Wolkenstein (c. 1376–1445), and the papal singer and composer Johannes Brassart (c. 1400–55), must not be omitted here. Politically speaking, their

---

3   See, for example, Jana Fantysova [Fantysová-Matějková], *Wenceslas de Bohême: un prince au carrefour de l'Europe* (Paris, 2013); Remco Sleiderink, *De stem van de meester: de hertogen van Brabant en hun rol in het literaire leven (1106–1430)* (Amsterdam, 2003). On the role of the Luxembourgs for the development of English, see Alfred Thomas, *Reading women in late medieval Europe: Anne of Bohemia and Chaucer's female audience* (New York, 2015).

revival of the imperial office after the sustained power vacuum left by the last Hohenstaufen, Frederick II (1194–1250), gave the imperial court at Prague a power and cultural glamour it never surpassed in later times. The Luxembourgs managed to stabilize the Empire through the promulgation of the Golden Bull (1356). Through a culture of efficient administrators, typically drawn from the ranks of the Church, they became involved with some of the leading lights of the cultural and intellectual life of their times (Petrarch, the Germanophone poet Heinrich von Mügeln, or the (arch)bishops Arnošt of Pardubice and John of Neumarkt come to mind). They played a significant role in the resolution of the Great Schism at the Council of Constance in 1417. Last, but not least, through their dynastic policies, they connected Hungary to the Habsburgs through the marriage of Sigismund's daughter Elizabeth with Duke Albert of Austria (1397–1439, King of Hungary 1437–9, King of the Romans 1438–9), thereby laying the foundation for the later succession of Habsburg Kings (of Hungary) and (Holy Roman) Emperors and, eventually, the Austro-Hungarian Empire – a cultural force the importance of which no European today will deny. It is no exaggeration, then, to claim that the Luxembourgs are a dynasty of truly European rank – their influence, albeit on different levels and in varying degrees of intensity, can still be felt in present-day England, Belgium, France, Luxembourg, Germany, the Czech Republic, Poland, Hungary, Romania, Austria, and Italy. Why, then, are they not more present in our collective consciousness? The contributors to this volume give their own, individual answers to this question, looking at it through the lenses of the various topics they chose for their essays. Encompassing a range of disciplines, including history, art history, literary history, and historical musicology, the texts assembled in this book complement each other chronologically, thematically, and methodologically. They frequently cross disciplinary boundaries, and jointly create a mosaic of studies that combine close readings with larger-scale overviews. Together, they invite readers to connect the essays they select for reading into a network of potential replies of their own, contingent with their personal research interests and intellectual curiosities. It is the authors' and the editors' fervent hope that this collection as a whole will contribute decisively to raising the Luxembourg profile in today's global public discourse, especially within the English-speaking world where, for reasons to be discussed shortly, Luxembourg studies still occupy an undeservedly marginal position.

TAKING STOCK

Luxembourg possessions and political interests straddled the Holy Roman Empire from west to east and from north to south. They therefore, by necessity, affected the Empire's neighbours in all directions, from the kingdoms of France and England to the west to those of Hungary and Poland further to the east, not to mention the papacy and its motley allies and foes on the Italian peninsula in the south. Indeed, the late-medieval history of the papacy as an institution complements the history of the Holy Roman Emperors in a way similar to a system of communicating vessels: having settled in Avignon at the very beginning of the Luxembourg period (1309), the papacy – next to the models of the late Capetians in France and the great Holy Roman and Roman Emperors of the past – provided a vital point of reference for the quasi-sacerdotal rulership style developed by Emperor Charles IV during the third quarter of the fourteenth century. In this political project – *sui generis* in his time – he was both inspired and advised by his erstwhile mentor, Pierre Roger (Pope Clement VI, r. 1342–52). When later in the course of the 'long Luxembourg century' the Church and the papacy underwent what was probably their greatest crisis ever in the form of the Great Schism (1378–1417), the Luxembourgs, from about 1400 onwards, became key players in the resolution of this conflict, smoothing the way for the papacy's final return to Rome (1417) by means of the interventions of Sigismund of Luxembourg. The Church held two large councils, significantly, on imperial territory (Constance 1414–17 and Basel 1433–49) during the Luxembourg period, again reflecting the political weight and influence of Luxembourg rulers, in this case Sigismund of Luxembourg.

But Church history is supranational history – so, with Bohemia as the linchpin (from the 1310s) and from the late 1340s to the 1400s effectively the centre of gravity of Luxembourg power in the geographical middle of Europe, did the Luxembourgs also play a major part in the late-medieval history of modern European nation states? The answer is yes – certainly, and emphatically so for the Czech Republic and Luxembourg, and to a considerable degree for present-day Germany and Austria. But Luxembourg influence can be felt in varying degrees across a much larger group of modern nation states.[4] This begs the question: Could the transnational nature of the Luxembourg Empire be part of the answer to the relatively low profile of the Luxembourgs today?

Like Europe itself, the Luxembourg domains were not only intensely 'multinational', but also intensely multilingual: for Charles IV, the main languages of his Empire were German, Italian, Slavonic (Czech) and Latin.[5] In modern terms, the Luxembourg territories included ancestral

---

4 From west to east: England (and by extension today's United Kingdom), Belgium, Luxembourg, France, Germany, Switzerland, Austria, the Czech Republic, the Slovak Republic, Poland, Hungary, Romania, Slovenia, Croatia, and Italy.
5 As codified in chapter 31 of the Golden Bull for the Empire (1356), in which Charles IV, for practical reasons, recommends that prince-electors teach their successors Latin, Italian, and Slavonic – which in this context meant Czech – in

versions of many more idioms than just these four – French, Dutch, Czech, German, Italian, Hungarian, Polish, Slovenian, Croatian, and Romanian, not to mention the languages used by the local Jewish and other diasporic communities. Latin was well-suited as the transnational medium and the tool of choice for communication among the educated segments of the population in such a conglomerate, but Luxembourg cultural and administrative policies also exerted significant influence on the evolution of German (through the work of the Prague court's chancellery), Czech (through its cultivation as the ancestral language of Bohemia), and – as already mentioned – English (through the English queen, Anne of Bohemia, who in all likelihood inspired, if not directly encouraged, the use of English at the court of her husband, Richard II, following the example familiar to her from Prague).[6] The Luxembourg contribution to the development of French, similarly, is hardly negligible. But as in the case of the nation states found today on the grounds of the former Luxembourg territories, the modern historiographers of these languages, with the possible exception of Czech, typically located their watershed events, such as the translation of the Bible into German by Martin Luther or the arrival of Shakespeare on the London stage, in periods either earlier or later than Luxembourg rule, even if a case could be made that decisions or practices established during the Luxembourg

---

addition to German, which they speak naturally (*naturaliter*). These four languages were considered by Charles the main languages of communication within the Empire. See Wolfgang D. Fritz (ed.), *Die Goldene Bulle Kaiser Karls IV. vom Jahre 1356* (Weimar, 1972), 90; Pierre Monnet, 'La Bulle d'Or de 1356, un texte dans la longue durée allemande et européenne', *Bulletin de l'Institut Historique Allemand de Paris* 15 (2010), 29–51. See also the essay by Václav Žůrek in this volume.

6   See Hans-Joachim Solms, 'Deutsch in Prag zur Mitte des 14. Jahrhunderts', in Heinz Sieburg and Amelie Bendheim (eds), *Prag in der Zeit der Luxemburger Dynastie: Literatur, Religion und Herrschaftskulturen zwischen Bereicherung und Behauptung* (Bielefeld, 2018), 37–52; Tomáš Velička, 'Die deutsche Sprache in den Kanzleien der ersten Luxemburger in Böhmen (1310–1378)', in Tomáš Velička (ed.), *Spätmittelalter in landesherrlichen Kanzleien Mitteleuropas: Alte Tradition und der mühsame Weg zu neuen Fragen und Antworten* (Berlin, 2020), 169–90 (for German); the essays by Matouš Jaluška (for Czech) and Václav Žůrek (for German and Czech) in this volume; and (for English) Alfred Thomas, *The Court of Richard II and Bohemian Culture: Literature and Art in the Age of Chaucer and the Gawain Poet* (Cambridge, 2020), in particular chapter 1 'Richard II and the Luxembourg court', 1–42, and chapter 2 'The familiar patron: collaboration and conflict in Chaucer and late medieval European court writing', 43–84; Peter Brown and Jan Čermák (eds), *England and Bohemia in the Age of Chaucer* (Cambridge, 2023). See also Ivan Hlaváček, 'Dreisprachigkeit im Bereich der Böhmischen Krone: Zum Phänomen der Sprachbenutzung im böhmischen diplomatischen Material bis zur hussitischen Revolution', in Anna Adamska and Marco Mostert (eds), *The development of literate mentalities in East Central Europe* (Turnhout, 2004), 289–310.

period enabled or at least contributed significantly to the making and the sustained influence of these events.

One answer to the Luxembourg 'problem' can therefore be found in the subsequent history of the lands formerly under Luxembourg rule, and in particular in the two cultural and political developments that have most profoundly affected every region of Europe since the late eighteenth century: the formation of nation states, and the concomitant establishment of national philologies alongside the constitution of related academic disciplines (art history, musicology) and institutions (academies and universities). This was usually shored up by the creation of 'national' canons of art, literature, and music designed to underpin monolithically conceived national identities. None of these developments have been kind to the survival and historiography of transnational and multilingual states or empires. Jointly, they disrupted our perception of the complexities of pre-modern cultural networks and dynastic legacies by rearranging the physical and intellectual map of Europe into national centres and peripheries, and into largely segregated disciplines of academic knowledge production. These traditional formations of scholarship have gradually been softened in recent years by the political and scholarly developments of the late twentieth and early twenty-first centuries, enabling first interdisciplinary, then multidisciplinary and now transdisciplinary practices of scholarship to be carried out in decidedly transnational, pan-European geographical and institutional frameworks such as the European Research Area (ERA) or, indeed, the objectives of the grant agency that stimulated the creation of this very volume, the European Research Council (ERC). The present volume is therefore not only one more effort to help overcome the distortions wrought by traditional, but ultimately anachronistic, perceptions of the pre-modern past, in this case focusing on the late-medieval Luxembourgs, but also a direct result of these changed research policies and priorities. The authors are representatives of multiple national and disciplinary traditions, and were encouraged by the editors to engage in disciplinary crossovers and the reassessment of traditional historiographies; while the results can – as ever – only be provisional, it is our collective hope that this volume may contribute to a more nuanced and contextualized view of the Luxembourg period in European history, and stimulate further research.

In the world of Anglophone scholarship, an additional obstacle presents itself by way of a long-standing tradition of medievalist scholarship that focuses much more on the Romance countries of medieval Europe than on central, northern, or eastern Europe. This is compounded by the indisputable circumstance that the bulk of Luxembourg scholarship is written in Czech or German, in addition to contributions in Dutch, French, Hungarian, and Polish. While the contributions of English-speaking scholars to Luxembourg research have been substantial and are fully represented in this volume, there is no denying the fact that engaging with the Luxembourgs from a native English-speaking linguistic and institutional perspective has its own, special challenges. By opening up a window on the riches of Luxembourg scholarship outside the realm of Anglophone scholarship, the authors and editors of this volume hope to help break down this very real barrier to further engagement. We wish to entice future generations of cultural and political historians from the English-speaking world to join the Luxembourg research community and take a fresh look at the fascinating world of the Luxembourgs and their courtly networks, cultural politics, and dynastic legacy.

NATIONAL HISTORIES AND LUXEMBOURG SCHOLARSHIP: LUXEMBOURG, THE CZECH REPUBLIC, AUSTRIA AND GERMANY, AND BEYOND

The one nation state that today carries the Luxembourg name, the Grand Duchy of Luxembourg, only recently established a university (2003). This institution has quickly become a 'hot spot' of current Luxembourg studies.[7] Meanwhile, the role played by the Luxembourgs in the late-medieval history of the Holy Roman Empire and of Bohemia – notably focused on Emperor Charles IV – gave rise to an intense (and continuing) interest from historians in Germany, the Czech Republic, and Austria, generating a fertile tradition of Luxembourg studies carried primarily by historians writing in both Czech and German; the results of their work are eloquently attested to in copious entries in this volume's bibliography.

Bohemia, the jewel in the crown of the Luxembourg Empire, by the late 1400s became an integral part of the Habsburg domains. The gravitational centre of Habsburg rulership, since late-medieval times, lay in and around Vienna – a development that put Prague, despite a glorious interlude under Rudolf II, into the position of a secondary city. Under the influence of nineteenth-century nationalism, however, exploring Luxembourg and Přemyslid history again became a favoured occupation of academics and researchers in Bohemia who were inspired by burgeoning Czech nationalism: after all, Charles IV was the son of a Přemyslid mother, Elizabeth of Bohemia (1292–1330), and therefore a direct descendant from the legendary founders of the dynasty, Přemysl and his wife Libuše. Moreover, his lineage included the martyred

---

[7] Through its Centre Luxembourgeois de Documentation et d'Études Médiévales (CLUDEM) which has become a centre of research focused in particular on the early parts of the Luxembourg period, i.e., the time of Henry VII and John of Bohemia.

Duke Wenceslas (c. 907–35, later canonized as St Wenceslas) – a point that Charles himself was more than content to make and reinforce, making him as Czech as could be. Meanwhile, the Luxembourgs also attracted the interest of German-speaking nationalist thinkers, both of Bohemian origin and from elsewhere in the German-speaking lands. To them, Luxembourg history was primarily part of the history of the Holy Roman Empire, while to Czechs, the Luxembourgs as Kings of Bohemia remained, and remain, inextricably intertwined to the present day with Czech national identity. This double claim by both Czech and Germanophone (mostly Austrian and German) scholarship still accounts for the overwhelming part of Luxembourg studies in history, and is marked by a subtle but important distinction relating to the position of the dynasty in the two complementary historical narratives: in the Bohemian and present-day Czech context, the Luxembourgs live on first and foremost as part of the ongoing line of the Kings of Bohemia. Conversely, in German-speaking lands, scholars tend to look at the Luxembourgs primarily within the context of the medieval empire where the Luxembourgs take their places in the succession of Kings of the Romans and Holy Roman Emperors.

Luxembourg contributions to the histories of present-day Hungary and Poland are complicated by the complex histories of both countries. To give but one example, Silesia changed overlords from the Luxembourgs (being part of the Kingdom of Bohemia) to the Habsburgs (who absorbed Silesia into their Austria-centred portfolio of territories) to the Hohenzollern of Prussia (1763), then became part of the newly founded German nation state (1871) and after 1945 of Poland. Similar histories prevail throughout the regions and territories formerly part of Central European monarchies – their territories now are typically part of independent nation states, some of them formed quite recently, including Slovakia (1993), Slovenia (1991), and Croatia (1991). With their coming-into-being as modern nation states in the twentieth century only, it seemed – and seems to remain – difficult to ascribe foundational character to events of the Luxembourg period. The one exception to this might have been the Grand Duchy of Luxembourg; but there, the long-standing link with the House of Orange, with the Kings of the Netherlands rulers of Luxembourg in personal union from 1815 until 1890, and the bilingual, indeed multilingual, nature of its population made construction of a separate national identity perhaps a less pressing problem than elsewhere on the European continent.[8] There has, of course,

---

8   For further details on the role of the Luxembourgs, and in particular John of Bohemia, in the construction of Luxembourg national identity during the late nineteenth, twentieth, and twenty-first centuries, see Pit Péporté, *Constructing the Middle Ages: Historiography, Collective Memory and Nation-Building in Luxembourg*

always been an interest in Luxembourg matters among French-speaking, Dutch-speaking, and Anglophone scholars as well. As our bibliography shows, however, their quantitative share in Luxembourg scholarship is – and remains – comparatively low. Compounded by the difficulty of accessing the dominant languages of Luxembourg scholarship – Czech and German – this relative paucity of academic research contributed to the phenomenon that Luxembourg scholarship in English remains a minority pursuit. As stated above, it is one of the explicit aims of this volume to help redress this imbalance by inspiring future students and historians in Anglophone institutions of higher learning around the world to engage with the late-medieval Luxembourgs.

LUXEMBOURG COURT CULTURE WITHIN THE FRAMEWORK OF THE ARTS-RELATED DISCIPLINES

There is one more reason for the eclipse of many important Luxembourg cultural achievements, and it must be sought in the construction of our modern academic disciplines. For example, in the history of nationalism, language formed an essential criterion for the assigning of identity.[9] This led to the early creation of academic disciplines exploring the 'modern languages' and their genesis from the medieval vernaculars. The impact of such an approach on any multilingual space is by necessity destructive, dissociating the interaction between, for example, Czech and German text production in Bohemia or, with similar impact, between French and Germanic idioms (both Dutch and German) in the Lotharingian lands in

---

(Leiden, 2011), 161–270; Jana Fantysová-Matějková, 'Der Pater Patriae und der Vater der luxemburgischen Geschichtsschreibung? Jean Bertholet über Johann von Luxemburg', in Lenka Bobková and Jan Zdichynec (eds), *Geschichte – Erinnerung – Selbstidentifikation, Die schriftliche Kultur in den Ländern der Böhmischen Krone im 14.-18. Jahrhundert* (Prague, 2012), 51–71; Pit Péporté, 'When "Jan Lucemburský" meets "Jean l'Aveugle": a comparison of King John of Bohemia's representation in the Czech lands and Luxembourg', *Husitský Tábor* 17 (2012), 29–49; Pit Péporté, 'Les débuts de la médiévistique au Luxembourg? L'oeuvre de Jean Schoetter (1823–1881) et la construction de la nation luxembourgeoise', in Isabelle Guyot-Bachy and Jean-Marie Moeglin (eds), *La naissance de la médiévistique: Les historiens et leurs sources en Europe au Moyen Âge (XIXe - début du XXe siècle)* (Geneva, 2015), 453–72; Dušan Zupka, 'Medieval Dynasties in Medieval Studies: A Historiographic Contribution', *Forum Historiae* 13 (2019), 89–101.
9   As confirmed, in the case of the Grand Duchy of Luxembourg, by the introduction of Luxembourgish as the national language by law in 1984. The same law made French and German official administrative languages of the country. See 'Loi du 24 février 1984 sur le régime des langues' (https://legilux.public.lu/eli/etat/leg/loi/1984/02/24/n1/jo, accessed 29 April 2023).

favour of a single dominant language and its evolutionary narrative, with corresponding centres which typically do not encompass the Luxembourg heartlands. Therefore, with the exception of Czech, written witnesses from the Luxembourg lands tended to end up at the perceived 'peripheries' of their respective modern nation states and national cultures, diminishing their chances of playing an important part in nineteenth- and twentieth-century discipline formations. They were also, by necessity, 'late', and therefore automatically assigned another handicap with regard to scholarly projects that were typically in search of the earliest, oldest, and purest witnesses of their respective objects of interest. The one great exception to this pattern may be found in the reception of literary works in French associated with the Luxembourgs, most notably the works of Guillaume de Machaut and Jean Froissart. The price for inclusion was, however, to seamlessly integrate the works of these authors into a Francocentric master narrative, thereby for the most part eliminating the complexities of their relationships with patrons, languages, and dynasties outside the *regnum Francorum*. Furthermore, these two 'late' authors also suffered for many years from the progressivist bias built into the traditional structure of the humanities. The same goes for Heinrich von Mügeln on the Germanophone side.

All of this has changed in recent decades, and it is one of the intentions of the present volume to showcase the important work conducted by literary scholars (mostly but not exclusively based in the Low Countries and, to a lesser extent, in Germany) who have recently highlighted the dynamic relationship between Dutch, French, and German in late-medieval Europe, and to enhance awareness for their work in the English-speaking world.[10] Concerning Bohemia and the eastern part of the Luxembourg lands, Václav Žůrek's essay in this volume provides an overview of the

---

10   The issue has been recognized by Anglophone scholars but treatment, so far, has been mostly confined to the relationship between English and French. See, for example, Ardis Butterfield, *The familiar enemy: Chaucer, language, and nation in the Hundred Years War* (New York, 2009). Recent decades saw the systematic exploration of French as a transnational medium of expression in late-medieval Europe; see, for example, Christopher Kleinhenz and Keith Busby (eds), *Medieval Multilingualism: The Francophone World and Its Neighbours* (Turnhout, 2010); David Murray, *Poetry in Motion: Languages and Lyrics in the European Middle Ages* (Turnhout, 2019); William Burgwinkle, Jane Gilbert and Simon Gaunt, *Medieval French Literary Culture Abroad* (Oxford, 2020); Elizabeth Eva Leach, 'Ripping Romance to Ribbons: The French of a German Knight in *The Tournament at Chauvency*', *Medium Ævum* 89 (2020), 327–49; David Murray, '"Ju, ich jag": A Three-Part Song in the Mönch von Salzburg Corpus in Translingual Perspective', *Oxford German Studies* 49 (2020), 1–26; and the project The Multilingual Dynamics of Medieval Flanders carried out from 2018 to 2023 at Utrecht University (https://multilingualdynamics.sites.uu.nl/, accessed 29 April 2023).

literary production in the three main languages of the kingdom – Czech, German, and Latin. However, a great deal of space remains for future exploration with regard to the interaction of languages in the Luxembourg domains east of the Rhine and south of the Alps, not least in the south-eastern parts of Europe.

The Luxembourg lands are also a strangely silent place, if we examine the track record of modern music scholarship. In the standard versions of late-medieval music history, France, England, and Italy take centre-stage during the 'long Luxembourg century', with Central Europe only coming into sight by the end of the Luxembourg period. It is a question not previously addressed by musicological scholarship why a dynasty of European importance like the Luxembourgs did not produce any music of rank that seems comparable to its political status, when their competitors in western Europe did. The issue is all the more puzzling as we know that at least some of the Luxembourg rulers were familiar with the musical styles (of mensurally composed polyphony) that have been fascinating musicologists for decades. The one big exception to this is of course Guillaume de Machaut, the former retainer of John of Luxembourg, but even Machaut's position vis-à-vis his patron remained poorly understood until now.[11] Two of the essays in this volume (Fantysová Matějková and Smilansky) provide important new material to assess the relationship between the Valois and the Luxembourgs, and where to place Machaut in all this. Another essay (Kügle) tackles the role and functions of sounds and music in Luxembourg cultural politics, taking into account the multilingual and multicultural environments over which the Luxembourgs ruled as well as their need to set themselves apart from their main political competitors. Prevailing models of late-medieval music history are based on arranging the music that has come down to us in our sources by increasing degrees of notational and musical complexity into a linear progression. This historiographic model, with seeming inexorability, leads to the imitative polyphonic style cultivated by Josquin Desprez and his contemporaries in the late-fifteenth century, but undervalues or even disregards the ongoing creation and sustained cultivation of monophonically notated traditions – of plainchant and of song – in the areas east of the Rhine. Conversely, music history and music cultures here are reconceived as a set of conscious

---

11   This gap in scholarship seems to be closing rapidly now. See, for example, the contributions by Andrew Wathey, 'Guillaume de Machaut and Yolande of Flanders', and Benjamin L. Albritton, '*Ex historia Guillelmi di Mascandio*: Machaut in the *Annales Hannoniae* of Jacques de Guise', both in Jared C. Hartt, Tamsyn Mahoney-Steel and Benjamin Albritton (eds), *Manuscripts, Music, Machaut: Essays in Honor of Lawrence Earp* (Turnhout, 2022), 111–26 and 127–50. Also Kevin Brownlee, 'Machaut as Poet Figure in the *Prise d'Alexandre*', in Hartt, Mahoney-Steel and Albritton (eds), *Manuscripts, Music, Machaut*, 207–17.

political choices designed to project cultural prestige and dynastic 'soft power' in relation to starkly divergent pre-existing cultural expectations and political intentions. This all happened within, and was conditioned by, the highly disparate cultural contexts, milieux, and networks that the Luxembourgs operated in in the different domains they ruled over.

Compared with the often-camouflaged presence of the Luxembourgs in the fields of literary and music studies (which many of the contributions in this volume proactively seek to bring into renewed visibility), the Luxembourgs have long been recognized as a major force in architectural and art history. While many Plantagenet and Valois period buildings were destroyed in subsequent centuries, the Luxembourgs, in Bohemia in particular, were luckier in this regard. As pointed out by Len Scales in the present volume, this may be more than a historical coincidence, however: as a reaction to the linguistically disparate nature of their domains, Luxembourg rulers, notably Charles IV, embraced the public accessibility of the non-verbal, visual arts (architecture, sculpture) as the medium that allowed them to convey messages to all their subjects; as Scales points out, Charles' investment as a founder of buildings and institutions was massive, and to some of his subjects oppressive. It stands to reason that a focus on less public visual art forms, such as manuscript painting in the case of Charles' successor Wenceslas, could have contributed to undermining the imperial claims of Luxembourg rulers by its lack of public visibility. At the same time, the books produced under and for Wenceslas rival in quality and quantity the patronage of many of his contemporaries, and may in fact have been inspired by the example of Wenceslas' French cousins, King Charles V and his three brothers, notably John of Berry. They are addressed in this volume in two complementary essays by Maria Theisen and Gia Toussaint dedicated to the so-called 'Wenceslas Bible' – a monumental witness to the theological ferment that prevailed in late-fourteenth-century Prague. The 'Wenceslas Bible' stands out through its intrinsic nature as an (intended) full translation of Holy Scripture into German (which in fact trails an earlier full translation of the Bible into Czech produced in Bohemia in the 1360s, as pointed out by Václav Žůrek). Furthermore, it is a vital witness to vigorous theological debates between Christian and Jewish scholars in the Bohemian capital in the time of Wenceslas of Bohemia, as demonstrated by Theisen. Toussaint's essay, meanwhile, explores the highly sophisticated play with visual symbolism used by artists active in Bohemia in the Luxembourg period. It continues to resist full understanding by modern art historians – a point also made evident in Lenka Panuškova's essay on the enigmas that are posed by the Vyšší Brod cycle of panel paintings from the middle of the fourteenth century. Probably used as part of the coronation ceremony of Charles and his first wife, Blanche of Valois, as King and Queen of Bohemia in 1347, the cycle eloquently illuminates the influence exerted on artists in Bohemia by colleagues from Italy, France, and the Low Countries, demonstrating that the centre of Europe was far from a backwater by then.

The contributions by Ingrid Ciulisová and Matouš Jaluška shed further light on the inner layers of Luxembourg court culture. The highly visible, static and monumental works of architecture, sculpture and panel painting were typically, and early on, seen by modern scholars as well-suited building blocks for the creation of narratives of national identity. They are therefore well-studied. However, Luxembourg rulers also had a profound impact on the creation of smaller, portable, decorative or ornamental artefacts. Traditionally disregarded, these works of art include elaborate goldsmith's objects encrusted with precious stones, which can be linked to the liturgy as *ornamenta*. Ciulisová´s investigation of the magnificent Reliquary Cross of Charles IV reveals that such marvellous objects possessed multiple meanings and served a diverse range of purposes. Another example of a marvellous object is a humble hazel bush, which, as Matouš Jaluška demonstrates, had a significant role in constructing Přemyslid-Luxembourg dynastic – and by extension, Czech historical – identity in the so-called Dalimil Chronicle – a text produced relatively early, during the reign of John of Luxembourg, but widely read and received in court circles under Charles IV.

LUXEMBOURG SCHOLARSHIP WITHIN THE CONTEXT OF RECENT WORK ON LATE-MEDIEVAL EUROPEAN COURT CULTURES

Despite the growing density of individual studies on the Luxembourg rulers prompted by the shift towards interdisciplinary work embodied in investigating multilayered performances of rulership, the picture of Luxembourg court culture is far from complete; we are at present far removed from a holistic understanding of the courts of the Luxembourgs.[12] In this volume, we have taken what may at first seem a conventional approach towards organizing the material in Parts I–III by anchoring each section around one of three successive generations of Luxembourg rulers. This approach does, however, allow us to bring home the very different personalities, personal histories, and reception histories – by contemporaneous chroniclers and modern scholars alike – extended to the periods of the four Luxembourg rulers who are given this kind

---

12 The only monograph to date that is dedicated to the Luxembourgs as a dynasty is Jörg K. Hoensch, *Die Luxemburger: eine spätmittelalterliche Dynastie gesamteuropäischer Bedeutung 1308–1437* (Stuttgart, 2000). The work focuses on political history.

of primary attention as chronological anchors in this volume: John of Bohemia, Charles IV, and his sons Wenceslas and Sigismund. By the same token, we have deliberately introduced elements into these sections and their headings that direct the attention away from the enthroned rulers as the centres of our narrative, instead re-casting them as historiographic markers for the years when their sustained presence on the throne, and the financial and political clout that came with it, enabled them (and, at least as importantly, those around them) to leave a significant imprint on the cultural record.

Thus, Part I, while dedicated to the time of John of Bohemia, in fact de-centres the King of Bohemia by focusing on the networks of aristocrats (Smilansky) and of retainers (Fantysová Matějková) that John and his retinue were part of. Given his frequent travels, it becomes clear that he (and similar rulers of his time) in fact depended on such administrators on the ground for the execution of day-to-day business as well as the accumulation of political and cultural capital, in John's case in the western part of the Luxembourg domains. Shifting the spotlight to the eastern domains, the analysis of the history of the Vyšší Brod cycle in the same section (Panušková) reveals that the head of the Rožmberk family was the primary agent behind the creation of this group of panel paintings, albeit in the service of the Luxembourg dynasty (in this case, preparing the coronation of John's successor, Charles, and his first wife Blanche of Valois as King and Queen of Bohemia in Prague in 1347). Similarly, Part II approaches the time of Charles IV not – as is so often the case – through discussion of Charles himself as the towering political agent that he no doubt was, but through various ways in which his fingerprint is reflected in the cultural production of Bohemia during the third quarter of the fourteenth century. Charles' famous Reliquary Cross emerges as a materialization of a network of interlocking narratives that focuses as much on the magical properties of gemstones and relics as on Charles' political programme, giving visibility to his claim of a genealogy of Christian emperors that reaches back to Roman times (Ciulisová). A survey of literary production during Charles' reign provides an overview of works in the three languages Charles and his courtiers cultivated (Czech, German, and Latin), thereby acknowledging the growing emphasis on medieval multilingualisms in current medieval and court studies (Žůrek). A study of the reception of the Dalimil Chronicle, produced again within the orbit of the Prague court during John of Luxembourg's reign, discusses the appropriation of Old Czech foundational legends into Caroline historiography (Jaluška). The second section is further unified by a focus on the marvellous embodied, on the one hand, in the materials used in the Reliquary Cross (Ciulisová) and, on the other, in the importance assigned a hazel bush connected with Charles' ancestry in the surroundings of Prague. By this focus on the supernatural and on multiplicities of languages and cultural practices, we again intend to deflect some of the engrained habits of thinking about Charles and his time.[13]

Part III, with Charles' sons and successors, Wenceslas and Sigismund, as chronological anchors, continues this indirect approach by focusing, in Wenceslas' case, on the key surviving bibliographical artefact of his time, the Wenceslas Bible. It is studied here from two contrasting, yet complementary, perspectives, focusing on the intellectual climate that gave rise to the project (Theisen), and the intricate symbolic language deployed in its illuminations (Toussaint). Again, it is worthwhile remembering that the Bible was not a direct commission by Wenceslas but was donated to him, and that therefore a relatively large circle of members and associates of the court must have been involved in its creation. At the same time, the extremely personal nature of some of its illuminations suggests that the manuscript was intended very much for Wenceslas' personal use, contributing to the esoteric atmosphere of his rulership. The two contributions that close Part III widen the circle of discussion by drawing on documents wholly external to the Luxembourg court. Both the reflection of the rulers' personae in the correspondences of ambassadors from various states in Italy during the reigns of Wenceslas and his half-brother Sigismund (Schmidt), and the records of the Imperial Abbey of Ellwangen (Whelan) in present-day southern Germany during the period of Sigismund, shine an indirect but no less penetrating light on what it meant to be King of the Romans and/or Holy Roman Emperor, in particular for those who had to manage the royal or imperial presence when constrained to interact with it directly.

Part IV, lastly, explicitly addresses a few aspects of Luxembourg studies that, in the editors' view, warranted particular, urgent attention. With the focus on the human, geographical and material 'periphery' of the Luxembourg rulers, the absence of studies on Luxembourg women becomes ever more glaring, and the essay appearing in our collection, while offering many details, is as much intended to be read as an invitation to further research as an attempt to offer some initial insights (Burkhardt). A revisionist reading of Charles' focus on statuary and architecture will further nuance the polished image of this emperor (Scales), and a first stab at the politics underlying the Luxembourgs' choices (and abstentions!) in their patronage of various musical styles and practices may help to

---

13 The same point was recently made independently by Filip Srovnal in his 'Der Trumphbogen für den kommenden Herrscher' (2019). Srovnal stresses the sustained involvement of the Nuremberg patriciate in the construction of the Frauenkirche, and critiques the exaggerated emphasis attributed to Charles IV directly in the traditional historiography of this important project.

re-balance the music history of late medieval Europe as more than the history of composed mensural polyphony (Kügle).

By devoting attention to objects, persons, and institutions from the orbit of the Luxembourgs we respond to the need for transcending the traditional historiographic model with its focus on individuals and in particular on male rulers; instead, our objective is to reconceive Luxembourg history as a multicentric and multilayered network of relationships between objects and people or between people. These networks are both horizontal and vertical; they run *among* the aristocracy, *between* the aristocracy and their retainers (clerical or otherwise), *among* the retainers; last, but not least, they encompass the ecclesiastic powers and career paths that existed both in parallel, in competition, and in complementarity with the late-medieval laity, be they members of the aristocracy or not. It is important to appreciate that the networks in question here are not neutral; far from it, they are not only marked by differences in power, but indeed constructed in such a way as to reinforce and perpetuate such power differentials. Next to social coercion and physical violence, therefore, synergetic networks of cultural production working together are the most powerful vehicles to generate political clout and persuasion. Together they produce the record of dynastic legacy studied in this volume. In sum, then, this collection of essays on the late-medieval Luxembourgs may serve as a blueprint for a novel approach to the study of pre-modern cultures that conceives of itself as a tapestry of interlocking narratives. None of these narratives claims exclusivity at the expense of any other; read together and against each other, however, they jointly may enable us to reach a new level in our efforts to regain the fullest understanding possible of the richness and diversity of the cultural experiences of the past.

PART I

JOHN THE BLIND AND HIS PROGENY IN FRANCE

CHAPTER 1

THE 'LUXEMBOURGNESS' OF THINGS: MACHAUT C, GLAZIER 52, AND DYNASTIC PRESENCE IN EARLY FOURTEENTH-CENTURY FRANCE[1]

URI SMILANSKY

Dynastic presence, feudal allegiances, and military cooperation between the house of Luxembourg and the late Capetian and early Valois kings of France are easy to demonstrate. Influence and individuals' identities, however, are much harder to substantiate, as they go beyond familial affiliation. Tags are often misleading. Indeed, this contribution characterizes as anachronistic the notion of a dynastic, genetic, definable 'Luxembourgness' which circulated across Europe with the movement of single family members. It is engaged with here as a means to consider the importance of affiliation and influence beyond the body of the ruler, and as applicable also to the agendas of rivals, courtiers, cultural creations,

---

1 This text was written at the University of Oxford in the context of the ERC project 'Music and Late Medieval European Court Cultures' (malmecc.music.ox.ac.uk). The project received funding from the European Research Council under the European Union's Horizon 2020 research and innovation programme (grant no. 669190). I would like to thank Karl Kügle and Jana Fantysová-Matějková for their advice regarding earlier versions of this contribution.

and even objects.² It is also tempting to use such tags for marking out certain materials and relationships as 'othered' or exotic. For those of us interested primarily in the Kingdom of France, for example, discussing 'Luxembourgness' can become part of a strategy to contain and manage materials or influences perceived as foreign, or perhaps as code for value judgements relating to the relationships between centre and periphery. My essay takes a wider, Francophone focus, and discusses the projection of communicable identities during the process of exchange as a coming together of categories, not as independent or isolated occurrences. It considers Guillaume de Machaut – and by extension, his cultural output – as a French-speaking retainer of a Luxembourg court. His activities are thus examined as part of larger geopolitical processes, in relation to contemporary Valois cultural production, and most importantly, through the prism of material engagement. Following a presentation of some historical background, the heart of the chapter offers a case study involving two coupled manuscripts used to probe the assumptions and mechanisms we often associate with ownership, influence, and the projection of (self-) identity. In particular, I will combine the examination of literary and book dedications and ownership with the cultural necessities surrounding inter-dynastic mingling, movement, and familial relationships. To what degree do patrons' personal, linguistic, familial, or geographic differentiators allow them to mould their hereditary or newly acquired social roles and functions? Was greater loyalty demanded by past or by present circumstances, to birth or marriage? How do courtly

---

2   Such constellations of meaning form the focus of many 'post-human' theories, including Latour's Actor-Network Theory and Barad's Agential Realism. As I deem the adoption of their terminologies more prohibitive than useful in this case, I have refrained from doing so. For examples of their applications, see John R.W. Speller, *Bourdieu and Literature* (Cambridge, 2011); Rita Felski, 'Latour and Literary Studies', *PMLA* 130:3 (2015), 737–42; Hans Ulrich Gumbrecht, *Stimmungen lesen: Über eine verdeckte Wirklichkeit der Literatur* (Munich, 2011); Stephen Ahern (ed.), *Affect Theory and Literary Critical Practice: A Feel for the Text* (London, 2019); or Marilynn Desmond and Noah D. Guynn (guest eds of special issue: *Category Crossings: Bruno Latour and Medieval Modes of Existence*), *Romanic Review* 111:1 (May, 2020). A recent, relevant exposition of the related notion of 'multimodality' (applied more to the current context of reading than to historical ones) can be found in Kate Maxwell, 'A Multimodal Reading of MS **C**: Order, Decoration, Mutation', in Lawrence Earp and Jared C. Hartt (eds), *Poetry, Art, and Music in Guillaume de Machaut's Earliest Manuscript (BnF fr. 1586)* (Turnhout, 2021), 133–53. See also Jane Gilbert, 'The Manuscript as Property and as Apparatus: Oxford, Bodleian Library, MS Bodley 264, and its Networks', in Karl Kügle (ed.), *The Networked Court: Transdisciplinary Perspectives on Late Medieval European Court Cultures* (forthcoming). Historiographic anachronisms relating specifically to Luxembourg are discussed below.

cultural artefacts perform within this field? What difference does changing our understanding of their early history make to that of wider politics and culture? What could 'Luxembourgness' mean beyond direct contact and presence? How should we engage with the blurred and shifting borderlines of political, linguistic, cultural, and dynastic affiliation?

My first object of interest comprises fols 23r–58v of the manuscript Paris, Bibliothèque nationale de France, f. fr. 1586, known to Machaut scholars as manuscript **C**.[3] I will differentiate this section from the manuscript as a whole by referring to it as **RemC**. The second artefact is the manuscript New York, Morgan Library, Glazier 52 (henceforth, **G52**).[4] **RemC** contains the earliest surviving version of Guillaume de Machaut's (1305–77) *Remede de Fortune* (henceforth, *Remede*), copied – like all other *dits* in **C** – on a physically separable set of gatherings.[5] It stands out from

---

3 The fully digitalized manuscript is available at https://gallica.bnf.fr/ark:/12148/btv1b8449043q. Its structure, contents and history are discussed (among others) in Lawrence Earp, *Guillaume de Machaut: A Guide to Research* (New York, 1995), 77–9; 'Scribal Practice, Manuscript Production and the Transmission of Music in Late Medieval France: The Manuscripts of Guillaume de Machaut' (unpublished PhD dissertation, Princeton University, 1983), 131–42, 371–3; Uri Smilansky, 'Creating MS C: Author, Workshop, Court', *Early Music History* 39 (2020), 253–304; and Lawrence Earp and Jared C. Hartt (eds), *Poetry, Art, and Music in Guillaume de Machaut's Earliest Manuscript (BnF fr. 1586)* (Turnhout, 2021).

4 Images of the 29 pages of this manuscript that contain an illumination (about a quarter of the total) are available at http://ica.themorgan.org/manuscript/page/1/76994, along with a partial bibliography (http://ica.themorgan.org/manuscript/description/76994). A particularly pertinent discussion appears in Lisa Daugherty Iacobellis, '"Grant peine et grant diligence": Visualizing the Author in Late Medieval Manuscripts' (unpublished PhD dissertation, Ohio State University, 2017), 127–34, 313.

5 For the *Remede* and its analysis, see its two current editions and bibliographies therein: James I. Wimsatt and William W. Kibler (text eds) with Rebecca A. Baltzer (music ed.), *Guillaume de Machaut: 'Le Jugement dou roy de Behaigne' and 'Remède de Fortune'* (Atlanta, GA, 1988); and R. Barton Palmer (text ed. and trans.), with Domenic Leo (art ed.) and Uri Smilansky (music ed.), *The Boethian Poems*, in R. Barton Palmer and Yolanda Plumley (eds), *Guillaume de Machaut: The Complete Poetry & Music*, vol. 2 (Michigan, 2019), along with its central position to many of the contributions in Earp and Hartt, *Poetry, Art, and Music*. Central contributions on Machaut's biography include, Earp, *Guide*, ch. 1; Roger Bowers, 'Guillaume de Machaut and his Canonry of Reims, 1338–1377', *Early Music History* 23 (2004), 1–48; Elizabeth Eva Leach, *Guillaume de Machaut: Secretary, Poet, Musician* (Ithaca, NY, 2011), 7–33; and Lawrence Earp, 'Introduction', in Lawrence Earp and Jared C. Hartt (eds), *Poetry, Art, and Music in Guillaume de Machaut's Earliest Manuscript (BnF fr. 1586)* (Turnhout, 2021), 21–55, building upon new discoveries subsequently detailed in Andrew Wathey, 'Guillaume de Machaut and Yolande of Flanders', in Jared C. Hartt, Benjamin Albritton and Tamsyn Mahoney-Steel (eds), *Manuscripts, Music, Machaut: Essays in Honor of Lawrence Earp* (Turnhout, 2022), 111–25. Important

the other contents of this lavish luxury book due to its even more elevated visual and material presentation.⁶ While sharing a scribe with other sections of **C**, its illuminator, decorator and pen-flourisher – all the best in the collection – worked only on this section. **G52** is a shorter manuscript of 56 leaves, containing a single work, yet again, in its earliest surviving copy. This is Jean de Vignay's (c. 1282/5–c. 1350?) *Livre de la moralité des nobles hommes et des gens du peuple sus le gieu des eschés* (henceforth, *Eschés*), a translation and amplification of Jacobus de Cessolis' (c. 1250–c. 1322) *Libellus de moribus hominum et officiis nobilium ac popularium super ludo scachorum*.⁷

---

further context for its discussion is provided in Jana Fantysová Matějková's contribution to this volume, including a justification of Machaut's revised birth date given here.
6   For the visual impact of the *Remede* in **C**, see François Avril, 'Les manuscrits enluminés de Guillaume de Machaut', *Actes et Colloques* 23 (1982), 117–33, at 119–20; Sylvia Huot, *From Song to Book: The Poetics of Writing in Old French Lyric and Lyrical Narrative Poetry* (Ithaca, NY, 1987), at 242–73; or more recently, Anne Stone, 'Made to Measure: On the Intimate Relations of Song and Parchment in Guillaume de Machaut's *Remède de fortune* in MS C', in Lawrence Earp and Jared C. Hartt (eds), *Poetry, Art, and Music in Guillaume de Machaut's Earliest Manuscript (BnF fr. 1586)* (Turnhout, 2021), 93–131, and Lenka Panušková, 'Machaut's Le Remède de Fortune und die höfische Gesellschaft in Bild', in Dana Dvořáčková-Malá, Kristýna Solomon and Michel Margue (eds), *Über den Hof und am Hofe: Literatur und Geschichtsschreibung im Mittelalter* (Dresden, 2021), 81–96.
7   Both author and work are much less studied in this case. The most detailed study of Vignay and his output remains Christine Knowles, 'Jean de Vignay, un traducteur du XIVe siècle', *Romania* 75 (1954), 353–83, based on Christine Knowles, *The Life and Work of Jean de Vignay* (unpublished PhD dissertation, University of London, 1953), with updates in Mattia Cavagna, 'Jean de Vignay: actualités et perspectives', *Cahiers de recherches médiévales et humanistes* 27 (2014), 141–9. See also Claudine A. Chavannes-Mazel, *The Miroir Historial of Jean le Bon: The Leiden Manuscript and its Related Copies* (Leiden, 1988), vol. 1, 167–72, 195–211. A critical edition of the *Eschés* appears in Carol S. Fuller, *A Critical Edition of* Le Jeu des Eschés Moralisé (unpublished PhD dissertation, Catholic University of America, 1974), using three other early manuscripts, not this one (see historiographical discussion below). To this day, a certain degree of confusion exists between the Latin original, Vignay's translation, and that of Jean Ferron (1347), a situation only compounded by the existence of a manuscript tradition that conflates both versions and was subsequently used by Caxton in his English version of 1476. See Christine Knowles, 'Caxton and His Two French Sources: The "Game and Playe of the Chesse" and the Composite Manuscripts of the Two French Translations of the "Ludus Scaccorum"', *The Modern Language Review* 49 (1954), 417–23. All these very popular and widely circulating works (along with other translations) were and are often referred to as the *Échecs moralisé*, not to be confused with the poetic *Échecs d'amours* (c. 1380) and its follow-up, the *Eschez amoureux moralises* by Evrard de Conty. For the wider cultural and behavioural importance of chess in the Middle Ages, see

It has long been recognized that the two sources share visual and material characteristics, having been created within the same Parisian, mid-century workshop.[8] These include folio size, layout, scribal hand, decorative flourishing, elevated use of colour (the use of alternating blue and gold for initials, and of blue rather than red *tituli*), shared models for their illuminations, and, perhaps, shared artists.[9] **Figure 1.1** presents both their opening pages, allowing for a direct comparison. The degree of 'Luxembourgness' of these books relies on the biographies of the authors whose works they contain; on their dedicatees and owners; on the works themselves; on their use as part of courtly and political performance; and finally, on their relationship with each other. Not all these questions can be answered here, yet in order to use these books in considering what any notion of 'Luxembourgness' might mean in this period, I will first introduce the dynastic intertwining of the houses of Luxembourg, Capet, and Valois, along with other personalities surrounding the manuscripts in question.

Emma Cayley, *Debate and Dialogue: Alain Chartier in his Cultural Context* (Oxford, 2006), 162–88, and more widely, Marilyn Yalom, *Birth of the Chess Queen: A History* (New York, 2004).

8   François Avril, 'Un Chef-d'œuvre de l'enluminure sous le règne de Jean le Bon: La Bible Moralisée manuscrit français 167 de la Bibliothèque Nationale', *Monuments et Mémoires de la Fondation Eugène Piot* 58 (1973), 91–125, at 100, rehearsed in Earp, 'Introduction', 25–7, and in more detail in Kyunghee Pyun, 'The Master of the *Remede de Fortune* and Parisian Ateliers c.1350', in Lawrence Earp and Jared C. Hartt (eds), *Poetry, Art, and Music in Guillaume de Machaut's Earliest Manuscript (BnF fr. 1586)* (Turnhout, 2021), 195–216. On the notion of 'workshop', see Richard H. Rouse and Mary A. Rouse, *Manuscripts and their Makers: Commercial Book Producers in Medieval Paris, 1200–1500* (London, 2000); John Lowden, 'Beauty or Truth? Making a *Bible Moralisée* in Paris around 1400', in Godfried Croenen and Peter Ainsworth (eds), *Patrons, Authors and Workshops: Books and Book Production in Paris around 1400* (Leuven, 2006), 197–222, and in the current context, Smilansky, 'Creating MS C', 263–7.

9   Domenic Leo, 'The Pucellian School and the Rise of Naturalism: Style as Royal Signifier?', in Kyunghee Pyun and Anna D. Russakoff (eds), *Jean Pucelle: Innovation and Collaboration in Manuscript Painting* (London, 2013), 149–70 (esp. 154–5; 167), associates the artist responsible for the opening illumination of **G52** with that responsible for **RemC**'s illumination, dating the former source to 1348. This, however, is not universally accepted. For an overview of relevant artistic identifications, see also Pyun, 'The Master of the *Remede de Fortune*', 199.

Figure 1.1. MS C, fol. 23r (above) and G52 fol. 1r (opposite) compared.

Ci commencent les rubriches du premier livre de la moralité des nobles hommes et des gens du peuple sus le jeu des eschés translatee de latin en françois par frere Jehan de Vignay de l'ordre de hault pas.

- Sous quel roy le jeu des eschés fu trouvé.
- Qui trouva le dit jeu.
- Des .iii. causes pourquoy il fu trouvé.
- De la fourme du roy et de ses meurs et de son estat.
- De la fourme de la royne et de ses meurs et de la maniere d'icelle.
- De l'estat et de l'office des alphins.
- De l'office et des meurs des chevaliers

et de l'ordre de chevalerie.
- De l'office et des meurs des rocs qui sont vicaires du roy.

Ci commencent les rubriches du second livre de l'estat et des condicions des gens du peuple qui sont deuises entre huit. Comme les offices de toutes les gens de tous mestiers et de toutes marchandises et tout applique as .viii. pionniers.

- De la fourme et la maniere de ceulx qui labourent les terres et nourrissent les bestes.
- De l'office de tous ceulx qui forgeur et de leur oeuvres.
- De l'office et du mestier des notaires tondeurs de linge et drapiers.
- De l'office des marchans et des changeurs.
- De l'ouvre et de l'usage des medicines des apoticaires et des epiciers.

CAPET–VALOIS–LUXEMBOURG RELATIONS, 1288 TO 1346

Had he stopped to take stock of his family's fortunes in early June 1288, prospects would have seemed bleak to the nine-year-old Henry of Luxembourg (c. 1278–1313), soon to be installed Count Henry VII. On 5 June, his father and three uncles perished during the Battle of Worringen, which marked the culmination of the War of the Limburg Succession.[10] With the Holy Roman Empire in a weakened state – the King of the Romans being preoccupied in the south and no emperor since the days of Fredrick II – the power struggle on its north-western edge eventually required the arbitration of the French king, Philip IV ('the Fair', 1268–1314). The Luxembourgs not only suffered a grave dynastic loss, but were fighting on the losing side: having not long hence bolstered their claim on Limburg by buying Reinald of Guelders' (1255–1326) claim to it,[11] both land and title were given in 1289 to the battle's victor, Duke John I of Brabant (1252/3–94). French preference for John was, perhaps, unsurprising. After all, John's first wife, Margaret of France (1254–71), was the king's aunt, and John's sister, Mary (1254/6–1321/2), was the French dowager queen and the king's stepmother (see genealogies). Both Philip IV and his father (Philip III, 1245–85) maintained a long-standing policy of opportunistic encroachment on the imperial border, ranging from the patient building of local allegiances to repeated attempts to offer French candidates for election as King of the Romans.[12]

With Henry's mother, Beatrice of Avesnes (c. 1260?–1321), acting as regent, both French influence and the smoothing of Luxembourg-Brabant relations were bolstered by offering tutelage to the young count within the French royal household.[13] This move was extremely effective. By the time

---

10 See Vera Torunsky, *Worringen 1288: Ursachen und Folgen einer Schlacht* (Cologne, 1988), with many relevant documents available in the 700-year anniversary exhibition book published as Werner Schäfke (ed.), *Der Name der Freiheit, 1288–1988: Aspekte Kölner Geschichte von Worringen bis heute* (Cologne, 1988). The most detailed English discussion to date can be found in Jan Müller, *The Battle of Worringen, 1288: The History and Mythology of a Notable Event* (unpublished MA thesis, University of Alberta, 1993). See also Bouko de Groot, 'The Battle of Worringen: The Charge of Six Thousand to Decide the Fate of Limbourg', *Medieval Warfare* 2:2 (2012), 42–6.
11 See attestation of sale in Schäfke, *Der Name der Freiheit*, 2.
12 See Fritz Kern, *Die Anfänge der französischen Ausdehnungspolitik bis zum Jahre 1308* (Tübingen, 1910). During the period discussed in this essay, the most important French candidacies included those of Philip III in 1273, Charles of Valois in 1308, and Charles IV of France in 1324.
13 See Welvert Eugène, 'Philippe le Bel et la maison de Luxembourg', *Bibliothèque de l'école des chartes* 45 (1884), 180–8. For the wider aristocratic practice of educating

of Henry's coming of age around 1293–4,[14] he married Margaret of Brabant (1276–1311), John I's daughter, and had affiliated himself with both French politics and culture. Indeed, having been knighted by the French king, one of his first acts as a major was to swear a pact of allegiance to France and offer military aid in its war against England in 1294–7.[15] Though extensive French-Luxembourg relations can be demonstrated earlier, 1288 can nonetheless be considered a step change in their personal intensity, one that was bolstered and institutionalized in 1294.[16] The following half century, however, did not see a unipolar focus to Luxembourgian political and dynastic attention. In 1308 Henry was elected King of the Romans as a compromise candidate, and was subsequently crowned Holy Roman Emperor in Rome in 1312. His son, John of Luxembourg (1296–1346, later 'the Blind'), was married in 1310 to Elizabeth of Bohemia (1292–1330), the Přemyslid heiress of that kingdom. These events shifted the political focus within the Luxembourg family back towards the Empire,

---

children in the courts of their feudal superiors, see Shulamith Shahar, *Childhood in the Middle Ages* (London and New York, 1990), ch. 10, and within a specifically royal context, Nicholas Orme, *From Childhood to Chivalry: The Education of the English Kings and Aristocracy, 1066–1530* (London, 1984), 28–9. On attitudes to childhood and emotionality in general, see the overview provided in Albrecht Classen, 'Philippe Ariès and the Consequences: History of Childhood, Family Relations, and Personal Emotions: Where do we stand today?', in Albrecht Classen (ed.), *Childhood in the Middle Ages and the Renaissance: The Results of a Paradigm Shift in the History of Mentality* (Berlin and New York, 2005), 1–65. Both this episode and the lasting relationship between Henry's son and a succession of French kings is usefully summarized in Philippe Contamine, 'Politique, culture et sentiment: Jean l'Aveugle et la royauté française', in Michel Pauly (ed.), *Johann der Blinde, Graf von Luxemburg und König von Böhmen 1296–1346* (Luxembourg, 1997), 343–61.
14 For the problem in assigning a specific date for this, see Georgina R. Cole-Baker, 'The Date of the Emperor Henry VII's Birth', *The English Historical Review* 35 (1920), 224–31.
15 Technically, Luxembourg remained an imperial fief, though the promise to protect France against any external aggressor undermined this. Such arrangements caused tension between France and the Empire. See Jörg K. Hoensch, *Die Luxemburger: Eine spätmittelalterliche Dynastie gesamteuropäischer Bedeutung 1308–1437* (Stuttgart, 2000), 25–8.
16 While the Romance vernacular later called 'French' had long been a major language in Luxembourg, it should be remembered that language borders – to the extent those existed within multilingual societies – did not match those of political units, especially not within the Empire. See Harald Völker, 'Altfranzösisch in deutscher Feder? Sprache und Verwaltung in der Grafschaft Luxemburg im 13. Jahrhundert', in Wolfgang Dahmen, Günter Holtus, Johannes Kramer, Michael Metzeltin, Wolfgang Schweickard and Otto Winkelmann (eds), *Schreiben in einer anderen Sprache: Zur Internationalität romanischer Sprachen und Literaturen* (Tübingen, 2000), 35–52. For ties between Henry V of Luxembourg (1216–81) and Louis IX of France (1214–70), see Hoensch, *Die Luxemburger*, 22–3.

specifically Central Europe, and, in a new development, to northern Italy.[17] Nevertheless, both Henry's son and grandson were sent to spend their formative years in Paris, and the first half of the fourteenth century saw a number of intermarriages, military cooperations and exchanges of personnel.[18] For example, in 1322, Henry's daughter, Mary of Luxembourg (1304–24), married King Charles IV of France (1294–1328) shortly after the latter's accession to the throne (see genealogies). Her brother, John of Luxembourg, took a French princess, Beatrice of Bourbon (d. 1383), as his second wife in 1334, four years after the death of Elizabeth of Bohemia.[19] Two of John's children followed suit, with Wenceslas/Charles of Luxembourg (1316–78, later Holy Roman Emperor Charles IV) marrying Blanche of Valois (1317–48), sister of the future King of France, Philip VI (1293–1350), in 1323, and Jutta/Bonne of Luxembourg (1315–49) wedding the then heir-apparent John of France, Duke of Normandy (1319–64, later

---

17 For Henry's punishing itinerary through the Empire following his election (and its practical and symbolic meaning), see Ellen Widder, 'Orte der Macht: Herrschaftsschwerpunkte, Handlungsräume und Öffentlichkeit unter Heinrich VII. (1308-1313)', in Ellen Widder and Wolfgang Kraut (eds), *Vom luxemburgischen Grafen zum europäischen Herrscher: Neue Forschungen zu Heinrich VII.* (Luxembourg, 2008), 69–145. For the securing of the Kingdom of Bohemia, see Robert Antonín, 'Der Weg nach Osten: Heinrich VII. und der Erwerb Böhmens für die Luxemburger', in Sabine Penth and Peter Thorau (eds), *Rom 1312: Die Kaiserkrönung Heinrichs VII. und die Folgen: Die Luxemburger als Herrscherdynastie von gesamteuropäischer Bedeutung* (Cologne, 2016), 9–22. For the complexity of discussing influence, western and eastern relations in this context, see Martin Kintzinger, 'Politische Westbeziehungen des Reiches im Spätmittelalter: Westliche Kultur und Westpolitik unter den Luxemburgern', in Joachim Ehlers (ed.), *Deutschland und der Westen Europas im Mittelalter* (Stuttgart, 2002), 423–55.
18 For the notion of an educational tradition, see Johannes Fried, *The Middle Ages* (Cambridge, MA, 2015), 393–4. Charles' upbringing in Paris is much better documented than John's, with the latter's presence there relying heavily on supposition. See, for example, Contamine, 'Politique, culture et sentiment', 346. On the unnecessary association of John's close ties with the Kings of France with prior acquaintance, see Michel Margue and Jean Schroeder (eds), *Un itinéraire européen: Jean l'Aveugle, comte de Luxembourg et roi de Bohême, 1296-1346* (Brussels, 1996), 57–8. Indeed, they discern a cooling relationship between France and Luxembourg following Henry's accession to the imperial throne, followed by a rekindled cooperation following John's failure to become emperor and distancing from the running of Bohemia. In particular, this took place in the context of political strife involving Luxembourg, Bar, and Verdun. As we shall see below, all these locations are also significant in relation to Machaut. See 55–66.
19 On John and Beatrice's marriage in the context of French-Luxembourg relations, see Jana Fantysová-Matějková, *Wenceslas de Bohême: Un prince au carrefour de l'Europe* (Paris, 2013), 18–24.

King John II), in 1332.[20] Both John and his son Charles joined the French against the English at the Battle of Crécy (1346), where John met his heroic death and Charles – only elected King of the Romans the previous month – escaped from the field wounded.[21] The personal and cultural exchanges that followed such (and other) movements fill the pages of this volume. The one most pertinent here relates to Guillaume de Machaut's extended service to John of Luxembourg and his presumed attachment to Bonne when seeking new patronage within the French fold, be that as early as the 1330s or following John's demise in 1346.

IDENTITY FORMATION BETWEEN INDIVIDUAL AND DYNASTY

For me, the essential parameter for contextualizing this assortment of data is a pattern that emerges when considering the reception, acceptance or rejection of members of the houses concerned following changes in their physical circumstances. This separates those who opted for assimilation (and were accepted by their peers and subjects alike) from those who decided against it – at times even ostentatiously so – and were resented and resisted. Interestingly, this separation crosses both gender and dynastic affiliation. For example, for about a decade between the mid 1330s and mid 1340s, Bohemia had both a Luxembourg king (John of Luxembourg) and heir-apparent (Charles of Luxembourg), both of whom were married to French princesses (Beatrice of Bourbon and Blanche of Valois respectively, both being of a similar age). The behaviour and acceptance of the two generations, however, was remarkably different. John and Beatrice – who did not speak Czech and spent the least amount of time possible in Prague – were treated with indifference or hostility; Charles and Blanche – who made a point of learning Czech and got involved in civic and institutional matters – were adopted and celebrated.[22] In the

---

20 For a wider context, see Amelie Fössel, 'Die Heiratspolitik der Luxemburger', in Sabine Penth and Peter Thorau (eds), *Rom 1312: Die Kaiserkrönung Heinrichs VII.*, 427–44. For a specifically French orientation, see Carl D. Dietmar, *Die Beziehungen des Hauses Luxemburg zu Frankreich in den Jahren 1247–1356* (Cologne, 1983).
21 See Walther Rose, 'König Johann der Blinde von Böhmen und die Schlacht bei Crécy (1346)', *Zeitschrift für historische Waffen- und Kostümkunde: Organ des Vereins für Historische Waffenkunde* 7 (1915), 37–60, with many necessary updates and further sources of testimony in Michael Livingston and Kelly DeVries (eds), *The Battle of Crécy: A Casebook* (Liverpool, 2015).
22 This is, of course, a crass simplification. Another (arguably more important) difference was that of blood: only Charles, through his mother, was linked directly to the Přemyslid dynasty. However, John's throne was not challenged upon the death of his Přemyslid wife, Elizabeth, allowing us to see this emphasis, too, as a cultural

other direction, John and Beatrice's son was born in Prague, and named Wenceslas (1337–83) after the patron saint of the Přemyslid dynasty. He remained in Prague as his French mother left for Luxembourg shortly after his birth, and inherited the County of Luxembourg only in 1353.[23] Nevertheless, and without demonstrating himself as a particularly effective or successful count or duke, his assimilation into the cultural melting pot of his Luxembourg-Low Countries-French charge saw him accepted as the 'local' feudal authority. Likewise, his half-sister Bonne (originally Jutta) was also born in Prague. Evidence concerning her upbringing is sparse, although scholars have suggested that up to the age of 11 she experienced a peripatetic education, for the most part away from both her parents. This likely included protracted periods spent in two different convents in and around Prague, and a year in Wartburg Castle at the house of a betrothed's family, before the arrangement fell through.[24] She spent the next five years in Luxembourg, likely at the Dominican nunnery of Marienthal. There she renewed her marriage preparations, originally expecting to wed the heir to the County of Bar (Henry of Bar, 1315–44, subsequently Henry IV; see genealogies), and finally marrying John of France. The military alliance to which her marriage contract was appended was signed in Fontainebleau in January 1332, some six months before the wedding itself.[25] Nevertheless,

---

construct designed to elevate one couple and denigrate another. It does not explain the different treatment of their two French wives.

23 This is not to say that he was not being prepared for his inheritance of Luxembourg in the intervening years, as the county was promised to the offspring of John's second marriage within its marriage contract. For his inheritance and relationship with his half-brother emperor, see Fantysová-Matějková, *Wenceslas de Bohême*, ch. 2, and Michel Pauly, 'Karl IV. und sein Halbbruder Wenzel: Das Herzogtum Luxemburg und Karls Politik im Westen des Reiches', in Amelie Bendheim and Heinz Sieburg (eds), *Prag in der Zeit der Luxemburger Dynastie* (Bielefeld, 2018), 13–36.

24 The convents suggested here are the Cistercian monastery of Königsaal/Zbraslav (1319–22) and the Benedictine convent of St George in Prague Castle (1323–5). See William G. Land, *The Prayer Book of Bonne of Luxembourg: A Personal Document* (Washington, 1984), 2–4; Joni M. Hand, *Women, Manuscripts and Identity in Northern Europe, 1350–1550* (Farnham, 2013), 12–13; Annette Ingebretson Lermack, 'Fit for a Queen: The Psalter of Bonne of Luxembourg at The Cloisters' (unpublished PhD dissertation, University of Iowa, 1999), 40–4. All, to varying degrees, rely on Raymond Cazelles, *Jean l'aveugle: comte de Luxembourg, roi de Bohéme* (Paris, 1947). Some of these monastic locations are inferred rather than recorded, and may well be problematic. See Michel Margue, '*Regum de stirpe*: Some aspects of the Monastic Policy of John of Luxembourg, King of Bohemia and Count of Luxembourg', in Klara Benešovska (ed.), *A Royal Marriage: Elisabeth Přemyslid and John of Luxembourg 1310* (Prague, 2011), 262–76, as well as Jana Fantysová-Matějková's contribution to this volume.

25 See Contamine, 'Politique, culture et sentiment', 349–52.

cultural, linguistic, and ideological assimilation allowed her to become integrated into the French queen's retinue and successfully assume the role of royal-consort-in-waiting.[26]

Accepting this pattern has clear implications for the question of personal and dynastic identity. It seems that pre-hereditary or pre-nuptial personal histories offered – and were understood as – but one of a range of anchor points on which an eventual, often cross-cultural identity was to be constructed. While personal circumstances would make their mark upon an individual's psyche, successful mastery of the duties of subsequent social and political roles often required such marks to be suppressed, even erased. Many of the nobles mentioned here – especially the women, but also Henry VII before 1308 and John before 1310 – could have had little confidence in predicting their final geopolitical and cultural environment, or gain the freedom to choose it. On the one hand, familial association was of central importance in marriage politics: it would have shaped not only a potential bride's dowry, but the political access and genealogical authority established by any union.[27] On the other, it is clear that privileging biological parentage above all other considerations in assigning 'Luxembourgness' and viewing it as a prime qualifier of identity is an anachronistic construct of later nationalistic historiography.[28] For example, before becoming Queen of France, Mary of Luxembourg was first engaged (aged four) to Ludwig (1297–1311), heir to the Duchy of Bavaria. Any preparations undertaken for this union were forsaken when Ludwig died, at which point she was sent to reside at Marienthal in the County of Luxembourg. In 1318, she and her sister were summoned to the monastery of Zbraslav outside Prague, so that the representatives of King Charles I

---

26 See Lermack, 'Fit for a Queen', ch. 3.
27 See Fössel, 'Die Heiratspolitik der Luxemburger'.
28 See, for example, Dušan Zupka, 'Medieval Dynasties in Medieval Studies: A Historiographic Contribution', *Forum Historiae* 13 (2019), 89–101, and with specific focus on Luxembourg, Pit Pérporté, *Constructing the Middle Ages: Historiography, Collective Memory and Nation-Building in Luxembourg* (Leiden, 2011); 'When "Jan Lucemburský" meets "Jean l'Aveugle": a comparison of King John of Bohemia's representation in the Czech lands and Luxembourg', *Husitský Tábor* 17 (2012), 29–49; 'Les débuts de la médiévistique au Luxembourg? L'oeuvre de Jean Schoetter (1823–1881) et la construction de la nation luxembourgeoise', in Isabelle Guyot-Bachy and Jean-Marie Moeglin (eds), *La naissance de la médiévistique: Les historiens et leurs sources en Europe au Moyen Âge (XIXe - début du XXe siècle)* (Geneva, 2015), 453–72; Jana Fantysová-Matějková, 'Der Pater Patriae und der Vater der luxemburgischen Geschichtsschreibung? Jean Bertholet über Johann von Luxemburg', in Lenka Bobková and Jan Zdichynec (eds), *Geschichte - Erinnerung - Selbstidentifikation, Die schriftliche Kultur in den Ländern der Böhmischen Krone im 14.-18. Jahrhundert* (Prague, 2012), 51–71, and the ample other studies referred to there.

of Hungary could choose one of them as their new queen.[29] Her younger sister having been chosen, Mary then remained in Prague. Cazelles asserts that following the rift between John of Luxembourg and Elizabeth of Bohemia in 1319, Mary was charged with taking care of her brother's children, although Peter of Zittau places her in Elizabeth's company for the years 1318–22, that is, until her short-lived marriage and queenship of France.[30] None of her pre-nuptial contexts necessitated engagement or association with local culture, or took heed of Mary's cultural preferences. While her familial background and dynastic position within the web of elite European aristocratic society marked her out as a potential queen, any previously learnt behaviours that came with her earlier experiences can be thought of as close to irrelevant to fulfilling her role, beyond the acquisition of cultural flexibility and the seemingly contradictory skills of dynastic representation and assimilation. The system was thus rather impersonal in terms of the positioning of the individuals within it, though character (together with health, ability, and chance) shaped their success or failure in inhabiting their allotted roles. The trumping of function over individuality seeped back into the personal and familial, as can be illustrated by the first will of Joan of Burgundy (1293–1349), Queen of France, dated 1329.[31] In it she bequeathed her coronation crown and best diadem to her daughter-in-law (that is, the future queen), whomever that was to end up being (her son, John, married Bonne of Luxembourg only in 1332). As the reuse of queens' coronation crowns was not common in France at this point, this act can be read as an attempt to transform a personal object to one of dynastic significance.[32]

---

29 See Cazelles, *Jean l'aveugle*, 106–10. For the context of the alliance with Charles I of Hungary, see Renáta Skorka, 'De Luxembourg à Oradea: Histoire de la reine Béatrice de Hongrie', *Mélanges de l'École française de Rome – Moyen Âge* 129:2 (2017), <http://journals.openedition.org/mefrm/3663>, accessed 16 March 2023.

30 For Mary's childcare responsibilities, see Cazelles, *Jean l'aveugle*, 74. For Peter of Zittau's text, see Josef Elmer (ed.), *Chronicon Aulæ Regiæ—Excerpta de Diversis Chronicis Additis Quibusdam Aulæ Regiæ Memorabilibus—Chronicon Francisci Pragensis—Chronicon Benessii de Weitmil*, Fontes Rerum Bohemicarum, vol. 4 (Prague, 1884), 261.

31 This Joan of Burgundy was the wife of King Philip VI of France, with the will written shortly after her coronation. She should not be confused with the Joan of Burgundy who was queen to Philip V, or with their daughter, Joan of France, Countess and Duchess of Burgundy, both of whom also figure in this essay. For their familial relationships, see the genealogies.

32 See Murielle Gaude-Ferragu, 'Les dernières volontés de la reine de France. Les deux testaments de Jeanne de Bourgogne, femme de Philippe VI de Valois (1329, 1336)', *Annuaire-Bulletin de la Société de l'histoire de France, 2007* (2007), 23–66, at 34–5. The uniqueness and specificity of crowning rituals were embedded into the identity of each medieval kingdom. Some, therefore, placed more emphasis

Naturally, this tendency affected actors throughout the social spectrum: the contrast between Machaut's single use of one word with Germanic origins and his repeated references to Central European occurrences has long been noted.[33] Linguistically and stylistically, he was unabashedly 'French'. Considering that his poetic career may well have begun outside France while on itinerant service to John of Luxembourg, should this be read as reflecting his personal prejudices, or those of his patron? A tolerant interpretation would see Machaut's output as a direct outcome of his courtly function, him being a French poet catering for the Francophone faction of his patron's court. After all, and regardless of his personal preferences, John of Luxembourg's feudal domains included a number of Francophone areas, and he held fiefs also from the counts of Hainaut and the King of France.[34] For example, in association with his marriage to Beatrice of Bourbon in 1334, John was given Mehun-sur-Yévre (in the environs of Bourges, now in the department Cher in central France) by Philip VI.[35]

---

on the queen's reuse of crowns than others. For an exploration of the concept of individuality in relation to the Middle Ages, see Franz-Josef Arlinghaus (ed.), *Forms of Individuality and Literacy in the Medieval and Early Modern Periods* (Turnhout, 2015).

33 See, for example, Earp, *Guide*, 12–14, or Uri Smilansky, 'Machaut and Prague: A Rare New Sighting?', *Early Music* 46 (2018), 211–23. A specific locus of interaction is considered in Albert Prioult, 'Un poète voyageur: Guillaume de Machaut et la "Reise" de Jean l'Aveugle, roi de Bohème, en 1328–1329', *Lettres Romanes* 4 (1950), 3–29. For the intersection between poetics and politics in Bohemian-French relations, see Martin Nejedlý, 'Deux poètes français du quatorzième siècle en Bohême. Rencontres et confrontations', *Prague Papers on the History of International Relations* 1 (1997), 30–53; 'La Bohême et ses habitants vus par quatre auteurs français du Moyen Age (Guillaume de Machaut, Eustache Deschamps, Jean Froissart, Jean d'Arras)', *Listy filologické / Folia philologica* 128 (2005), 21–34. See also the contributions by Claude Gauvard, Waldemar Voisé, Malgorzata Wozna, Vaclav Černy, Jitka Snízková and Ladislav Vachulka in Jacques Chailley, Paul Imbs and Daniel Poirion (eds), *Guillaume de Machaut, poète et compositeur: Colloque–table ronde organisé par l'Université de Reims (Reims, 19–22 avril 1978)* (Actes et colloques, 23) (Paris, 1982).

34 In this context, it should be remembered that (after Latin) French acted as an international *lingua franca*, and that the French monarchy enjoyed great transnational prestige at this time. John's behaviour, therefore, can be seen as cultivating ties with the most powerful kingdom around following his failure to secure the emperorship for himself, rather than as a petulant disinterest in Bohemian affairs. See also Karl Kügle's and Jana Fantysová Matějková's contributions to this book, as well as Uri Smilansky, 'The *Ars Subtilior* as an International Style', in Stefan Morent, Silke Leopold and Joachim Steinheuer (eds), *Europäische Musikkultur im Kontext des Konstanzer Konzils* (Memmingen, 2017), 225–49.

35 See Earp, 'Introduction', 33 and Margue and Schroeder, *Un itinéraire européen*, 69, 71, who contextualize the donation within the wider financial dealings between the two kings. The castle was confiscated from Robert III of Artois in 1332, and was

Indeed, as discussed in Jana Fantysová Matějková's contribution, Machaut seems likely to have been stationed primarily in John's western areas of influence, also looking after his interests there when the King of Bohemia was occupied elsewhere. A less kindly and perhaps more sensationalist view might interpret Machaut's output as the performance of difference from his patron's Bohemian environment, its language, and its culture, in support of a king often at loggerheads with his subjects, and who chose to spend much of his time outside his kingdom.[36] Either way, analysis of his actions, attitudes, and artistic output (or anyone else's, for that matter) has to be tempered with awareness of both the habits of his locus and the external expectations relating to his role, including the implied appropriateness of cultural engagement.

While such a view of poets' positions can be considered divisive, culture also offers a unique locus of performance in smoothing over the contradictions and transitions of role and geography. A luxury book, for example, performs beyond economic power, projecting also aesthetic, cultural, linguistic, intellectual, and genealogical authority through a combination of its materiality and binding, illumination, content, and use. Before delving into my case study, however, it is also worth noting that cultural influence often resulted from subtler relationships operating on a completely different level. For example, the French, royal 'Pucellian' school of manuscript illumination – upon which the naturalistic, 'Post-Pucellian' style of **RemC** and **G52** depends – is characterized by an integral Italianate influence.[37] This, however, has little to do with the biographical histories of any of the royal patrons who commissioned books from workshops

---

reintegrated into the royal holdings following John of Luxembourg's death. It later became part of the Duchy of Berry, created in 1360 for John of France (1340–1416), son of John II and Bonne. Thereafter, it soon became the site of a famous princely and royal residence. For that incarnation, see Harry Bober, 'André Beauneveu and Mehun-sur-Yèvre', *Speculum* 28:4 (1953), 741–53.

36 For John and Elizabeth's relationship, his inheritance and status as an absent ruler, see Michel Pauly (ed.), *Die Erbtochter, der fremde Fürst und das Land: Die Ehe Johanns des Blinden und Elisabeths von Böhmen in vergleichender europäischer Perspektive = L'héritière, le prince étranger et le pays: le mariage de Jean l'Aveugle et d'Elisabeth de Bohême dans une perspective comparative européenne* (Luxembourg, 2013). Perhaps as a middle way – and in my eyes less convincingly, considering the linguistic constellation of John's holdings – scholars have used this characterization of Machaut's output to support a distancing between the poet and John himself, and for Machaut's early affiliation with the French royal court. See, most recently, Earp, 'Introduction', 21.

37 On Pucelle, see Kathleen Morand, *Jean Pucelle* (Oxford, 1962); Kyunghee Pyun and Anna D. Russakoff (eds), *Jean Pucelle: Innovation and Collaboration in Manuscript Painting* (London, 2013). Leo, 'The Pucellian School and the Rise of Naturalism', is perhaps most relevant here.

promulgating this fashion.[38] It was these commissions that established the reputation of 'Pucellian' visual tropes, not their geographic, temporal, and political point of origin, or, for that matter, their actual artistic content.

BOOKS, POLITICS, IDENTIFYING PATRONAGE

All this leads us back to the careers and activities of Guillaume de Machaut and Jean de Vignay, their patrons, and their books. Both the *Remede* and the *Eschés* are likely the product of the early 1340s.[39] By this point, Vignay was well into his sixth decade, and having completed a number of large-scale royal commissions, was closely associated with the intellectual endeavours of Philip VI and his first wife, Joan of Burgundy. Reconstructing Machaut's whereabouts during this time has created more difficulties. Nevertheless, a growing body of opinion suggests his continued service to John of Luxembourg up to the latter's death in 1346, with a recent discovery of a subsequent direct employment

---

38 Such workshops served many members of the French royal family. Particularly important books are linked to Joan of Évreux, Joan of Burgundy, Charles IV, Philip VI, John II, and Bonne of Luxembourg.

39 In dating the *Eschés*, Knowles, 'Jean de Vignay', combines stylistic grounds and the dating of other translations to place it after 1335. Her association of the work with John II while still Duke of Normandy and his mother, Joan of Burgundy, provided a *terminus ante quem* of 1349 (Joan's death) for the commission, and 1350 (John's inheriting the crown) for its presentation. While some of these associations are challenged below, the dating of the work is not affected. An annotation to the manuscript Lunel, Bibliothèque municipale, MS 8 supplies the date 1340, though this source's own late date and general unreliability problematizes this (reasonable) assertion. For the *Remede*, see Yolanda Plumley, *The Art of Grafted Song: Citation and Allusion in the Age of Machaut* (Oxford, 2013), 197–318, where Plumley demonstrates that Machaut began writing ballades c. 1339, meaning the *Remede* (which contains two) could not have taken the form in which it came down to us before this point. The suggestion that the *Lyon* – intrinsically dated to 1342 – post-dates the *Remede* would give at least a tentative end-date for composition, although its reliance on manuscript order representing chronology and the treatment of certain poetic themes is problematic. See Wimsatt and Kibler, *Guillaume de Machaut*, 33–4. On the importance of copying practicalities on dating this source and its components, Smilansky, 'Creating MS C'. Fantysová Matějková's somewhat later chronology of Machaut's *dits* places the *Remede* between 1346 and 1349, chiming with Earp, 'Introduction', which revises his earlier view. However, as both rely to a large degree on the *dit*'s association with Bonne, their arguments are of lesser weight within my discussion. On the possibility of musical revision (now invisible) taking part before MS C was created, see Karen Desmond, 'Traces of Revision in Machaut's Motet *Bone Pastor*', in Lawrence Earp and Jared C. Hartt (eds), *Poetry, Art, and Music in Guillaume de Machaut's Earliest Manuscript (BnF fr. 1586)* (Turnhout, 2021), 397–432.

being dated 1349, that is, comfortably later than his association with John.[40] It is by now clear that he did not choose to reside in Reims immediately after obtaining his canonry there in 1338. Still, it is likely that at least the later services Machaut provided to John had to do with the latter's western interests and took place on both sides of the border between France and the Empire. These may have been undertaken within John's entourage during periods he spent in that area, or more independently when he was away, or where the services required were more ambassadorial in nature.[41] For example, while no direct evidence of this survives, it is possible that following the recall of John's eldest son, Charles of Luxembourg, from Paris in 1330 or in preparation for John's daughter Bonne's arrival there in 1332, Machaut was tasked with furthering Luxembourg interests at the French court.[42] Lawrence Earp (among others) relied on this evidential ambiguity to suggest a close association with Bonne during this period (and through her, also with her husband), relying mostly on literary conflations between her and

---

40 See Bowers, 'Guillaume de Machaut'; Leach, *Guillaume de Machaut*, 12–26; and Jana Fantysová Matějková's contribution to this volume. See, however, Earp, 'Introduction', which advocates a separation from John from as early as 1338. Wathey, 'Guillaume de Machaut', provides evidence of Machaut's direct employment between 1349 and 1353 at the service of Yolanda of Flanders (1326–95), Countess of Bar.

41 Some interesting parallels are offered by a courtier whom we now recognize as the owner of one of Machaut's 'collected works' manuscripts. Aubert de Puychalin's stated duties at the court of Aragon – associated with the representation of the interests of John of Berry (Jean de Berry, 1340–1416) and his nephew, Charles VI of France (1368–1422) – ranged from the safeguarding of financial interests, through the provision of military assistance, to ensuring that a royal relative was well treated (in this case, Yolanda of Flanders' granddaughter and the king's cousin, Yolanda of Bar = Violant de Bar, 1365–1431, following her widowhood in 1395). See Yolanda Plumley and Uri Smilansky, 'A Courtier's Quest for Cultural Capital: Notes on the Early Ownership of the Machaut Manuscripts F-G' (forthcoming). It is worth noting that the courtiers discussed there operated as practical enablers, not as part of the performance of staged diplomacy, where official emissaries from the highest echelons of the aristocracy were required. The latter were usually dispatched for formal ratification at the conclusion of a political process, not for open-ended, extended durations of representation or negotiation. Machaut, having no high aristocratic pedigree, could therefore suitably operate as a functional representative of John's interests on the ground.

42 John of Luxembourg spent nearly all of 1332 in France, allowing for a smooth hypothetical transition of Machaut's from service within John's itinerant retinue to more distant service within a defined geographical and cultural orbit. See Fantysová Matějková, *Wenceslas de Bohême*, 18–19, or Contamine, 'Politique, culture et sentiment', 349–52.

characters within Machaut's *dits* (including the *Remede*).[43] It is thus often taken for granted that following her father's death, she 'inherited' Machaut's services and became his next major patron.

Considering Bonne as Machaut's first port of call when searching for patronage in France may seem to us natural, indeed, rather tempting.[44] It would also be easy enough to imagine how Machaut's, Bonne's, and John of France's agendas – while operating on different social strata and independently from one another – could have converged around the object of a luxurious copy of the *Remede*. The performance of **RemC** is, after all, rather extreme. The *Remede*'s interpolation of multiple musical works proclaiming novelty and sophistication is matched in **RemC** with the use of exceptionally expensive materials and the highest quality illuminations, a number of which are over-sized. Indeed, Anne Stone recently proposed that the work was composed with the layout of this specific manuscript in mind.[45] Its contents offer a new 'art of love' and tuition in courtliness and etiquette.[46] Regardless of the level of actual interaction, such an object would have had great potential as a prop in the performance of cultural capital.[47] As we have seen, by the late 1330s and early 1340s, all three were

---

43 See, for example, Daniel Poirion, *Le poète et le prince: L'évolution du lyrisme courtois de Guillaume de Machaut à Charles d'Orléans* (Paris, 1965), 194, 201; Wimsatt and Kibler, *Guillaume de Machaut*, 33–6, 53; and Lawrence Earp, 'Genre in the Fourteenth-Century French Chanson: The Virelai and the Dance Song', *Musica Disciplina* 45 (1991), 123–41, and 'Introduction', which states explicitly (32) that 'what I seek, first, is grounds to positing a term of service to Bonne of Luxembourg.' In relation to the *Remede*, I hope to expand on the current analysis and revisit many of these associations and perceived dedicatory techniques in a monograph, *Cultural Performance and the* Remède de Fortune: *Events, Texts, Books* (forthcoming).
44 For my own recent succumbing to this temptation, see Smilansky, 'Creating MS C', 298–304.
45 See Stone, 'Made to Measure'.
46 See Douglas Kelly, *Machaut and the Medieval Apprenticeship Tradition: Truth, Fiction and Poetic Craft* (Cambridge, 2014), 23–7. For an interpretation centred on the art of memory, see Jody Enders, 'Music, Delivery, and the Rhetoric of Memory in Guillaume de Machaut's *Remède de Fortune*', *PMLA* 107:3 (1992), 450–64. For one providing an 'art of rhetoric', see Jordan Stokes, 'In Search of Machaut's Poietics: Music and Rhetoric in *Le Remede de Fortune*', *The Journal of Musicology* 31 (2014), 395–430. For its status as a psychological 'art of wellbeing', see Tamsyn Mahoney-Steel, 'From Socially Distant to Socially Engaged: Exploring the Soundscape and Material Environment of Guillaume de Machaut's *Remede de Fortune*', *Digital Philology* 10:1 (2021), 64–94. These interpretations are discussed, evaluated, and expanded in Smilansky, *Cultural Performance*.
47 Important here is the notion of a 'rhetoric of ornament', where the external ornamentation of a text – in this case, musically, visually, and materially – acts as both surrogate and guarantor of the authority of its content. See Margaret Goehring, 'Artifice and Ornament in the *Dit de lyon* Garden Miniature', in Lawrence Earp

well established in their respective positions: John, as the first natural heir to the French throne after the crises of the early fourteenth century; Bonne, as future queen and producer of the next generation of male heirs (having given birth to four sons between 1338 and 1342); and Machaut, as a well-respected and sought-after retainer, enjoying independent means through a service career at the court of Bonne's father.[48] Nevertheless, John of France – now in his late teens and early twenties and already having overcome a number of bouts of serious illness – had to contend with the constant tensions between the Tancarville and Harcourt factions within his personal holdings as Duke of Normandy and Count of Anjou and Maine, as well as with the first battles of the Hundred Years' War.[49] Like any heir-apparent, his courtly performance would have been measured against that of his father, as well as those of other ducal courts. As the intended second Valois king, he had an important role in establishing the new dynastic identity, balancing tradition and continuity with newness and uniqueness. His book-commissioning and acquisitions have long since been associated exactly with this kind of cultural positioning.[50] Bonne, of course, would have been integral to the dynastic performance. Beyond the bearing of sons, it would have been expected of her – and vital to her Valois family – to assimilate culturally, in terms of both linguistic and institutional environments. Neither her preparation nor her previous circumstances were conducive to this. We have already noted her predominantly Empire-oriented upbringing and periods of residency in convents. With John of France often absent and Bonne's near-constant state of pregnancy from 1336 onwards (including periods of confinement), she spent most of her time alongside other royal ladies at the court of her mother-in-law, Joan of

---

and Jared C. Hartt (eds), *Poetry, Art, and Music in Guillaume de Machaut's Earliest Manuscript (BnF fr. 1586)* (Turnhout, 2021), 217–37, esp. 221–6.

48 See overviews in Raymond Cazelles, 'Jean II le Bon: Quel homme? Quel roi?', *Revue historique* 251 (1974), 5–26; and Lermack, 'Fit for a Queen', ch. 3 and 6. For Machaut's reputation and the circulation of his works at the point of the creation of C, see Elizabeth Eva Leach, 'Machaut's First Single-Author Compilation', in Helen Deeming and Elizabeth Eva Leach (eds), *Manuscripts and Medieval Song: Inscription, Performance, Context* (Cambridge, 2015), 247–70, revised and updated in Lawrence Earp and Jared C. Hartt (eds), *Poetry, Art, and Music in Guillaume de Machaut's Earliest Manuscript (BnF fr. 1586)* (Turnhout, 2021), 59–91 (to which subsequent page numbers refer).

49 See François Neveux and Claire Ruelle, *La Normandie royale: des Capétiens aux Valois, XIIIe-XIVe siècle* (Rennes, 2005), 491–7; François Neveux, *La Normandie pendant la guerre de Cent ans (XIVe-XVe siècle)* (Rennes, 2008) ; and Françoise Autrand, *Charles V, le Sage* (Paris, 1994).

50 See, for example, Léopold Delisle, *Le Cabinet des Manuscrits de la bibliothèque Impériale* (Paris, 1868), 15–18.

Burgundy, either in Paris or Vincennes.[51] This context diminished (though not entirely) her opportunities for both independent courtly performance, and for being seen as acting in the traditional role as intercessor to her husband. Any external opportunities to assert dynastic and personal authority would have been attractive. Pressure was likely increased by her need to contend with the memories of her aunt Mary's and brother Charles' earlier residences at the royal court.[52] Regardless of their precise position, poets were always on the lookout for opportunities to project their credentials, especially when moving between courts and offering literary and musical novelties. It is even possible to read John and Bonne's patronage of Machaut as an intentional counterbalance to the association of other notable cultural figures (for example, Vignay, or Philippe de Vitry) with the courts of Charles IV and Philip VI: the up-and-coming generation asserting their identity, sophistication, and courtliness by promoting an independent source of cultural capital.[53]

Before succumbing to the allure of this image, however, it is worth noting that if such tenuous grounds suffice for suggesting a long-standing relationship, it is possible to propose many other patrons for both the *Remede* and **RemC**.[54] For example, Wimsatt and Kibler emphasize the mention of the Park of Hesdin in the *Remede* as the 'one undisguised – and very suggestive – proper name in the work', but discuss it only in relation to royal visits there, and not in relation to its actual owners at the time.[55] Joan of France (1308–47), Duchess of (French) Burgundy through marriage (which also made her sister-in-law to Philip VI's queen, Joan), but in her own right Countess of (Imperial) Burgundy and Artois, was the

---

51 See Lermack, 'Fit for a Queen', 44–56.
52 Mary was at the French court in 1322–4, Charles in 1323–30, with Bonne arriving in 1332. Margue and Schroeder, *Un itinéraire européen*, 71, however, claim Charles could still be considered a resident there when Bonne arrived.
53 Such a notion is weakened by evidence of John's later ties with Vitry, but could still have contributed to courtly optics in the 1330s and 1340s. See, most recently, Andrew Wathey, 'Philippe de Vitry, Bishop of Meaux', *Early Music History* 38 (2019), 215–68. For more details on Vitry's earlier career, see, for example, Andrew Wathey, 'The Marriage of Edward III and the Transmission of French Motets to England', *Journal of the American Musicological Society* 45 (1992), 1–29. Furthermore, there is much potential for anachronism in our privileging of novelty as an unquestionably positive signifier. For a reappraisal of the source of authority and relationship with the past in relation to the poetic *formes fixes*, see Yolanda Plumley, 'Guillaume de Machaut and the Advent of a New School of Lyric c.1350: The Prestige of the Past', in Lawrence Earp and Jared C. Hartt (eds), *Poetry, Art, and Music in Guillaume de Machaut's Earliest Manuscript (BnF fr. 1586)* (Turnhout, 2021), 315–40.
54 Especially if we accept the idea that the work was composed with this version in mind, as suggested in Stone, 'Made to Measure'.
55 Wimsatt and Kibler, *Guillaume de Machaut*, 35.

daughter of Philip V (c. 1293–1322) and (yet another) Joan of Burgundy and Artois (1292–1330).⁵⁶ She inherited Hesdin as a personal holding from her maternal grandmother, Mahaut of Artois (1268–1329), a famous cultural patron who greatly enhanced Hesdin's prestige.⁵⁷ Any visitor there between 1330 and 1347 would have known who the lady of the castle was, and reference to the County of Artois had particular political implications in this period: Philip VI assembled his army in Arras – including a contingent sent by John of Luxembourg – before embarking on his first military campaign as king in 1328. He also presided over the contested inheritance of the county between Mahaut and her nephew, Robert III of Artois (1287–1342; the dispute lasted some 30 years), which was seen by contemporaries to have eventually led to the outbreak of war with England.⁵⁸ Likewise, a number of the ensuing campaigns and battles took place in Artois and its immediate surroundings, involving Philip VI, John of Luxembourg, and Joan's husband, Odo IV, Duke of Burgundy (1295–

---

56   As the tags suggest, the neighbouring Duchy and County of Burgundy did not share feudal allegiance, the duchy being a fiefdom of the Kings of France and the county of the Holy Roman Empire. Joan of France's own daughter-in-law's second marriage was to John II of France following Bonne's death (1350). See genealogies. I consider these relationships and their implications for the *Remede* more fully in my forthcoming monograph.
57   Mahaut has already been a focus for scholarly interest since the nineteenth century. See Jules-Marie Richard, 'Une petite nièce de saint Louis: Mahaut, comtesse d'Artois et de Bourgogne (1302–1329)', *Étude sur la vie privée, les arts et l'industrie, en Artois et à Paris au commencement du XIVe siècle* (Paris, 1887); 'Les Livres de Mahaut, Comtesse d'Artois et de Bourgogne, 1302–1329', *Revue des questions historiques* 40 (1886), 135–41. See also Régine Page, 'The Patronage of Mahaut d'Artois and Three Fourteenth-Century Altarpieces', in Paul Binski and Elizabeth A. New (eds), *Patrons and Professionals in the Middle Ages: Proceedings of the 2010 Harlaxton Symposium* (Donington, 2012), 199–215; or Susan Groag Bell, 'Medieval Women Book Owners: Arbiters of Lay Piety and Ambassadors of Culture', *Signs* 7 (1982), 742–68. For Hesdin more specifically, see Anne Hagopian Van Buren, 'Reality and Literary Romance in the Park of Hesdin', in Elisabeth Blair Macdougall (ed.), *Medieval Gardens* (Washington, DC: Dumbarton Oaks Research Library and Collection, 1986), 115–34; Sharon Farmer, 'Aristocratic Power and the "Neutral" Landscape: The Garden Park at Hesdin, ca. 1291–1302', *Speculum* 88 (2013), 644–80; Elly R. Truitt, 'The Garden of Earthly Delights: Mahaut of Artois and the Automata at Hesdin', *Medieval Feminist Forum* 46 (2010), 74–9; *Medieval Robots: Mechanism, Magic, Nature, and Art* (Philadelphia, 2015), esp. 122–40; or more recently Goehring, 'Artifice and Ornament'.
58   See William H. TeBrake, *A Plague of Insurrection: Popular Politics and Peasant Revolt in Flanders, 1323–1328* (Philadelphia, 1993); and Dana L. Sample, 'Philip VI's Mortal Enemy: Robert of Artois and the Beginning of the Hundred Years War', in Andrew Villalon and Donald Kagay (eds), *The Hundred Years War (Part II): Different Vistas* (Leiden, 2008), 261–84.

1349, Queen Joan's brother).⁵⁹ It would perhaps have been more natural to associate a poem from this period set in this estate with its feudal lady, rather than with a visitor, however illustrious.

Even if a visiting royal dedicatee is preferred to the owner of Hesdin, other ladies with direct links to John of Luxembourg can be suggested. His second wife, Beatrice of Bourbon, left Prague for good some two weeks after her coronation on 18 May 1337, and spent the remaining 46 years of her life in Luxembourg and France.⁶⁰ A *dit* by her husband's retainer representing her as the figurehead of an ideal court would have been useful both as a gift within the royal couple, and for propaganda value towards outsiders. Alternatively, the reigning French monarchs, Philip VI and Joan, shared many contextual elements with the situation described above regarding their son John of France and his Luxembourg wife, Bonne. John of Luxembourg was on very good terms with Philip VI and his predecessor, Charles IV, and may well have spent more time in their company than in that of his own daughter.⁶¹ Also, Philip VI and Joan had already demonstrated interest in consuming and commissioning vernacular literature, while the younger John and Bonne were still an unknown cultural quantity.⁶² As a result, Machaut – as a member of John's inner retinue – may have had better access to the personnel and institutions of the French royal court than to those of the ducal court of Normandy. In this context, it is important to note that during periods of conflict, numerous separations could develop between the administrative running of feudal institutions, geography, and the physical body of their figureheads. For example, I have mentioned the regular residency of Bonne at her mother-in-law, Queen Joan's, court, resulting primarily from the political and military instability in the north of the Kingdom of France. Especially when John was also at the royal court, the administration of

---

59 For the early events and politics of the war, see Jonathan Sumption, *The Hundred Years War I: Trial by Battle* (London and New York, 1990). As a Peer of France and close ally of Philip VI and John II, Odo also took part in the 1328 campaign and was involved in the Artois dispute.
60 See Fantysová Matějková, *Wenceslas de Bohême*, 37.
61 See Margue and Schroeder, *Un itinéraire européen*, 62–86; summarized in Earp, *Guide*, 8–16 and more fully in Contamine, 'Politique, culture et sentiment'.
62 See Plumley, *The Art of Grafted Song*, part II, which discusses, for example, Watriquet de Couvin and Jehan de Le Mote. Vignay's commissions have already been mentioned. Lermack, 'Fit for a Queen', 224–30, traces a pattern from Joan of Burgundy to John II of France by which serious book collecting and commissioning only began after being crowned, and thus considers the preoccupation an element of royal duty. For the queen's books in particular, see Claudine A. Chavannes-Mazel, 'De boeken van Jeanne de Bourgogne, koningin van Frankrijk (r. 1328–1349)', in Robert W. Scheller (ed.), *Representatie: kunsthistorische bijdragen over vorst, staatsmacht en beeldende kunst* (Amsterdam, 2004), 84–110.

their Duchy of Normandy would have operated from beyond its borders. Furthermore, active campaigning would separate many courtly functions from its male ruler. In 1338, Philip VI officially invested Joan with all royal powers and responsibilities (other than waging war) during his frequent military absences.[63] At such times, the wider institutions of the royal court would have officially focused on her person, rather than his.

If Machaut wrote the *Remede* while still in the service of John of Luxembourg, its dedication likely represented his patron's interests first, and his own second. Indeed, a dedication of either *dit* or book may just as easily have been offered on the instruction of John as patron rather than on Machaut's own initiative. Such presentations could then be considered a tool in the patron's demonstration of 'soft power', akin to other forms of gift-giving.[64] Its target was as likely to be an external power capable of furthering John's cause as it was a relation already under his familial authority. Securing the allegiance of a queen holding temporal power may have been a more pressing need than supporting his daughter's position as expected spouse of the future monarch. From Machaut's point of view, continuing employment with John and income from multiple benefices divorces the act of dedication from a search for new patronage, or from an expectation that it would result in a long-term association. Furthermore, there is no compelling reason for the conflation between the *Remede*'s subject matter and the recipients of a book containing it. Why should a royal patron familiar with, even fond of, Hesdin not appreciate receiving a book purportedly about the place and its owner (especially if this is a close family member)?[65] Any reciprocating gesture from the recipient could just as well be directed solely towards John of Luxembourg rather

---

63 See André Poulet, 'Capetian Women and the Regency: The Genesis of a Vocation', in John Carmi Parsons (ed.), *Medieval Queenship* (London, 1998), 93–116 (esp. 112–13).

64 See Uri Smilansky, 'Texts on the Move: Book Presentations Between Social Networks, European Politics, and Literary Performance', in Karl Kügle (ed.), *The Networked Court: Transdisciplinary Perspectives on Late Medieval European Court Cultures* (forthcoming), especially the discussion of the social appropriateness of such gifts, suggesting that the use of the author (or some other book-practitioner) as an intermediary in the presentation was an essential part of the performance. See also Brigitte Buettner, 'Past Presents: New Year's Gifts at the Valois Courts, ca. 1400', *The Art Bulletin* 83 (2001), 598–625; Gadi Algazi, Valentin Groebner and Bernhard Jussen (eds), *Negotiating the Gift: Pre-Modern Figurations of Exchange* (Göttingen, 2003).

65 Another example within Machaut's output would be the *Prise d'Alexandre*, which chronicles Peter I (1328–69), King of Cyprus' crusading efforts. As it also describes Peter's assassination, it could not have been presented to (and was likely not even commissioned by) its subject.

than to Machaut as poet.[66] Of course, weighing the likelihood of these (and other) possibilities can in itself be problematic, as the evidence relied upon is often not only partial, but also unspecific.[67] Knowing authors' momentary locations or administrative contacts does not limit their wider, contemporaneous literary relevance, and fame as a literary patron does not in itself raise the likelihood that single works with no (or ambivalent) internal dedication should be associated with this or that patron.[68]

JOINT MATERIALITY? LINKING VIGNAY AND MACHAUT

In what follows, I continue this thought experiment only in the direction of Philip VI and Joan as potential alternative recipients of the *Remede*, as this is where the relationship between **RemC** and **G52** can make an interesting contribution, and where a change in our historical narrative may have the potential to affect the perception of the *Remede*'s 'Luxembourgness'. On the face of it, the coupling of the two texts contained in these sources seems to enhance the association with the younger Valois, as the prologue to Vignay's translation dedicates the work to John of France as Duke of Normandy. Thus, John's coronation in 1350 is often taken as the *terminus ante quem* for the *Eschés*.[69] However, not all is as it seems. The said prologue does not appear in **G52**. Instead, the text concludes with a unique epilogue which specifies Philip VI as its intended recipient.[70] This association does

---

66 It should be remembered here that not all presentations and dedications resulted in the acceptance of service and subsequent patronage. See, for example, Smilansky, 'Texts on the Move', which considers Froissart's use of both book-giving and literary reading to facilitate momentary access rather than ongoing employment or patronage.

67 For example, Wathey's recent discovery of the substantial patronage of both Guillaume and Jean de Machaut by Yolanda, Countess of Bar opens the possibility of earlier links with her as patron as well. See Wathey, 'Guillaume de Machaut'. The County of Bar straddled the border between France and the Holy Roman Empire just south of Luxembourg and, like it, was elevated to a duchy in the early 1350s. As a result, and especially during her widowhood 1344–53, Yolanda's position as an independent female figure of political authority with established, regular dealing with John of Luxembourg, Philip VI, and their heirs cannot be in doubt. See Michelle Bubenicek, *Quand les femmes gouvernent. Droit et Politique au XIVe siècle: Yolande de Flandre* (Paris, 2002).

68 See, in this regard, the temptations of a 'Great Court Theory', challenged in Andrew Tomasello, 'A Footnote on Aragonese Mass Manuscripts and the Decline of the Great Court Theory of Music History', *Musica Disciplina* 49 (1995), 95–119.

69 Some qualifiers to this are discussed below.

70 He is not described by name, but as the royal nephew of Philip the Fair, that is, Philip IV. The **G52** epilogue is transcribed in Iacobellis, "'Grant peine et grant

not require an adjustment of the dating of the work, but it brings the *Eschés* into line with all of Vignay's other known dedications, and makes sense of his most substantial divergence from the Latin original. At the beginning of the section dedicated to the queen, Vignay adds a set of historical anecdotes on the foundation and independence of the Kingdom of France, preparing it with a justification of male primogeniture.[71] As this was the basis for Philip VI's claim to the throne, such references would have been more urgent for the king than for his son.

G52 was late to resurface. It was purchased by William Simon Glazier in 1958, to later be loaned (1963), then gifted (1984), to the Pierpont Morgan Library. The lasting influence on Vignay scholarship of Knowles' work from the early 1950s resulted in the awareness of this source's unique textual features remaining minimal.[72] Their implications have not yet been fully considered. But what should we make of the *Eschés*' double dedication? We do possess evidence of the creation of multiple luxury manuscripts of single works within a similar temporal and geographic context.[73] Indeed, two copies of another of Vignay's translations, the *Miroir historial*, were apparently created (at least partially under his supervision) for and presented to both Joan of Burgundy and her son John of France around 1333.[74] The two sources even contain discrepancies in the text of their prologues. In that pair, however, it is John's copy that carries a textual association of the work with his mother, a specification that is missing

---

diligence'", 313, and is discussed in 132–4.

71 This section is discussed in Fuller, 'A Critical Edition', 78–81, as are other changes which support a political, pro-Valois interpretation. On Vignay's special treatment of the chapter on the queen and its association with Joan of Burgundy, see Knowles, 'The Life and Works', 30–1. This is strengthened by the dedication of **G52** to Joan's husband, a fact Knowles could not have known.

72 For example, it seems likely that the absence of **G52** from Fuller's 1974 edition was the outcome of her being unaware of its existence rather than a decision to ignore it. While discussing this source and quoting Iacobellis, Earp, 'Introduction', 25–7 does not refer to the epilogue or the specific dedication it contains. Stone, 'Made to Measure', 126–7 acknowledges this (fn 37), yet only after emphasizing the association of the translation with John. For similar historiographical influence on the reception of **C**, see Leach, 'Machaut's First', 59–62.

73 For a detailed case study, see Rouse and Rouse, *Manuscripts and their Makers*, ch. 7. The books discussed there, however, are not of new works, and the differences between them relate to presentation, not text. They do not include personal dedications, let alone conflicting ones.

74 See Claudine A. Chavannes-Mazel, 'Problems in Translation, Transcription and Iconography: The *Miroir historial*, Books 1–8', in Monique Paulmeir-Foucart, Serge Lusignan and Alain Nadeau (eds), *Vincent de Beauvais: intentions et receptions d'une œuvre encyclopédique au Moyen Âge* (Montreal, 1990), 345–74.

from her own.⁷⁵ Nevertheless, both contain frontispiece-illuminations that make Joan's role as the commissioner clear. While the books were dedicated to different patrons, the dedication of the translation itself did not change. It was clearly not a problem to present John of France with a new book of a new translation that was commissioned by and dedicated to his mother. Indeed, it is likely that she initiated both translation and gift as an educational coming-of-age present to her son. To this familial relationship should be added proximity, as the royal and ducal households mostly cohabitated at Vincennes.⁷⁶ In this context, it is easy to imagine how the presentation of duplicate books where each object was dedicated to a different generation of the family was considered unproblematic. Conversely, it problematizes any attempt at claiming that the contents of such duplicated items – that is, the texts themselves – were individually commissioned by two different patrons sharing the same space.⁷⁷ I am, therefore, not convinced by Iacobellis' suggestion that **G52** had a lost double which included the dedication to John of France, and on which all subsequent copies of the *Eschés* relied.⁷⁸ Such a textual difference, in the context of cohabitating father and son, would have to be considered a transparent fabrication on Vignay's part, instead of celebrating a joint cause or project shared by both generations. After all, Philip and John would have known who initiated the translation.

Rather, I contend that it would have been politically risky for Vignay to remove the dedication to Philip VI while the king was still alive. Thus, I consider the re-dedication to have occurred later, probably at a few years'

---

75   Perhaps establishing dynastic prestige and authority was more important for the non-commissioning younger generation. Joan, after all, knew about and expected the translation. For the dynastic parameter of book-collection and presentation, see Deborah McGrady, *The Writer's Gift or the Patron's Pleasure? The Literary Economy in Late Medieval France* (Toronto, 2019), ch. 1, and Joan A. Holladay, 'Fourteenth-Century French Queens as Collectors and Readers of Books: Jeanne d'Evreux and Her Contemporaries', *Journal of Medieval History* 32 (2006), 69–100. For a mirroring of unspecified dedications in the visual language of books, see John Lowden, 'The Royal / Imperial Book and the Image and Self-Image of the Medieval Ruler', in Anne J. Duggan (ed.), *Kings and Kingship in Medieval Europe* (London, 1993), 213–40. Here, Lowden understands the avoidance of portraiture as a suggestion of intimacy rather than distance.
76   For the joint residency, see, for example, Françoise Lehoux, *Jean de France, Duc de Berry: sa vie, son action politique (1340–1416)* (Paris, 1966–8), 7.
77   Conflicting simultaneous dedications seemed to have become more common only later in the century, a process in which Christine de Pizan apparently took an important lead. See J.C. Laidlaw, 'Christine de Pizan: A Publisher's Progress', *Modern Language Review* 82 (1987), 35–75.
78   Iacobellis, '"Grant peine et grant diligence"', 133.

remove and after Philip's death in August 1350.[79] At this point, it would have made little sense to reproduce the earlier dedication to Philip VI. This, along with the uniqueness of **G52**'s epilogue, suggests a copying date before John's coronation to be more likely.[80] In addition, Vignay's involvement in manuscript production would have offered flexibility and dexterity in revising works for new patrons. I therefore conclude that the original dedicatee and commissioner of the translation is more likely to have been Philip VI, not John of France. John only conferred the Duchy of Normandy on his son, Charles of France (1338–80, the future Charles V), in 1355, so referring to him as duke remained viable until that date.[81] As the mention of Normandy was important to Vignay in setting out his own Norman roots (and thus, his feudal affinity with John of France as patron), this could have been retrospectively engineered using a technique not dissimilar to that used by Machaut when dating his *dits* or dedicating the *Navarre*, and despite the availability of a higher, royal title.[82] Thus, the procedure makes sense even after John's ascent to the throne, and I can think of no reason why Vignay would have undertaken a re-dedication in the other direction, even without considering the relative dating of the *Eschés*' surviving sources. Vignay enjoyed established ties with Philip VI, and there is no reason to believe that the prologue would have offended the king, or that he would have resented receiving a copy of a work commissioned by and dedicated to his son and heir.

At this point it is important to assess the meaning we assign to the **RemC-G52** link. It is, of course, entirely possible that it is but an accidental by-product of a temporally close production history. The noticeable

---

79 On the practicalities and cultural context of presentation and re-presentation, see Smilansky, 'Texts on the Move'.
80 My implied earlier date for **G52**'s illumination chimes with the recent conclusions in Earp, 'Introduction', and Pyun, 'The Master of the *Remede de Fortune*', that **C** was likely mostly decorated already in the 1340s, as opposed to the suggestion in Avril, 'Un Chef-d'œuvre', 99, 114–18, that both these sources were illuminated between 1350 and 1356.
81 See Autrand, *Charles V*, 166–7. It should be remembered that Vignay's date of death is a conjecture based on the dedicatees of his translations and the dating of some of his manuscripts. We have no secure date for him later than 1333, although that marker is associated with a 'middle period' translation, which was followed by a number of others, including the *Eschés*. He may thus still have been active in the early 1350s. See Knowles, 'Jean de Vignay', 356.
82 See overviews in R. Barton Palmer (text ed. and trans.), with Domenic Leo (art ed.) and Uri Smilansky (music ed.), *The Debate Poems: Le Jugement dou Roy de Behaigne, Le Jugement dou Roy de Navarre, Le Lay de Plour*, in R. Barton Palmer and Yolanda Plumley (eds), *Guillaume de Machaut: The Complete Poetry & Music*, vol. 1 (Michigan, 2016). On the dating and re-dating of this work, see Bowers, 'Guillaume de Machaut', 10–13, and Lawrence Earp, *Introductory Study* in *Guillaume de Machaut, The Ferrell-Vogüé Machaut Manuscript* (Oxford, 2014), 35–7.

differences between **RemC** and the rest of its host manuscript, however, problematize this suggestion.[83] The thematic combination of the two works also makes sense, suggesting that their shared visuality, if not denoting actual joint presentation, was intended to link them in their owner-viewer's mind. Vignay's own contributions to the *Eschés* strengthen the moralistic qualities of his Latin original, emphasizing its essential quality as a 'mirror of princes' and weakening its already minimal usefulness as a playing manual.[84] The royal and regal game of chess becomes but a pretext for the provision of moral and behavioural advice appropriate to the social strata represented by each of the various playing pieces. As a result, just as the *Remede* teaches etiquette and courtliness, the *Eschés* teaches morals and government, with the two working in a complementary manner as a pair.[85] Stereotypically, the latter befitted the role of a male ruler, while the former that of his female consort.[86] The two manuscripts had, therefore, the potential for a double-presentation to a royal couple.[87]

83 Potential explanations for these differences range from an attempt to highlight this section of the manuscript as a commemoration to Bonne (subsequently undermined by the manuscript's final ordering), to a realization that maintaining such a high material standard for the whole collection would be unaffordable. None are externally substantiated. See overview in Smilansky, 'Creating MS C'.
84 See Fuller, 'A Critical Edition', 77–89.
85 At the very least, the emphasis on literary piety and improvement would have allowed the linking, and to portray **RemC** as more than indulgent secular entertainment. On the usefulness of this association for creating aristocratic appeal, see Hélène Haug, 'Fonctions et pratiques de la lecture à la fin du Moyen Âge. Approche sociolittéraire du discours sur la lecture en milieu curial d'après les sources narratives françaises et bourguignonnes (1360–1480)' (unpublished PhD dissertation, Université de Louvain, 2013) and summary in '*Ains les lisoie entre mes dens*. Figures d'auteurs-lecteurs (XIVᵉ-XVᵉ siècles): une réaction face au succès mitigé des *nouvelletez* littéraires en contexte curial?', *Fabula* (2014) <http://www.fabula.org/colloques/document2402.php> [accessed 16 March 2023]. See also Smilansky, *Cultural Performance*.
86 See, for example, Murielle Gaude-Ferragu (trans. Angela Krieger), *Queenship in Medieval France, 1300–1500* (London, 2016). In my forthcoming monograph, I hope to offer a more detailed discussion of these stereotypes as role-specific rather than necessarily person- or gender-specific; of the gendering and non-gendering of chess, courtliness, and governance treatises; and an exploration of the flexibility of gendered association with regards to both these works. For considerations of female political power and its associated stereotypes, opportunities, and dangers from a Luxembourg angle, see Julia Burkhardt's contribution to this volume. A relevant analysis of the French context is available in Poulet, 'Capetian Women and the Regency', and wider contextualizations in Heather J. Tanner (ed.), *Medieval Elite Women and the Exercise of Power, 1100–1400: Moving Beyond the Exceptionalist Debate* (London, 2019).
87 The gendering suggested here would not necessitate a separation into different audiences. After all, women often assumed governance responsibilities, making

This, however, requires an understanding of **RemC** as existing independently, before **C**, with the larger collection being constructed around **RemC** at its core. To date, commentators – myself included – have only used the links between **RemC** and **G52** to date manuscript **C** and bolster its association with both Parisian production and the patronage of John and Bonne. To my knowledge, none have yet to engage seriously with the separability of **RemC** from its host manuscript. For my part, I have previously argued that the copying of *dits* in **C** on independent gathering-structures was a practical solution for an author approaching the creation of his first 'collected works' manuscripts.[88] While that argument holds, it does not contradict (and I did not seriously entertain) the possibility that the differences between **RemC** and the rest of **C** arose from an independent early history. Doing so, however, has some considerable advantages. For example, seeing **RemC** as the first presentation copy of the newly composed *Remede* designed for independent circulation makes more sense of the unusual elements in its presentation and organization as discussed by Stone.[89] Indeed, we *must* assume this state of affairs if we want to treat the coupling of **RemC** and **G52** as going beyond their production history to also encompass their presentation.[90]

RemC's subsequent incorporation into the 'complete works' manuscript **C** can then be imagined as either a change of plan before a presentation occurred, or as a reciprocal gesture by the recipient following a successful presentation. For current purposes, the latter option offers more interesting narratives: viewing **RemC** as a post-1346 attempt at securing patronage, whereby Machaut was attempting to 'piggy-back' on Vignay's established connections at the royal court, would see such a reciprocation as directed towards Machaut as author. While tempting, this scenario implies that, for whatever reason, the completed manuscript **C** did not result in the

---

relevant advice particularly useful. Likewise, even didactic works specifically written for a queen could be more useful when listened to by the king and his advisors than by the dedicatee herself. For both these elements, see Rina Lahav, 'A Mirror of Queenship: The *Speculum dominarum* and the Demands of Justice', in Karen Green and Constant J. Mews (eds), *Virtue Ethics for Women, 1250–1500* (Dordrecht, Heidelberg, London and New York, 2011), 31–44; or Kathleen Ashley, 'The *Miroir des Bonnes Femmes*, Not for Women Only?', in Kathleen Ashley and Robert L.A. Clark (eds), *Medieval Conduct* (Minneapolis, 2001), 86–105.
88   Smilansky, 'Creating MS C', 273–8.
89   Stone, 'Made to Measure'. These relate to the matching of the work's interpolated music with the placement of over-sized illuminations in **RemC**, and to its wider gathering-structure. On the independent circulation of new *dits* before the collation of **C**, see Leach, 'Machaut's First', 59–62.
90   One can go so far as to suggest an original intention to bind **RemC** and **G52** together as one book, but I cannot offer any evidence for this, and the possibility does not affect the rest of my argument.

hoped-for royal patronage, with Machaut instead establishing an affiliation with the Duchess of Bar by mid 1349 at the latest (that is, before both Bonne's and Joan's deaths). Alternatively, viewing **RemC** as an offering from within John of Luxembourg's service allows its coupling with **G52** to become a political comment on the closeness of Valois-Luxembourg relations. The cultural reciprocation of turning it into a larger collection of text and music associated with Luxembourg patronage can then be seen as an homage directed towards the King of Bohemia (or his children, if undertaken in commemoration after John's death). Manuscript C becomes a physical manifestation of a much-valued political relationship and a focus of dynastic memory.[91] It need have little to do with personal patronage of the author or his future career prospects. Nevertheless, once the decision to transform the single-work book into a larger collection was made, it would have been only natural to return to that author for further materials, and to use the same workshop that made such a good job of **RemC** when commissioning the rest of the work, especially considering its existing links with royal patronage. Technically, there is little ground to rule out such a procedure.

We are thus placed at an interpretative crossroads. The privileging of the mentioning of Hesdin within the *Remede* can be taken literally as referring to the estate's owner (Joan of France), more loosely as referring to one of a number of royal visitors there, or as a geographical reference point which associated the story with the geopolitics of France's north-eastern border. Machaut's textual word play has often been interpreted (somewhat problematically in my opinion) to conflate the beloved lady of the *Remede* with Bonne of Luxembourg and, by implication, with Bonne as the intended recipient of the text.[92] Still, none of these readings necessarily anchors

---

91 For other cases of separation between textual content and books' usefulness as artefacts in social and political performance, see Smilansky, 'Texts on the Move'. Earp, 'Introduction', 26–8, recently hypothesized that **C** may have been a commission by Joan of Burgundy, intended for her daughter-in-law, Bonne, following a similar pattern of commissioning she applied in relation to her son.

92 Wimsatt and Kibler, *Guillaume de Machaut*, 34–5. Earp, 'Introduction', 22–4, strengthens the reliance on this word play by comparing it to the opening verses of the *Arbre d'amours*, dated internally to 23 April 1345. In that context, however, the word play appears as part of an opening exultation of a patron, and is made specifically in relation to a lady of that name who takes a position external to the narrative (and alongside the mentioning of other external figures, such as her father, John of Luxembourg). This is not the case in the *Remede*. Earp goes further and suggests that the date cited in the poem affects the likely time of Machaut's use of the pun (and by implication, delaying the composition date of the *Remede*). To my eyes, this pun is not subtle or unique enough to require a joint context or linear poetic inspiration. Even if this was the case, Machaut could well have had other sources for the pun. For example, Peter of Zittau's chronicle uses a Latin variant of

the recipient of **RemC** as the identified female protagonist of the story. An alternative privileging of visuality and materiality enables an original association between **RemC** and **G52**. While in itself precarious, such an association – combined with Vignay's biography and the new reading of the *Eschés*' dedication – suggests that the first recipient of this copy of the *Remede* may not have been Bonne, but her mother-in-law, Queen Joan. Yet, the two are not inherently contradictory. Just as we have seen Bonne's husband accepting a book containing a new work commissioned by and dedicated to his mother, why should we not accept Joan of Burgundy, reigning Queen of France, as the first recipient of a book containing a story relating to either her son's or her brother's wife? Indeed, if we consider the *dit* as representing John of Luxembourg's interests rather than Machaut's emotions and as didactic rather than (pseudo-auto-)biographical, it would not be a problem for the unnamed lady in the story to conflate elements of both these close relatives.

***

I wholeheartedly admit that the materials presented here fall far short of constituting proof. Nevertheless, I consider the ideas they contain worth entertaining for two primary reasons. First, they act as a reminder of how shaky the foundations are of nearly every interpretation we impose on our surviving evidence, as well as of the advantages and dangers of combining literary, material, and historical evidence. Second, the central role assigned to Machaut in the crystallization of Francophone poetic, narrative, musical, and notational practice means that any adjustment to the reconstruction of his biography, or to the patronage networks that supported and consumed his work, has considerable implications for our wider cultural-historical narratives. The emphasis given here to Philip VI and Joan of Burgundy as the major players in the Valois-Luxembourg cultural exchange (rather than it being symbolized by Bonne's marriage to their son) is a case in point. Perhaps due to a subconscious collective historiographical preference to characterize Machaut as the voice of a new, vernacular, younger art (one which links to both literary and musical production of the later fourteenth and fifteenth centuries), or due to a need to separate Machaut from the sphere of influence of his more established

---

the same pun when lamenting the death of Bonne's grandmother, Guta (Judith) of Habsburg (1271–97). See Jana Fantysová Matějková, 'Guillaume de Machaut und die Königsaaler Chronik', in Dana Dvořáčková-Malá and Kristýna Solomon (eds), *"Über den Hof und am Hofe": Geschichtsschreibung und Literatur* (Dresden, 2021), 147–62 (esp. 161). The gap between Machaut's use and Chaucer's adaptation of this technique some decades later (discussed in Wimsatt and Kibler, *Guillaume de Machaut*, 33–5) also warns against relying on such similarities for the purposes of dating.

and near contemporary, Philippe de Vitry, this royal generation has, until recently, been conspicuous mostly by its historiographical absence within Machaut scholarship.[93] Also in terms of book ownership and commissioning, while we know both Philip and Joan were active in this sphere, their efforts are usually consigned to a footnote in comparison with the activities of their grandson Charles V.[94] The gap in musical survival between the interpolated Fauvel manuscript (Paris, Bibliothèque nationale de France, f. fr. 146) and manuscript **C** has relegated the intervening years to vague obscurity, even when evidence of musical and poetic activities in this period abounds.[95] Only in the area of research into queenship and gender politics has Joan featured since early on in the discipline.[96] Despite

---

93 Earp, *Guide*, for example, mentions Philip VI a number of times, but for the purposes of historical background and for his early links with John of Luxembourg, Philippe de Vitry and Guillaume de Trie, not as a patron of literature and music. He does not appear in the index of Leach, *Guillaume de Machaut*, and neither mention Joan of Burgundy. As the footnotes here attest, the beginnings of a transition become evident in a number of contributions in Earp and Hartt, *Poetry, Art, and Music*, although as a whole, analyses remain very much Bonne-oriented.

94 This is a feature of, for example, Deborah McGrady, *The Writer's Gift*, where this royal couple's bookish activities are noted (twice), but only in passing. However, Rouse and Rouse, *Manuscripts and the Makers*, 194, counter the Charles V 'orthodoxy', exemplifying the existence of a royal book collection already in the late Capetian period. Lermack, 'Fit for a Queen', ch. 6, discusses early Valois book patronage as a self-aware and intentional continuation of earlier practices, and offers overviews of the habits of Philip VI, Joan of Burgundy, John II and Bonne of Luxembourg. See also Holladay, 'Fourteenth-Century French Queens'.

95 For the centrality of this Fauvel manuscript to modern musicological narratives, see Margaret Bent and Andrew Wathey (eds), *Fauvel Studies: Allegory, Chronicle, Music and Image in Paris, Bibliothèque Nationale MS Français 146* (Oxford, 1998); or Emma Dillon, *Medieval Music Making and the Roman de Fauvel* (Cambridge, 2002). For the notion of a 'lacuna' here, see Wulf Arlt, 'Machaut in Context', in Jacqueline Cerquiglini-Toulet and Nigel Wilkins (eds), *Guillaume de Machaut 1300–2000* (Paris, 2002), 99–114, or more recently Desmond, 'Traces of Revision'. A number of scholars have attempted to fill this musical gap; for example, Plumley, *The Art of Grafted Song* or Felix Diergarten, *Komponieren in den Zeiten Machauts: Die Liedsätze des Codex Ivrea* (Würzburg, 2021).

96 See, for example, Catharine Mary Charlton Bearne, *Lives and Times of the Early Valois Queens: Jeanne de Bourgogne, Blanche de Navarre, Jeanne d'Auvergne et de Boulogne* (London and New York, 1898). On Joan's negative image, see Aline Vallée-Karcher, 'Jeanne de Bourgogne, épouse de Philippe VI de Valois: une reine maudite?', *Bibliothèque de l'École des chartes* 138 (1980), 94–6. Especially when considering literary patronage, however, she is still often eclipsed by figures such as Joan of Evreux. See, for example, Holladay, 'Fourteenth-Century French Queens'. A more even-handed assessment of the literary patronage of the two queens as they relate to a single book can be found in Anna Russakoff, 'Portraiture, Politics, and Piety', *Studies in Iconography* 37 (2016), 146–80.

their known interest and patronage in the production and collection of vernacular works, minimal attention is paid to Philip VI and Joan. Instead, multiple attempts have been made to associate John and Bonne with such activities, even where a relative dearth of supporting materials necessitates increasing levels of creativity in interpretation. To me, this suggests a re-evaluation of royal patronage patterns in the 1330s and 1340s may be due, and that Machaut (and by extension, his patron, John of Luxembourg) may have paid more attention to the King and Queen of France than to the daughter of the King of Bohemia.

Although the linking of Joan of Burgundy and **RemC** (and by extension, with Machaut and the *Remede* text) is presented here as a thought experiment undertaken within an examination of Valois-Luxembourg cultural links, its acceptance or rejection would offer more than a biographical footnote. For example, this scenario suggests a greater cultural continuity in the first half of the fourteenth century than is currently allowed for, literary as well as musical. The appealing notion of a break – between this and the next generation of royal patrons and consumers; between Vitry and Machaut – has long seemed more illusory than actual.[97] The alternative would only tie strands together, joining 'older' patrons with 'newer' production as a counterbalance to current trends pushing chronologically later the dates at which 'new' practices have become established, and create a smoother, multilayered and mixed contour to mid-century cultural consumption and meaning.[98] This does, however, diminish somewhat the link between Machaut, the *Remede*, or at the very least **RemC**, and Bonne. Does this reduce Machaut's, the *dit*'s or the book's 'Luxembourgness'? Do Machaut's continued association with John of Luxembourg, the extensive cohabitation of Joan and Bonne at Vincennes, and Bonne's need to perform a French rather than a Luxembourgish or Bohemian identity suggest any Luxembourg

---

97 See, for example, Wathey, 'Philippe de Vitry', and the above discussion of royal living arrangements during this period.
98 For the notion of musical development and the dating of various elements within it, see Wulf Arlt, 'Aspekte der Chronologie und des Stilwandels im französischen Lied des 14. Jahrhunderts', *Basler Beiträge zur Musikgeschichte* 3 (1982), 193–280, with recent developments discussed in Karen Desmond, *Music and the Moderni, 1300–1350: The Ars nova in Theory and Practice* (Cambridge, 2018); 'Traces of Revision'; and Anna Zayaruznaya, 'Old, New, and Newer Still in Book 7 of the *Speculum musice*', *Journal of the American Musicological Society* 73 (2020), 95–148. An example of the still diverging opinions on this matter can be found in the neighbouring articles by Karen Desmond, '"One is the loneliest number…": The Semibreve Stands Alone', *Early Music* 46 (2018), 403–16; and David Catalunya, 'Insights into the Chronology and Reception of Philippe de Vitry's Ars Nova Theory: Revisiting the Mensural Treatise of Barcelona Cathedral', *Early Music* 46 (2018), 417–37.

associations not to have been affected by an alternative recipient for this book? Would an association with Joan reduce our notion of Bonne's independent cultural contribution to the Valois image? Perhaps. Would this impact on the Luxembourg contribution more widely? In my eyes, not necessarily. After all, Machaut's own Luxembourg affiliation can make a dedication or presentation to Joan be understood as an extension of his role as the King of Bohemia's representative, and so, as politically Luxembourgish as can be. It can, therefore, demonstrate the continuous strengthening of Luxembourg-French diplomatic and cultural ties at the highest levels. Similarly, would the new first dedication of the *Eschés* make it less relevant for Luxembourg cultural consumption despite its subsequent reworking for John of France as Duke of Normandy? Would the cultural performance of the coupled manuscripts **RemC** and **G52** be intrinsically different according to which choice we make? Would their joint performance have changed, were they to be inherited by any subsequent princely couple? Is it more important to discern which royal couple acted as patron here, or whether the similarities between the two sources were – or were perceived as – intentional rather than accidental?

I suggest that the overarching problem here is actually that of approach, that is, with our need to construct a narrative based on either geographic or dynastic focus. Our differing emotionality with regard to medieval attitudes to familial relationships (through blood or contract), and medievals' propensity to move around and adjust their behaviour to role and place, should act as warning signs in this endeavour. We have seen multiple examples of enmities ameliorated through marriage, or of education within one context in preparation for one cultural-political affiliation being seemingly cast aside with a change of circumstance as wedding plans are revised, appointments made, or inheritances received. Taking on the role of 'Queen of France-in-waiting' trumps personal, familial, geographic, and linguistic history. Still, it does not invalidate them, which is where cultural performance comes in. Books, with their intrinsic multilayered visual, material, textual, and linguistic performativity, can perhaps demonstrate both inclusion and difference more easily than other objects. As such, they can be used to smooth the process of transition. The resulting image requires us to concentrate on momentary influences, needs and choices – good and bad – of members of an exclusive yet dynamic and flexible elite. Rather than seeing the Valois, Luxembourgs, or indeed, Brabants, Bars, Burgundys, and many others as nuclear families in the modern sense, they can be seen as loose factions or groupings within a larger aristocratic clan, each focusing on the cultural, linguistic, and military needs and opportunities available within their shifting geographical network of influences.[99] Individuals' transitions between such factions can cause rupture and friction, bring them closer together, or remain invisible due to successful assimilation. Viewing the creation and consumption of cultural objects within this framework may help us to characterize their meaning as they change through time and movement, both as material artefacts, and as conveyers of textual and musical content.

While 'Luxembourgness' is offered as a porous entity operating within a network of shifting individual and collective agendas, it is clear that its relevance reverberated beyond the presence of family members or the borders of personal holdings. As a result, Luxembourg power and politics – both soft and hard – needs to be integrated also into what we may consider to be French or English culture, as do the influences of its other neighbours and interests, from its immediate borderlands, via the papacy, to Angevin territories around Europe.

---

99 For similar approaches, see, for example, Juan José Carreras and Bernardo García García (eds) (English version by Tess Knighton (ed.) and Yolanda Acker (trans.)), *The Royal Chapel in the Time of the Habsburgs: Music and Court Ceremony in Early Modern Europe* (Woodbridge, 2005), or more recently, Karl Kügle (ed.), *The Networked Court* (forthcoming).

CHAPTER 2

GUILLAUME DE MACHAUT AT THE COURT OF JOHN OF LUXEMBOURG: DEFINING A SOCIAL MILIEU[1]

JANA FANTYSOVÁ MATĚJKOVÁ

The life and works of Guillaume de Machaut, one of the most significant poet-composers of the fourteenth century, have been widely studied.[2] It is well known that Machaut started his career in the

---

1   The present study was written within the project 'John of Luxembourg and Bonne of Luxembourg as patrons of Guillaume de Machaut. Intention and reception of Machaut's work in the historical context', funded by GAČR under the No 19-07473S and realized at the Masaryk Institute and Archives of the Czech Academy of Sciences (CAS). It has been produced with the assistance of the database Czech Medieval Sources online (http://cms.flu.cas.cz/en/researchers/czech-medieval-sources-on-line.html), provided by the LINDAT/CLARIAH-CZ Research Infrastructure (https://lindat.cz), supported by the Ministry of Education, Youth, and Sports of the Czech Republic (project no. LM2018101). Last, but not least, many thanks to Karl Kügle and Uri Smilansky for their very helpful comments, which contributed significantly to the final form of this text.
2   For older literature, we will refer to Lawrence Earp, *Guillaume de Machaut: A Guide to Research* (New York and London, 1995); Elizabeth Eva Leach, *Guillaume de Machaut: Secretary, Poet, Musician* (Ithaca, NY and Leuven, 2011); for Machaut's works, we refer to the editions and translations of R. Barton Palmer et al. (eds), *Guillaume de Machaut: The Complete Poetry and Music*, vol. 1, The Debate Series

service of John the Blind, King of Bohemia and Count of Luxembourg (1296–1346). The aim of this article is to reconsider Machaut's biography from the perspective of the court of Luxembourg-Bohemia. The court is a complicated and changeable structure with the prince and his family members at its heart, their everyday needs being met by their respective households around whom further administrative, political, juridical, diplomatic, social, cultural, and other activities provided by the corresponding personnel were organized. Yet neither the court of John of Luxembourg nor his chancery (relevant to Machaut)[3] have ever been subject to such comprehensive research.[4] What we have is a general idea of how John's court looked, a few particular studies, and a set of questions to be raised with respect to Guillaume de Machaut. These are: For what purpose did John need someone like Machaut? What was the geographical area of Machaut's activities? What was Machaut's working environment like, and who were his colleagues? These are certainly questions that can be answered by the tools of traditional historical research, supplemented by comparative prosopography and comparative literary analysis. There can be no doubt that the historical, social, and cultural context of the court of Luxembourg-Bohemia is highly relevant to our understanding of Machaut's work and his own articulations in his *dits*.

This article is based on well-known sources, administrative as well as literary ones, that have been largely discussed with regard to Machaut's

---

and vol. 2, The Boethian Poems (Kalamazoo, 2016 and 2019); R. Barton Palmer (ed.), *Guillaume de Machaut: La Prise d'Alixandre (The Taking of Alexandria)* (New York, 2002); Ernst Hoepffner (ed.), *Œuvres de Guillaume de Machaut*, 3 vols (Paris, 1908–11).

3   For a recent summary see Dana Dvořáčková-Malá, 'Role kanceláře', in ead. (ed.), *Dvůr jako téma: Výzkum panovnické společnosti v českém středověku – historiografie, koncepty úvahy* (Prague, 2020), 123–31. About John's chancery and its personnel see Ferdinand Tadra, *Kanceláře a písaři v zemích českých za králů z rodu Lucemburského Jana, Karla IV, a Václava IV, 1310–1420: Příspěvek k diplomatice české* (Prague, 1892), 11/83–18/90 (the pages have two numbers); Peter Moraw, 'Über den Hof Johanns von Luxemburg und Böhmen', in Michel Pauly (ed.), *Johann der Blinde, Graf von Luxemburg und König von Böhmen 1296–1346* (Luxembourg, 1997), 93–120; and Nicolas van Werveke, *Étude sur les chartes luxembourgeoises du Moyen Age* (Luxembourg, 1889).

4   However, new research about the court and chancery of John of Luxembourg is currently in progress at the University of Luxembourg. It includes a conference volume entitled *Die Luxemburger: Dynastisches Programm und Herrschaftsbildung in globaler und lokaler Hinsicht / Les Luxembourg: projet dynastique et construction de la domination entre perspectives globales et locales. Tagungsband zur Tagung vom 28.-30. November 2018 an der Universität Luxemburg* (in preparation) and the edition and digitization of pertinent princely charters within the framework of the TRANSSCRIPT project (http://telma.irht.cnrs.fr/chartes/en/transscript/page/transscript-project, accessed 31 March 2023).

biography. Yet many of them have either not been fully exploited or not correctly understood, for they have not been placed in the full historical framework of the court of John of Luxembourg. In what follows, I conceive the historical context of these sources mainly in terms of the social milieu of John's court. In order to answer the above-mentioned questions, two hierarchic levels of this social structure will be examined, the second one depending on the first. The first level can be called the dynastic one. It is aligned with the marriage-related aspects of the politics of John, King of Bohemia and Count of Luxembourg, and comprises the network of John's relatives and their entourage at kindred Francophone courts of western Europe, especially in Paris, Hainaut and the Bourbonnais. The second level can be called administrative; it consists of the personnel of a court employed in order to realize the dynastic policy of the prince. In the present study, my interest in this milieu at John's court is limited to the aspects relevant to the life of Guillaume de Machaut.

SOURCES

Before delving into the socio-historical context, it seems useful to review the documentary sources that we have, and to revisit the most influential of Machaut's literary articulations about King John of Bohemia in the *Confort d'Ami* and in the *Prise d'Alixandre*.

The earliest and most informative archival sources connecting Guillaume de Machaut with the court of John the Blind are four papal bulls from the 1330s nominating Machaut to canonicates *sub expectatione prebendae* (further referred to as *s.e.p.*). In these bulls, Machaut is characterized as cleric, familiar, member of the household, almoner (1330), notary (1332, 1333) and secretary (1333, 1335) of the King of Bohemia,[5] and mentioned as a holder of the following benefices: a chaplaincy in Houdain (before 1330, to 1338), a canonicate *s.e.p.* in Verdun (1330–5), a canonicate *s.e.p.* in Arras (1332–5), and canonicates in Saint-Quentin (1335) and Reims (*s.e.p.* 1333–8), where he became beneficiary of a life-long prebend in 1338.[6] Other documents from this period show Machaut as a member of John's chancery, signing a deed of John's homage to the Count of Hainaut

---

5   Antoine Thomas, 'Extraits des archives du Vatican pour servir à l'histoire littéraire', *Romania* 10 (1881), 321–33, at 330–3: 'pro te, clerico, elemosinario et familiari suo domestico' (1330); 'pro te, domestico, familiari, notario suo' (1332); 'pro te familiari et domestico, notario suo secretario' (1333 and 1335).

6   Anne Walters Robertson, *Guillaume de Machaut and Reims: Context and Meaning in his Musical Works* (Cambridge, 2002); Roger Bowers, 'Guillaume de Machaut and His Canonry of Reims, 1338–1377', *Early Music History* 23 (2004), 1–48.

for La Roche and Durbuy (1 May 1334);[7] as a well-known person at the court of Hainaut, mentioned by his full name in the accounts and receiving a gilded cup as a gift (14 July 1341);[8] as a member of the King of Bohemia's retinue in Reims, testifying to John's homage to the abbot of St Rémy (30 May 1344);[9] as an executor of a canonicate *s.e.p.* at St Mary Magdalen in Verdun granted on 4 December 1345 to Johannes, son of Egidius, arbalester of Luxembourg, who was a cleric and secretary of the King of Bohemia by that time.[10] Sources from Reims show that on 28 January 1338 Guillaume de Machaut was too busy to be inducted into his canonicate in Reims in person[11] – perhaps John the Blind needed him in Paris or in Luxembourg[12] – and that he was present at the enthronement of Archbishop Jean de Vienne on 13 April 1340,[13] when John the Blind was in Paris.[14] Most likely, the poet-composer is also identical with 'G. de Machau', who – according to the accounts of the city of Reims going

---

7   Alphonse Verkooren (ed.), *Inventaire des chartes et cartulaires du Luxembourg*, t. II (Brussels, 1915), 160, no. 699.
8   Earp, *Guillaume de Machaut*, 14, 1.5.4a–b; Hendrik Gerard Hamaker, *De rekeningen der grafelijkheid van Holland onder het Henegouwsche huis*, t. III (Utrecht, 1878), 49.
9   Transcription by Bowers, 'Guillaume de Machaut', 9, n. 22: 'Roye de boheme [margin]. L'an mil CCC xliiij le iour de la trinitet. Reprist de monsigneur de S[aint] Remy de Reins nobles princes et puissans messires Johans roye de bohe[me] tout ce qu'il tenoit en foy et hommaige de l'eglise S[aint] Remy de Reins et en entra en la foy [et] en l'omage dou dit monsigneur l'abbe, present monsigneur Ernoul d'augimont, monsigneur Jeh[an] de Trugny, Guill[aum]e de machaut chenoine de Reins, Jeh[an] frere dou dit Guill[aum]e chenoine de Verdun, Gilequin de Rodem[ac], Jeh[an] dit des pres de landres, Pensart lauribi de montois, Pierre de saumaise' (Reims, Archives départementales de la Marne, MS 56 H 74, piece A, fol. 30v).
10 Earp, *Guillaume de Machaut*, 23, 1.7.1.b–c; Bowers, 'Guillaume de Machaut', 9 and n. 22; Leach, *Guillaume de Machaut*, 16–17.
11 Bowers, 'Guillaume de Machaut', 7, n. 9: 'Nunc Guillermus de Machaudio receptus fuit per procuratorem anno domini M' CCCo tricesimo septimo feria quarta post conversum sancti pauli' (Reims, Archives départementales de la Marne, 2 G 1650, fol. 54v).
12 For the most recent itinerary of John of Luxembourg see Zdeněk Žalud, 'Česká šlechta na dvoře Jana Lucemburského' (PhD thesis, Charles University Prague, 2007), https://is.cuni.cz/webapps/zzp/detail/24435/ (accessed 31 March 2023), 135–47 and 196–203, at 198.
13 Bowers, 'Guillaume de Machaut', 8 (quoting Reims, Archives départementales de la Marne, MS 2 G 323, piece 13). See also Earp, *Guillaume de Machaut*, 19–20, 1.6.1.g–1.6.1.h, and Leach, *Guillaume de Machaut*, 28–9.
14 For John the Blind in Paris and Vincennes in March-April 1340 (together with Charles) see Josef Emler (ed.), *Regesta diplomatica nec non epistolaria Bohemiae et Moraviae*, t. III–IV (Prague, 1890–2; further quoted as *RBM*) t. IV, 304–6, nos 766, 769, 772, 775.

from 1 March 1340 to 21 February 1341 – sold a packhorse to Hue le Large, alderman of Reims.[15]

The administrative documentation can be complemented by Machaut's literary testimonies, yet not without caution and a critical approach. Treating these sources as purely literary and therefore unreliable would not seem entirely appropriate. Machaut's works – or at least selected verses in them – do at times demonstrably display important historical references. 'In most of his narrative poems, the persona performs a function within the fictional event that is somewhat analogous to the poet's functioning in his historical situation', in the words of R.B. Palmer.[16] Also, Machaut's *dits* often refer to real time and space. Such references are worth examining, even though they are not entirely specific. Last, but not least, Machaut gives two versified, historical accounts of his service to King John in his *Confort d'Ami* (1357) and the *Prise d'Alixandre* (c. 1370). John's exemplary portrait in the *Confort* (henceforth: *CA*), especially the part recounting historical events (*CA*, vv. 2989–3079), was usually understood as resulting from Machaut's personal experience. For this reason, it was used to complete Machaut's biography. Nevertheless, a close comparison with the *Chronicon Aulae regiae* compiled at the Cistercian monastery of Zbraslav (Latin: Aula regia; German: Königsaal), nowadays ordinarily called the *Zbraslav Chronicle* and further referred to in this study as *ZC*, by Otto of Thuringia (d. 1314) and Peter of Zittau (d. 1339),[17] suggests that John's exemplary portrait seems to a significant extent to depend on Peter's chapters dealing with John of Luxembourg.[18] Although Machaut tends to complete Peter of Zittau's historiographical base line with his own information, he sticks to the chronicle in a relatively rigorous way, so that it is possible to establish a concordance between both sources.[19] A comparative reading of both texts allows us to hypothesize Machaut's horizon of knowledge, his grasp of the facts, and the way he reconceptualizes John's image provided by the chronicle in terms of chivalric virtues. As I shall argue, there is therefore no reason to posit Machaut's direct, personal involvement in the reported

---

15   Pierre Varin (ed.), *Archives administratives de la ville de Reims*, II/2 (Paris, 1843), 831–3.
16   R. Barton Palmer, 'Introduction', in R.B. Palmer (ed. and trans.), *The Judgement of the King of Bohemia* (New York and London, 1984), xiii–xlix, at xxv.
17   'Petra Žitavského Kronika zbraslavská', in Josef Emler (ed.), *Fontes rerum Bohemicarum*, t. IV (Prague, 1884), 2–337, further referred to as *ZC*.
18   This is discussed in detail in Jana Fantysová Matějková, 'Guillaume de Machaut und die Königsaaler Chronik', in Dana Dvořáčková-Malá and Kristýna Solomon (eds), *'Über den Hof und am Hofe': Geschichtsschreibung und Literatur* (Dresden, 2021), 147–62.
19   The story of John's acquisition of the throne of Bohemia starts in Book I, ch. I/108–10 of the *ZC*.

exploits of the King of Bohemia beyond his explicit testimony, which I suggest we accept as believable.

To what events does Machaut claim to testify as an eye witness? In the *CA*, the poet asserts that the King of Bohemia either nourished him or brought him up (*CA*, v. 2936); that John was very generous with material resources (vv. 2930–50) and that he entrusted him with the distribution of soldiers' pay, a task that Machaut carried out more than 50 times (vv. 2945–6); that he was at Křivoklát Castle,[20] where it is cold even in the summer (vv. 3013–16); that he saw 13 dukes of Silesia render homage to John of Bohemia, when the latter acquired Wrocław (German: Breslau) from Duke Boleslas (vv. 3023–7) on 9 May 1329; and that he participated in the crusade in Prussia and Lithuania (vv. 3049–50) in 1328–9.[21]

Thus, Machaut explicitly claims to have been physically present only at a selection of the events he discusses in his account of John's accomplishments; and as a cleric of John's court, he was no doubt familiar with information circulating in this milieu and with the basic facts of John's rule and biography. This can be illustrated by his verses about John's acquisitions of the Duchy of Wrocław and the allegiances of the dukes of Silesia:

De la s´en ala en **Pouleinne**,	Thence he proceeded to Poland,
Et la conquist a moult grant peinne.	After much struggle conquering it.
Aussi **conquist il Breselau**,	He also won Breslau,
Qui estoit le duc Boselau,	Which belonged to Duke Boleslas,
Et .xiij. dus qui tout hommage	And thirteen dukes there gave him
Le firent par son vasselage.	Their complete loyalty because of his valor.
Je le vi, pour ce le tesmong,	I saw this, and so I bear witness,
Car partout en seray tesmong.	And everywhere I'll attest to it.
Bien .x. ans roys s'en appela.	More than ten years he called himself its king.
Et puis il s'en ala de la	And afterward he went
Droit en roiaume de Cracoe	Straight to the kingdom of Krakow
Et par les glaces en Letoe.	And across the ice into Lithuania.[22]

The first three verses of this sequence (*CA*, vv. 3021–3) refer to Peter of Zittau's chapter II/19, in which the *ZC* chronicler reports on the events of 1327, i.e., John's expedition against the King of Poland, which gained

---

20 Křivoklát (central Bohemia), Pürglitz or Bürglitz in German, *Bruguelis* in Machaut's verse, is the castle where Henry of Habsburg (1299–1327), John's prisoner after the Battle of Mühldorf (1322), was kept more than one year.
21 *CA*, in Palmer et al. (eds), *Guillaume de Machaut*, vol. 2, 468–73. The scholarly consensus on Machaut's report on the crusade is that it is genuine. See Werner Paravicini, *Adlig leben im 14. Jahrhundert: Weshalb sie fuhren* (= *Die Preußenreisen des europäischen Adels*, t. 3), (Göttingen, 2020), 65–6.
22 *CA*, vv. 3021–32, trans. R.B. Palmer in Palmer et al. (eds), *Guillaume de Machaut*, vol. 2, 470–3. All quotations from *CA* follow Palmer's edition and spelling.

him favour and the homages of the dukes of Upper Silesia, called dukes of Poland ('duces Polonie'), and John's acquisition of hereditary rights to the Duchy of Wrocław from Duke Henry of Wrocław, brother of Boleslav of Legnica and Brzeg (*CA*, v. 3021–32):

Tempore isto, quo rex Johannes moratus est in regno Boemie, venit ad ipsum **Henricus VI, dux Silesie, dominus civitatis Wratizlauie, habuitque cum rege tractatum de ducatus sui resignacione.**	At this time, when King John was staying in the Kingdom of Bohemia, **Henry VI, Duke of Silesia, Lord of the city of Wrocław**, came to him **and conducted negotiations with the King about his stepping down from the Duchy.**
Eodem tempore **multi duces Polonie** ad Johannem, regem Boemie, **visitantem eorum terminos venerunt eique fidem et dexteram sub forma homagii ultronei prebuerunt.** Erat enim tunc rex sub tali intencione, quod **Cracouiam cum regno Polonie** sibi ablatam cuperet in manu valida recuperare. **Incipiebant namque iam premissi exercitus ipsam Cracouiam civitatem hostiliter impugnare.**	At that same time, **many dukes of Poland** came to John, King of Bohemia, who was visiting their lands, and voluntarily swore him fidelity and gave him their right hand in the form of homage. Indeed, the King's intention at the time was to regain by force **Krakow together with the kingdom of Poland** which had been taken away from him. For the troops he sent in advance had already started to attack the city of Krakow with hostile intention.[23]

Strikingly, Machaut asserts that John of Luxembourg conquered Poland, which the king did not. Quite the contrary, not only was his expedition against Ladislas the Short (1327) unsuccessful, he even conceded the title of King of Poland and the corresponding rights to the Kingdom of Poland, which he had inherited from the Přemyslids, to Casimir III the Great (1335). This was sharply criticized by Peter of Zittau in chapter III/11 ('*Qualiter Johannes, rex Boemie, alienavit regnum Polonie*'). Machaut's idea of John's conquest of Poland probably stems from John's chancery, which consistently titled the King of Poland as 'King of Krakow'. Therefore, the kingdom ruled by Ladislas the Short and Casimir III was 'roiaume de Cracoe' (*CA*, v. 3031) and not Kingdom of Poland. This allows Machaut to create a flattering story about John's policy towards Poland and to dissipate Peter's criticism. However, his mention of John's acquisition of Poland can refer only to the fact that John of Luxembourg became overlord of the dukes of Upper Silesia (*duces Poloniae*) in 1327 (and possibly also of Lower Silesia, which was seen as a part of the Kingdom of Poland too).

---

23 *ZC*, II/19, 285. All translations from *ZC* are by this author.

Furthermore, in Machaut's verses, the acquisition of Wrocław by John of Luxembourg that took place in 1327 is then conflated with a second, related event that the poet saw as an eye witness on 9 May 1329 in Wrocław on the way back from Prussia. During a public ceremony in front of the cathedral of St John the Baptist, John of Luxembourg received a 'second wave' of oaths of allegiance mostly from the dukes of Lower Silesia, including Boleslav, Duke of Legnica and Brzeg, the brother of Henry VII of Wrocław.[24] At that time, Boleslav also renounced his possible hereditary rights to Wrocław, which is explicitly mentioned by Machaut (*CA*, vv. 3024–8):

Qui estoit le duc Boselau,	Which belonged to Duke Boleslas,
Et .xiij. dus qui tout hommage	And thirteen dukes there gave him
Le firent par son vasselage.	Their complete loyalty because of his valor.
Je le vi, pour ce le tesmong.	I saw this, and so I bear witness.[25]

This is not explicitly specified by Peter of Zittau, who merely says:

Eodem anno [1329] mense Mayo **Boleslaus, dux Slesie, dominus Brigensis civitatem Lignicz** cum suis pertinenciis, quam a fratre suo Wladizlao clerico vi abstulit et sue dicioni subdidit, a Johanne, rege Boemie et Polonie, iure feodali quasi coactus suscipit et ad eius obsequia perpetuo cum suis heredibus se astringit. **Duces quoque Polonie et Slesie, quorum numerum nunc nescio pre multitudine**, fere omnes eodem tempore eiusdem regis serviciis se mancipant, fidem prestant.	In the same year [1329], in the month of May, **Boleslav, Duke of Silesia and Lord of Brzeg,** was forced by the King of Bohemia and of Poland to subject **the city of Legnica** with its dependencies – which he had forcibly taken away from his brother Wladislaw who was a cleric, and subjected to his rule – to accept [Legnica] in accordance with feudal law [from John as overlord] and to pledge him [the King] perpetual obedience in his name and in the name of his heirs. Also, nearly all **the Dukes of Poland and of Silesia – the present number of whom I do not know, for they are too many** – bound themselves to the service of the above-mentioned King and swore him fidelity.[26]

Machaut's account here is therefore more precise, supporting his claims to have been an eye witness to this event, whereas Peter of Zittau's words make it evident that, clearly, he was not.

---

24 See Lenka Bobková, *Jan Lucemburský, otec slavného syna* (Prague, 2018), 308–11.
25 *CA*, vv. 3021–32, trans. R.B. Palmer in Palmer et al. (eds), *Guillaume de Machaut*, vol. 2, 470–3.
26 *ZC*, II/22, 300.

Finally, the poet adds a summary of what he knew about the matter: Henry VI of Wrocław died on 24 November 1335 and John of Luxembourg inherited the Duchy of Wrocław as a direct fief of Bohemia, which means that he ruled over Wrocław as King of Bohemia from the end of 1335 up to his death in August 1346, i.e., for ten years ('Bien dis ans roys s'en appella', *CA*, v. 3029). This verse in turn seems to be based on indirect knowledge. Machaut merely gives the length of the period between the acquisition of Wrocław and John's death; meanwhile, the narration of Peter of Zittau describes the specific circumstances and emphasizes the role of Charles of Luxembourg:

Eodem anno [1335] in die beate Katherine absque heredibus obiit Henricus, dux Slesie, dominus Wratislauiensis. Quo mortuo mox Johannes, rex Boemie, Karolum, filium suum, misit, qui se patris nomine de civitate Wratislauiensi et de aliis cunctis ad ducatum eundem pertinentibus sine contradiccione qualibet intromisit; sic enim dux Heinricus idem disposuerat adhuc vivus.	In the same year [1335], on Saint Catherine's day, Henry, Duke of Silesia, Lord of Wrocław, died without heirs. Immediately after his death, John, King of Bohemia, sent his son Charles, who took possession in the name of his father of the city of Wrocław and of all other dependencies of the Duchy without any opposition; for so it had been arranged by Duke Henry when he was alive.[27]

This amalgam of what was experienced directly and what was known by Machaut from secondary sources about John's acquisition of the Silesian duchies is followed in the *CA* by verses about the crusade to Prussia and Lithuania, which in turn are described in chapters II/20 and II/21 of the *ZC*. Interestingly, Machaut prioritized the succession of Zittau's chapters over his own experience and placed the second series of homages (1329) in Wrocław, which Peter of Zittau does not even mention, before the crusade, contrary to historical reality and his personal experience (see Table 2.1).

The comparison with the *Zbraslav Chronicle* also allows us to identify to a fuller extent the localities of John's exploits, some of which have been already suggested by other scholars:

---

27 *ZC*, III/10, 330. The spelling difference Henricus-Heinricus follows the quoted edition.

Table 2.1. The policy of John the Blind towards Poland and Silesia. Comparison between Machaut's *CA* and the *ZC* by Peter of Zittau.

Vv. 3021-22 De la s'en ala en **Pouleinne** / Et la conquist a moult grant peinne [*sic*].	II/19: 1327 Eodem tempore **multi duces Polonie** ad Johannem, regem Boemie, **visitantem eorum terminos venerunt eique fidem et dexteram sub forma homagii ultronei prebuerunt.** Erat enim tunc rex sub tali intencione, quod Cracouiam cum **regno Polonie** sibi ablatam cuperet in manu valida recuperare. **Incipiebant namque iam premissi exercitus ipsam Cracouiam civitatem hostiliter impugnare.**
V. 3023: Aussi **conquist il Breselau**	II/19, 1327: Tempore isto, quo rex Johannes moratus est in regno Boemie, venit ad ipsum **Henricus VI, dux Slesie, dominus civitatis Wratizlauie, habuitque cum rege tractatum de ducatus sui resignacione.** Huic rex provinciam Glacensem ad tempora vite ducis possidendam pro ducatu assignat, sibique deputat mille marcas argenti annis singulis a fisco regio, quoad vixerit percipiendas. Igitur in die beati Ambrosii episcopi rex cum duce Wratizlauiam pervenit et se de civitate et omni ducis dominio accedente plurium consilio iure perpetuo intromisit, ita sane, quod dux ducatum suum regis nomine ad vitam suam debeat possidere. Herede quidem masculino tunc dux caruit, filias tantum habuit, plus **quoque regi de ducatu quam Bolezlao proprio fratri suo favit.** Querebat enim idem Bolezlaus dux de Brega omni tempore, qualiter Henricum dictum fratrem suum eiceret de suo dominio vi vel fraude.
Vv. 3024-28: Qui estoit le duc Boselau, Et treize dus qui tout hommage / Li firent, par son vasselage. *Je le vi, pour ce le tesmong. Car partout en seray tesmong.*	II/22, 1329: Eodem anno mense Mayo **Boleslaus, dux Slesie, dominus Brigensis civitatem Lignicz** cum suis pertinenciis, quam a fratre suo Wladizlao clerico vi abstulit et sue dicioni subdidit, a Johanne, rege Boemie et Polonie, iure feodali quasi coactus suscipit et ad eius obsequia perpetuo cum suis heredibus se astringit. **Duces quoque Polonie et Slesie, quorum numerum nunc nescio pre multitudine,** fere omnes eodem tempore eiusdem regis rerviciis se mancipant, fidem prestant.
V. 3029: Bien dis ans roys s'en appella.	III/10, 1335: Eodem anno in die beate Katherine absque heredibus obiit Henricus, dux Slesie, dominus Wratislauiensis. Quo mortuo mox Johannes, rex Boemie, Karolum, filium suum, misit, qui se patris nomine de civitate Wratislauiensi et de aliis cunctis ad ducatum eundem pertinentibus sine contradiccione qualibet intromisit; sic enim dux Heinricus idem disposuerat adhuc vivus.

CA, vv. 3061-4

Que fist il devant Basenouve,	What did he accomplish before Poznań,
A Senouain et a Lendouve,	At Znojmo and at Landau,
Et devant La ou fu li Hongres	And before Laa where the Hungarians
A .c. mille hommes (c'est li nombres)?	Were a hundred thousand men (that's the figure)?[28]

These lines refer to the siege of Poznań (German: Posen) in October 1331 (*ZC*, II/28); the military conflict at the Austro-Moravian border next to Znojmo (Latin: Snoma, Znoyma; German: Znaim) in November 1328 (*ZC*, II/20); the expedition against the Emperor Louis of Bavaria and the Duke of Austria, including the confrontation near Landau an der Isar in 1336 (*ZC*, III/13); and the military campaign in Laa an der Thaya (Lower Austria) in 1331 (*ZC*, II/28). Interestingly, the siege of Poznań and the campaign next to Laa are reported in two letters written by 'Henricus incliti domini Johannis, regis Boemie, notarius', one of Machaut's colleagues in John's chancery.[29] His letters dated 27 October 1331 in Brno and 26 November 1331 in Laa were integrated by Peter into chapter II/28 'Epistola de processibus et successibus regis Johannis'.[30] The letter from Laa enumerates all the soldiers of all the armies of Bohemia, Austria and Hungary, the total number of which was reaching the 100,000 evoked by Machaut: There were 50,000 Hungarians (3500 helmets), 21,800 Austrians (1800 helmets), and the army of Bohemia amounted to 20,000 soldiers and 1500 heavy-armoured warriors (*viri galeati*).

The influence of the *ZC* on Machaut's portrait of John of Luxembourg is not limited to the historical parts of the portrait. Peter of Zittau was a poet too, and his chronicle contains some 4000 verses that comment on the events described in prose. One of his verse sequences is similar to Machaut's opening of the portrait of John the Blind (*CA*, v. 2923-9):

---

28 The translation by R.B. Palmer in Palmer et al. (eds), *Guillaume de Machaut*, vol. 2, 472-3, is emended with the geographical names researched by Henri Grappin, 'IV. Basenuove = Poznań', *Revue des études slaves* 14 (1934), 81-2; Václav Černý, *Staročeská milostná lyrika a další studie ze staré české literatury* (Prague, 1948; reprint: 1999), 194 for Landau; and by Fantysová Matějková, 'Guillaume de Machaut', 156 for Znojmo (Znaim).
29 Ferdinand Tadra (*Kanceláře*, 15/87, no. 11) and Peter Moraw ('Über den Hof', 93-120 at 118, nos III/7, 9) suggest identifying him with Heinrich Schatz of Nuremberg, cleric of the diocese of Bamberg: Heinrich Schatz of Nuremberg is called *clericus* and *notarius* of the king in the supplication of John of Luxembourg from 24 July 1330; see Zdeňka Hledíková (ed.), *Monumenta Vaticana res gestas Bohemicas illustrantia. Tomus prodromus: Acta Clementis V. Johannis XXII. et Benedicti XII. 1305-1342* (further quoted as *MVB TP*) (Prague, 2003), 481, no. 877.
30 *ZC*, II/28, 309-11 and 314-15.

Pren garde au bon roy de Behaingne,	Take as your model the good king of Bohemia,
Qui en **France** et en **Alemaingne**,	Who in France and Germany,
En Savoie et en Lombardie,	In Savoy and Lombardy,
En Dannemarche et en Hongrie,	In Denmark and Hungary,
En Pouleinne, en Russe, en Cracoe,	In Poland, Russia, Krakow
En Masouve, en Prusse, en Letoe	In Masovia, Prussia, and Lithuania
A la pris et honneur conquerre.	Did venture to win glory and honor.[31]

Peter of Zittau invites his public to observe John's military deeds in a less enthusiastic way:

Hunc peto cerne virum, qui perpetrat undique mirum.	Please, see this man, who carries out amazing deeds everywhere.
Hic nisi bellare solet et pugnis inhiare, Qui quasi torpescit, a bellis cum requiescit.	When he is not accustoming himself to warfare and looking out for battles, he becomes sort of stiff, while having a rest from wars.
Est raro terra, que sit per eum sine guerra,	There is hardly a country that would not be involved in a war by him,
Hoc **Germania, Francia, Flandria** monstrat aperte.	which is sufficiently demonstrated by Germania,[32] France and Flanders.[33]

More interestingly, Machaut used the ZC also for the sake of what could be called heroization or mythologization of John's chivalric attitudes. John's portrait in the CA is organized around the key concept of honour, which is mentioned seven times throughout the portrait. Two verse sequences in the CA relate to three specific episodes narrated by the chronicler of the ZC. Machaut abstracts from John's attitude that he showed within particular, singular historical circumstances, and reconceives it in more general terms emblematic of the honour, and personal virtue, of his master.

---

31   Palmer et al. (eds), *Guillaume de Machaut*, vol. 2, 466–7.
32   In his chronicle, Peter of Zittau uses the term Germania (situated between the Rhine and Vistula rivers), which includes the Kingdom of Bohemia. Germany, i.e., the German-speaking territories of the Holy Roman Empire, is called 'Alemania' (cf. Machaut's 'Allemaingne' in the verses quoted above). The inhabitants of 'Alemania' are 'Alemani', while 'Teutonici' are German-speaking people, who also inhabit the Kingdom of Bohemia. See especially Peter's discourse on the regicide in chapter I/100, where he uses all these terms (ZC, 147).
33   ZC, II/20, 290.

I. (*CA*, v. 2976–81)

Qu'il estoit en si haut sommet	He remained at such a pinnacle
D'onneur qu'il n'avoit si haut homme	Of honor there was no nobleman so great
Voisin, ne l'empereur de Romme,	Among his neighbors, not even Rome's emperor,
Que s'il li vosist mouvoir guerre	Whom he would not seek out
Ou faire qu'il ne l'alast querre	Right in the middle of his country
Tout en milieu de son païs.	If he wished to attack or make war upon him.

II. (*CA*, v. 2985–8)

Et adés si bien se chevi	And he so quickly moved to act
Qu'onques encor signeur ne vi	There was never a lord I saw
Qui telle force avoir peüst	With sufficient might
Qu'en sa terre une nuit geüst.	To spend even a single night in his territory.[34]

The neighbours mentioned in the first segment are Albrecht and Otto of Habsburg, Dukes of Austria, whose castles north of the Danube were conquered by the King of Bohemia in April 1336 and who fled from their military camp so that John, who wanted to engage them in a fight, could not find them (*ZC*, III/12). In July 1336, John – compared by Peter of Zittau to a roaring lion – moved his troops to Landau an der Isar (cf. *CA*, v. 3062: 'A Senouain et a Lendouve') in order to fight against the Emperor Louis IV and the Duke of Austria, who attacked John's ally and son-in-law Henry of Lower Bavaria and intended to attack the King of Bohemia too:

Quo audito Johannes, rex Boemie, qui tunc erat in metis Austrie, quasi leo rapiens et rugiens et veluti aquila sumptis sibi pennis velocibus gressibus cum paucis primo transiens per Budweys, Cambiam, in Struwingam in subsidium genero suo venit Henrico, duci Bauarie. Cum toto suo, qui ipsum secutus fuerat, exercitu iuxta Landaw prope flumen Ysaram in campestribus satis tutis tentoria sua fixit …	Having heard this news, the King of Bohemia, who was at the Austrian border by that time, like a ravening and roaring lion and like an eagle on his wings moved his small troops, making a rapid march first through Budějovice (German: Budweis), [and] Cham to Straubing in order to help his son-in-law Henry, Duke of Bavaria. He encamped with all his army that followed him next to Landau upon the river Isar on plains that were secure enough … [35]

The Emperor and the Duke of Austria did not offer resistance.

The second segment comes from the letter sent by John's notary Heinrich from Laa an der Thaya on 26 November 1331 (*ZC*, II/28) stating practically the same as Machaut: 'Despite the above-mentioned multitude

---

34 Palmer et al., *Guillaume de Machaut*, vol. 2, 470–1.
35 *ZC*, III/13, 331–3.

of our enemies, they did not dare to spend two nights at our borders.'[36] Compare this to Machaut: 'There was never a lord I saw / With sufficient might / To spend even a single night in his territory.'[37]

ZC, II/28 (1331)	CA, vv. 2986–8
Quamvis autem **maxima**, ut dictum est, **multitudo hostium fuerit**, nunquam tamen **pernoctare duabus noctibus in nostris terminis** ausa fuit.	Qu'onques encor signeur ne vi Qui telle force avoir peüst Qu'en sa terre une nuit geüst.

Machaut generalizes John's attitudes in singular moments in order to create an almost mythical image of the dauntless King of Bohemia. Interestingly, the poet seems to prefer to rely on the authority of a written text even though he would probably have been able to create a convincing portrait of an exemplary warrior based on his personal experience and the existing literary stereotypes alone.

Machaut's mentions of the episodes of 1336 show that in 1357, the date of completion of the *CA*, he had knowledge of information also contained in the full version of the chronicle, which includes the chapter III/14 about John's second crusade to Prussia in 1337 (cf. *CA*, v. 3051; the first expedition took place in 1328–9). The last chapter of the *ZC* is III/15, the last reported event of which took place in February 1338. In the following year, Peter of Zittau died. The first author to use Peter's chronicle as a source for his own work and write a continuation was Francis of Prague (d. 1362), confessor to the Bishop of Prague, Jan IV of Dražice (d. 5 January 1343). The first redaction of Francis' *Chronicle* dedicated to the bishop was written during 1341–2; in that version, the last chapter of the *ZC* used by Francis was III/11 discussing the year 1335. The second redaction was written in the 1350s and dedicated to Charles IV. This second version also included the last chapters of the *ZC*.[38]

Machaut's suggested use of the *ZC* would account for the somewhat strange distribution of the reported facts in the *Confort*. It was noticed by many scholars that Machaut gives details about events that happened a long time ago, sometimes even before his coming to John's court, on the one hand; on the other, he is rather concise about the last decade of John's rule (the mid 1330s to mid 1340s), which was far closer to his time of writing the *CA*, and also to his own personal experience and recollection

---

36 Ibid., 311.
37 Palmer et al., *Guillaume de Machaut*, vol. 2, 470–1, vv. 2986–8.
38 Jana Zachová (ed.), *Fontes rerum Bohemicarum, Series nova, t. I: Chronicon Francisci Pragensis* (Prague, 1998).

of events.³⁹ Furthermore, Machaut deliberately sums up only John's deeds on the right bank of the Rhine and not those which occurred on his side, the left bank, allegedly because many pilgrims, knights, and ladies, i.e., his assumed public, know very well that there was nothing blameworthy about them.

CA, vv. 3083–6

De ce qu'il fist dessa le Rin	Of what he did on the other side of the Rhine,
Me taïs, car maint bon pelerin,	I will say nothing, but many good pilgrims,
Maint chevalier et mainte dame	Many knights and many ladies,
Scevent qu'il n'i ot point de blame.	Know that nothing was blameworthy.⁴⁰

Interestingly, Machaut hints most likely at the 'blame' in Peter of Zittau's Book II and III, threatening John's memory with dishonour.⁴¹ Peter's criticism is unleashed in chapter II/6, 'De discordia inter regem et reginam Bohemiae', according to which the king attacked the queen on the basis of a false accusation and caused the disruption of their marriage: 'Uxorem suam vivam, nullo crimine obnoxiam quasi repudiavit, ipsam suis liberis privavit et in pluribus gravaminibus conturbavit. Ecce quos Deus coniunxit, consilium iniquum disiunxit' ('He almost repudiated his living wife, who perpetrated no crime, deprived her of her children, and disquieted her with many troubles. This way what God brought together, ill advice brought apart').⁴² It contains a very sharp passage, which was subject to self-censorship by Peter of Zittau in his autograph of Book II.⁴³ It states that the king behaved 'as if the bridle of his reason had ruptured', suggesting that he succumbed to all kinds of distortions and vices and acted like a tyrant:

---

39 Hoepffner, *Œuvres de Guillaume de Machaut*, t. I, XVIII; Earp, *Guillaume de Machaut*, 1.3, 8–9 and 12–14.
40 Palmer et al., *Guillaume de Machaut*, vol. 2, 474–5.
41 For John's image in the chronicles of Bohemia, see Peter Hilsch, 'Johann der Blinde in der deutschen und böhmischen Chronistik seiner Zeit', in Pauly (ed.), *Johann der Blinde*, 21–35.
42 ZC, II/6, 251.
43 The passage was nevertheless copied into the chronicle of Francis of Prague, who most likely had the autograph in hand in 1341. See Marie Bláhová, 'Osudy Zbraslavské kroniky', *Studia historica Brunensia* 62 (2015), 143–54. The autograph is Vatican Library, Palatini Latini, 950 (available online at https://digi.ub.uni-heidelberg.de/diglit/bav_pal_lat_950/0028, accessed 31 March 2023). See Zdeňka Hledíková, *Paleograficko-kodikologické etudy* (Prague, 2021), chapter 'Peter von Zittau: Das Beispiel des Autorenautographs und Eventualität des Autographenatlanten', 239–54.

ZC, II/6 (1319)

Porro rex quasi rupto iam freno racionis et cassato vinculo matrimonialis dileccionis totus effrenis efficitur, voluptate vincitur, voluntate perversa regitur ac in ipso perfecte tyrannidis operacio reperitur. Ludit in alea, nec solvit officia, irascitur et ludendo patitur mala verba. Nocturno contentus quandoque solo famulo discurrit tempore per vicos et plateas in Pragensi civitate; plus ridiculosis quam religiosis intendit moribus et dictis. Si aliquando missarum non ex devocione sed compulsione humane verecundie interest officio, non instat oracionibus sed confabulacionibus et cachinno. Verba huius pro folio arboris reputantur, et privilegia, quantum cera in sigillo ponderat, sic curantur.[44]	Then the King – as if the bridle of his reason had now ruptured and the bond of marital love broken – succumbs to pleasure, is ruled by corrupted desire and exhibits the behaviour of a perfect tyrant. He plays dice and does not fulfil his duties; he gets angry and tolerates wicked conversation while playing. In the night, being satisfied with just one servant every now and then, he roams the streets and squares of the City of Prague; he pays more attention to ridiculous manners and sayings than to religious ones. If he sometimes attends to the duty of [going to] Mass, it is not out of piety, but because he is compelled out of shame in front of the people; he does not pursue prayers, but conversations and loud laughter. His words are considered as leaves on a tree and the privileges that he issues have as much value as the wax on his seal.

This indictment is followed by a complaint about his rough tax policy towards burghers, especially of the city of Prague: 'Cives suos aggravat; Praga in exemplum prodeat, que hoc anno tredecim milia marcarum exaccionata compulsaque persolvit' ('He overburdens his burghers; Prague may serve as an example, which was forced and obliged to pay thirteen thousand marks that year').[45] The chapter closes with a verse sequence discussing how a perfect youth ('puer angelicus') can turn into an unkind and unjust ('iniquus') adult, which is the reason why the chronicler changes the tone of his narration.[46] The lack of reason for which the king is reproached by Peter of Zittau also concerns John's military exploits in chapter II/20, for the judgement of 'all wise people' is that 'John, King of Bohemia, is more helped by fortune than by reason': 'Ab omnibus sapientibus iudicatur, quod Johanni, regi Boemie, plus fortuna quam racio in suis actibus suffragatur.'[47]

The Silesian policy of the years 1327–9 celebrated by Machaut in the *CA* is seen by Peter of Zittau in a more realistic light, i.e., by acknowledging that the homage of Boleslas of Legnica and Brzeg was a consequence

---

44 *ZC*, II/6, 251.
45 Ibid.
46 *ZC*, II/6, 251.
47 Ibid., II/20, 290.

of coercion, and stating clearly that the duke was *forced* by the king to submit to feudal law ('iure feodali quasi coactus suscipit').[48] Chapter II/29 (1332) suggests that the degraded state of the Kingdom of Bohemia is due to the fact that Elizabeth Přemysl married a foreigner ('sibi alienigenam pro maritali consorcio copulasse').[49] The animosity toward foreigners also negatively affected John's second spouse Beatrice of Bourbon and her son Wenceslas (*ZC*, III/14): Wenceslas' birth (1337) did not give pleasure to many, because he did not have Přemyslid blood: 'In nativitate huius pueri non multi gaudebant, quia ipsum processisse non de stirpe Boemica asserebant.' The subsequent departure of Beatrice of Bourbon for Luxembourg was allegedly more enjoyed by the public than her arrival: 'In hujus regine recessu plus omnis letatur populus quam adventu.'[50]

Douglas Kelly convincingly showed that Machaut was capable of telling 'a falsehood or fiction in order to relate his hidden truth'.[51] Having said that, Machaut – like all late medieval authors – obviously did not deem factual precision as important as we do today. In the *CA*, he ostensibly adapts reality in order to satisfy the requirements of rhythm and rhyme: he says that Esslingen is situated in Thüringen, while it is in Swabia; that 'Breselau' belonged to 'Boselau', which it did not; and when compiling John's achievements in Italy on the basis of the *ZC* (chapter II/27), he replaces Brescia, where John celebrated a significant success, with Pietrasanta, belonging to Lucca at that time, presumably for no other reason than to rhyme 'plus que cent' and 'Pietrecent' (*CA*, vv. 3057–8).[52] His figures are largely overstated compared to those of Peter of Zittau: when the *ZC* says 'novem milliam marcarum argenti' (II/12), Machaut says 'cent mille mars' (*CA*, v. 3018); when Peter of Zittau estimates the number of baptized pagans to 3000 – 'circiter tria milia gentilium baptizata'

---

48 Ibid., II/22, 300.
49 Ibid., II/29, 312.
50 Ibid., III/14, 334–5.
51 Douglas Kelly, *Machaut and the Medieval Apprenticeship Tradition: Truth, Fiction and Poetic Craft* (Cambridge, 2014), 297–9.
52 Machaut gives the same information as Peter of Zittau about the ownership of Lucca and Brescia/Pietrasanta, i.e., 'Lucka et Brixia huic regi prestant subieccionis perpetue iuramentum' vs. 'il fu sirez de Pietrecent, / Et de Luques'. Machaut shortens Zittau's enumeration of the Lombard towns acquired by John ('Brixia, Pergamus, Cremona, Placencia, Cume, Parma, Regium, Modena, Lucka cum omnibus earum districtibus et castellis; item Mediolanum, Nauarria, Papia'), but gives the correspondent number of 12: 'Après conquist en Lombardie / Parme, Rege, Mode, Pavie / Et jusques a douze citez' (*CA*, vv. 3053–6 vs. *ZC*, II/27, 307). Peter also explains John's peace-making policy in considerable detail (*ZC*, II/27, 308) while Machaut summarizes it by means of the topos of the 'roy paisible' (*CA*, v. 3060).

(II/21) – Machaut says 'plus de sis mille' (CA, v. 3034).⁵³ He also at times quite frankly admits to inventing amounts.⁵⁴ In this light, his verse 'je fu ses clers ans plus de .xxx.', rhymed with 'entente' (PA, vv. 785–6), which would mean that Machaut was attached to John's court already before 1316,⁵⁵ is most likely exaggerated or at least to be taken with a pinch of salt too. The papal bull from 1335 affirms that Machaut had been John's cleric for 12 years or so ('duodecim annis vel circa'), which gives the year 1323. Most likely, then, Machaut's verses about his employment at the court of Luxembourg-Bohemia were intended to prove that his service was long and important enough to entitle the poet to interpret John's character and deeds.⁵⁶

WHEN DID MACHAUT ENTER JOHN'S SERVICE?

There are two historiographical lines, each supporting a different date for Machaut's entry into John's service. The date 'before 1316' results from Machaut's own words, 'je fu ses clers ans plus de .xxx.' (PA, v. 785); it is usually linked to Machaut's studies that the king supposedly arranged for him in France or in Paris. Paul Imbs connected this verse with another one from the *Prise d'Alixandre*, where Machaut describes John as the good

---

53 Six thousand is probably a more precise figure, for Peter of Dusburg gives the same number of baptized pagans in his *Chronicon Terrae Prussiae*. See Theodor Hirsch, Max Töppen, Ernst Strehlke (eds), *Scriptores rerum Prussicarum: Die Geschichtsquellen der Preussischen Vorzeit* (Leipzig, 1861), t. I, 215. However, according to W. Paravicini, *Adlig leben*, 65–6, Machaut largely overstates the extent of the ravaged territory.

54 Cf. the exorbitant sum of '.ij. .c. mille livres' (CA, v. 2941) that John of Luxembourg was able to distribute among his *gens d´armes*: 'Je ne di pas en si grant somme / Com dessus le devise et somme. / Einsois le di par aventure.' ('But not, I should add, with so great a sum / As I have described and mentioned above. / That was a random example'). See Palmer et al, *Guillaume de Machaut*, vol. 2, 468–9, and CA, vv. 2947–9.

55 Alternatively, it could mean that he continued serving John after his death (1346) up to 1353 or even beyond.

56 Palmer (ed.), *Guillaume de Machaut: La Prise d'Alixandre*, 72–3, vv. 785–92: 'je fu ses clers ans plus de .xxx. / si congnui ses meurs et sentente / sonneur son bien sa gentillesse / son hardement et sa largesse / car jestoie ses secretaires / en trestous ses plus gros affaires / sen puis parler plus clerement / que maint autre et plus proprement' ('I was his clerk for more than thirty years / And knew well his manner and his beliefs / His honor, his virtue, his gentility, / His courage and his generosity, / For I was then his secretary / In all his most important dealings. / Thus I can speak more properly / And truly about him than can many others'). Cf. Bernard Ribémont, 'Dire le vrai et chanter des louanges', *Cahiers de recherches médiévales* 10 (2003), 155–72.

king who ensured his material support and education ('li bons roys qui me norri', v. 831).[57] This statement also appears earlier, in the *Confort* (vv. 2935-6): 'De son bien tous li cuers me rit, / Et pour ce aussi qu'il me nourrit' ('My whole heart rejoices at his virtue / And also because he supported me').[58] Should we, then, suppose that Guillaume studied at John's expense for seven years before he entered his service and that by 1323 he was a fully operational officer with a *magister* degree? In fact, in the context of John's court, such a chronological sequence would be both unusual and unlikely. It neither corresponds with the career patterns of the clerics found at John's court, nor fits the political context of John's reign.

First, let us have a look at the careers of three of Machaut's colleagues in the king's chancery who held *magister* degrees: Guillaume Pinchon (d. 1363), Johannes of Pistoia (d. 1371), and Welislas of Sedlčany (d. 1367). None of them acquired a university degree before entering John's service. Guillaume Pinchon[59] appeared in John's chancery in 1324, i.e., roughly the same time as Machaut (according to Benedict XII's bull).[60] On 24 November 1324, when receiving his first canonicate *s.e.p.* in Avranches, he resigned his previous benefice *s.e.p.*, a collation of the Benedictine priory of Saint-Martin-des-Champs near Paris. F.J. Felten suggests a connection of this 'Clunyan' prebend with Pinchon's studies,[61] in analogue to how Machaut's biographers understand Machaut's chaplaincy in Houdain, a collation of the abbot of Saint-Rémy of Reims, another Benedictine house. Prebends that were collations of Benedictine abbots were relatively usual among John's clerics: e.g., on 19 May 1326, Nicolas Efficax of Luxembourg, notary of the King of Bohemia, received benefices *s.e.p.* that were collations of St

---

57 As quoted in Václav Černý, 'Guillaume de Machaut au service du roi de Bohème', in Jacques Chailley et al. (eds), *Guillaume de Machaut, poète et compositeur: Colloque-table ronde organisé par l'Université de Reims (Reims, 19-22 avril 1978)* (Paris, 1982), 67-8. See also Earp, *Guillaume de Machaut*, 12, 1.5.2; Robertson, *Guillaume de Machaut*, 36-7.
58 Palmer et al., *Guillaume de Machaut*, vol. 2, 466-7.
59 John of Luxembourg had in his service several other members of the Pinchon family named Radulphus, Nicolas, and Thomas. See Franz J. Felten, 'Johann der Blinde und das Papsttum', in Pauly (ed.), *Johann der Blinde*, 383-418, at 406-7 and 410-13. The documents relating to Radulphus, Nicolas, and Thomas show an affiliation to the diocese of Coutances; see Guillaume Mollat, *Jean XXII: Lettres communes*, 14 vols (Paris, 1309-21), t. VI, 27, no. 23651; 195, no. 25349; and 415, no. 27520. Thomas Pinchon was vicomte of Avranches; see Léopold Delisle (ed.), *Actes normands de la Chambre des comptes sous Philippe VI de Valois (1328-1350)* (Rouen, 1871), 348, no. 198; and bailli of Cotentin in the 1350s.
60 Werveke, *Étude*, 88; Kerstin Hitzbleck, *Exekutoren: Die außerordentliche Kollatur von Benefizien im Pontifikat Johannes' XXII.* (Tübingen, 2009), 402-4.
61 Mollat, *Jean XXII*, t. V, 263, no. 21090; Felten, 'Johann', 410.

Willibrord of Echternach and of Saint-Laurent in the vicinity of Liège;[62] on 4 January 1333, Jean de Machaut and Henry Ha(i)lle[63] received benefices *s.e.p.* that were collations of the abbots of Notre-Dame of Montebourg in the diocese of Coutances (Jean de Machaut) and of Notre Dame in Le Bec-Hellouin in the diocese of Rouen (Henry Ha(i)lle).[64] However, there is no direct evidence that these benefices were related to their studies.

In 1325, Guillaume Pinchon was called *clericus*, *secretarius* and *familiaris* of the king and served as *nuncius regius* at the curia in Avignon.[65] Pinchon, who became Archdeacon of Avranches in October 1329, is mentioned as *magister* for the first time on 21 September 1330. Five months later, on 17 February 1331, he is called *cancellarius regis Bohemiae* for the first time, although he seems to have already been the factual head of John's chancery earlier.[66] In the 1320s, the importance of Pinchon's role was most likely expressed by the title of *secretarius*.[67] During the first two decades of the rule of John of Luxembourg, this designation was used only in a few cases, for Guillaume Pinchon and three other high-ranking individuals: magister Nicolas of Ybbs, Bishop of Regensburg, who was also a counsellor of the king (1313); Philip of Rathsamhausen, Bishop of Eichstätt (1313) and also John's counsellor; and Johannes of Nassau, a relative (*consanguineus*) of the king (1326). In the 1330s and 1340s, John had about a dozen secretaries of Pinchon's rank (approximatively), including Guillaume and Jean de Machaut, who were often, but not always, notaries at the same time.[68] This qualitative shift in the social status of individuals designated as secretaries and the – presumably concomitant – changes in the function of these

---

62 Mollat, *Jean XXII*, t. VI, 195, no. 25353; *RBM* III, 468, no. 1201. The original wording is 'prope Leodium'.
63 This name appears in two orthographic variants, Halle or Haille.
64 Thomas, 'Extraits', 333, no. V; *MVB TP*, 562, no. 1035.
65 Siegmund Riezler (ed.), *Vatikanische Akten zur deutschen Geschichte in der Zeit Kaiser Ludwigs des Bayern* (Innsbruck, 1891), 351, no. 924; for Pinchon between 25 October 1325 and 28 July 1330, see ibid., 248–9, no. 563; 269–70, no. 627; 275, no. 646; 290–1, no. 708; 355–6, no. 938; 431, no. 1225; 472–3, no. 1358; 566, no. 1659.
66 This assumption appears repeatedly in the bibliography from Tadra (1892) until Marie Bláhová, 'Kancléři na dvoře Jana a Karla', in František Šmahel and Lenka Bobková (eds), *Lucemburkové: Česká koruna uprostřed Evropy* (Prague, 2012), 414–19. For Pinchon as Archdeacon of Avranches, see Hitzbleck, *Exekutoren*, 402; as *magister*, see Riezler (ed.), *Vatikanische Akten*, 482, no. 1386a; as *cancellarius*, see Eduard Winkelmann (ed.), *Acta imperii inedita*, t. 2 (Innsbruck, 1885), 798–800, no. 1135.
67 March 1325; Mollat, *Jean XXII*, t. 5, 338, no. 21893.
68 Moraw, 'Über den Hof', 116–17, does not include John's *secretarii* among the chancery staff (*Kanzleibeamte*).

people at John's courtly establishment have not been sufficiently explained and require further research.[69]

Johannes of Pistoia, John's *clericus, familiaris, capellanus, notarius* and *secretarius*, entered John's and Charles' service at the beginning of 1332 in Italy.[70] He was married and had a son Guillaume (*Guilielmus* in Latin) in Pistoia. Johannes did not benefit from any prebends before moving to Avignon and becoming *familiaris* and *registrator* of Clement VI in 1342.[71] In 1346, he is mentioned as *magister* and moves up to the position of chaplain of the pope (*capellanus commensalis*, 1347) and later *abbreviator* in the papal chancery.[72] Welislas of Sedlčany was a notary, secretary and diplomat of John and of John's son Charles from about 1325. He gained a *magister* degree before 19 June 1347 (within one year of Charles' election), probably because the King of the Romans needed to promote him to the highest positions in the imperial chancery, as Spěváček assumes.[73]

The *magister* degree played a crucial role in the careers of these three colleagues of Machaut, but neither a degree nor a similar promotion can be observed in the poet's case. Furthermore, the two papal graces issued on 30 July 1330 simultaneously with Machaut's nomination to his first expectative in Verdun are addressed to Johannes of Arlon, *in utroque iure perito*, and to Nicolas Mensdorf of Luxembourg, *magistro*; the absence of a degree of Machaut's in this document is not an omission.[74] Hypothetically, Machaut could have studied during his service, as others of John's administrators obviously did, without obtaining a university degree. He could also have obtained it later in life. The earliest mention of Machaut

---

69   Zbyněk Sviták, 'Česká královská kancelář ve středověku', in Waldemar Chorążyczewski and Janusz Tandecki (eds), *Belliculum diplomaticum II Thorunense* (Toruń, 2007), 25–55, at 36, observes that the function of secretaries is unclear.
70   Jiří Spěváček, 'Die Anfänge der Kanzlei Karls IV. auf italienischem Boden in den Jahren 1332–1333', *Mitteilungen des Instituts für Österreichische Geschichtsforschung* 76 (1968), 299–326, at 306–8.
71   Tadra, *Kanceláře*, 16/88, no. 14; Ursmer Berlière (ed.), *Suppliques de Clément VI (1342–1352): Textes et analyses*, t. I. (Rome – Bruges – Paris, 1906), 35, no. 171 and 39, no. 194. He was canon in Beauvais (1345), see Riezler (ed.), *Vatikanische Akten*, 801–2, no. 2217, and dean of the St Salvator chapter in Utrecht (1346), ibid., 819–20, no. 2253.
72   For Johannes as *magister* on 22 April 1346, see Riezler (ed.), *Vatikanische Akten*, 819–20, no. 2253; for his role at the curia, ibid. passim; as *capellanus* of the pope, ibid., 844, no. 2320.
73   Jiří Spěváček, 'Významní notáři-diplomaté prvních Lucemburků v Čechách', *Československý časopis historický* 21 (1973), 711–60, at 725–7, n. 41–2. It is neither known where he studied nor whether his degree was in liberal arts or theology.
74   *MVB TP*, 488, nos 886–8.

among *magistri* dates from 18 August 1352, but it is inconclusive whether the title applies also to him.[75]

How old was Guillaume de Machaut when arriving at John's court, if we assume that he had not attended university first? A point of reference is the minimum legal age of 25 for a minor benefice enacted by the Third Lateran Council (1179).[76] Unfortunately, we lack the supplications for the benefices mentioned in the first bull issued by John XXII for Guillaume de Machaut on 30 July 1330, i.e., for his chaplaincy *sine cura* in Houdain and his canonicate *s.e.p.* in Verdun. We therefore do not know when Machaut obtained the chaplaincy *sine cura* that he held in July 1330 and whether it was preceded by the usual supplication form asking for a church benefice 'cum cura vel sine cura', for only in the case of 'cum cura' was the minimal legal age required. As already mentioned, the chaplaincy of Houdain was a collation of the abbot of the Benedictine house of Saint-Rémy at Reims. The abbot was most likely familiar with Machaut, as Machaut was probably educated at the cathedral school in Reims, as Anne Walters Robertson suggests. This does not exclude Machaut having possible ties to the Benedictines of Saint-Rémy and of Saint-Nicaise during this time. His completion of these initial studies would have earned him the title *clericus*.[77] As for the canonicate *s.e.p.* at the cathedral of Verdun, it would be sufficient for Machaut to be just 25 years old. Based on these considerations, Machaut's date of birth can be shifted to 1305, so that he would have been 18 years old in 1323, when he – according to the bull of Benedict XII – entered John's service. If this is the case, he entered John's service as a young *clericus Remensis diocesis*, similarly to his brother Jean.[78] After initial training in Reims he would have continued his education by

---

75 Cf. Earp, *Guillaume de Machaut*, 7, 1.2.8 and 23, 1.7.1.f; See also Bowers, 'Guillaume de Machaut', 23, n. 61.

76 Canon 3. Canonicates are not explicitly mentioned, however. See the codification of Boniface VIII (1298): *Corpus iuris canonici. Liber sextus.* Titulus VI. De electione et electi potestate. Cap. VII: 'Inferiora etiam ministeria, ut puta decanatum, archidiaconatum, et alia, quae curam animarum habent annexam, nullus omnino suscipiat, sed nec parochialis ecclesiae regimen, nisi qui iam vigesimum quintum annum aetatis attigerit, et scientia et moribus commendandus exsistat' ('Further, with regard to the inferior ministries, for instance that of dean or archdeacon, and others which have the care of souls annexed, let no one at all receive them, or even the rule of parish churches, unless he has already reached his twenty-fifth year of age, and can be approved for his learning and character'; translation quoted from https://www.papalencyclicals.net/councils/ecum11.htm, accessed 31 March 2023). See also Bernard Guillemain, *La Politique bénéficiale du Pape Benoît XII, 1334–1342* (Paris, 1952), 134; and Earp, *Guillaume de Machaut*, 4, 1.2.1.

77 Robertson, *Guillaume de Machaut*, 35–6.

78 Ibid., 19; Thomas, 'Extraits', 333, no. V.

gaining practical experience as a junior clerk at John's court, and in this way was nurtured by the king (as he repeatedly asserts).

The second argument as to why Machaut was not employed by John the Blind by 1316 is that the policy and the needs of the King of Bohemia did not justify such a step. The cordial relationship between the dynasties of Luxembourg and France was renewed only after the death of Philippe V (on 3 January 1322), who was relatively hostile towards the Count of Luxembourg.[79] There is no evidence that John of Bohemia entered French territory before the coronation of Charles IV le Bel. During the first decade of his reign in Bohemia, he was primarily focused on the stabilization of his kingdom, which Machaut laconically describes as:

CA, vv. 2991–6

Par force d'armes et d'amis	Through the force of arms and allies
En subjection les a mis.	He did subject these people.
Comment qu'il li fussent rebelle	Though they all rebelled
Tuit, mais il gaaingna la querelle,	Against him, he prevailed in the war,
Et maintes fois se combati,	Fighting many battles,
Dont maint grant orgueil abati.	And thus humbling many a great pride.[80]

A turning point of his policy in Bohemia occurred in 1318–19, when John had to make peace with the most powerful faction of the nobility of the kingdom that also sought to destroy the political power of the queen, Elizabeth Přemysl.[81] John's deal with the nobility set considerable limits on royal power in Bohemia and implied profound changes in his political strategy. The king became more oriented towards expansion into the so-called 'lands adjoining the Bohemian crown' (especially Bautzen and Görlitz, later called Upper Lusatia, and the duchies of Silesia), the development of the County of Luxembourg, and different policies leading to the regaining of the imperial throne, including a close collaboration with France from 1322.[82] The new Francophone personnel at his court, the

---

79 For Philip V's alliance with the prince-bishop of Liège against John of Luxembourg, see Jules Viard (ed.), *Les Journaux du Trésor de Charles IV le Bel* (Paris, 1917), col. 1055, n. 2.
80 Palmer et al., *Guillaume de Machaut: The Complete Poetry and Music*, vol. 2, 470–1.
81 For John's relationship with Elizabeth, see, e.g., Michel Margue, 'L'épouse au pouvoir: le pouvoir de l'héritière entre 'pays', dynasties et politique impériale à l'exemple de la maison de Luxembourg (xiiie–xive s.)', in Éric Bousmar, Jonathan Dumont, Alain Marchandisse and Bertrand Schnerb (eds), *Femmes de pouvoir, femmes politiques durant les derniers siècles du Moyen Âge et au cours de la première Renaissance* (Brussels, 2012), 269–310, at 287–95.
82 The most recent biography of John of Luxembourg is by Lenka Bobková, *Jan Lucemburský*; see also Johannes Abdullahi, *Der Kaisersohn und das Geld: Freigebigkeit und Prachtentfaltung König Johanns von Böhmen (1296-1346)* (Luxembourg,

presence of which is perceptible from around 1323, was mostly required by this new Franco-Imperial policy and the new dynastic bonds between the Luxembourgs and the French royal dynasty which were tied under the reigns of Charles le Bel and Charles' successor, King Philip VI of Valois. It should be pointed out that the new Francophone staff, including Machaut, was attached to John's Francophone domains, especially the County of Luxembourg, which – apart from German-speaking parts – included Francophone domains (e.g., *quartier roman*), but also fiefs in Hainaut provided to the Luxembourgs by the counts of Hainaut in the years 1321–34 and 1343–83.[83] From December 1334, John also held different domains inside the Kingdom of France, which were either his personal fiefs from Philip VI, such as Mehun-sur-Yèvre (1334–46), or belonged to his second wife Beatrice of Bourbon, such as Creil-sur-Oise.

It is possible that John's return to grace at the court of France was mediated by Guillaume I/III (c. 1286–1337), Count of Hainaut, Holland and Zealand from 1304 to 1337, and his wife Jeanne of Valois, second-eldest daughter of Charles of Valois. In December 1320, they hosted the King of Bohemia, Jean of Hainaut and Beaumont (d. 1356), and Guy de Châtillon, Count of Blois (husband of Jeanne's sister Marguerite of Valois), in Binche.[84] John of Luxembourg was the son of the Emperor Henry VII and the reason for his welcome at the court of France mostly resided in the matters of the Holy Roman Empire, the interest in which he shared with Charles of Valois, the uncle of the King of France, Charles le Bel. Charles of Valois, who earlier (1308) had harboured ambitions towards the imperial crown, followed closely the juridical process that Pope John XXII launched against Louis of Bavaria, King of the Romans, in 1323; the year 1324 also saw the first indication that the Luxembourgs might be ready

---

2019); for Luxembourg under John's rule, see Winfried Reichert, *Landesherrschaft zwischen Reich und Frankreich: Verfassung, Wirtschaft und Territorialpolitik in der Grafschaft Luxemburg von der Mitte des 13. bis zur Mitte des 14. Jahrhunderts* (Trier, 1993), 2 vols. See also Wojciech Iwańczak, *Jan Luksemburski, dzieje burzliwego żywota i bohaterskiej śmierci króla Czech i hrabiego Luksemburga w 21 odsłonach* (Warsaw, 2012); Michel Margue (et al.), *Un Itinéraire européen: Jean l'Aveugle, comte de Luxembourg et roi de Bohême, 1296–1346* (Luxembourg, 1998); Michel Pauly (ed.), *Johann der Blinde, Graf von Luxemburg und König von Böhmen 1296–1346* (Luxembourg, 1997); Klára Benešovská (ed.), *King John of Luxembourg (1296–1346) and the Art of his Era* (Prague, 1998).

83 For the administration of the Francophone domains of Luxembourg see Reichert, *Landesherrschaft*, t. II, 637–44. The Hainaut fiefs included Aymeries, Dourlers, Pont-sur-Sambre, Quartes, and Raismes, localities now situated in France, région Hauts-de-France, Département Nord.

84 H.J. Smit (ed.), *De rekeningen der graven en gravinnen uit het henegouwsche huis*, t. I: *Rekeningen van Jan II en Philippine van Luxemburg, Johanna van Valois en Willem IV* (Amsterdam, 1924), 85.

to grant the imperial kingdom of Arles and Vienne to the Valois, if they acceded once more to the Roman throne.[85]

WHY WAS GUILLAUME DE MACHAUT EMPLOYED AT JOHN'S COURT?

The question of why and how Guillaume de Machaut entered the service of the King of Bohemia has been the subject of a great number of rather unsatisfactory hypotheses. This is due to the lack of sources and resultant lack of proof. R.B. Palmer seems to have been the last one to articulate a suggestion: 'Jean had frequent dealings with the archbishop of Reims, a see with which Machaut may have been associated at an early age, and the archbishop perhaps effected an introduction.'[86] Unfortunately, John's frequent dealings with the archbishop (which would have left traces in the sources) also remain unsubstantiated. Nonetheless, the supposition that Machaut was familiar with Reims and that Reims played a certain role in the activities of John the Blind seems correct; and it is consistent with the historical data. The recent discovery by Benjamin L. Albritton of a history of the counts of Rethel written by Guillaume de Machaut suggests that the poet-composer also had important ties to the County of Rethel, situated between the County of Luxembourg and Reims.[87]

When Charles le Bel became King of France, he was supposed to ensure heirs and successors to the kingdom and therefore had to come to terms with his current marriage with Blanche of Burgundy, who had been condemned for adultery and imprisoned at Château Gaillard. Charles'

---

85 Joseph Petit, *Charles de Valois (1270–1325)* (Paris, 1900), 200–1.
86 R.B. Palmer, 'Introduction', in Palmer et al. (eds), *Guillaume de Machaut: The Complete Poetry and Music*, t. 1, 3.
87 Benjamin L. Albritton, '*Ex historia Guillermi de Mascandio*: Machaut in the *Annales Hannoniae* of Jacques de Guise', in Jared C. Hartt, Tamsyn Mahoney-Steel and Benjamin L. Albritton (eds), *Manuscripts, Music, Machaut: Essays in Honor of Lawrence Earp* (Turnhout, 2022), 127–49. The last member of the local dynasty of Rethel, Joanna, Countess of Rethel, died in 1328 and was succeeded by her son, Louis I of Flanders from the house of Dampierre. The extinction of a local dynasty and the accession of a foreign one is a typical occasion for writing such a history. The next dynastic change in Rethel took place only after Machaut's death (the last members of the house of Dampierre, Louis II and his daughter Marguerite of Flanders, died in 1384 and 1405 respectively). Therefore, the possibility that the history of the counts of Rethel was Machaut's earliest work (from the early 1330s) and not his latest (dating from 1369–77) should not be neglected (cf. Albritton, ibid., 137–44). The death of Joanna of Rethel created an opportunity for John of Luxembourg to buy the castle of Orchimont desired by the counts of Luxembourg already in the thirteenth century. See Reichert, *Landesherrschaft*, t. II, 614–15.

uncle, Charles of Valois, arranged the annulment of the marriage by the pope (19 May 1322), arguing that it had been concluded in contradiction with canon law.[88] In the summer, the young King of France decided to marry Marie of Luxembourg (c. 1305–24), the eldest daughter of Emperor Henry VII and the younger sister of John of Bohemia. John, who was fighting at the Battle of Mühldorf am Inn at the time (cf. *CA*, vv. 3008–10: 'Et a desploïe baniere / Et compaingnie noble et riche / Desconfit le duc d'Osteriche'[89]), could not be present at her marriage with Charles le Bel on 21 September 1322 in Provins. Marie was accompanied by her uncle Baldwin, Elector-Archbishop of Trier, and her retinue was welcomed by the French constable Gaucher de Châtillon-Porcien (1249–1329), previously entrusted by the King of France with a mission to the King of Bohemia and the Count of Bar.[90] Therefore, it is quite possible that Machaut entered John's service upon recommendation of the Châtillon-Porciens as R. Bowers suggested, but he could also have met the Châtillons later, at John's court, for Gaucher's son Jean de Châtillon worked as a mediator for the King of France in the conflicts between the counts of Luxembourg and Bar.[91] Jean de Châtillon's daughter Jeanne (c. 1320–85; sister of Hugues, canon of Reims) married Egidius (IV) of Rodemack (c. 1320–81) from a high-ranking noble family of Luxembourg (probably in the 1340s).[92] Egidius figures among the witnesses of John of Bohemia's homage to the abbot of Saint-Rémy of Reims (1344), and his name in the listing of witnesses to this event comes right after those of Guillaume and Jean de Machaut.[93]

In the context of Marie's wedding, Charles le Bel provided his brother-in-law with an income, an annual pension (*fief-rente*) consisting of 4000 *livres tournois* from the Trésor. This is mentioned in the document by Philip of Valois, by then King Philip VI of France, endowing John the Blind with Mehun-sur-Yèvre (December 1334).[94] On the occasion of

---

88   Petit, *Charles de Valois*, 200.
89   'And with unfolded banner / And a host noble and powerful / He defeated the Duke of Austria.' Palmer et al., *Guillaume de Machaut*, vol. 2, 470–1. Translation amended by this author.
90   Jules Viard (ed.), *Les Journaux ... de Charles IV*, t. II, col. 294, no. 1668 and col. 159, no. 791.
91   Marville, 13 August 1329; http://telma.irht.cnrs.fr/chartes/en/transscript/notice-acte/115 (accessed 31 March 2023); the same in *RBM* III, 621, no. 1583, and Verkooren (ed.), *Inventaire*, 143–4, no. 677.
92   Reichert, *Landesherrschaft*, t. II, 980–9; Alain Atten, 'Rodemack et son château', Les cahiers lorrains 4 (1979), 97–105, at 98.
93   See above. In June 1349, Egidius provided some service to Bonne of Luxembourg; see Jules Viard (ed.), *Les Journaux du Trésor de Philippe VI de Valois suivis de l'Ordinarium thesauri de 1338–39* (Paris, 1899), col. 274, no. 1486.
94   Jean Bertholet, *Histoire ecclésiastique et civile du Duché de Luxembourg et Comté de Chiny*, t. VI (Luxembourg, 1741), pièces justificatives, XXIV–V; Philippe

John's second wedding with Beatrice of Bourbon, the treaty of which was signed on 18 December 1334 at Vincennes, Philip VI replaced John's lifelong *fief-rente* from the Trésor with the same income from the castle and *châtellenie* of Mehun-sur-Yèvre (Dép. Cher), and the lands of Faillouël and Condren not far from Saint-Quentin. The marriage treaty designated the future son of the couple, i.e., Wenceslas (b. 1337), as the presumptive heir of the County of Luxembourg; and Philip VI declared John's French fiefs to be hereditary in the line of the counts of Luxembourg (i.e., not the kings of Bohemia). The French *fief-rente* was implicitly connected with the military engagement of the holder in the conflicts of the kings of France: John of Bohemia was therefore expected to participate in the war of Gascony against the English in 1325 together with the Count of Hainaut (this campaign did not take place).[95] In 1328, John similarly sent 500 soldiers ('quingentos galeatos viros bellicos') to Cassel, who fought under the command of John of Hainaut and Beaumont within the army of Hainaut.[96]

After John's death at Crécy in 1346, the feudatory of 4000 *livres* was theoretically, but not in fact, inherited by John's son Wenceslas, Count (and from 1354 Duke) of Luxembourg.[97] After the enthronement of Charles V in 1364, the hypothetical income of 4000 *livres* held by Wenceslas was transformed into a rent of 6000 francs per year from the Trésor.[98] The principal French officer operating transactions related to this rent was Jacques la Barbe, *receveur* of the King of France in Reims.[99] While we do not have accounts for the time of John the Blind, it is possible that transactions between Luxembourg and France were already carried

---

Contamine, 'Politique, culture et sentiment dans l'Occident de la fin du Moyen Âge: Jean l'Aveugle et la royauté française', in Pauly (ed.), *Johann der Blinde*, 343–61, at 353; Reichert, *Landesherrschaft*, t. I, 224–5, n. 219.

95 Pierre Chaplais, *English Medieval Diplomatic Practice*, 2 vols, t. I (London, 1982), 282–3, no. 153a and 283–6, no. 153b.

96 ZC, II/20, 290; 'Chronique anonyme de Flandres', in Siméon Luce (ed.), *Chroniques de Jean Froissart*, t. I (Paris, 1869), 302: 'La huitième bataille estoit conduite par Monseigneur le comte de Heinaut à XVII banières; et y avoit une esle de messire Jehan de Heinaut, son frère, qui menoit les gens du roy de Behaigne' ('The eighth troop was conducted by Monseigneur the Count of Hainaut and counted 17 banners; and it had a flank of Messire Jean of Hainaut, his brother, who led the people of the King of Bohemia'; translation by this author).

97 Mehun-sur-Yèvre instead passed to Bonne of Luxembourg. Faillouel and Condren had been conceded to Guillaume Roger de Beaufort, brother of Clement VI, in the context of Charles' election to the Roman throne. See Jana Fantysová Matějková, *Wenceslas de Bohême, un prince au carrefour de l'Europe* (Paris, 2013), 73, n. 22, and 75.

98 Ibid., 212.

99 For Jacques la Barbe see ibid., 386, 473–4, 507–8.

out by an officer of the King of France in Reims in John's times. This hypothesis could explain why John needed clerics familiar with Reims and why Guillaume de Machaut and his brother Jean appear to have had something to do with John's finances. Not only was Guillaume the king's almoner before April 1332 and replaced by his brother Jean in this function (before January 1333),[100] but also, by his own admission, he was in charge of distributing payment to 'gens d'armes'.[101] The poet recalls that, during his years in John's service, he distributed money to soldiers more than 50 times, which is a lot (even if overstated). Thus, it seems that the Machaut brothers might have been placed in employment for the initial purpose of managing John's financial transactions with France. This also means that they were affiliated with the Luxembourgian rather than with the Bohemian part of John's domain, which is supported further by additional details. The need for someone to administer soldiers' pay can also probably account for Machaut's participation in the crusade to Prussia and Lithuania of 1328–9. As for the Kingdom of Bohemia, the pay of the 'stipendiarii' was the subject of permanent lamentations by Peter of Zittau, who was interested in the flow of finances, especially those coming from the kingdom.[102]

From January 1332, John of Luxembourg was bound to the Valois by far-reaching military obligations defined in the treaty of Fontainebleau. He promised to serve in the regions of Champagne, Vermandois, and Amiens with 400 'hommes d'armes' at his own cost. Even in the more remote regions, he was supposed to deliver a few hundred soldiers at any

---

100 For Jean de Machaut as *elemosinarius* see Thomas, 'Extraits', 333, no. V. See also Elizabeth Eva Leach, 'Guillaume de Machaut, Royal Almoner: *Honte, paour* (B25) and *Donnez, signeurs* (B26) in Context', *Early Music* 38:1 (2010), 21–42. There is currently no study dedicated to almoners at the court of John of Luxembourg.
101 *CA*, 2940–51. 'Gens d'armes' means soldiers or mercenaries. Cf. s.v. 'Arme' in: *Dictionnaire du Moyen Français* (DMF 2020), http://www.atilf.fr/dmf (accessed 31 March 2023). The Latin equivalent of the term used by the *ZC* is 'stipendiarii'.
102 E.g., *ZC*, III/12, 332: 'Igitur copiosa pecunia, scilicet viginti milia marcarum, ut dicitur, per Johannem regem subito congregata cito dispergitur, stipendiariis pars solvitur, pars alias emittitur et totaliter dissipatur' ('Then an abundant amount of money, namely twenty thousand marcs – as it is said – hastily collected by John, King of Bohemia, got dispersed right away; part of it was paid to soldiers, part of it spent in other ways and totally squandered'). See also the letter of the notary Heinrich, ibid., II/28, 309: 'die decimo Wratislauiam pervenit, in qua civitate paucis sub diebus plus quam duodecim milia marcarum diversis extorsionum modis tam a christianis obtinuit quam iudeis. Hanc quidem pecuniam quasi totam stipendiariis deputavit' ([John of Luxembourg] 'arrived on the tenth day [after his departure from Prague] to Wrocław, in which city he obtained by different means of extortion from Christians as well as from Jews more than twelve thousand marcs within a few days. Almost all this money was ascribed to the soldiers').

time that any member of the French royal lineage was 'en ost'.[103] If one of Machaut's most important preoccupations at John's court consisted of distributing soldiers' pay and John was primarily obliged to defend Champagne, Vermandois, and Amiens, the location of Machaut's prebends in Reims (1333/1335), Saint-Quentin (c. 1334) and Amiens (1343)[104] might have been a strategic choice.

The account of the French *fief-rente* extant for the years 1373–80 (under Duke Wenceslas) was written by Jean de Raing, *châtelain* and *receveur* of Aymeries and Raismes, the Hainaut fiefs of the Luxembourg family. Jean de Raing is also mentioned as a secretary of the under-age King of France, Charles VI, in 1381.[105] In other terms, his activities covered Luxembourg, France, and the Hainaut fiefs, which seem also to have been the principal perimeter of the Machauts' activities. The Hainaut fiefs had belonged to John's grandmother Beatrice of Avesnes and Beaumont, and were subject to the oath of allegiance sworn by John to the Count of Hainaut on 11 September 1321, after Beatrice's death.[106] The Hospital of Sainte-Marie-de-Houdain, where Machaut held a chaplaincy, was situated some 80 kilometres from Raismes; his expectative in Arras (1332) was only 60 kilometres from this locality. Leuze-en-Hainaut, where Jean de Machaut held a canonicate (before 1342), is some 30 kilometres from Raismes.[107] John also inherited some of his grandmother Beatrice's entourage, especially her chaplain Nicasius de Wavrechain, a native of Hainaut (d. 1349),[108] who appears as John's chaplain in the same series of papal graces as Guillaume de Machaut (from 17 April 1332[109] and from 4 January 1333[110]). Both series also include Robert du Palais, *clericus parisiensis diocesis*, notary, and secretary to the king. The latter comprises Jean de Machaut in the function

---

103 Contamine, 'Politique', 349–53; *RBM* III, 727, no. 1867.
104 Earp, *Guillaume de Machaut*, 20, 6.2.1.i., quoting Glenn Piers Johnson, 'Aspects of Late Medieval Music at the Cathedral of Amiens', 2 vols (PhD dissertation, Yale University, 1991). See also Pierre Desportes and Hélène Millet (eds), *Fasti Ecclesiae Gallicanae. Répertoire prosopographique des évèques, dignitaires et chanoines de France de 1200 à 1500*, t. I, Diocèse d'Amiens (Turnhout, 1996), 120.
105 For Jean de Raing see Fantysová Matějková, *Wenceslas*, 212, n. 9; 386, n. 18; 434; 466, n. 113; 470–1; 474–5; 507–8.
106 *RBM*, t. III, 296, no. 722–3.
107 Ladislav Klicman (ed.), *Monumenta Vaticana res gestas bohemicas illustrantia: t. I Acta Clementis VI. Pontificis Romani: 1342–1352* (Prague, 1903) (further quoted as *MVB* I, 63–4, nos 109–10.
108 Friedhelm Burgard, *Familia Archiepiscopi: Studien zu den geistlichen Funktionsträgern Erzbischofs Balduins von Luxemburg (1307–54)* (Trier, 1991), 226; Arnold Fayen (ed.), *Lettres de Jean XXII (1316–1334). Analecta Vaticano-Belgica*, 3 vols (Rome, 1908 and 1912), t. I, 173, no. 262.
109 Felten, 'Johann', 414–15; Hitzbleck, *Exekutoren*, 403–4.
110 *MVB TP*, 560–2, nos 1030–5.

of John's almoner, Henri Ha(i)lle, and Peter of Waben. Henri Ha(i)lle and Peter of Waben are listed as clerics and familiars of the king without any explicitly mentioned functions.

Guillaume de Machaut's connection with Hainaut appears repeatedly, and in various types of sources: he issued and signed a document settling the feudal bonds between the counts of Luxembourg and Hainaut regarding La Roche and Durbuy on 1 May 1334 in Noyon.[111] The Hainaut accounts record a gift received by Machaut on 14 July 1341, when the court of Guillaume IV and Jeanne of Brabant was in Binche.[112] Machaut's works in turn evince traces of the influence of the poets Jehan de le Mote and Nicole de Margival,[113] both connected with the house of Avesnes-Beaumont; and Machaut's verse 'Einsi comme on torche Fauvain'[114] indicates that his public was familiar with the stories of Fauvel or Fauvain the Horse, i.e., with the *Roman de Fauvel* by Gervais du Bus and Chaillou de Pesstain, and/or the *Histoire de Fauvain* by Raoul le Petit, works related not only to Charles of Valois, but also to his daughter Jeanne of Valois and the family of the counts of Hainaut.[115] Interestingly, the interpolated version of the *Roman de Fauvel* (Bibliothèque nationale de France, fr. 146) contains a direct allusion to John of Bohemia as a member of the Virtues tournament team, for it mentions the heraldry of Bohemia: 'de gueles à lions / Rampans d'argent ....'[116] This reference might well have been added at a very late stage of the compilation, in 1322.[117] Thus, John of Luxembourg

---

111 Verkooren (ed.), *Inventaire*, 160, no. 699.
112 Earp, *Guillaume de Machaut*, 14, 1.5.4.b.
113 Janet F. van der Meulen, 'De panter en de almoezenier: Dichtkunst rond het Hollands-Henegouwse hof', in Frank Willaert (ed.), *Een zoet akkoord: Middeleeuwse lyriek in de Lage Landen* (Amsterdam, 1992), 93–108, at 101; and Janet F. van der Meulen, '"Sche sente the copie to her daughter": Countess Jeanne de Valois and Literature at the Court of Hainault-Holland', in Suzanna van Dijk et al. (eds), *'I have heard about you': Foreign Women's Writing Crossing the Dutch Border: From Sappho to Selma Lagerlöf* (Hilversum, 2004), 61–83 (for Nicole de Margival see esp. 69, n. 33).
114 Guillaume de Machaut, 'Dit dou Lyon', in Hoepffner (ed.), *Œuvres de Guillaume de Machaut*, t. II, 151–237, at 219, v. 1716.
115 Yolanda Plumley, *The Art of Grafted Song: Citation and Allusion in the Age of Machaut* (Oxford, 2013), *passim*; Janet van der Meulen, 'Le manuscrit Paris, BnF, fr. 571 et la bibliothèque du comte de Hainaut-Hollande', *Le Moyen Âge* 113 (2007), 501–27.
116 Malcolm Vale, 'The World of the Courts: Content and Context of the Fauvel Manuscript', in Margaret Bent and Andrew Wathey (eds), *Fauvel Studies: Allegory, Chronicle, Music, and Image in Paris, Bibliothèque Nationale de France, MS Français 146* (Oxford, 1998), 591–8, at 595.
117 It was suggested by Margaret Bent that the compilation and new compositions of the interpolated *Roman de Fauvel* could have extended as late as 1322. See 'Early

was explicitly included in the milieu that displayed an incredible effort in order to present Enguerrand de Marigny as a deterrent example.[118]

Guillaume de Machaut was probably a usual member of John's retinue during the king's visits at the court of Hainaut as well as during other events, feasts, or tournaments, which gave occasion to different interactions between the Avesnes-Beaumonts and the Luxembourgs. Count Guillaume I/III of Hainaut, Zealand and Holland and his siblings John of Beaumont and Marie, Countess of Clermont and Duchess of Bourbon, were children of Philippa of Luxembourg, daughter of John's great-grandfather Henry V, Count of Luxembourg. (John's grandmother Beatrice of Avesnes and Beaumont was their cousin.) These multiply related courts and their personnel should be considered as the milieu Machaut was familiar with, and that also functioned as his public.

BETWEEN LUXEMBOURG, PARIS, AND HAINAUT

It is relatively difficult to form an idea of what the court of the King of Bohemia looked like when residing in Luxembourg. The lack of accounts has a considerable impact on any attempt at reconstruction. John's court in the west was always missing the Countess of Luxembourg, i.e., the Queen of Bohemia Elizabeth Přemysl, who stayed in Central Europe. This might have been a serious diplomatic and social handicap. Therefore, the presence of other members of the royal family in Luxembourg was probably more important. One might think of the four-month sojourn of John's sister Marie in 1322, and the extended stay of John's daughter Bonne (1326–32). Blanche of Valois, the first wife of John's first-born son, Charles of Luxembourg, and John of Luxembourg's second wife Beatrice of Bourbon also spent a significant amount of time there in 1330–4 (Blanche of Valois), and in 1335–6 and 1337–40/46 (Beatrice of Bourbon). Beatrice might have resided mostly elsewhere in the 1340s, for she was entrusted with the administration of the French domains of Mehun-sur-Yèvre, Marsy, Paudy, and Creil-sur-Oise.[119] Alternatively, she could have also resided in Damvillers (Luxembourg), her marital dower, or in Paris. At some moment in the 1340s, most likely in 1342, John's youngest son Wenceslas, born in 1337 in Prague, was taken from Bohemia

---

Papal Motets', in Richard Sherr (ed.), *Papal Music and Musicians in Late Medieval and Renaissance Rome* (Oxford, 1998), 5–43, at 12.
118 Andrew Wathey, 'Gervès du Bus, the Roman de Fauvel, and the Politics of the Later Capetian Court', in Bent and Wathey (eds), *Fauvel Studies*, 599–613.
119 On 30 November 1340 in Verdun. See Alphonse Huillard-Bréholles, *Titres de la Maison ducale de Bourbon* (Paris, 1867) t. I, 391, no. 2274.

to Luxembourg. When he was seven years old, he had Joffrid of Rodemack as his cleric.[120]

John's sister Marie of Luxembourg was escorted from Prague to Luxembourg in April 1322,[121] and John's itinerary shows that the king was in the County of Luxembourg from April to June.[122] It also seems that John was content to dwell in France in the company of his sister and Charles le Bel, often accompanied by Philip of Valois, the eldest son of Charles of Valois and, from 1328, King Philip VI of France. In 1323, John of Luxembourg organized a tournament in Cambrai, an imperial town at the French border, 'amore regis and regine Francie', i.e., in order to express his love for Marie of Luxembourg and Charles IV.[123] John's presence in France is also attested in the first months of the years 1323 and 1324, before Marie's death in March 1324. From 1323, Marie supervised the education of her nephew Wenceslas (1316–78, the later Emperor Charles IV), at the time the presumptive heir of the Kingdom of Bohemia.[124] Wenceslas arrived in Paris in 1323, at the age of seven, and left for Luxembourg in 1330, when he was 14. During the feast of Pentecost 1323, when Marie was crowned Queen of France in the Sainte-Chapelle, Wenceslas was confirmed, took the name of Charles, i.e., the name of King Charles le Bel alluding to Charlemagne, and was betrothed to the youngest daughter of Charles of Valois, Blanche (1317–48). After Marie's death, John of Luxembourg seems to have visited France much less frequently; he was there only at Christmas 1324 and at a few special occasions. He attended the coronation of Jeanne d'Évreux, Charles le Bel's third wife, as Queen of France, in May 1326 in Paris, with a becoming retinue ('cum decenti frequenca familie sollempniter interfuit'), and displayed his military skills at a tournament.[125] He hurried to Paris after the death of Charles le Bel in February 1328 and offered his support to Philip of Valois (= Philip VI of France), who rewarded him with a residence in Paris, later called the Hôtel de Bohême.[126] The King of Bohemia also appeared at Philip's coronation in Reims in May 1328 and was staying in Paris, perhaps in his hôtel, on a few insufficiently documented later occasions.

---

120 November 1344; *MVB* I, 261, no. 440.
121 *ZC*, II/11, 261.
122 Between 18 April and 19 May 1322; see *RBM* III, 313, no. 771 and 317, no. 780. In May and June, a war between the Count of Luxembourg and the Count of Bar took place. In July 1322, John of Luxembourg was back in Prague. Cf. *ZC*, II/11, 261.
123 Henri Moranvillé (ed.), *Chronographia regum Francorum*, 3 vols (Paris, 1891–7), t. I, 274–5.
124 *ZC*, II/12, 264–5.
125 Ibid., II/17, 279.
126 The donation took place at the Louvre. See Contamine, 'Politique', 348.

John's daughter Bonne (b. 1315) had already moved from Prague to Luxembourg on 6 April 1326 with respect to her engagement to the young son of the Count of Bar.[127] She was living in Luxembourg for six years, up to 1332. The first two years of Bonne's sojourn in Luxembourg (1326–8) correspond with a period of very intense contacts between John of Luxembourg and the court of Hainaut. John visited Jeanne of Valois in Valenciennes in April and again at the Ascension (2 May) 1326, also meeting Godefroi, Guillaume and Walerand, princes of Juliers (Jülich), Walerand of Luxembourg-Ligny and John of Beaumont. In August 1327 he came to Le Quesnoy and in December 1327 to Valenciennes, where he met the English envoys and several counts and knights from the Empire, who gathered there in order to escort Philippa of Hainaut to England. John also participated at tournaments in Condé-sur-l'Escaut (1327) and 's-Gravenzande (1328).[128] In April 1328, he dined with John of Beaumont and the English envoys in Le Quesnoy, and in June he met with John of Beaumont in Le Quesnoy again and appeared also in Valenciennes, where a tournament took place on 10 June.[129] Jean Froissart reports on the tournaments and the relationship between John of Luxembourg and his relatives of Avesnes-Hainaut and Beaumont, including the Duke of Bourbon.[130] The chronicler Johann of Victring refers to the same period when talking about the wedding of John of Luxembourg and Beatrice of Bourbon, who admired her future husband as a tournament champion and allegedly attracted his attention by means of some precious tournament accessories.[131] In the summer of 1328, the king had to leave for Bohemia because of the war at the Austro-Moravian border, after which he undertook the crusade to Prussia and Lithuania with Guillaume de Machaut in his company (1328–9). He was back in Luxembourg in October 1329. His presence in Hainaut is also documented in June 1334 in Mons[132] and after his wedding ceremony with Beatrice (on 6 January

---

127 ZC, II/17, 279.
128 Evelyne van den Neste, *Tournois, joutes et pas d'armes dans les villes de Flandre à la fin du Moyen Âge (1300–1483)* (Paris, 1996), 126 and 218, no. 22; for the tournament in 's-Gravenzande see Joseph-Marie-Bruno-Constantin Kervyn de Lettenhove (ed.), *Œuvres de Froissart. Chroniques* (Brussels, 1867–77), t. II, 101–2.
129 Smit (ed.), *De rekeningen*, t. I, 85, 90, 159–60, 275, 375–6, 384, 388.
130 Kervyn de Lettenhove (ed.), *Œuvres de Froissart. Chroniques*, t. II, 98–9.
131 The Chronicle of John of Victring is published in Johann Friedrich Böhmer (ed.), *Fontes rerum Germanicarum. Geschichtsquellen Deutschlands*, t. I (Stuttgart, 1843), 271–450, at 413: 'Fertur hanc in dilectione habuisse speciali, quia ei jocalia pretiosa, ad opera militaria necessaria et ad tornetas direxerit, ejusque amicitiam fuerit sic venata quod illectus extitit et abstractus.'
132 *RBM* IV, 19, nos 52–4.

in Luxembourg) in February and March 1335, when they participated in a tournament at Condé-sur-l'Escaut.[133]

It is possible to hypothesize that Bonne of Luxembourg (born 1315), who was some two years younger than Philippa of Hainaut (born c. 1314) and of a similar age as Beatrice of Bourbon (born c. 1314) and Blanche of Valois (born 1316), was introduced to courtly society at these or similar occasions.[134] In 1330, Bonne was joined in Luxembourg by Blanche of Valois.[135] After the death of Elizabeth Přemysl, Queen of Bohemia, on 28 September 1330, John of Luxembourg's youngest daughter Anne (born 1323) left Prague on 8 April 1331 to join her sister Bonne and her sister-in-law Blanche in Luxembourg. From this moment on, the entire royal family was absent from Bohemia, a circumstance which Peter of Zittau complained about.[136] Apparently, the female members of the Luxembourg family held court in Luxembourg between 1326 and 1334; they were occasionally joined there by John of Luxembourg and by Charles of Luxembourg (1330–1). This seems to imply that the Luxembourg household in Luxembourg also maintained a household account which was probably similar to the one of the *hôtel* of Jeanne of Valois and her children.[137] Bonne, who was only 11 years old in 1326, might have been staying in Luxembourg under the supervision of her aunt Marguerite of Luxembourg, prioress of the Dominican nunnery in Marienthal, but that arrangement would most likely not have been an obstacle to her participating in courtly life when her father was in the west.

In 1332, Bonne was married to Philip VI's eldest son, the future John the Good, which probably required some personnel serving John of Luxembourg and his relatives in Paris. We know that *magister* Henry

---

133 On Ash Wednesday 1334, i.e., 1 March 1335, John acknowledged his debt towards Guillaume of Hainaut for expenses related to the tournament in Condé. See Kervyn de Lettenhove (ed.), *Œuvres de Froissart. Chroniques*, t. II, 510 and http://telma.irht.cnrs.fr/chartes/en/transscript/notice-acte/24999 (accessed 31 March 2023).
134 The accounts of Hainaut mention a trumpeter of the King of Bohemia: 'A 1 ménestrel le roy de Behangne ki trompa devant medame 40 s.' (7 September 1330); see Smit (ed.), *De rekeningen*, t. I, 526.
135 According to the *Vita Karoli*, ch. 3–4, in Josef Emler (ed.), *Fontes rerum Bohemicarum*, t. III. (Prague, 1882), 324–417 at 340–1. According to older historians, Blanche had already left for Luxembourg in 1329; see Petit, *Charles de Valois*, 248–9; Johann Friedrich Böhmer (ed.), *Regesta Imperii (1314–1347): Die Urkunden Kaiser Ludwigs des Baiern, König Friedrichs des Schönen und König Johanns von Böhmen. Additamentum primum* (Frankfurt am Main, 1841), 298.
136 *ZC*, II/27, 308–9.
137 Smit (ed.), *De rekeningen*; see also Thérèse de Hemptinne and Valeria Van Camp, 'Gens, maisnie, ou hôtel? Le personnel à gages à la cour de Guillaume I/III de Hainaut et Hollande/Zélande et de son épouse Jeanne de Valois (1304–1337)', Bulletin de la Commission royale d'Histoire 178 (2012), 23–64.

of Jodoigne (from Brabant, d. 1352) served simultaneously John of Luxembourg, Marie of Luxembourg, and Charles le Bel (1324).[138] John of Luxembourg and his daughter Bonne probably shared the secretary Henry Ha(i)lle from the diocese of Rouen, who came into John's service by 1328 and became the subject of a joint supplication of the King of Bohemia and his daughter in 1343.[139] Therefore, it is not impossible that Machaut was employed in a similar way, in spite of the fact that there is no direct evidence of his service to Bonne apart from his own assertion: 'moult la servi / mais onques si bonne ne vi' ('having performed much service for her. / But never did I lay eyes on any woman this "good"').[140] Machaut's first possible connections to the court of Paris can be guessed from the fact that he received a prebend in the royal collegiate chapter of Saint-Quentin from King Philip VI (= Philip of Valois) at some time between 4 January 1333 and 17 April 1335. The nomination so far has been mostly discussed with respect to Machaut's signature on a document of John of Bohemia's dated 1 May 1334 in Noyon. In the previous days, the kings of France and of Bohemia sojourned at the Abbey of Notre-Dame at Ourscamp, where a multitude of other princes were also present, such as Guillaume I of Hainaut; Adolph de La Marck, Prince-bishop of Liège; Renaud, Count of Guelders; Louis, Count of Loos and Chiny; and others.[141] The discussion between John of Luxembourg and Philip VI concerned Louis of Bavaria and resulted in further negotiations of their respective envoys in Avignon.[142] Hypothetically, their meeting gives an occasion for Machaut to receive a nomination to the canonicate of Saint-Quentin directly from the King of France, although this was not necessarily the case. As David Fiala reminds us, the first cleric of John of Luxembourg who received a canonicate in Saint-Quentin was Nicasius of Wavrechain in 1332.[143] Therefore, a possible connection between these benefices for

---

138 Fayen (ed.), *Lettres de Jean XXII*, t. I, 472, no. 1276 (26 January 1324).
139 *MVB* I, 41, no. 75 (1342); *MVB* I, 141–2, no. 230 (1343).
140 Palmer (ed. and trans.), *Guillaume de Machaut. La Prise d'Alixandre*, 72–3, vv. 769–70.
141 On 29 April 1334. See *RBM* IV, 13, no. 34; for the presence of Philip VI at Ourscamp, see Jules Viard, 'Itinéraire de Philippe VI de Valois', *Bibliothèque de l'École des Chartes* 74 (1913), 74–128 and 525–619, at 114.
142 *RBM* IV, 20–1, nos 62–3, 65.
143 David Fiala, 'La collégiale royale de Saint-Quentin et la musique', in Camilla Cavicchi, Marie-Alexis Colin and Philippe Vendrix (eds), *La Musique en Picardie du XIVe au XVIIe siècle* (Turnhout, 2012), 188–227, at 202. Nicasius of Wavrechain also seems to have been a member of the retinue of the King of Bohemia during his travels in May and June 1334. His presence is attested by a document issued by John of Luxembourg in Valenciennes on 16 June 1334; see http://telma.irht.cnrs.fr/chartes/en/transscript/notice-acte/25014 (accessed 31 March 2023).

John's clerics, King John's military obligations in Vermandois (1332), and his fiefs next to Saint-Quentin (December 1334) should not be excluded.

It is up for discussion how much attention should be paid to other possible patrons of Guillaume de Machaut who are never mentioned by the poet himself, such as John's second wife, Beatrice of Bourbon (c. 1314–83). In fact, Beatrice appears to have been keen on music, for she chose sirens as *attendants* of her heraldic shield. On the exemplar of her seal from 1351, the sirens even play musical instruments, a vielle and a harp.[144] Later in her life, Beatrice enjoyed the services of the minstrel Jean d'Ivoix (or d'Avignon), who also worked for her son Wenceslas.[145] It is unclear to what extent John and Beatrice inhabited Mehun-sur-Yèvre, but the charter from 17 May 1346 that seems to be the only document issued by John of Luxembourg at the castle is highly significant in the cultural context: on the request of the Dominican Petrus de Castro Reginaldi, John confirmed that the assertion found in a number of *romans*, chronicles and motets ('romancie, cronice et moteti') that his father Emperor Henry VII had been poisoned by the Dominican Bernardus de Montepulciano was false.[146] Such assertions appear in the *ZC* in chapter I/115, in which Peter of Zittau shares the testimony of Henry VII's physician, *magister* Nicolas of Fulda. They are also raised in the interpolated version of the *Roman de Fauvel* (Paris, Bibliothèque nationale de France, fr. 146) in the motet *Scariotis Geniture / Jure quod in opere / Superne matris*, and in the poem *De l'Ipocrisie des Jacobins* by Jehan de Condé, a poet from Hainaut.[147] This reminds us that we have a tendency to underestimate the political impact of such texts, which were obviously able to harm one's public image for many decades.

---

144 René Laurent, *Les sceaux des princes territoriaux belges du Xe siècle à 1482* (Brussels, 1993), 3 vols, t. I/2, 499–500; t. II, 268, nos 57–8.
145 Fantysová Matějková, *Wenceslas*, 475.
146 Karl Zeumer (ed.), *Monumenta Germaniae Historica. Constitutiones et acta publica imperatorum et regum*, t. 8, Inde ab a. MCCCXLV usque ad a. MCCCXLVIII (Hannover, 1982), 58–60, no. 37.
147 For the motet see BnF, ms fr. 146, fol. 2r and Leo Schrade (ed.), *Polyphonic music of the fourteenth century*, t. I, *The Roman de Fauvel; the Works of Philippe de Vitry; French Cycles of the Ordinarium Missae* (Monaco, 1956), 8–9; for the poem see Auguste Scheler (ed.), *Dits et contes de Baudouin de Condé et de son fils Jean, d'après les manuscrits de Bruxelles, Turin, Rome, Paris et Vienne*, t. 3 (Brussels, 1867), no. 55, 181–8 and 373–6. See also the chapter by Karl Kügle in this book.

MACHAUT'S POSSIBLE ROLES AS CLERIC, NOTARY, AND SECRETARY

The chancery of John, King of Bohemia and Count of Luxembourg, contained two kinds of chancellors. The first one was the *cancellarius regni Bohemiae*, which was a traditional honorific function of the Kingdom of Bohemia connected with the post of the provost of the chapter of Vyšehrad.[148] In Machaut's time, the function of the provost of Vyšehrad was held by Jan Volek (d. 1351), an illegitimate half-brother of Queen Elizabeth Přemysl. He served as chancellor between 1315 and 1334 (with a short break 1322–5 when he fell in disgrace). He was succeeded by Pierre de Mortemart (1334–5), Bishop of Auxerre and cardinal-priest of St Stephen in Coelio Monte; and by Berthold of Lipa from a high-ranking noble family of Bohemia (1335–45). The Luxembourgian historian Nicolas van Werveke saw John's chancery as one entity,[149] but it is unclear whether the activities of these chancellors of Bohemia and provosts of Vyšehrad also covered John's territories outside the Kingdom of Bohemia, i.e., the County of Luxembourg, Italy, and his Francophone fiefs. This is probably the reason why there was a second chancellor, a *cancellarius regis*. Between 1331 and 1342, the title was used by *magister* Guillaume Pinchon, Archdeacon of Avranches, who was probably a superior of Machaut and his colleagues. On several occasions, the nomination bulls for their benefices were issued by the pope when Pinchon was in Avignon; on some other occasions, Pinchon is mentioned among the executors of their benefices. Guillaume de Machaut was nominated to his canonicate of Verdun when Pinchon was in Avignon (1330), and Pinchon is named among the executors of his canonicates *s.e.p.* in Arras (1332) and in Reims (1335).[150]

The notaries of John's chancery were specialized in terms of languages and lands (regions). It is possible to make a rough distinction between two groups of personnel: 1) clerics, notaries, and secretaries originating from the Kingdom of Bohemia (e.g., Welislas of Sedlčany), Germany, called *Allemania* in the medieval sources (e.g., Heinrich Schatz of Nuremberg) and Luxembourg (e.g., Nicolas Efficax) who held benefices within the Kingdom of Bohemia, the neighbouring regions and/or in the dioceses of Trier or Liège; 2) Francophone clerics originating from dioceses within the Kingdom of France (Reims, Rouen, Paris, Coutances) who held benefices in Lotharingia, northern France and/or Paris. This second group also included the public notary Johannes of Pistoia and Peter of Waben,

---

148 Sviták, 'Česká královská kancelář', 36.
149 Werveke, *Étude*, 84–93.
150 Hitzbleck, *Exekutoren*, 402–4, ch. 3.5.3.

who is however never mentioned as a notary.¹⁵¹ Yet if a specialization of John's officers in terms of lands and languages can be perceived with clarity, assignments of specific tasks or functions are far less obvious. The Francophone personnel are usually mentioned in more than one function, typically as notaries and secretaries, but also as chaplains or *receveurs*. Let us remind ourselves that the Machaut brothers were also almoners, and that Jean de Machaut is never mentioned as a notary. From the viewpoint of prosopography, there was therefore an overlap between the chancery, the chapel, and the financial administration at John's court.

The only evidence of Machaut's activity as a notary is the chancery note, 'Par le roy, Guillaume de Machau', on a charter dating from 1 May 1334 in Noyon.¹⁵² Given the rarity of chancery notes at John's court, it is quite fascinating that there is another document with the same date issued from the same negotiations with William I of Hainaut and signed by Machaut's colleague Robert du Palais: 'Par le … roy, Rob[ert] du Pal.'¹⁵³ The nominations of Robert du Palais to papal benefices paralleled those of Machaut from 16–17 April 1332, 3–4 January 1333 and 17 April 1335: his function at John's court is described by the same words, but unlike Machaut he did not seem to give up his other benefices *s.e.p.* in 1335. He held prebends only as a chaplain of Suzanne and of Acy-Romance in the diocese of Reims; his canonicates in Noyon and Meaux were expectative.¹⁵⁴ He seems to have been connected to Meaux in more than one way, for he was promised another benefice in Meaux in June 1334, when Pinchon was in Avignon.¹⁵⁵ We do not know whether Robert du Palais, whose name

---

151 For Peter of Waben see Reichert, *Landesherrschaft*, t. II, 1020–2. Waben is situated not far from Montreuil (region Pas-de-Calais, Département Hauts-de-France) in Flanders. Peter of Waben, John's *dilectus familiaris et domesticus* (1333) and secretary (1337, cf. Verkooren (ed.), *Inventaire*, 179, no. 726), was appointed to the post of *receveur* of the County of Luxembourg during John's absence in 1341. See *MVB TP*, 561, no. 1033; Verkooren (ed.), *Inventaire*, 222, no. 793 (15 May 1341); 228, no. 803 (25 June 1341); 229, no. 804 (27 June 1341); 236, no. 812 (4 August 1341).

152 Verkooren (ed.), *Inventaire*, 160, no. 699.

153 Werveke, *Étude*, 88–9. Unfortunately, Werveke does not indicate his original source and it is unclear where it should be. Werveke also mentions two other original documents signed R (10 June 1334 in Mons and 6 March 1338 in Paris), see http://telma.irht.cnrs.fr/chartes/en/transscript/notice-acte/136 [accessed 31 March 2023]), which might mean Robert du Palais in analogue to the ones signed w (Welislas of Sedlčany) or Pe (Peter of Brno). See Spěváček, 'Významní notáři-diplomaté', 726 and 731. A chancery note 'Robert du Pal. s[cripsit]' is preserved on a document issued by John of Luxembourg on 15 May 1332 in Poilevache. See http://telma.irht.cnrs.fr/chartes/en/transscript/notice/23667 [accessed 31 March 2023].

154 *MVB TP*, 560–1, no. 1030.

155 On 23 June 1334. See Mollat, *Jean XXII*, t. 13, 156, no. 63410; Riezler (ed.), *Vatikanische Akten*, 566, no. 1659.

is mentioned by two anonymous Latin motets,[156] ever was successful at receiving his prebend in the capital of Brie.

John's clerics and notaries were active both in his presence[157] and independently representing his interests: in the accounts of Hainaut, a visit of the people of the King of Bohemia is mentioned in 1320, and on 5 January 1334 in Valenciennes a charter was issued in John's name in his absence.[158] On 23 September 1336, Dietmar Maul of Schlotheim (also called of Meckbach) wrote to Boemund of Saarbrücken, Archdeacon of Trier, that John intended to send Nicolas Efficax and Joffrid of Leiningen to Paris and to Avignon in order to look into the political situation.[159] From this we can see that John's clerics led busy lives, accomplishing missions here and there and being on the road a lot of the time. In his supplication from 1345, John the Blind explains that Peter of Waben cannot be in residence at the parish church of St Nicolas in Ghent because he must travel to diverse regions on a daily basis ('ipsum oportet cotidie per diversas discurrere regiones'); the otherwise unknown Gobelinus de Catheneyn from the diocese of Metz explains in his supplication (1342) that he had served Johannes of Pistoia for many years in Bohemia, in France, in Germany ('Alamania') and at the curia.[160]

The King of Bohemia was accompanied by clerics and notaries not only during his diplomatic and administrative travels, but also during military campaigns. We know from the ZC that the notary Heinrich was with John of Luxembourg in Wrocław, Głogów, Poznań, Brno, and Laa in autumn 1331.[161] Guillaume de Machaut travelled with him in the crusade of 1328–9 to Lithuania. Guillaume Pinchon was accompanying John at Brescia and Cremona (1331) and probably also elsewhere in Italy, where Johannes of Pistoia entered the service of the Luxembourgs.[162] Christian of Limburg was reporting from John's military camp on his success against the Duke of Austria in April 1336 to Nicolas Efficax, who forwarded the information to Baldwin of Trier.[163] Johannes of Pistoia and Henry Ha(i)lle were staying with John during the siege of Tournai by the English in the military camp

---

156 Lawrence Earp, 'Introduction', in Lawrence Earp, Jared C. Hart and Domenic Leo (eds), *Poetry, Art, and Music in Guillaume de Machaut's Earlies Manuscript (BnF fr. 1586)* (Turnhout, 2021), 21–55, at 39.
157 For Welislas of Sedlčany and Peter of Louny present in Trenčín and Visegrád in 1335 and 1336, see Spěváček, 'Významní notáři-diplomaté', 728 and 732.
158 Werveke, *Étude*, 207–8.
159 Burgard, *Familia*, 115–16, n. 94.
160 Berlière (ed.), *Suppliques de Clément VI*, t. I, 218, no. 883 and 39, no. 194.
161 *ZC*, II/28, 309–11 and 314–15.
162 Spěváček, 'Die Anfänge', 301–8.
163 Burgard, *Familia*, 115–16, n. 94.

of Bouvines in September 1340, when the blind king let Johannes write his testament.[164]

Furthermore, John's notaries and secretaries usually had other clerics in their service. Christian of Limburg worked for Nicolas Efficax; Gobelinus de Catheneyn for Johannes of Pistoia; and Johannes, son of the Luxembourgian arbalester Egidius, for Peter of Waben.[165] It is possible that the Machaut brothers were similarly affiliated with Guillaume Pinchon. This would account for the fact that Jean, a *clericus remensis*, was granted his first benefice *s.e.p.* in the diocese of Coutances (1333); Guillaume obtained his first canonicate *s.e.p.* in Verdun on 30 July 1330, when Pinchon was in Avignon together with two other envoys of the King of Bohemia, Joffrid of Leiningen and Nicolas Mensdorf from Luxembourg. As far as we know, the principal subject of their negotiations concerned a new project of reconciliation between Pope John XXII and the Emperor Louis of Bavaria, which was presented also by the ambassadors of Otto of Habsburg and of Baldwin of Trier. John XXII confirmed the reception of John's embassy and of his envoy's documents on 28 July 1330.[166] Three days later, he issued a document rejecting the political project put forth by the three delegations.[167] By this time, in July and August 1330, three series of nominations to benefices were issued for the people from John's court and from Bohemia. The first series dates from 24 July and includes benefices for Heinrich Schatz of Nuremberg, Herman of Prague, and Nicolas Efficax[168] (among others). These have Guillaume Pinchon named as executor.[169] The second series from 30 July 1330 includes Johannes of Arlon, Guillaume de Machaut, and Nicolas Mensdorf, who was a member of Pinchon's delegation.[170] These three prebends were treated separately from the previous series and were connected with at least one member of the delegation on the ground in Avignon at the time. Guillaume Pinchon held a prebend in the cathedral chapter of Verdun[171] and could have

---

164 For the latest edition of the testament of John of Luxembourg, see Anne-Katrin Kunde, '"Hec autem est nostra ultima voluntas": Das Testament König Johanns von Böhmen, Graf von Luxemburg. Kommentar und Neuedition', *Hémecht* 73 (2021), 336–57. Guillaume Pinchon is designated as one of the executors of John's last will.
165 *MVB* I, 143, no. 233; Earp, *Guillaume de Machaut*, 23, 1.7.1.c.
166 Riezler (ed.), *Vatikanische Akten*, 472–3, no. 1358; cf. *RBM* III, 654, no. 1669; *In extenso: MVB TP*, 483, no. 883.
167 *MBV TP*, 484–7, no. 884; *RBM* III, 654, no. 1671.
168 He was nominated to a canonicate *s.e.p.* in Prague cathedral; *RBM* III, 654, no. 1667.
169 *MVB TP*, 481–2, nos 877–81.
170 *MVB TP*, 488–9, nos 886–8. For Nicolas Mensdorf see Burgard, *Familia*, 25–33.
171 Guillaume Pinchon was granted the prebend of the defunct Sanso de Calvemonte on 19 May 1326. Fayen (ed.), *Lettres de Jean XXII*, t. I, 540–1, nos 1454–5, and t. III, 45–6, no. 1757.

wished to have his younger colleague, Guillaume de Machaut, in the same institution. A third series of prebends was issued on 8 August and the beneficiaries were people from Bohemia.[172]

Given Machaut's personal testimony on the pay of the 'gens d'armes', we might surmise his presence on occasions connected with John's finances in the context of the Hundred Years' War, such as in August 1337 at Maubuisson-lès-Pontoise;[173] in August-September 1338 at Amiens;[174] in December 1338 and January 1339 in Languedoc;[175] at the siege of Cambrai and at Buironfosse (near Saint-Quentin) in September and October 1339;[176] and possibly also in Vincennes in December 1339, when Charles of Luxembourg received 1468 *livres parisis* from the Trésor;[177] again in September 1340 at the siege of Tournai; and perhaps also during the war of Liège in June 1346 and in the French army during the campaign of Crécy. It was most likely in the context of the Hundred Years' War that Guillaume Pinchon progressively integrated himself into the administration of the King of France. In July 1339, when Edward III was preparing for the Thiérache campaign (which resulted in the siege of Cambrai and the presence of a French and an English army at Buironfosse without, however, daring to join battle), Guillaume Pinchon, *maître des requêtes de l´hôtel du roi*, and Jehan d'Ynteville, counsellor of the King of France responsible for the fortification and garrison of Reims, were exchanging information with the Marshal of France, Mathieu de Trie (d. 1344), who commanded the French garrison in Tournai.[178] In August, Pinchon, Ynteville, and the baillis of Vitry(-le-François) and of Vermandois received instructions from the King of France regarding the city of Reims and the chapter of Notre Dame, refusing to pay their tax subsidies related to the defence.[179] (By that time, Machaut was a non-resident canon of the chapter and participated at the enthronement of Jean de Vienne as Archbishop of Reims on 13 March 1340). According to a fragment of an account of the bailliage of Caen, Pinchon sent letters to the King of France to inform him about the

---

172 *MVB TP*, 491–3, nos 894–9.
173 *RBM* IV, 186–7, nos 453–4.
174 Viard, 'Itinéraire', 83 and 528; *RBM* IV, 238, no. 613.
175 Claude Devic, *Histoire générale de Languedoc*, t. I (Toulouse, 1840), 123.
176 *RBM* IV, 186–7, no. 453; 244, no. 631; 248, no. 640; 288, no. 744. See also http://telma.irht.cnrs.fr/chartes/en/transscript/notice-acte/25007 (accessed 31 March 2023).
177 Jules Viard and Aline Vallée (eds), *Registres du Trésor des Chartes*, Paris, Arch. nat., *Règne de Philippe de Valois* (Paris, 1984), t. III, 2e partie, 177, no. 4387.
178 Varin (ed.), *Archives*, 812–13, no. CDLVII, and 816, no. CDLIX. Mathieu de Trie was the older brother of Guillaume de Trie, Archbishop of Reims 1324–34, who crowned Philippe VI in 1328 and was the subject of Machaut's motet M18.
179 Varin (ed.), *Archives*, 816–18, nos CDLIX and CDLXI.

state of the region ('l'estat du pays', i.e., Normandy) in 1341 or 1342; and in 1343, he participated in the collection of tax subsidies in Normandy.[180]

Given the participation of John the Blind in the military campaigns of 1339 and 1340, it is possible that the 'G. de Machaut' mentioned in the accounts of the city of Reims (from 1 March 1340 to 21 February 1341) was indeed Guillaume de Machaut.[181] The account states that 'G. de Machaut' sold a packhorse to Hue le Large, alderman of Reims, because a horse for lease was not available, when Hue was in the military camp of the King of France.[182] The scholarly discussion surrounding Machaut's sale of the horse concerned the question of whether Guillaume de Machaut had taken up residence at Reims by that time; it was, however, based on an erroneous supposition, namely that the purchase of the packhorse took place in Reims. The record says clearly that it happened when Hue le Large was in the military camp of Philippe VI.[183] According to the account, the camp was near 'Escaudemire'[184] (called 'Escaduevre' by Jean le Bel and Escaudoeuvres today), i.e., the episode occurred during the siege of Thun-l'Évêque, and specifically between 18 and 23 June 1340 when the castle surrendered.[185] The neighbouring castle of Escaudoeuvres, less than five kilometres from Thun-l'Évêque, had been taken by John, Duke of Normandy, in the second half of May 1340. Both castles were situated in the Cambrésis, which belonged to the Empire, and were under the command of Guillaume of Hainaut and John of Beaumont.[186] Machaut's potential presence in the military camp of the King of France during the campaign against Hainaut opens up a new bunch of questions, which cannot be discussed here.

180 Delisle (ed.), *Actes normands*, 266 and 288.
181 The other person who is a candidate for this transaction was 'G. de Machau', a ropemaker (*cordier*) settled in Reims. See Varin (ed.), *Archives*, 824.
182 Varin (ed.), *Archives*, 831–3: '*Item*, xxiii liv. pour un cheval acheteit à G. de Machaut, pour ce que on ne peust recouvrer de cheval à louier, pour porter la male H. le Large, quant il fust en l'ost devant Estantdemire, pour parler au roy, pour le cris qui fust fais en ceste ville que chascuns alast en l'ost'. Trans. by Earp, *Guillaume de Machaut*, 22, 1.7.1: 'Item, 23 *livres* for a horse purchased from G. de Machaut, because a horse to lease could not be found, to carry the trunk of H. le Large, when he was with the army at Estantdemire (*recte* Estaudemire?), in order to speak to the king on account of the proclamation made in this town that everyone was about to be mustered.'
183 This is the reason why the alderman had to borrow the amount to be paid for the horse from a third person, as another mention in the same account shows. See Varin (ed.), *Archives*, 834.
184 Cf. Delisle (ed.), *Actes normands*, 267.
185 Viard, 'Itinéraire', 84 and 537.
186 Jules Viard and Eugène Déprez (eds), *Chronique de Jean le Bel* (Paris, 1904), 169–77.

Guillaume Pinchon's involvement in the war-related duties of John of Luxembourg was rewarded (among other tokens of gratitude) by a gift of an English prisoner-of-war of the king at some unknown moment of the first phase of the Hundred Years' War (no specific date is available). The prisoner was subsequently exchanged for a French prisoner-of-war called Guillaume d'Argouges, who in consequence owed 1400 *livres tournois* of ransom to Guillaume Pinchon. On 30 October 1349 in Caen, John, Duke of Normandy, issued a confirmation statement related to this settlement.[187] In 1342, Guillaume Pinchon was called not only *cancellarius* of the King of Bohemia, but also counsellor of Philippe de Valois.[188] Most likely, he was also advancing the imperial interests of the Luxembourgs in France. On 4 April 1346 in Avignon, Pinchon received an annual income of 100 *livres parisis* from John's first-born son, Charles of Luxembourg (= Charles IV), then Margrave of Moravia. This information comes from a vidimus and confirmation of Charles' document by Philip VI issued in January 1347 at Vincennes. Philip VI confirmed Charles' document for two reasons. The first one was the request from Charles, the second the king's desire to reward Guillaume Pinchon for the services he performed for the French crown. Pinchon's income was financed from Charles' *fief-rente*, which in turn came from the Trésor.[189] The fact that Charles had an annual income from the King of France at the time was probably also one of the motives for his participation in the Battle of Crécy on 26 August 1346. It is nevertheless unclear whether his units continued participating in the war afterwards.[190] However, it is clear that Pinchon's service to the Luxembourgs was not interrupted by John's death.

---

187 Aline Vallée (ed.), *Registres du Trésor des chartes t. III, règne de Philippe de Valois, 3e partie JJ 76 à 79B: Inventaire analytique et index généraux* (Paris, 1984), 199, no. 7350. The document refers to Guillaume Pinchon as Archdeacon of Avranches, *Maître des requêtes de l´hôtel du roy* and Chancellor of John, King of Bohemia.

188 *MVB* 1, 50–1, no. 90 (16 August 1342). According to Françoise Autrand, *Naissance d'un grand corps de l'Etat: les gens du parlement de Paris, 1345–1454* (Paris, 1981), 96, Guillaume Pinchon was also counsellor at the Parliament of Paris between 1345 and 1347.

189 Vallée (ed.), *Registres du Trésor*, t. III, 3e partie, 21, no. 6271.

190 Cf. Heinz Thomas, 'Die Beziehungen Karls IV. zu Frankreich von der Rhenser Wahl im Jahre 1346 bis zum Grossen Metzer Hoftag', *Blätter für deutsche Landesgeschichte* 114 (1978), 165–201, at 177. Thomas does not mention the fact that Pinchon's annual income from Charles of Luxembourg came from the French Trésor. As this *fief-rente* was given to Charles before the death of John of Luxembourg, it is not identical with the French fief of his father (i.e., Mehun-sur-Yèvre), which Charles transferred to his sister Bonne after their father's death (ibid., 176; and Johann Friedrich Böhmer and Alfons Huber (eds), *Regesta Imperii VIII. Die Regesten des Kaiserreichs unter Kaiser Karl IV. 1346–1378* (Wien, Köln, Weimar, 1877) 25, nos 262–3).

In 1342, Johannes of Pistoia was deputized to coordinate the imperial policy of the Luxembourgs in Avignon,[191] and at some unknown moment Nicolas Efficax was integrated into the court of Cardinal Gui de Boulogne (nominated by Clement VI in September 1342) as a *familiaris*, and associated with the court of Clement VI as an 'apostolice sedis capellanus'.[192] These steps were mostly required in the careful pursuit of the greatest political objective of the Luxembourgs: the recovery of the imperial throne. It is not clear to what extent Machaut was involved in these diplomatic activities, for in the 1340s he seems to have been preoccupied with his literary work: the *Dit dou Lyon* contains an intra-textual date of 2 and 3 April 1342;[193] and the sojourns of John of Luxembourg at Durbuy, i.e., the circumstances of the *Jugement dou roy de Behaingne*, are attested by the sources only in the 1340s, in August 1343 and 1344.[194] The latest document connecting Guillaume de Machaut with the court of John of Luxembourg is the nomination of Johannes, son of Egidius, arbalester of Luxembourg, to the canonicate *s.e.p.* at St Mary Magdalen in Verdun, dating from 4 December 1345. It mentions Machaut as one of the three executors of this benefice, the two others being Johannes of Pistoia and the abbot of Altmünster in Luxembourg. As one of the executors usually came from the curia of the pope (i.e., Johannes of Pistoia), another from the region or (arch) diocese concerned (i.e., the abbot of Altmünster), and the third from the direct milieu of the candidate, it is possible to conclude that Guillaume de Machaut was still active as a secretary of John of Luxembourg.[195]

Guillaume Pinchon (who did not resign his function as *maître des requêtes* to the King of France) was appointed provost of the cathedral chapter of Mainz in 1350. He most likely owed this dignity to Charles, King of the Romans, and he continued working for him.[196] Similarly, Johannes of Pistoia (who was promoted by Clement VI to the episcopal sees of Trent

---

191 Tadra, *Kanceláře*, 16/88; for the documents from Pistoia's negotiations, see Riezler (ed.), *Vatikanische Akten*, passim.
192 Ladislav Klicman, 'Mikuláš řečený Efficax z Lucemburka a Mikuláš, levoboček krále Jana', *Český časopis historický* 4 (1879), 246–9, at 248–9.
193 Guillaume de Machaut, 'Dit dou Lyon', 160, vv. 32–3 and 163, v. 140. At this time, John of Luxembourg was in the County of Luxembourg. See *RBM* IV, 443–6, nos 1097, 1102, 1107.
194 *RBM* IV, 807, no. 2072, and 577, no. 1422. See also Fantysová Matějková, 'Guillaume de Machaut'.
195 Ursmer Berlière and Philippe Van Isacker (eds), *Lettres de Clément VI (1342–1352), t. I (1342–1346)* (Rome, 1924), 644, no. 1736.
196 Thomas, 'Die Beziehungen', 168.

in 1348 and Spoleto in 1349)[197] reappeared later in the service of Charles IV and benefited from new incomes.[198] In this context, the new exciting discoveries of Andrew Wathey regarding the employment of Guillaume and Jean de Machaut at the court of Yolande of Bar between 1349 and 1353 are extremely valuable.[199] The Machaut brothers, canons in Verdun (in Guillaume's case only *s.e.p.* 1330–5), a city where the *droits de garde* were shared between the Count of Luxembourg and the Count of Bar (from 1337), must have already been familiar with the affairs between the counties of Luxembourg and Bar during their service to John.[200] Guillaume de Machaut could also have had experience with the military units of Henry IV, Count of Bar (1336–44), who participated in the Hundred Years' War on the French side in a similar way as John of Luxembourg. However, in the light of the careers of Machaut's colleagues, it does not seem likely that the Machaut brothers severed their ties with Charles IV after John's death. Charles took over the County of Luxembourg, which served as a pawn to secure the enormous debt created by his election at Rhense as a counter-king of the Romans on 11 July 1346. As King of the Romans and later Emperor, Charles had a specific policy towards the County of Bar (part of which belonged to the Holy Roman Empire) and the Kingdom of France, which had usurped imperial rights in Lotharingia that Charles aimed to regain (especially in the years 1346–56). Charles IV also strongly supported his nephews, Charles of France and John of Berry, during the crisis following the captivity of their father John II, King of France, at the Battle of Poitiers (1356–64) and even afterwards.[201] The exact relationship of Charles IV towards Charles of Évreux, King of Navarre, is unclear but, as Raymond Cazelles puts it, the former servitors of John of Luxembourg

---

197 For further references and information about Johannes of Pistoia, see Kunde, '"Hec autem est nostra ultima voluntas"', 348, n. 56.
198 Tadra, *Kanceláře*, 13/85, no. 3 and 16/88, no. 14; see also Winkelmann (ed.), *Acta imperii inedita*, t. 2, 569, no. 887.
199 Andrew Wathey, 'Guillaume de Machaut and Yolande of Flanders', in Jared C. Hartt et al. (eds), *Manuscripts, Music, Machaut*, 111–25. The documents relate specifically to the years 1349, 1350 and 1353 and therefore they do not exclude Bowers' hypothesis about Machaut's first residential year in Reims in 1351-2 (Bowers, 'Guillaume de Machaut', 7–8, 19).
200 The same appears to be true for Guillaume Pinchon, who was canon of Verdun from 1326 (see above). He was a mediator in the conflict between Bar and Lorraine (1350–1) after 2 November 1351. See *MVB*, t. I, 729, no. 1408 and Heinrich Volbert Sauerland, *Vatikanische Urkunden und Regesten zur Geschichte Lothringens* (Metz, 1905), t. II, 105–6, nos 1106–9.
201 Heinz Thomas, *Zwischen Regnum und Imperium: Die Fürstentümer Bar und Lothringen zur Zeit Kaiser Karls IV.* (Bonn, 1973); František Šmahel, *The Parisian Summit, 1377–78. Emperor Charles IV and King Charles V of France* (Prague, 2015); see also Fantysová Matějková, *Wenceslas*, passim.

(i.e., the Pinchon family and the Machaut brothers) appear close to the 'parti navarrais'. The King of Navarre was also involved in the attempted 'fugue du dauphin' (i.e., the 17-year-old Charles' abscondment from the French royal court) in 1355. The aim was to escort his brother-in-law Charles of Valois, the eldest son of King John II of France, to the Emperor, who would grant him investiture for the Dauphiné of Viennois, a fief of the Empire. This idea certainly sprung from the draft treaty of a mutual alliance addressed by Emperor Charles IV to John II, King of France, on 26 August 1355. The proposal was drafted by Guillaume Pinchon but was officially rejected by John II on 6 January 1356.[202]

In the period following the death of John of Luxembourg and possibly also before, Machaut's engagement at the court of one prince does not automatically exclude his service to other princes (and princesses, for that matter). His appearance at the courts of Yolande of Bar and of Charles of Navarre should be understood in the context of the social milieu and courtly network within which Machaut operated in the previous decades. It is certainly not a coincidence that Guillaume de Machaut also refers to John of Luxembourg and Charles IV in his narrative poetry in the following decades.

CONCLUSIONS

In 1322, the house of Luxembourg and the court of France (re-)established close mutual bonds. These renewed bonds included an annual income provided to the Count of Luxembourg by his brother-in-law, Charles IV le Bel, King of France. John's *fief-rente*, which tied him closely to the French monarchy, implied military obligations of the Count of Luxembourg towards the King of France. John's income from the King of France was most likely administered by the royal *receveur* in Reims and an officer of the Count of Luxembourg.

Guillaume de Machaut entered Luxembourg service at approximately the same time (c. 1323). There is no evidence to suggest any connection between the commencement of Machaut's service and the diplomatic rapprochement between France and the house of Luxembourg. Machaut was employed within the Francophone segment of John's chancery and financial administration. His tasks probably included the ongoing cultivation and social curation of John's feudal obligations, such as homage to the Count of Hainaut. He and his brother Jean de Machaut,

---

[202] Raymond Cazelles, *Société politique, noblesse et couronne sous Jean le Bon et Charles V* (Geneva, 1982), 87–8; Françoise Autrand, *Charles V* (Paris, 1994), 150–73, and *Naissance*, 98; see also Fantysová Matějková, *Wenceslas*, 139–51.

who is documented in Luxembourg service from 1333 onwards, reported to Guillaume Pinchon, chancellor of the king during the 1330s and 1340s.

Like the other clerics in John's service in the Luxembourgs' geographically dispersed domains, Guillaume de Machaut travelled a lot. However, most of the time, his itinerary was different from that of the King of Bohemia as depicted in Machaut's *Comfort d´Ami*. Machaut probably did visit Bohemia, as he asserts in the *CA*, but the only reliable information about his transrhenanian travels with the king concerns John's expedition to Prussia and Lithuania in 1329 and their subsequent journey back to Bohemia via Wrocław.[203] As demonstrated above, a considerable part of Machaut's portrait of the King of Bohemia as an *exemplum* of kingship and chivalry in the *CA* can be traced to the narrative established by Peter of Zittau (+ 1338) in his *ZC*.[204]

Rather than from Machaut's poetry, therefore, the radius and extent of Machaut's physical whereabouts must be reconstructed on the basis of archival documents which demonstrably involve him. These documents show him as a beneficiary of a chaplaincy, and of canonries with a prebend or without; as King John's cleric, *familiaris*, almoner, notary, secretary, and legal witness of homage; and as an executor of his colleague Johannes Arbalestarius' benefice. The archival materials show clearly that Machaut was intimately familiar with an important number of ecclesiastical institutions, dignitaries, and prelates from the archdioceses of Reims and Trier. He most likely accompanied John of Luxembourg whenever possible while the king dwelled in his Francophone domains, or travelled to Francophone regions. He also undertook diverse missions on King John's behalf when the king was away. In this capacity, Machaut's moves can be situated mainly in the northern regions of the Kingdom of France and in the Francophone parts of the Empire (County of Luxembourg, Cambrésis, Hainaut). It is also possible to speculate about repeated sojourns in Paris, with or without King John, for the abbot and the monks of Sainte-Geneviève in Paris figure among the executors of his benefice in Reims (1333 and 1335).[205]

Three sources hint at Machaut's direct or indirect relationship to the first Valois King of France, Philip VI. These are (1) Machaut's chancery note on a document prepared at Noyon in 1334, where John of Luxembourg

---

203 For John's itinerary, see footnote 12. No specific information is available about the route taken by Machaut. It would, however, be dangerous to assume that Machaut was with the king at all times.
204 A detailed French-Latin parallel comparison of both texts is attached to my recent article "'S'en puis parler plus clerement": Guillaume de Machaut jako dvorský úředník a básník na dvoře Jana Lucemburského (ca 1323–1346)', *Český časopis historický* 120 (2022), nos 3–4, 541–606, esp. 597–604.
205 Thomas, 'Extraits', 331–3, nos III and IV.

met with Philip of Valois; (2) his prebend in the royal collegiate chapter of Saint-Quentin (to which he was admitted in 1335 or before); and (3) his presence in the French military camp near Escaudoeuvres in 1340.[206]

It is also possible to speculate about Machaut's journeys to Avignon. His nomination bull issued by Benedict XII (1335) evokes not only information provided by John of Luxembourg, but also an assertion by Machaut himself ('tu, sicut asseris'). This expression might imply that he was personally present at the curia in April 1335 when the bull was produced.[207] Furthermore, the homage of John of Luxembourg to the abbot of Saint-Rémy witnessed by Machaut on 30 May 1344 took place during King John's journey back from Avignon via the Bourbonnais. The witnesses of this homage might have already been in the King of Bohemia's retinue before the date appearing on the document, allowing for the possibility that Machaut took part in John of Luxembourg's and his son Charles' journey to Avignon in March and April 1344.[208]

Machaut's *dits* written during the lifetime of John of Luxembourg seem to fall into the 1340s and might be the result of changes in John's political and cultural practices necessitated by his blindness. This is a subject that requires further research. There can be no doubt, however, that the network of contacts that Machaut established during his more than 20 years of service to King John of Bohemia (1323–46), and his resulting identity as a (former) servitor of this most illustrious of monarchs of his time, in combination with his canonry at Reims (1338), provided him with a solid base for his further career.

---

[206] For the document and events at Noyon and Ourscamps, see footnotes 111, 141 and 152; for the canonry at Saint-Quentin, see the bull edited by Thomas, 'Extraits', 332–3, no. IV, and footnote 143; for Machaut's presence at Escaudoeuvre, see footnote 182.

[207] Thomas, 'Extraits', 332–3, no. IV.

[208] For the document witnessed by Machaut, see footnote 9; for John of Luxembourg at the castle of La Bruyère de Laubespin on 1 May 1344, see Huillard-Bréholles, *Titres*, t. I, 408, no. 2370. For the visit to Avignon, see Bobková, *Jan Lucemburský*, 430–1. One of the highlights of these negotiations was the elevation of the Prague episcopal see to the level of an archbishopric.

CHAPTER 3

THE VYŠŠÍ BROD CYCLE AND ITS ANONYMOUS PAINTER: FRENCH AND BOHEMIAN COURT CIRCLES IN THE 1340s[1]

LENKA PANUŠKOVÁ

The group of nine panel paintings known as the Vyšší Brod Cycle (Figs 3.1A–I) is considered one of the masterpieces of medieval art in Bohemia. It received its designation after the Cistercian abbey in Vyšší Brod (Hohenfurth, southern Bohemia), on the premises of which it was discovered in the nineteenth century.[2] Assumed to have originated in the 1340s in Prague, it shows the history of salvation from the Annunciation to Pentecost in the order of the liturgical year. From a theological perspective, the cycle consists of three units. Whereas the first

---

1   This study was written within the framework of the project 'John the Blind and Bonne of Luxembourg as Patrons of Guillaume de Machaut: Intention and Reception of Machaut's Work in Historical Context', funded by the Czech Science Foundation (project no. 19-07473S). I dedicate this study to Hana Hlaváčková, whose research in book illumination and panel painting in late medieval Bohemia was a great inspiration for my work.
2   Jan Erazim Wocel, 'Bericht über eine kunstarchäologische Reise in Böhmen und Mähren', *Mittheilungen der k.k. Central-Commission zur Erforschung und Erhaltung der Baudenkmale* 3 (1858), 169–96, at 176. See also Jan Loriš, 'Mistr vyšebrodského cyklu: Devět desek s výjevy ze života a utrpení Kristova', in Antonín Matějček (ed.), *Česká malba gotická: Deskové malířství 1350–1450* (Prague, 1938), cat. no. 3, 44–9.

Fig. 3.1 A–I. Vyšší Brod Cycle, National Gallery in Prague, inv. nos. O 6786–O 6794, c. 99 cm x 93 cm.

A: Annunciation.

B: Nativity.

C: Adoration of the Magi.

D: Christ on the Mount of Olives.

E: Crucifixion.

F: Lamentation.

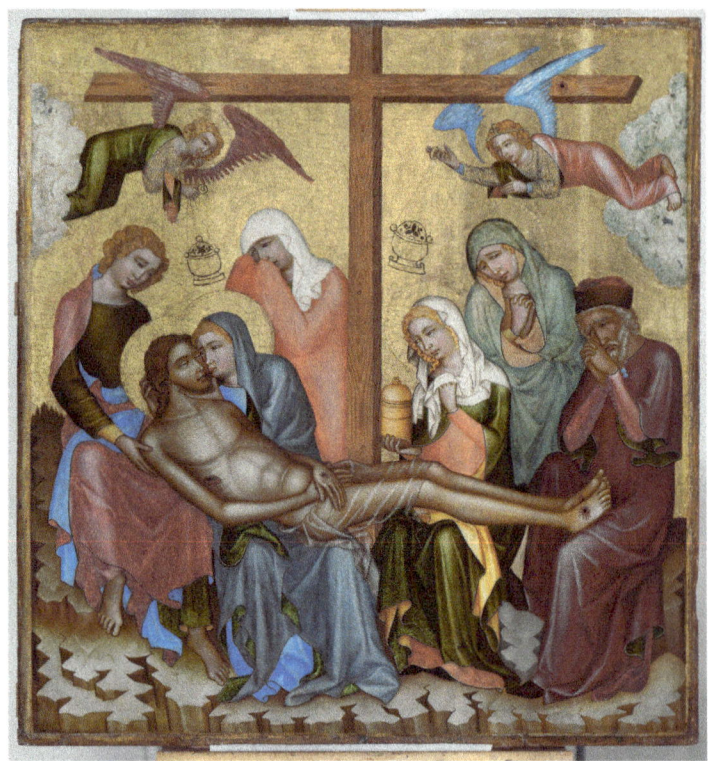

G: Resurrection.

H: Ascension.

I: Descent of the Holy Spirit.

triad covers the events of the Incarnation (Annunciation, Nativity, and the Adoration of the Magi; Figs 3.1A–C), the second unit deals with the story of Christ's suffering (Christ on the Mount of Olives, the Crucifixion, and the Lamentation; Figs 3.1D–F). The concluding triad celebrates the Resurrection and the Ascension of the Saviour in its first two panels. It ends with the Descent of the Holy Spirit (Figs 3.1G–I), who hovers as a dove above the illusionistic architecture under which the Apostles are gathered, with the Virgin Mary in the middle.

Generally, scholars agree that the cycle is a work of at least three, possibly four, main painters with the first four panels being assigned to the master painter.[3] The identity of this master painter has been debated in

---

3   In the only monograph dealing with the cycle, Jaroslav Pešina distinguished three painters. See Jaroslav Pešina, *The Master of the Hohenfurth Altarpiece* (Prague, 1989), 54–7. More recently, Wilfried Franzen suggested that four main painters were active together with a handful of assistants; see Wilfried Franzen, 'Mistr Vyšebrodského cyklu s dílnou: Christologický cyklus z Vyššího Brodu, zv. Vyšebrodský', in Jiří Fajt (ed.), *Karel IV. Císař z Boží milosti: Kultura a umění za vlády Lucemburků 1310–1437*, exhibition catalogue (Prague, 2006), cat. no. 9, 87–8. Researchers also pointed out a great disparity in the quality of the individual panel paintings. Franzen emphasized that the cycle as a whole is more consistent than

a number of papers dealing with his origin and training. In a monograph published in 2018, Aloysia Berens suggested that the Vyšší Brod master was also responsible for the Genealogical Cycle at Karlštejn Castle.[4] After finishing his work, according to Berens, he returned to Paris. There, he would have accepted another commission: two frontispieces which introduce the so-called manuscript A (Paris, Bibliothèque nationale de France, MS français 1584) containing the collected works of Guillaume de Machaut.[5] Although a connection between the Genealogical Cycle[6] and

---

the individual Vyšší Brod panels. This observation may, however, rather serve as an argument that the main painters worked under pressure to finish in time for the coronation ceremony. See below for further details.

4   Aloysia R. Berens, *Maître de Vyssi Brod et de Guillaume de Machaut, peintre et enlumineur au XIVe siècle: étude sur Jean de Bondol et son rapport avec l'art en Bohême* (Luxembourg, 2018).

5   The manuscript fr. 1584 has received enormous attention from researchers dealing with Guillaume de Machaut and his poetic œuvre. It contains a prescriptive index of works as well as the *Prologue*, a versified exposition of Machaut's poetics. Two large-format illustrations accompany the *Prologue* (ff. Dr and Er). Attributed by François Avril to the Master of the Bible of Jean de Sy, both the images show the poet receiving visitors. On f. Dr, Love introduces his children Sweet Thought, Pleasure, and Hope. Fol. Er shows Nature bringing *Sens*, Rhetoric, and Music. For the images see https://gallica.bnf.fr/ark:/12148/btv1b84490444/f15m [accessed 22 March 2023]. See François Avril, *L'enluminure à la Cour de France au XIVe siècle* (Paris, 1978), 28, 36; idem, 'Les manuscrits enluminés de Guillaume de Machaut', in *Guillaume de Machaut: Colloque – Table ronde, Université de Reims* (Paris, 1982), 117–34; idem, 'Un chef d'œuvre de l'enluminure sous le règne de Jean le Bon: la Bible moralisée, manuscript français 167 de la Bibliothèque nationale', *Monuments et mémoires de la Fondation Eugène Piot* 58 (1972), 91–125. More recently, see Domenic Leo, '"The Beginning is the End": Guillaume de Machaut's Illuminated *Prologue*', in Yolanda Plumley, Giuliano Di Bacco and Stefano Jossa (eds), *Citation, Intertextuality and Memory in the Middle Ages and Renaissance*, vol. 1 (Exeter, 2011), 96–112, and Elizabeth Eva Leach, 'Seeing *Sens*: A Picture of Two Guillaumes and Two Brothers?', in Jared C. Hartt, Tamsyn Mahoney-Steel and Benjamin L. Albritton (eds), *Manuscripts, Music, Machaut: Essays in Honor of Lawrence Earp* (Turnhout, 2022), 291–307. The master (*fl.* 1355–80) thought responsible for these illuminations worked on a number of manuscripts commissioned by the French king Charles V himself or by other members of the royal court. Stylistic parallels to his work have been observed with the Genealogical Cycle in the Karlštejn Castle. See Jaromír Homolka, 'Umělecká výzdoba paláce a menší věže hradu Karlštejna', in Jiří Fajt (ed.), *Magister Theodoricus: Dvorní malíř císaře Karla IV. Umělecká výzdoba posvátných prostor hradu Karlštejna* (Prague, 1998), 95–154. I will return to this issue below.

6   On the Luxembourg Genealogical Cycle and the identity of its painter, see Antonín Friedl, *Mikuláš Wurmser: Mistr královských portrétů na Karlštejně* (Prague, 1956); more recently, Jiří Fajt and Wilfried Franzen, 'Nové dvorské umění: od napodobování k císařskému stylu', in Jiří Fajt and Markus Hörsch (eds), *Císař Karel IV. 1316–2016: První česko-bavorská zemská výstava* (Prague, 2017), 139–46.

French book painting is widely accepted,[7] the idea of a single, ingenious master responsible for crucial stylistic changes from the 1340s to the 1370s does not sit well with present-day understanding of medieval workshop practices. Nevertheless, this notion still permeates the art-historical discourse among a significant number of Czech researchers; it can be observed, perhaps with excessive emphasis, in Berens' work as well. For the purposes of this paper, I suggest that there was a single workshop in Prague around the 1340s responsible for the production of panel paintings.[8] In this workshop, several high-quality painters worked side by side on the most prestigious commissions, using model-books to design the iconographic layout of a given scene.[9] The topic has most recently been discussed by Hana Hlaváčková,[10] suggesting, for example, a connection of the Vyšší Brod Cycle with the workshop that produced manuscripts for the royal court in Prague. She concluded, however, that contemporaneous panel and wall painting had best be investigated in a separate study in the future. Building on Hlaváčková, this paper proposes that, in the 1340s, panel paintings were produced in Prague by an atelier working independently of the Prague illuminators but that they mutually exchanged motifs, materials, or craftsmen.

Simultaneously, this paper aims to place the Vyšší Brod Cycle into a wider context – networks of artists and their workshops, active particularly for the French and Bohemian royal courts. It seeks to establish an interrelation both in style and motifs transmitted from Paris to Bohemia

---

7   Stylistically, it is necessary to differentiate between 'French art' and 'French-inspired art'. The second designation particularly applies to the murals at Karlštejn Castle. Here, inspiration from French book painting of the 1350s can certainly be observed but mingles with local artistic practices and style. Therefore, Jaromír Homolka's labelling of the 'French' aspects in the Genealogical Cycle as 'parallels' to contemporaneous French book painting defines the style of the Genealogical Cycle rather more precisely than does Aloysia Berens. See Homolka, 'Umělecká výzdoba', and Berens, *Maître de Vyssi Brod et de Guillaume de Machaut*, 33–58. Moreover, Berens fails to recognize other sources of French motifs, which are to be observed, e.g., in Sienese panel painting, and book painting of the Trecento.
8   By the term workshop, I mean a group of painters working together on commissions assigned to the workshop.
9   For this practice, see Robert W. Scheller, *Exemplum: Model-Book Drawings and the Practice of Artistic Transmission in the Middle Ages (ca. 900 – ca. 1470)* (Amsterdam, 1995).
10 Hana Hlaváčková, 'Pražské iluminátorské dílny doby Karla IV. a jejich styl', in Kateřina Kubínová and Klára Benešovská (eds), *Imago/Imagines: Výtvarné dílo a proměny jeho funkcí v českých zemích od 10. do první třetiny 16. století* (Prague, 2019), vol. 2, 540–71.

and back by other channels than individual masters.[11] In doing so, special attention will be devoted to the reconstruction of the Vyšší Brod Cycle as well as to the place for which it was originally intended. In this context, I shall also discuss the recently discovered painting of the Annunciation that copies the Vyšší Brod image in almost every single detail (Fig. 3.2).[12] Finally, I shall review Aloysia Berens' hypothesis from the perspective of workshop networks and links between Paris and Prague.

THE VYŠŠÍ BROD CYCLE: ITS DONOR AND PLACE OF ORIGIN

The second panel of the Vyšší Brod Cycle with the Nativity scene proves significant for establishing the identity of the donor (Fig. 3.1B). At the bottom right-hand corner, a kneeling figure with a church model can be identified as Lord Peter I of Rožmberk (German: Rosenberg, d. 1347). A coat of arms displaying a five-petalled rose lying in front of him proves Peter's identity. At the royal court of John of Luxembourg, he acted as regent during the absences of the king. Later, as Lord Chamberlain, Peter was in charge of organizing the coronation ceremony of Charles IV and his wife Blanche of Valois that took place in the old St Vitus Basilica at Prague Castle in 1347. Most scholars at present agree that the cycle was commissioned by Peter for the Cistercian abbey in Vyšší Brod, to which Peter retreated shortly before his death in 1347. However, the iconography of the Annunciation, the very first panel of the cycle, in particular includes details which might point to a significant influence from the French court

---

11   It has to be noted that medieval Bohemian art of the fourteenth century benefited from various sources of inspiration – not only from France (Paris) and Avignon but in particular also from Sienese production, represented, for example, by Duccio, or Pietro and Ambrogio Lorenzetti. This Italo-French synthesis also decisively informed the works by Simone Martini in the papal palace at Avignon. For more research on the Sienese inspirations in Central European art, see Gerhard Schmidt, 'Zur Datierung des "kleinen" Bargello-Diptychons und der Verkündigungstafel in Cleveland', in Albert Châtelet and Nicole Reynaud (eds), *Études d'art français offerts a Charles Sterling* (Paris, 1975), 47–63.
12   For the circumstances of this discovery, see Martin Vaněk, 'Národní galerie a nákup století', Artalk.cz https://artalk.cz/2019/09/02/narodni-galerie-a-nakup-stoleti/ [accessed 22 March 2023]. The panel was acquired by the Foundation of Richard Fuxa and offered to the National Gallery in Prague; see Hana Hlaváčková, 'Vyšebrodský mistr ve středověké Evropě', *Art Antique*, March 2020, https://www.artantiques.cz/vysebrodsky-mistr-ve-stredoveke-evrope [accessed 22 March 2023]. See also Jan Klípa, 'The Enthroned Madonna from Dijon: A Recently Discovered Painting from the Workshop of the Master of the Vyšší Brod Altarpiece', *Umění* 67 (2019), 215–25.

instead, and therefore to a connection with the coronation ceremony. They include the blue overcoat of the archangel covered with golden fleur-de-lys as well as the golden sphere in his left hand (Fig. 3.1A). On the basis of these motifs, Jaroslav Pešina suggested that the cycle was intended to commemorate the events of the coronation and subsequently reached Vyšší Brod because of Peter's involvement with the monastery, which was founded in 1259 by Peter's ancestor Vok I of Rožmberk and served as the family's burial place. However, as Hana Hlaváčková[13] pointed out, the remarkably well-preserved monastery archives do not include any reference to the panel paintings, nor have any plausible placements for the panels within the monastery's architectural framework been proposed.[14] Therefore, the cycle might have reached the monastery at a much later time, for example, as a result of the secularization and Church reform instigated by Joseph II (r. 1765–90).[15] At the same time, Hlaváčková elaborated further on Pešina's suggestion that the paintings were employed in the coronation ceremony.[16] She proposed that the Vyšší Brod Cycle was indeed commissioned by Peter I of Rožmberk – however, not for the monastery church, but very probably for St Vitus Cathedral at Prague Castle. She argued that the old basilica, being in the process of demolition, hardly offered an appropriate space for the coronation of the Bohemian king and queen.[17] Therefore, movable panel paintings would have appeared an excellent option for decorating the church interior while concealing any construction activity. Moreover, since Peter acted as the chief organizer (and possibly financial sponsor of the cycle), it seems

---

13   Hana Hlaváčková, 'Panel Paintings in the Cycle of the Life of Christ from Vyšší Brod (Hohenfurth)', in Klára Benešovská (ed.), *King John of Luxembourg and the Art of His Era* (Prague, 1998), 244–55, at 251.
14   Xaver M. Millauer, *Fragmente aus dem Nekrolog des Zistercienser-Stiftes Hohenfurt* (Prague, 1819); Mathias Pangerl, *Urkundenbuch des Cistercienserstiftes Beatae Mariae Virginis zu Hohenfurt in Böhmen*, Fontes rerum Austriacarum II, vol. 23 (Vienna, 1865).
15   In the Habsburg domains, about a third of the monasteries ceased to exist at that point in time because they were not engaged in useful work for the community (care of the sick, education, and above all agriculture). See, e.g., P.G.M. Dickson, 'Joseph II's Reshaping of the Austrian Church', *The Historical Journal* 36 (1993), 89–114. Due to the reform, the Cistercians in Vyšší Brod lost a large part of their property and were not allowed to accept any more novices. For more on this episode in the history of the monastery, see https://www.klastervyssibrod.cz/EN/History/Joseph-II-s-monasteries-abolition [accessed 22 March 2023].
16   See Pešina, *The Master of the Hohenfurth Altarpiece*, 27–8; Hlaváčková, 'Panel Paintings', 251.
17   The foundation stone of the new cathedral was laid in 1341. See Anežka Merhautová (ed.), *Katedrála sv. Víta* (Prague, 1994), esp. the chapter by eadem, 'Basilika sv. Víta, Václava a Vojtěcha', 16–24.

logical that he was keen to see himself being made visible within the cycle. In contrast to previous reconstructions arranging the panels into a square altarpiece, Hlaváčková also proposed their alignment in a single row on the rood screen of the cathedral behind the altar of the Holy Cross. This altar stood presumably in front of the wall of the second crypt built in 1256. Reinforcing her hypothesis, the central triad of the cycle showing the Passion of Christ (Figs 3.1D–F) was damaged by candles, as the restoration account stated, whereas the other panels were not.

ALTARPIECES IN CISTERCIAN MONASTERIES: THE IMPORTANCE OF MARIOLOGY

Hlaváčková's hypothesis was not accepted by Czech scholars, except by a few of her students,[18] despite the fact that her detractors proposed no relevant counterarguments. In his most recent study on the Vyšší Brod Cycle, Jan Royt referred to Hlaváčková's hypothesis.[19] In order to support the idea that the panels used to form a square altarpiece, he pointed to Passion altarpieces preserved in Cistercian monasteries. The Passion altar in Heilsbronn (diocese of Eichstätt) from around 1350 provides, according to Royt, a close parallel to the Vyšší Brod Cycle both in terms of origin and arrangement.[20] However, only the left wing of this altarpiece is preserved, depicting Longinus and some Jews under the Cross on the outer side. The inner panel is divided into four compartments and shows the Kiss of Judas, Christ before Herod, the Resurrection, and the Ascension. Peter Strieder assumes that in the central part of the altarpiece a screen housed sculptures in a way similar to the much smaller Passion Altarpiece of the same workshop, now kept in Nuremberg, that contained relics and was intended for private devotion.[21] Since only a fragment survives,

---

18 For example, Petr Jindra, 'K ideovému obsahu vyšebrodského cyklu' (Masters thesis, Institute for Art History, Faculty of Arts, Charles University Prague, 2008). See also idem, 'The Iconography of Christ in the Resurrection Panel of the So-Called Hohenfurth Cycle in an Exegetic View', *Bulletin of the National Gallery in Prague* 25 (2015), 6–37.
19 Jan Royt, 'Poznámky k rekonstrukci a k ikonografii Vyšebrodského oltáře', in Aleš Mudra and Michaela Ottová (eds), *Ars videndi: Professori Jaromír Homolka ad honorem* (Prague, 2006), 175–83. See also Annegret Laabs, *Malerei und Plastik im Zisterzienserorden: Zum Bildgebrauch zwischen sakralem Zeremoniell und Stiftermemoria 1250–1430* (Petersberg, 2000).
20 For a more detailed description of the Heilsbronn altar, see Peter Strieder, *Tafelmalerei in Nürnberg 1350–1550* (Königstein im Taunus, 1993), 12–17, esp. 14 (with images).
21 Strieder, *Tafelmalerei*, 14. For the Heilsbronn Passion Altarpiece, see Strieder, *Tafelmalerei*, cat. no. 1, 166. The smaller Passion Altarpiece is kept in the

the reconstruction of the Heilsbronn Passion Altarpiece remains highly hypothetical. Therefore, in my opinion, it cannot serve as a corresponding analogy without further evidence. Besides, the Vyšší Brod panels are single-side paintings, suggesting rather a different arrangement than a winged altarpiece. On those grounds, the examples of winged altarpieces either painted or sculpted on both the inner or outer sides which Royt enumerates in his study do not offer relevant comparands. This applies, among other examples, to the sculpted altarpiece in the so-called Torkapelle of Kloster Hude near Oldenburg (around 1320), which includes 24 reliefs representing Jesus' childhood and Passion. Further on, Royt brings up the iconographic qualities of the cycle. He claims that the cycle accentuates the Virgin Mary and thus corresponds with the traditional Marian dedication of all Cistercian monasteries. However, Hlaváčková pointed out that the Vyšší Brod Cycle is strictly Christological; the Virgin there acts merely as the mediator of the Incarnation.[22]

THE ICONOGRAPHY OF THE VYŠŠÍ BROD ANNUNCIATION PANEL

An inscription in a golden circle surrounds the half-figure of the Lord in the upper left corner of the first panel (Fig. 3.1A). Milena Bartlová managed to decipher it as follows: *RORATE CELI DESUPER ET NUBES PLUANT IUSTUM APERIET TERRA.*[23] She identified it correctly as the passage from Isaiah 45:8 that speaks of the coming of the Messiah born of a virgin. The dew falling from Heaven recalls either the story of the dew on Gideon's fleece in Judges 6:37–40 as a symbol of Mary's virginity or the manna from Heaven sent by the Lord to the Israelites in the desert (Exodus 16:14–15). In the latter case, the episode pre-figures the Eucharist that brings to mind the sufferings of Jesus Christ on the Cross. The pair of peacocks which flank the canopy of the Virgin's throne in the panel (Fig. 3.1A) symbolizes the incorruptibility of Christ's body that was resurrected from the dead as well as immortality and eternal life.[24] Within the framework of biblical typology, the two books open in

---

Germanisches Nationalmuseum; see Strieder, *Tafelmalerei*, cat. no. 3, 167.
22 On this theological point, see also the essay by Matouš Jaluška in this volume, which demonstrates the relevance of these thoughts to Charles IV's self-representation.
23 Milena Bartlová, "'Rorate celi desuper et nubes pluant iustum': New Additions to the Iconography of the "Annunciation" from the Altarpiece of Vyšší Brod', *Source: Notes in the History of Art* 13:2 (1994), 9–14.
24 This meaning of the peacock goes back to the *Physiologus*, a didactic Christian text written originally in Greek in the second century AD. It includes descriptions of

front of the Virgin stress the complementarity of the Old and the New Testament. Contemporary Marian hymns and invocations contain the same symbolism, but the iconography of the Annunciation must of course be seen in the context of the whole cycle.[25] According to Hlaváčková, the Vyšší Brod Crucifixion panel (Fig. 3.1E) represents the central axis of the cycle, Salvation. Only with all nine panels arranged in a single line do they produce meaningful pairings. First, Hlaváčková mentions the episode on the Mount of Olives (Fig. 3.1D) which can be paired with the Lamentation panel (Fig. 3.1F).[26] She links the sleeping Apostles in the Mount of Olives panel with the two triads of mourners in the Lamentation panel; both are connected by the horizontal body of the Saviour. Hlaváčková recognizes an even clearer correspondence in the second pair created by the Adoration of the Magi (Fig. 3.1C) and the Resurrection (Fig. 3.1G) panels. The three Marys visiting the empty tomb echo the three kings presenting their gifts to the new-born child. Here, Jesus sits on the lap of the Virgin Mary, symbolizing the Throne of Wisdom, and thus establishes a theological counterpart to the resurrected Saviour enthroned on the tomb; typologically, both recall an altar as well as the Ark of the Covenant. The next pair of panels with the Nativity (Fig. 3.1B) and the Ascension (Fig. 3.1H) visualizes the doctrine of Incarnation and the physical departure of Christ to Heaven after his resurrection. Moreover, the iconography of both panels conveys the hypostatic union of Christ's humanity and divinity. In this context, the naked upper body of the Child together with the physical features of the ascending Saviour, whose feet can still be observed by the Apostles, underline Christ's human nature stressed earlier by the motive of the footprints that he left on the Mount of Olives (Fig. 3.1D). Finally, the panels with the Annunciation (Fig. 3.1A) and Pentecost (Fig. 3.1I) do not depict Jesus Christ in his humanity but rather are of a symbolic character, with the Holy Spirit shown as the *spiritus agens* of the Trinity. Thus, the Virgin Mary represents, on the one hand, the *mediatrix* of the Incarnation through the Holy Spirit; on the other hand, she symbolizes the Holy Church that was established on the very day when the promised

---

various animals, stones, and plants together with their moral and symbolic qualities. For an edition see Francis Carmody, *Physiologus: The Very Ancient Book of Beasts, Plants and Stones* (San Francisco, 1953). See also Anna Dorofeeva, 'Miscellanies, Christian Reform and Early Medieval Encyclopaedism: A Reconsideration of the Pre-Bestiary Latin *Physiologus* Manuscripts', Historical Research 90:250 (2017), 665–82.

25 See Royt, 'Poznámky k rekonstrukci a k ikonografii Vyšebrodského oltáře', 179–81.

26 See Hlaváčková, 'Panel Paintings', 248.

Comforter descended upon the Apostles.[27] This interpretation of the Vyšší Brod Cycle as a whole within the medieval theological discourse affirms its Christological meaning.

COPYING THE ANNUNCIATION PANEL

The recent discovery of a copy of the Annunciation panel (91.8 cm x 79.5 cm, Fig. 3.2) complicates the proposed hypothesis that the Vyšší Brod Cycle was commissioned by Peter I of Rožmberk with the intent to decorate the choir screen of Prague Cathedral for the coronation ceremony.[28] Hana Hlaváčková called the second Annunciation panel a later 'adaptation' of the Vyšší Brod Annunciation. She argued that its typological significance made the Vyšší Brod panel worth reproducing. Despite some minor alterations (e.g., the crystalline terrain with trees instead of the lily; compare Fig. 3.1A and Fig. 3.2), the newly discovered painting in my opinion originated in the same workshop as the Vyšší Brod Annunciation, even though it was not painted by the same hand as the Vyšší Brod panel that served as its model. In comparison with the Vyšší Brod Cycle, which was extensively restored in 1948–60, the recently discovered panel painting manifests severe deteriorations in the layers of the paint.[29] Nevertheless, the newly discovered painting corresponds to its under-drawing in every detail. Since this panel survives significantly reduced in thickness, the original appearance of the back panel cannot be determined.[30] For that reason, it is not possible to discuss the ways in

---

27 'And I will pray to the Father, and he shall give you another Comforter, that he may abide with you for ever; Even the Spirit of truth; whom the world cannot receive, because it seeth him not, neither knoweth him: but ye know him; for he dwelleth with you, and shall be in you' (John 14:16-17), cited after the King James Version of the Bible; see https://www.bibelwissenschaft.de/online-bibeln/king-james-version/lesen-im-bibeltext/bibel/text/lesen/stelle/53/140001/149999/ch/ce58a38a09e8225880d293f85b3e8789/ [accessed 22 March 2023].

28 The newly discovered Annunciation panel was publicly presented at the National Gallery in Prague in spring 2019. See above, n. 12. For further information, see the discussion in Artalk.cz https://artalk.cz/2019/10/29/zvestovani-panne-marii-pujde-do-aukce-jednani-s-ngp-zrejme-selhala/ [accessed 22 March 2023].

29 For technical aspects of the Vyšší Brod panel paintings, see Mojmír Hamsík, 'Malířská technika Vyšebrodského cyklu', *Umění* 10 (1962), 388–400. See also the unpublished restoration report of the newly discovered Annunciation panel by Adam Pokorný, National Gallery Prague, 2018. I thank Jan Klípa (researcher at the Department of Medieval Art, Institute of Art History, Czech Academy of Sciences) for a copy of the report.

30 The restoration report estimates that the wooden panel was originally 20 millimetres thick and only later cut to the present 13 millimetres. The same fate met the Vyšší Brod Cycle, which was also trimmed in this way.

Fig. 3.2. Annunciation, Private Collection, c. 1350, 91.8 cm x 79.5 cm.

which the painting might have been displayed or presented to its viewer/s. According to its current dimensions (91.8 cm x 79.5 cm) it appears of comparable size to the panels of the Vyšší Brod Cycle (99 cm x 93 cm).

For the purposes of this study, the issue of the workshop organization is decisive and therefore has to be addressed more thoroughly. Obviously, the newly discovered panel painting, despite its deterioration, is a work of another anonymous and very skilful painter who, I suggest, worked side by side with the Vyšší Brod master.[31] Thus, in my assessment, current

---

31 See Hlaváčková, 'Vyšebrodský mistr ve středověké Evropě'; Klípa, 'The Enthroned Madonna from Dijon'. Also Franzen, 'Mistr Vyšebrodského cyklu s dílnou'.

theories assuming that the most skilful painter was automatically also the head of the workshop responsible for the most prestigious commissions – to which the Vyšší Brod Annunciation (Fig. 3.1A) painting undoubtedly belongs – do not necessarily find confirmation.[32] It has been noticed earlier in this study that the Vyšší Brod panels are the work of at least three painters.[33] More particularly, the last two panels in the cycle, the Ascension and the Descent of the Holy Spirit (Figs 3.1H–I), differ significantly from the first triad (Figs 3.1A–C) in style; the last two panels of the cycle (Figs 3.1H–I) manifest a strong influence of French court painting. Hlaváčková claims that both the Ascension and the Descent of the Holy Spirit might have originated later than the first group of three panels.[34] Concerning their style in colour modelling, she assigns them to painters trained very probably in Cologne. A very similar combination of stylistic elements both from France and the Lower Rhine region manifests itself in the newly discovered Annunciation panel (Fig. 3.2). These observations provide us with arguments to hypothesize that Prague housed a group of highly skilled professionals from various areas of western Europe (including France and the Lower Rhine) and central Italy (Siena), along with local illuminators who jointly were able to reflect the latest visual trends.[35] This heterogeneous group of craftsmen very probably worked together on larger orders such as the cycle of nine panels. Indeed, as we shall see next, the group responsible for the Vyšší Brod Cycle produced several other panel paintings of excellent quality made for esteemed members of the Prague royal court.

32 Although previously some scholars following Jaroslav Pešina insisted on the theory of a main master and his assistants, the panels with Christ praying on the Mount of Olives, the Crucifixion, and the Lamentation, thought to be the work of assistants, are in my view of the same high quality as the panels of the first group ascribed to the painter called the main master of the workshop. Some decline in quality may be observed in the Crucifixion; still, the painting as a whole retains the high level of quality that marks the entire cycle.
33 For further details see above, including bibliography on the topic.
34 I discussed these issues thoroughly with Hana Hlaváčková on numerous occasions, for which I am highly grateful to her.
35 The Italianate orientation of the workshop responsible for the Vyšší Brod Cycle is usually inferred from comparing the cycle to the panel paintings of Klosterneuburg. See Gerhard Schmidt, 'Malerei bis 1450: Tafelmalerei – Wandmalerei – Buchmalerei', in Karl M. Swoboda, *Gotik in Böhmen: Geschichte, Gesellschaftsgeschichte, Architektur, Plastik und Malerei* (Munich, 1969), 167–321, at 171–9.

THE MADONNA OF KŁODZKO AND OTHER PRODUCTIONS OF THE VYŠŠÍ BROD CYCLE GROUP OF PAINTERS

In 1344, almost simultaneously with the first three panels of the Vyšší Brod Cycle, the Madonna of Kłodzko (Czech: Kladsko; German: Glatz) in Lower Silesia was commissioned by Ernest of Pardubice after being ordained the first Archbishop of Prague (Fig. 3.3). The iconographic details in the painting refer to a handful of Marian invocations that led scholars to compare it with the *Akathistos* hymn, the most popular Marian hymn in the Eastern liturgy.[36] Similar in kind to the symbols used in both the Annunciation paintings (Figs. 3.1A and 3.2), these signs were readily accessible to a highly educated audience. Following this line of reasoning, Hlaváčková argues that the lily, being the most common attribute of the Virgin in the Annunciation scene, was deliberately omitted in the second Prague Annunciation panel (Fig. 3.2). Instead, the painter focused on the more sophisticated typological motives deployed in the Vyšší Brod panel (Fig. 3.1A), which in turn made it attractive for reuse in a new painting. A few decades later, a third Annunciation panel, kept today in the Cleveland Museum of Art (Fig. 3.4),[37] evidently restated the principal composition of both the Prague Annunciations (Figs 3.1A and 3.2) but failed to match their complicated symbolism. These observations suggest some form of exchange among the craftsmen involved, all of whom were operating in Prague.

Within the same group of craftsmen, several more panel paintings originated. They typically show a picture of the Mother of God holding the baby Jesus in her arms. Examples include the Strahov Madonna (Fig. 3.5) and the Veveří Madonna. The Madonna of Zbraslav[38] shares the elaborate mise-en-scène of the Virgin's hair covered by a veil, as well as the

---

36 The dating of the panel can be established on the basis of the archbishop's insignia, which are laid down at the footsteps of the Virgin's throne. Ernest of Pardubice was ordained on 30 April 1344. Robert Suckale suggested an earlier dating for the painting shortly before Ernest's ordination. See his 'Die Glatzer Madonnentafel des Prager Erzbischofs Ernst von Pardubitz als gemalter Marienhymnus: Zur Frühzeit der böhmischen Tafelmalerei', *Wiener Jahrbuch für Kunstgeschichte* 46/47 (1993/4), 737–56. For the meaning of the *Akathistos* hymn in the Eastern Church, see Egon Wellesz, 'The "Akathistos": A Study in Byzantine Hymnography', *Dumbarton Oaks Papers* 9/10 (1956), 141–74; Nancy Patterson Ševčenko, 'Icons in the Liturgy', *Dumbarton Oaks Papers* 45 (1991), 45–57.
37 Cleveland Museum of Art, Mr and Mrs William H. Marlatt Fund 1954.393, c. 1380, France or Netherlands, 40.3 x 31 cm.
38 National Gallery Prague, Madonna of Strahov, inv. no. O 539, and Madonna of Zbraslav, inv. no. VO 2.116. The Madonna of Veveří, 79.5 x 62.5 cm, has been kept in the Diocesan Museum of Brno since 2016.

Fig. 3.3. Madonna of Kłodzko, Berlin, Staatliche Museen, Gemäldegalerie, inv. no. 1624, 186 cm x 95 cm.

Fig. 3.4. Annunciation, Cleveland Museum of Art, Mr and Mrs William H. Marlatt Fund 1954.393, c. 1380, France or the Netherlands, 40.3 cm x 31 cm.

Fig. 3.5. Madonna of Strahov, Picture Gallery of the Premonstratensian Monastery in Strahov, inv. no. O 539, 94 cm x 84 cm.

transparent shirt that her child is wearing, with the Madonna of Kłodzko (Fig. 3.3). The combination of plain calligraphy with soft light and shade modelling for volume supports the theory of domestic artists learning and adopting new stylistic forms. At the same time, as Hlaváčková demonstrates for the Prague illuminators in the course of the long fourteenth century, older artistic generations remained active alongside younger painters who came from other regions as well as from Bohemia. The Prague production included not only larger panels, but also small portable objects exemplified by the Virgin and Child panel painting at the National Gallery Prague, known as the Madonna of Rome, that once might have formed a diptych

Fig. 3.6. Diptych of Karlsruhe, Staatliche Kunsthalle, Karlsruhe, inv. no. 2431a-b, 20 cm x 14.5 cm.

similar to the diptych in the Staatliche Kunsthalle Karlsruhe (Fig. 3.6).[39] The small Prague painting copied the Madonna of Zbraslav in all details. Copying important images and devotional models on varying scales and for different types of audiences was nothing unusual in medieval artistic production.[40]

THE FRANCO-ITALIAN ORIENTATION OF ART DURING THE LUXEMBOURG CENTURY: SOURCES AND MEDIATORS

In view of the evidence and argument presented above, it seems highly unlikely that the creator responsible for the Vyšší Brod Cycle of nine panel paintings covering the history of Salvation from the Annunciation to the Descent of the Holy Spirit was a single person. At the same time,

39 Inv. no. 2431a-b.
40 For ways of transmission and exchange of motives, ideas, and forms among medieval workshops, see Scheller, *Exemplum*.

the Vyšší Brod Cycle did not appear suddenly in medieval Bohemia but was deeply rooted in the local artistic tradition. It is necessary to bear in mind that ateliers in Prague may have also worked continuously during the era of John of Luxembourg, although very little has been preserved that can be assigned to the 1310s, 1320s, and 1330s with certainty.[41] Due to the negative statements of chroniclers and John's contemporaries who repeatedly pointed to the king's frequent absences from Bohemia and his neediness in terms of financial resources, modern-day scholars have tended to connect significant art commissions primarily with Charles IV and prominent members of Charles' court. In the words of Lenka Bobková, one of the most prolific Czech medievalists, who published a complex monograph on John of Luxembourg with the subtitle *Father of a Famous Son*, King John did not enjoy any particular favour in Czech historiography.[42] But governing simultaneously over the County of Luxembourg and the Bohemian kingdom enabled John to combine a

---

41 Here, we need to point to the Passional of Abbess Kunigunde (Prague, Národní knihovna České republiky, MS XIV.A.17), the illuminations of which combine French courtliness with Italianate ornamentics. For iconographic as well as stylistic correspondences with the Kaufmann Crucifixion, see the catalogue entry by Jiří Fajt and Robert Suckale, 'Kaufmann Crucifixion', in Jiří Fajt (ed.), *Karel IV. Císař z Boží milosti: Kultura a umění za vlády Lucemburků 1310–1437*, exhibition catalogue (Prague, 2006), cat. no. 1, 77–8. Cf. Jiří Fajt and Robert Suckale, 'Kaufmann Crucifixion', in Barbara D. Boehm and Jiří Fajt (eds), *Prague: The Crown of Bohemia 1347–1437* (New York, 2005), cat. no. 1, 132–3. Generally, artistic production at the turn of the thirteenth and early fourteenth centuries in Bohemia excelled, for example, in reliquaries which – similarly to the Passional – were made for the aristocratic Benedictine nunnery of St George at Prague Castle. See the exhibition catalogue and the introductory study in Klára Benešovská (ed.), *A Royal Marriage: Elisabeth Přemyslid and John of Luxembourg* (Prague, 2011), with further bibliography. Another example is provided by the façade of the Stone Bell House in the Old Town of Prague, whose sculptural programme is preserved in fragments. The building served as a temporary residence for the royal couple of John of Luxembourg and Elizabeth of Bohemia (= Přemyslid) shortly after their marriage and John's arrival in Prague. For more on the architecture and sculptural decorations, see Klára Benešovská, 'The Arrival of John of Luxembourg and Elisabeth in Prague in December 1310: The Stone Bell House as the Royal City Residence', in Benešovská (ed.), *The Royal Marriage*, 54–69 and 80–125. See also eadem, 'The House at the Stone Bell: Royal Representation in Early-Fourteenth-Century Prague', in Zoë Opačić (ed.), *Prague and Bohemia: Medieval Art, Architecture and Cultural Exchange in Central Europe* (Leeds, 2006), 48–53, with further bibliography. Most recently on the topic, see Mateusz Grzęda, 'Façade of the House at the Stone Bell in Prague and a new Paradigm of Representation', *Umění* 65 (2017), 214–25. For art production in thirteenth-century Bohemia in a wider context, see Antonín Hejna (ed.), *Umění 13. století v českých zemích* (Prague, 1983).
42 Lenka Bobková, *Jan Lucemburský: otec slavného syna* (Prague, 2018).

long-standing affinity to the French royal court with imperial ambitions. In his efforts to secure the imperial throne for the house of Luxembourg, John repeatedly intervened in imperial politics, taking the side of Louis of Bavaria at one time, of the pope in Avignon at another.

The cultural impact of John's rule in the Czech lands still awaits a thorough re-evaluation. Nevertheless, it would not be too daring to assume that some form of cultural exchange of the Bohemian kingdom with other royal courts and with the papal curia took place. One of the Luxembourgs' main supporters and the predecessor of Ernest of Pardubice, John IV of Dražice, spent 11 years in Avignon at the papal curia (1318–29).[43] After his return to Bohemia, John of Dražice immersed himself in reform activities which were accompanied by intensified funding of monasteries and building projects in central Bohemia. His commissions might have included the enigmatic Kaufmann's Crucifixion panel painting (Fig. 3.7) that, according to Robert Suckale, introduced crucial stylistic and iconographic elements to Bohemian works of art that were to be copied until the early fifteenth century.[44] Together with Jiří Fajt, Suckale argued for the Bohemian origin of Kaufmann's Crucifixion and suggested a date after 1330, coinciding with the bishop's return to Prague. Suckale pointed out that the Franco-Italian orientation dominated Central European art as early as the 1330s when Italianate elements became reflected across today's Germany, particularly in the Upper Rhine region. With this hypothesis, Suckale disputed Gerhard Schmidt's theory according to which the light-and-shade modelling of volume, which is so significant for the artistic production of the 1340s, goes back to lost paintings originating around Jean Pucelle and his Parisian followers.

---

43 Zdenka Hledíková, 'Jan IV. z Dražic a Avignon', in Michal Svatoš (ed.), *Scientia Nobilitas: Sborník prací k poctě prof. PhDr. Františka Kavky, DrSc.* (Prague, 1998), 31–9; eadem, *Biskup Jan IV. z Dražic (1301-1343)* (Prague, 1991), esp. 99–123.
44 Berlin, Staatliche Museen, Gemäldegalerie, inv. no. 1833. See Jiří Fajt and Robert Suckale, 'Kreuzigung', in Fajt (ed.), *Karel IV. Císař z Boží milosti*, cat. no. 1, 77–8.

Fig. 3.7 Kaufmann's Crucifixion, Berlin, Staatliche Museen, Gemäldegalerie, inv. no. 1833.

THE VYŠŠÍ BROD GROUP OF PAINTERS, THE MASTER OF THE BIBLE OF JEAN DE SY, AND JEAN BONDOL[45]

Among the Parisian workshops which members of the French royal court repeatedly entrusted with their commissions, Aloysia Berens identified the anonymous master to whom she attributed the two most crucial cycles of fourteenth-century paintings in Bohemia, i.e., the Vyšší Brod Cycle and the Genealogy of the Luxembourgs at Karlštejn Castle. Only two manuscript copies of the Genealogy, dating from the sixteenth century, have been preserved.[46] The original wall paintings dated back to 1355–7 when Charles, having received the imperial crown, returned from Rome. According to Berens, the anonymous master arrived in Prague at the beginning of his career after receiving basic training in Paris. She recognizes him in a certain Johannes Ga[l]licus, a French member of the Prague guild of painters, sculptors, and goldsmiths. Johannes' name is given in various versions in Czech, German, or Latin, and he is listed in 1365 and again in 1375 in the *Zechenbuch* of the Prague painters' guild; however, the *Zechenbuch* does not specify his profession.[47] Matthias Pangerl, the *Zechenbuch*'s editor, suggested that he was a goldsmith since his name features among other goldsmiths. In addition, he donated to the guild a piece of gold – '*Monsier Johannes Galicus dat aurum pro toto*'[48] – which Pangerl interpreted as confirming his suggestion that Johannes Gal[l]icus was a goldsmith, not a painter.

---

45   See the bibliographical summary in Lawrence Earp, *Guillaume de Machaut: A Guide to Research* (New York and London, 1995), 133–4. In his later work, François Avril reaffirmed Delaissé's opinion that Jean Bondol was a painter, not a manuscript illuminator. See Earp, *Guillaume de Machaut: A Guide*, 134. See also above, n. 5.
46   See Berens, *Maître de Vyssi Brod et de Guillaume de Machaut*. The wall paintings were copied by Matouš Ornys of Lindperg in his *Obrazy z české historie*, 1569–75. The work is preserved in two manuscripts. The first was prepared for Emperor Maximilian II and is now the 'Codex Heidelbergensis', Archiv Národní galerie v Praze, Varia, no. AA 2015. The second is kept in Vienna, Österreichische Nationalbibliothek, Cod. 8330, ff. 6r–59r. See Karel Stejskal, 'Die Rekonstruktion des Luxemburger Stammbaums auf Karlstein', *Umění* 28 (1978), 535–65; idem, 'Noch einmal über die Datierung und Zuschreibung der Karlsteiner Malereien', in Jiří Fajt (ed.), *Court Chapels of the High and Middle Ages and Their Artistic Decoration* (Prague, 2003), 343–50; Kaja von Cossart, '*Codex Heidelbergensis* s kopiemi nástěnným maleb lucemburského rodokmenu na hradě Karlštejn', in Fajt and Hörsch (eds), *Císař Karel IV. 1316–2016*, 408–9.
47   A 'Zechenbuch' contained basic rules of a medieval *Zeche* (German *Zunft*), a guild, including a list of its members. It also gathered further information of the guild, e.g., new members and events organized by the group. See Matthias Pangerl, *Das Buch der Malerzeche in Prag* (Vienna, 1878), 85–6.
48   Pangerl, *Malerzeche*, 86.

Although artists of various countries settled in Prague and its close surroundings in the fourteenth century, the career Berens suggests for the anonymous painter appears far too ambitious to be managed in a single lifetime. Besides his work for Emperor Charles IV, the master, meanwhile identified by Berens with Jean Bondol, later worked on the frontispiece miniatures to Machaut's manuscript compilation A (Bibliothèque nationale de France, MS fr. 1584), and last but not least oversaw the production of the Angers tapestry of the Apocalypse. In fact, Berens' idea goes back to such authorities among art historians as Charles Sterling.[49] He was one of the first who recognized stylistic similarities between the Master of the Bouquetaux, known later also as the Master of the Bible of Jean de Sy,[50] and the Master of the Luxembourg Genealogy. Czech scholarship dealing with Karlštejn Castle and particularly with the Cycle of the Luxembourg Genealogy accepted Sterling's suggestion that the painter was of Franco-Flemish origin.[51] In Czech research, moreover, his identity became connected with Nicholas Wurmser, a citizen of Strasbourg who received an unencumbered farm in Mořina, a village near Karlštejn, in reward for his services to the emperor.[52] Despite previous theories proposing

---

49   Charles Sterling, *La peinture médiévale à Paris 1300–1500* (Paris, 1987), vol. 1, 180–92, with bibliography.
50   The Master of the Bible of Jean de Sy was active in Paris c. 1350–80. He contributed to illuminated manuscripts made for French kings John II the Good and Charles V. He received the name after his early work: illuminations in a copy of Jean de Sy's French translation of the Latin Bible made for John the Good, MS fr. 15397. See Sterling, *La peinture médiévale à Paris 1300–1500*, 176–9; also Henry Martin, *La Miniature française du XIIIe siècle au XVe siècle* (Paris, 1923), 44–54, who was the first to recognize the master as an individual and who called him 'Maître aux Bouqueteaux'. For images see https://gallica.bnf.fr/ark:/12148/btv1b84471814/f1.planchecontact [accessed 22 March 2023]. See also Earp, *Guillaume de Machaut: A Guide* with further references to studies on this anonymous artist by François Avril, p. 134.
51   Jan Krofta, 'K problematice karlštejnských maleb,' *Umění* 7 (1958), 2–30, esp. 4–5. Also Homolka, 'Umělecká výzdoba'.
52   Preserved archival materials concerning Karlštejn Castle mention the same farm in Mořina as being given by the emperor to Theodorik, another painter and *familiaris* of Charles'. See the original documents edited in Jiří Fajt (ed.), *Magister Theodoricus, Court Painter of Emperor Charles IV: The Pictorial Decoration of the Shrines at Karlštejn Castle* (Prague, 1998), 341–9. Thus, in the Czech literature, two ingenious painters were established whose names encapsulate the chefs-d'oeuvre of Bohemian art production in the decades from the 1350s to the 1370s. This line of research was fostered by the exhibition catalogues and monographs produced by Jiří Fajt, and therefore became widespread in European medieval studies. See Barbara Drake Boehm and Jiří Fajt (eds), *Prague: The Crown of Bohemia, 1347–1437* (New York, 2005); Fajt, *Karel IV. Císař z Boží milosti*; and Fajt and Hörsch (eds), *Císař Karel IV. 1316–2016*. In addition, in a recently published monograph, Fajt

Wurmser as the Master of the Luxembourg Genealogy, simultaneously working on the Apocalypse cycle at Prague Castle, I share the view proposed by Kateřina Kubínová that Wurmser was a member of a larger workshop operating first solely at Karlštejn Castle and soon afterwards in the Emmaus monastery in the New Town of Prague.[53]

The Karlštejn workshop's activities coincided almost exactly with the production of the Bible of Jean de Sy in Paris, dated on written evidence to 1355–7.[54] Therefore, the stylistic correspondence of these artworks resides exclusively in their contemporaneity and not in their production by a single artist. Commissioned by the supreme representatives of power in France, and in Bohemia and the Holy Roman Empire, respectively, the centre of which was in Prague, the Caroline productions reflected the most up-to-date tendencies in mid fourteenth-century visual arts in Central Europe. Considering the tight relations between Prague and Paris in matters of family and politics as well as between Prague and the papacy in Avignon,[55] mutual exchange of forms and models in art and culture seems unsurprising. Hence, the presence of the so-called Master of the Bible of Jean de Sy in Prague as suggested by Berens is not a requirement to account for the creation of the two works of art considered here.

In addition, Berens and other scholars, represented mainly by Jiří Fajt, do not consider another factor that proves to be crucial for a full understanding of the complex cultural interchange between the Kingdom

---

elaborated further on Charles IV's court painters by constructing an identity for Sebald Weinschrötter, another master painter active in the services of the Holy Roman Emperor in Nürnberg. See Jiří Fajt, *Nürnberg als Kunstzentrum des Heiligen Römischen Reiches: Höfische und städtische Malerei in der Zeit Karls IV. 1346–1378* (Berlin, 2019). However, Fajt's hypothesis of the imperial style of Charles IV represented by the works of Nicholas Wurmser of Strasbourg, Master Theodoric, and recently by Sebald Weinschrötter has received much criticism in Czech scholarship, most recently by Kateřina Kubínová in her review in *Umění* 69 (2021), 357–64.

53 Kateřina Kubínová, *Emauzský cyklus* (Prague, 2012).
54 Sterling, *La peinture médiévale*, 176–9. For the identification of the master's œuvre with a complete bibliography, see 'Master of the Bouqueteaux', in Colum Hourihane (ed.), *The Grove Encyclopedia of Medieval Art and Architecture* (Oxford, 2012), vol. 2, 389. See also Avril, 'Un chef d'œuvre'.
55 For artistic exchanges between Prague and Avignon, see the classical work by Eugen Dostál, 'Čechy a Avignon: Příspěvky k vzniku českého iluminátorského umění v XIV. století', *Časopis Matice moravské* 46 (1922), 1–106. See also Lubomír Slavíček, '"Případ Dostálův": K polemice Eugena Dostála a Antonína Matějčka na téma Čechy a Avignon', *Sborník prací Filozofické fakulty Brněnské university* 41 (1997), 49–100. Also Ferdinand Tadra, *Kulturní styky Čech s cizinou až do válek husitských* (Prague, 1897), available online at https://kramerius5.nkp.cz/view/uuid:eff97370-8e0b-11dd-a227-000d606f5dc6?page=uuid:b9835705-c3d4-4a22-9093-8ec702ec1409 [accessed 22 March 2023].

of France, the French-influenced Low Countries, and Bohemia. This factor is the Brabant court of Wenceslas of Bohemia in Brussels, which Charles Sterling mentions as a potential inspiration for the cycles of wall paintings at Karlštejn Castle.[56]

BRUSSELS – PRAGUE – PARIS

In 1352, King John's son from his second marriage to Beatrice of Bourbon, Wenceslas, married Joanna of Brabant, heiress to the Duchy of Brabant. A year later, in 1353, his half-brother, Holy Roman Emperor Charles IV, installed him as Count and, from 1354, as Duke of Luxembourg. Although practically nothing has been preserved in the realm of visual arts from the period of Wenceslas' reign which could unmistakably be linked to the court in Brussels and its members, a different situation applies to the written arts, as the Duke of Brabant and Luxembourg was a distinguished patron of Jean Froissart. He figures as a main character in several of Froissart's poetic works, notably *Meliador* and *La Prison Amoureuse*. The court in Brussels, due to its geographical position at the crossroads between England and the Continent, attracted artists and craftsmen from both sides of the North Sea.[57] Furthermore, Wenceslas cultivated a close relationship to Emperor Charles IV as well as to the French king Charles V, the first-born son of Bonne of Luxembourg. Bonne was the elder sister of Emperor Charles IV, and a half-sister of Wenceslas. Later, the Duke of Brabant played a crucial role in the negotiations between England and Bohemia regarding the marriage between Anne of Bohemia, Charles IV's daughter, and the English king Richard II. The *Grandes Chroniques de France* refer to a number of occasions when luxurious gifts were exchanged among European princely courts, more particularly between the French royal court and the Holy Roman Emperor, while he was visiting the country. Although the emperor's journey to the Parisian summit took place in 1377–8, some 20 years later than the Genealogy of Luxembourg at Karlštejn Castle, it still provides a good reason to reflect further about cultural exchanges among these three courts, not least because the Brabant court also played a significant role in imperial politics.

An active interchange of models and forms took place among workshops employed by these courts, including itinerant artists. A number of foreign,

---

56 See also the essay by Jana Fantysová Matějková in this volume.
57 Jana Fantysová Matějková, 'Wenceslas de Bohême, duc de Luxembourg et de Brabant, entre le Saint Empire romain et la France 1337–1383' (unpublished PhD thesis, Université de Paris-Sorbonne, 2007); eadem, *Wenceslas de Bohême: un prince au carrefour de l'Europe* (Paris, 2013), with further readings. See also the essay by Karl Kügle in this volume.

or non-Bohemian, craftsmen were present in Prague during the fourteenth century. More than one work may be ascribed to them, as Berens surmised of the anonymous master whom she considers responsible for the two greatest masterworks of Bohemian medieval art in the middle decades of the fourteenth century. Considering the range of panel painting production in the 1350s in Prague, practical reasons suggest that a single person could not be in charge of managing the tasks of being a member of a Prague workshop and simultaneously taking part in decorating activities at Karlštejn Castle, each of which was particularly demanding in its own right. Similarly, painters working in the 1350s at Karlštejn Castle probably cooperated under one or even more leading masters who decided on models and compositions to be applied in the wall paintings. However, despite the relationships between the Bohemian and the French royal court, it was not common practice that a single, genius master travelled from one place to another to assist in the creation of the most prestigious works of art, especially if these diverge significantly in their techniques – from panel painting, to wall painting, to book illumination, to tapestry. Scepticism towards Berens' identification of the anonymous masters of Vyšší Brod and of the Genealogy of Luxembourg is therefore justified, both considering the historical circumstances and on the basis of our current understanding of medieval workshop organization.

PART II

MARVELLOUS OBJECTS AND CULTURE AT THE COURT OF CHARLES IV

CHAPTER 4

CHARLES OF LUXEMBOURG AND HIS RELIQUARY CROSS: THE SIGNIFICANCE OF PRECIOUS STONES[1]

INGRID CIULISOVÁ

Charles of Luxembourg (1316–78), King of Bohemia (r. 1346–78) and Holy Roman Emperor (r. 1355–78), is considered one of the most capable and effective rulers of the fourteenth century. The eldest son of John of Luxembourg (1296–1346), he was the second Luxembourg king to rule Bohemia and the second of his line to achieve the status of Holy Roman Emperor (his grandfather, Henry VII of Luxembourg, was Holy Roman Emperor in 1312–13). He held his royal throne and imperial position for 32 years. From the beginning of his reign, Charles made every effort to secure his status by associating his personal accomplishments with a prestigious imperial past. Links with the past were also emphasized

---

1 This article was made possible thanks to funding received from the European Union's Horizon 2020 research and innovation programme (under Marie Skłodowska-Curie grant agreement no. 786156) and the Slovak Academy of Sciences (under project no. SoE/2017/72.C/MOCAHIC). I am indebted to Gervase Rosser and Martin Henig for their steadfast support and valuable comments on earlier versions of the present text. Also, my thanks go to Gia Toussaint for all the comments and suggestions she kindly gave me.

in the funeral oration delivered on the occasion of his death in 1378,[2] in which Charles was praised as *alter Constantinus* and his large-scale programme of assembling holy relics celebrated.[3]

Indeed, there are several parallels between Charles and Constantine the Great (r. 306–37). Each of them is credited with establishing a new capital for the empire he ruled. Constantine built a new imperial residence at Byzantium and in 330 renamed the city Constantinople, which became the capital of the Roman Empire (and remained the capital of the Eastern Roman Empire for more than a thousand years). Charles' complex refurbishment of Prague from the 1340s, which transformed a rather provincial city into a new centre of the Holy Roman Empire, was one of the greatest achievements of his artistic patronage. Charles re-drew the religious map of Central Europe by amassing a huge number of important holy relics in Prague, thus making the city the spiritual centre of the Holy Roman Empire, and conferring on it a status that at that time was rivalled only by Paris and Rome. In this he followed Constantine, who after founding Constantinople made Jerusalem the spiritual centre of the Roman world by ordering the construction of Christian holy sites there.[4] Moreover, Emperor Constantine is credited with developing an interest in the collecting and, crucially in the context of the present study, reuse of valuable objects of the past in the ceremonial objects that he commissioned for his personal use. Such recycling of objects from earlier periods in order to serve a new purpose had a long history in Roman artistic practices and had even become a widespread characteristic of late Roman art. Constantine created perhaps the most magnificent example of an ancient composite object: the Arch of Constantine in Rome, a major

---

2   See Josef Jireček, Josef Emler and Ferdinand Tadra (eds), *Fontes rerum Bohemicorum / Prameny českých dějin* 3 (Prague, 1882), 421–32, esp. 429; Rudolf Chadraba, 'Tradice druhého Konstantina a řecko-perská_antiteze v umění Karla IV', *Umění* 16 (1968), 567–602; František Šmahel, 'Kdo pronesl smuteční řeč při pohřbu císaře Karla IV.?', *Studia mediaevalia Bohemica* 2 (2010), 215–20.

3   On the importance of Emperor Constantine as a role model for Charles IV, see Heike Johanna Mierau, in Andreas Goltz and Heinrich Schlange-Schöningen (eds), *Konstantin der Große: Das Bild des Kaisers im Wandel der Zeiten* (Cologne, Weimar, and Vienna, 2008), 109–38; Kateřina Kubínová, 'Karl IV. und die Tradition Konstantins des Großen', in Jiří Fajt and Andrea Langer (eds), *Kunst als Herrschaftsinstrument: Böhmen und das Heilige Römische Reich unter den Luxemburgern im europäischen Kontext* (Berlin and Munich, 2009), 320–7.

4   The foundation of Constantinople took the imperial centre to the east of the Mediterranean and demanded a re-drawing of the political map quite as radical as that of the religious map – according to which Jerusalem became the privileged spiritual centre of the Roman world. See Jaś Elsner, 'Constantine – Perspectives in Art', in Noel Lenski (ed.), *The Cambridge Companion to the Age of Constantine* (Cambridge, 2006), 255–77, esp. 265.

Fig. 4.1. Ambo of Henry II, Treasury of Aachen Cathedral, c. 1024. Ivory, copper plate, gemstones, agate and rock crystal vessels, agate and chalcedony chess figures, oak parapet, height 146 cm. Photo © Archive of the author.

triumphal arch celebrating Constantine's victory over his rival Maxentius at the Battle of the Milvian Bridge in 312.[5] Numerous fragments taken from earlier Roman monuments and mounted in the arch perpetuated the majesty of Constantine, honouring and acclaiming his stature. Subsequently, the Roman practice of appropriating and recycling objects from different times and places became a common feature of numerous medieval religious dedications of various kinds.

Two of these tokens of devotion are of particular interest here: sumptuous composite objects that Charles of Luxembourg had seen and perhaps might even have had the opportunity to observe in detail. One is the eleventh-century golden pulpit (or ambo) (Fig. 4.1) with its monumental *crux gemmata* commissioned by Henry II, Holy Roman Emperor (r. 1014–24),

---

[5] The Arch of Constantine is today considered to be the first surviving public monument to boast the juxtaposition of objects from different periods. On this topic I have consulted Jaś Elsner, 'From the Culture of *spolia* to the Cult of Relics: The Arch of Constantine and the Genesis of Late Antique Forms', *Papers of the British School at Rome* 68 (2000), 149–84; Elsner, 'Constantine', 256–60; and Jaś Elsner, 'Late Antique Art: The Problem of the Concept and the Cumulative Aesthetic', in Simon Swain and Mark J. Edwards (eds), *Approaching Late Antiquity: The Transformation from Early to Late Empire* (Oxford, 2004), 271–309, esp. 288–92.

Fig. 4.2. Cross of Lothair, Treasury of Aachen Cathedral, c. 1000 (cross), fourteenth century (base). Oak core, gold, silver, gemstones, cameos, height 50 cm. Photo © Domkapitel, Aachen, Pit Siebigs, Aachen.

and donated by him to Charlemagne's Palatine Chapel in Aachen,[6] the city where most German kings anointed to reign over the Holy Roman Empire were crowned King of the Romans (emperors-elect),[7] including Charles himself. Remarkably, the pulpit brings together various extraordinary objects, incorporating gemstones provenant from ancient Rome, Coptic Alexandria, and Fatimid Egypt. The other intriguing object is the Lothair cross. Made of oakwood covered in sheets of gold and of gilt silver and encrusted with gems and pearls, it is dated c. 1000, and supported by a later base. It is now kept in the treasury of Aachen Cathedral (Fig. 4.2). The cross, embellished with a Roman cameo of Emperor Augustus (first century AD) (Fig. 4.3), was thought to be a gift from one of the Ottonian rulers, possibly the Emperor Otto III, to Aachen Cathedral.[8] Scholars have assumed that both the pulpit and the cross served as ceremonial objects during the coronation rituals of the kings of the Romans; their primary purpose was thus to convey a message of power.[9]

Charles of Luxembourg was crowned as *rex Romanorum* at Aachen on 25 July 1349, and records of his itinerary indicate that he visited the city

---

[6] Erika Doberer, 'Studien zu dem Ambo Kaiser Heinrichs II. im Dom zu Aachen', in *Karolingische und ottonische Kunst: Werden, Wesen, Wirkung* (Wiesbaden, 1957), 308–59; Horst Appuhn, 'Das Mittelstück vom Ambo König Heinrichs II. in Aachen', *Aachener Kunstblätter* 32 (1966), 70–3; Ernst Günther Grimme, 'Der Aachener Domschatz', *Aachener Kunstblätter* 43 (1972), cat. 27, 38–43; Gia Toussaint, 'Cosmopolitan Claims: Islamicate *spolia* During the Reign of King Henry II, 1002–24', *The Medieval History Journal* 15 (2012), 299–318.

[7] This was the king's title after being elected emperor by the German princes (and then crowned in Aachen), before being crowned as emperor in Rome by the Pope. It designated the heir to the imperial throne between his election as emperor (usually during the lifetime of a sitting emperor) and his succession to the imperial throne after the death of the current emperor; but not all kings of the Romans made the journey to Rome for their coronation, and therefore retained their initial title throughout their reign. The practice of papal coronations ended in 1508. See Barbara Stollberg-Rilinger, *Holy Roman Empire: A Short History* (Princeton, 2018).

[8] Another remarkable stone recycled in the cross is the rock crystal intaglio of Otto's Carolingian predecessor, Lothar II, King of Lotharingia (r. 855-69), after whom the cross is named. Ginevra Kornbluth, 'The Seal of Lothar II: Model and Copy', in *Francia* 17 (1990), 55–68. On the Lothair cross, see Grimme, 'Der Aachener Domschatz', cat. 22; Norbert Wibiral, '*Augustus partem figurat*: Zu den Betrachtungsweisen des Zentralsteines am Lotharkreuz im Domschatz zu Aachen', *Aachener Kunstblätter* 60 (1994), 105–30; Georg Minkenberg, 'Lotharkreuz', in M. Kramp (ed.), *Krönungen: Könige in Aachen – Geschichte und Mythos*, exhibition catalogue, vol. 1 (Mainz, 2000), 342–3.

[9] Eliza Garrison, *Ottonian Imperial Art and Portraiture: The Artistic Patronage of Otto III and Henry II* (Farnham and Burlington, 2012), 96.

Fig. 4.3. Portrait of the Roman Emperor Augustus. Cameo at the centre of the Cross of Lothair, Treasury of Aachen Cathedral, first century, sardonyx. Photo © Genevra Kornbluth.

repeatedly.[10] He bequeathed various precious objects to the treasury of Aachen Cathedral and in 1362 commissioned the altar there dedicated to St Wenceslas.[11] In the light of these facts, Charles presumably had many

---

10 On Charles IV and Aachen, see Hans P. Hilger, 'Der Weg nach Aachen', in Ferdinand Seibt (ed.), *Kaiser Karl IV.: Staatsmann und Mäzen* (Munich, 1978), 324–6, 331–4, 461; Thomas R. Kraus, 'Studien zur Vorgeschichte der Krönung Karls IV. in Aachen', *Zeitschrift des Aachener Geschichtsvereins* 88/89 (1981/2), 43–93; František Kavka, 'Karl IV. (1349–1378) und Aachen', in Kramp (ed.), *Krönungen*, vol. 2, 477–84; Jiří Fajt, 'Karl IV. – Herrscher zwischen Prag und Aachen: Der Kult Karls des Großen und die karolinische Kunst', in Kramp (ed.), *Krönungen*, vol. 2, 489–500; Franz Machilek, 'Karl IV. und Karl der Große', *Zeitschrift des Aachener Geschichtsvereins* 104/5 (2002/3), 113–45.

11 The altar was founded by Charles on 20 December 1362. See Bedřich Mendl and Milena Linhartová (eds), *Regesta diplomatica nec non epistolaria Bohemiae*

opportunities to acquaint himself with earlier votive offerings preserved in Aachen Cathedral, including the pulpit and the cross, and these may well have served him as models for his own votive objects.

THE HISTORY OF THE CORONATION CROSS

One of the commissions that Charles of Luxembourg is believed to have ordered was the jewelled reliquary cross kept today in the treasury of St Vitus Cathedral in Prague (Figs 4.4, 4.5).[12] Surprisingly, the fourteenth-century inventories of the treasury do not tell us anything about this object; but it is known that in 1480 the cross was in deposit at Helfenburk Castle in Bohemia, which had once been owned by the Archbishop of Prague, Jan Očko of Vlašim, who maintained a close relationship with Charles.[13] By the beginning of the sixteenth century, the cross was preserved at Karlštejn Castle near Prague. The cross, thenceforth, was removed only on special occasions, such as for the coronations of Bohemian rulers. For this reason, the cross is today called the 'Coronation Cross of Bohemia'.[14]

At the end of the nineteenth century, scholars began to pay attention to this object.[15] It was studied predominantly on the basis of formal criteria, by which scholars were able to categorize the object in terms of its age and style.[16] However, during the fourteenth century these criteria were of little

---

et Moraviae VII/5, 1358–1363 (Prague, 1963), no. 1290; Percy E. Schramm and Hermann Fillitz, *Denkmale der deutschen Könige und Kaiser, Bd. II: Ein Beitrag zur Herrschergeschichte von Rudolf I. bis Maximilian I., 1273–1519* (Munich, 1978), 37–8.
12 Inv. no. K 25 (97).
13 At Helfenburk, a detailed description of the cross was included in the inventory of the objects kept there in 1480. See Václav Schulz, 'Popis velikého kříže zemského z roku 1480', *Věstník královské české společnosti nauk, třída filosoficko-historicko-jazykozpytná* (1897), 7–9.
14 František Fišer, *Karlštejn: Vzájemné vztahy tří karlštejnských kaplí* (Kostelní Vydří, 1996), 242, 261.
15 Franz Bock, 'Der Schatz von St. Veit zu Prag: I. Abtheilung', *Mittheilungen der K.K. Central-Commission zur Erforschung und Erhaltung der Baudenkmale* 14 (1869), 9–35, esp. 27–31; Antonín Podlaha and Eduard Šittler, 'České korunovační kříže v pokladu Svatovítském', *Památky archaeologické a místopisné* 20 (1902), 1–14, esp. 1–9; Antonín Podlaha and Eduard Šittler, *Chrámový poklad u sv. Víta v Praze: Jeho dějiny a popis* (Prague, 1903), 167–74.
16 The cross was analysed in detail especially in the seminal writings of Emanuel Poche. See Emanuel Poche, 'Einige Erwägungen über die Kameen Karls IV', in Jaroslav Pešina (ed.), *Sborník k sedmdesátinám Jana Květa* (Prague, 1965), 82–93; Emanuel Poche, 'K otázce ostatkových křížů Karla IV', *Sborník Národního muzea v Praze / Acta Musei Nationalis Pragae, Series A – Historia* 21 (1967), 239–46; Emanuel Poche, 'Umělecká řemesla gotické doby', in *Dějiny českého výtvarného umění 1/2* (Prague, 1984), 440–79. See also Schramm and Fillitz, *Denkmale der deutschen*

Fig. 4.4. Coronation Cross, front side. Gold, pearls, gemstones, rock crystal, glass, relics, with a new base made of gilded copper added in the 1520s, 62.5 cm x 41.5 cm. Treasury of St Vitus Cathedral, Prague. Photo © Courtesy of Prague Castle Administration/Jan Gloc.

Fig. 4.5. Coronation Cross, back side. Gold, pearls, gemstones, rock crystal, glass, cameos, and relics. Base of gilded copper added in the 1520s; overall dimensions 62.5 am x 41.5 cm. Treasury of St Vitus Cathedral, Prague. Photo © Courtesy of Prague Castle Administration/Jan Gloc.

concern to those who viewed it. By the late twentieth century, scholars focused almost exclusively on the history of the relics incorporated into the body of the cross, regarding it as 'the most prestigious reliquary from the Bohemian medieval past';[17] their approach has been primarily to explore the sacred and devotional aspects of the object, based mostly on its iconography.[18] The considerable number of precious stones encrusted in the cross were implicitly downplayed or neglected in these studies.[19]

In the present essay, the Coronation Cross will be investigated from a different perspective: instead of the relics and the reliquary function of the cross, I shall focus on the carved gemstones, especially on the cameos, in an attempt to demonstrate that precious and semi-precious stones were not just ornamental elements decorating the cross, as is usually claimed. On the contrary, they significantly contributed to the talismanic character of the cross as a powerful apotropaic object, and crucially informed the construction of the visual message that the cross was intended to convey – a visual message that may have been linked to Charles, who presumably was responsible for commissioning the cross and who in all likelihood acquired and deliberately selected the gemstones displayed on this object. My intention in what follows is to analyse the cross not solely within the

---

Könige und Kaiser, 65 (with earlier literature); Hans R. Hahnloser and Susanne Brugger-Koch, *Corpus der Hartsteinschliffe des 12. – 15. Jahrhunderts* (Berlin, 1985), 130, cat. 150. Most recently, the object was examined by Karel Otavský, 'Zlatý relikviářový kříž', in Jiří Fajt and Barbara D. Boehm (eds), *Karel IV. Císař z Boží milosti: Kultura a umění za vlády posledních Lucemburků 1310-1437*, exhibition catalogue (Prague, 2006), 111–14; idem, 'Goldenes Reliquienkreuz', in Jiří Fajt, Markus Hörsch and Andrea Langer (eds), *Karl IV. Kaiser von Gottes Gnaden: Kunst und Repräsentation des Hauses Luxemburg 1310-1437* (Munich, 2006), 111–14. See also Karel Otavský, 'Zlatý relikviářový kříž', in Ivana Kyzourová (ed.), *Svatovítsky poklad* (Prague, 2012), no. 1; and Karel Otavský, 'Relikvie, relikviáře a královské insignie', in František Šmahel and Lenka Bobková (eds), *Lucemburkové: Česká koruna uprostřed Evropy* (Prague, 2012), 532.

17 Josef Cibulka, *Korunovační klenoty království českého* (Prague, 1969), 87–8; and Ivo Hlobil, *České korunovační klenoty: pamětní vydání ke vzniku České republiky* (Prague, 1993), 66–7.

18 See especially Fišer, *Karlštejn*, 246–52; Karel Otavský, 'K relikviím vlastněným císařem Karlem IV., k jejich uctívání a jejich schránkám', in *Court Chapels of the High and Late Middle Ages and Their Artistic Decoration: Proceedings from the International Symposium* (Prague, 2003), 392–8, esp. 394–5); Otavský, 'Zlatý relikviářový kříž', 111–13. One exception are texts devoted to technical analysis and conservation of the cross. For this aspect, see Jaroslav Bauer, 'Korunovační kříž ostatkový ze Svatovítského pokladu', *Technologia artis* 2 (1994), and the conservation report of 2003 written by Andrej Šumbera. The report is preserved at the archive of Prague Castle, nos 405.480/02, 405.611/02.

19 See for example, Otavský, 'Zlatý relikviářový kříž' (Prague 2006), 111–14.

context of visual history, but also as a material object.[20] In the absence of written evidence, this is crucial. Although the material analysis cannot provide the same level of information as a written historical record, it helps us to develop a better understanding of the long-lost and obscure ways in which exquisite objects functioned, and of how it was perceived in specific social settings in the distant past.

Furthermore, it should be noted that despite an impressive and valuable body of scholarly work on Charles of Luxembourg and his patronage, most of the studies related to the topic are dominated by nation-state narratives and mono-disciplinary perspectives, disregarding the multicultural features that are characteristic of the objects created in Charles' time. Studies of this type tend to interpret individual elements of the objects in isolation and ignore their composite nature. In contrast, my approach has been transnational and interdisciplinary, exploring the Coronation Cross as an amalgam of various elements while drawing upon sources in a range of disciplines – principally, those of history, history of art, material culture, and archaeology.

THE COMPOSITE CHARACTER OF THE CORONATION CROSS

Close inspection of the cross reveals details about how this object evolved over time. Its current dimensions are 62.5 cm × 41.5 cm; it should be noted, however, that the cross has not retained its original form. Its original base disappeared before 1480 and a new one, made of gilded copper, was added later, probably in the 1520s. Thus, the object was partially redesigned, especially in its lower part.[21] In spite of this, the cross still possesses much of its initial composite character, retaining many of its original components which were in turn deliberately compiled from different periods and cultural contexts.

One such component is the gold body of the cross itself. The cross is shaped in the form of earlier medieval crosses, with its fleur-de-lys

---

20   On this topic I have consulted Chris Tilley et al. (eds), *Handbook of Material Culture* (London, 2006); Caroline Walker Bynum, *Christian Materiality: An Essay on Religion in Late Medieval Europe* (New York, 2011); Michael Yonan, 'Toward a Fusion of Art History and Material Culture Studies', *West 86th: A Journal of Decorative Arts, Design History, and Material Culture* 18 (2011), 232–48; 'Notes from the Field: Materiality', *The Art Bulletin* 95 (2013), 10–37; Philippe Cordez, 'Die kunsthistorische Objektwissenschaft und ihre Forschungsperspektiven', *Kunstchronik* 67 (2014), no. 7, 364–73.
21   Emanuel Poche, *České umění gotické 1350–1420: Katalog uměleckého řemesla* (Prague, 1970), no. 427.

terminals dating to the thirteenth century. This indicates either that the cross is a fourteenth-century object deliberately designed in a thirteenth-century shape that originated with the Capetian kings of France, associated especially with the saintly King Louis IX of France, who was regarded as the most Christian king of that era, or that it is a thirteenth-century cross, remade about one hundred years later. In addition, the object follows the model of sumptuously jewelled early medieval crosses, *cruces gemmatae*, which were developed as part of the veneration of the Holy Cross at the beginning of the fifth century to signify the divine authority of Christ and of Christian emperorship.[22]

Noteworthy historical documents indicate that from 1350 onward Charles temporarily owned one prestigious *crux gemmata*: the Imperial Cross (1025–30, Vienna, Kunsthistorisches Museum, inv. no. WS XIII 21) – a precious reliquary (the cross accommodated particles of the True Cross and the Holy Lance), and one of the most remarkable jewelled crosses of this period. In his role as Holy Roman Emperor, Charles guarded the cross and other imperial relics, and therefore must have had first-hand knowledge of them. His deeper interest in this object is demonstrated by his commission in 1352 of a new foot for the cross, made of gold-plated silver over a wooden core, engraved with a donatory inscription, and adorned with royal and imperial emblems, which emphasize Charles' personal connections with this precious object.[23] Like the Imperial Cross, the Coronation Cross incorporates portable objects that originally served different purposes: relics and gemstones. Both share one essential quality: in Charles' time, they were understood to possess divine power.[24]

---

22 Ilder Garipzanov, 'The Sign of the Cross in Late Antiquity', in *Graphic Signs of Authority in Late Antiquity and the Early Middle Ages, 300–900* (Oxford, 2018), 92. On jewelled crosses in the Middle Ages, see Theo Jülich, 'Gemmenkreuze: Die Farbigkeit ihres Edelsteinbesatzes bis zum 12. Jahrhundert', *Aachener Kunstblätter* 54/55 (1986–7), 99–258. Recent work on jewelled reliquaries includes Martina Bagnoli, 'The Stuff of Heaven: Materials and Craftsmanship in Medieval Reliquaries', in Martina Bagnoli, Holger A. Klein and Charles G. Mann (eds), *Treasures of Heaven: Saints, Relics, and Devotion in Medieval Europe* (Baltimore, 2010), 137–47; Gia Toussaint, *Kreuz und Knochen: Reliquien zur Zeit der Kreuzzüge* (Berlin, 2011); Cynthia Hahn, *Strange Beauty: Issues in the Making and Meaning of Reliquaries, 400–circa 1204* (University Park, PA, 2012), esp. 73–109; Ginevra Kornbluth, 'Active Optics', *Different Visions* 4 (2014); and Karen Overbey, 'Seen Through Stone: Materiality and Place in a Medieval Scottish Pendant Reliquary', *Res* 65/66 (2014/15), 243–58.
23 On the imperial insignia, see Hermann Fillitz, *Die Insignien und Kleinodien des Heiligen Römischen Reiches* (Vienna, 1954).
24 On this topic, see especially Christel Meier-Staubach, *Gemma spiritalis: Methode und Gebrauch der Edelsteinallegorese vom frühen Christentum bis ins 18. Jahrhundert*,

THE RELICS

Charles of Luxembourg was one of the most avid collectors of holy relics in Christendom. Relics were objects of paramount importance, priceless treasures, and became central to his project of sacralizing the monarchy and himself.[25] Relics believed to have been in direct contact with Christ's body during his Passion formed the most precious part of his remarkable collection. Charles commissioned several of these to be incorporated into the Coronation Cross.[26] In the West during the medieval period, holy relics were much-desired commodities, sought after by resourceful men and women both within and outside the Church. Charles, one of the most powerful men in late medieval Europe, was no exception. Even though relics possessed no intrinsic material value, he sought them out in great quantity,[27] primarily because they were regarded almost universally as being important sources of personal supernatural power, for good or for ill, via possession and close contact with them.[28] That is why Charles and other medieval rulers amassed relics: not only to manifest their piety, but also to harness their sacred power for personal advantage and thus to bolster

---

vol. 1 (Munich, 1977); Patrick J. Geary, *Thefts of Relics in the Central Middle Ages* (Princeton, 1978).

25 On the topic of the immense significance for Charles of the cult of saints and their physical remains, there exists a considerable body of literature. See especially Wolfgang Schmid, 'Vom Rheinland nach Böhmen: Studien zur Reliquienpolitik Kaiser Karls IV', in Ulrike Hohensee, Mathias Lawo, Michael Lindner, Michael Menzel and Olaf B. Rader (eds), *Die Goldene Bulle: Politik–Wahrnehmung–Rezeption* (Berlin, 2009), 431–64; Martin Bauch, *Divina favente clemencia: Auserwählung, Frömmigkeit und Heilsvermittlung in der Herrschaftspraxis Kaiser Karls IV.* (Cologne, Weimar, and Vienna, 2015), 182–6; and David C. Mengel, 'Bohemia's Treasury of Saints: Relics and Indulgences in Emperor Charles IV's Prague', in Marie-Madeleine de Cevins and Olivier Marin (eds), *Les saints et leur culte en Europe centrale au Moyen Age (XIe–début du XVIe siècle)* (Turnhout, 2017), 57–76.

26 The Coronation Cross contains fragments of the following major Passion relics: the Crown of Thorns, the True Cross, the sponge, a holy nail, and rope. On the relics and the Coronation Cross, see most recently Otavský, 'Goldenes Reliquienkreuz', and Otavský, 'Zlatý relikviářový kříž'.

27 According to Martin Bauch, the number of identifiable relics in Prague rose from 77 at Charles' accession to the throne to 605 at his death. He may have commissioned about 400 new reliquaries for them, costing around 40,000 gulden. See Bauch, *Divina favente clemencia*, 311–12.

28 Patrick Geary, 'Sacred Commodities: The Circulation of Medieval Relics', in Arjun Appadurai (ed.), *The Social Life of Things: Commodities in Cultural Perspective* (London, New York, and Cambridge, 1986), 169–91, esp. 175–6); Patrick Geary, 'Reliquien und Macht', in Falko Daim and Thomas Kühtreiber (eds), *Sein und Sinn, Burg und Mensch: Niederösterreichische Landesausstellung im Schloss Ottenstein und Schloss Waldreichs vom 5. Mai bis 4. November 2001*, exhibition catalogue (St Pölten, 2001), 353–4.

their authority. It is therefore plausible that the idea of consolidating the most holy relics of Christendom into a single object such as a cross might have occurred to Charles. The ownership of such a powerful object would have enabled him not only to demonstrate his devotion to God and to increase his prestige as a pious Christian sovereign, but also to participate in what was understood to be the relics' divine powers.

In Charles' time this idea, though not a new one, circulated widely through royal circles. One other extant example of such an object is the fourteenth-century reliquary called the Libretto of Louis of Anjou, today kept in the Museo dell'Opera del Duomo in Florence[29] (Fig. 4.6). The donatory inscription on the verso indicates that the reliquary was commissioned by Charles V of Valois, King of France (r. 1364–80), as a gift for his brother, Louis I, Duke of Anjou (1339–84), presumably around the year 1370. This small-scale object was created in the form of a book (dimensions, closed: 7.5 cm × 6.3 cm), its primary materials being gold, precious stones, painted parchment, and enamel, and also incorporating many holy relics. A considerable number of these are believed to be drawn from the most powerful relics of Christendom kept in the royal foundations of Sainte-Chapelle and Saint-Denis, such as the fragments of the True Cross, of the thorns from the Crown of Thorns, and of the nails and lance of the Crucifixion. These relics are set in the middle part of the reliquary, framed by pearls and rubies in enamelled compartments shaped like the objects from which they came, and therefore easily recognizable. The wooden fragment of the Holy Cross, the most important relic of all in the ensemble, dominates this central section. The libretto itself is foldable, and thus could be kept comfortably close to its owner wherever he went. Charles V's great-great-grandson, Charles VIII of France (r. 1483–98), is known to have possessed a powerful talismanic object identical, or almost identical, to that owned by Louis of Anjou. Charles V also commissioned similar reliquaries for other members of his family, and one of them

---

29   Giovanni Poggi, 'Il Reliquiario del "libretto" nel Battistero fiorentino', in *Rivista d'arte* 9 (1916), no. 3, 239–49; Rodolfo Gallo, *Il tesoro di San Marco e la sua storia* (Venice and Rome, 1967), 105–7; Bruno Donzet and Christian Siret (eds), *Les Fastes du gothique: Le siècle de Charles V*, exhibition catalogue, Galeries nationales du Grand Palais, 9 octobre 1981–1 février 1982 (Paris, 1981), no. 211, 260–2; Bertrand Jestaz, 'Le reliquaire de Charles V perdu par Charles VIII à Fornoue', *Bulletin monumental* 147 (1989), 7–10; Eva Kovács, *L'âge d'or de l'orfèvrerie parisienne au temps des princes de Valois* (Dijon, 2004), 174–9; Susie Nash, *Northern Renaissance Art* (Oxford, 2008), 230–2; and Beate Fricke, 'Reliquien und Reproduktion: Zur Präsentation der Passionsreliquien aus der Sainte-Chapelle (Paris) im "Reliquiario del Libretto" (Florenz) von 1501', in Jörg Probst (ed.), *Reproduktion: Techniken und Ideen von der Antike bis heute. Eine Einführung* (Berlin, 2011), 34–55.

Fig. 4.6. Reliquary called the Libretto, front side. Gold, enamel, pearls, rubies, parchment, c. 1370. Museo dell'Opera del Duomo, Florence. Photo © Age Fotostock/Nicolò Orsi Battaglini.

is listed in the will of his youngest brother, Philip the Bold, Duke of Burgundy (1342–1404).[30]

Charles of Luxembourg was closely connected by marriage to the French royal house. His sister, Bonne of Luxembourg (1315–49), married the future King John II of France (r. 1350–64); their children included Charles V of France, Louis of Anjou, and other princes of the blood. Charles himself spent his formative years at the French court, married Blanche of Valois (1317–48), a sister of Philip VI of France (r. 1328–50), and certainly had opportunities to observe and become familiar with the enshrined relics preserved in the treasury of Saint-Denis in Paris. Similarly, his nephew Charles V of France might have known about the artefacts commissioned by his uncle, Emperor Charles of Luxembourg, after being crowned Holy

---

30 It is 'un precieux tableau que me donna mons. mon frere le roy Charles, dont Dieu ayt l'ame, ouquel a de toutes les reliques de la sainte chapelle du Palais et des reliques de l'église de mons. Saint Denys …'; see Bernard Prost and Henri Prost, *Inventaires mobiliers et extraits des comptes des ducs de Bourgogne de la Maison de Valois (1363–1477), 2. Philippe le Hardi* (Paris, 1908), 225, no. 1409.

Roman Emperor.[31] Diplomatic gifts played an important role here. For example, in 1377, Charles V, King of France, ordered a payment to Jehan (Jean) du Vivier, one of his goldsmiths, for two gold reliquaries given 'à nostre très chier oncle l'empereur de Rome', one of which contained 'une piece du fust de la vraye croix' (a piece of the wood of the True Cross).[32]

As mentioned above, the Coronation Cross similarly incorporated some of the most precious relics of Christendom, including thorns from the Crown of Thorns and pieces of the True Cross.[33] The latter are prominently positioned in the very centre of the front and back of the Coronation Cross. Moreover, the fragment of the True Cross in the front is lavishly embellished with precious gemstones and might have originally served as a pectoral as there is a loop at the top through which a cord or chain could be passed. A second fragment, the more substantial of the two, is framed in gold and dominates the back side of the cross. Both items were thought to have come from the True Cross on which Jesus was crucified. The True Cross was reportedly discovered by Helena, mother of the first Christian emperor, Constantine; its remains were sent by her to him to serve as a symbol of his authority.[34] For this reason, relics of

---

31 Charles IV supported Charles V, French regent and the Emperor's nephew as son of John the Good and Bonne of Bohemia, throughout the difficult time when his father, King John II, was a prisoner in London. See Jana Fantysová Matějková, 'Bourbonský vévoda na dvoře Karla IV. (1357–1359): Poznámka k říšsko-francouzským vztahům v době zajetí francouzského krále Jana II. Dobrého', *Historie-Otázky-Problémy* 3 (2011), 77–87.

32 'Charles V ordonne de faire payer 116 francs d'or à nostre orfévre et varlet de chambre Jehan du Vivier, pour deux reliquiaires d'or garniz de cristaulz et de quatre grosses perles, c'est assavoir l'un pour mettre une piece du fust de la vraye croix, et l'autre pour mettre autres reliques, lesquiex reliquiaires nous avaon … donnez à nostre très chier oncle l'empereur de Rome.' Léopold Delisle, *Mandements et actes divers de Charles V (1364–1380): recueillis dans les collections de la Bibliothèque nationale* (Paris, 1874), 795, no. 1602.

33 Podlaha and Šittler, *Chrámový poklad*, 167–70; Anatole Frolow, *La relique de la Vraie Croix: Recherches sur le développement d'un culte* (Paris, 1961), 513, cat. 731.

34 Jan Willem Drijvers, *Helena Augusta: The Mother of Constantine the Great and the Legend of Her Finding of the True Cross* (Leiden, 1992). On the relics of the True Cross, see Holger A. Klein, *Byzanz, der Westen und das 'wahre' Kreuz: Die Geschichte einer Reliquie und ihrer künstlerischen Fassung in Byzanz und im Abendland* (Wiesbaden, 2004); Holger A. Klein, 'Eastern Objects and Western Desires: Relics and Reliquaries between Byzantium and the West', *Dumbarton Oaks Papers* 58 (2004), 283–314; Barbara Baert, *A Heritage of Holy Wood: The Legend of the True Cross in Text and Image* (Leiden, 2004). Constantine is said to have put some of the relics from his possessions under the honorific column with his colossal gilded bronze statue that adorned the Emperor's Forum of Constantinople. These relics included the crosses of the two thieves crucified alongside Christ, the alabaster vase with the perfume with which Mary Magdalene anointed Christ, and the object

the True Cross, including the ones acquired by Charles of Luxembourg, possessed both a special religious and historical potency. The religious potency signified redemption, while the historical one referred to imperial and regal legitimacy. Furthermore, in the medieval period it was believed that the True Cross had yet another special spiritual potency: it was used to guarantee the truth of statements or oaths. According to *The Golden Legend*, a collection of saints' lives written in the thirteenth century by Jacobus de Voragine and one of the most widely read devotional books during the fourteenth century, the True Cross also possessed a power to cause the motion of water and the healing of the sick.[35] In addition, due to Constantine's legendary vision of the Cross and his miraculous victory in battle against Maxentius under the protection of the Cross in 312, the relics of the Holy Cross were highly prized as an apotropaic device and a source of protection and divine power. For this reason, the relics of the True Cross were part of the battle equipment of royal and imperial rulers, and were immensely coveted as amulets.[36]

THE GEMSTONES

In addition to relics, Charles of Luxembourg also sought ancient coins, manuscripts, rare fabrics, jewels, objects of curiosity and, especially, precious gemstones, many of which he subsequently adapted to religious purposes in innovative ways. Charles' interest in these precious objects was driven in large part by the fact that, in his time, gemstones, like the holy relics of Christendom, were regarded as a source of spiritual power.[37] Despite the Christian Church's opposition to instrumental magic

---

identified as the *palladium* of Athena. See Jean Ebersolt, *Constantinople: Recueil d'études, d'archéologie et d'histoire* (Paris, 1951), 71–3; and Holger A. Klein, 'Sacred Relics and Imperial Ceremonies at the Great Palace of Constantinople', in Franz A. Bauer (ed.), *Visualisierungen von Herrschaft* (Istanbul, 2006), 79–99, esp. 81.

35 Jacobus de Voragine, *The Golden Legend: Readings on the Saints*, trans. William Granger Ryan (Princeton, 2012), 278.

36 Byzantine emperors had carried such relics in battle since the sixth century. See Michael McCormick, *Eternal Victory: Triumphal Rulership in Late Antiquity, Byzantium, and the Early Medieval West* (Cambridge, 1986), 216, 247.

37 See mainly Fernand de Mély, 'Du role des pierres gravées au Moyen Âge', *Revue de l'art chrétien* 42 (1893), ser. 4, 14–24, 98–105; George F. Kunz, *The Curious Lore of Precious Stones* (Philadelphia and London, 1913); Joan Evans, *Magical Jewels of the Middle Ages and the Renaissance Particularly in England* (Oxford, 1922); Christel Meier-Staubach, *Gemma Spiritalis: Methode und Gebrauch der Edelsteinallegorese vom frühen Christentum bis ins 18. Jahrhundert* (Munich, 1977); Theo Jülich, 'Sakrale Gegenstände und ihre Materialien als Bedeutungsträger', *Rheydter Jahrbuch für Geschichte, Kunst und Heimatkunde* 19 (1991), 254–6; Lorraine Daston and

in nearly all its forms (the Church seems to have tolerated the tradition of the medicinal amulet),[38] precious stones were widely valued for their divine power when attached to limbs, hidden in clothing, hung around the neck, or simply kept in the house. Numerous medieval texts, in particular lapidaries, encyclopaedic compendia about gemstones, described in detail their appearance, their origins, and their perceived thaumaturgical and healing virtues. Lapidaries flourished at medieval courts, and some texts about gemstones emanated directly from imperial circles.[39] In addition, gemstones occupied an important place in medieval astrology as repositories of planetary forces. They were seen as part of the God-given order – symbols of the divine power of God – and were understood to have properties connected directly to Him. The foundation stones of the heavenly Jerusalem were said in scriptural texts to comprise various gemstones, including sapphires, chalcedonies, emeralds, and sardonyx; other biblical texts referred to gems used for the sumptuous decoration of the breastplate of Aaron the High Priest.[40]

Katharine Park, *Wonders and the Order of Nature, 1150–1750* (New York, 2001), 75–6; Edina Bozoky, *Charmes et prières apotropaïques* (Turnhout, 2003); Gia Toussaint, 'Heiliges Gebein und edler Stein: Der Edelsteinschmuck von Reliquiaren im Spiegel mittelalterlicher Wahrnehmung', *Das Mittelalter* 8 (2003), 41–66; Brigitte Buettner, 'From Bones to Stones – Reflections on Jeweled Reliquaries', in Brigitte Reudenbach and Gia Toussaint (eds), *Reliquiare im Mittelalter* (Berlin, 2005), 43–59; Elena Di Venosa, *Die deutschen Steinbücher des Mittelalters: Magische und medizinische Einblicke in die Welt der Steine* (Göppingen 2005). On ancient gems in the Middle Ages, see Erika Zwierlein-Diehl, *Antike Gemmen und ihr Nachleben* (Berlin and New York, 2007).

38 John M. Riddle, *Marbode of Rennes' (1035–1123) De lapidibus: Considered as a Medical Treatise* (Wiesbaden, 1977); Francis B. Brévart, 'Between Medicine, Magic, and Religion: Wonder Drugs in German Medico-Pharmaceutical Treatises of the Thirteenth to Sixteenth Centuries', *Speculum* 83 (2008), 1–57.

39 One of them was *Otia Imperialia*, an encyclopaedic work written 1210–14 by an English cleric, Gervasius of Tilbury (c. 1150–c. 1235), and dedicated to his patron, Emperor Otto IV (1175–1218). In his work, Gervasius made consistent reference to objects that caused wonder, including gemstones. *Otia Imperialia* was translated into French and much read in the fourteenth century. See Shelag E. Banks and James W. Binns (eds and trans.), *Gervase of Tilbury Otia Imperialia: Recreation for an Emperor* (Oxford, 2002); Thomas B. Mueller, 'The Marvellous in Gervase of Tilbury's *Otia Imperialia*' (D.Phil. thesis, University of Oxford, 1990); Fritz P. Knapp, '"Wahre" und "erlogene" Wunder: Gervasius von Tilbury und der Höfische Roman', *Beiträge zur Geschichte der deutschen Sprache und Literatur* 132 (2010), 230–44.

40 Revelation 21:19–21; Exodus 39:8–14. For English translations, see https://www.biblegateway.com/passage/?search=Ufunuo+21&version=KJV and https://www.biblegateway.com/passage/?search=Exodus+39&version=KJV [accessed 31 March 2023].

Charles of Luxembourg, a well-educated man, was undoubtedly aware of the spiritual properties of gemstones. He may already have been acquainted with them at the court of his father, John of Luxembourg, King of Bohemia. The fourteenth-century Latin *Epistola de cautela a venenis ad Johannem, regem Bohemie*, devoted to various forms of protection against poisoning, contains an example of this.[41] The text was written in the form of a letter by Johannes Hake (Johann von Göttingen, c. 1280–1349), a respected physician of his time who had studied medicine at the universities of Paris and Montpellier.[42] From 1324 Hake served as chaplain, personal physician, and *familiaris domesticus* to John of Bohemia, to whom the text was addressed. Hake had a good reputation as a doctor and had served from 1314 to 1318 as the personal physician of Louis IV of Bavaria (who was later crowned Holy Roman Emperor); in 1335, he was the personal physician of Pope Benedict XII. Hake is believed to have written his treatise around 1330, just before John of Luxembourg's campaign to gain territory in Italy in 1330–1; its chief purpose was to offer John of Luxembourg information about the best possible protection against poisoning. Hake especially recommended the use of an emerald (*smaragdus*). He described in detail the emerald's magical properties and explained how the stone could be recognized, where it could be found, and how it should be properly used by people who had been poisoned.[43] Charles of Luxembourg joined his father on the journey to Italy and in his

41 Prague, Národní knihovna České republiky, XI.E.9, fol. 272r–277v, chart. saec. XIV et XV ff. 340, 21.5×15 cm. d. m.; see Josef Truhlář, *Catalogus codicum manu scriptorum latinorum qui in C. R. bibliotheca publica atque universitatis Pragensis asservantur. Pars posterior: Codices 1666–2752 forulorum IX–XV et Bibliothecae Kinskyanae – Adligata 2753–2830* (Prague, 1906), 157–8, no. 2056: 'Johannis de Göttingen, capellani Johannis regis Bohemiae, ad eundem regem tractatus de cautela a venenis. 'Gloriosissimo principi … Johanni … Bohemie Polonieque regi' … 'una nux magna bene sana et electa' (158). On the content, see Milada Říhová and Martin Steiner, '"Gloriosissimo principi": Epistola de cautela a venenis ad Johannem, regem Bohemiae', *Acta Universitatis Carolinae – Philologica* 2 (2004), 169–200; and Milada Říhová et al., *Lékaři na dvoře Karla IV. a Jana Lucemburského* (Prague and Litomyšl, 2010), 67–73, 97–103. For a complex evaluation, see Franck Collard, 'Une voie germanique de la "vénénologie" à la fin du Moyen Âge? Recherches sur quelques écrits latins spécialisés en provenance de l'Empire', *Francia: Forschungen zur westeuropäischen Geschichte* 40 (2013), 57–77, esp. 62–9).
42 On Johann Hake, see Karl Wenck, 'Johann von Göttingen, Arzt, Bischof und Politiker zur Zeit Kaiser Ludwigs des Bayern', *Archiv für Geschichte der Medizin* 17 (1925), 141–56; Arend Mindermann, *Der berühmteste Arzt der Welt: Bischof Johann Hake, genannt von Göttingen (um 1280–1349)* (Bielefeld, 2001).
43 Říhová, *Lékaři na dvoře*, 97–103.

autobiography reported how in Pavia a number of men from his entourage were poisoned while Charles miraculously survived.[44]

Charles himself owned at least one magical gemstone, contained within a seal ring. It was a powerful amulet with healing properties that Charles had inherited from his grandfather, Henry VII of Luxembourg, and which he used to seal a letter that he sent to the Metropolitan Chapter in Prague in 1354. In this letter, Charles described the ring as enclosing a ruby-coloured stone that possessed the power to stop bleeding.[45] In addition, as mentioned above, Charles had possession of the imperial crown, the magnificent jewelled object believed to have belonged to Charlemagne.[46] The lavishly decorated crown was reputed to have contained a wondrous stone, presumably a large opal, whose uniqueness earned it its own name – *lapis orphanus*, or 'orphan stone'. The gemstone was already renowned in the thirteenth century; the German Dominican philosopher and friar Albertus Magnus (1200–80) wrote in his *De Mineralibus* (*Book of Minerals*) (c. 1248–52) that the stone with a hue of 'gleaming white snow' was said to preserve the royal honour.[47] The exclusivity of this object was

---

44 'Život císaře Karla IV.', in Jireček, Emler and Tadra, *Fontes rerum Bohemicorum*, 342.

45 In the letter sent by Charles IV to the Prague Chapter on 17 February 1354, this ring is described as follows: '… unum annulum … cum gemma habente colorem quasi rubini, cuius virtute et tactu restringitur sanguinis fluxus.' See Podlaha and Šittler, *Chrámový poklad*, 32.

46 Kunsthistorisches Museum Vienna, Schatzkammer, WS XIII 1. The imperial crown dates from the second half of the tenth century. The cross is an addition from the early eleventh century; see Robert Folz, *Le souvenir et la légende de Charlemagne dans l'empire germanique médiéval* (Paris, 1950), 454. For further on the imperial crown, see Gunther G. Wolf, *Die Wiener Reichskrone* (Vienna, 1995); Hermann Fillitz, 'Die Reichskleinodien: Ein Versuch zur Erklärung ihrer Entstehung und Entwicklung', in Hermann Fillitz, *Thesaurus mediaevalis: Ausgewählte Schriften zur Schatzkunst des Mittelalters*, ed. Franz Kirchweger and Werner Telesko (Ostfildern, 2010), 15–26.

47 'Orphanus est lapis qui in Corona Romani Imperatoris est, neque unquam alibi visus est, propter quod etiam Orphanus vocatur: est autem colore quasi vinosus, subtilem habens vinositatem, et hoc est sicut si candidum nivis candens seu micans penetraverit in rubeum, clarum, vinosum, et sit superatum ab ipso. Est autem lapis perlucidus, et traditur quod aliquando fulsit in nocte, sed nunc tempore nostro non micat in tenebris. Fertur autem quod honorem servat regalem.' I quote according to *DE MINERALIBUS ET REBVS METALICIS LIBRI QVINQVE. Alberto Magno summe Philosopho. COLONIAE An. M.D.LXIX.*, 167–8. The passage has been translated as follows: 'Orphanus is the stone in the crown of the [Holy] Roman Emperor, and has never been anywhere else, and therefore is called the orphan. Its colour is like wine, of a delicate wine-red, as if gleaming or shining white snow were mingled with clear red wine, and were overcome by it. It is a brilliant stone, and tradition says that at one time it used to shine by night; but nowadays it does not shine in

also emphasized in the inventory of imperial relics provided to Charles in 1350, indicating that Charles was familiar with the special power imputed to this gem.

It is therefore not surprising that the Coronation Cross incorporated not only several relics but also a group of precious and semi-precious gemstones. However, the description of the cross dating to 1480 reveals that, in Charles' time, the decoration of the cross was slightly different from what we see today. In addition to the sapphires, there were emeralds placed at the very top of each central fleur-de-lys. Thus, the cross was encrusted with precious stones which, from the fifth century at least, were reserved exclusively for use by emperors and their families.[48] The special status of these gems would probably have been maintained by their presumed magical properties. According to Albertus Magnus' *Book of Minerals*, a 'smaragdus' (emerald) 'increases wealth and confers persuasive speech in (pleading) causes; and suspended from the neck, cures hemitertian fever and epilepsy', while a sapphire 'makes a man chaste and cools internal heat, checks sweating, and cures headache and pain in the tongue .... They say that invigorates the body, and brings about peaceful agreements, and makes one pious and devoted to God, and confirms the mind in goodness.'[49] Both emeralds and sapphires are mentioned in the Bible; they adorn the New Jerusalem and are present in the High Priest's breastplate.

On the Coronation Cross, the precious gemstones are shaped mostly in the rounded form of cabochons, carefully polished and secured by simple claws made of gold. The gems themselves are set in such a way that each fleur-de-lys terminal of the cross is surrounded by stones and white pearls. This type of framing follows the model of the early medieval mounting of gems, such as the mounting of the intaglio portrait of Julia, daughter of the emperor Titus (Fig. 4.7), a large aquamarine engraved with the head of a woman and signed by the Greek engraver Evodos, made about AD 90, which decorated the summit of the Crest of Charlemagne in the

---

the dark. It is said to preserve the royal honour.' See Albertus Magnus, *Book of Minerals*, trans. Dorothy Wyckoff (Oxford, 1967), 111. Albertus' work has also been known as *Mineralia, Lapidarius, Liber de mineralibus et lapidibus*, or *De mineralibus et rebus metallicis*. On the orphanus, see Estelle Morgan, '"Lapis Orphanus" in the Imperial Crown', *The Modern Language Review* 58 (1963), 210–14; Gunther Wolf, 'Der "Waise": Bemerkungen zum Leitstein der Wiener Reichskrone', *Deutsches Archiv für Erforschung des Mittelalters* 41 (1985), 39–65; Arno Mentzel-Reuters, 'Die Goldene Krone: Entwicklungslinien mittelalterlicher Herrschaftssymbolik', *Deutsches Archiv für Erforschung des Mittelalters* 69 (2004), 135–82, esp. 147–63).

48 Gerda Friess, *Edelsteine im Mittelalter: Wandel und Kontinuität in ihrer Bedeutung durch zwölf Jahrhunderte (in Aberglauben, Medizin, Theologie und Goldschmiedekunst)* (Hildesheim, 1980), 63.

49 See Albertus Magnus, *Book of Minerals*, 120, 115.

Fig. 4.7. Portrait of Julia, daughter of Emperor Titus, Italy, Rome, before 90 CE. Mount: France, ninth century. Aquamarine (intaglio); gold, sapphire, pearls (mount); 10.5 cm x 9.5 cm. Paris, Bibliothèque nationale de France, Département des Monnaies, Médailles et Antiques. Photo © BnF, Paris.

abbey church of Saint-Denis, Paris.[50] The preferred early medieval form of the reliquary cross was strongly influenced by the Carolingian mounting

---

50 Poche, 'Einige Erwägungen', 85–6; Blaise de Montesquiou-Fezensac and Danielle Gaborit-Chopin, 'Camées et intailles du Trésor de SaintDenis', *Cahiers Archéologiques: Fin de l'Antiquité et Moyen Âge* 24 (1975), 137–62, esp. 141); Peter Lasko, *Ars Sacra 800–1200* (New Haven, 1994), 18–19; Marue L. Vollenweider and Mathilde Avisseau-Broustet, *Camées et intailles II: Les portraits romains du Cabinet*

of gems, and Charles' famous namesake remained throughout his life a potent model of imperial rulership for the Luxembourg emperor. Charles' profound interest in Charlemagne may be reflected in the design of the Coronation Cross.[51]

THE GEMSTONES AND THEIR IMAGES

On the verso of the Coronation Cross are cameos – gemstones with carved images. They serve as lids of small boxes protecting the relics. Generally ignored by previous scholarship, these small carvings have never been examined in any detail despite there being nine of them. Three cameos of this collection are Byzantine; they depict the Crucifixion (onyx, twelfth–thirteenth century), the archangel Michael (chalcedony, twelfth century), and a figure of Christ blessing (sardonyx, thirteenth century). Four of the gemstones are Western Medieval; these are carved in the form of another Christ blessing (amethyst, thirteenth century), a facing male bust (sapphire, thirteenth century), a pair of standing rulers (agate, twelfth century), and a portrait of Frederick II of Hohenstaufen, Holy Roman Emperor (sardonyx, after 1220). Finally, there are two magnificent Roman imperial pieces, both made of sardonyx.[52] Scholars have assumed that the first of the two portrays Alexander the Great, but it may well be an idealized portrait of Claudius, created during his reign. The second one is a portrait cameo of Antonia Minor, mother of the emperor Claudius (Fig.

---

des Médailles (Paris, 2003), 128–9, no. 145; Erik Inglis, 'Expertise, Artifacts, and Time in the 1534 Inventory of the St-Denis Treasury', *Art Bulletin* 98:1 (2016), 14–42.
51 The Holy Roman Emperors, including Charles IV, asserted their lineage from Charlemagne, who was also a holy figure, and believed that they were divinely sanctioned to lead Christendom. On the relationship between Charlemagne and Charles of Luxembourg, see Marie Bláhová, 'Nachleben Karls des Grossen in der Propaganda Karls IV', *Das Mittelalter* 4 (1999), 11–25; Machilek, 'Karl IV. und Karl der Große', 113–45; and Zoë Opačić, 'Karolus Magnus and Karolus Quartus: Imperial Role Models in Ingelheim, Aachen and Prague', in Ute Engel and Alexandrea Gajewski (eds), *Mainz and the Middle Rhine Valley: Medieval Art, Architecture and Archaeology* (Leeds, 2007), 221–46.
52 On the cameos, see Hans Wentzel, 'Mittelalterliche Gemmen: Versuch einer Grundlegung', in *Zeitschrift des deutschen Vereins für Kunstwissenschaft* 8 (1941), 45–98, esp. 8, 51, 74–7, 82–3; Jiří Frel, 'Les portraits antiques en Tchécoslovaquie', in Jaroslav Pešina (ed.), *Sborník k sedmdesátinám Jana Květa* (Prague, 1965), 48–9; Jan Bouzek, Marie Dufková and Karel Kurz, *Antický portrét*, exhibition catalogue, National Museum in Prague (Prague, 1972), 38; and most recently Ingrid Ciulisová and Martin Henig, 'An Imperial Portrait Cameo of Antonia Minor in a Fourteenth-century Reliquary Cross in Prague', *Journal of the British Archaeological Association* 174 (2021), 6–15 (OA https://doi.org/10.1080/00681288.2021.1924984).

4.8).⁵³ Most intriguing, however, is the fact that this cameo of Antonia was re-employed by Charles to commemorate a Christian saint. The original portrait was supplemented with a linear halo around the head and a monogrammatic inscription on either side. New palaeographical analysis confirms that the monogram shows 'S. CA', consistent with St Catherine of Alexandria, and that the gothic majuscule appears to be from the fourteenth century. Thus, in the fourteenth century, the ancient imperial cameo of Antonia Minor was rededicated to St Catherine, Charles of Luxembourg's heavenly protectress.⁵⁴ According to *The Golden Legend*, St Catherine was born a princess and, as such, was usually pictured as a crowned, luxuriously dressed woman.⁵⁵ As a result, the image of St Catherine not only corresponded with the existing cameo portrait of Antonia but also helped connect the cross directly with Charles and his strategy of self-promotion as a pious ruler.

According to Wentzel, the nine cameos' historical associations collectively link them to both the Eastern Roman and the Western Latin worlds. The Byzantine past is exemplified by the amethyst cameo depicting Christ blessing (depicted here as Pantokrator, ruler of all), the central image of the Eastern Orthodox Church. The Western Latin world is evoked by the stone of Frederick II of Hohenstaufen (Figs 4.9, 4.10).⁵⁶

---

53 See Wolf-Rüdiger Megow, *Kameen von Augustus bis Alexander Severus* (Berlin, 1987), 290–1, and most recently Ciulisová and Henig, 'An Imperial Portrait Cameo'. The Prague cameo of Antonia Minor is comparable with the cameo of Antonia Minor preserved in the National Archaeological Museum in Florence (first century AD, and later additions. Sardonyx; height 49 mm).

54 Ciulisová and Henig, 'An Imperial Portrait Cameo'. Charles was keen on St Catherine, one of the most popular early Christian virgin martyrs in medieval devotion, and especially venerated her. According to his autobiography, he believed that it was St Catherine who ensured his victories in battles at San Felice near Modena in 1332 and again in 1340 when Charles took the Penede Castle, close to Lake Garda in Italy. Charles established a new Augustinian nunnery with the church dedicated to this saint in the New Town in Prague and was personally present at its consecration in 1367. Moreover, in his private oratory chapel at Karlštejn Castle, he had the picture of St Catherine painted on the stone mensa of the central altar. See Balázs Nagy and Frank Schaer, *Karoli IV Imperatoris Romanorum vita ab eo ipso conscripta et Hystoria nova de Sancto Wenceslao Martyre: Autobiography of Emperor Charles IV and His Legend of St. Wenceslas* (Budapest, 2001), 44, 150; Johann Friedrich Böhmer, *Regesta Imperii VIII: Die Regesten des Kaiserreichs unter Kaiser Karl IV. 1346–1378*, ed. Alfons Huber (Hildesheim, 1968, reprint of the edition Innsbruck, 1877), 372; František Ekert, *Posvátná místa král. hl. města Prahy*, 2 (Prague, 1884), 170–82.

55 Jacobus de Voragine, *Golden Legend*, 720–7.

56 Wentzel, 'Mittelalterliche Gemmen', 76–7; Hans Wentzel, 'Staatskameen im Mittelalter', *Jahrbuch der Berliner Museen* 4 (1962), 42–77, esp. 54–5); Rainer Kahsnitz, 'Staufische Kameen', in Reiner Haussherr (ed.), *Die Zeit der Staufer:*

Fig. 4.8. Imperial portrait cameo of Antonia Minor, first century CE, sardonyx, height 3.7 cm. Incorporated into Coronation Cross, Treasury of St Vitus Cathedral, Prague. Photo © Courtesy of Prague Castle Administration/Jan Gloc.

Geschichte-Kunst-Kultur, vol. 5. *Supplement: Vorträge und Forschung*, exhibition catalogue (Stuttgart, 1979), 477–520, esp. 478–9); and *Die Zeit der Staufer: Geschichte-Kunst-Kultur*, vol. 1 (Stuttgart, 1977), cat. 860, 676–7.

Fig. 4.9. Christ blessing, thirteenth century, amethyst, height 3.2 cm. Incorporated into Coronation Cross, Treasury of St Vitus Cathedral, Prague. Photo © Courtesy of Prague Castle Administration/Jan Gloc.

The first of these two cameos shows Christ holding a book, most probably the Gospel, and blessing with his right hand. The purple colour of the amethyst stone clearly signifies the imperial status of the figure. Although this medieval cameo was clearly inspired by Byzantine models, it was created in the Western Latin world.[57] And notably, the imperial seal

---

57 Gerda Friess, *Edelsteine im Mittelalter: Wandel und Kontinuität in ihrer Bedeutung durch zwölf Jahrhunderte (in Aberglauben, Medizin, Theologie und Goldschmiedekunst)* (Hildesheim, 1980), 63. On the Christ Pantokrator, see Nancy Patterson, 'Types of Christ', in *The Oxford Dictionary of Byzantium*, vol. 1 (New York and Oxford, 1991), 438. For supposed Byzantine models, see for instance the cameo

Fig. 4.10. Frederick II of Hohenstaufen, Holy Roman Emperor, after 1220, sardonyx, height 3.8 cm. Incorporated into Coronation Cross, Treasury of St Vitus Cathedral, Prague. Photo © Courtesy of Prague Castle Administration/Jan Gloc.

of Frederick of Hohenstaufen (1194–1250), made around 1220, served as a model for the anonymous master who created the cameo of Frederick now mounted on the Coronation Cross.[58] As on the seal, we see him in a frontal position, seated in majesty on a throne with his insignia: the crown, the sceptre topped with the cross in his right hand, and the orb in his left.

In Charles' time, both the reference to the Eastern Christian Church[59] and to Frederick would surely have resonated powerfully. Charles, like Frederick before him, was actively attempting to resolve what had been for a long time a burning political and religious issue: the Great Schism and the reunion of the Eastern Church with the West. In 1355, shortly after his coronation as Holy Roman Emperor, Charles was in touch with the Byzantine emperor John V Paleologos (1332–91), one of the principal initiators of political negotiations about this matter at the time; and some scholars have suggested that the Byzantine ruler also sent Charles a piece of the Holy Cross.[60] Frederick II is generally considered to be one of the most controversial imperial figures, well known for his clash with the papacy, his excommunications, and his persistent claims to universal power. Nevertheless, it was Frederick who in 1212 issued the charter of great significance for the Bohemian king, Ottokar I Přemysl, confirming that the royal title of the Bohemian kings was hereditary and thus perpetuating the hereditary form of the Bohemian monarchy.[61]

---

showing Blessing Christ (bloodstone, c. tenth–eleventh century) from the collections of the Victoria and Albert Museum, London, inv. no. A 160-1978; Paul Williamson, 'A Byzantine Bloodstone Carving in the Victoria and Albert Museum', *The Burlington Magazine* 122 (1980), 66–9.

58   Rainer Kahsnitz, 'Staufische Kameen', in Reiner Haussherr (ed.), *Die Zeit der Staufer*, 478–9.

59   Helen C. Evans pointed out that Charles' interest in Eastern images may also have been inspired by his desire to emulate Emperor Constantine, founder of the Christian state that was still called 'the Empire of the Romans' in the fourteenth century and is today known as Byzantium. See Helen C. Evans, 'The Madonna of Most', in Barbara Drake Boehm and Jiří Fajt (eds), *Prague: The Crown of Bohemia 1347–1437*, exhibition catalogue, Metropolitan Museum of Art, New York (New Haven and London, 2005), cat. 27, 156.

60   On this issue, see Miroslav Hroch and Věra Hrochová, 'Karel IV. a otázka obrany Balkánu proti Osmanům v polovině 14. století', in Václav Vaněček (ed.), *Karolus Quartus* (Prague, 1984), 205–14. For a wider context, see Joseph Gill, *Church Union: Rome and Byzantium 1204–1453* (London, 1979). On the piece of the Holy Cross sent to Charles IV by John V Paleologos, see Otavský, 'K relikviím vlastněným císařem Karlem IV', 395.

61   Zdeněk Měřínský and Jaroslav Mezník, 'The Making of the Czech State: Bohemia and Moravia from the Tenth to the Fourteenth Centuries', in Mikuláš Teich (ed.), *Bohemia in History* (Cambridge, 1998), 39–58; and Martin Wihoda and Josef Žemlička (eds), *Zlatá bula sicilská: Mezi mýtem a realitou* (Prague, 2016). In

Apparently, Charles sought to benefit from the potency of the deliberately selected stones bearing these images. The relics gave the cross the character of a powerful apotropaic object, but the stones, particularly the cameos, imparted a narrative that was just as important. Supplementing the rarity of the gemstones and the spiritual and magical properties they were thought to possess, the cameos imbued the cross with tangible connections to the past. While the fundamental spiritual message conveyed by the relics was the legendary story of the True Cross, the cameos' multiple historical and artistic connections induced another discourse, the primary significance of which was to establish continuity between Charles' reign, the ancient Roman emperors, and in particular the Christian Rome of Constantine the Great. Medieval emperors regarded themselves as successors of the old Roman emperors and took seriously the topos of 'translatio imperii', understood here as an unbroken link between antiquity and modernity.[62] In their entirety, the cameos would have effectively supported Charles' imperial status and thus the special position of Bohemia and the Luxembourgs within the Holy Roman Empire.

Charles was a man of good education, literate and proficient in several languages, with a wide range of literary and theological interests acquired in his early youth in Paris, and later developed on his numerous travels around Europe. His learned interests embracing theology, history, liturgy, and more, found reflection in his own Latin writings.[63] However, a crucial

---

spite of the ongoing papal antipathy toward Frederick and his legacy, for Charles IV, Frederick's art commissions remained an important source of inspiration. On connections between the Tower of Old Town Bridge built in Prague in Charles IV's time and the Capua gate near Naples commissioned by Emperor Frederick II in the 1230s, see Willibald Sauerländer, 'Two Glances from the North: The Presence and Absence of Frederick II in the Art of Empire: The Court Art of Frederick II and the *Opus Francigenum*', in William Tronzo (ed.), *Intellectual Life at the Court of Frederick II. Hohenstaufen*, Studies in the History of Art, vol. 44, Center of Advanced Study in the Visual Arts, Symposium Papers (Hannover and London, 1994), 188–209, esp. 197–200); and Ján Bažant, 'Karel IV., "Staroměstská mostecká věž" a "pons animarum"', *Listy filologické / Folia philologica* 120 (1997), 46–59.

62 Werner Goez, *Translatio imperii: Ein Beitrag zur Geschichte des Geschichtsdenkens und der politischen Theorien im Mittelalter und in der Frühen Neuzeit* (Tübingen, 1958), esp. 237–57; Peter Hutter, *Germanische Stammväter und römisch-deutsches Kaisertum* (Hildesheim, Zürich, New York, 2000), 26.

63 Charles' writings include his autobiography (*Commentarius de Vita Caroli* or *Vita*), a new life of St Wenceslas (*Hystoria nova de sancto Wenceslao martyre, duce Bohemorum*), a coronation Ordo (*Ordo ad coronandum regem Bohemorum et Ordo ad benedicendum reginam*), and an introduction to his *Majestas Carolina* prepared in 1350-1. See Bernd-Ulrich Hergemöller, 'Carolus quartus latinus: Karl IV. als literarisches Ego, als gestaltender Urheber und als geistige Autorität', in Bernd-Ulrich Hergemöller, *Cogor adversum te: Drei Studien zum literarisch-theologischen Profil Karls IV. und seiner Kanzlei* (Warendorf, 1999), 221–418; Anežka Vidmanová (ed.),

question remains to be answered: Was Charles aware of the visual message conveyed by the gemstones? The correspondence of Francesco Petrarca (1304–74), the illustrious poet, scholar, and antiquarian of exceptional curiosity and competence, offers a possible answer. A letter written by him in 1355 states that a selection of gold and silver coins bearing portraits of ancient emperors was presented to Charles by Petrarch, by then a well-known collector of Roman coins in his own right, when the two met in Mantua in December 1354.[64] This letter also relates that, on the occasion of their meeting, Petrarch gave Charles a brief outline of the great events in the life of each of the Roman emperors depicted on the coins, and that Charles studied these coins in detail (we even know that he later disputed the authenticity of one of them).[65] The actual coins have disappeared, but Charles was undoubtedly capable of distinguishing between the ancient images, and of reading the inscriptions on the coins. It seems that the cameos which came into his possession were later deliberately and by his explicit order re-employed on the Coronation Cross.

Karel IV.: Literární dílo (Prague, 2000); Eva Schlotheuber, 'Karl als Autor – Der "weise Herrscher"', in Jiří Fajt and Markus Hörsch, *Kaiser Karl IV. 1316–2016: Erste bayerisch-tschechische Landesausstellung*, exhibition catalogue (Prague, 2016), 69–78; and Martin Bauch, '"Et hec scripsi manu mea propria" – Known and Unknown: Autographs of Charles IV as Testimonies of Intellectual Profiles, Royal Literacy, and Cultural Transfer', in Sébastien Barret, Dominique Stutzmann and Georg Vogeler (eds), *Ruling the Script in the Middle Ages: Formal Aspects of Written Communication (Books, Charters, and Inscriptions)* (Turnhout, 2016), 25–47.

64 Charles met Petrarch in December 1354, during his imperial journey when he travelled to Rome to receive the crown. Petrarch's letter from 25 February 1355 was addressed to Lello di Pietro Stefano dei Tosetti, a Roman noble and intimate friend of the poet. See Francesco Petrarca, *Epistolae de rebus familiaribus et variae. Vol. 2*, ed. Iosephi Fracassetti (Florence, 1862), 520. On Petrarch as an antiquarian, see Roberto Weiss, 'Petrarch the Antiquarian', in Charles Henderson (ed.), *Classical, Medieval and Renaissance Studies in Honor of Berthold Louis Ullman* (Rome, 1964), 199–209; and Angelo Mazzocco, 'The Antiquarianism of Francesco Petrarca', *The Journal of Medieval and Renaissance Studies* 7 (1977), 203–24. For a wider context, see Charles C. Bayley, 'Petrarch, Charles IV, and the "Renovatio Imperii"', *Speculum* 17 (1942), 323–41.

65 See Charles' correspondence with Petrarch's student Niccolò Beccari of Ferrara (c. 1315–before 1374), a poet and presumably a tutor of Charles' younger son, Sigismund. See Karel Hrdina, 'Niccolò Beccari, Ital na dvoře Karla IV', in Bedřich Jenšovský and Bedřich Mendl (eds), *K dějinám československým v období humanismu: Sborník prací věnovaných Janu Bedřichu Novákovi k 60. narozeninám 1872–1932* (Prague, 1932), 159–77; Hanno Helbling, 'Le lettere di Nicolaus de Beccariis (Niccolò da Ferrara)', *Bullettino dell'Istituto storico Italiano per il medio evo e Archivio Muratoriano* 76 (1964), 241–89.

Fig. 4.11. Charles raising his reliquary cross with his third wife, Anne of Schweidnitz (?), before 1360. Fresco, gold, gemstones. Chapel of St Catherine, Karlštejn Castle. Photo © The National Heritage Institute, Prague.

THE CORONATION CROSS AND ITS PURPOSE

The Coronation Cross is thought to have been made or remade in the late 1350s or 1360s, most likely shortly after Charles' imperial coronation in 1355. However, this object is not identical with the cross several times depicted in the small and the high tower of Karlštejn. Emanuel Poche argued that there probably existed two different crosses containing a similar set of Christ's Passion relics.[66] The first was the altered thirteenth-century cross with distinctive fleur-de-lys terminals, most probably one of the crosses Charles owned personally and later used during coronations. The second was the massive cross with quadrilobes painted at Karlštejn and celebrated as the Bohemian Cross (Fig. 4.11). This cross almost certainly found its temporary resting place on the altar of the Chapel of the Instruments of Christ's Passion, Charles' private oratory located on the

---

66 Poche, 'K otázce ostatkových křížů Karla IV', 239–46. According to Poche, the cross is comparable with crosses of Sens, Saint-Omer, and Gosse. See Jean Taralon, *Les trésors des églises de France*, exhibition catalogue, Musée des arts décoratifs (Paris, 1965), ill. nos 118, 120, 124. See also Jaroslav Pešina et al., *České umění gotické* (Prague, 1970), 337–8.

second floor of the Lesser Tower of the castle, and later dedicated to St Catherine.⁶⁷ In the course of time, the Bohemian Cross disappeared, as did the original base of the Coronation Cross after the object was offered as security for a loan by Vladislas II, King of Bohemia, in the 1470s.⁶⁸ In any case, it is evident that each of the two ornaments served both as precious reliquaries connecting the owner with Christ and as awe-inspiring multi-purpose objects – protective devices similar to the ancient cult object, the Palladium, the purpose of which was to repel enemies, ward off natural disasters, and guarantee divine protection – in this case to the Luxembourgs as rulers.

In addition to the Coronation Cross, at least two fourteenth-century gem-based objects traditionally linked to Charles of Luxembourg have survived and are extant today.⁶⁹ One of them is a silver crown with 22 cameos and intaglios. The other is the reliquary bust of Charlemagne on which the silver crown rests (Fig. 4.12); both are now kept in the treasury of Aachen Cathedral. Many of the cameos and intaglios that adorn the silver crown have Roman origins.⁷⁰ Notably, both the Aachen crown and the Coronation Cross are lavishly decorated with precious stones, including Roman cameos, and both display fleur-de-lys ornamentation. The magnificent silver bust of Charlemagne is ornamented with a large number of gemstones, many of them carved, and there are also numerous carved gemstones of different sizes mounted on his tunic. The Aachen silver crown is thought to be Charles' private crown, made in Prague for his coronation in Aachen in 1349 in the absence of the royal insignia of the kings of the Romans kept at this time in the hands of Louis of Brandenburg (1316–61), the eldest son of Charles' rival, Louis IV of Bavaria.⁷¹ The crown is closely linked to the bust of Charlemagne and seen as analogous to

---

67 Jaromír Homolka, 'Umělecká výzdoba paláce a menší věže hradu Karlštejn', in Jiří Fajt (ed.), *Magister Theodoricus, dvorní malíř císaře Karla IV.: Umělecká výzdoba posvátných prostor hradu Karlštejna* (Prague, 1998), 96–153; Paul Crossley, 'The Politics of Presentation: The Architecture of Charles IV of Bohemia', in Sarah Rees Jones, Richard Marks and Alastair J. Minnis (eds), *Courts and Regions in Medieval Europe* (York, 2000), 141.
68 Fišer, *Karlštejn: Vzájemné vztahy tří karlštejnských kaplí*, 261.
69 Poche, 'Einige Erwägungen', 87–9; Karel Stejskal, *Umění na dvoře Karla IV* (Prague, 1978), 85, 90.
70 Hans Peter Hilger, 'Anmerkungen zu der Reliquienbüste Karls des Grossen im Domschatz zu Aachen', *Aachener Kunstblätter* 48 (1978/9), 17–24; Ján Bažant, 'Medusa, Ancient Gems, and the Holy Roman Emperor Charles IV', *Anodos: Studies of the Ancient World* 13 (2013), 35–50.
71 On the death of Louis IV in 1347, the imperial treasure was in possession of his son, Louis of Brandenburg, who refused to relinquish it. Charles formally received the imperial relics and regalia on 12 March 1350 in Munich. They were brought to Prague by Jan Očko of Vlašim and Guillaume de Landstein. See Robert Folz, *Le*

Fig. 4.12. Reliquary bust of Charlemagne, second half of the fourteenth century, oak wood, silver, gilded silver, gemstones, cameos, and intaglios, Treasury of Aachen Cathedral. Photo © Bildarchiv Foto Marburg.

the reliquary of St Wenceslas upon which Charles placed the royal Bohemian crown after his coronation as King of Bohemia in 1347.[72] Even the Coronation Cross is considered by some scholars as an alternative coronation cross for the kings of the Romans, created to complement the Aachen silver crown.[73] Charles' first coronation took place in Bonn in 1346, after he had been elected Rival King of the Romans in opposition to the Bavarian emperor Louis IV. This coronation took place in Bonn as neither Aachen nor Cologne would open their gates to Charles. Thus, one can speculate that all this was done presumably for a single particular purpose: to legitimize *ex post* the status of the Aachen silver crown and thus make the act of Charles' coronation as King of the Romans justifiable and thus acceptable. While this hypothesis may seem convincing, it is also true that no direct written evidence has survived to corroborate it. It should be openly acknowledged that no written historical record exists to confirm Charles of Luxembourg's having commissioned the Aachen silver crown, the reliquary bust of Charlemagne, or the Coronation Cross. However, there is non-textual, material evidence that can be used in much the same way as documents, offering insights at least as significant as those afforded by the traditional study of written sources, and thus shedding light on Charles' likely engagement in the creation of these objects.

Recent scholarship has already revealed that, in addition to the reliquary cross, the numerous Roman cameos displayed on the Aachen silver crown might have been re-employed on this object in order to link Charles of Luxembourg to his illustrious Roman imperial predecessors.[74] The same can be said about the Roman portrait cameos on the cross, including the cameo of Antonia Minor, which Charles re-dedicated to his preferred saint, Catherine of Alexandria. At the very least, this indicates that before their reuse the gemstones would have been selected deliberately, and that

---

Souvenir et la Légende de Charlemagne dans l'Empire germanique médiéval (Paris, 1950), 453.

72 On the reliquary bust of Charlemagne, see Ernst Günther Grimme, 'Mittelalterliche Karlsreliquiare: Die Verehrung Karls des Großen, dargestellt anhand von Aachener Reliquienbehältern und anderen Werken der Goldschmiedekunst', *Aachener Kunstblätter* 16 (1957), 30–6; Ernst Günther Grimme, 'Der Aachener Domschatz', cat. 69; Hilger, 'Anmerkungen zu der Reliquienbüste', 17–24; Percy E. Schramm and Hermann Fillitz, *Denkmale der deutschen Könige und Kaiser. Bd. II: Ein Beitrag zur Herrschergeschichte von Rudolf I. bis Maximilian I., 1273–1519*, no. 30, 58; Karel Otavský, 'Aachener Goldschmiedearbeiten des 14. Jahrhunderts', in Anton Legner (ed.), *Die Parler und der schöne Stil 1350–1400: Europäische Kunst unter den Luxemburgern*, 4 (Cologne, 1980), 77–82; M. Fritz, *Goldschmiedekunst der Gotik im Mitteleuropa* (Munich, 1982), cat. 84, 196–7; Georg Minkenberg, Die Büste Karls d. Gr. im Aachener Domschatz (Heidelberg, 2008).

73 Poche, 'Einige Erwägungen', 87–9; Stejskal, *Umění na dvoře Karla IV*, 85.

74 Bažant, 'Medusa', 35–50.

the act of selecting the stones required the personal participation of a knowledgeable patron or his learned advisers.[75]

Equally important is the status of ancient cameos as rare and costly objects during the late medieval period. One example is Le Grand Camée de France, which was valued so highly that in early 1340 Philip of Valois, King of France, sent it from the Sainte-Chapelle to Pope Clement VI to Avignon as security for a loan.[76] Even in the fifteenth century, the valuations attached to precious stones significantly varied in comparison to paintings. Whereas the engraved gemstones of the Medici collections were valued between 400 and 1000 florins each, and the famous sardonyx cameo Tazza Farnese at 10,000 florins, the price of an average painting by a master of the stature of Filippo Lippi or Sandro Botticelli would have ranged between 50 and 100 florins, and a large fresco cycle, such as Ghirlandaio's *Story of Saint John the Baptist* in Santa Maria Novella in Florence, would only have cost about 1000 florins.[77] Clearly, only the most powerful and resourceful individuals, mostly imperial and royal founders, could afford to own ancient cameos.[78] Charles was one of them. He assembled a considerable number of cameos and, as can be seen in the medieval inventories of St Vitus Cathedral, he incorporated many of them into precious liturgical vessels to serve as ecclesiastical *ornamenta*.[79]

CONCLUSION

As the preceding analysis of the Coronation Cross has shown, the following conclusions can be drawn: First, the cross is a deliberately fashioned composite object into which various highly valuable elements

---

75 On Charles IV and his possible advisers, see Flaminia Pichiorri, 'Die Rekrutierung diplomatischen Personals unter Karl IV.: Zeitphasen und Verfahrensweisen', in Ulrike Hohensee, Mathias Lawo, Michael Lindner, Michael Menzel and Olaf B. Rader (eds), *Die Goldene Bulle*, 835–68; Václav Žůrek, 'Entre la cour et la ville: les gens de savoir au service de l'empereur Charles IV à Prague', in Léonard Courbon and Denis Menjot (eds), *La cour et la ville dans l'Europe du Moyen Age et des Temps Modernes* (Turnhout, 2015), 313–23.
76 Ernest Babelon, *Catalogue des camées antiques et modernes de la Bibliothèque nationale* (Paris, 1897), no. 264, 125–6.
77 Ernst H. Gombrich, 'The Early Medici as Patrons', in Ernst H. Gombrich, *Norm and Form: Studies in the Art of the Renaissance* (London, 1978), 35–57, esp. 52.
78 Hans Peter Hilger, 'Die Reliquienbüste Karls des Grossen und ihre Krone im Domschatz zu Aachen', *Sborník mezinárodní vědecké konference Doba Karla IV. v dějinách národů ČSSR, Materiály ze sekce dějin umění*, ed. M. Svatoš (Prague, 1982), 269–73, esp. 272.
79 Antonín Podlaha and Eduard Šittler, *Chrámový poklad u sv. Víta v Praze: Jeho dějiny a popis* (Prague, 1903), iii–xxx.

of disparate origins were incorporated.⁸⁰ The special character of these elements, the spiritual features assigned them, and the message that they conveyed together indicate that all these components in all likelihood were acquired and purposely selected by Charles of Luxembourg himself. Second, my analysis revealed that the Coronation Cross was designed according to a pre-existing learned programme in which Charles was personally involved. The materialization of the programme was made possible by the reinvention of the *crux gemmata*, an early medieval type of cross lavishly decorated with gemstones. Basing their work on *crux gemmata* models, medieval craftsmen were able to supplement a group of holy relics incorporated into the cross with gemstones, including ancient and medieval cameos. The gems supported and reinforced the perceived supernatural power of the relics, imbued the object with multicultural features, and, moreover, created specific spiritual, geographical, historical, and artistic connections with the past that helped promote Charles' political agenda.

These findings confirm that the images of the cameos also effectively advertised more specific messages. The choice of the fleur-de-lys decorations on the cross was thoughtful, as that heraldic symbol linked the object with the kings of France, in particular St Louis IX, viewed at the time as the embodiment of the ideal Christian king. By employing that motif, a close bond between Charles of Luxembourg and the saintly royal authority of France could be made explicitly manifest. Finally, it is very likely that the Coronation Cross was originally one of the crosses owned by Charles personally; as such, it would have been seen only by a small group of courtiers entitled to enter the inner core of the royal castle, or by privileged and distinguished visitors such as foreign envoys who might have been in need of being convinced of the special divine protection conferred upon Emperor Charles of Luxembourg.

Overall, the preceding examination demonstrates that the Coronation Cross was not simply an ecclesiastical ornament, a reliquary designed to manifest Charles' piety, as it has usually been perceived, but rather is best understood as a multi-purpose object. It served the royal and imperial ambitions of Charles but also made him visible as a learned ruler who was

---

80   On this topic, see especially William Heckscher, 'Relics of Pagan Antiquity in Medieval Settings', *Journal of the Warburg Institute* 1 (1938), 204–20; Avinoam Shalem, *Islam Christianized: Islamic Portable Objects in the Medieval Church Treasuries of the Latin West* (Frankfurt am Main, 1996); Stefania Gerevini, 'The Grotto of the Virgin in San Marco: Artistic Reuse and Cultural Identity in Medieval Venice', *Gesta* 53 (2014), 197–220. On Charles of Luxembourg as a collector of gems, see Ingrid Ciulisová, 'The Power of Marvellous Objects: Charles IV of Luxembourg, Charles V of Valois and their Gemstones', *Journal of the History of Collections* 33 (2021), 1-13 (OA https://doi:10.1093/jhc/fhaa023).

well acquainted with the past of his illustrious predecessors. Furthermore, due to the presence of the relics and the gemstones, the cross was a powerful talismanic device.

Magnificent objects like the Coronation Cross can enlighten us about a period as a whole. As such, they often occupy a significant position in grand historical narratives. But grand stories require solid foundations. The in-depth examination of this kind of object helps us to avoid simple generalizations and revise accepted narratives. It also contributes to a better and more nuanced understanding of their ability to proclaim power and authority, here specifically of Emperor Charles and the Luxembourgs, including their spiritual connectedness both to antiquity and to the Christian world – a model that can be applied on a broader scale both to pre-modern Europe and beyond.

CHAPTER 5

CHARLES IV AND THE PATRONAGE OF MULTILINGUAL LITERATURE AT HIS COURT AND BEYOND

VÁCLAV ŽŮREK

The Prague court of Bohemian King and Holy Roman Emperor Charles IV of Luxembourg (r. 1346–78) was a multilingual and cosmopolitan environment where Latin, German, and Czech existed side-by-side. Such a trilingual environment was a fundamental characteristic of life in late-medieval Prague, and in the Lands of the Bohemian Crown in general.[1]

The commonplace nature of a trilingual environment at the Prague court and within the inner circle of the Luxembourg dynasty is succinctly illustrated by the trilingual Bible that Anne of Bohemia, Charles IV's daughter, is said to have brought with her to England, where she came to marry King Richard II in 1382. This manuscript allegedly used by Queen Anne was used as an argument by John Wyclif when he defended the right to an English vernacular translation of the Bible.[2]

---

1   This statement leaves aside the Jewish community in the Kingdom of Bohemia, which for the purposes of this essay cannot be included in the discussion due to reasons of scope.
2   John Wyclif, 'De triplici vinculo amoris', in Rudolf Buddensieg (ed.), *John Wyclif's Polemical Works in Latin*, vol. 1 (London, 1883), 151–98, at 168: *Nam possibile est, quod nobilis regina Anglie, soror cesaris, habeat ewangelium in lingwa triplici exaratum, scilicet in lingwa boemica, in lingwa teutonica et latina, et hereticare ipsam propterea implicite foret luciferina superbia* [For it is lawful for the noble queen of England, the sister of the emperor, to have the gospel written in three languages,

Princess Anne came to England from the Prague court, where trilingual functioning was seen as a normal part of everyday life as well as of literary creation.³ The reign of her father, Charles IV, is associated with intensive literary production in Latin, German, and Czech, and much of this production can be placed in the context of the court.⁴

What was the role that the cosmopolitan court, and especially the monarch and other patrons in his proximity, could have played in this development? Can an impulse towards multilingualism genuinely be identified in this environment, and to what extent do the surviving sources support this role of the monarch and his associates? This essay will examine the role of Emperor Charles IV in promoting the production of Latin texts and in the development of vernacular – German and Czech – textual production. It will not be assumed a priori that the monarch himself was the sole instigator of these activities, although this is often the appearance created in older scholarship. Therefore, this study will include an analysis of the role of Charles' chancellor John of Neumarkt, who was probably the most active promoter and author of vernacular literary

---

that is, in Czech and in German and in Latin: and it would savour of the pride of Lucifer to call her a heretic for such a reason as this!]. English translation is quoted from Margaret Deanesly, *The Lollard Bible and Other Medieval Biblical Versions* (Cambridge, 1966), 248.

3   See Alfred Thomas, *Anne's Bohemia: Czech Literature and Society, 1310-1420* (Minneapolis, 1998); Michael van Dussen, *From England to Bohemia: Heresy and Communication in the Later Middle Ages* (Cambridge, 2012), 12-36, esp. 18, where he explains the context of the information about this manuscript. See also Alfred Thomas' latest book, in which he presents Queen Anne as a promoter of vernacular literature with an emphasis on multilingual literary production, which was commonplace within the milieu from which she originated, unlike the French princesses who typically became English queens before her and were used to support French literature. Alfred Thomas, *The Court of Richard II and Bohemian Culture: Literature and Art in the Age of Chaucer and the Gawain Poet* (Cambridge, 2020), 1-41.

4   For some basic orientation concerning multilingual production in the Bohemian literary landscape during the Luxembourg era, see Václav Bok, 'Zur literarischen Situation im Böhmen des 14. Jahrhunderts', in Joachim Heinzle, L. Peter Johnson and Gisela Vollmann-Profe (eds), *Literatur im Umkreis des Prager Hofs der Luxemburger*, Schweinfurter Kolloquium 1992, Wolfram-Studien, 13 (Berlin, 1994), 10-27; Winfried Baumann, *Die Literatur des Mittelalters in Böhmen: Deutsch-lateinisch-tschechische Literatur vom 10. bis zum 15. Jahrhundert* (Munich, 1978); Lenka Jiroušková, 'Prague', in David Wallace (ed.), *Regeneration: A Literary History of Europe, 1348-1418*, vol. 2 (Oxford, 2016), 617-51. An introduction to the multilingual aspects of literary life in the Czech lands in the fourteenth and fifteenth centuries is offered by Jakub Sichálek, 'Vícejazyčnost literárního života v českých zemích 14. a 15. století. Sedm tematických exkurzů v rámci bohemistiky', *Česká literatura* 62:6 (2014), 711-44.

output at the imperial court and beyond during the third quarter of the fourteenth century.

The role of Emperor Charles IV in promoting the production of Latin texts and the development of vernacular textual production can be debated, but in one respect the emperor's contribution was unquestionable: many sources provide evidence of Charles' efforts to recruit people into his service by attracting them to Prague and providing them with a Church prebend as a living. This is demonstrated, for example, by numerous requests to the Roman curia, which resulted in the granting of benefices to individuals who wrote various works for the emperor or his court.[5] A number of clerical *literati* from various regions of Europe figure among members of Charles' court.[6] Some of them, particularly theologians, were drawn from learned members of the religious orders, especially the mendicants.[7]

A well-known example is that of the Italian poet Petrarch, whom Charles tried to recruit into his service and persuade to move to Bohemia. The poet visited Prague in 1356 but did not accept the offer; however, he remained in correspondence with the emperor.[8] In other cases,

---

5   František Kavka, *Am Hofe Karls IV.* (Leipzig, 1989), 149–60. Portraits of many of them can be found in Ferdinand Seibt (ed.), *Karl IV. und sein Kreis*, Lebensbilder zur Geschichte der böhmischen Länder, 3 (München, 1982). Cf. also S. Harrison Thomson, 'Learning at the Court of Charles IV', *Speculum* 25 (1950), 1–20, and Hubert Herkommer, 'Kritik und Panegyrik. Zum literarischen Bild Karls IV. (1346–1378)', *Rheinische Vierteljahrsblätter* 44 (1980), 68–116.

6   Many of them were referred to as chaplain (*cappelanus*), companion (*comensalis*), or generally as *familiaris*.

7   During the 1350s and 1360s, the university founded in Prague by Charles in 1348 was still relatively young and still developing. It was not yet producing many graduates, and the emperor had to help provide teaching scholars. Rather than the university acting as a supplier of learned scholars for the emperor to engage with, we therefore find, instead, primarily the professors there at his service. František Šmahel, 'Die Anfänge der Prager Universität. Kritische Reflexionen Zum Jubiläum Eines "Nationalen Monuments"', in idem, *Die Prager Universität im Mittelalter/ Charles University in the Middle Ages* (Leiden and Boston, 2007), 1–50. Cf. also Hans-Joachim Schmidt, 'Power through Poverty: Mendicant Friars at the Imperial Courts in the 14th Century', in Gert Melville and James D. Mixson (eds), *Virtuosos of Faith: Monks, Nuns, Canons, and Friars as Elites of Medieval Culture* (Münster, 2020), 189–208, here 198–203; Václav Žůrek, 'Karl IV. und seine Mönche. Klöster als Orte des Wissens im mittelalterlichen Prag', in Julia Becker and Julia Burkhardt (eds), *Kreative Impulse: Innovations- und Transferleistungen religiöser Gemeinschaften im mittelalterlichen Europa* (Regensburg, 2021), 397–412. These are mainly professors of theology at the University of Prague, thanks to whom it was possible to begin the courses at all.

8   Petrarch won the esteem of the emperor, who made him a Count Palatine and a councillor. Cf. Eva Schlotheuber, 'Petrarca am Hof Karls IV. und die Rolle der

however, he was more successful, attracting writers, poets, scholars, and church dignitaries to his service, even if in some cases only temporarily. Examples include the chronicler Giovanni Marignolli, the lawyer Bartolus of Sassoferrato, the theologian Conrad of Halberstadt the Younger, or the poet Heinrich von Mügeln. The result of these efforts was a concentration of scholars and writers whose works contributed to the construction of the image of Charles IV as a pious and wise monarch. This image became established among Charles' contemporaries and influenced the perception of the emperor in the following centuries until today. As potential patrons, authors, and readers, but also as recipients of the systematic patronage of the emperor and his inner circle, this group of men changed fundamentally and permanently the literary landscape of Bohemia and the whole Lands of the Bohemian Crown, and even of Central Europe.

From the extensive testimony of the sources, especially contemporary chronicles, we can assume that Charles IV of Luxembourg was interested in language and its use both for educational purposes and as an element of symbolic communication. He himself, according to several witnesses, spoke several languages.[9] The emperor's interest in languages was also a characteristic part of the emperor's self-representation. He described his own linguistic skills in the *Vita Caroli*:

> *Ex divina autem gracia non solum Boemicum, sed Gallicum, Lombardicum, Teutunicum et Latinum ita loqui, scribere et legere scivimus, ut una lingua istarum sicut altera ad scribendum, legendum, loquendum et intelligendum nobis erat apta.*
>
> [By divine grace therefore we know how to speak, write, and read not only Czech, but French, Lombard (Italian), German, and Latin so that we are able to write, read, speak, and understand any one of these languages as well as another.][10]

Humanisten', in Heinrich C. Kuhn (ed.), *Sammelpublikation der Vortragsreihe des SS 2004 an der LMU München* (Munich, 2004), available online at http://www.phil-hum-ren.uni-muenchen.de/SekLit/P2004A/Schlotheuber.htm (consulted 26 March 2023); Jiří Špička, 'Francesco Petrarca travelling and writing to Prague's court', *Verbum: Analecta Neolatina* 12:1 (2010), 27–40.

9   These testimonies are listed in Václav Žůrek, 'Der Weise auf dem Thron. Zu einem wichtigen Aspekt des Herrschaftsstils Karls IV', in Martin Bauch, Julia Burkhardt, Tomáš Gaudek and Václav Žůrek (eds), *Heilige, Helden, Wüteriche. Herrschaftsstile der Luxemburger (1308–1437)*, Forschungen zur Kaiser- und Papstgeschichte des Mittelalters – Beihefte zu J. F. Böhmer, Regesta Imperii, 41 (Cologne/Weimar/Vienna, 2017), 325–39, esp. 332–4.

10 Balázs Nagy and Frank Schaer (eds), *Karoli IV Imperatoris Romanorum Vita Ab Eo Ipso Conscripta; Et, Hystoria Nova de Sancto Wenceslao Martyre* (Budapest, 2001), 68; the translation is quoted from the same book, 69.

This statement echoes literary portraits of the ideal prince, who was supposed to possess wisdom, which included, for example, education in languages.[11]

Symptomatically, the future Archbishop of Prague, John of Jenštejn, in his eulogy at the funeral of the emperor, drew attention to the linguistic skills of the emperor when he wanted to emphasize the personal wisdom of the late ruler:

> *Secundo: ipse habuit in se spiritum intellectus. Unde ipse intellexit fere omnia idiomata tocius christianitatis. Optime istas scivit linguas, videlicet bohemicam, que est naturalis, teutonicam, latinam, francigenam, lombardicam, thuscanicam et quam plures particulares linguas et ab hiis descendentes perfecte scivit ac intellexit. Unde verus fuit Christi apostolus, quia in omnem terram exivit sonus eius et talis debuit toti universo preesse, qui dispartitis linguis loqueretur sapienciam et cuilibet responderet in lingua sua, in qua natus est (Acta II cap.).*
>
> [Secondly, he had the spirit of reason in him. Therefore, he understood almost all the language of Christendom. His knowledge of the languages, namely, Czech, which was his native tongue, German, Latin, French, Lombard, Tuscan, and too many other languages and languages derived from them, he knew and understood perfectly. And so he was a true Apostle of Christ, for 'his voice went out into all the earth' (Psalm 18:5), and such a one should stand at the head of the whole world, speaking wisdom in various tongues, and answering every man 'in his own language, in which he was born' (Acts 2:8).][12]

Charles was thus perceived by chroniclers and scholars not only as a polyglot, as is often mentioned, but also as a *rex litteratus*, a king who even wrote his own texts, as we shall see later. The emperor's keen interest in the use of language in everyday politics and government also emerges from chapter 31 of *The Golden Bull for the Empire* (1356), in which Charles IV recommends for practical reasons to prince-electors to teach their children not only German, which they speak naturally (*naturaliter*), but also Latin, Italian, and Slavonic, which in this context probably meant Czech:

---

11 The importance of wisdom for the individual's personal representation and style of government, along with the emphasis on knowledge of languages, is analysed by Žůrek, 'Der Weise auf dem Thron', where he also reviews other testimonies.
12 *Sermo factus per dominum Johannem archiepiscopum pragensem post mortem imperatoris Caroli IV*, in Josef Emler (ed.), *Fontes rerum Bohemicarum*, vol. 3 (Prague, 1882), 427 (translation by author).

> *Quapropter statuimus, ut illustrium principum, puta regis Boemie, comitis palatini Reni, ducis Saxonie et marchionis Brandemburgensis electorum filii vel heredes et successores, cum verisimiliter Theutonicum ydioma sibi naturaliter inditum scire presumantur et ab infancia didicisse, incipiendo a septimo etatis sue anno in gramatica, Italica ac Slavica lingwis instruantur, ita quod infra quartum decimum etatis annum existant in talibus iuxta datam sibi a deo graciam eruditi; cum illud non solum utile, ymmo ex causis premissis summe necessarium habeatur, eo quod ille lingue ut plurimum ad usum et necessitatem sacri Romani imperii frequentari sint solite et in hiis plus ardua ipsius imperii negocia ventilentur.*

> [Wherefore we decree that the sons, or heirs and successors of the illustrious prince electors, namely of the king of Bohemia, the count palatine of the Rhine, the duke of Saxony and the margrave of Brandenburg – since they are expected in all likelihood to have naturally acquired the German language, and to have been taught it from their infancy, – shall be instructed in grammar (= Latin), the Italian and the Slavic tongues, beginning with the seventh year of their age. So that, before the fourteenth year of their age, they may be learned in the same according to the grace granted them by God. For this is considered not only useful, but also, from the aforementioned causes, highly necessary, since those languages are wont to be very much employed in the service and for the needs of the holy empire, and in them the more arduous affairs of the empire are discussed.][13]

These four languages were considered the main languages of communication within the empire.

It can even be said that Charles aspired to the image of a wise king, who not only emphasizes education and knowledge of languages, but also, for example, the promotion of education, in the first place at Prague University, the institution which he personally helped to establish in the form of four faculties of the *studium generale* on the Parisian model. Part

---

13 Wolfgang D. Fritz (ed.), *Die Goldene Bulle Kaiser Karls IV. vom Jahre 1356*, MGH Fontes Iuris Germanici, 11 (Weimar, 1972), 90. The translation is an adapted version of the text given in Ernest Henderson (ed. and trans.), *Select Historical Documents of the Middle Ages* (London, 1905), 261. For the meaning 'Latin' of the original word 'gramatica', see Jan Frederik Niermeyer (ed.), *Mediae Latinitatis lexicon minus*, vol. I, A–L (Leiden and Boston, 2002), 618. See also the recent interpretation of this chapter in Pierre Monnet, *Charles IV: Un empereur en Europe* (Paris, 2020), 73.

of this image was also the idea of a wise king who was himself educated, knew languages, and understood complex subjects such as theology.[14]

LATIN: LEGITIMIZING RULERSHIP THROUGH NARRATING THE PAST

In search of traces of the emperor's patronage, let us begin with the Latin production.[15] In terms of assessing the active role of the emperor in commissioning the writing of literary works, several chronicles offer the most promising material. The literary rendering of the past for contemporaries and possibly the present for future generations played a crucial role in Charles' cultural policy, and accordingly literary production dealing with the past was very rich. We know of at least five chronicles written for Charles IV (ascribed to, or 'authored by', Francis of Prague, Beneš Krabice of Weitmil, Přibík Pulkava of Radenín, Giovanni de' Marignolli, and Abbot Neplach).[16] Besides these five explicitly commissioned historiographical works, several other authors dedicated their historical works to the emperor, who was known to have a weakness for this type of literature (e.g., Conrad of Halberstadt the Younger or Marco Battagli).[17] The importance of the past and its instrumentalization in the context of regal and dynastic representation was one of the key components of the rulership style of King and Emperor Charles IV, alongside ostentatious piety and the construction of the image of the wise king.[18]

---

14   Žůrek, 'Der Weise auf dem Thron', 329-39.
15   Jana Nechutová, *Die lateinische Literatur des Mittelalters in Böhmen* (Cologne, 2007).
16   All these chronicles were published in the series Fontes rerum bohemicarum (hereafter FRB) during the second half of the nineteenth century: Josef Emler (ed.), *Iohannis Neplachonis Chronicon*, FRB, 3 (Prague, 1882), 451-84; Josef Emler (ed.), *Iohannis de Marignolis Chronicon Bohemorum*, FRB, 3 (Prague, 1882), 492-604; *Cronica Francisci Pragensis*, 4 (Prague, 1884), 347-456; Josef Emler (ed.), *Cronica ecclesiae Pragensis Benessii Krabice de Weitmile*, FRB, 4 (Prague, 1884), 459-548. The chronicle of Francis of Prague was re-edited in recent years: Jana Zachová (ed.), *Chronicon Francisci Pragensis*, FRB, series nova, 1 (Prague, 1997). For the edition of Pulkava's chronicle, see below.
17   For more details on the historiographical culture at the court and the chroniclers writing for Charles IV, see, above all, the studies of Marie Bláhová, 'Die Hofgeschichtsschreibung am böhmischen Herrscherhof im Mittelalter', in Rudolf Schiefer and Jaroslaw Wenta (eds), *Die Hofgeschichtsschreibung im mittelalterlichen Europa* (Toruń, 2006), 51-73; eadem, 'Zur Fälschung und Fiktion in der offiziellen Historiographie der Zeit Karls IV', in *Fälschungen im Mittelalter*, vol. 1, *Schriften der MGH* 33:1 (Hannover, 1988), 377-94.
18   For the notion of rulership style, see Martin Bauch, Julia Burkhardt, Tomáš Gaudek, Paul Töbelmann and Václav Žůrek, 'Heilige, Helden, Wüteriche,

The chronicles served several purposes, the first of which was to legitimize the dynasty's position on the Bohemian and imperial thrones. But we must not forget other, rather topical issues as well. It is evident from the surviving chronicles that the political agenda of Charles' reign was reflected in these works. At the same time, the authors strove to define and formulate this agenda. It is thanks to these chronicles that the image of Charles IV's reign as that of a pious, wise and, above all, successful monarch has remained dominant for centuries.[19]

A good example that clearly illustrates the role of Charles as patron is the *Chronicon Bohemiae* written by Přibík Pulkava of Radenín. He was the rector of the school at the St Egidius church in Prague Old Town and most likely began writing in the 1360s or early 1370s. The oldest extant manuscript bears the date 1374.[20]

Pulkava conceived his chronicle as a synthesis of various accounts about the history of the *gens Bohemorum* from the arrival of the Czechs in Bohemia to the reign of John of Luxembourg. The work was reworked and enlarged several times by the author as well as by later copyists and therefore has a relatively complicated textual history. In the final authorial redaction, completed by Pulkava before 1380, the narration covers the history of the Czechs from their arrival in the Bohemian basin until the death of Charles IV's mother, the Přemyslid princess Elizabeth of Bohemia, in 1330.[21] Apart from the introductory *origo gentis*, Pulkava concentrated on the history of the ducal and later royal house of the Přemyslids, starting with the election of the mythical figure of Přemysl the Ploughman as Bohemian duke.

Pulkava narrates that the Slavs travelling with forefather Czechs did not only occupy Bohemia; their offspring continued on their travels further to the north and east and colonized 'the land of Moravia, and similarly

---

Eine konzeptionelle Skizze zu "Herrschaftsstilen" im langen Jahrhundert der Luxemburger', in Martin Bauch, Julia Burkhardt, Tomáš Gaudek and Václav Žůrek (eds), *Heilige, Helden, Wüteriche*, 11–27.

19 Cf. Wojciech Iwańczak, 'L'empereur Charles IV et son attitude face à l'histoire', in Chantal Grell, Werner Paravicini and Jürgen Voss (eds), *Les princes et l'histoire du XIVe au XVIIIe siècle*, Pariser historische Studien, 47 (Bonn, 1998), 141–9. A comprehensive analysis of historiography at Charles' court is still lacking; however, recently, a few studies (cited below) have considered not only the contents but also other aspects of these texts, such as the materiality of the surviving manuscript texts or the narrative strategies of the authors and their political context. In general, recent research on medieval chronicles is very diversified but usually focused on individual works, environments, or genres. For a comprehensive record of current scholarship on chronicle writing, see the studies published in the yearbook *The Medieval Chronicle* 1–14 (1999–2022).

20 Krakow, Muzeum Narodowe, Biblioteka książąt Czartoryskich, MS 1414.
21 Prague, Národní knihovna České republiky, MS I D 10.

[settled] in the principalities of Meissen, Bautzen, Brandenburg, and Lusatia',[22] which geographically correspond to the Luxembourg territorial expansion. Despite the evident fact that a great part of the inhabitants of the regions listed here were predominantly German-speaking in the fourteenth century (whereas, in Bohemia and Moravia, German speakers were a significant minority), Pulkava mentions only Slavs. This way, writing in the service of the court, he constructs a common origin for the inhabitants of the Central-European Luxembourg territories in order to create a basis for a common memory and identity, and to strengthen the Luxembourg claims to the throne of Bohemia.[23]

The formal arrangement of the work indicates the tight connection to the court. The author was allowed to work with documents from the royal archive, a collection of key documents relating to the status of the Kingdom of Bohemia, founded by Charles IV. Pulkava frequently took advantage of this collection and, in order to make his text more convincing, he copied many charters from the archive into it.

Pulkava probably strove to amass the greatest quantity of information available to him when compiling his narrative. He rewrote the chronicle several times after obtaining access to new sources, especially old chronicles. He describes this procedure very accurately in the epilogue, which closes the most complete redaction of Pulkava's text:

> *Scitoque tamen istud, quod omnes res fabulose et non vere ac fidei dissimiles sunt omisse et reiecte, sed quod verum et certum est, de eis excerptum, hoc est in hac cronica mandato predicti imperatoris positum. Nam illas omnes res certas et veras ac gesta seu facta sue terre Boemie idem imperator, quam pervalide super omnes alias suas terras dilexit, solus omnibus cronicis monasteriorum et baronum visis et cum summa diligencia perlectis memorato Przibiconi demandavit ex eis unam cronicam veram et rectam conscribere et in unum volumen redigere, quod et, prout cernis, fecit.*[24]

[You should know that all invented, untrue, and implausible things were left out and rejected; and [only] what is true and

---

22 Přibík Pulkava, *Chronicon Bohemiae*, ed. Josef Emler, FRB, 5 (Prague, 1893), 5: *... regionem, que terra Morauia dicitur, nec non similiter Misnam, Budissinensem, Brandemburgensem, et Lusaciam principatus inhabitare ceperunt*. See Václav Žůrek and Pavlína Rychterová, 'Slavonic and Czech identity in the *Chronicon Bohemiae* by Přibík Pulkava of Radenín', in Pavlína Rychterová (ed.), *Historiography and Identity VI: Competing Narratives of the Past in Central and Eastern Europe, c. 1200 – c. 1600* (Turnhout, 2021), 225–56. The translation is quoted from p. 240.
23 Žůrek and Rychterová, 'Slavonic and Czech identity'. See also the essay by Matouš Jaluška in this volume.
24 Přibík Pulkava, *Chronicon Bohemiae*, ed. Josef Emler, 207.

certain was written down and included in this chronicle at the order of the aforementioned emperor. The emperor in fact went through and carefully read all the chronicles from monasteries and of noblemen, and [he] asked Přibík to write down in one true and right chronicle [and] in one volume all these certain and true things, actions, and deeds of his country, which he loved above all others. Which, as you can see, [he] did.]²⁵

According to the author's own words in the epilogue, the task that he endeavoured to accomplish was to compile a chronicle from all the available histories, at the orders of Emperor Charles.²⁶ Pulkava also emphasizes the active role of the emperor, whose motivation is interpreted as love for his country:

> *Et sic sepedictus imperator propter pervalidam huius terre dileccionem et ipsius magnam exaltacionem habensque ad eam specialem caritatem libenter in eam tocius mundi gloriam induxisset.*
>
> [And so the often mentioned emperor, out of a particularly great love for this country, because of its great promotion and because he also has a special care (caritatem) for it, liked to bring into it the glory of the whole world.]²⁷

According to Pulkava's epilogue, Charles IV was not only a patron, but also a 'conceptor' of the chronicle.²⁸ Some notes in the extant manuscripts suggest that Charles IV significantly contributed to the conception of the work – even occasionally naming the emperor as the author of the chronicle.²⁹ The case of this chronicle demonstrates that Charles was active

---

25   Translation is quoted from Žůrek and Rychterová, 'Slavonic and Czech identity', 229.
26   Přibík Pulkava, *Chronicon Bohemiae*, 207: '*Explicit cronica Boemorum quam de anno Domini millesimo trecentesimo septuagesimo quarto ad mandatum serenissimi ac invictissimi principis et domini, domini Karoli quarti, divina favente clemencia Romanorum imperatoris ac Boemie regis, Przibico de Tradenina, arcium liberalium doctor, congregavit ac composuit [...] ex omnibus cronicis omnium monasteriorum et quorundam baronum, ubicunque potuit conquirere.*' ('This is the end of the chronicle of the Czech people, which was brought together and composed by Přibík of Radenín, doctor of liberal arts in the year 1374 out of chronicles from all monasteries and certain noblemen wherever he could collect on the order of the bright and invincible prince and master, Charles IV, Roman emperor and king of Bohemia by the favour of divine mercy.')
27   Přibík Pulkava, *Chronicon Bohemiae*, 207. Translation is my own.
28   For the use of the term in an art-historical perspective, see the essay by Maria Theisen in this volume.
29   Cf. for instance the incipit in Wrocław, Biblioteka Uniwersytecka, MS R 199, fol. 1r: *Incipit cronica serenissimi principis Karoli, regis Boemorum et imperatoris*

as a patron of Latin chronicles and literally sought to move the writing of history from the monasteries to the court, where it could be written under the supervision of the monarch and serve to glorify his rule as political propaganda.[30] This also applies, for example, to the universal chronicle of Giovanni Marignolli written in the 1350s at the court of Prague.[31] The chronicle was written in Latin, but vernacular translations also contributed to its later impact. Only later was Pulkava's chronicle translated into Czech (before 1400) and twice into German during the fifteenth century.[32]

However, the role of Charles IV was more complex than being only the patron of Latin chronicles; he entered the literary discourse at his court himself, as an author. Emperor Charles IV composed an autobiography from his birth (1316) to his election as King of the Romans in 1346. He conceived this text, traditionally called *Vita Caroli (Quarti)*, as a theologically tinged and instructive narrative of how he was elected (anti-) king of the Romans and asserted himself with the help of God in spite of all adversities, handling difficult circumstances, and demonstrating that he was both brave and prudent.[33]

The *Vita Caroli* is an exceptional literary text, not only because it is a work written – or at least significantly co-written – in Latin by a reigning monarch, but also because it is rather exceptional in its content.

Romanorum et semper Augusti, quam ipse composuit et diligenter compilavit. ('Here begins the chronicle of the most serene prince Charles, the king of Bohemia, the Roman emperor and at all times an increaser of the realm, which he himself composed and carefully compiled.').

30 Inspiration from the French environment may have played a role here, where the young Charles may have observed increased interest in the systematic support of the royal court for chronicle production. For this broader phenomenon, cf. for example, Isabelle Guyot-Bachy and Jean-Marie Moeglin, 'Comment ont été continuées les Grandes Chroniques de France dans la première moitié du XIVe siècle', *Bibliothèque de l'École des chartes* 163:2 (2005), 385–433.

31 Anna-Dorothee von den Brincken, 'Die universalhistorischen Vorstellungen des Johann von Marignola OFM', *Archiv für Kulturgeschichte* 49:3 (1967), 297–339; Václav Žůrek, 'Godfrey of Viterbo and his Readers at the Court of Emperor Charles IV', in Thomas Foerster (ed.), *Godfrey of Viterbo and his Readers: Imperial Tradition and Universal History in Late Medieval Europe* (Farnham, 2015), 87–102; cf. also Irene Malfatto, 'John of Marignolli and the Historiographical Project of Charles IV', *Acta Universitatis Carolinae : Historia Universitatis Carolinae Pragensis* 55:1 (2015), 131–40.

32 Vlastimil Brom, 'Aus der offiziellen böhmischen Historiographie Karls IV. – Die Pulkava-Chronik in drei Sprachversionen', *Brünner Beiträge zur Germanistik und Nordistik* 15:1–2 (2010), 5–19.

33 For basic information about the *Vita*, see Eugen Hillenbrand, 'Die Autobiographie Karls IV. Entstehung und Funktion', in Hans Patze (ed.), *Kaiser Karl IV. 1316-1378. Forschungen über Kaiser und Reich*, Blätter für Deutsche Landesgeschichte, 114/1978, 39–72. See also the essay by Matouš Jaluška in this volume.

It offers not a history of the reign, or a description of the great deeds of the monarch, but a biographical account of the youth of the future king and emperor at a time when he had not yet ascended the throne. It is also worth noting some formal specifics of this work, such as the fact that it is written in the first-person plural, thus imitating the diction of official acts written in the royal chancery.[34] A controversial issue remains the dating, which is also related to the motivation for writing the autobiography. The most probable date seems to be around 1350, which was the date favoured by the German expert and editor of the text Eugen Hillenbrand.[35] Other historians prefer the period around 1374 and consider the text a legacy written for his successors, just as the opening sentence of the work says.[36] This is not the only literary work that can be directly attributed to Charles; besides his autobiography, he is also considered the author of a collection of moralistic lessons, the *Moralitates*, and of the Legend of St Wenceslas.[37]

The Legend of St Wenceslas is a short text which takes the form of twice six breviary lections from the Office of St Wenceslas, the first dealing with his life and the second with the saint's death and miracles. The author drew much of his inspiration from earlier legends, but attributed to his saintly ancestor precisely the conception of government that he himself held. St Wenceslas, an early-medieval prince of the tenth century, is described in the legend as the ideal ruler of the fourteenth century: a learned and humble Christian monarch. He (like Charles himself) is characterized by spectacular, and above all active, piety. When Henry I offers him a reward, he characteristically chooses a relic of St Vitus. On all these points, the construction of the figure of the saint corresponds directly to the idea of Charles himself as formulated at the Prague court.[38]

---

34   See the summary of the recent literature by Eva Schlotheuber, 'Die Autobiographie Karls IV. und die mittelalterlichen Vorstellungen vom Menschen am Scheideweg', *Historische Zeitschrift* 281 (2005), 561–91. For the broader context of medieval autobiographical texts, cf. Pierre Monnet and Jean-Claude Schmitt, 'Introduction', in eadem (eds), *Autobiographies souveraines* (Paris, 2012), 7–32. An inspiring reading of autobiography in the fourteenth century is offered by Laurence De Looze, *Pseudo-Autobiography in the Fourteenth Century: Juan Ruiz, Guillaume de Machaut, Jean Froissart, and Geoffrey Chaucer* (Gainesville, 1997).
35   Hillenbrand, 'Die Autobiographie Karls IV.'.
36   Marie Bláhová, 'Literární činnost Karla IV', in *Kroniky doby Karla IV.* (Prague, 1987), 560–2; cf. Jiří Spěváček, 'Karel IV. a jeho Vlastní životopis', in *Karel IV. Vlastní životopis. Vita Karoli Quarti* (Prague, 1979), 170–8.
37   For the *Moralitates*, see the recent analysis and edition by Jana Nechutová, 'Die Moralitates im literarischen Werk Karls IV', *Graeco-Latina Brunensia* 23:1 (2018), 139–67.
38   Anton Blaschka, *Die St. Wenzelslegende Kaiser Karls IV.* (Prague, 1934); an edition is provided on pp. 64–80. The English translation of the legend is published in *Karoli IV Imperatoris Romanorum Vita*, 185–209. Cf. Zdeněk Uhlíř, *Literární*

It is clear, then, that with regard to Latin text production we can identify the emperor in an active role as an author, but above all as a patron who took a lively interest in literary production and was personally involved in approaching at least some of the authors concerned, and shaping the works they produced under his aegis.[39]

GERMAN: PRAISING THE EMPEROR AND TRANSLATING IN HIS SERVICE

In the following, we shall examine whether the same can also be said with regard to the vernacular; a closer look at the production in the individual languages concerned will help to reveal any possible connections between the sovereign and multilingual texts from the immediate and more distant milieu of the Prague court.

Text production in German and Czech was an important part of cultural life at the court of Charles IV. Mention should be made in this context that French texts played a very limited role at the Prague court; this phenomenon came to an end with the death of King John at the latest. This is somewhat surprising, especially given that King John of Luxembourg was culturally strongly influenced by Francophone literature from the time spent at the French court during his youth and later; however, as far as we know, the only Francophone author linked with the Prague court in any way at all was the king's long-time secretary Guillaume de Machaut, who was also a prolific writer and poet-musician.[40] King John became a literary figure thanks to Machaut, but his works were of limited, if any, relevance to the Prague court and its production. This is also true of Emperor Charles IV, who spent seven years of his childhood at the court in Paris, was educated there and prided himself on his knowledge of French. However, we cannot find any traces of Francophone literature in Prague during Charles' time.[41]

---

prameny svatováclavského kultu a úcty ve vrcholném a pozdním středověku (Prague, 1996), 23–4, 132–3; Bernd-Ulrich Hergemöller, *Cogor adversum te. Drei Studien zum literarisch-theologischen Profil Karls IV. und seiner Kanzlei* (Warendorf, 1999), 233–53.
39   This is true not only of the chronicles, where the evidence for his involvement is very convincing, but also for other works written for him; see Nechutová, *Die Lateinische Literatur*.
40   For more on this topic, see the contributions of Uri Smilansky, Jana Fantysová Matějková and Karl Kügle in this volume.
41   On Charles' childhood at the French court, see František Šmahel, *The Parisian Summit, 1377–78* (Prague, 2014), 18–33. Some awareness in Bohemia of the *Roman de Fauvel* written in Paris in the orbit of Charles of Valois in the late 1310s is assumed by Martin Nejedlý, 'Otec české královny Blanky z Valois a jeho knížecí zrcadlo', *Český časopis historický* 119 (2021), 32–73.

The Prague court had a strong tradition of supporting German poetry since the thirteenth century, when German Minnesingers created works for the Přemyslid kings. Around 1300, poets writing in Czech also joined in.[42] The role of vernacular production in the overall context of the court of Charles IV increased significantly.[43]

The importance of the German language is underscored by two non-artistic aspects of the functioning of the Prague court under Charles IV. First of all, it should be remembered that in the Bohemian Crown Lands (a state formation proclaimed in 1348, which included, in addition to Bohemia and Moravia, Silesia, Upper and Lower Lusatia and small territories in the German-speaking parts of the empire) there was a large German minority population; in some parts of the crown lands, for example Lusatia or Silesia, they were in fact in the majority. This was also true of the larger cities, mining towns, and, above all, Prague.[44]

The administrative agenda, and the composition of the court, also played a role in the use of the German language. Charles IV became King of the Romans as early as 1346 and emperor in 1355. The chancery and court were common to both Charles' hereditary lands and the imperial administration, so that the chancery staff was largely made up of German speakers. According to the surviving sources, especially charters, the administrative language was not only Latin, but also to a large extent German.[45] Moreover, many representatives of imperial cities and princes resided in Prague as the political and administrative centre of the empire.

---

42 Cf. Hans-Joachim Behr, *Literatur als Machtlegitimation. Studien zur Funktion der deutschsprachigen Dichtung am böhmischen Königshof im 13. Jahrhundert* (Munich, 1989). For the oldest Czech epic compositions, see Jan Lehár, *Nejstarší česká epika. Dalimilova kronika, Alexandreida, první veršované legendy* (Prague, 1983).
43 Bok, 'Zur literarischen Situation'; Baumann, *Die Literatur des Mittelalters in Böhmen*.
44 There is no comprehensive study of the use of German in medieval Bohemia at present, so only some preliminary analyses can be quoted. Cf. Zdeněk Masařík, *Die mittelalterliche deutsche Kanzleisprache Süd- und Mittelmährens*, Opera Universitatis Purkynianae Brunensis, Facultas philosophica, 110 (Brno, 1966); Hans-Joachim Solms, 'Deutsch in Prag zur Mitte des 14. Jahrhunderts', in Amelie Bendheim and Heinz Sieburg (eds), *Prag in der Zeit der Luxemburger Dynastie Literatur, Religion und Herrschaftskulturen zwischen Bereicherung und Behauptung* (Bielefeld, 2018), 37–51.
45 Tomáš Velička, 'Die deutsche Sprache in den Kanzleien der ersten Luxemburger in Böhmen (1310–1378)', in idem (ed.), *Spätmittelalter in landesherrlichen Kanzleien Mitteleuropas. Alte Tradition und der mühsame Weg zu neuen Fragen und Antworten* (Berlin, 2020), 169–90; Cf. also Ivan Hlaváček, 'Dreisprachigkeit im Bereich der Böhmischen Krone: Zum Phänomen der Sprachbenutzung im böhmischen diplomatischen Material bis zur hussitischen Revolution', in Anna Adamska and Marco Mostert (eds), *The development of literate mentalities in East Central Europe*

It is therefore a very likely assumption that German was the main language of communication of the Luxembourg dynasty. This is already very probable for Charles' parents, Elizabeth and John. Three of Charles' wives came from German-speaking families. His first wife, Blanche of Valois, came from France but her entourage was soon sent back from Prague. Blanche learned German in the first place, according to the testimony of the local chronicler Peter of Zittau:

> *Ut autem hominibus benignius possit convivere, lingwam Teutunicam incipit discere et plus in ea solet se quam in ligwaio Boemico exercere, nam in omnibus civitatibus fere regni et coram rege conmunior est usus ligwe Teutunice quam Boemice ista vice.*[46]

> [In order, however, to make her more friendly with the people, she begins to learn the German language, and exercises herself more in it than in the Czech language; for in almost all the towns of the kingdom and before the king the German language is more generally used at this time than the Czech.]

The importance of the German language for members of the Prague court is further illustrated by an anecdote from the visit of Emperor Charles IV to Paris in the winter of 1377–8. The author of the continuation of the *Grandes Chroniques de France* describes how during the emperor's visit, the emperor and his entourage heard from King Charles V in French the reasons for the conflict with the English king, and how Emperor Charles IV himself briefly interpreted in German to his entourage, whose members did not understand French:

> *Et en briefves paroles l'Empereur dist en alemant à ses gens, qui presens estoient et qui n'entendoient pas françois, ce que le Roy luy avoit dit, et leur exposa les lectres que sur ce avoit oy lire, et fist response au Roy tele comme il s'ensuit, c'est assavoir qu'il dist que très bien avoit entendu ce que le Roy avoit dit très sagement…*

> [After that, the emperor, in a short speech in German, told his people who had been present and had not understood the French what the king had said, and also elucidated the content of the

---

(Turnhout, 2004), 289–310; and Mathias Lawo, 'Sprachen der Macht – Sprache als Macht. Urkundensprachen im Reich des 13. und 14. Jahrhunderts (mit editorischem Anhang)', in Ulrike Hohensee, Mathias Lawo, Michael Lindner, Michael Menzel and Olaf B. Rader (eds), *Die Goldene Bulle: Politik – Wahrnehmung – Rezeption*, vol. 1 (Berlin, 2009), 517–62.

46 Anna Pumprová, Libor Jan, Robert Antonín, Demeter Malaťák, Lukáš Švanda and Zdeněk Žalud (eds), *Cronica Aule regie. Die Königsaaler Chronik*, MGH, Scriptores, 40 (Wiesbaden, 2022), 512. The spellings 'ligwaio' and 'ligwe' are given according to the edition.

papers which he had heard read on it. He then gave the king such an answer as follows, i.e. that he had very carefully listened to everything that the king had very wisely presented ...]⁴⁷

This leaves us with the question to what extent the relationship between German-language literature at court and the emperor as patron can be clarified. In the context of Middle High German literature written at the Prague court under and for Charles IV, the work of Heinrich von Mügeln stands out. Heinrich's poem *Der Meide Kranz* (*The Garland of the Virgin*) is a monumental project that addresses the conflict between the sciences and the virtues not in Latin – as one might expect – but in a vernacular language.

It remains unclear whether the author chose the German language in order to appeal to a particular audience (such as German-speaking students in Prague), or whether it was poetic self-confidence, demonstrating his ability to address such material in a vernacular language. Another motive may have been the wish to be understood by much of Charles' imperial court. While these details remain open to debate, the poem's connection to the emperor is indisputable. It is not only dedicated to Charles, but, in a sophisticated way, the emperor becomes a character in it: in the first part of the poem, Emperor Charles appears by name as the judge who should decide which of the sciences is of the greatest importance and to which goes the garland of victory.⁴⁸ From the beginning, the author is open about the fact that one of the aims of his poem is praising the wise emperor. He makes this clear in the opening of the first book:

> *uf den spruch ein nuwes ticht / ich schepf uß sinnes wage sicht / in lop dem keiser Karlen ho, / durch schult in allen landen, wo / gelesen wirt min krankes ticht, / sint mich sin gabe hat gericht: / wie das min kunst unwirdik was, / doch mild er nach genaden maß.*

---

47 Quotation from Roland Delachenal (ed.), *Chronique des règnes de Jean II et de Charles V (Les Grandes Chroniques de France)*, vol. II, 1364–80 (Paris, 1916), 255–6. The translation is quoted from Šmahel, *Summit*, 219.

48 The literature on the poem is extensive. In the context of Charles' court, see especially Karl Stackman, '"Der meide kranz": Das "nuwe ticht" Heinrichs von Mügeln', *Zeitschrift für deutsches Altertum und deutsche Literatur* 135 (2006), 217–39; Christoph Huber, 'Karl IV. im Instanzensystem von Heinrichs von Mügeln 'Der meide Kranz', *Beiträge zur Geschichte der deutschen Sprache und Literatur* 103 (1981), 63–91. For a recent analysis of the role of Charles' literary representation in *Der Meide Kranz* and other contemporary works, see Alexandra Urban, *Poetik der Meisterschaft in 'Der meide kranz'. Heinrich von Mügeln auf den Schultern des Alanus ab Insulis*, Deutsche Literatur. Studien und Quellen, 44 (Berlin and Boston, 2021), 135–82.

[In accordance with (the teaching of) that dictum, I scoop and create a new poem out of the shallow waves of the mind, duly praising the noble Emperor Charles throughout all the lands where my poor poem might be read, given that his bounty has benefitted me. Although my art was unworthy, he applied a generous measure, in accordance with mercy.][49]

An important theme in the work is the emperor's ability to judge and decide justly while respecting the principles of how decision-making works at court and in the monarchy. This is how the poet speaks of Charles in the prologue:

kunk Karlen. das sin leben kunt: / er mochte brechen und enbricht: / des gab im got sin war gericht, / das er in volle geben mak / der tugnde Ion und bruches slak.

[His life proclaims the following: he could break (the Law) and yet he refrains from doing so. For that reason, God gave him his true jurisdiction, so that he may fully provide the reward of virtue and the chastisement of vice.][50]

The poem, probably written soon after Charles' return from the imperial coronation in Rome in 1355, rhetorically interacted not only with the scholars working at the recently founded university (1348), but also addressed the community of readers at court. It was closely linked to the idea of Emperor Charles as a learned ruler. In the text, the emperor also seeks the advice of Heinrich von Mügeln, the author of the poem. Although Heinrich tends to grant primacy among the sciences (*artes*) to philosophy, the emperor clearly prefers theology, to which he also attributes the victory.

The theme of the relationship between the emperor and theology was elaborated, probably under the influence of reading this Mügeln poem, by another key author and figure of Charles' court, John of Neumarkt. In a letter addressed to the emperor, he praised not only the emperor's wisdom but also his interest in scholarship combined with piety, which resulted in the emperor obtaining the pope's permission to establish a theological faculty at the University of Prague, which was an exceptional

---

49 Heinrich von Mügeln, *Der meide kranz. A Commentary*, ed. Annette Volfing (Tübingen, 1997), 31. The English translation is quoted from the same book, p. 31.
50 Volfing (ed.), *Der meide kranz*, 14; also the commentary on this passage on pp. 27–8. See also Lena Oetjens, 'Charles IV and learned order: The discourse on knowledge in "Der meide kranz"', *Acta Universitatis Carolinae. Historia Universitatis Carolinas Pragensis* 55:1 (2015), 141–52.

privilege at the time.⁵¹ Its foundation in Prague and its collaboration with the mendicants' schools in the Bohemian capital played a very important role in learned theological debate in Prague and found its reflection in the devotional activities at Charles' court.⁵²

John of Neumarkt (c. 1310–80), an important author and scholar, was the head of Charles' chancery from 1353 to 1374 and became Bishop of Litomyšl (1353) and later Olomouc (1364).⁵³ John had a major influence on the style of Latin and German charters issued by the imperial chancery, and he himself corresponded with Petrarch and Cola di Rienzo, admiring their rhetorical style, which he tried to emulate. His influence, however, was most evident in the production of literary texts in German.⁵⁴ He was engaged in translations from Latin into German, and from the surviving sources it is clear that his translations were intended for the court.

From the Italian campaign to Rome in 1354/5, on which he accompanied Charles IV, John brought back the manuscript of the *Soliloquium anime ad deum* attributed to pseudo-Augustine, which he translated into German at the emperor's direct request in 1357–63 under the title *Buch der Liebkosung* (*The Book of Caress*). In the German prologue, he mentions both the emperor's commissioning of the work and his support, and states that the emperor's motivation for translating the Latin text into German was to enable those who did not understand Latin to have access to the work:

> ... mein gnediger herr, von gnaden des almehtigen got so vil uernunft hat vnd sich auch so fleiszicleich geubt hat in den heiligen schriften, das er des groszen achpern lerers sancti Augustini buch der liepkozung, doryn er sich in got mit tyfen synnen suszicleich erlustet, vnd auch ander seine buch wol vernemen mug in latein, als si beschriben vnd begriffen sind, doch ist so groz sein angeborne

---

51 Urban, *Poetik der Meisterschaft*, 141–7; Michael Stolz, 'Vivus est sermo tuus. Religion und Wissen in der Prager Hofkultur des 14. Jahrhunderts', in Klaus Ridder and Steffen Patzold (eds), *Die Aktualität der Vormoderne. Epochenentwürfe zwischen Alterität und Kontinuität*, Europa im Mittelalter, 23 (Berlin, 2013), 267–94.
52 Šmahel, 'Die Anfänge der Prager Universität'.
53 The basic work on John is still Joseph Klapper, *Johann von Neumarkt. Bischof und Hofkanzler. Religiöse Frührenaissance in Böhmen zur Zeit Kaiser Karls IV.*, Erfurter Theologische Studien, 17 (Leipzig, 1964); more recent findings are recounted in Marie Bláhová, 'Osobnost Jana ze Středy', in Pavel Brodský, Kateřina Spurná and Marta Vaculínová (eds), *Liber viaticus Jana ze Středy. Vol. 2, komentářový svazek ke zmenšené reprodukci rukopisu XIII A 12 Knihovny Národního muzea* (Prague, 2016), 35–69.
54 Benedikt Konrad Vollmann, 'Johann von Neumarkt: Lateinischer und deutscher Stil', in Wolfgang Harms and Jan-Dirk Müller (eds), *Mediävistische Komparatistik. Festschrift für Franz Josef Worstbrock zum 60. Geburtstag* (Stuttgart and Leipzig, 1997), 151–62; John M. Clifton-Everest, 'Johann von Neumarkt und Cola di Rienzo', *Bohemia* 28 (1987), 25–44.

*tugent vnd di besunder lib, di er als ein cristenleicher furst hatt czu seinem ebencristen, das er begeret vnd mir Johannes von gots gnaden bischof czu dem Luthomuschyl, seinem obersten schreiber, gepoten hat vnd wolt das mit seinen keyserleichen gnaden, das ich das egenant buch der lipkozung von wort czu worte czu deutscher czung bringen vnd keren sold, auf di red das von diser deuhtschen schrift manig mensch getrost werd, das sich in dem latein niht verrichten kond...*⁵⁵

[... my dear lord, by the grace of the almighty God, has so much understanding and has also so diligently studied the Holy Scriptures that he has learnt the great book of love, the book of Saint Augustine, in which he rejoices in God in a profound sense, and may well understand other of his books in Latin, as they are written and understood. Yet he is so great in his inherent virtue and special love that he as a Christian prince, has for his fellow Christians, that he has requested and granted to me John by the grace of God, bishop of Litomyšl, his chief scribe, and wishes to do so with his imperial graces, that I bring and turn the book of love from word to word to the German tongue, so that many people will be comforted by this German writing, which could not be done in Latin...]⁵⁶

With the work of John of Neumarkt, we can see a purposeful vernacularization of religiously educative knowledge at the Prague court as well as of the emperor's interest in this effort. John was also the author of dozens of German prayers that were very popular and have survived in many manuscripts.⁵⁷ John of Neumarkt had a great interest in literature in general, and was an author, promoter, and instigator of Latin and vernacular literature at court.⁵⁸

The idea of promoting vernacular literary production and translation of devotional texts is also relevant to another work that John was involved in disseminating in the courtly environment. It is a set of three letters, the

---

55   Joseph Klapper (ed.), *Buch der Liebkosung*, Vom Mittelalter zur Reformation. Forschungen zur Geschichte der deutschen Bildung, 6/1, Schriften Johanns von Neumarkt, 1 (Berlin, 1930), 7–8.
56   The translation is made by the author.
57   Kathrin Chlench-Priber, *Das Korpus der Gebete Johanns von Neumarkt und die deutschsprachige Gebetbuchkultur des Spätmittelalters* (Wiesbaden, 2020).
58   From the point of view of historical research, we must also add that the collection of his Latin and German letters is, moreover, a very useful and colourful source of information about the court of Charles IV and the cultural and political life there. See the edition of his letters *Briefe Johanns von Neumarkt*; Josef Bujnoch, 'Johann von Neumarkt als Briefschreiber', in Ferdinand Seibt (ed.), *Karl IV und sein Kreis* (Oldenburg, 1978), 67–76.

so-called *Letters of St Jerome*, which he first compiled for his sovereign, or rather adapted on the basis of the texts of Giovanni d'Andrea and other texts he brought from Italy. He dedicated the work in the prologue to Emperor Charles:[59]

> *Propter quod ego, licet insufficiens et indignus, maiestatis tamen vestre sedulus et fidelissimus venerator, magis attendens in hys obsequi maiestati cesaree [...] tres epistolas in hunc libellum ordinaui multa deliberacione conscribi, que sunt a viris excellentibus edite in laudem Jeronimi gloriosi.*[60]

> [Therefore I, though imperfect and unworthy, the one who attentively and faithfully reveres your majesty, listening very carefully in his service to the imperial dignity [...] I have composed and very deliberately written down the three letters, which were written by excellent men in praise of renowned Jerome.]

The *Letters of St Jerome* circulated at court at first in Latin, but John took it upon himself to translate them into German. He dedicated his translation to Margravine Elisabeth of Oettingen, wife of the emperor's brother John Henry of Luxembourg, who, as Margrave of Moravia, resided in Brno.[61]

---

59   Joseph Klapper (ed.), *Hieronymus. Die unechten Briefe des Eusebius, Augustin, Cyrill zum Lobe des Heiligen,* Vom Mittelalter zur Reformation, 6, Schriften Johanns von Neumarkt, 2 (Berlin, 1932). For its transmission, see Soňa Černá, 'The Letters of St Jerome of the Prague Chancellor and Notary John of Neumarkt: A Transmission History', in Pavlína Rychterová (ed.), *Pursuing a New Order. Vol. I. Religious Education in Late Medieval Central and Eastern Central Europe* (Turnhout, 2019), 47–74.
60   *Hieronymus. Die unechten Briefe*, 3–4.
61   Amalie Fößel, 'Bücher, Bildung und Herrschaft von Fürstinnen im Umkreis des Prager Hofes der Luxemburger', *Zeitschrift für Literaturwissenschaft und Linguistik* 40:3 (2010), 35–56. See the dedication letter addressed directly to Elisabeth, edited in Paul Piur (ed.), *Briefe Johanns von Neumarkt. Sammlung mit einem Anhang: Ausgewählte Briefe an Johann von Neumarkt, urkundliche und briefliche Zeugnisse zu seinem Leben,* Vom Mittelalter zur Reformation, 8 (Berlin, 1937), no. 127, pp. 194–6: *Der durchlewchtigen furstynn und frawen, frawen Elizabeth, margrauynn czu Merhern, meiner gnedigen suenderleichen frawen, enbiet ich Johannes, von gots gnaden bischof czu Olmuncz, des romischen keisers kanczler, mein demuetiges gepet in dem heiligen namen des allemechtigen gots. [...] Dovon, durchleuhtige furstynn vnd gnedige fraw, hab ich in disem buch gearbeitet mit rechten trewen vnd mit ernstleichem fleisze czu wirden dem allemechtigen got, sant Jeronimus czu eren vnd czu getrewem dinst ewern furstenleichen gnaden.* (I, John, by the grace of God, bishop of Olomouc, the Roman emperor's chancellor, offer my humble prayer in the holy name of the Almighty God to the noble princess and lady, Lady Elizabeth, Margravine of Moravia, my gracious [and] incomparable lady. [...] Therefore, my dear princess and gracious lady, I have worked in this book with true loyalty and with a sincere desire to serve the Almighty

The symbolism of St Jerome as the alleged translator of the Bible not only into Latin, but also into the Slavonic language, naturally played a role in the interest of the Prague court in this Church Father.[62] Jerome was also venerated in one of Prague's *lieux de savoir*, the so-called Slavonic or Emmaus monastery, where the Benedictine monks were allowed to celebrate mass in Church Slavonic and whose scriptorium was supported by the emperor. The monastery also became an important place for the development of vernacular literature: manuscripts written in a special alphabet, the Glagolitic script, preserved not only texts in Church Slavonic but also many Old Czech translations, which will be discussed next.[63]

With regard to text production in German, Charles IV no longer appears as an active initiator or even participant, as in the case of some Latin texts. Rather, his role is first and foremost that of a recipient of dedications. The active role was played primarily by courtiers such as John of Neumarkt, whose letters – frequently apologizing for the delay in translation – demonstrate that the emperor kept a close eye on this kind of cultural activity.[64]

If the role of patron of vernacular literature in German cannot therefore be denied Charles, was this also the case for Czech? In the last part of this essay, let us see how far it is possible to trace a direct or indirect relationship between the emperor and Czech literary production.

God, Saint Jerome, and to be faithful to your princely graces.) Cf. also the dedication to Elisabeth in the German translation of the *Letters* published in *Hieronymus. Die unechten Briefe des Eusebius, Augustin*, 6–9.

62 Ricarda Bauschke, 'Johann von Neumarkt: "Hieronymus-Briefe". Probleme von Epochengrenzen und Epochenschwellen am Beispiel des Prager Frühhumanismus', in Nicola McLelland, Hans-Jochen Schiewer and Stefanie Schmitt (eds), *Humanismus in der deutschen Literatur des Mittelalters und der Frühen Neuzeit. Vol. XVIII. Anglo-German Colloquium Hofgeismar 2003* (Berlin, 2008), 257–82.

63 See Julia Verkholantsev, *The Slavic Letters of St. Jerome. The History of the Legend and Its Legacy, or, How the Translator of the Vulgate Became an Apostle of the Slavs* (DeKalb, 2014), 63–115; Julia Verkholantsev, 'St. Jerome as a Slavic Apostle in Luxemburg Bohemia', *Viator* 44 (2013), 251–86; Klára Benešovská and Kateřina Kubínová (eds), *Emauzy. Benediktinský klášter Na Slovanech v srdci Prahy* (Prague, 2008).

64 See the edition of this letter in *Briefe Johanns von Neumarkt*, no. 29, pp. 51–2.

CZECH: SEARCHING FOR A CONNECTION TO THE COURT

Ever since the fifteenth century, Charles IV has been considered by scholars as a great patron of literature in the Czech language.[65] Indeed, during the second half of the fourteenth century, literary production in Bohemia was distinguished by a remarkable flourishing of vernacular production in Czech, which developed with a certain phase delay and under the inspiration of literary production in German. Texts in Czech are mainly translations or adaptations, however, with few original works.[66]

Some of these works may serve to clarify the meaning of the emperor's patronage and his court in general. In the first place, we must mention the Bible, a complete translation of which into Czech was made sometime between 1350 and 1360. There are scholarly disputes about the authorship of such an extensive project; it was certainly not the work of a single individual, but of a group of translators. Some scholars argued that the translation might be linked with the Prague Dominicans or with the Augustinian Canons of Roudnice nad Labem, a monastery founded and supported by Archbishop Ernest of Pardubice. It is also possible that the translation was made with the help of the aforementioned Benedictine monastery of the Slavonic Rite in the New Town of Prague.[67]

In the case of the full translation of the Bible, we can only speculate about the level of support extended by the court. Emperor Charles IV issued a decree in Lucca on 17 June 1369 in which he endorsed the Inquisition in the northern, German-speaking parts of the Holy Roman Empire and called on the lay princes to assist the inquisitors in seeking out sermons and theological commentaries in German. The decree was issued in the context of the papacy's struggle against the Beghard and Beguine movements in the Low Countries and present-day northern

---

65 As already articulated by Jan Hus; see Pavlína Rychterová, 'The Vernacular Theology of Jan Hus', in Ota Pavlíček and František Šmahel (eds), *A Companion to Jan Hus* (Leiden and Boston, 2015), 170–213. This image was in modern times transformed into the idea of a broad support of Czech literature at his court, which is also widespread in modern scholarship on medieval literature. See Jiří Hasil, 'Karel IV. a čeština', *Studie z aplikované lingvistiky* 8 (2017), 23–33.
66 Jiroušková, 'Prague'.
67 Vladimír Kyas, 'Die alttschechische Bibelübersetzung des 14. Jahrhunderts und ihre Entwicklung im 15. Jahrhundert', in Reinhold Olesch and Hans Rothe (eds), *Kuttenberger Bibel bei Martin von Tišnov. Kommentare* (Paderborn, 1989), 9–52; Jakub Sichálek, 'European Background: Czech Translations', in Elizabeth Solopova (ed.), *The Wycliffite Bible: Origin, History and Interpretation* (Leiden, 2017), 66–84. For the later German translation of the Bible sponsored by Martin Rotlev and intended for the court of Wenceslas IV, see the essays by Maria Theisen and Gia Toussaint in this volume.

Germany, whose use of vernacular treatises was considered by the Church a vehicle potentially instigating interpretations of Church doctrine.[68] This, however, does not prevent the emperor's support of the vernacular translation of the Bible into Czech or German. Charles' position in this matter seems rather pragmatic and motivated by the most recent political developments; therefore, it cannot be deduced that he opposed translation projects in Bohemia as a matter of principle. The aforementioned effort of the Inquisition and the support of the emperor was not targeted primarily at the translations of the Bible, but particularly at the vernacular commentaries, which denied the authority of the Church.[69]

If the link between the Czech Bible and the emperor's court remains opaque, it is possible to suggest some other indirect connections between the imperial court and Old Czech translations. A plausible connection with the Czech Bible translation may be found in an anonymous Dominican translator and, more generally, in the Dominican milieu.[70]

The anonymous Dominican, who according to linguistic analysis contributed to the first Czech translation of the Bible, in the 1350s translated and partly adapted into Czech a contemporary bestseller – the collection of legends compiled by Jacobus de Voragine and widely known under the title *Legenda Aurea*. The Czech adaptation was called *Pasionál* (*Passional*). As the surviving Latin manuscripts of this work copied in Bohemia show, this very popular text was quite often supplemented with regional, mainly Bohemian, saints (for example, Wenceslas, Ludmila, and Procopius). This had already occurred shortly after 1300. Later, a set of 166 legends was created, most of which were translated into Czech by the aforementioned anonymous Dominican, including legends of Bohemian saints. This collection also included the legend of St Wenceslas, whose author was Charles IV himself and which, apart from being copied separately, was also inserted in the aforementioned *Chronicle* compiled by Pulkava.[71] The

---

68 For the decree, see Johann F. Böhmer and Alfons Huber (eds), *Regesta Imperii. Die Regesten des Kaiserreichs unter Kaiser Karl IV. (1346–1348)*, vol. 8 (Innsbruck, 1889), no. 7287, p. 759; cf. Richard Kieckhefer, *Repression of Heresy in Medieval Germany* (Liverpool, 1979), 34–8; Michael Tönsing, 'Contra hereticam pravitatem. Zu den Luccheser Ketzererlassen Karls IV. (1369)', in Friedrich Bernward Fahlbusch and Peter Johanek (eds), *Studia Luxemburgensia. Festschrift Heinz Stoob zum 70. Geburtstag* (Warendorf, 1989), 285–312. See also Maria Theisen's article in this volume.
69 Olivier Marin, *L'archevêque, le maître et le dévot. Genèses du mouvement réformateur pragois (années 1360–1419)* (Paris, 2005), 513–14.
70 Vendula Rejzlová, 'K tzv. Dominikánovi a českým dominikánům doby Karlovy', *Česká literatura* 63:3 (2015), 435–47.
71 Anežka Vidmanová, 'Spletitá cesta Zlaté legendy do české literatury', in eadem (ed.), *Jakub de Voragine, Legenda aurea* (Prague, 1998), 9–36, here 28–36; Anežka Vidmanová, 'La branche tchèque de la Legende dorée', in Brenda Dunn-Lardeau

last-mentioned circumstance points to an indirect connection with the imperial court, but it is not necessarily a conclusive sign of direct imperial patronage. The text of the St Wenceslas legend also circulated separately in Latin and Czech manuscript versions, so the translator and compiler of the Czech *Pasionál* could therefore have accessed that text directly. He need not have resorted to a version of Pulkava's *Chronicle*, and could even have included it in the collection from a source with a pre-existing translated version of the legend of the popular saint.[72] Although this particular text did not enjoy wide circulation, it was especially popular among court circles; for example, John of Neumarkt had the Wenceslas legend copied in Latin into his richly decorated and illuminated personal manuscript, *Liber Viaticus*.[73]

Another, even closer, connection to the court and the political programme of Charles IV is the inclusion of the 'Life of St Arnulfus' in the *Pasionál*. This seventh-century Bishop of Metz (d. 640) had no previous connection with Bohemia. However, part of his *vita* in Czech is incorporated in the *Pasionál*. It includes a genealogy of the Merovingian rulers, which, significantly, literally coincides with the genealogical portrait gallery that adorned the imperial residence of Karlštejn Castle.[74] This legend, which probably was not included in the Latin manuscripts of the *Pasionál* produced in fourteenth-century Bohemia, provides a narrative that fits well with the idea that Emperor Charles IV was part of a line of rulers that, beginning with Noah and continuing through Roman gods (Jupiter and Saturn), Trojan heroes, Merovingian and Carolingian rulers (including Charlemagne) to the dukes of Brabant and Luxembourg, predestined his lineage for the imperial dignity. This idea was visualized on the walls of the great hall of Karlštejn.[75]

(ed.), *Legenda aurea. Sept siècles de diffusion. Actes du colloque international sur la Legenda aurea: texte latin et branches vernaculaires* (Montréal, 1986), 291–8.
72 Blaschka, *Die St. Wenzelslegende Kaiser Karls IV*.
73 Prague, Knihovna Národního muzea, MS XIII A 12, fols 313r–317v. Cf. the facsimile of this splendid manuscript by Pavel Brodský, Kateřina Spurná and Marta Vaculínová (eds), *Liber viaticus Jana ze Středy. Vol. 1* (Prague, 2016).
74 Prague, Národní knihovna České republiky, MS XVII D 8, fols 167v–174v. Its edition prepared by Andrea Svobodová is digitally published on https://vokabular. ujc.cas.cz/moduly/edicni/edice/c3369146-5b9e-4a93-9279-7b6e65dd9d20/plny-text/s-aparatem/folio/167v (consulted 26 March 2023).
75 For the genealogical gallery and its meaning, see Marie Bláhová, 'Herrschergenealogie als Modell der Dauer des politischen Körpers des Herschers im mittelalterlichen Böhmen', in Andreas Speer and David Wirmer, *Das Sein der Dauer*, Miscellanea Mediaevalia, 34 (Berlin and New York, 2008), 380–97, at 393–7; Karel Stejskal, 'Noch einmal über die Datierung und Zuschreibung der Karlsteiner Malereien', in Jiří Fajt (ed.), *Court Chapels of the high and late Middle Ages and their artistic decoration* (Prague, 2003), 47–58, here 53–7.

However, it would be premature to conclude that the emperor was the direct patron of the work of the anonymous Dominican. There is, however, another candidate for patronage who already appeared more often in the present context, namely chancellor John of Neumarkt. It was already suggested in earlier research that he was associated with this Old Czech cycle of legends. According to some indirect evidence, especially the inclusion of the 'Life of St Hedwig', who was a favourite saint of John of Neumarkt, it is believed that John was the co-initiator of the translations leading to the creation of the Old Czech *Pasionál*.[76]

However, this is not the end of the connection between Charles' court and the Czech vernacular translations produced during the reign of Charles IV. The anonymous Dominican, in addition to his contribution to the Czech Bible translation and the creation of the Old Czech *Pasionál*, also authored the *Život Krista Pána* (*The Life of Christ the Lord*). This Old Czech text was based on the *Meditationes vitae Christi* attributed to pseudo-Bonaventure. However, the translator treats it very freely.[77] The author identifies himself in the prologue of the text as a member of the Dominican Order:

> *Ale jež jest pamět člověčie u prodlení časa k zapomnění hotova, protož já, predikátorového zákona nedóstojný duchovný, jal sem sě po to dielo, počen psáti o počátku našeho spasenie.*[78]

> [But since the memory of man is ready to forget in time of delay, I, a spiritual man unworthy of the Order of the Preachers, went after this work, and began to write about the beginning of our salvation.]

The hypothesis of Emperor Charles' commission and his influence on the composition of this work gradually gained ground only later. In a copy dated 1497 we find this expressed directly, instead of identifying the author as a Dominican in the same passage:

> *Ale jenž jest pamět člověčie u prodlení času k zapomnění hotova, protož já, neduostojný, přikázaním ciesaře Karla, krále českého, jal sem se pro toto dielo, počav psáti o počátku našeho spasenie.*[79]

---

76   Anežka Vidmanová, 'K původní podobě a textové tradici staročeského Pasionálu', *Listy filologické* 108 (1985), 16–45, esp. 39–40, where she dates its origin to 1357.
77   For the edition, see Martin Stluka (ed.), *Život Krista Pána* (Brno, 2006). The connection between the two texts was proved by Jan Vilikovský, 'Staročeský Passionál a Život Krista Pána', in idem, *Písemnictví českého středověku* (Prague, 1948), 141–60. The anonymous Dominican, for example, copied eight articles from the *Life of Christ the Lord* for the *Pasionál*.
78   *Život Krista Pána*, 4.
79   *Život Krista Pána*, 279.

[But since the memory of man is ready to be forgotten by the delay of time, therefore I, unworthy, by the commandment of Emperor Charles, King of Bohemia, began to write for this work, having begun to write about the beginning of our salvation.]

Even in the prologue of the original text, however, the translator pays tribute to and praises the (unidentified) initiator of this work, who made him write it in Czech, without specifying who was the initiator:

A to sem umyslil s pomocí Ducha svatého pořád psáti, aby u budúcích časiech bohobojní křestěné na těchto knihách čtúc, v Jesu Christu sě kochajíc, buoha chválili, jeho miléj matcě čest i chválu vzdávajíc, za toho, jest to kázal česky psáti, buoha prosili a s nim sě všickni buohu dostali věky věkóm. Amen.[80]

[And this I have purposed, with the help of the Holy Spirit, to write continually, that in the times to come the God-fearing Christians, reading these books, and delighting themselves in Jesus Christ, may praise God, and give honour and praise to his dear mother, and pray to God for him who has ordered to write this in Czech, and with him all God will be received forever and ever. Amen.]

The translator himself remains unidentified. Despite all efforts, any attempts to link a specific member of the Dominican community to this individual have so far remained unconvincing.[81] The socio-cultural environment and presumptive audience for which these translations were produced can, however, be identified more clearly. Very probably, they were created for women's monasteries, for example, the Dominican Sisters in the Old Town or the very privileged Benedictine monastery of St George at Prague Castle, which was usually headed by a member of the royal family, and whose nuns were also recruited exclusively from noble women. At this stage of the vernacularization of religious literature, readers from such communities were no doubt interested in these kinds of texts but did not usually know enough Latin to access them in the original versions.

In contrast, the first Czech-Latin dictionaries, glossaries, collections of proverbs and riddles were written for a slightly different environment. From an acrostic (*Magister Bohemarius Bartholomeus de Solencia dictus Claretus*; Master Bartholomeus of Chlumec called Claret, author of the *Bohemarius*), we can more closely identify the most prolific author of this

---

80 *Život Krista Pána*, 4.
81 Thomas, *Anne's Bohemia*, 41–2.

group of texts as Bartholomeus de Solencia (Bartoloměj of Chlumec).[82] From indirect sources and references in his works, it seems plausible that he produced some of his Latin-Czech glossaries in the orbit of Charles' court, or rather of his courtiers, and with their support. Claretus worked at the school of the Metropolitan Chapter located at Prague Castle, and mentions many members of the court, so it can be assumed that he was in regular contact with them. Valuable additional testimony is provided by his book *Glossarius*. Thanks to the fact that Claretus mentions his contemporaries alongside book authorities at the end of each chapter, it is possible to date the *Glossarius* rather precisely to the years 1359/60–1363/4. In the verse references at the end of the chapters, the author successively mentions many members of the Prague court, whom he thus identifies as possible inspirers and patrons.

As the relevant verses indicate, the main initiators of Claretus' Czech-Latin *Glossarius* included important persons at the court, such as Archbishop Ernest of Pardubice[83] and chancellor John of Neumarkt.[84] Besides these and other personalities, the emperor himself is also mentioned; Claretus describes him with the words: '*Karolus hiis sanus, rex, caesar, ator, Elianus*' ['Wise Charles, King, Emperor, Elias-like instigator'].[85] Claretus systematically dealt with linguistic tools that facilitated education, consciously insisting that it was important and necessary in this respect to include Czech in the predominantly Latin curriculum in schools like the one at the Metropolitan Chapter where he was teaching, so that students could understand the meaning of Latin words but also know and be able to use their Czech equivalents. He himself expressed this conviction in the prologue to another work, *Vocabularius*: 'Utilitas iuvenum me compulit edere metrum:/ Vocibus imposita que dantur signa secunda,/ Hec pro posse meo resignabo sermone Boemo:/ Nam sine vocabulis mens inscita dicitur omnis.' ['The utility of youth compels me to translate to the best of my ability in the metre words into Czech, since without a knowledge of vocabulary every

---

82 Bohumil Ryba, 'K rukopisným latinsko-českým slovníkům ostřihomským', *Listy filologické* 75 (1951), 89–123; Anežka Vidmanová, 'Mistr Klaret a jeho spisy', *Listy filologické* 103 (1980), 220. *Bohemarius* is the title of his dictionary, but it can also be read as an honorary title for an author's services to the Czech language.
83 Václav Flajšhans (ed.), *Klaret a jeho družina*, vol. I (Prague, 1926), 196, v. 2495: *Firmet hec Arnestus archipresul, auctor honestus.*
84 *Klaret a jeho družina*, vol. I, 192, v. 2383: *(Hec) Olomucensis data presulis aucta Iohann(i)s.*
85 *Klaret a jeho družina*, vol. I, 194, v. 2437; for the explanation of this identification, see Anežka Vidmanová, 'Ator Elianus', *Listy filologické* 102 (1979), 157–60.

man is considered a fool.'].⁸⁶ The fact that the work of an author who contributed substantially to the development of the Czech vocabulary in many areas mentions leading men of the imperial court led by Charles IV himself could be read as a confirmation of the author's efforts to reach a courtly audience (a number of Czech nobles are also mentioned), but this can scarcely confirm the direct patronage of all these men.

In comparison with the Latin text production, the number of Czech works that we can associate with Charles IV as a direct or indirect patron is close to nil. However, here we need to remind ourselves of the historical context. For many decades the university and the Prague religious schools functioned only in Latin, and vernacular works that were not epic and lyric compositions only very gradually entered the public discourse through the vernacularization of religious educational texts. These were intended to contribute to religious education and enlightenment for those whose education was not predicated on the knowledge of Latin. Czech translations were therefore primarily intended for members of female monastic communities.⁸⁷ Gradually, they also came to involve the more affluent members of civic communities and members of noble Bohemian (Czech-speaking) families, whose leading representatives were naturally present at the imperial court. In this respect, the monarch's court acted as an element whose support of vernacular translations and original texts contributed significantly to their development. These efforts would become even more pronounced during the reign of Charles' son, Wenceslaus IV (1378–1419).⁸⁸

CONCLUSION

In this essay I have attempted to look at the literary patronage emanating from the Prague court from the perspective of the possible contributions of Emperor Charles as a primary patron who stimulated literary production in multiple languages. The chosen languages played a role not only in these works, but also in Charles' political programme. The Prague court thus became a space of contact and interference, in which the increased density created by parallel production, competition, and imitation of various text types led to the development of a multilingual text production

---

86 *Klaret a jeho družina*, vol. I, vv. 1–4.
87 As indicated, for example, by Josef Vintr, 'Komu byl určen první český překlad bible z poloviny 14. století a další otázky s tím spojené', *Listy filologické* 142 (2019), 333–67, esp. 354–9.
88 Cf. for instance Robert Novotný, 'Das Mäzenatentum am Hof Wenzels IV', in Petr Elbel, Alexandra Kaar, Jiří Němec and Martin Wihoda (eds), *Historiker zwischen den Zeiten: Festschrift für Karel Hruza zum 60. Geburtstag* (Vienna, 2021), 249–68.

that influenced the literary landscape for the following final decades of the Middle Ages and for centuries beyond.[89]

Although the emphasis on the Slavic origin of the Czech people and half of Charles' family was part of Charles' political programme,[90] a programmatic promotion of Czech as a literary language cannot be noted. In the case of German, the contemporary text production proves the emperor's ongoing and sustained interest in the German language through the translation efforts of John of Neumarkt and the emperor's role in the career of Heinrich von Mügeln. But the emperor was by far the most evident patron in the case of works in Latin, especially with regard to the production of chronicles, and his own authorial activities. The different kinds of involvement of the emperor as a patron in the process of the creation of literary works is probably related to the different intended audiences and purposes which in turn reflect the roles assigned by Charles and his courtiers to the different languages and thus the different impacts they would have on the imperial court.[91]

---

89   Michael Stolz, 'Prag als diskursiver Interferenzraum im Spätmittelalter', in Richard Němec and Peter Knüvener (eds), *König und Kaiser Karl IV. und die Oberlausitz – Schöpfer und Herrscher* (Berlin, 2021), 98–114.
90   Žůrek and Rychterová, 'Slavonic and Czech identity'.
91   This study was supported by grant no. 19-28415X 'From Performativity to Institutionalization: Handling Conflict in the Late Middle Ages (Strategies, Agents, Communication)' from the Czech Science Foundation (GAČR).

CHAPTER 6

MIRACULOUS OBJECTS AND FOUNDATIONAL SINS: VERBAL AND MATERIAL REALITY IN THE *DALIMIL CHRONICLE*, THE CHRONICLE OF PŘIBÍK PULKAVA OF RADENÍN, AND CHARLES IV'S AUTOBIOGRAPHY

MATOUŠ JALUŠKA

Emperor Charles IV strove to have himself portrayed as a *rex litteratus*, a wise and literate king able to use his intellectual powers decisively for the benefit of the whole realm. In the texts written under his patronage with various degrees of his participation, he often defined what to him were the ingredients of a proper exercise of sovereign power.[1] Given the

---

1   František Šmahel, 'Duchovní život, kultura a umění za vlády Lucemburků', in František Šmahel and Lenka Bobková (eds), *Lucemburkové: Česká koruna uprostřed*

pivotal role of ostentatious personal piety and religious paradigms in Charles' construction of the royal persona and the representation of the world around him, it seems fair to speak in his case about a personal 'political theology' that connected him as an actor with the *general* history of salvation of humankind.[2] On the other hand, Charles' subjects were engaged in a range of *particular* discourses, using various languages which, especially in the case of Czech and German within the Lands of the Bohemian Crown, sometimes entered in conflict with each other. The literate king needed to accommodate these tensions so that he would be able to successfully communicate his achievements to his subjects. Through this process of accommodation, the function of *rex litteratus* is enriched with elements associated with the paradigm of 'peacemaker king' (*rex pacificus*), another role that Charles aspired to.[3]

In this chapter I will examine traces of this strategy in a cluster of texts whose origin is customarily placed in the orbit of the Prague court in the third quarter of the fourteenth century. This cluster consists of the emperor's biography, the *Vita Caroli*, conventionally dated to around 1350, a collection of moral sentences and short exegeses known as the *Moralitates Caroli quarti imperatoris* (1370s), and the last and most successful of Bohemian chronicles sponsored by Charles, the *Chronicon Bohemiae*[4] of Přibík Pulkava of Radenín (finished probably in 1374). All of them were written in Latin – a supra-regional tongue 'cut from the embodied concerns of the vernacular'[5] and suitable for negotiations between various linguistic communities. As such, they will be read against a slightly older

---

Evropy (Prague, 2012), 257–82, at 263–6. Cf. Robert Antonín, *The Ideal Ruler in Medieval Bohemia* (Leiden, 2017), 288–94.

2   Šmahel, 'Duchovní život', 263. In Šmahel's use the term does not point to Carl Schmitt, but rather to Ernst Kantorowicz, cf. William Chester Jordan, 'Preface (1997)', in Ernst H. Kantorowicz, *The King's Two Bodies* (Princeton, NJ, 2016, orig. 1957), xxv–xxxi, at xxv. For a detailed discussion on performative aspects of Charles' sacred kingship and the role of relics in it, see Martin Bauch, *Divina favente clemencia: Auserwählung, Frömmigkeit und Heilsvermittlung in der Herrschaftspraxis Kaiser Karls IV.* (Cologne, 2015), esp. 63–170.

3   For an overview of the function of the peacemaker paradigm in narrative sources from medieval Bohemia, see Antonín, *The Ideal Ruler*, 285–8.

4   The naming of this chronicle in manuscripts and among historians is inconsistent. I adopt the title used by Václav Žůrek and Pavlína Rychterová, 'Slavonic and Czech Identity in the *Chronicon Bohemiae* by Přibík Pulkava of Radenín', in Pavlína Rychterová and David Kalhous (eds), *Historiography and Identity VI: Competing Narratives of the Past in Central and Eastern Europe, c. 1200–c. 1600* (Turnhout, 2021), 225–56.

5   Nicholas Watson, 'The Idea of Latinity', in Ralph J. Dexter and David Townsend (eds), *The Oxford Handbook of Medieval Latin Literature* (Oxford, 2012), 124–48, at 137.

vernacular account of the history of the Czech people running from their mythical beginnings to the accession of John of Luxembourg in 1310; it was composed in Old Czech a few years after King John's enthronement and today it is known as the *Dalimil Chronicle*.[6]

All these texts interacted with each other throughout Charles' reign, providing their audiences with historical narratives linked (in one way or the other) to the history of the Bohemian lands and, implicitly, to the archetypal Latin chronicle of the Czechs written by Cosmas, canon of Prague, in 1125 and known as the *Chronica Boemorum* (or *Bohemorum*; Bertold Bretholz, author of the fundamental critical edition of the text, uses the spelling without the 'h'). They have been preserved in various versions in the three principal languages of Bohemia – Latin, Czech and German – and testify to the steady increase of literary life that came about in the era of the last Přemyslid kings and reached full bloom under the Luxembourg dynasty. Another feature they have in common is that they attempt to ground or even contain the mixed feelings that the Czech-speaking and increasingly literate indigenous nobility had about the accession of a non-native dynasty to the Prague throne.[7]

The texts will be examined through close reading, taking into account the processes through which their authors sought authority and validation for their words in the material sphere. Scholars have studied the texts considered in this essay mainly as historiographical sources, with the objective to underline the 'historicism' of Charles' ideological project.[8]

---

6   For a comprehensive introduction and a French translation in prose, see Éloïse Adde-Vomáčka, *La Chronique de Dalimil: Les débuts de l'historiographie nationale tchèque en langue vulgaire au xive siècle* (Paris, 2016).

7   Marie Bláhová, 'Písemná kultura', in František Šmahel and Lenka Bobková (eds), *Lucemburkové: Česká koruna uprostřed Evropy* (Prague, 2012), 559–69, at 563–7. Cf. Lenka Jiroušková, 'Prague', in David Wallace (ed.), *Europe: A Literary History. 1348–1418*, 2 vols (Oxford, 2016), vol. 2, 617–51. For the overview of gradual textualization of the Land Law as evidence of Czech nobles' literacy as well as their determination to resist a monarch, see Jiří Kejř, 'Die Urkunde als Beweismittel im Gerichtsverfahren im mittelalterlichen Böhmen', in Anna Adamska and Marco Mostert (eds), *The Development of Literate Mentalities in East Central Europe* (Turnhout, 2004), 51–8. For a new assessment of a medieval German translation of the pronouncedly anti-German *Dalimil Chronicle*, see Vlastimil Brom, 'The Rhymed German Translation of the Chronicle of the So-Called Dalimil and its Strategies of Identification', in Rychterová and Kalhous (eds), *Historiography and Identity VI: Competing Narratives*, 257–80.

8   This point of view was, in recent decades, represented mainly by the prolific output of Marie Bláhová. In addition to her texts focused on particular problems cited elsewhere in this chapter, see a more general overview of late medieval Bohemian historiography in Bláhová, *Staročeská kronika tak řečeného Dalimila v kontextu středověké historiografie latinského kulturního okruhu a její pramenná*

More recently, they were interpreted as testimonies to an ideal of sovereign power that Charles strove to enact.[9] The reading that follows will take a slightly different perspective, informed by recent calls for reading medieval chronicles as literary artefacts.[10] Instead of the ideal ruler I shall focus on a particular shape or, rather, a texture of the world created by the texts examined, in which the sovereign can perform his role and where Charles' self-representational project attains its fullest meaning, of which manipulating past forms is an inseparable part. How do the participants in this world communicate? How do they express the difference between effective and ineffective interactions? And, in particular: what is the role of 'marvellous objects' that people look at with awe, subsequently sharing their astonishment verbally with each other in this textual universe?

Charles' affinity for such objects, especially the relics of saints, and their connection to his self-representation strategy is well known.[11] In his contact with material holiness, Charles as the undisputed hegemon (the *mundi monarcha*) acts as the most prominent representative of the (lay) people regarding the sphere of the sacred. This way, he eventually transcends his lay position and transforms himself into a chosen guide who leads his subjects towards salvation.[12] He is able to enact this role precisely through his persona as the *rex litteratus* who is able to act effectively in the verbal sphere, at the same time counting on the support provided by physical items, whose validity he sometimes confirms by means of words inscribed by his own hand in their substance.[13]

---

hodnota (Prague, 1995), 134–40. In English, see Julia Verkholantsev, *The Slavic Letters of St. Jerome: The History of the Legend and Its Legacy, or, How the Translator of the Vulgate Became an Apostle of the Slavs* (DeKalb, 2014), 76–116.
9   Antonín, *The Ideal Ruler*, 54–5.
10 Cf. Jan Lehár, *Nejstarší česká epika: Dalimilova kronika, Alexandreida, první veršované legendy* (Prague, 1983), 12–29; Vojtěch Bažant, 'Kronikář ve svém díle: Problematika autora a vypravěče', *Mediævalia historica Bohemica* 20 (2017), 141–57. Compare also Éloïse Adde's reading of Dalimil as a conscious creator of Czech literature in her *Le Chronique de Dalimil*, 49–50.
11 See, e.g., Eva Schlotheuber, 'Der weise König', *Revue d'histoire luxembourgeoise* 63 (2011), 265–79. For the connection between wisdom, sanctity, and Charles' quest for symbolic capital, see Bauch, *Divina favente clemencia*, 31–41.
12 Václav Žůrek, *Karel IV.: Ideál středověkého vládce* (Prague, 2018), 167–72. Martin Bauch, 'Hegemoniales Königtum jenseits von Politik- und Verfassungsgeschichte: Zur sakralen Herrschaftspraxis Karls IV.', in Christine Reinle (ed.), *Stand und Perspektiven der Sozial- und Verfassungsgeschichte zum römisch-deutschen Reich: Der Forschungseinfluss Peter Moraws auf die deutsche Mediävistik* (Affalterbach, 2016), 97–110.
13 See, for example, Charles' signature which he added to a fragment of a purported autograph of the Gospel of St Mark's in 1354. See Martin Bauch, 'Et hec scripsi manu mea propria: Known and Unknown Autographs of Charles IV as

It is the connection between the material and verbal sphere as a negotiating strategy that is the focus of what follows. In this work I turn to a basic theological framework of late medieval intellectual discourse in which Emperor Charles participated. In particular, I refer to the writings of Augustine of Hippo (St Augustine) about the nexus between spiritual and material reality in miraculously or sacramentally signifying objects such as the Eucharist or holy relics.[14] According to Zdeněk Kalista and Bernd-Ulrich Hergemöller, Charles' ideological project is imbued with Augustinianism.[15] This is not unusual in Charles' time. There was much debate at the time about Augustine's legacy and (in a narrower sense) who were his true heirs – the Augustinian canons or their mendicant cousins, the Augustinian hermits. At the heart of the controversy lies Augustine's tomb in Pavia, where the young Charles experienced a miracle involving the Eucharist that saved him from poison (see below in the section on the *Vita Caroli*).[16] During the fourteenth century we can observe the process of Augustine's gradual transformation from a 'mere' father of the Church into a model Christian. He became a saint capable of combining an eremitical life of reflective detachment from the world (*vita contemplativa*) with active engagement in human communities (*vita activa*), thus providing his followers with a model of the perfect Christian life.[17] It is mainly this possibility of synthesis of spiritual and material means towards salvation that I am interested in in this chapter.

The second focus of Augustinian inspiration that I find in the texts under study is the ambivalent relationship to words as signs, which emerges most prominently from Augustine's *De magistro* and will become apparent below in the dialogue between the *Dalimil Chronicle* and *Chronicon Bohemiae* of Přibík Pulkava. As revealed in *De magistro*, proper learning, according to

---

Testimonies of Intellectual Profile, Royal Literacy, and Cultural Transfer', in Sébastien Barret, Dominique Stutzmann and Georg Vogeler, *Ruling the Script in the Middle Ages: Formal Aspects of Written Communication (Books, Chapters, and Inscriptions)* (Turnhout, 2016), 25–48, at 32–6, 40–1, and 46–7.

14   Elena Lombardi, *The Syntax of Desire: Language and Love in Augustine, the Modistae, Dante* (Toronto, 2007), 30–1.

15   Zdeněk Kalista, *Karel IV.: Jeho duchovní tvář* (Prague, 2007), 49–66; idem, *Karel IV. a Itálie* (Prague, 2004), 145–88. Bernd-Ulrich Hergemöller, *Cogor adversum te: Drei Studien zum literarisch-theologischen Profil Karls IV. und seiner Kanzlei* (Wahrendorf, 1999), 240.

16   Kaspar Elm, 'Augustinus Canonicus – Augustinus Eremita: A Quatrocento Cause Célèbre', in Timothy Verdon and John Henderson (eds), *Christianity and the Renaissance. Image and Religious Imagination in the Quattrocento* (New York, 1990), 83–107. See also Kalista, *Karel IV. a Itálie*, 148.

17   Eric Leland Saak, *Luther and the Reformation of the Later Middle Ages* (Cambridge, 2017), 64–82, at 67.

Augustine, is to be done by looking at things, not signs.[18] Unless one sees the thing itself (*res ipsa*), one has learned nothing. For Augustine 'vision precedes signification and is its epistemic foundation'. Hence, a 'wise' exercise of royal power entails presentation of salutary visible things to the subjects and also distribution of narratives about successful or failed processes of signification and their consequences.[19]

A NOTE ON THE SOURCES

The number of known manuscript witnesses to Charles' biography hovers around 20.[20] In my choice of a particular codex for this study I proceed from the need to supplement the *Vita* with the *Moralitates*, a collection of moral sentences and short exegeses of a type similar to the meditative chapters of the biography. This collection was traditionally ascribed to Charles; its roots in the *Liber philosophorum moralium antiquorum* by John of Procida were only recently discovered by Jana Nechutová.[21] The *Moralitates* survives in only two medieval codices, in Vienna (Österreichische Nationalbibliothek, ms. 556, fols 53r–69r) and in Prague (Národní knihovna České republiky, ms. XIX B 5, fols 151r–156r); in both sources it follows the *Vita Caroli* as a sequel.

For this reason, I choose as the basic manuscript for the *Vita* and *Moralitates* (as well as for the *Chronicon Bohemiae* of Přibík Pulkava) the Prague manuscript XIX B 5, a paper miscellany of 243 numbered folios, written exclusively in Latin by at least four different hands. Here, the biography and the moral sentences are grouped together with other writings that relate to Charles IV under the heading 'Dicta imo vita Caroli IV. Romanorum imperatoris', written by a later, probably nineteenth-century, hand.[22] This 'Caroline' section was copied as a whole by a single, early fifteenth-century scribe; it comprises 34 folios of the manuscript

---

18 *De magistro* x.32–36, in Augustinus Hipponensis, *Contra academicos. De beata vita. De ordine. De magistro. De libero arbitrio*, ed. W.M. Green and K.D. Daur (Turnhout, 1970), 190–4.
19 Phillip Cary, *Outward Signs: The Powerlessness of External Things in Augustine's Thought* (New York, 2008), 91–7, quote at 95.
20 Marie Bláhová, 'Soudobé kroniky o Karlovi IV.', in Marie Bláhová, Zuzana Lukšová and Martin Nodl, *Karel IV. v soudobých kronikách* (Prague, 2016), 31–64, at 40.
21 Jana Nechutová, 'Die Moralitates im literarischen Werk Karls IV', *Graeco-Latina Brunensia* 23 (2018), 139–67 (see also a new critical edition of the text at 151–67). For the connection between *Vita* and *Moralitates*, see e.g. Jiří Hasil, 'Karel IV. a čeština', *Studie z aplikované lingvistiky*, special issue (2017), 23–33, at 27.
22 Ms. XIX B 5, fol. 134r. See also the description in Bláhová, 'Recepce České kroniky', 63.

and begins with the *Vita* (fols 134r–151r), immediately followed by the *Moralitates* (fols 151r–156r). Then it continues with a complete Latin version of the *Ordo ad coronandum regem Bohemorum* with the *Ordo ad benedicendum reginam* (fols 156v–163r) and ends with a sermon by the Prague Archbishop John of Jenštejn (d. 1400), delivered at Charles' funeral in 1378 (fols 163r–167v).

The Caroline section is preceded by two historical narratives, written by different hands datable to the end of the fourteenth century. In first position there is the *Chronicon imperatorum et pontificum* of Martin of Troppau (fols 1r–85v), supplemented with tables of nations of the Empire, rulers of Bohemia (beginning with Přemysl the Plowman), Prague bishops, and Christian kingdoms and bishoprics in Rome's jurisdiction (inserted at fols 11r–13r). The second place belongs to Přibík's *Chronicon Bohemiae*, followed by a table of contents (fols 86r–129r and fragment on f. 135v).

The rest of the manuscript contains various historical texts and notes, among which stand out two anti-Hussite texts (fols 170r–173v), a version of Einhard's *Vita Karoli Magni* (fols 178r–222r), a collection of letters and notes touching on the topic of papal supremacy, concluded by a note on the Council of Basel (fols 222v–227v), and, finally, a version of Charles IV's Golden Bull (fols 229r–243v).[23]

In the case of the *Dalimil Chronicle* I follow critical consensus and cite the text from the Vienna Codex (Vienna, ÖNB, Cod. Series nova 44). This source transmits the text in a form that is considered closest to the assumed archetype from the beginning of the fourteenth century and as such has the longest history of reception.[24] The manuscript itself is a carefully executed parchment codex, written probably in the first years of the fifteenth century, perhaps for Charles' son and successor, Wenceslas; the chronicle is the sole text contained within.

Overall, the *Dalimil Chronicle* was preserved in 13 medieval manuscripts (including fragments) in various codicological contexts that testify to its popularity.[25]

---

23 For an exhaustive description of the codex, see Alena Richterová, *Děčínské rukopisy ze sbírky Františka Martina Pelcla (1734–1801), nyní ve fondech Národní knihovny České republiky* (Prague, 2007), 128–34.

24 Jiří Daňhelka, Karel Hádek, Bohuslav Havránek and Naděžda Kvítková (eds), *Staročeská kronika tak řečeného Dalimila. Vydání textu a veškerého textového materiálu*, 2 vols (Prague, 1988), vol. 1, 31–3.

25 For a detailed discussion of the Vienna Codex and its role in the first years of the fifteenth century, see Radko Šťastný, 'Vídeňský rukopis Dalimilovy kroniky a doba Václava IV. (jeho podoba, literární kontext a význam)', *Česká literatura* 33 (1985), 389–407. The chronicle's popularity and the ecosystem of its manuscript tradition are summarized in Éloïse Adde, 'Environnement textuel et réception du texte médiéval: La deuxième vie de la Chronique de Dalimil', *Médiévales* 73 (2017),

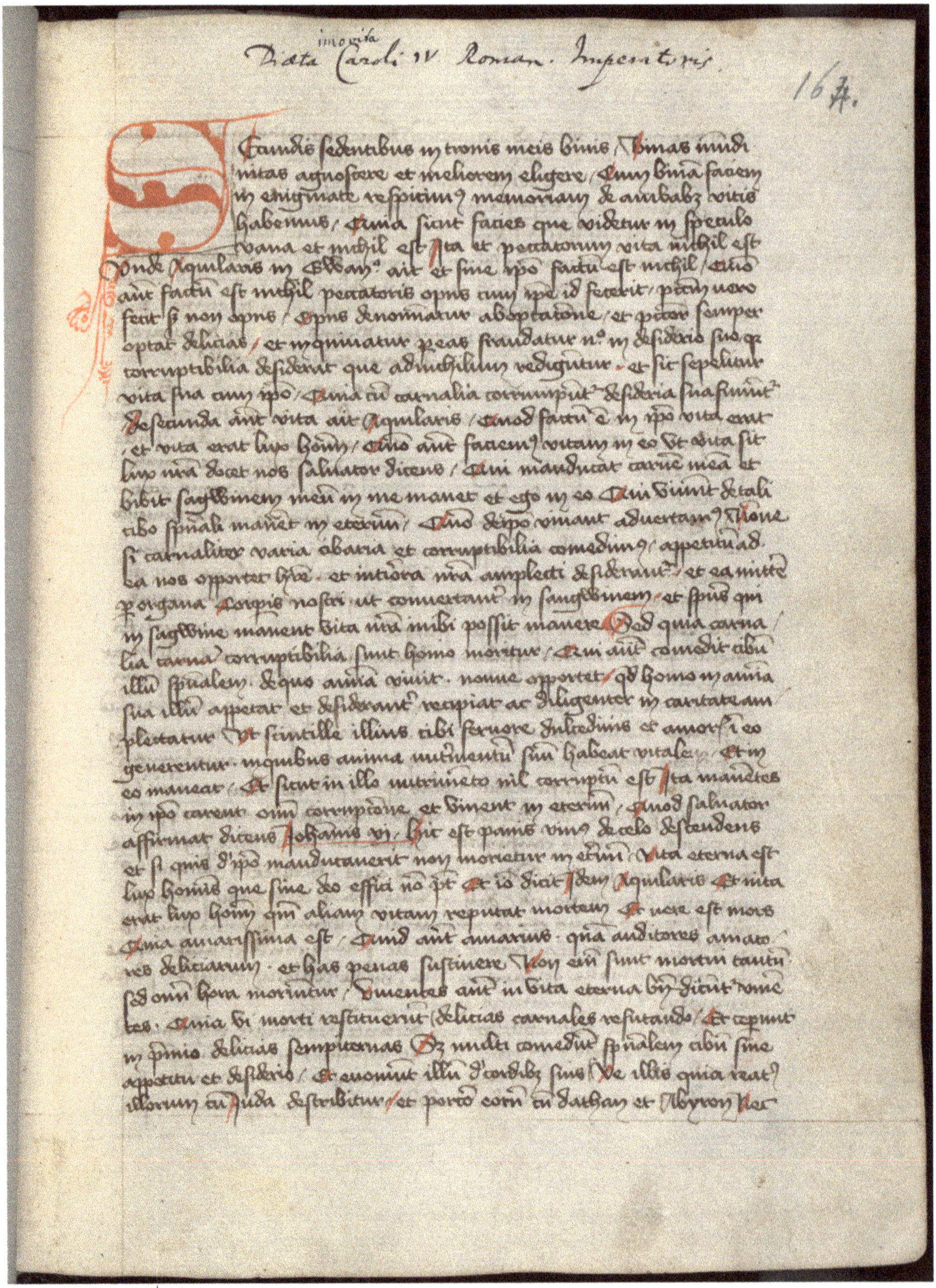

Dicta Caroli IV Roman. Imperatoris [*ima vita* interlinear]

Fig. 6.1. Prague, Národní knihovna České republiky, ms. XIX B 5, fol. 164r. Beginning of the *Vita Caroli*.

VITA CAROLI: REALITY AND NOTHINGNESS

The Latin narrative portraying the first 30 years in the life of Charles IV, usually referred to as *Vita Caroli* (*Karoli*) or *De vita sua*, consists of 20 chapters, of which the first 14 are written in the first person singular and serve as the basis for the standard interpretation of the *Vita* as the emperor's autobiography.[26] After the first two chapters, which serve as a prologue, Charles asserts his ancestral heritage from both his father's Luxembourg and mother's Přemyslid sides. After briefly recounting his childhood years in France (chapter 3), he focuses on his experiences during his father's battles in Italy (chapters 4–7), his first attempts to rule Bohemia (chapter 8), the help he gave his family in Tyrol (chapters 9–10), his final return to Bohemia, and further activities in Central Europe (chapters 11–14). In chapters 11–13 the narration is interrupted by a more reflexive and meditative subject matter when Charles expounds upon Jesus' parables about the Kingdom of Heaven (Matthew 13:44–50). The remaining six chapters are written in the third person and lead up to Charles' election as King of the Romans in 1346.

According to its 'sermon-like' prologue,[27] the purpose of the *Vita Caroli* is to transmit knowledge to future rulers occupying Charles' 'double throne', i.e., ruling Bohemia and the Empire. The prologue's initial set of topics is, however, formulated in a rather general manner. Instead of the rule of a monarch over their subjects, it is concerned with the rule of individual human beings over themselves, problems of self-control, and the art of choosing the right path in life. Here, Charles' heirs are bound to 'consider the double life of this world' and 'select the better one' from two possible options ('binas mundi vitas agnoscere et meliorem eligere').[28] As it turns out, these two options mean either succumbing to one's own vices or behaving properly as is expected of a Christian. Up to here, this

---

169–92. New insights into the late medieval reception and reworking of the chronicle are offered by Vojtěch Bažant, 'Formy a funkce narativu o českých dějinách v 15. století', in Pavlína Cermanová and Pavel Soukup (eds), *Husitské re-formace: Proměna kulturního kódu v 15. století* (Prague, 2019), 226–51.

26 I follow Nagy's advice to 'stick to the authorship of the Czech ruler, accepting the fact that not all the problematic points can be explained'; see Balász Nagy, 'Memories of the Self: The Autobiography of Charles IV in Search of Medieval Memories', in Rafał Wójcik (ed.), *Culture of Memory in East Central Europe in the Late Middle Ages and the Early Modern Period* (Poznań, 2008), 161–6, at 162. For a general introduction to the *Vita Caroli*, see e.g. Martin Nodl, 'Vita Caroli', in Šmahel and Bobková (eds), *Lucemburkové*, 240–2.

27 See Nagy, 'Memories of the Self', 162.

28 Ms. XIX B 5, fol. 134r. Cf. Josef Emler (ed.), *Fontes rerum Bohemicarum III* (Prague, 1883), 336. All transcriptions and translations are mine unless stated otherwise. For the sake of clarity, I add modern punctuation.

is hardly surprising. What is specific to the *Vita Caroli*, however, is that the difference between the path of Christian virtue and the path of sin is very consistently linked to the difference between material existence and nothingness, and that Charles' heirs are being led to the recognition that in solving dilemmas encountered in real life a human being should constantly renew the moral lessons impressed into their memory at an earlier stage in life through maintaining close contact with material, tangible objects that have the power to support remembrance. Both features are made evident in an exemplary *enigma* with which the *Vita Caroli* begins:

> Cum binam faciem in enigmate respicimus, memoriam de ambabus vitis habemus. Quia sicut facies, que videtur in speculo, vana et nichil est, ita et peccatorum vita nichil est. Unde Aquilaris in evangelio ait: Et sine ipso factum est nichil. Quomodo autem factum est nichil peccatoris opus, cum ipse id fecerit? Peccatum uero fecit, sed non opus.[29]

> [We remember the notion of double life by using the parable of the two faces. The face we see in a mirror is empty and nothing; similarly, the life of sinners is nothing. That is why John says in the Gospel: 'and without him was not anything made'. But how is it possible to turn a sinner's work into nothing although he himself performed it? The answer is: he produced a sin, but not a work.]

A cherished medieval topos of a human being who stands at the crossroads of life and needs to remind itself about the original virtuous inclinations of its own soul as well as about the end it aspires to in order to select the best way towards salvation is reformulated here as the choice between being and obliteration.[30] The nature of this choice is demonstrated through an exemplary object, the mirror. The author of the prologue can count on a venerable literary tradition of exempla in which mirrors produce illusory images that obscure the truth (cf. 1 Corinthians 13:12) and can be outright dangerous (as is the case in various versions of the Narcissus myth).[31] At the same time, however, the mirror is still an easily accessible material

---

29 Ms. XIX B 5, fol. 134r. Cf. Josef Emler (ed.), *Fontes rerum Bohemicarum III* (Prague, 1883), 336.
30 Eva Schlotheuber, 'Die Autobiographie Karls IV. und die mittelalterlichen Vorstellungen vom Menschen am Scheideweg', *Historische Zeitschrift* 281 (2005), 561–91. For a more general discussion of this topos, see Eva Schlotheuber, 'Der Mensch am Scheideweg: Personkonzeptionen des Mittelalters', *Querelles: Jahrbuch für Frauen- und Geschlechterforschung* 10 (2005), 71–96.
31 Schlotheuber, 'Die Autobiographie Karls IV', 565–7. For an overview of the various strains of medieval 'specular' tradition, see Nancy M. Frelick, 'Introduction', in Nancy M. Frelick (ed.), *The Mirror in Medieval and Early Modern Culture:*

object which the reader or listener of this passage can look at – and in looking recollect the moral obligation stated here. The exemplary object is thus present in the real life as an aid to remembrance.

In the parable, real, material and living existence is identified with the side of the living beholder who looks into the mirror and sees his or her own face. The author concentrates on the 'emptiness' of the image beheld on the surface and presents it as an analogy of sin, which, although visible, lacks a true being, because it was committed without the help of God, who alone is able to create. The *Vita Caroli* follows tradition that connects being with goodness and sees the highest degree of both in God. Everything else, on the other hand, was created by this God out of nothing and, as such, tends to dissolve into nothingness once again.[32]

In the following, etymological part of the prologue, the author connects the word 'opus' (work) with 'optatio' (wish) and states that the nature of a thing has much to do with the desire of its maker. Thus, the difference between 'uti' and 'frui', 'use' and 'enjoyment', formulated by Augustine in his *De doctrina christiana*, comes into play and with it a possibility of morally assessing people by examining their ability to seek the highest, 'intransitive' enjoyment in God alone and to orientate the lowlier desires in accordance with the Holy Spirit.[33]

If human agents sinfully desire only their own pleasure in this body, they direct their works towards eventual annihilation. According to the prologue, the temporary existence of things in the world is passing and precarious; however, the author does not advise the audience to leave the world, but to find a way in it that will enable them to enact the role of a ruler as an 'image of Christ the King' and to fulfil the maxim 'to rule is to serve God' ('Deo servire est regnare'), attributed to Augustine.[34] Charles uses this maxim later in the *Vita*, in the second sermon out of three (chapter 12 in the *Vita*) based on parables from the Gospel of Matthew

---

Specular Reflections (Turnhout, 2016), 1–29. Interplay between the Pauline and the 'narcissistic' tradition is discussed at 4–9.

32 Hergemöller, *Cogor adversum te*, 238. Augustine's privational theory of evil belongs to the same tradition. Cf. Jesse Couenhoven, 'Augustine', in Keith L. Johnson and David Lauber (eds), *T&T Clark Companion to the Doctrine of Sin* (London, 2016), 181–98. The sequence of the two modes of living in the prologue, where the sinful life goes first and the virtuous one follows, can also be traced back to Augustine, e.g. to his *Contra Julianum*. See Schlotheuber, 'Die Autobiographie Karls IV.', 566.

33 *De doctrina christiana* i.3–4. Corpus Christianorum Series Latina 32, 8. Cf. Eugene Vance, *Marvelous Signals: Poetics and Sign Theory in the Middle Ages* (Lincoln, NE, 1989), 34–50. Lombardi, *The Syntax of Desire*, 25–7, 66–76.

34 The sentence paraphrases various of Augustine's authentic assertions. See e.g. *De civitate Dei* xix.14–15. Corpus Christianorum Series Latina 48, 380–2.

concerning the Kingdom of Heaven – the parables of the hidden treasure, of the pearl and of the fishing net.[35]

All three exegeses that form chapters 11–13 of the *Vita Caroli* demonstrate the ability of material objects to illuminate a spiritual reality, whereas words are assigned the duty to reflect this connection or to serve as a medium of confession in which the speakers themselves are turned into objects of reflection. If done properly, this enables the establishment of another material link between the heavenly and the earthly realms, through which human beings find support for their actions in the divine creator of all existing things – embodied in material form in the sacrament of the Eucharist.[36] This is highlighted already in the prologue:

> In nutrimentum animarum vestrarum cibum illum desiderate recipere et sine ipso nolite vivere, ut in eternum vivatis. Et non in solo pane vivit homo, sed ex omni verbo, quod procedit ex ore dei. Nam panis celestis non solum est panis, sed et caro et verbum, que si sola esset, non haberet nutrimentum vite eterne. Quomodo autem ille panis sit caro, ait salvator: Panis, quem ego dabo, caro mea est. Que caro verbum est, prout Iohannes in evangelio ait: Et verbum caro factum est. Quod verbum deus erat, de quo idem: Et deus erat verbum. Et sic iste panis caro, verbum et deus est.[37]
>
> [Seek to feed your souls with this food and do not live without it, so you shall live forever. 'Man does not live by bread alone; but man lives by every word that proceeds from the mouth of the Lord.' For the bread of heaven is not only bread, but also flesh and word, and if it were only flesh, it would not feed us for eternal life. But the Saviour says in which way the bread is flesh: 'The bread that I will give is my flesh.' As John says in the Gospel, this flesh is the word: 'And the word became flesh.' The word was God, as the same says: 'And God was the word.' And in such a manner this bread is simultaneously flesh, word, and God.]

Hearing the 'word of God' thus coincides with receiving the body of Christ. Both forms of the word are present here – the word as a means of proclaiming the Gospel and the word as Christ himself, as present in the Eucharist – and demand confirmation in practice. In Charles' case,

---

35 Ms. XIX B 5, fol. 145r. Cf. Emler (ed.), *Fontes rerum Bohemicarum III*, 357.
36 See Ian Christopher Levy, 'The Eucharist and Canon Law in the High Middle Ages', in Ian Christopher Levy, Gary Macy and Kristen van Ausdall (eds), *A Companion to the Eucharist in the Middle Ages* (Leiden, 2012), 399–446, at 407.
37 Ms. XIX B 5, fol. 134v. Cf. Emler (ed.), *Fontes rerum Bohemicarum III*, 337.

this is the practice of proper execution of royal duty, not least in its 'literary' aspect.

Similar Johannine emphasis is also present in the Latin *Moralitates*, where the key verse 'In the beginning was the Word' connects meditative praise of the Virgin Mary, filled with standard material images of Mary as the 'well of salvation' or 'beryl of virginity', with Charles' homily on the Lucan pericope about the ten lepers.[38] The narrator in the *Vita Caroli* concludes the first chapter with a reflection on the toponym of Bethlehem as the 'house of bread' in which 'Christ, who is the real bread' was born. Based on what has been discussed above, this etymological conclusion again shows that objects and activities in this world can link us with eternal life through words and texts. The importance of material objects (mirror, bread, chalice, cross, Bethlehem) goes through the whole prologue and, eventually, becomes the key to the whole of the *Vita Caroli*.

The second chapter of the biography forms the transition from theological considerations to the central narrative and strengthens the already established link between the eternal word and the sublunar world. The narrator concludes his meditation on the nature of human existence[39] with an explicit rejection of simple contempt for the world, attributing the notion of the temporary realm as a meritless scene for transitory human affairs to people 'that have no faith' ('impii').[40] His readers and successors, on the contrary, have to act as material images of the perfectly valid word of Jesus Christ as the King of Heaven. As such, again, they can participate in His permanence even in this world, if only they follow His commandments in real life.

In the third chapter of the *Vita Caroli* the narrative proper begins. It has been repeatedly stated that Charles makes of himself and the ordeals that he survived a model for his descendants.[41] This exemplarity also includes his own life on the border between emptiness and fullness, between a word filled with the body of God and the empty word of sinners. Charles'

---

38 Nechutová, 'Die Moralitates', 160. For the importance of Luke 17:11–19 for the latter part of the *Moralitates*, where the compiler highlights the difference between the natures of human beings and angels that enables humanity to keep faith in its salvation, see Bernd-Ulrich Hergemöller, 'Black Sabbath Masses: Fictitious Rituals and Real Inquisitions', in Christoph Auffarth and Loren T. Stuckenbruck (eds), *The Fall of the Angels* (Leiden, 2004), 176–91, at 185–9.
39 Cf. Nagy, 'Memories of the Self', 162.
40 Emler (ed.), *Fontes rerum Bohemicarum III*, 337.
41 Cf. Hergemöller, *Cogor adversum te*, 76–7; Zdeněk Vašek, 'Výchova urozených dětí v českých zemích pozdního středověku v díle čtyř dobových autorů', *Acta universitatis Carolinae – Historia universitatis Carolinae pragensis* 56 (2016), 47–63, at 52–3; Tomáš Borovský, 'Život krále jako exemplum', in *Vita Caroli quarti* (Brno, 2016), 147–77.

rescue from death by poisoning in the fourth chapter points emphatically in this direction:

> In die autem pasche [...] intoxicata fuit familia mea, et ego divina me gracia protegente evasi, quia missa magna prolixe agebatur, et Communicaveram in eadem et nolui comedere ante missam. Cum autem irem ad prandium, dictum fuit michi, quod familia mea subito in infirmitatem ceciderit. Et specialiter illi, qui ante prandium comederant [...] Et sic aspiciens, vidi hominem pulchrum et agilem, quem non cognovi, qui deambulabat coram mensa fingens se mutum. De quo habita suspicione ipsum captivare feci. Qui post multa tormenta tercia die locutus est, et confessus fuit, quod ipse in coquina cibariis toxicum immiserat.[42]

> [On Easter Sunday [...], my retinue was poisoned. I escaped with my life under the gracious protection of God, because the solemn Mass continued for a long time and I went to receive the sacrament, so I did not want to eat before it. When I came to lunch, I was told that my retainers had suddenly fallen ill, and especially those who ate something before lunch [...] And as I looked around, I saw an attractive man whom I did not know, walking around the table in quick movements, pretending to be a mute. I began to suspect him and ordered his capture. After much torture, he broke silence on the third day and confessed to mixing poison into the meals in the kitchen.]

At the beginning, the young prince prefers the bread of God's word, obtained through the Mass and palpably present in the Eucharist, to a mundane meal, which, as it turns out, was poisoned by an agent of Azzo Visconti disguised as a mute servant. The mask of the poisoner is thus placed in the sphere of human speech and marked by an absence – a dumb person does not need to answer questions about intentions or motives and can move freely through Christian society, in which dumbness primarily means the inability to act proactively, to be 'mute as a stone' or a 'mute idol' that cannot do good or harm. Isidore of Seville characteristically connects the word 'mutus' with 'mitis', 'docile' ('Mitis, lenis et mansuetus et cedens inprobitatibus et ad sustinendam iniuriam tacens, quasi mutus').[43] Charles, instilled with the word of God which he

---

42 Ms. XIX B 5, fols 137r–137v. Cf. Emler (ed.), *Fontes rerum Bohemicarum III*, 342.
43 *Etymologiae* x.168. Isidore of Seville, *Etymologiarum sive originum libri XX*, ed. W.M. Lindsay (Oxford, 1911), vol. I, unpaginated. See also 2 Corinthians 12:2 and cf. Karl Steel, 'Muteness and Disembodied Difference: Three Case Studies', in Richard H. Godden and Asa Simon Mittman (eds), *Monstrosity, Disability, and the Posthuman in the Medieval and Early Modern World* (Cham, 2019), 305–14.

received through Communion, demonstrates his ability to 'cure' the 'mute' man, making him speak and proclaim his true allegiance, in a strikingly secular and ironic parallel to the miracles of curing the deaf or exorcising demons in the synoptic Gospels.[44] Human will is weak when connected not to the eternal sphere but to a body that feels pain. The determination to fake muteness, which can also be read as a parody of a regular vow of silence,[45] is eventually broken.

The real danger here did not stem from verbal simulacra but from the material reality of the poison used against the retainers – who did not show a proper ability to discern the importance of the materialized word of the Sacrament. The weakness of the verbal mask used by the assassin in comparison with the bodies and materials that surrounded him is demonstrated by Charles' ability to identify him based on his physical appearance (the prince had never seen him among his courtiers before) and by the confession made (perhaps timed symbolically) on the third day of bodily torture.

Another Eucharistic miracle which shows the inefficiency and emptiness of human speech when not anchored in an object is recounted in the fifth chapter, when a group of representatives of Verona, Parma, Reggio, and Modena conspire against John and Charles in 'a small chapel in the Diocese of Reggio':

> Fecerunt legere missa [*sic*] volentes iurare super corpore Christi illos tractatus firmos tenere. Actumque est, cum sacerdos sacramentum confecisset, cum elevacione in eadem missa obscuritas cum turbine venti valde magna facta est in ecclesia, ita quod omnes territi fuerunt. Et postquam lux reversa fuit, sacerdos ante se in altari corpus Christi non recepit. Tunc dolenter stabant omnes stupefacti. Et sic alterum inscipientes inventum est corpus domini ante pedes Marsilii de Rubeis, qui erat caput et doctor istius tractatus. Et tunc omnes una voce dixerunt: quod facere decrevimus deo non placet. Et sic dimisso quilibet ad propria remeavit.[46]

> [They ordered a Mass to be read and intended to swear their mutual fidelity on the body of Christ. And it came to pass, when the priest had sanctified the Sacrament at Mass, that there was a great darkness at the moment of the Elevation and the wind was blowing in the church, so that they were all afraid.

---

44 E.g., Mark 5:1–20, 7:36–7.
45 Cf. Alan R. Press, 'Quelques observations sur la chanson V de Guillaume IX: "Farai un vers pos mi sonelh"', in *Études de civilisation médiévale (IXe-XIIe siècles): Mélanges Edmond-René Labande* (Poitiers, 1974), 603–9.
46 Ms. XIX B 5, fols 138r–138v. Cf. Emler (ed.), *Fontes rerum Bohemicarum III*, 344.

And when there was light again, the priest did not find the body of Christ on the altar. So they all stood there miserably, wondering and looking at each other. The body of the Lord was found at the feet of Marsilius de Rubeis, who was the head and instigator of this pact. At that moment they all cried out: God does not like our intentions. And so they parted and returned to their dwellings.]

The conspiracy fell apart, its actors continued to serve Charles and eventually confessed their intentions to him, for which they were not punished in any way, and the prince kept silent about all this 'as if he knew nothing'. The intervention of the incarnate Word here means a sufficient guarantee of safety for the ruler and future fidelity by his subjects and allies.

Charles' devotion to the Eucharist is usually interpreted in the context of his conception of the holiness of the royal and imperial office and is often counted among the factors that influenced the onset of the Czech Reformation.[47] The point of the 'textocentric' reading presented here is to demonstrate that it also served as a paradigmatic object to speak about and to support and regulate human speech. In both examples, consideration of the incarnate Word in the form of the Eucharist stopped the processes that could have led to Charles' death, while standard human language repeatedly demonstrated its emptiness. It was shown that false muteness (and other discursive tricks) can be revealed by a turn away from speech to a particular body. The oath that was meant to connect a treacherous word with the Word of God fails and the Word of God itself, transformed in an object, miraculously rectifies the situation.

The empty and non-binding nature of human language is demonstrated further in the sixth chapter, in the case of John of Luxembourg:

> Post hec inimici treugas seu pacta minime tenuerunt. Et sic perditum fuit Castrum Papiense, quia non permiserunt ipsum inimici fulcire victualibus, prout promiserant. Sicque pater noster cum gentibus suis propter blanda verba et falsa promissa in pecuniis et expensis defecerunt.[48]
>
> [Subsequently, the enemies did not keep the truce and agreements, and so the castle of Pavia was taken, because the enemies would not allow it to be supplied with food, although

---

47   Cf. David R. Holeton, 'The Bohemian Eucharistic Movement in Its European Context', *Bohemian Reformation and Religious Practice* 1 (1996), 23–48; Olivier Marin, *L'archevêque, le maître et le dévot: Genèses du mouvement réformateur pragois (années 1360–1419)* (Paris, 2005), 458–66.
48   Ms. XIX B 5, fol. 139v. Cf. Emler (ed.), *Fontes rerum Bohemicarum III*, 346.

they had promised to do so. Thus, our father and his army lost
money and equipment through flattery and false promises.]

Charles' father put his trust in 'beautiful words' of flattery, that would
be broken as soon as John's enemies saw fit. Any damage caused to
the Luxembourg party in Pavia is nonetheless counterbalanced by the
motivation for prayer offered by this experience to the narrator of the *Vita
Caroli*. Similar dynamics can also be observed in the enigmatic first part
of the *Moralitates*, where a series of 16 'virtues of a believer' is ascribed to
an authoritative voice of a certain Sedechias, who 'was the first to receive
God's law and comprehend the wisdom' ('Sedechias primus fuit, per quem
nutu Dei lex recepta fuit et sapiencia intellecta').[49]

Although, as Jana Nechutová has shown, this Sedechias was not
originally meant to be identified with Zedekiah, the last king of Judah,
who saw his sons executed moments before his own eyes were put out, and
was held in Babylonian captivity for the rest of his life,[50] it is the image of
this king who was 'doing what was evil in the eyes of the Lord' and was
punished accordingly that might have come to the mind of an audience
confronted with this passage. As a witness to this association stands a
partial translation of the *Moralitates* into Czech, written probably in the
last quarter of the fourteenth century,[51] where Sedechias is unambiguously
referred to as a 'king':

> [Počíná se] skládanie veliké múdrosti a strachu božieho skrze
> téhož ciesaře šlechetného a krále českého, jimžto učí krále i
> kniežata i všecky obecně, a na potvrzenie všie šlechetnosti
> přivodí krále Sedechiáše.[52]

> [Here begins a treatise on the great wisdom and fear of God,
> written by the same noble Emperor and King of Bohemia, from
> which kings and princes and all others are to learn. And to
> confirm the value of this text, he brings in King Zedekiah.]

In the context of Charles' evaluation of material experience as the
foundation of verbal activity, the presence of this Old Testament king
who felt God's justice on his own body, was given time to contemplate
his misdeeds after his punishment, and thus became wise, makes a good
exemplum.[53]

---

49 Ms. XIX B 5, fol. 153r. Cf. Nechutová, 'Die Moralitates', 153.
50 Kings 25:1–7. Cf. Nechutová, 'Die Moralitates', 146–7.
51 Josef Emler (ed.), *Spisové císaře Karla IV.* (Prague, 1878), xix–xx.
52 Prague, Library of the National Museum (Knihovna Národního muzea), ms. V B 24, fol. 189v. Cf. Emler (ed.), *Spisové císaře Karla IV.*, 121.
53 Cf. Alois M. Haas, *Geistliches Mittelalter* (Freiburg, 1984), 242–6; Anneke B. Mulder-Bakker and Liz Herbert McAvoy, 'Experientia and the Construction of

THE *DALIMIL CHRONICLE* – FOUNDATIONAL SIN AND PERPETUAL COMPETITION

Mnozí pověsti hledají, / v tom múdře a dvorně činie, / ale že své země netbají, / tiem svój rod sprostenstvím vinie. / Nebo ež by sě do nich které cti nadieli, / své země by skutky jměli, / z nichž by svój rod vešken zvěděli, / a odkud by přišli, věděli. / Jáz těch kněh dávno hledaji / a veždy toho žádaji, / aby sě v to někto múdrý uvázal / a vše české skutky v jedno svázal. / A dotad sem toho žádal, / donidž sem toho právě nezbádal, / že sě v to nikte nechce otdati. / Pro to sě sám v to musím uvázati.[54]

[Many seek a reputation for themselves, and this is a courtly and wise endeavour. However, when people neglect their own land, they impute their kin with baseness. For if they had knowledge of the glorious deeds of their compatriots, they would be interested in them. For a long time, I searched for books and longed for someone to collect Czech deeds in one place. And my longing ended when I understood that no one was ready to do so. For this reason, I must burden myself with this task.]

With these lines begins the prologue to the rhymed *Dalimil Chronicle*, an anonymous Old Czech poem of 5569 lines (in the critical edition).[55] Completed probably between 1312 and 1314, it is the first text written in Old Czech that has come down to us from the beginnings of the Luxembourg rule in Bohemia.[56]

Experience in Medieval Writing: An Introduction', in Anneke B. Mulder-Bakker (ed.), *Women and Experience in Later Medieval Writing: Reading the Book of Life* (New York, 2009), 1–24.

54 Cod. Series nova 44, fol. 1r. Cf. Daňhelka et al. (eds), *Staročeská kronika*, vol. 1, 83. For the sake of clarity I follow Daňhelka's punctuation and diacritics and break the text into verses, signalled in the manuscript by a simple period. An alternative translation of this passage, together with a general introduction to it, is available in Pavlína Rychterová, 'The Chronicle of So-Called Dalimil and Its Concept of Czech Identity', in Pavlína Rychterová and David Kalhous (eds), *Historiography and Identity VI: Competing Narratives of the Past in Central and Eastern Europe, c. 1200–c. 1600* (Turnhout, 2021), 171–206.

55 Jiří Daňhelka, Karel Hádek, Bohuslav Havránek and Naděžda Kvítková (eds), *Staročeská kronika tak řečeného Dalimila: Vydání textu a veškerého textového materiálu*, 2 vols (Prague, 1988), vol. 1, 8.

56 Although the *Dalimil Chronicle* predates Charles' era, it remained popular through the rest of the Middle Ages, where it served various political purposes, and persisted into the age of printing with the edition prepared by Pavel Ješín of Bezdězec in 1620. The rich tradition of historical research on the Old Czech chronicle is recapitulated in Marie Bláhová, *Staročeská kronika tak řečeného*

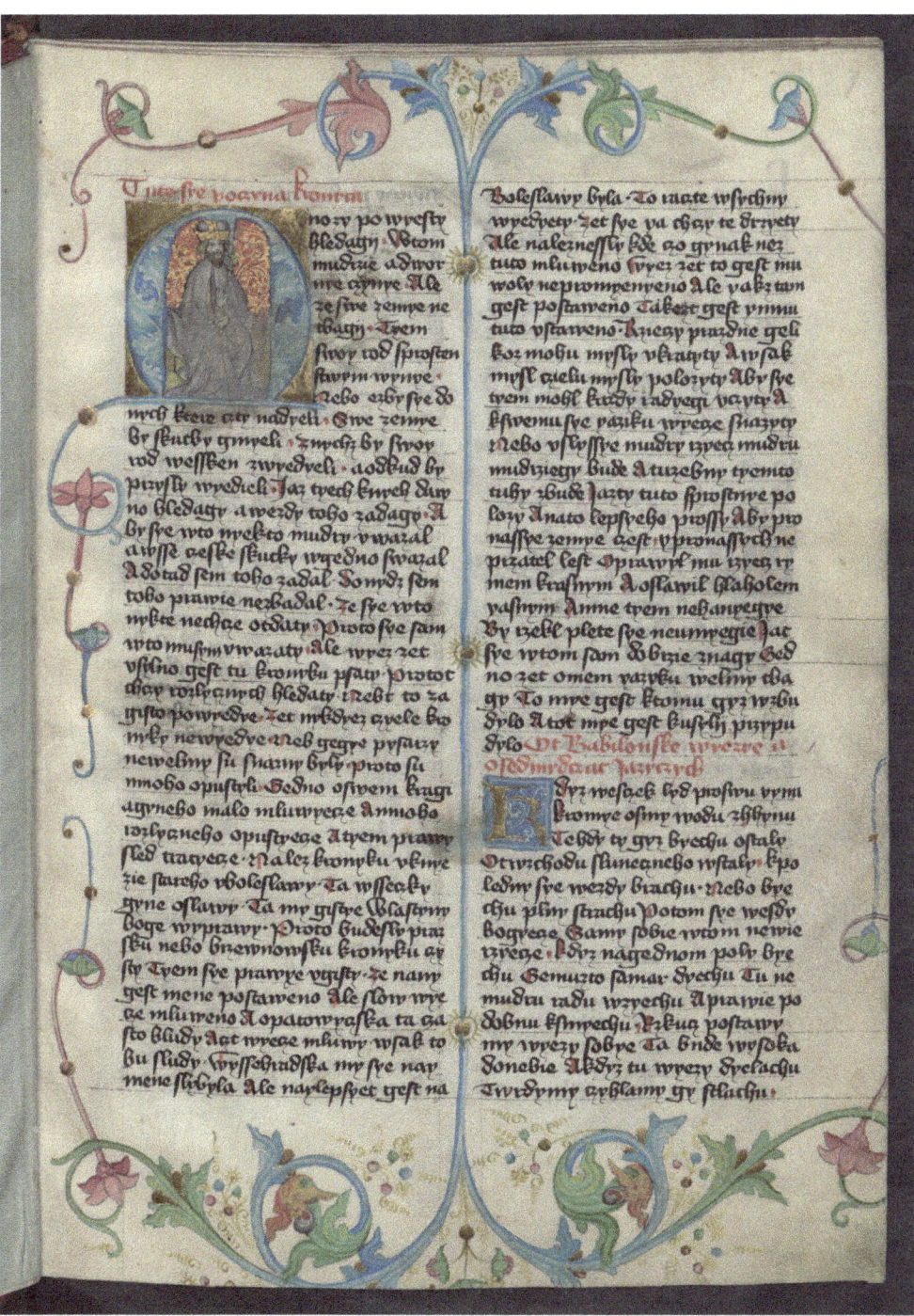

Fig. 6.2. Vienna, Österreichische Nationalbibliothek, Cod. Series nova 44, fol. 1r. Beginning of the *Dalimil Chronicle*.

As is evident already in the cited opening passage of the prologue, the anonymous author of the Old Czech chronicle, since the seventeenth century conventionally known as Dalimil,[57] introduces the readers to a world conceived as a sphere of perpetual discursive competition between individual actors. The key word of the prologue is a polyvalent term: 'pověst', which, as Jan Lehár points out (following a groundbreaking study by Miloslav Šváb), is most likely a genitive singular, not the accusative of the plural form.[58] As such, the term does not denote a narrative ('a story about something'), but 'one's reputation', that is, fame as the subject of conversation between people that enters a discursive sphere, a close equivalent of the Latin term 'fama'.[59] According to both scholars, the unnamed 'many' who 'seek a reputation for themselves' at the beginning of the prologue are in the first instance the poets, who, instead of Czech history, retell stories about Alexander the Great and other generic material and thus diminish the dignity of their own nation.

However, in addition to the producers of texts, their presumed addressees, in the case of the *Dalimil Chronicle* the Bohemian nobility,[60] can strive for 'reputation' as well – and thus they stand in the non-specific position of the 'many' in the first line. If we read the prologue in this way, it turns into a much more general critique of those who neglect their own history as a source of this 'reputation', even though they still wish to assert themselves in the discursive sphere, attaining a good name and surpassing their rivals' social standing. Such behaviour deserves criticism, partly because the anonymous author of the *Chronicle* is convinced about

---

Dalimila v kontextu středověké historiografie latinského kulturního okruhu a její pramenná hodnota (Prague, 1995). In English see, e.g., Marie Bláhová, 'Vernacular Historiography in Medieval Czech Lands', *Medievalia* 19 (2016), 33–65.

57 The inconclusive discussion about Dalimil's identity in Czech historiography is summarized in Adde-Vomáčka, *La Chronique de Dalimil*, 19–24. The name 'Dalimil of Meziříčí, canon of Boleslav' was for the first time listed by a priest, historian and 'the first true Czech author' Václav Hájek of Libočany among the sources of his imaginative chronicle printed in 1541. See Václav Hájek z Libočan, *Kronika česká*, ed. Jan Linka (Prague, 2013), 32. Tomáš Pešina of Čechorod (1629–80) then connected Hájek's Dalimil with the hitherto anonymous rhymed Old Czech chronicle.

58 Jan Lehár, *Nejstarší česká epika*, 74; Miloslav Šváb, *Prology a epilogy v české předhusitské literatuře* (Prague, 1966), 172–5. For the accusative reading, see e.g., Éloïse Adde-Vomáčka, *La Chronique de Dalimil*, 239: 'Beaucoup d'hommes collectent les histoires.'

59 Cf. Francesco Migliorino, 'La Grande Hache de l'histoire: Semantica della fama e dell'infamia', in I. Lori Sanfilippo and A. Rigon (eds), *Fama e publica vox nel Medioevo* (Rome, 2011), 3–22; Gianni Guastella, *Word of Mouth: Fama and Its Representations in Art and Literature from Ancient Rome to the Middle Ages* (Oxford, 2017), 53–65.

60 Adde-Vomáčka, *La Chronique de Dalimil*, 123–9.

the advantage of possessing definite knowledge of one's own history, and partly because discursive competition is not limited to individual human beings, but also includes families and communities. These communities, like persons, can be unjustly held in disdain, accused of 'baseness', inferiority or rudeness.[61] Such reluctance to use information about one's own origins in the competitive struggle of European politics weakens the position of all members of the community in question, because the fame of the tribe is easily forgotten if people remain silent about it.

In this way, the prologue turns out to be a meditation on a crime of the tongue based on an act of defaming one's own family, conditioned by ignorance of the past – a shortcoming that is disseminated so widely in the author's community that it requires a book to be written for it to be remedied. In the second part of the prologue the author turns towards the difference between fullness and emptiness in a way similar to the *Vita Caroli*. But this time the object of distinction is not a way of life, but words:

> Řěči prázdné, jelikož mohu, myšli ukrátiti, / a však mysl cělú myšli položiti, / aby sě tiem mohl každý radějí učiti / a k svému sě jazyku viece snažiti. / Nebo uslyšě múdrý řěč múdrú, múdřějí bude / a túžebný tiemto túhy zbude.[62]

> [I intend to reduce the empty words as much as I can. However, I want the meaning to be preserved in its entirety, so that everyone can learn from it and more strenuously work for their nation. Because if a wise man hears a wise speech, he becomes even wiser, and in the same way a sad man gets rid of his grief.]

The author desires to achieve the fullness of meaning, the chief feature of which, in contrast to emptiness, lies in the effect his words have on the audience. Here, the prologue returns to the topic of the pragmatic usefulness of language in a competitive world, mentioned in the first lines referring to reputation and its acquisition.[63] A chronicle composed of 'full' or 'wise' words motivates the recipients to read and apply what they read, encouraging them to defend their linguistic community ('jazyk', i.e., literally, their 'tongue') and changing them for the better, adding wisdom to the wise and relieving the sad from their sadness. This dual purpose emerges from the prologue as the principal reason for the chronicler's project.

---

61 Jaromír Bělič, Adolf Kamiš and Karel Kučera, *Malý staročeský slovník: Příručka ke studiu na filozofických a pedagogických fakultách* (Prague, 1979), 471.
62 Cod. Series nova 44, fol. 1r. Cf. Daňhelka et al. (eds), *Staročeská kronika*, vol. 1, 84.
63 Cf. Alfred Thomas, *Anne's Bohemia: Czech Literature and Society 1310–1420* (Minneapolis, MN, 1998), 50.

Then, in a way similar to the prologue of the paradigmatic oldest chronicle of the Czech lands, *Chronica Bohemorum*, written by Cosmas of Prague in 1119–25, the author constructs a *captatio benevolentiae* focused on his inability to write in an adorned style, inviting more proficient readers to correct and refine his text.[64] However, Cosmas sees the purpose of his work in ensuring that the events of individual years do not fall into oblivion. He creates a reservoir of historical memory imbued with Classical learning that connects the history of Bohemia to a wider Latinate context. The anonymous author of the *Dalimil Chronicle*, on the other hand, endeavours to motivate his listeners to take action in the discursive sphere.

Again, in a way already established by Cosmas' *Chronica Bohemorum*, the *Dalimil Chronicle* begins at the Tower of Babel, adding peculiar emphases to the well-known biblical story. The story is presented as the particular example of the power of language that the anonymous author tries to tap into:

> Když vešcek lid pro svú vinu / kromě osmi vodú zhynu, / tehdy ti, již biechu ostali, / od vzchodu slunečného vstali, / k poledni se veždy brachu; / nebo biechu plni strachu. / Po tom sě vešdy bojiece, / sami sobě v tom nevěřiece.[65]
>
> [When all but eight people perished for their sins in the water, the survivors moved from the east to the south. After the hardships they experienced, they were permanently afraid and did not believe in themselves.]

The survivors of the flood are afraid and insecure. Only gradually do they bolster their courage by taking joint action – the construction of a tower at the field of 'Samar'. According to the author, this collective decision was 'unwise' ('nemúdrá') and 'indeed ridiculous' ('právě podobná k smiechu'), yet it seemed to ameliorate the situation for the time being, as it allowed them to unite around building a solid artefact. Although they used bricks and mortar, the anonymous author emphasizes that the most powerful binding agent between them was human language itself, because it enabled them to cooperate.

This was made evident by God's intervention. Neither the building project itself nor familial ties between people could survive linguistic confusion, when everyone 'started to speak his own language'.[66] At that

---

64 Cosmas of Prague, *Chronica Boemorum*, ed. Bertold Bretholz (Berlin, 1923), 1–4. Cf. Šváb, *Prology a epilogy*, 177.
65 Cod. Series nova 44, fol. 1r. Daňhelka et al. (eds), *Staročeská kronika*, vol. 1, 98.
66 Cf. Vojtěch Bažant, 'Představy o počátcích národů v historické kultuře 14. a 15. století' (unpublished PhD thesis, Charles University Prague, 2020), 66–7.

moment, the competition of 'language communities' (roughly equivalent to Latin *nationes*)[67] and 'families' began. Since then, the situation, in the eyes of the chronicler, has been getting worse day by day. The general decline is illustrated in the third chapter, when a Croatian nobleman named Czech leaves his country after committing murder, leaving his six brothers there and taking a significant part of their servants and livestock with him. He is 'Forefather Czech', the founder of the community that the anonymous author writes for.

The story arc of the *Dalimil Chronicle* can be broadly conceived as a story of the eventual ascendancy of the Czech tongue. Following its migration to Bohemia, the community first establishes political institutions, adopts Christianity, and acquires royal dignity for its rulers. The original version of the chronicle most likely had 103 chapters, which can be meaningfully divided into four quarters of roughly equal size, marked by changes in the status of the Czech political community. The first quarter (chapters 1–24) depicts pagan antiquity, the second (chapters 25–49) encompasses the period of the princely reign until the time of Vratislav, who is crowned in chapter 50 when 'the Czechs received the greatest honour'. They are allowed to choose their own kings and are given a white lion with a single tail for their coat of arms. Then comes the third quarter, the conflict-filled epoch of kings and princes. Here, the chronicler focuses in particular on affinities and antipathies in a triangle set up between the rulers, the indigenous Czechs, and the German settlers in the country. At the coronation of the third Přemyslid king (Přemysl Ottokar I, crowned 1198, d. 1230) in chapter 75, the lion in the Bohemian coat of arms receives a second tail and for the remaining part of the text the situation noticeably changes. In this last quarter, rulers are no longer praised or condemned primarily according to their relationship to the Germans. Instead, in the stories of the last five Přemyslid kings we follow a regular rhythm of rise and subsequent decline and fall, the latter usually associated with the acceptance of the royal crown from the Emperor. After the assassination of Wenceslas III (r. 1305–6), the chronicler takes the reader through the final crisis. This ends with the coronation of John of Luxembourg, the new 'noble king'. In the last chapter, the author gives this king advice based on

---

67   David Kalhous, '"…rogans eum sibi in auxilium contra superbiam Teutonicorum": The Imaging of Theutonici in Bohemian Medieval Sources between the Ninth and Fourteenth Centuries', in Andrzej Pleszczynski and Grischa Vercamer (eds), *Germans and Poles in the Middle Ages: The Perception of the 'Other' and the Presence of Mutual Ethnic Stereotypes in Medieval Narrative Sources* (Leiden, 2021), 81–97.

the ancient prophecy of Princess Libuše, mentioned at the beginning of the chronicle.[68]

In various guises, the Czech actors in the *Dalimil Chronicle* replicate the events from the plain of Samar, establishing consulting bodies, offering advice to each other, and deliberating about the future course of events. The word 'counsel' ('rada') is repeated 75 times in the established text, almost twice more often than simple 'speech' ('řěč').[69] But these counsels usually end badly, leading to discord or demonstrating the inability of human actors to understand each other and transform words into positive action.

An exemplary account about such failure is placed at the beginning of the author's narrative of the War of the Maidens, the foundational conflict in the self-representation of the Czech community. In Cosmas' short, 'playful', and highly sexualized version of this story, based on Livy's account of the rape of the Sabine women,[70] the war leads to the definitive establishment of male dominance in gender relationships among the Czech people. The *Dalimil Chronicle*, on the other hand, offers a significantly expanded retelling in much darker colours:

> Po tom jejie kniené válku počechu / a právě podobnú k smiechu. / Nebo tomu za právo chtiechu, / aby takéž dievka zemí vládla / a mužie drželi by sě rádla. / Chtiece své řěči užiti, jechu sě hradu staviti. / Dievky hradu Děvín vzděchu / a Vlastu za knieni vzěchu. / Ta po všie zemi dievkám posla posly / řkúc: "Podbímy pod sě ty bradaté kozly!" [...] Kněz Přěmysl chtieše toho brániti, / páni řkú: "Pokusímy, co dievky mohú učiniti." / Vecě Přěmysl: "Viděch ve sně dievky, krev ločíce / a po všiej zemi jako vsteklé běhajíce. / Pro ten sen boji sě v zemi zlého." / Páni na smiech obrátichu sen knězě svého.[71]

> [After [Libuše's death], her ladies started a ridiculous war. They demanded that a maiden rule the country and that men plough the fields. Not wanting to engage in idle talk, the maidens set about building a castle and elected Vlasta as their Duchess.

---

68 In the Cod. Series nova 44, the first quarter covers fols 1r–6v, the second 6v–14r, the third 14r–22v, the fourth 22v–30v. Fols 29v–30v contain four additional chapters about the course of John's reign added by another author. Cf. Daňhelka et al. (eds), *Staročeská kronika*, vol. 1, 10–13 and 51–73.
69 Adde-Vomáčka, *La Chronique de Dalimil*, 399.
70 Lisa Wolverton, *Cosmas of Prague: Narrative, Classicism, Politics* (Washington, DC, 2015), 130–2. See also her English translation of the paragraph in question in Cosmas of Prague, *The Chronicle of the Czechs*, 50–2. Cf. Cosmas of Prague, *Chronica Boemorum*, 20–1.
71 Cod. Series nova 44, fols 2v–3r. Cf. Daňhelka et al. (eds), *Staročeská kronika*, vol. 1, 161–2.

> Then she sent envoys to maidens all around the country with the message: "Let's subdue those bearded bucks". [...] Duke Přemysl wanted to confront the maidens, but the lords said, "Let them try and see what they can do." Přemysl replied, "I saw in a dream a girl who drank blood and ran across the ground like a rabid animal. I am afraid that it brings an ill omen for the country." However, the lords laughed at their Duke's dream.]

This passage, the ninth chapter of the established text, is framed by two instances of laughter and speech. The ridiculous nature of the war itself, proclaimed at the beginning, is mirrored in the derisive laughter of the Czech lords in reaction to Přemysl's ominous dream about a girl drinking blood. This reaction renders the duke's warning to the nobles futile and his word powerless. As a result, war ensues. The maidens, on the other hand, are able to avoid idle talk, and proceed to action. They build a castle and organize an assembly, where they successfully elect an able leader, Vlasta, who then stirs the opposition to Přemysl's rule by her mere words. Her verbal acumen serves as another example of the potential of speech to bind objects and people together, but also to direct them towards evil – an aggression started for a wrong reason and in a wrong direction that enfeebles the wider community made up of both men and women.[72]

The foundational sin of pride invested in words results in a demonstration of the empowering potential of speech. But it is immediately followed by a (divinely sanctioned) collapse. It remains in force throughout the text and the chronicler is not going to provide any remedy to it – in the latter part of the *Dalimil Chronicle* the author observes how the speakers of the Czech language compete with Polish and (especially) German speakers, showing how fragile is their unity when faced with these external threats. Calls for action and admonishing tirades by nobles and dukes eventually fail in the same way as did Přemysl's warning against the rebellious maidens. It becomes evident that the situation necessitates a different solution. The use of narratives about the ancient history of Bohemia in the Latin chronicle of Přibík Pulkava (dated to the 1370s) represents an attempt at finding it.

---

72 For an interpretation of a later version of the *Dalimil Chronicle* through the lens of gender, cf. Martin Šorm, 'Reading About Men and For Men: Daughters Against Fathers, Violence and Wisdom in One Medieval Manuscript', in Daniela Rywiková and Michaela Antonín Malaníková (eds), *Premodern History Through the Prism of Gender* (Lanham, 2021), 161–95, at 165–72.

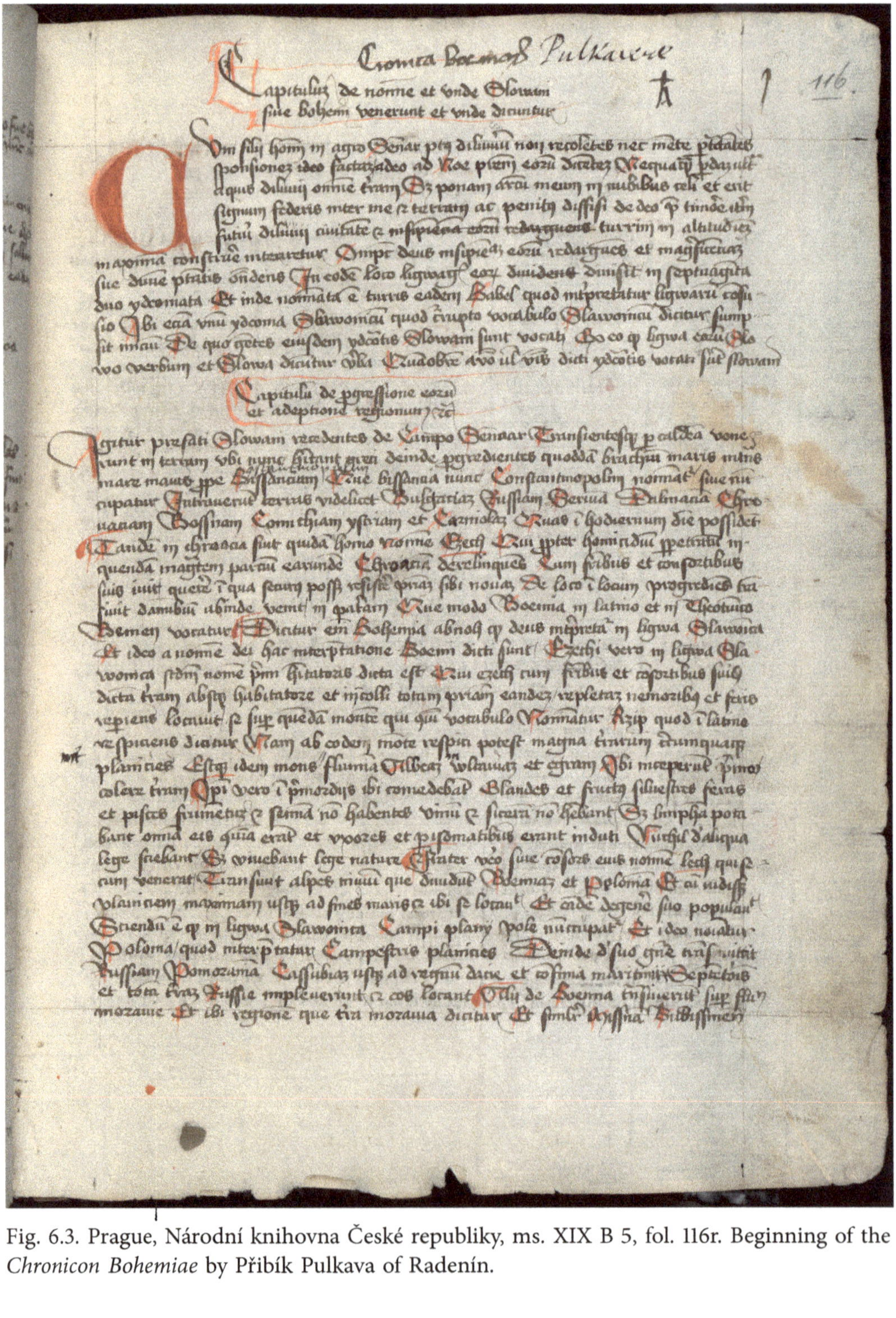

Fig. 6.3. Prague, Národní knihovna České republiky, ms. XIX B 5, fol. 116r. Beginning of the *Chronicon Bohemiae* by Přibík Pulkava of Radenín.

THE *CHRONICON BOHEMIAE* OF PŘIBÍK PULKAVA: MATTER AND MEMORY

A discrepancy, or even mutual exclusivity, between the ideological project of Charles IV and the confrontational linguistic 'nationalism' of the *Dalimil Chronicle* is evident and has often been noted by scholars.[73] For Dalimil, writing in Czech in the second decade of the fourteenth century, the struggle between the linguistic communities sharing the space of the Bohemian basin constitutes one of the basic elements of a conflicted world order that cannot be overcome. Conversely, the Latin texts produced at the court of Charles IV, the 'wise' and 'peace-making' king,[74] aim at a reconciliation of the particular communities around an active, embodied force, e.g., the mobile Eucharist in the story about the unsuccessful conspiracy in the fifth chapter of the *Vita Caroli*.

In Charles' autobiography it became clear that in the verbal sphere this unifying agent might well be Charles himself – as a king who is able, 'by the grace of God', to 'speak, write and read not only Czech, but also French, Lombard, German and Latin' and is 'as adept at each of these languages as at another' ('divina autem gracia non solum Boemicum, sed Gallicum, Lombardicum, Teutonicum et Latinum Ita loqui, scribere et legere scivimus, vt una lingwa istarum sicut altera ad scribendum, legendum, loquendum et intelligendum nobis erat apta.').[75] The opposing tongues can be learned and mastered by a sovereign human actor backed by God's grace, who can then use his power to put an end to strife.

I will now move on to a different, more general method of powerful, pacifying words – in particular, the 'full' words that the author of the *Dalimil Chronicle* was so keen to convey to the readers. This method was employed in the *Chronicon Bohemiae*, commonly ascribed to Přibík Pulkava of Radenín (d. before 1380), a schoolmaster at the collegiate church

---

73 Cf. Martin Nodl, *Tři studie o době Karla IV.* (Prague, 2006), 65–106. For a more extreme view, presenting the Cambridge Manuscript of the *Dalimil Chronicle* as a direct opposite to the *Maiestas Carolina*, see Radko Šťastný, 'Cambridžský rukopis Dalimilovy kroniky a doba Karla IV.', *Česká literatura* 31 (1983), 385–400, at 394 and 399. See also Daňhelka's sober-minded critique of Šťastný's thesis in Daňhelka et al. (eds), *Staročeská kronika*, vol. 1, 29.

74 Eva Schlotheuber, 'Der Ausbau Prags zur Residenzstadt und die Herrschaftskonzeption Karls IV.', in Markéta Jarošová (ed.), *Prag und die grossen Kulturzentren Europas in der Zeit der Luxemburger (1310–1437): Internationale Konferenz aus Anlaß des 660. Jubiläums der Gründung der Karlsuniversität in Prag, 31. März – 5. April 2008* (Prague, 2008), 601–21. Lena Oetjens, 'Charles IV and Learned Order: The Discourse of Knowledge in *Der meide kranz*', *Acta Universitatis Carolinae – Historia Universitatis Carolinae Pragensis* 55 (2015), 141–51, at 142. Cf. Antonín, *The Ideal Ruler*, 293.

75 Ms. XIX B 5, fol. 140v. Cf. Emler (ed.), *Fontes rerum Bohemicarum III*, 348.

of St Giles in Prague, but according to some manuscripts also to Charles himself.[76] Přibík uses the Old Czech *Dalimil Chronicle* as the principal source for his narrative about the pagan prehistory of Bohemia. In his reworking of Dalimil's material, his quest for common points is grounded in material reality. This resonates with the notion of materiality as the essential component of an effective speech evident in the *Vita Caroli*, but in Přibík it takes on a more secular tinge.

In terms of popularity, Přibík's *Chronicon Bohemiae* is without doubt the most successful historical text produced in Luxembourg Bohemia. A recent survey by Marie Bláhová counts no fewer than 44 manuscript witnesses divided between six redactions of the Latin text, an Old Czech translation (prepared most probably already in the 1370s, quite possibly by the author himself), two fifteenth-century German translations, and various abridged versions in Czech and Latin.[77] Of these manuscripts, 37 were written before 1526, the year of ascension of the Habsburg dynasty to the throne that customarily marks the end of the Middle Ages in Bohemia. The rest are more recent copies that (together with the reception of the chronicle by historians between the fifteenth and eighteenth centuries) testify to its unparalleled and durable impact on the literature in and about the Czech lands.

Being a chronicler of the Czechs, Přibík follows roughly the same sequence of events as Dalimil. At first glance it becomes obvious that he paid more attention to telling the ancient history of Bohemia, in contrast to his treatment of more recent history. At the beginning of the chronicle, he richly depicted pagan antiquity as well as the time of the first Christian princes and saints, weaving the legend of St Wenceslas, written by Charles IV himself, into his text.[78] With the passage of time, his text becomes less interesting in terms of narrative and contains increasing numbers of documents copied directly from the archive of the Bohemian Crown, to which the author had access thanks to Charles' patronage.[79] As a storyteller, Přibík makes his presence felt again at the end of the chronicle, when he recounts the adventures of Elisabeth, the future wife of John of Luxembourg. In some manuscripts, which according to Marie Bláhová represent the fifth and sixth redaction, this final part, after the murder of Wenceslaus III and the extinction of the Přemyslids in the

---

76 Žůrek and Rychterová, 'Slavonic and Czech Identity in the *Chronicon Bohemiae*', 228. Cf. Bláhová, 'Recepce České kroniky', 54–5.
77 Bláhová, 'Recepce České kroniky', 53–72. Cf. Žůrek and Rychterová, 'Slavonic and Czech Identity in the *Chronicon Bohemiae*', 227.
78 Jana Nechutová, *Die lateinische Literatur des Mittelalters in Böhmen* (Köln, 2007), 166.
79 Žůrek and Rychterová, 'Slavonic and Czech Identity in the *Chronicon Bohemiae*', 228–9.

male line, forms a separate, second book of the *Chronicon*.[80] The most comprehensive version of the text reaches up to the year 1330 and, besides Czech history, incudes brief notes on the history of Brandenburg, a new crown land which Charles acquired in 1374. In the Prague manuscript XIX B 5, the *Chronicon* is brought up to the year 1326.

The pivotal difference between the *Dalimil Chronicle* and the *Chronicon* reveals itself early on, in Přibík's retelling of the Babel myth, where the author, in comparison with Dalimil, points to another sort of failure:

> Cum filii hominum in agro Sennar post diluvium non recolentes nec mente pertractantes sponsionem factam a deo ad Noe, patrem eorum, dicentem: Nequaquam perdam ultra aquis diluvii omnem carnem Et ponam arcum meum in nubibus celi, et erit signum federis inter me et terram: ac penitus diffisi de deo pre timore iterum futuri diluvii civitatem et turrim in altitudinem maximam construere niterentur; Omnipotens deus insipienciam eorum redarguens et magnificam sue divine potestatis ostendens In eodem loco linguas eorum divisit in septuaginta duo ydiomata.[81]

> [The sons of men who settled in Sennar after the flood forgot and did not reflect on the promise that their ancestor Noah had received from God when God said, "I will not destroy all the flesh with the waters of the flood, but will build my rainbow in the clouds of heaven, and it will be the sign of the Covenant between me and the earth." On the contrary, they were thoroughly separated from God, and for fear of a new flood they tried to build a city with a very high tower. God Almighty disapproved of their folly and showed the majesty of His power at that place when He divided their tongues into seventy-two languages.]

In this version of the story, based on the exegetical tradition which follows Josephus Flavius and his *Antiquitates Judaicae* (which was in Přibík's time widely disseminated by the *Postillae perpetuae* of Nicholas of Lyra),[82] the

---

80 Bláhová, 'Přibíka Pulkavy z Radenína Kronika česká', 573–7.
81 Ms. XIX B 5, fol. 153r. Cf. Josef Emler and Jan Gebauer (eds), 'Přibíka z Radenína řečeného Pulkavy Kronika česká', in *Fontes rerum Bohemicarum V* (Prague, 1893), 1–326, at 3–4. I follow the punctuation of the edition while keeping the capitalization of the manuscript.
82 Flavius Josephus, *Opera: Græce et latine*, ed. Guilelmus Dindorfius (Paris, 1845), vol. 1, 13–14. Cf. Phillip Michael Sherman, *Babel's Tower Translated: Genesis 11 and Ancient Jewish Commentary* (Leiden, 2013), 153–94. For an overview of the wide reception of the *Antiquitates* in the Middle Ages, see Karen M. Kletter, 'The Christian Reception of Josephus in Late Medieval Antiquity and the Middle Ages', in Honora H. Chapman and Zuleika Rodgers (eds), *A Companion to Josephus*

fracture of the unity of humankind was caused primarily by humanity's obliviousness and its resulting inability to act in accordance with God's word as represented by the divine promise of a flood-free future. Přibík puts this obliviousness in an even worse light by including a selective citation of Genesis 9:11–13, where God establishes the rainbow as an eternal symbol, and then showing that people are not able to conform to their post-diluvial relationship with the Lord even though this visual sign arises again and again before their eyes, reminding them that God is still determined to keep his promise.[83]

In the *Dalimil Chronicle*, the Tower of Babel was put forward as the principal artefact erected through the sheer power of human speech, but left unfinished, thereby demonstrating the inability of people to use the instrument of language well. Přibík, on the other hand, places the rainbow, the product of a divine utterance, at the beginning of history. Instead of being unable to speak, people are unable to listen and take note.

As in the *Dalimil Chronicle*, the situation of humanity gradually worsens in Přibík's narrative. In Dalimil's text, the breakdown of the binding power of language leads to the disintegration of societies and families. It initiates the universal competition among humans that spreads in an ominously inconsistent manner, sometimes seemingly abating, then flaring up again with renewed vigour. For Přibík, such disintegration and decay affect language itself. The name of the community that lies in the spotlight of his text serves as an exemplar of this process at the end of the first chapter: 'There [i.e., at the Tower of Babel] originated also the singular Slavonic language, which is called Slavonic by corruption, which is why the peoples who speak this same language are called Slowanii because their language renders "verbum" as "slovo" and "verba" as "slova"' ('Ibi eciam unum ydioma Slawonicum, quod corrupto vocabulo Slawonicum dicitur, sumpsit inicium, De quo gentes eiusdem ydiomatis Slowani sunt vocati [...] per lingwa eorum Slowo verbum et Slowa dicuntur verba').[84] The original vowel is lost and replaced by another, which moves the shape of the Latin form of the word further from its Czech etymology. When speech moves between different languages, it evolves towards unintelligibility and unreliability.

(Chichester, 2016), 368–81. An early modern edition of Nicholas' commentary on Genesis is available online: <http://digital.ub.uni-duesseldorf.de/urn/urn:nbn:de:hbz:061:1-34622> [accessed 9 March 2023]. Here see fol. 59r.

83 Cf. John Stewart, *The Emergence of Subjectivity in the Ancient and Medieval World: An Interpretation of Western Civilization* (Oxford, 2020), 62.

84 XIX B 5, fol. 86r. Cf. Emler and Gebauer (eds), 'Přibíka z Radenína řečeného Pulkavy Kronika česká', 4.

A similar process is present in the next chapter, which deals with Forefather Czech/Bohemus, his crime in Croatia, and his search for a new land:

> Dicitur enim Bohemia a buoh, quod deus interpretatur in lingua Slawonica. Et ideo a nomine Dei hac interpretatione Boemi dicti sunt. Czechi vero in lingwa Slawonica secundum nomen primi habitatoris dicta est. Qui Czech [...] locavit se super quendam montem, qui communi vocabulo Nominatur Rzip quod in latino respiciens dicitur.[85]

> [The name Bohemia stems from 'buoh', which is how the word 'deus' is translated into the Slavonic language. Thus, according to this interpretation, the Bohemians took their name from the name of God. Then, they have the name 'Czechi' in the Slavonic language after its first inhabitant. Czech [...] climbed on a mountain that is by a common name called Rzip, which in Latin means 'looking around'.]

The current language, then, appears as a corrupted and ambivalent entity. The names of natural phenomena are usually explained by Přibík as stemming from their material features, e.g., Rzip (Říp, a mountain to the north-west of Prague) from its suitability for looking around or Polonia from the word for field, 'pole', whereas names of human entities and communities are closely connected to the verbal sphere shared by various tongues and speakers where nothing, however, is certain. Thus, in one language the same community can be denoted by God (through the word 'buoh' in 'Bohemus') and by a fugitive murderer (through the connection to the 'forefather Czech' and his story).

A solution for linguistic ambivalence and the general instability of the discursive sphere lies in the imitation of God's initial act of transmuting a word into a sensually perceptible object that would serve as a material symbol. As was shown in the case of the rainbow, a mere visualization is not enough. Forgetful and fallen humanity needs something that can be touched and/or consumed. This connects Přibík's notion with Charles' emphasis, in the *Vita Caroli*, on the Eucharist as the most productive and useful embodied form of the Word available to inhabitants of this world. This is demonstrated compellingly in the chronicler's version of the War of the Bohemian Maidens. It is, again, based largely on the *Dalimil Chronicle*, but with a few conspicuous twists:

> Defuncta lybussa et Sepulta in dicto castro, elevavit se in fastum quedam virgo nomine Wlasta, que cupiditate dominandi, prout

---

85   XIX B 5, fol. 86r. Cf. Emler and Gebauer (eds), 'Přibíka z Radenína řečeného Pulkavy Kronika česká', 4.

quondam lybussa, domina sua, rexerat, secrete convocavit ad se alias virgines et dominas dicens eis: Domina nostra Lybussa rexit istud regnum, dum viveret; quare ego non regerem una vobiscum terram et regnum? Nam omnia secreta sua scio, et sortilegia et auguria sororis sue Tetcze, et medicinas et herbas sanitatis et infirmitatis agnosco velut biela, soror eius. [...] Si nunc vultis mecum coniurare et me iuvare, Spero, quod dominabimini viris in omnibus. Tunc omnes responderunt: Placet, tunc dedit eisdem virginibus confectum potum, ut odio haberent maritos, fratres et amicos et quidquid masculini sexus esset.[86]

[When Libuše died and was buried in said castle [Libuš], a maiden named Vlasta arose, motivated by pride and longing to rule in the same way as her mistress, the deceased Libuše. She secretly summoned the other ladies and maidens and said to them: While our Lady Libuše lived, she ruled in this kingdom. Why should I not rule with you in the land and the kingdom? I know all her secrets, as well as the magic and prophecies of her sister Tetka, together with her medicines and herbs of health and of sickness like her sister Běla. [...] Because of that, if you want to ally with me now and support me, I have hope that you will subjugate the men in every manner. All replied: Agreed. So, she gave a skilfully crafted potion to the maidens, making them hate their husbands, brothers and friends and all male creatures.

The initial part of the story remains the same in all redactions of Přibík's *Chronicon Bohemiae*.[87] The identification of pride on the part of the maidens as the principal cause of war remains the same as in the *Dalimil Chronicle*. So does their nostalgia for Libuše's reign. The maidens remember the days when Libuše led the people without her male consort Přemysl, the first duke, accompanied only by her two sisters. This mnemonic feat alone makes them more powerful than their male adversaries. In comparison with Dalimil, the motif of a council where women deliberate on Vlasta's arguments, and their oratory skill, gathers even more emphasis in the *Chronicon Bohemiae*. The political and moral aspect of the matter is nevertheless immediately diluted by the use of the potion with the effect of stirring up the female community and thereby making war inevitable. In later redactions of the text, the materiality of Vlasta's potion is established

---

86 Ms. XIX B 5, fol. 87v. Cf. Emler and Gebauer (eds), 'Přibíka z Radenína řečeného Pulkavy Kronika česká', 9.
87 Cf. Marie Bláhová, 'Translations of Historiographical Writings Composed and Read in the Czech Lands up to the Hussite Revolution and Their Audience', *Prague Papers on the History of International Relations* (2018), 44–57, at 48–9.

even more firmly by an emphasis on its sensory properties – it is its 'taste' ('sapor') that causes the virgins to stubbornly hate all males.[88]

In the recounting of the events that lead to the war between Vlasta's virgins and the males led by the duke Přemysl in the seventh chapter of the *Chronicon Bohemiae*, the magical potion is immediately complemented with the chalice of blood in Přemysl's oneiric vision that was already present in the *Dalimil Chronicle*. This chalice, however, remains an intangible image enclosed in one man's dream. It depends on Přemysl's communication skills whether or not this omen can successfully be used to warn the community. In Přibík's version, the duke fails in the same way as in the Old Czech text ascribed to Dalimil. In contrast with the maidens, the Bohemian lords are evidently unable to remember the days of Libuše's female rule and therefore underestimate the danger that Vlasta poses for their status.

In both chronicles, as well as in Cosmas' original version, the men finally prevail not through their military strength but thanks to a ruse devised by Přemysl, which in the *Chronicon Bohemiae* forms a neat *inclusio* with Vlasta's initial use of the potion. In Dalimil's Old Czech rhymes, the men pretend to negotiate for peace, lure the maidens inside Vyšehrad Castle, violate them, and deprive them of their courage through the violent imposition of male sexual dominance. Vlasta is then overcome with rage and leads the female army into an ill-prepared battle where she is defeated and killed.[89]

Přibík's version is less overtly sexualized but more radical. Instead of sadistic sensuality, it emphasizes eating, drinking, and gluttony. The female envoys are not raped but made passive at tables laden with drinks and delicacies that they discover in the seemingly empty castle. When the drunkenness makes the maidens forget their military training and neutralizes the effect of Vlasta's potion ('ebrietatis sunt vicio pregravate'), the men rush out of their hideouts and at Přemysl's command execute all the maidens.[90] This particular retelling of the War of the Maidens thus

---

88 See, e.g., the manuscript I D 10 of the National Library (Národní knihovna České republiky) in Prague, which contains the most complete and probably final Latin version of the *Chronicon Bohemiae* (fol. 111v): 'Que Wlasta debitum nacta tempus virginibus propinavit potum artificiose confectum, cuius saporis virtute omnes eedem virgines quosque viros, fratres, consanguineos et amicos, quidquid masculini sexus erat, immaniter usque ad mortem odire ceperunt.'
89 Daňhelka et al. (eds), *Staročeská kronika*, 233 and 237–8. Cf. John M. Klassen, *Warring Maidens, Captive Wives, and Hussite Queens: Women and Men at War and Peace in Fifteenth-Century Bohemia* (Boulder, CO, 1999), 18–19; Thomas, *Anne's Bohemia*, 60–1.
90 Ms. XIX B 5, fol. 89r. Cf. Emler and Gebauer (eds), 'Přibíka z Radenína řečeného Pulkavy Kronika česká', 12.

ends with a demonstration that the word of an exemplary political speaker and role model for future rulers of Bohemia, Duke Přemysl, is eventually catalysed into material reality. The catalyst takes the form of food and alcohol that act on the bodies of the girls and finally cause their demise.

Dalimil had already written about drinks affecting a person. In his chronicle, Vlasta instructs her maidens to maintain 'moderation in drinking' ('v pití smieru'), and also exhorts them not to be afraid of men who 'get drunk every night' ('zapíjejí sě na každú noc'). Initially, Dalimil's version of the girls' war thus appears as a conflict of sober, temperate women against drunken men, likened in their intemperance to 'bearded he-goats' ('Podbímy pod sě ty bradaté kozly!').[91] In contrast to Dalimil, Přibík's chronicle is more about the competition between two drinks in a woman's body. Alcohol prevails over Vlasta's magical potion and as such serves as a paradoxical antidote to a competing material object on the side of the enemy. The prerequisite to this success lies in a new, successful connection of material reality and memory among Přemysl's subjects. The Bohemian lords eventually start to take female strength seriously when they see the carnage of war all around. The maidens, on the other hand, become susceptible to Přemysl's might when they are given something to drink.

PŘEMYSL'S HAZEL – A PERPETUAL MIRACLE

How the thoughts outlined in the initial, exemplary part of Přibík's chronicle can be solved in the extratextual world in the context of Charles' self-representational project can be demonstrated by a privilege given in Prague on 12 May 1359.[92] In it, the king exempts a group of peasants in the village of Stadice near Ústí nad Labem and all their future heirs from levies and other obligations. Three tracts of land in their tenancy are reserved for the royal domain and identified as the field that was once tilled by the founder of the Přemyslid dynasty, Přemysl the Ploughman –

---

91 All quotations from Cod. Series nova 44, fol. 3r. Cf. Daňhelka et al. (eds), *Staročeská kronika*, vol. 1, 161 and 172.

92 Original lost, copy preserved in the National Museum Archive (Archiv Národního muzea) in Prague, collection Stadice. See Bedřich Mendl and Milena Linhartová (eds), *Regesta diplomatica nec non epistolaria Bohemiae et Moraviae* VII/1 (Prague, 1954), 138–9. Cf. Kateřina Engstová, 'Marignolova kronika jako obraz představ o moci a postavení českého krále', *Mediaevalia historica Bohemica* 9 (1999), 77–94, at 78–9; Robert Antonín, '"De sublimacione principum seu rectorum": Paměť o počátcích panovnického rodu Přemyslovců v proměnách věků', *Český lid* 101 (2014), 335–58, at 351; Marie Bláhová, 'The Genealogy of the Czech Luxembourgs in Contemporary Historiography and Political Propaganda', in E. Kooper and S. Levelt (eds), *The Medieval Chronicle IX* (Amsterdam and New York, 2014), 1–32, at 9.

the future Duke Přemysl of the chronicles – when envoys came to acknowledge him as the first Czech duke. One of the magical acts that the new ruler performed at that moment was to drive the hazel-wood prod with which he commanded his oxen into the ground, in accordance with the prophecy of Libuše, who had instructed the envoys regarding the signs by which they were to recognize their duke. The prod immediately turned green and grew into a hazel bush, which, in accordance with the privilege, still flourishes at that place.

The privilege is composed as a response to a request from two brothers, whose family had allegedly lived in Stadice from time immemorial, cultivating the land connected with Přemysl's legend. 'According to the testimonies of the chronicles and books of the Bohemian land and kingdom' ('prout hec in gestis et libris cronicis terre et regni Bohemie'), this family had been free from all feudal duties since the time of Přemysl, the first Czech duke, 'called from a plough and solemnly promoted to his position as Duke of Bohemia' ('de post aratro assumpti et in ducem Bohemie magnifice sublimati'). The situation changed only recently, with the brothers being deprived of their liberties 'unjustly and perhaps also because of gross and lazy ignorance' ('per iniuriam et forte ignoranciam forsitan crassam et supinam') on the part of the 'prince of good memory', John, the King of Bohemia, and the supreme marshal of the Kingdom of Bohemia Henry of Lipá. Charles' privilege manifestly reinstates their ancient freedom. The only obligation of the beneficiaries is to nurture Přemysl's hazel and to supply its entire yield every year 'to us and to our successors, the Kings of Bohemia'.[93]

Therefore, ordinary nuts are to be regularly consumed at the summit of the pyramid of power. Every year, they shall renew afresh the bond of the Czech kings to Stadice, which Charles' father had forgotten.

The product of Přemysl's wonder-working with a rod becomes 'mirandum', an object to be looked at and sensually perceived.[94] This 'mirandum', connected to the sphere of worldly dominion, forms an analogue to the sacral miracles, which, according to Augustine's conception, serve to remind humanity of the power of God as demonstrated through the creation of the world out of nothing. People buried under the weight of habit and ignorance tend to forget the miraculous nature of everything

---

93 'Volumus postremo et statuimus perpetuo, ut prefati heredes ipsorumque liberi et heredes omnes et singulas nuces, quas dicte virge coruli produxerint, nobis et successoribus nostris, Bohemie regibus, teneantur annis singulis fideliter presentare.' Mendl and Linhartová (eds), *Regesta*, 139.
94 For illustration of an analogous process in French sources, see Martin R. Kauffmann, 'The image of St Louis', in Anne J. Duggan (ed.), *Kings and Kingship in Medieval Europe* (London, 1993), 265–86.

that is, and their memory needs perpetual refreshing.[95] The nuts similarly remind their consumers about the miraculous roots of the Bohemian monarchy and of the salvific paradigms of government associated with Přemysl, the original legislator of the Bohemian polity.

The story of Přemysl the Ploughman formed a part of the vivid cultural milieu of fourteenth-century Bohemia. Stadice served as a 'place of memory' that was widely known and referred to.[96] Přibík Pulkava reveals the importance of Přemysl's hazel for Charles' project, connecting it explicitly not only with a unique miraculous occurrence but also with the continuous production of the 'miranda' each autumn. He does so when he assures the readers that Přemysl's rod 'immediately bloomed' and sprouted three branches:

> Ex quibus ramis duo mox arefacti sunt et tercius crevit ac dilatatus est valde, prout usque in presentem diem videri potest, fructum nucum annis singulis producens, cuius fructus per multos annos non deperit nec putrescit, nec eciam unquam vermis in eisdem nucibus invenitur.[97]

> [Two of the branches soon withered and the third grew and became very large. It can still be seen today. Every year it bears nuts. Its fruit does not spoil or rot for many years, nor can any worm ever be found in it.]

However, apart from being a place of memory, Stadice and its hazel bush have also become a place of guilt and one of the principal examples of the foundational sin at work during the reign of King Wenceslas I (r. 1230–53):

> Pak sě kněz korunova / a svú čest tiem vši osnova. / I poče král se psy honiti / a se psy v svém domu za obyčej bydliti. / Honě v lesě, oko ztrati / a v lesě jě sě přěbývati. / Na Křivokláte přěbýváše / a o Praze nic netbáše. / Ale že se psy rád honieše, / a snad pro to jej noha i boléše. / Jakž sě na královstvo světi, / jě sě svým rodem styděti. / Káza s Stadic svój rod rozehnati / a tu ves Němcóm dáti. / Páni pod sobú větev podtěchu, / že

---

95 Cf. Benedicta Ward, *Miracles and the Medieval Mind: Theory, Record and Event, 1000–1215* (Aldershot, 1987), 3–19; Chris Gousmett, 'Creation Order and Miracle According to Augustine', *Evangelical Quarterly* 60 (1988), 217–40.
96 Cf. Nodl, *Tři studie o době Karla IV.*, 81–2; Vojtěch Bažant, 'Příběhy stadického krále: Několik pohledů na jednu událost', in Eva Doležalová and Petr Sommer (eds), *Středověký kaleidoskop pro muže s hůlkou: Věnováno Františku Šmahelovi k životnímu jubileu* (Prague, 2016), 13–25, at 14–16.
97 Ms. XIX B 5, fol. 87r. Cf. Emler and Gebauer (eds), 'Přibíka z Radenína řečeného Pulkavy Kronika česká', 7.

královi z toho nic nevececbu. / Neb uzřě, že počě péčě nejmieti
na pány; / rozděli Němcóm své dědiny v lány.⁹⁸

[Then the prince crowned himself and thus established his
glory. He was often hunting with dogs and lived with them
in one house; he even lost one eye during a hunt. He stayed
in the woods, especially at Křivoklát Castle, and did not
care about Prague. His fondness for dwelling with dogs was
perhaps the reason for his pain in a leg. As soon as he became
King, he became ashamed of his family, ordered the Czechs to
be expelled from Stadice, and gave the village to the Germans.
The Lords did not admonish the King for that and in that
way they cut the branch on which they were sitting, because
when the King saw that there was no need for him to consider
the Lords' counsel, he distributed his hereditary land to the
Germans.]

Ignorance of one's own history, bringing shame on the family, and
obliviousness to important matters and the duties of a ruler combine
in this story, which strongly resonates with the prologue of the *Dalimil
Chronicle*. Charles' conception of kingship, on the other hand, combines
sacral and secular histories and duties in a mission that ultimately points
towards the salvation of the kingdom. In order for this to be achieved, the
eradication of such ignorance attains paramount importance. Apart from
the *Vita*, this is also pointedly expressed in his *Ordo ad coronandum regem
Bohemorum*, in a prayer for God's uplifting grace that will enable the
king's subjects to 'feel His (i.e., God's) coming through him (i.e., the king)'
('per eum tuum in nobis adesse senciamus adventum').⁹⁹ The inadequate
use of human language, which is as powerful as it is destructive, along
with the universal and perpetual strife that informs the discursive sphere
of the *Dalimil Chronicle*, represent a challenging obstacle, especially in
the multilingual environment of the Kingdom of Bohemia that Charles
attempted to cultivate. In confrontation with it, the Emperor demonstrates
that his power feeds from two sources – his universal, imperial ambitions
and a local base, secured by his Přemyslid lineage. In other words, the
efficacy of his word as a ruler, teacher, and preacher facing the sins of
his community rests on two miraculous objects: the Word that regularly

---

98   Cod. Series nova 44, fol. 23r. Daňhelka et al. (eds), *Staročeská kronika*, vol. 2, 304.
99   Ms. XIX B 5, fol. 157v. Cf. Josef Cibulka, *Český korunovační řád a jeho původ* (Prague, 1934), 78. For the late fourteenth-century Old Czech translation, see Martina Jamborová (ed.), *Korunovační řád Karla IV.* (Prague, 2020), 88. Cf. Václav Žůrek, 'Korunovační řád Karla IV. jako ritualizovaný panovnický program', *Časopis národního muzea – řada historická* 176 (2007), 105–43, at 132.

becomes flesh during the Mass, and the nuts produced by a hazel bush in a field somewhere in the north-west of Bohemia that find their way to the royal table.[100]

---

[100] This essay was written with the support of Research Development Program RVO 68378068 and finalized with the support of the Czech Science Foundation as part of project GA ČR 23-07559S (Verbal Efficacy in Literature of Medieval Bohemia). During the work on this text, use was made of the Czech Literary Bibliography (ORJ identifier: 90243; https://www.vyzkumne-infrastruktury.cz/en/social-sciences-and-humanities/czech-literary-bibliography/) and of the Czech Medieval Sources online database (http://cms.flu.cas.cz/en/researchers/czech-medieval-sources-on-line.html) provided by the LINDAT/CLARIAH-CZ Research Infrastructure (https://lindat.cz) supported by the Ministry of Education, Youth, and Sports of the Czech Republic (project no. LM2018101).

PART III

WENCESLAS AND SIGISMUND: ART, POLITICS, AND DIPLOMACY

CHAPTER 7

THE MAKING OF THE WENCESLAS BIBLE, WITH SPECIAL CONSIDERATION OF THE THEOLOGICAL CONCEPT OF ITS GENESIS INITIAL

MARIA THEISEN

The Wenceslas Bible (Vienna, Österreichische Nationalbibliothek, Cod. 2759–2764) is the most famous of the manuscripts prepared and lavishly illuminated for King Wenceslas IV of Bohemia (1361–1419). This vernacular Bible – preserving a German translation of Scripture and therefore considered by some a heretical threat – provides an important insight into the pressing problems of its time. To understand its historical significance and its unique pictorial programme, it is necessary to briefly recall the political and ecclesiastical circumstances at the time of the manuscript's creation, as well as the king's position within that context.

From 1376 until 1400, Wenceslas was King of the Romans, and in 1378 he succeeded his father, Emperor Charles IV (1316–78), on the throne. From the start of his reign, the Church was divided by the Great Papal Schism, and more and more voices within the clergy as well as the laity claimed that the Empire and the Church urgently needed reform. The priest and professor of theology at Prague University, Jan Hus (c. 1370–1415), a strong advocate of Church reform, soon became the leading representative of a movement in Bohemia known as Hussitism today. Like the Oxford professor John Wyclif (c. 1330–84), whose treatises Hus had studied in depth, Hus advocated fundamental religious renewal and institutional reform of the Church.¹ According to his convictions, neither the clergy nor the pope, nor any dogmas, should be authoritative in matters of faith, only the Holy Scriptures themselves. Consequently, the Bible was the only *lex divina* that every believer should know.

With this claim, Hus picked up on a tendency that had already developed well before him: the translation of the Holy Scriptures into the vernacular languages, so that lay people could read and hear the true Word of God in their own language without any mediation by the priesthood. The oldest known translation of a full Bible into Czech, the so-called Dresden Bible, dates from around 1360.² The author of this translation was probably an Augustinian canon from Roudnice nad Labem/Raudnitz an der Elbe or a Dominican, since the manuscript itself was intended for the Dominican nuns of Prague.³ Parallel to this, German-language translations of the Bible were also undertaken in the spirit of promoting contemporary forms of piety among lay believers.⁴ The text that became the basis of

---

1 František Šmahel, *Jan Hus. Život a dílo* (Prague, 2013); František Šmahel, 'Was there a Bohemian Reformation?', in Kateřina Horničková and Michal Šroněk (eds), *From Hus to Luther: Visual Culture in the Bohemian Reformation (1380–1620)* (Turnhout, 2016), 7–16, at 7–10; Franz Machilek, *Jan Hus (um 1372–1415): Prediger, Theologe, Reformator* (Münster, 2019).
2 The Dresden Bible was destroyed by fire in 1914; the first redaction of the Czech Bible nevertheless survives in two copies from the fifteenth century: the so-called Litoměřice-Třeboň Bible (dated 1411–14; Litoměřice, Státní oblastní archiv, BIF 3/2, BIF 3/1, and Třeboň, Státní oblastní archiv, A 2), prepared for Jan Hus' friend Peter of Zmrzlík ze Svojšína, and the Olomouc Bible (dat. 1417; Olomouc, Státní vědecká knihovna, M III 1); cf. Vladimír Kyas, První český překlad *Bible* (Prague, 1971); Pavel Spunar, 'The first Old-Czech translation of the Holy Script', in *The Bible in Cultural Context* (Brno, 1994), 321.
3 A collective Bible translation by Augustinians, Dominicans, and Franciscans at the cathedral school on Hradčany is also considered possible. See Vladimír Kyas (ed.), Staročeská Bible drážďanská *a olomoucká*, vols 1–3 (Prague, 1981–8); Hans Rothe and Reinhold Olesch (eds), Staročeská Bible drážďanská *a olomoucká*, vol. 4 (Leiden, 1996); Jaroslava Pečírková et al. (eds), Staročeská Bible drážďanská *a olomoucká*, vol. 5 (Prague, 2009); Jakub Sichálek, 'European Background: Czech Translations', in Elizabeth Solopova (ed.), *The Wycliffite Bible: Origin, History and Interpretation* (Leiden, 2017), 66–84, at 80–2.
4 Early examples of this are provided by the translations of the so-called 'Austrian Bible Translator' from the Duchy of Austria. In the first half of the fourteenth century, he translated the Old Testament, the Gospels, and the Commentary to the Psalms into German (his work is currently being investigated and edited at the Bavarian Academy of Sciences, <https://bibeluebersetzer.badw.de/das-projekt.html> [accessed 31 March 2023]). The oldest New Testament in the German language is the Augsburger Bibelhandschrift from 1350 (Staats- und Stadtbibliothek Augsburg, 2°

the Wenceslas Bible, an (aspirational) full Bible translation financed by the royal mint master Martin Rotloew (d. 1392), must have been produced around 1380.⁵ Towards the end of the fourteenth century, Jan Hus and the circles representing the Wyclif wing at Prague University are thought

---

Cod. 3), followed by the Codex Teplensis (from Tepl Abbey near Cheb, in German: Eger, in Bohemia; Prague, Národní knihovna České republiky, Teplá b 10), which was created at about the same time as the Wenceslas Bible; cf. Elke Donalies, *Die Augsburger Bibelhandschrift und ihre Überlieferung* (Münster and New York, 1992); Manja Vorbeck-Heyn, *Die deutschsprachige Evangelientradition im 14. und 15. Jahrhundert und ihre Textgliederungsprinzipien*, Berliner Sprachwissenschaftliche Studien, 11 (Berlin, 2008), 52–4 (siglum 'Te').

5   The German text of the Wenceslas Bible does not stem from a single source. Rather, it is based partly on a translation made for Martin Rotloew, and partly on additions and interpolations that were either written especially for the king or taken from other sources. It is possible that the original was never completed, although the preface implies this. Rotloew's commission survived in several copies and variants; scholars therefore speak of a 'Prague Rotloew branch' of the textual tradition. One manuscript copy (Stuttgart, Würtembergische Landesbibliothek, HB II 7, fol. 5v; dat. 1455) still proudly names him as follows: 'Her Mertein Rotleb der so saß zu Prage und der gepaut hat das collegium zu Prage und die Biblihu hat man im zu teusch gemacht' ['Mr Mertein Rotleb, who sat in Prague and who had built the College in Prague and the Bible was made in German for him']. Martin Rotloew was master of the mint of Kutná Hora/Kuttenberg from 1379, following the death of his father John, and one of the wealthiest citizens of Prague. The Stuttgart copy explicitly associates him with the (later) *collegium*, and thus intends to trace its translation back to learned university circles. In 1383, because of a dispute, Rotloew had to cede a house to the king, who then donated it to the university. Perhaps Wenceslas also took over the still unfinished translation of the Bible at that time, cf. Heimo Reinitzer, 'Die Wenzelsbibel', in *Die deutsche Literatur des Mittelalters, Verfasserlexikon*, vol. 10 (2010), coll. 869–75, at col. 871. In comparison to the Stuttgart copy, the Wenceslas Bible offers some derivations and interpolations, including the part of the prologue dedicated to Wenceslas as an addendum, for which reason Reinitzer and also Mentzel-Reuters dated its text a little later; cf. Arno Mentzel-Reuters, '"Oufsliessen deiner schrifte tor": Mitteldeutscher Biblizismus und die Wenzelsbibel', in Joachim Heinzle, L. Peter Johnson and Gisela Vollmann-Profe (eds), *Wolfram-Studien 13: Literatur im Umkreis des Prager Hofs der Luxemburger. Schweinfurter Kolloquium 1992* (Berlin, 1994), 174–206, esp. on the Wenceslas Bible and Hussitism at 178–80. Taking into account Rotloew's career, Hedwig Heger assumed that this translation was written around 1380; cf. Hedwig Heger, 'Philologischer Kommentar zur Wenzelsbibel', in *Die Wenzelsbibel. Vollständige Faksimile-Ausgabe der Codices Vindobonenses 2759–2764 der Österreichischen Nationalbibliothek Wien*, Codices Selecti, 70 (Graz, 1998), 51–123. Hana Hlaváčková, 'K dataci a emblematice Bible Václava IV / On the Dating and Emblematics of the King Wenceslaus IV's Bible', *ARS* [Bratislava] 51:1–2 (2018), 42–50, on the other hand, argues for a dating of the translation before 1376 (the year of Wenceslas' and Johanna's coronation as King and Queen of the Romans) and places the beginning of the actual work on King Wenceslas' illuminated Bible towards the end of the 1370s.

to have been involved in the second redaction of the Czech Bible. Among other achievements, the introduction of the diacritical marks into the written Czech language is connected to their efforts.

Translations of the Bible and of Bible commentaries were subject to the interpretive privilege of the official Church. Uncontrolled versions of the Bible, coupled with an increasing emancipation of the laity from the Church, were soon recognized as threats by the Church authorities. In 1369, Emperor Charles IV, at the request of Pope Urban V, therefore issued a ban on the distribution of vernacular bibles to non-theologians.[6] This was intended to prevent misinterpretations of the Holy Scriptures by lay persons. However, strict compliance with this imperial (not papal) restriction could hardly be controlled, was not prosecuted, and ultimately remained ineffectual. Nevertheless, the vernacular Bible remained a contested issue; this is shown by the circumstance that the ban issued by Charles IV was ostentatiously lifted by the commissioning of a large German Bible in the 1380s by his son Wenceslas IV, by virtue of his dignity as King of the Romans. This encouraged further translation campaigns in the two vernacular languages spoken in his kingdom, Czech and German – with the German branch being driven by a less radical spirit than the Czech one.[7] At the time Wenceslas apparently believed that he, as King of the Romans, could shape the reformation of the Church and of the Holy Roman Empire in line with his own views. Moreover, his German Bible, as we shall see in what follows, provides information about his attitude and self-perception.[8] He obviously could not imagine that he himself would soon be dethroned, nor how vehemently the question of 'reform' would be fought out some 20 years later.

After a brief introduction to the unfinished manuscript of the Wenceslas Bible, I look at its process of creation. We shall see – especially on the pages that were never illuminated – that the passages intended for illumination were originally provided with Latin instructions addressed to the illuminators. Paraphrasing the Vulgate, these instructions were not inserted by an artisan from an illuminators' workshop, but by a

---

6   Johann F. Böhmer and Alfons Huber (eds), *Regesta Imperii. Die Regesten des Kaiserreichs unter Kaiser Karl IV. (1346–1348)*, vol. 8 (Innsbruck, 1889), no. 7287 (p. 759); Carl Mirbt, *Quellen zur Geschichte des Papsttums und des römischen Katholizismus* (Tübingen, 1924), at 226; Martin Leutzsch, 'Bibelübersetzung als Skandal und Verbrechen', in Rainer Dillmann (ed.), *Bibel-Impulse: Film, Kunst, Literatur, Musik, Theater, Theologie* (Berlin, 2006), 46–8.
7   Mentzel-Reuters, '"Oufsliessen deiner schrifte tor"', 181.
8   Tomáš Gaudek, 'Reprezentace objednavatelů českých iluminovaných rukopisů doby Lucemburské', in Kateřina Kubínová and Klára Benešovská (eds), *Imago Imagines II. Výtvarné dílo a proměny jeho funkcí v českých zemích od 10. do první třetiny 16. století* (Prague, 2019), 416–17.

person (or two) with a sophisticated theological background, who took the role of *conceptor*, i.e., of a kind of artistic director responsible for the entire pictorial programme of the king's Bible. I trace the *conceptor*'s intentions and intellectual horizon, additionally taking into account the fully illuminated pages and miniatures for which the instructions are no longer visible. I approach the underlying scholarly debates from the context established by the vivid theological discourse in Prague at a time marked by calls for a return to the early Church.

The illuminations of the Days of Creation provide particularly rich grounds for this kind of analysis. They reveal ideas that are extremely erudite: not only about space and time, and the creation of the angels and of the four elements, but also about the then much-discussed themes of sin and redemption, and the understanding of the crowned king himself as Adam's successor, as reflected in the miniatures of the first, second and sixth days of creation. Using texts by Ambrose, Aquinas, Pseudo-Methodius, and others discussed at Prague University in the late 1300s, as well as apocryphal texts and rabbinic literature, I sketch a milieu that included scholars from Prague University and the Prague Jewish community, with its chief rabbi Avigdor Kara. The intense scholarly discussions of late fourteenth-century Prague seem to have profoundly influenced the *conceptor* of the pictorial programme and, presumably, the royal commissioner himself, who seems to have shared the interest in the topical search for the roots of Christianity. In fact, Wenceslas himself was seeking to take a leading role in Church reform and – as we know from the prologue – intended to donate this vernacular Bible to *all* Christendom (meaning the Holy Roman Empire). While the conclusions, starting from visual evidence, must in the end remain conjectural, the iconological approach adopted in this study opens a new hermeneutic window on the creation of the Wenceslas Bible which we can now see as deeply embedded within the context of the cultural and theological milieus of Prague in the final years of the fourteenth century.

THE BIBLE OF KING WENCESLAS AT A GLANCE

Although the Wenceslas Bible is one of the best-researched manuscripts of its period,[9] many fundamental questions still remain unanswered: we

---

9   Codicological benchmarks: Cod. 2759: 240 fols (according to court librarian Peter Lambeck [d. 1680]: 1–240; nineteenth century (before 1864): 1–239, skipped fol. 134, corrected as fol. 133* in the twentieth century), 535 x 370 mm, one scribe (according to the philologist Hermann Menhardt [d. 1963]: hand 1); Cod. 2760: 182 fols (Lambeck: 241–422; twentieth century: 1–182), 535 x 370 mm, one scribe (Menhardt: hand 1); Cod. 2761: 144 fols (Lambeck: 1–144), 535 x 370 mm, three

do not know the identity of the translator of this German Bible, nor are we certain exactly when its translation was made. It is unknown when the scribes (*ingrossatores*) started copying the text. We cannot determine exactly how many scribes were involved, and how many persons illuminated the biblical text. Hermann Menhardt distinguished three scribal hands; art historians assume that at least nine illuminators and their assistants worked on the precious artistic decoration. The style of the illuminations suggests that the production of the Bible continued throughout the last decade of the fourteenth century, and perhaps longer.[10]

The prologue clearly indicates that the intention is not to present an abbreviated or revised version of the Bible, but a complete translation of the Holy Scriptures.[11] Its author emphasizes that he aims to provide

---

scribes (Menhardt: hand 1 fols 1ra–6vb, 8ra–128vb, 137ra–144vb; hand 2 fols 129ra–131vb; hand 3 from 1447 fols 7ra–7vb, 132ra–136vb); Cod. 2762: 211 fols (according to Lambeck: 145–355), 535 x 370 mm, three scribes (Menhardt: hand 1 fols 148ra–211vb; hand 2 fols 11ra–146ra; hand 3 from 1447 fols 1ra–10va, 147va–147vb); Cod. 2763: 206 fols (Lambeck: 1–206), 535 x 370 mm, two scribes (Menhardt: hand 1 fols 2ra–186vb, 193ra–206vb; hand 3 from 1447 fols 1v, 187ra–192vb); Cod. 2764: 231 fols (according to Lambeck: 207–437; twentieth century: 1–231), 535 x 370 mm, three scribes (Menhardt: hand 1 fols 1ra–123vb, 131ra–138vb; hand 2 fols 153ra–224vb; hand 3 from 1447 fols 124ra–130vb, 139ra–152vb, 225ra–231ra). All volumes are written in *textura* on parchment, with the text laid out in two columns and 36 lines per page. The Bible was bound in three volumes in 1447 and divided into six volumes around 1790. In the course of the production of the facsimile edition during the 1980s, the Bible was split into eight parts, but its old shelfmarks were retained. Selection of art-historical literature: Julius von Schlosser, 'Die Bilderhandschriften Königs Wenzel I., ein Interimskommentar zur Faksimile-Ausgabe der Wenzelsbibel', *Jahrbuch der Kunsthistorischen Sammlungen des Allerhöchsten Kaiserhauses* 14 (1893), 215–308; Karel Chytil, 'Bible Václava IV. a díla příbuzná', *Památky archeologické* 13 (1885), 205–18, 311–16; Hermann Menhardt, *Verzeichnis der altdeutschen literarischen Handschriften der Österreichischen Nationalbibliothek*, vol. 1, Veröffentlichungen des Instituts für deutsche Sprache und Literatur. Deutsche Akademie der Wissenschaften zu Berlin, 13 (Berlin, 1960), 266–8; Josef Krása, *Die Handschriften König Wenzels IV.* (Vienna, 1971); Gerhard Schmidt, 'Kunsthistorischer Kommentar', in *Die Wenzelsbibel*, 239–42; Hana Hlaváčková, 'Old Testament Scenes in the Bible of King Wenceslas IV', in *The Old Testament as Inspiration in Culture. International academic symposium Prague, September 1995* (Třebenice, 2001), 132–9; Gerhard Schmidt, 'Wenceslas IV's Books and Their Illuminators', in Barbara Drake Boehm and Jiří Fajt (eds), *Prague: The Crown of Bohemia 1347–1437* (New York, 2005), 220–4; Ulrike Jenni and Maria Theisen, *Mitteleuropäische Schulen IV (ca. 1380–1400). Hofwerkstätten König Wenzels IV. und deren Umkreis* (Vienna, 2014), 158–211 (with further literature). <https://e-book.fwf.ac.at/o:571> (text), <https://e-book.fwf.ac.at/o:572> (tables) [accessed 10 March 2023].

10 Jenni and Theisen, *Mitteleuropäische Schulen IV*, 158–211.
11 The books of Maccabees I and II, Daniel, the Minor Prophets and the New Testament are, however, missing. Cf. Reinitzer, 'Die Wenzelsbibel', col. 871.

direct access to the biblical text not only to clerics, but also to lay people. Therefore, he expressly gave priority to a translation that stays as close as possible to the original Latin text. We also know from the prologue that King Wenceslas and his wife intended to donate the Bible:

> wer nu diser schrifte hort / wil lesen und ir suzen wort / der schol nu dancken dem vrumen / von dem dicz gestift ist kumen / dem hochgeborne kunig wenczlab vein / und der durchluchtigisten kuniginne sein / den dicz durch gotes wirdigkeit / frümet aller cristenheit / Got gebe in dorumbe czu lone / des edeln himelriches crone. / Amen.[12]

For unexplained reasons, however, the king's German Bible with its ambitious comprehensive pictorial programme was never finished.[13] The text, written and only partially illuminated up to the Book of Ezekiel, remained unbound during the lifetime of King Wenceslas. In the middle of the fifteenth century, under Emperor Frederick III of Habsburg (1415–93), the Bible was bound in three volumes. Around 1790, the bulky volumes had to be rebound and were divided into six parts. Two of these volumes contain no illuminations at all (2762 and 2764), and two others are not fully illuminated (2761 and 2763). All in all, a total of 19 historiated initials and 635 framed miniatures were completed; a further 900 were planned. Had the text been completed and illustrated in the same density, the king's Bible would have contained about 2000 miniatures: the largest project of its kind in Bohemia around 1400.

---

12 '[They] who now shall read this treasure of Scripture and its sweet words, let them give thanks to the pious one, to the high-born King Wenceslas and his most noble queen, by whom this [work] was donated, for through [adding to] God's dignity this benefits all Christendom. May God therefore give them [the donors] the crown of the noble Heavens as [their] reward' (translation by Karl Kügle). Vienna, ÖNB, Cod. 2759, fol. 2r; it remains unclear which of Wenceslas' two wives was meant by *kuniginne sein*. Wenceslas IV was married to Johanna of Bavaria-Straubing from 1376 to 1386, and to Sophia of Bavaria-Munich from 1389 to 1419, both Wittelsbach princesses.

13 The termination of the work is most probably connected with King Wenceslas' failed attempt to travel to Rome in 1402, which, despite his deposition, was intended to help him obtain the imperial crown. Since the entire picture programme of the Bible was oriented towards Wenceslas as King of the Holy Roman Empire, a continuation of the work on this costly Bible after 1402 must have become meaningless.

A MAGNIFICENT GERMAN BIBLE FOR THE KING AS DEFENDER OF CHRISTENDOM

As King of Bohemia and of the Romans, Wenceslas 'by God's grace' saw himself in a key position between God and the Christian community: a position, particularly important at the time of the Papal Schism, which divided the Church and with it all European courts into two camps until 1417. It was also a time marked by various reform efforts. While Jan Hus advocated a Church in poverty, and Communion under the *species* of both bread and wine for all believers, a group of Augustinian canons in Bohemia proclaimed the necessity of adherence to strict observance in the monasteries, the improvement of worship and pastoral care, and the increased cultivation of the arts and sciences that man owed to Divine Creation. The starting point of this strong ecclesiastical reform movement in Bohemia was the Augustinian canonry in Roudnice, expressly recommended by the Archbishop of Prague as a model for other convents in 1398.[14] Wenceslas, however, sympathized more with Hus' fundamental criticism regarding the clergy and the demand for Church poverty. He could have made convenient use of Church properties to fill his own empty coffers after his father had spent more than was available and, besides increasing taxes, had transferred villages and land to the Church. In the climate of reform efforts, Wenceslas therefore hoped not only to expand his sphere of influence, but also to regain some of his income. The dispute with the Prague Archbishop John of Jenštejn over the rich abbey of Kladruby in 1393 (which resulted in the death of the archbishop's vicar-general John of Nepomuk and the archbishop's flight to Rome) provides some insight into this constellation of difficulties.[15] Here, Wenceslas' sense of reform inevitably took a very different shape from that of Hus, who ultimately undermined the authority of the king by his refusal to recognize the pope as the Head of the Church. The importance of the king as defender of the faith was severely challenged by these developments. Perhaps precisely for this reason royal authority is frequently asserted by royal emblems worked into the border decorations of his Bible and also

---

14 Franz Machilek, 'Die Augustiner Chorherren in Böhmen und Mähren', in *Archiv für Kirchengeschichte von Böhmen, Mähren, Schlesien* 4 (1976), 107–44; Franz Machilek, 'Kirchliche Reformen des 14./15. Jahrhunderts', in Winfried Eberhard and Franz Machilek (eds), *Kirchliche Reformimpulse des 14./15. Jahrhunderts in Ostmitteleuropa*, Forschungen und Quellen zur Kirchen- und Kulturgeschichte Ostdeutschlands (Köln – Weimar – Vienna, 2006), 26–8.
15 For details on the circumstances of this episode, including older literature, cf. Klara Hübner, 'Herrscher der Krise – die Krise des Herrschers: König Wenzel IV. als Projektionsfläche zeitgenössischer Propaganda', *Biuletyn Polskiej Misji Historycznej* 11 (2016), 294–320, at 307–11.

in some miniatures and initials in the text itself. Examples are found in the depiction of King Wenceslas himself, his emblems, and his coats of arms in the introductory initials of the Books of Kings,[16] or in a miniature depicting Wenceslas (in contemporary courtly dress, peeking out of a tent decorated with his *W* and *e* monograms) watching the collection of donations for the Tent of Revelation (Fig. 7.1).[17] Most of the images thus represent unique compositions, especially designed for the Bible of King Wenceslas.[18]

PLANNING AN ILLUSTRATION PROGRAMME

As was common practice with extensive miniature cycles, a cohesive workflow between all persons involved had to be ensured by a coordinator or *conceptor*; Marcel Thomas once compared his function with that of an editor.[19] This person held a key position between patron, scribes, and illuminators. He was responsible for the storyline of the entire illustration programme and the correct insertion of the pictures. He communicated with the illuminators by giving written instructions on the margins next to each planned miniature (Fig. 7.2). These instructions were partially painted over or erased in the illuminated parts of the Wenceslas Bible, yet are still clearly legible in the non-illuminated parts. Thus, the fewer pictures were inserted, the more instructions remained visible; conversely,

---

16 Cod. 2760, fol. 33r (Regum I: King Wenceslas enthroned with insignia on the central letter bar. Behind him two Wild Men, who are holding the Luxembourg tournament helmet); Cod. 2760, fol. 74r (Regum II: King Wenceslas enthroned, with the imperial insignia, within the letter 'E'. Below, two bath attendants presenting the coat of arms of the Empire and the coat of arms of Bohemia, both connected with the king by a torque); Cod. 2760, fol. 108r (Regum III: Bath attendant with scroll 'thoho bzde thoho' and a kingfisher. At her feet, the imperial and the Bohemian coats of arms).

17 Unfortunately, the pictorial instructions at the bottom of the page were thoroughly erased before the artist painted over the respective area with tendrils. Vienna, ÖNB, Cod. 2759, fol. 93r; Maria Theisen, 'Texte und Bilder einer Zeitenwende', in Sára Balász (ed.), *Quelle und Deutung, vol I.1* (Budapest, 2014), 105–45, at 132 (Fig. 7).

18 Only a few of them quote old models, such as Jacob's dream of the Ladder to Heaven (Cod. 2759, fol. 24r). This composition is almost identical to a composition from around 1360, which was handed down in the *Liber viaticus* (Prague, Knihovna Národního muzea, XIII A 12, fol. 289v) of the Litomyšl bishop and councillor of Emperor Charles IV, John of Neumarkt/Jan ze Středy (1310–1380).

19 Marcel Thomas and Gerhard Schmidt, *Die Bibel des Königs Wenzel: Mit 32 Miniaturen im Originalformat nach der Handschrift aus der Österreichischen Nationalbibliothek* (Graz, 1989), at 92.

Fig. 7.1. Vienna, ÖNB, Cod. 2759, fol. 93r – Wenceslas watching the collection of donations for the Tent of Revelation.

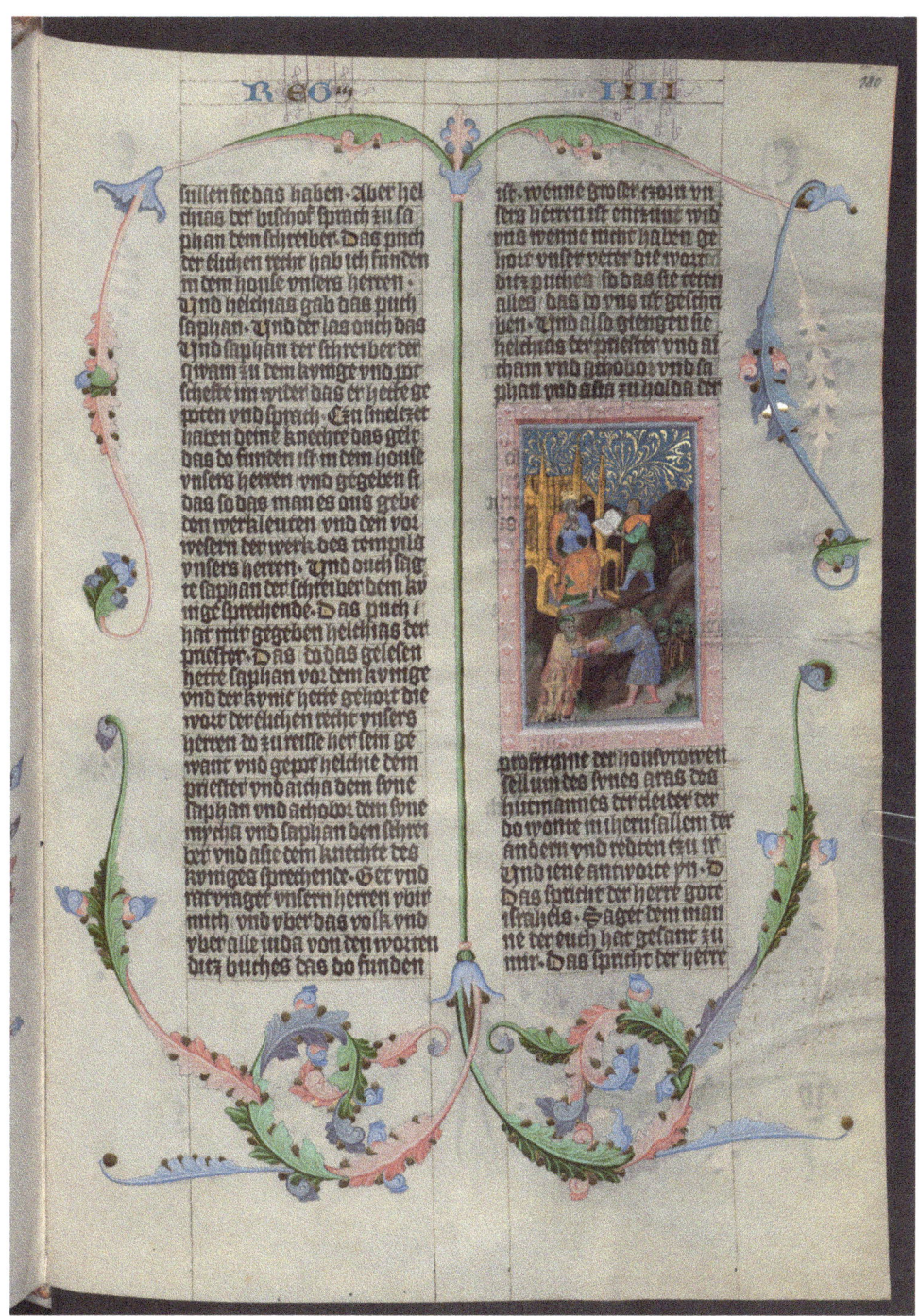

Fig. 7.2. Vienna, ÖNB, Cod. 2760, fol. 180r – faded seven-line painters' instruction in the right-hand margin.

the more pictures were inserted, the fewer instructions are preserved.[20] The instructions vary in their level of detail and also in the way they are formulated (some address the illuminators in the present tense, some relate the episodes – like the biblical texts – in the past tense). We can therefore assume that two people conceived the picture programme in the course of the approximately ten to 15 years it may have taken to produce this Bible. Nevertheless, we can say with certainty that the instructions do not contain information about the exact placement of the figures or the colouring, but rather follow the text of the Vulgate. As an example, let us take a closer look at the instruction for a miniature in Cod. 2761, fol. 137r, which should have shown Tobias and the fish (Fig. 7.3). The instruction reads:

> hic ponas postquam recessisset Thobias, insecutus est cum cane et mansit iuxta aquam Tygris et Thobias exivit ad flumen ad lavandum pedes et ecce piscis horribilis exivit de aqua, volens devorare eum; mox Thobias clamavit voce magna ad angelum et Thobias arripuit piscem et traxit eum ad litus et evisceravit et assavit eum igni.[21]

In comparison, the Bible (Tobias 6:1–3) reads as follows:

> 1 profectusque est Tobias et canis secutus est eum et mansit prima mansione iuxta fluvium Tigris
> 2 et exivit ut lavaret pedes suos et ecce piscis inmanis exivit ad devorandum eum
> 3 quem expavescens clamavit voce magna dicens Domine invadet me![22]

The *conceptor* first freely followed the Vulgate, and in the second part of his account summarized the essential points of the whole episode as a series of actions. A mere instruction for illuminators could have been

---

20 Still legible instructions were published by Julius von Schlosser, 'Die Bilderhandschriften Königs Wenzel I', as early as 1893; see also Stanko Kokole, '"Hic ponas". Hierher setze das Bild', *Imagination* 10:2 (1995), 7–10.
21 'Put here when Tobias went forward, followed by his dog, and he stayed near the waters of the Tigris, and Tobias went to the river to wash his feet, and, behold, a monstrous fish leaped out of the water, wanting to devour him; then Tobias cried out with a loud voice unto the angel, and he took hold of the fish, and drew it to the shore, and gutted it, and roasted it upon the fire' (transl. by the author).
22 'And Tobias went forward and the dog followed him and he lodged the first night by the river of Tigris. And he went out to wash his feet and, behold, a monstrous fish came up to devour him. And Tobias being afraid of him cried out with a loud voice, saying: Sir, he cometh upon me! (…)'. This and the following Bible citations in English are quoted according to *The Holy Bible: Douay-Rheims Version, Biblia Sacra iuxta Vulgatam Clementinam* [English-Latin Bible] (London, 2008).

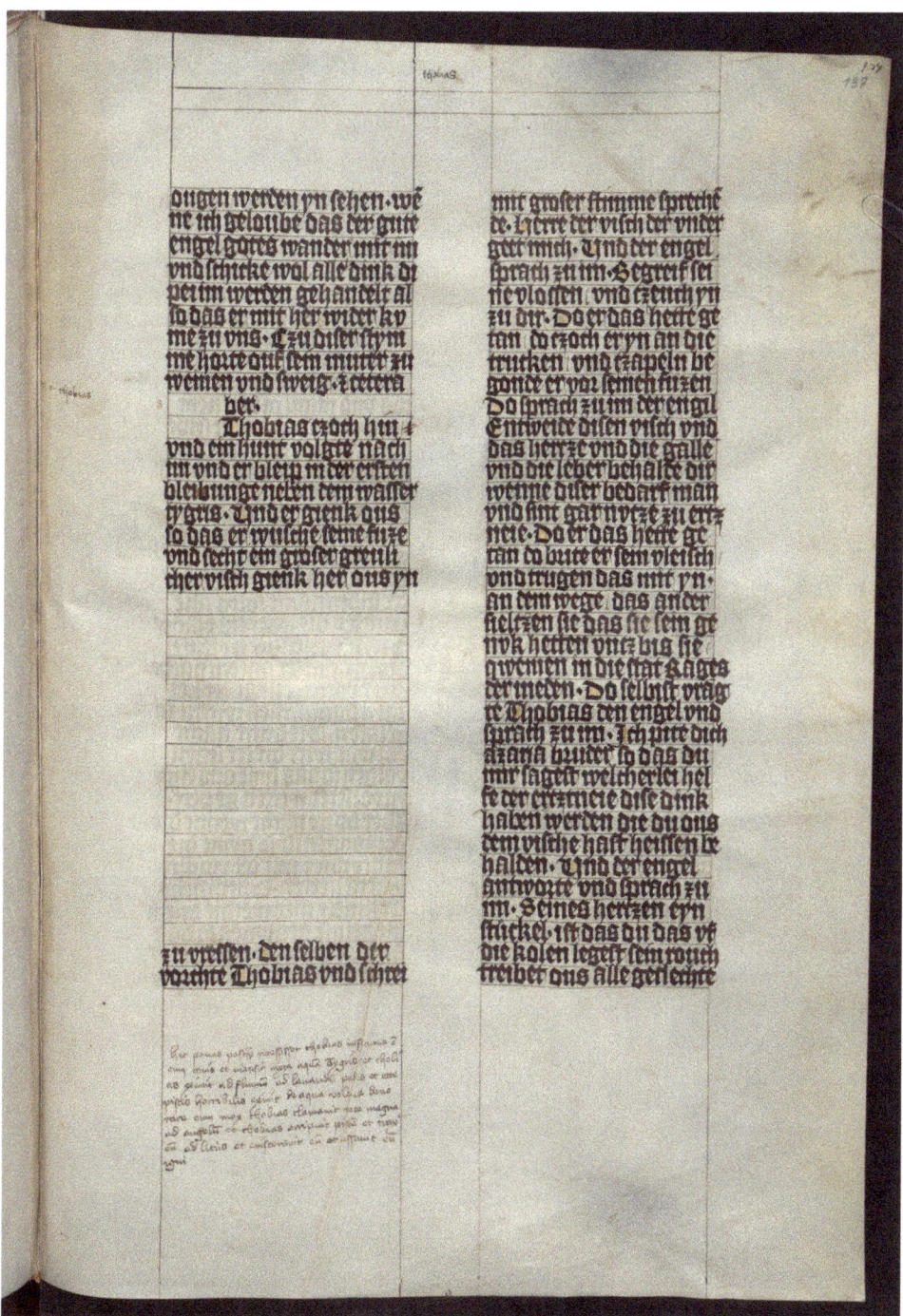

Fig. 7.3. Vienna, ÖNB, Cod. 2761, fol. 137r – non-executed miniature and painters' instruction in the lower margin.

much simpler: 'Paint the angel and Tobias here with a big fish on the bank of a river.' In view of this, we may conclude that this instruction was most likely not given by an artist, but by a theologian.

In order to ensure that the images illustrated the German text correctly, and to avoid the risk of heretical interpretations, the *conceptor* turned to the illuminators in Latin, with the help of quotations from the Vulgate and lengthy explanations. From this, we may conclude that he was highly interested in representing the true Word of God. Consequently, he (or they) also gave cross-references and further facts, metaphors, indirect speech, and sometimes information about different spatial environments. A good example for indirect speech is Cod. 2762, fol. 181r (the corresponding miniature was not realized):

> hic ponas Job, quomodo Dominus plagat eum cum maligno spiritu Sathan, qui eum cruciat ulceribus plenum, et Job sedit et deponit saniem et immundiciam de corpore cum una testa figuli. Videns autem hec uxor eius inquit: adhuc tu permanes in simplicitate tua et ipse ad uxorem ait: una de stultis mulieribus es et sic in hunc modum contendunt. Job vero dicit uxori: si bona suscepimus de manu domini, mala autem etc.[23]

In this case, the *conceptor* assumed that the illuminator was familiar with this scene and ended the dialogue with an 'etc.', probably noticing at the point where he placed the 'etc.' that a miniature can depict a dialogue scene in general, but not its specific content.

Despite these complicated instructions, the illuminators seldom made mistakes. They often divided their image fields into two or three zones in order to depict several scenes showing the main character in various environments and actions within one frame. In this way, they were able to tell a continuous story in images – called a *maeren hort* ('a wealth of stories') in the prologue. In some cases, they used banners with Latin inscriptions as additional aids inside the miniatures, e.g., in Cod. 2760, fol. 40v: 'Samuel inter civitatem Masphat et Bethcar ponit lapidem et vocat nomen loci illius lapis adiutoris quia victoria ibi facta est per Judeos et Filisteos.'[24] This repeats almost verbatim 1 Samuel 7:12: 'tulit

---

23 'Here put Job, how the Lord tormented him with the malicious spirit of Satan, who tortures him, full with ulcers, and Job sat down and scraped the pus and dirt from his body with a shard of clay. When his wife saw this, she asked him: do you still hold fast (to faith) in your simplicity? And he answered his wife: you are one of the foolish wives, and in this way they contended. Verily Job said to his wife: If we accept from God the good, then also the bad, etc.' (transl. by the author).
24 'Samuel took a stone and laid it between Masphat and Bethcar and he called the place the Stone of the Helper, where victory was gained by the Jews and (!) the Philistines' (transl. by the author).

autem Samuhel lapidem unum et posuit eum inter Masphat et inter Sen et vocavit nomen eius lapis Adiutorii dixitque hucusque auxiliatus est nobis Dominus.'[25] Only rarely were the banners inside the miniatures in German, e.g., in Cod. 2760, fol. 30r, showing Ruth and Boas, the latter with a banner saying: 'kum unde is mit myr.'[26] The German translation of the Bible itself was cited as authoritative for the illuminators only in very exceptional cases, for example in the Psalter, Cod. 2763, fol. 31v: 'hic ponas quod pagani circumvallant civitatem, que dicitur Ceyla; cum David audisset, accessit ad eos cum exercitu magno et processit a civitate, prout in rubrica clarius continetur; quod restet illuminandum, lege rubricam.'[27] Similarly on fol. 48r: 'hic ponas quod filii Israel captivantur et Salmanasar, rex Assirie, captivavit decem tribus et duxit eas captivas. Eodem tempore Asaph compilavit hunc psalmum; legas in rubrica et plenies invenies.'[28] The content was thus stated; exactly how the illuminator was to portray the Assyrians and the Jews or even Asaph in concrete terms was obviously no longer a concern of the *conceptor*. Hana Hlaváčková argued that precisely because the miniatures are so closely related to the text, not much interest in exegetical interpretation can be observed.[29] And yet it is remarkable that the explanations in the margins are far more concerned with the text than with telling the illuminators how to 'translate' it into pictorial compositions.

---

25 'And Samuel took a stone, and laid it between Masphath and Sen: and he called the place, the Stone of help. And he said: Thus far the Lord hath helped us' (quoted according to *The Holy Bible: Douay-Rheims Version*).
26 'Come and eat with me' (transl. by the author). The two miniatures were designed by different illuminators, the so-called Simson Master (Latin banner) and the Ruth Master (German banner).
27 'Put here, as the heathens besiege the city that is called Ceyla; when David heard about this, he attacked them with a strong army, and advanced to the city, as is clearly written in the [German] rubric; what is yet to be illuminated, read in the [German] rubric' (transl. by the author).
28 'Put here how the sons of Israel were captured, and Salmanasar, king of Assyria, took ten tribes captive and led them into captivity. It was during this time that Asaph wrote this Psalm; read [about it] in the [German] rubric and make up the rest' (transl. by the author). Concerning the authorship of these painter's instructions, the possibility that this section was prepared by a second *conceptor* is tantalizing. A precise analysis of the scribes' hands is still pending. In addition, the switch from Latin to German provides evidence that the illuminators were not just literate, but capable of working with painter's instructions in Latin as well as German-language rubrics. I only briefly mention in this context the depiction of the Altar of Incense by court illuminator Frana (Cod. 2759, fol. 86v), who obviously kept to the German text; more on this in Theisen, 'Texte und Bilder', 126 (Abb. 6), 127.
29 Hlaváčková, 'Old Testament Scenes', 132–9; also Reinitzer, 'Die Wenzelsbibel', col. 874.

Having said this, it would be particularly interesting to know the instruction next to the unconventional miniature on fol. 175r in today's Cod. 2763, which was intended to illustrate Jesus Sirach 24 (Fig. 7.4). For what we see here is Mary, the Mother of God, enthroned with the Jesus Child and surrounded by seven virgins. According to Jesus Sirach, Wisdom – God's daughter from Solomon's Book of Proverbs – took up residence among the people of Israel in Jerusalem. Wisdom was interpreted by Jesus Sirach as the testament between God and the people of Israel, and was therefore seen in rabbinical Judaism as a messenger of God in the form of a book, namely the Book of the Torah. John the Evangelist, by commencing his Gospel with a well-known verse alluding to Genesis, 'In the beginning was the Word, and the Word was with God, and God was the Word', drew this line to Jesus, the incarnated Logos and Divine Wisdom. Solomon thus embodied in the Old Testament a part of what Christ embodied in the New Testament, namely the aspect of Wisdom that dwells in a human being and comes from God himself. This idea has been introduced into Mariological literature, prayers, and iconography, in which Mary is considered the personified vessel of Divine Wisdom, a thought that was clearly expressed in the Lauretanian Litany ('sedes sapientiae, ora pro nobis'), and in artistic depictions of Mary and Child in the so-called 'sedes sapientiae' type. The inscription on the base of the throne of the Madonna, now in Berlin but sculpted in central Italy by Presbyter Martinus at some time during the twelfth century, leaves no doubt about its meaning: 'In gremio matris fulget sapientia patris.'[30] The seven virgins in our miniature probably stand for the seven characteristics of Divine Wisdom as described in Proverbs 8. This miniature, as one of the last to be completed, proves that the concept of the pictorial programme of this Bible was indeed theologically quite sophisticated.[31]

---

30 'In the womb of the Mother shines the wisdom of the Father' (transl. by the author); Berlin, Bodemuseum, Ident. Nr. 29.
31 Although the Lauretanian Litany received its name after the Italian pilgrimage site of Loreto only in the sixteenth century, its roots can be traced back to the Greek *Hymnos Akathystos* of the ninth century. Latin versions have come down to us from France (Île-de-France) from the twelfth century onwards. The text experienced its golden age in the late Middle Ages and early modern period. On the history of the Marian resp. Lauretanian Litany, cf. Walter Dürig (ed.), *Die Lauretanische Litanei: Entstehung, Verfasser, Aufbau und mariologischer Inhalt* (Sankt Ottilien, 1990), 9–11, 13–14 (Walter Dürig on the early Latin versions); Balthasar Fischer, 'Litanei. I.3 Anrufungslitaneien', in Walter Kasper (ed.), *Lexikon für Theologie und Kirche*, vol. 6 (Freiburg/Breisgau, 1997), col. 955; on the cult of the Virgin Mary promoted in Bohemia by Emperor Charles IV and the Prague Archbishop Arnošt of Pardubice, their French connections and strong relations to the Eastern Orthodox Church in Slavic countries, and the establishment of a *Collegium mansionarium* (or *speciales ministri Beatae Mariae Virginis*) at the Metropolitan Chapter in 1343, cf. Tomáš

Fig. 7.4. Vienna, ÖNB, Cod. 2763, fol. 175r – Madonna and Child enthroned, surrounded by seven virgins.

Fig. 7.5. Vienna, ÖNB, Cod. 2759, fol. 2v – Genesis initial depicting God's work of creation within an architecturally designed frame.

As it is not possible to discuss all miniatures of the Bible in this study, we will now concentrate on the large initial of the Genesis as an example of the *conceptor's* interpretative work (Fig. 7.5). The Genesis initial represents the actual beginning of the Holy Scriptures and was therefore traditionally given prominence. The initial here extends over the entire left-hand column of the text and shows God's work of creation within an architecturally designed frame.[32] Prophets, Evangelists and Apostles (often only distinguished by the attribute of a book as wise men and authors of the Old and the New Testament)[33] are sitting in the niches of this frame and either converse with each other or draw the viewer's attention to the scenes of Divine Creation in their midst. Colourful acanthus tendrils emanate from the frame, held by winged angels, and are furthermore decorated with the emblems and coats of arms of King Wenceslas and the Queen. Due to the abundance of ornaments and figures presented here, more than one glance is needed to realize that this is actually the initial letter 'I' of the Holy Scriptures. No painting instructions for this lavish initial have survived, providing all the more reason to take a closer look at the illustrations and their sources.

THE ICONOGRAPHIC DESIGN OF THE GENESIS INITIAL

'In principio creavit deus cælum et terram' are the first words of the Vulgate. In illuminated bibles the first letter 'I[n]' traditionally formed the frame for the representation of God's Creation by the 'Word of the Lord' as sung

---

Slavický, 'Czech Rorate Chants, Missa Rorate, and Charles IV's Foundation of Votive Officium in Prague Cathedral: The Testament of Choral Melodies to the Long-Term Retention of Repertoire', *Hudební věda* 55 (2018), 239–64, at 244–5. This knowledge was, among other things, reflected in corresponding Marian iconography, which also included the depiction of the Virgin Mary as 'sedes sapientiae' as known from the Lauretanian Litany, for example in the panel painting of Our Lady, which Arnošt of Pardubice donated to the Augustinian canons of Kłodzko around 1350 – here, with seven angels, cf. Jan Royt, 'Maria', in Stefan Samerski (ed.), *Die Landespatrone der böhmischen Länder: Geschichte, Verehrung, Gegenwart* (Paderborn and Munich, 2008), 180.

32 The structure of the initial as a multi-storey building with niches and windows, in which its earthly witnesses appear, follows Italian models such as those known from Bologna. See, for example, Albenga, Biblioteca capitolare, ms. 6 (written and illuminated in Bologna towards the end of the thirteenth century).

33 From their attributes as seen in Fig. 7.5, we can identify Peter (with key) and Paul (with sword), as well as John the Evangelist (with chalice), the Apostle Philip (with cross), and the two alleged cousins of Jesus, the Apostles Simon Zelotes (with saw) and Judas Thaddeus (with club).

in David's Psalm 33.³⁴ Early examples of 'I[n]' initials, filled with scenes of God's Divine Creation, date from the last quarter of the eleventh century. The initial type had its heyday in the twelfth and thirteenth centuries – 'oscillating between text, image and diagram'³⁵ – and remained the most widespread until the late fifteenth century. Countless variations depicted the works of God's Creation or, in larger concepts, referred to the Old and the New Testament, to the Fall and to Redemption, as well as to possible donors or to the then current history, which was understood as a continuation of the history of salvation.

According to Genesis, Heaven, the world, and all life on it are the work of Almighty God, who created everything in six days. On the seventh day God rested and 'saw that it was good'. But how can this Creation be imagined in concrete terms? Did God create everything in the beginning and then leave it to further development? Or was everything already precisely predefined? After all, the *creatio ex nihilo* – God's Creation from nothing – is difficult to understand. The question of the Divine Creation and its nature thus shaped theological and scientific discourse throughout the Middle Ages.³⁶ Not least, the great variety of images accompanying the first famous verses of Genesis in illuminated bibles are (as are the countless exegetical texts) eloquent witnesses of a lively search for answers to the basic questions of human existence, the divine origin of mind and body. Illustrations therefore do not necessarily follow the text word by word, but seek out its deeper meaning. The design of this first initial as realized in a particular milieu in late fourteenth-century Prague depended partly on the templates used; it also depended on the layout and space dedicated to illumination. But beyond that and above all, it was contingent on the theological discourse.

THE FIRST DAY

> *In anegenge schepfte got himel und erde. Die erde was aber unnucz und lere und vinsternisse warn auf der gestalt der abegrund und gotes geist wart gefurt auf den wassern. Und got sprache. Es werde ein liecht. Und es wart ein liecht. Und got sach*

---

34 'Verbo Domini cæli firmati sunt, et spiritu oris ejus omnis virtus eorum' ('By the word of the Lord the Heavens were established; and all the power of them by the spirit of his mouth', Psalm 33:6).
35 Andrea Worm, 'Das illuminierte Wort: Bildprogramme und Erzählstrukturen historisierter Initialen zur Genesis', in Susanne Ehrich and Julia Ricker (eds), *Mittelalterliche Weltdeutung in Text und Bild* (Weimar, 2008), 99–132, with regard to the Bible of King Wenceslas IV at 107.
36 Andrew J. Brown, *The Days of Creation: A History of Christian Interpretation of Genesis 1:1–2:3* (Blandford Forum, 2014).

das liecht das es gut was und schid das liecht von der vinsternisse und nante das liecht tack und die vinsternisse nacht. Und wart gemacht abent und morgen. Ein tag. (Cod. 2759, fol. 2v)[37]

The Creator appears with two planets in his hands, the sun and the moon, although according to the Bible the creation of these two heavenly bodies should be depicted in the fourth medallion. If we do not want to assume that the *conceptor* misunderstood the text, we can suggest that sun and moon should be interpreted as symbols of light and darkness, as is written in the first lines of Genesis (Genesis 1:5): 'God called the light day and the darkness night.'

In order to communicate this idea, other, earlier images show the Creator with two spheres, symbolizing the separation of light and darkness. In the mosaic at the west narthex of the Basilica di San Marco in Venice, dating from around 1220, for example, we see the separation of light and darkness represented by a red and a blue disc or sphere – an idea taken from the late-antique Cotton Genesis.[38] Johannes Zahlten substantiated this interpretation with an interesting reference to an eleventh-century ivory showing the Creator with the Dove above the waters on the first day. Next to the Dove there are two discs, one of which is inscribed 'LUX' and the other 'TEN[ebrae]'. As a further example, Zahlten mentioned an ivory altar from Salerno, made in the twelfth century. The two circular discs there are inscribed 'LUX' and 'NOX'.[39] Moreover, the identifications of 'Nox' with a personified 'Luna' and 'Dies' with 'Sol' were well-known models from antiquity – adopted by the illustrators of the Velislav Bible in Prague around 1340.[40] From this we can conclude with some certainty

---

37 'In the beginning God created heaven, and earth. And the earth was void and empty, and darkness was upon the face of the deep; and the spirit of God moved over the waters. And God said: Be light made. And light was made. And God saw the light that it was good; and he divided the light from the darkness. And he called the light Day, and the darkness Night; and there was evening and morning one day.' (Gen 1:1–5, quoted according to *The Holy Bible: Douay-Rheims Version*.) The transcription and modern edition of the text of the Wenceslas Bible are still pending. The project 'The Wenceslas Bible – Digital Edition and Analysis', started in February 2022 at Salzburg's Paris Lodron University in cooperation with the Austrian National Library and the Austrian Academy of Sciences, is currently dedicated to this task. See <https://www.plus.ac.at/germanistik/forschung/foschungsprojekt-die-wenzelsbibel-digitale-edition-und-analyse/> [accessed 10 March 2023].
38 Kurt Weitzmann and Herbert L. Kessler, *The Cotton Genesis: British Library, Codex Cotton Otho B VI* (Princeton, 1986).
39 Johannes Zahlten, Creatio Mundi: *Darstellungen der sechs Schöpfungstage und naturwissenschaftliches Weltbild im Mittelalter* (Stuttgart, 1979), 119–22, at 121.
40 Prague, Národní knihovna České republiky, XXIII C 124 (Genesis: fols 1r–52v); Karel Stejskal (ed.), *Velislai Biblia picta* (Prague, 1970); Hana Hlaváčková, 'Druhý den stvoření. Personifikace v českém středověkém umění', in Milena Bartlová (ed.),

that the *conceptor* of King Wenceslas' Bible was also familiar with the principle of the ancient 'Luna-Sol concept' for the first day of Creation.

The cycles of sun and moon are ultimately decisive for our perception of light and darkness, of day and night, of growth and decay. God holds both in his hands and is therefore the Lord of Time – with which everything began and with which everything will end. Another aim of this image, therefore, was to convey the concept of time, which for some authors began with the first day of Creation.[41] Furthermore, since antiquity the sun (god Sol) and the moon (goddess Luna) stood for the male and female principle, for the interplay of reason and feeling.[42] The joint representation of these two heavenly bodies therefore also symbolized the all-encompassing power of a good ruler. In Christian art, they were associated with God, particularly with depictions of Christ on the Cross, who sacrificed himself in order to atone for Original Sin and who reopened the door to Paradise and eternal life in the presence of God (i.e., leading mankind through darkness into light).[43] In this interpretation, the sun stands for salvation and the moon for damnation. Both were darkened and mourned for the Saviour at the death of Jesus, and according to Revelation 6:12, these two heavenly bodies will again be darkened at the announcement of the Last Judgement, i.e., the end of time.[44]

Dějiny umění v české společnosti: otázky, problémy, výzvy. Příspěvky přednesené na Prvním sjezdu českých historiků umění (Prague, 2004), 91–5; Zdeněk Uhlíř, *Velislavova bible* (Prague, 2007); Lenka Panušková, 'Die Velislav-Bibel in neuem Licht', *Umění* 56 (2008), 106–18, at 110f.

41 This opinion was expressed, e.g., by Rabbi Yehuda's son Simon (called 'Rabbi Simon' in the Jerusalem Talmud and Midrash, which were originally handed down orally, and in written form from c. 70 AD onwards); cf. Moritz Eisler, *Vorlesungen über die jüdischen Philosophen* (Vienna, 1876), 73. The sun and moon are also depicted in the first medallion of the Latin Bible of Andrew of Austria, painted in 1391 by a court illuminator of King Wenceslas IV (New York, The Metropolitan Library, MS M 833, fol. 5r), see <https://www.themorgan.org/manuscript/158986> [accessed 10 March 2023]. However, the addition of stars alludes to the creation of the heavenly bodies in general here, whereas in the Wenceslas Bible the focus on the sun and moon appearing by God's power allows further exegetical interpretation.

42 *Lexikon der christlichen Ikonographie*, vol. 4 (Freiburg, 1994/2004), coll. 178–80.

43 'Ego sum lux mundi: qui sequitur me, non ambulat in tenebris, sed habebit lumen vitæ' ('I am the light of the world: he that followeth me, walketh not in darkness, but shall have the light of life', John 8:12).

44 Such a depiction of God as Lord of Time must have been the first choice particularly in Prague, which during the reign of King Wenceslas IV had developed into a centre of astronomy, astrology and clockmaking. A well-known example of this is the clock of Prague's Old Town Hall, whose hands are provided with a sun and a moon disc, and which was originally designed by the mathematician and astronomer Jan Šindel (c. 1375–between 1455 and 1458). See Alena Hadravová, 'Jan Šindel a jeho traktát Pravidla pro výpočet zatmění Slunce a Měsíce / Jan Šindel

The Psalms reveal yet another aspect of the first day of Creation, namely the creation of the Heavens and the heavenly bodies – such as sun and moon – by divine intellectual power, i.e., the Word of God: 'By the word of the Lord the Heavens were made, and all their host by the breath of his mouth' (Ps 33:6).[45] This thought is also expressed by the beginning of John's Gospel, which again emphasized the power of the divine Word or Logos: 'In the beginning was the Word' (incarnated in Christ). In this way, our *conceptor* wanted to show nothing less than an immaterial, spiritual primeval state, which already encompassed everything that followed. In order to visualize this thought he was prepared to transfer the two symbols of infinite divine power, the sun and the moon, from the fourth to the first scene. 'And the Spirit of the Lord hovers over the waters': Water here is invoked as an essence that gives life without having its own form, but will be formed by the power of God's Spirit. We see this famous verse depicted almost literally in the small white dove – the symbol of the Holy Spirit – above the waters (underneath the sun), making the scene unmistakably recognizable as 'the first day'. God the Father looks towards the sun and at the same time towards St Peter on the left-hand side of the viewer, reminding us of Christ's words 'upon this rock I will build my Church' (Matthew 16:18), with Peter identified through his attribute, the key to Heaven. His counterpart is St Paul in the right niche, also marked by his attribute, the sword. The two apostolic prefects of the New Testament are thus assigned a particularly privileged position in this composition.

THE SECOND DAY

> *Und got sprach. Es werde ein vestenunge in der mitte der wasser und teilte die wasser von den wassern. Und got machte ein firmament und schied die wasser die do waren unter dem firmament von den die do waren auf dem firmament. Und es geschach also. Und got nante das firmament himel und wart gemacht abent und morgen, der ander tag.* (Cod. 2759, fol. 2v)[46]

---

and his Treatise Canones pro eclipsibus Solis et Lune', in *Astronomie ve středověké vzdělanosti / Astronomy in Medieval Learning*, Scripta Astronomica 10 (Prague, 2003), 53–70; Alena Šolcová, 'Mistr Jan Šindel – pravděpodobný tvůrce matematického modelu pražského orloje', *Pokroky matematiky, fyziky a astronomie* 54:4 (2009), 307–17.

45 This meaning is inherent in the language, as demonstrated by the Greek word *pneuma*, which can be translated both as 'spirit' and as 'breath'.

46 'And God said: Let there be a firmament made amidst the waters: and let it divide the waters from the waters. And God made a firmament, and divided the waters that were under the firmament, from those that were above the firmament, and it was so. And God called the firmament, Heaven; and the evening and morning

Since the biblical text speaks of the Firmament of Heaven and the waters below and above the Firmament, the discrepancy between text and image seems to be even greater in the second medallion than in the first one. Instead of a depiction of 'waters', we see God the Father standing in blessing in front of two small figures with halos. A little disc divided into four segments appears at their feet; each segment is painted differently (starting from the top left, clockwise): a beige surface (air), a grey stone formation (earth), red flames (fire), and olive-green waves (water). Undoubtedly, this is the representation of the four elements, and we may well assume again that the *conceptor* brought his knowledge of other texts about God's Creation into this picture.

Certainly, the Book of Wisdom was one of these texts: 'These [four elements] are so closely connected that no element can exist separately from another. They hold together so firmly that they are called the Firmament' (Sap 19:18). This is why, according to our Prague *conceptor*, the four elements had to be placed exactly at this point, because God used these elements in order to create the Firmament.[47] The four-element doctrine supported and explained the notion that all beings and all things consisted of these basic elements.

The depiction was based on doctrines that had already been developed by the Greek philosopher and naturalist Empedocles in the fifth century BC, and which had subsequently become more and more differentiated. Empedocles' contemporary, Zenon of Ela, attributed four qualities to the four elements: heat, cold, humidity and dryness. At the same time, Hippocrates developed his theory of temperaments, which he connected with the four elements as well. About a century later, Plato argued that everything emerged from one eternal *materia prima*, and saw four divine causes as the origin of things. He explained that the working cause is God himself, the formal cause is the Wisdom of God, the purpose is his Goodness, and as material cause, he set the four elements.[48] He then

---

were the second day' (Gen 1:6–8, quoted according to *The Holy Bible: Douay-Rheims Version*).

47 Zahlten does not give any explanation for the unusual fact that the disc of four elements is depicted in the second medallion in the Wenceslas Bible. According to Zahlten, the motif of the disc appears mostly in images of the first or the third day of creation; cf. Zahlten, Creatio Mundi, at 135.

48 Quoted and translated after Gregor Maurach and Adolf Walter (comm. and eds), 'Daniel of Morley's (c. 1140–c. 1210) Philosophia', *Abhandlungen der Braunschweigischen Wissenschaftlichen Gesellschaft* 44 (1993), 187–232, at 202. Another popular reading was Plato's *Timaios*, a fictitious argument between Plato's teacher Socrates, Timaios, and Hermokrates, in which the question was explored as to whether God had executed Creation abruptly or successively; Otto Apelt (ed.), 'Timaios und Kritias, Sophistes, Politikos, Briefe', in *Platon: Sämtliche Dialoge, unveränderter Abdruck der Ausgabe Hamburg 1922*, vol. VI (Hamburg, 2004), 29–187,

explained how God placed these four elements: '(...) God placed water and air in the middle between fire and earth (...)' (Plato, *Timaios* 7).[49]

The four-elements doctrine of Greek natural philosophy played an important role for Judeo-Christian commentaries on the Bible. In Hellenistic Judaism in particular, Greek and Jewish traditions merged and connected theology with the teachings of Plato and Aristotle, by giving these elements a spiritual meaning. The same applies to early Christian commentaries. Church Father Ambrose of Milan (339–97) propagated the four-elements doctrine in his *Hexameron* (itself based on Bishop Basil's preachings, d. 379), by saying that God, at the moment when he decided to bring into existence the non-existent, also created the corresponding matter together with form. He formed fire, water, and air as he wished, and made things come into being.[50] The *Hexameron* by St Ambrose was compulsory reading for every theologian in the late Middle Ages. (Lavishly illuminated copies of this text have been preserved from Bohemia, e.g., the *Exameron Ambrosii* of Prague Cathedral chapter, the illumination of which even provided the name for its anonymous artist.)[51] Augustine (354–430), who assumed that Plato might have even known the writings of the Jewish prophets, went into detail about Plato's *Timaios*. In his *De civitate dei*, he pointed out that the four elements must have already been laid out in their primordial form on the first day of Creation.[52] Furthermore, he attributed

---

at 49–50; a fundamental study concerning Platonic influences in the design of medieval Genesis initials is Harry Bober, 'In principio: Creation Before Time', in Millard Meiss (ed.), *De artibus opuscula XL: Essays in Honour of Erwin Panofsky*, vol. 1 (New York, 1961), 13–28.

49 Jonathan Barnes (ed.), *Aristoteles: Physics*, translated by R. P. Hardie and R. K. Gaye in Oxford 1930 (Princeton, 1984); Wolfgang Class, *Aristotle's Metaphysics: A Philological Commentary*, 4 vols (Saldenburg, 2014–18).

50 Carl Schenkl (ed.), *Ambrosius Mediolanensis: Hexaemeron, Opera 1*, Corpus Scriptorum Ecclesiasticorum Latinorum, 32:1 (Vienna, 1897); on the possible influence of the *Exameron Ambrosii*, especially on the emblematic programme in the margins of King Wenceslas' Bible, cf. Hana Hlaváčková, 'Courtly Body in the Bible of Wenceslas IV', in *Künstlerischer Austausch: Akten des 28. Internationalen Kongresses für Kunstgeschichte* (Berlin, 1993), 371–82; Hlaváčková, 'Old Testament Scenes', 132–9, at 135.

51 Prague, Knihovna metropolitní kapituly, Sign. A CXXXI; Antonín Podlaha, *Die Bibliothek des Metropolitankapitels* (Prague, 1904), 133–5; Robert Suckale, 'Die Buchmalerwerkstatt des Prager Hexameron. Ein Beitrag zur Kenntnis der Prager Buchmalerei um 1400–1440', *Umění* 38 (1990), 401–18.

52 Augustinus, *De civitate dei*, liber VIII, chapter 11; cf. Bernhard Dombart and Alfons Kalb (eds), *Sancti Augustini Opera, De civitate dei, Pars 14,1, Libri I–IX*, Corpus Christianorum Series Latina, 47 (Turnhout, 1955), at 227f.; Raymond Klibansky, *The Continuity of the Platonic Tradition during the Middle Ages* (London, 1939 and Munich, 1981); Therese Fuhrer, 'Die Platoniker und die Civitas Dei (Buch VIII–X)', in Christoph Horn (ed.), *Augustinus Civitate Dei* (Berlin, 1997), 87–108.

spiritual significance to the elements by interpreting them according to their allegorical content.[53] Augustine continued to influence the work of many early medieval authors. In particular, John Scotus (c. 815–77), like Augustine, made a significant contribution to the cultural transfer between Greek philosophy and Latin Christianity. He combined his idea of Creation with the teaching of the four elements and an underlying quintessence according to Aristotle. In addition, John took up the idea of *pneuma*, understood by the Stoics as a kind of 'fiery breath of air' that penetrates everything and thus complements the four elements as a cosmic force.

The Benedictine monk Honorius Augustodunensis (c. 1080–1150), whose texts were widely read in late medieval Bohemia, explained in his *Elucidarium* that the creation of the elements took place in the first three days, whereas in the following three days, all things and living beings that consist of these elements were created.[54] Peter Lombard (1095–1160), the director of the cathedral school of Paris, added: 'On those days the four elements of the world were distinguished and classified by their places, on the following three days they were decorated.'[55] This view was shared by Peter Comestor (c. 1100–78), who together with Peter Lombard and Stephan Langton was one of the three masters of the Paris School. Peter owed his epithet "Comestor" (the "Devourer") to the fact that he processed all the sources available to him, from antiquity, Judaism, and the Church Fathers to his immediate predecessors and contemporaries. His *Historia scholastica*, completed between 1169 and 1173 and approved by the pope during the Fourth Lateran Council in 1215,[56] was a paraphrase of the biblical story, commented on and supplemented by the wealth of sources known to Peter.[57] It became the most widespread complementary

---

53   Helen Bergin, 'Searching out the Holy Spirit via Earth's Elements', *New Blackfriars* 83:973 (March 2002), 136–47; Ludwig Fladerer, *Augustinus als Exeget. Zu seinen Kommentaren des Galaterbriefes und der Genesis* (Vienna, 2010).
54   On the dissemination of this text in Bohemia and its translation into Czech, see Jaroslav Svátek, 'Les manuscrits de l'*Elucidarium* originaires de Bohême: un nouveau recensement', *Scriptorium* 73 (2019), 126–43; the author traces 36 manuscripts of the *Elucidarium* written in Bohemia during the fourteenth and fifteenth centuries. Four of those belonged to the Czech College library of Prague University, cf. 131.
55   'Quatuor ergo mundi elementa illis diebus, suis locis distincta sunt et ordinata. Tribus autem sequentibus diebus ornata sunt illa quatuor elementa.' Cf. Petrus Lombardus, 'De rerum corporalium et spiritualium creatione', in Jean Aleaume (ed.), *Petri Lombardi Novariensis, cognomine Magistri Sententiarum, espiscopi Parisiensis, Sententiarium Libri Quatuor* (Paris, 1841), coll. 171, Liber secundus, Dist. XIV.
56   James H. Morray, 'Petrus Comestor: Biblical Paraphrase, and the Medieval Popular Bible', *Speculum* 68:1 (1993), 6–35.
57   Brown, *Days of Creation*, 70; Louis H. Feldman, *Studies in Hellenistic Judaism* (Leiden – New York – Cologne, 1996), 317–50 ('The Jewish Sources of Peter

reading to the biblical text, recommended for every student, and translated into French, Italian, English, German, and Czech during the fourteenth century.[58] Peter Abelard (1079–1142), who taught theology at the Church of Saint-Hilaire in Paris, also studied the theory of the elements and assigned the two light elements, air and fire, to the Heavens, the heavier elements to the earth.[59] The same ideas lived on in medieval cosmographies or *Imago Mundi* schemes, for which Honorius' *Imago Mundi* treatise, written around 1120, was an important precursor. The most widespread astronomical-cosmological manuscript of the Middle Ages was certainly the treatise *Liber de sphaera* (or *De sphaera mundi*) written around 1250 by the Parisian university professor Johannes de Sacrobosco (1195–1256), a work that was also used in teaching at Prague University.[60]

There is much to suggest that the *conceptor* took into account yet another text, namely an exegetical, apocryphal text originally called *m'arrat gazzê* ('Cave of Treasures'). This is a biblical retelling reaching from Creation to Pentecost and written in the fourth century by an author who called himself 'Ephrem the Syrian'.[61] He added some further aspects to the

---

Comestor's Commentary on Genesis in his *Historia Scholastica*' at 317).
58 The earliest Czech translation of the *Historia scholastica* was probably written in the Slavonic monastery in Prague (in Glagolitic and Old Czech) at the end of the fourteenth century; cf. Ludmila Pacnerová (ed.), *Staročeský hlaholský Comestor* (Prague, 2002); Sichálek, 'European Background: Czech Translations', 81.
59 Furthermore, texts by William of Conches (c. 1085–after 1154), Peter's contemporary and an early representative of the School of Chartres who had studied Plato's *Timaios* in depth and sought to interpret Creation with the help of *ratio*, become tangible in Prague. A sumptuously illuminated edition of his *Dragmaticon Philosophiae* is now kept at the Biblioteca Nacional de España, Madrid. Its illuminations point to a commissioner from the immediate circle of King Wenceslas IV (Madrid, BNE, Ms. Res. 28, dat. 1402); Italo Ronca and Josep Pujol (eds), *Guillelmi de Conchis Dragmaticon Philosophiae, vol. 1: Summa de Philosophia in Vulgari*, Corpus Christianorum, 62 (Turnhout, 1997). For more on William of Conches, see Eric M. Ramírez-Weaver, 'William of Conches, Philosophical Continuous Narration, and the Limited Worlds of Medieval Diagrams', *Studies in Iconography* 20 (2009), 1–41; Petra Aigner, 'Wilhelm von Conches (Guilelmus de Conchis)', *Biographisch-Bibliographisches Kirchenlexikon* 41 (Hamm, 2020), coll. 1539–54.
60 Petr Hadrava and Alena Hadravová, *Sféra Iohanna de Sacrobosco - středověká učebnice základů astronomie Iohannes de Sacrobosco* (Prague, 2019). The schematic representation of the four elements and heavenly spheres in King Wenceslas' Munich astrological manuscript follows this tradition (BSB, Clm 826, fol. 1v); Maria Theisen, *Kunsthistorischer Kommentar zur Faksimile-Edition der Handschrift der Bayerischen Staatsbibliothek (Clm 826): Astronomisch-astrologischer Codex König Wenzels* (Stuttgart, 2017), 41–4.
61 Therefore, Alexander Toepel placed this book among the genre of the 'rewritten Bible'-literature. See Alexander Toepel, *Die Adam- und Seth-Legenden im syrischen*

respective sections of God's daily works, and explained the nature of the Firmament and its individual layers as follows: 'And on the Second Day God made the Lower Heaven, and called it REKI`A [that is to say, 'what is solid and fixed,' or 'firmament']. This He did that He might make known that the Lower Heaven doth not possess the nature of the heaven which is above it, (...) for the heaven above it is of fire. And that second heaven is NÛHRA (i.e., Light), and this lower heaven is DARPITIÔN (...) it hath the dense nature of water (...) and the ascent of these waters which were above Heaven took place on the Second Day.'[62]

Albrecht Götze was able to prove that the *Cave of Treasures* became particularly popular in the Middle Ages due to the writings of Pseudo-Methodius: 'The *Revelationes* were one of the most widely read books of the Middle Ages (...). Pseudo-Methodius is the channel through which the legends from the beginning of the Syrian Cave of Treasures found their way into the history bibles of Western countries and also into the chronographies.'[63] The *Revelationes*, as tradition shows, were also among the literature considered fundamental by theologians in Bohemia.[64]

Prague had long been a centre of arts, literature, and sciences thanks to the court of the Přemyslid kings. Since the foundation of Prague University by Emperor Charles IV in 1348, and especially during the reign of his son, King Wenceslas IV, Prague turned into an important centre for the study of theology and natural sciences, such as mathematics, cosmology and astronomy/astrology, geography, medicine, and pharmacy. The University

---

Buch der Schatzhöhle: eine quellenkritische Untersuchung (2006), at 3f. On the author's identity, Sergey Minov, 'The Cave of Treasures and Formation of Syriac Christian Identity in Late Antique Mesopotamia: Between Tradition and Innovation', in Brouria Bitton-Ashkelony and Lorenzo Perrone (eds), *Between Personal and Institutional Religion* (Turnhout, 2013), 155–94, at 158f.

62 *The Cave of Treasures of St. Ephrem the Syrian, trans. from the Syriac by E. A. Wallis Budge* (London, 1927) <https://archive.org/details/stephrembookofthecaveoftreasure> [accessed 10 March 2023].

63 Quoted and translated after Albrecht Götze, 'Die Nachwirkungen der Schatzhöhle', *Zeitschrift für Semitistik und verwandte Gebiete* 2 (1923), at 55; Willem J. Aerts and Georg Arnold A. Kortekaas (eds), *Die Apokalypse des Pseudo-Methodius. Die ältesten griechischen und lateinischen Übersetzungen* (Leuven, 1998), at 6, 12, 19, 57; Benjamin Garstad (ed.), *Apocalypse of Pseudo-Methodius / An Alexandrian World Chronicle* (Cambridge, MA, 2012).

64 See, for example, the manuscripts Prague, Národní knihovna České republiky, I C 14; XIII G 18; XV E 4; XIX B 26; Prague, Knihovna Metropolitní kapituly, B XXVIII; Třeboň, Státní oblastní archiv, A 16. Marc Laureis and Daniel Verhelst, 'Pseudo-Methodius, Revelationes: Textgeschichte und kritische Edition. Ein Leuven–Groninger Forschungsprojekt', in Werner Verbeke, Daniel Verhelst and Andries Welkenhuysen (eds), *The Use and Abuse of Eschatology in the Middle Ages* (Leuven, 1988), 112–36. I thank Michal Dragoun for this reference.

of Prague attracted scholars from all over Europe, and they ensured the mediation and public disputation of the most important texts of ancient scientific, medical, and philosophical treatises, for which Arabic texts in Latin translation often formed the starting point.[65] Most scholars in the field of astronomy were theologians, such as canon Nicholas from St Vitus Cathedral on the Hradčín,[66] Jan Hus, and Conrad of Vechta (c. 1370–1431), a close friend to King Wenceslas IV and Archbishop of Prague after the resignation of Sigismund Albicus (Czech: Zikmund Albík z Uničova, c. 1359–1427). Albicus, the personal physician of the king, was also very well-versed in astrology.[67]

There is no doubt that the *conceptor* of the Genesis initial for the king's Bible had studied ancient literature, also regarding the four-elements doctrine and the related theological discourses. The second medallion of the Genesis initial shows God the Father, who created the four elements in order to create the Firmament. The same idea underlies, for example,

---

65 Marie Bláhová discussed, as one of many examples, the *disputatio* of 1411, organized by Jan Hus on works by Abenragel (Abu l-Hasan, d. c. 1040), Alkabitius (al-Qabīṣī, d. 967) and Averroës (Abū l-Walīd, d. 1198); cf. Marie Bláhová, 'Spuren des arabischen Wissens im mittelalterlichen Böhmen', in Andreas Speer and Lydia Wegener (eds), *Wissen über Grenzen: Arabisches Wissen und lateinisches Mittelalter* (Berlin, 2006), 133–42, at 139; concerning readings and quodlibets on Aristotle, Zeno, Plato and other ancient philosophers at Prague University, cf. František Šmahel, *Charles University in the Middle Ages: Selected Studies* (Leiden and Boston, 2007). Famous graduates and then professors of Charles University whose research was devoted to mathematical astronomy included Křišťan z Prachatic (Christian of Prachatice) (d. 1439), teacher of Jan Hus, Dean of the Faculty of Liberal Arts and Rector of Charles University, who is today known to a wider public mainly through his treatise on the construction of astrolabes, and the younger Jan Šindel (d. between 1455 and 1458), who was also the king's personal physician. Šindel is generally associated with the construction of the astrological clock for Prague's Old Town Hall. However, he was better known to Prague and Viennese students of the fifteenth century through his lectures on Claudius Ptolemy. See Pavel Spunar, *Repertorium auctorum bohemorum provectum idearum post universitatem Pragensem conditam illustrans*, vol. 1 (Wrocław, 1985), 97–150, at 103–40.
66 He was the scribe of the astronomical manuscript Vienna, ÖNB, Cod. 2378, an immediate predecessor manuscript to Cod. 2352, prepared for King Wenceslas IV. Cf. Jenni and Theisen, *Mitteleuropäische Schulen IV*, 69–89 and 89–122 (with further literature).
67 Milada Studničková, 'An den Rändern der Bibel des Konrad von Vechta', in Jeffrey F. Hamburger and Maria Theisen (eds), *Unter Druck: Mitteleuropäische Buchmalerei im 15. Jahrhundert,* Tagungsband zum internationalen Kolloquium in Wien, Österreichische Akademie der Wissenschaften, 13.1.–17.1.2016 (Petersberg, 2018), 12–21, at 14; Lenka Panušková, 'Die Vorliebe König Wenzels IV. für Astronomie und Astrologie: Was steht hinter den Diagrammen des Codex Clm 826?', in Milada Studničková and Maria Theisen (eds), *Art in an Unsettled Time. Bohemian Book Illumination before Gutenberg* (Prague, 2018), 82–97.

the corresponding representation in the Paris Fécamp Bible.[68] There, however, God stands within the elements, whereas in the Wenceslas Bible, his figure was placed firmly outside, communicating that his existence is not connected to any element or matter. The same is true of the two little figures who rise in front of him and who most probably represent spiritual beings.[69] These two figures, together with the four elements, lead us back to the ideas connected with the creation of all being from 'matter'.

Like Plato, Aristotle proposed that everything originates from a formless primordial substance (*materia prima*) from which all matter emerges. Only in metaphysics, pure existence itself is conceivable without matter and without any certain form (the quintessence). The work of Aristotle was of fundamental importance for generations of Jewish, Arabic, and Catholic philosophers and theologians.[70] Augustine (354–430) explained that the primordial substance contains the potency to all things.[71] Also, according to Solomon Ibn Gebirol from Málaga (eleventh century) and Maimonides (Rabbi Moshe from Córdoba, 1138–1204), God created matter, and matter emanating from God is present in the spiritual world: everything is based on a *materia universalis*, except the deity (as depicted in the second medallion).[72] The Parisian scholastics took up these ideas. Albertus Magnus (1200–80), who edited and commented on the works of Aristotle and thereby supported the integration of antique philosophers into the Catholic school of philosophy, explained: 'Materia est primum

---

68   London, British Library, Yates Thompson 1, fol. 4v (third quarter of the thirteenth century).
69   These are also mentioned by Johannes Zahlten, but unfortunately remained unexplained; cf. Zahlten, Creatio Mundi, at 135. The Morgan Bible undoubtedly shows two angels (with wings) in the second medallion, but does not emphasize their importance in the process of Creation, since God does not explicitly turn to them. Moreover, angelic figures are shown in the backgrounds of all seven medallions within this Genesis initial (New York, The Pierpont Morgan Library, MS M 833, fol. 5r). Therefore, it is precisely the reduction of the figures shown in the respective medallion of the Wenceslas Bible that reveals which aspects were particularly important to its *conceptor*.
70   Sven Müller, *Naturgemäße Ortsbewegung: Aristoteles' Physik und ihre Rezeption bis Newton* (Tübingen, 2006); also see manuscripts written at Charles University, e.g., *Jenko Wenceslai de Praga, Expositiones super libros Aristotelis* (Prague, Národní knihovna České republiky, VIII G 30, c. 1375); Anonymous, *Miscellany of medical and astronomical treatises*, Charles University, with texts by Euclid, Abu al-Hasan ben Ridvan, Hippokrates, Abu Zakaria Yuhana Ibn Masawaih, Theophilus Philaretus and others (Prague, Národní knihovna České republiky, VIII G 27, c. 1400/25).
71   *Confessiones* XII, 8; 40; *De civitate dei* XXII, 2; Christoph Horn (ed.), *Augustinus, De civitate dei* (Berlin, second edition, 2015).
72   Moritz Eisler, *Vorlesungen über die jüdischen Philosophen*, vol. 1 (Vienna, 1876), 62ff.

subiectum eius quod est', i.e., 'matter is the basis of all beings and things.' The primordial matter is *potentia inchoationis formae*,[73] it carries all form within itself. Thomas Aquinas (c. 1225–74) distinguished between different matter from which different beings – including spiritual beings such as angels – emerge. In his *Summa theologiae* he also mentioned a 'materia sensibilis and intelligibilis'.[74] Bonaventura (1221–74) believed that spiritual beings are pure *materia prima*.[75] Although the creation of angels is not mentioned in Genesis, it seemed clear from the Scriptures that they were God's creatures, created from *materia* before Adam, but the question remained: on which day?

Ephrem the Syrian[76] and Augustine were convinced that angels were created from a primordial substance on the first day and interpreted the famous words 'Fiat Lux!' as the creation of the spirit (enlightenment). In his *Confessiones*, Augustine speaks of 'spiritualis et intellectualis creatura' on the first day of Creation: 'it is light.'[77] In Ephrem's *Cave of Treasures*, we read:

> At the beginning, on the First Day, which was the holy First Day of the Week, the chief and firstborn of all the days, God created the heavens, and the earth, and the waters, and the air, and the fire, and the hosts which are invisible (that is to say, the Angels, Archangels, Thrones, Lords, Principalities, Powers, Cherubim and Seraphim), and all the ranks and companies of spiritual beings, and the light, and the night, and the day-time, and the gentle winds and the strong winds. All these were created on the First Day. And on the First Day of the Week

---

73 Albertus Magnus, 'Summa theologiae sive de mirabili scientia dei II, Q. 4'; Henryk Anzulewicz, 'Summa theologiae sive de mirabili scientia dei, libri 1–2', in Michael Eckert, Eilert Herms, Bernd Jochen Hilberath and Eberhard Jüngel (eds), *Lexikon der theologischen Werke* (Stuttgart, 2003), 681f.
74 Thomas Aquinas, *Summa theologica* I, Q. 44; online edition <http://www.logicmuseum.com/wiki/Authors/Thomas_Aquinas/Summa_Theologiae/Part_I/Q44> [accessed 10 March 2023].
75 Bonaventura, *Commentaria in Quatuor Libros Sententiarum* II, D. 3; online edition <https://franciscan-archive.org/bonaventura/sent.html> [accessed 10 March 2023].
76 In his extended description of the creation of Adam, Ephrem the Syrian once again refers to the existence of the previously created angels and to the meaning of the four elements.
77 Augustine, *Confessiones*, Liber XIII, chapter 2, 3; Jacques-Paul Migne (ed.), 'Sancti Aurelii Augustini, Hipponensis episcopi, Confessiones', *Patrologia Latina* 32 (Paris, 1861); James J. O'Donnell (ed.), *The Confessions of Augustine* (Oxford, 1992), electronic edition: <https://faculty.georgetown.edu/jod/conf/> [accessed 10 March 2023].

the Spirit of Holiness, one of the Persons of the Trinity, hovered over the waters (…).[78]

Accordingly, Peter Comestor reckoned that the creation of the angels, just like the four elements, took place on the first day.[79]

The problem was of course also discussed by Jewish theologians, and some rabbis believed that the angels were not created on the first, but on the second day. Rabbi Jochanan (Jerusalem, d. c. 80)[80], for example, was convinced that the angels were created on the second day, by quoting Psalm 103:4: 'Who makest thy angels spirits: and thy ministers a burning fire.' Rabbi Hanina (Galilee, d. c. 75)[81], however, by comparing Genesis 1:20 to Isaiah 40:26, said that the angels must have been created on the fifth day.[82] There also existed the kabbalistic idea that God created angels every day, but only the angels created on the second day would live on forever. Angels created on other days would 'perish, like those created on the fifth day who sang their anthem to God's praise, then ceased to be'.[83] It is, therefore, very likely that the two figures in the second medallion of our Genesis initial are such never-ceasing holy angels, who were created before the actual creation of the world, according to Rabbi Jochanan, on the second day. The two figures in our medallion could possibly refer to the

---

[78] *The Cave of Treasures of St. Ephrem the Syrian, trans. from the Syriac by E. A. Wallis Budge* (London, 1927) <https://archive.org/details/stephrembookofthecaveoftreasure> [accessed 10 March 2023].

[79] 'In principio creavit deus celum et terram. (…) id est celum empyreum et angelica natura. terram vero materiam omnium corporum id est quatuor elementa (…).' ('In the beginning God created heaven and earth […], that is, the empyrean heaven which is of angel-like nature, and the earth which is the matter of which consist all physical objects, in other words the four elements […]' ; translation by Karl Kügle); cf. Georg Husner (impr.), *Scholastica historia Magistri Petri Comestoris seriem brevem nimis et obscuram elucidans* (Strasbourg, 1500), a3.

[80] Rabbi Jochanan (ben Zakkaj – the Wise) is considered the head of the Jews after the destruction of the Temple in 70 AD and the founder of the House of Teachings in Jabne. The anachronistic title Rabban was a sign of the reverence and respect that later generations felt for him, since rabbinic law, rabbinic worship, and even the role of the rabbi in Jewish life can be traced back to him. Cf. Jacob Neusner, *A life of Yohanan ben Zakkai, ca.1–80 C.E.* (Leiden, 1970).

[81] Rabbi Hanina (also 'Chanina', ben Dosa) was a disciple of Jochanan. His title is likewise an honorary title; cf. Jonathan Kaplan, 'Ḥanina ben Dosa', in *Encyclopedia of the Bible and Its Reception* 11 (Boston, 2015), coll. 229–31.

[82] Bereishit Rabbah 1; cf. digital edition <https://www.sefaria.org/Bereishit_Rabbah.1.3?lang=bi> [accessed 10 March 2023]; *Midrash Rabbah*, trans. Rabbi Dr H. Freedman and Maurice Simon, with a foreword by Rabbi Dr I. Epstein (London, third edition, 1961), at 5.

[83] Herbert Lockyer, *All the Angels in the Bible: A Complete Exploration of the Nature and Ministry of Angels* (Peabody, MA, 1995), 11–15, at 13f.

two archangels Michael – who defended the Heavens – and Lucifer – who, later on, was damned to Hell and led Adam and Eve to break God's law: they are both God's creatures and define the further fate of mankind.[84] Peter Comestor, who says that, 'according to the Hebrew tradition', Lucifer was created on the second day, gives a hint at this interpretation.[85] The two wingless figures are archetypes of angels and correspond to the first biblical accounts in which angels appear as men or young men. They are quite different from those winged angels who are described in the younger writings of the Tanakh (especially those of the Babylonian Exile – such angels are shown in the frame of the initial, and thus belong to a different sphere of time).

How could King Wenceslas' *conceptor*, however, know of such rabbinical considerations? The king himself is said to have frequently granted audiences to Avigdor Kara ben Isaac (d. 1439),[86] the chief rabbi of the Prague community, and to have had extensive discussions with him on religious matters. Avigdor Kara impressed with his excellent knowledge of the Holy Scriptures; he was known as a Kabbalist, author of theological writings, and a poet. There is no concrete evidence that he was in the service of King Wenceslas, as was assumed by Jacob Moellin (c. 1360–1427),[87] but there is no doubt that he was willing to discuss theological issues in detail with the king and dignitaries of the Catholic Church. This way, rabbinical considerations also proved to be particularly influential for the newly formed group of Church critics around the theologian Jan Hus, who searched for the roots of the Christian faith. Thus, the creation of the holy angels on the second day may indeed have been a view impressed by Avigdor Kara, Jacob Moellin, or other contemporary Jewish authorities on the *conceptor* of the king's Bible. Many other miniatures

---

84 Maria Bettetini, 'Die Wahl der Engel: Übel, Materie und Willensfreiheit', in Christoph Horn (ed.), *Augustinus, De civitate dei*, Klassiker Auslegen, 11 (Berlin, second edition, 2015), 131–56.

85 (...) *tradunt enim hebrei: que hac die angelus factus est diabolus sathanael. id est lucifer*; cf. Husner, *Scholastica historia Magistri Petri Comestoris* (Strasbourg, 1503), a4.

86 He was the son of Isaac Kara, who died in the synagogue during the Easter pogrom of 1389. In memory of the dead of the pogrom, Avigdor wrote the elegy *Et Kol ha-Tela'ah asher Meẓa'atnu*. Milan Žonca, 'Několik poznámek k intelektuálnímu profilu Avigdora Kary', in Daniel Boušek, Magdalena Křížová and Pavel Sládek (eds), *Dvarim meatim: Studie pro Jiřinu Šedinovou* (Prague, 2016), 35–56; his possible connections to the court and courtiers are discussed at 45–7.

87 Jacob ben Moses Moellin (c. 1360–1427) was head of the Jewish communities in Germany, Austria, and Bohemia; Sidney Steiman, *Custom and Survival: A Study of the Life and Work of R. Jacob Molin* (New York, 1963); Martin Przybilski, *Kulturtransfer zwischen Juden und Christen in der deutschen Literatur des Mittelalters* (Berlin and New York, 2010).

of the Wenceslas Bible also show remarkably good knowledge of Jewish liturgical utensils like chalices, bowls, and censers,[88] which goes far beyond other contemporaneous representations as known, for example, from the Commentary on the Bible by Nicholas of Lyra.[89] This proves that Hana Hlaváčková was justified when she noted that the influence of the Jewish community on intellectual life, not least mirrored by the Wenceslas Bible, is investigated far too little.[90]

THE THIRD DAY

> Got vorwar sprach. Die wasser die under dem himel sind sammen sich an ein stat und erscheine die trucken und es geschach also. Und got name die trucken erde und die sammenunge der wasser nante her die mer. Und got sach das es gut was und sprach. Gebere die erde grunende wurcze und machende samen und ein opfeltragendes holcz und mache frucht noch seinem geslechte des same in im selbir sei auf der erden. Und es geschach allso. Und furbrachte die erde grundende wurcze die samen trug noch irem geslechte und holcz das do machte frucht und hette samen ein yetliches noch seinem geslechte. (…) (Cod. 2759, fols 2v/3r)[91]

In this medallion, the representation focuses on the very detailed biblical account of the creation of the plants, following the previous separation

---

88 It is perhaps no coincidence that most of these miniatures were created by court illuminator Frana, who in the late nineties of the fourteenth century ran a workshop right at the entrance to Prague's Jewish town; Václav Vladivoj Tomek, *Dějepis města Prahy*, vol. 2 (Prague, 1871), at 218; vol. 3 (1875), at 22; vol. 5 (1881), at 55; Maria Theisen, 'Picturing Frana', in Zoë Opačić and Achim Timmermann (eds), *Image, Memory and Devotion. Studies in Gothic Art* (London, 2010), 103–12.
89 King Wenceslas also seems to have owned volumes of this biblical commentary. Unfortunately, only one volume of the complete set has survived: the commentary on the Psalter. It was written at the same time as the Wenceslas Bible and contains a classical psalter illustration cycle with small historiated initials at the beginning of the major psalms (Salzburg, University Library, M III 20); cf. Theisen, 'Texte und Bilder', 105–45, at 135–9 (Fig. 79, 10).
90 Hlaváčková particularly remarked on the Hebrew inscriptions in some miniatures – to examine those more closely remains a desideratum; cf. Hlaváčková, 'Old Testament Scenes', 132–9, at 136 and 138.
91 'God also said: Let the waters that are under the heaven, be gathered together into one place: and let the dry land appear. And it was so done. And God called the dry land, Earth; and the gathering together of the waters, he called Seas. And God saw that it was good. And he said: Let the earth bring forth the green herb, and such as may seed, and the fruit tree yielding fruit after its kind, which may have seed in itself upon the earth (…)' (Gen 1:9–12, quoted according to *The Holy Bible: Douay-Rheims Version*).

of water and land.⁹² The miniature corresponds to Genesis 1:11 (and thus also to Petrus Comestor's *Historia scholastica*), saying: 'Produxit enim de terra herbam virentem, et facientem semen', and to the last verse of the description of the third day in the *Cave of Treasures*: 'And on this third day God commanded the earth, and it brought forth herbs and vegetables, and it gave birth in its midst to trees and seeds and plants and roots.'

THE FOURTH DAY

> *Got aber sprach. Es werde liecht an dem firmament des himels und teilen tag und nacht (...) und erleuchten die erde und es geschach also. Und got machte czwei grose liecht (...) und stern und saczte sie an des himels firmament so das sie leuchten auf der erden (...) und got sach das es gut was und wart gemacht abend und morgen der vierde tag.* (Cod. 2759, fol. 3r)⁹³

Instead of showing the creation of the sun and the moon on this day, which, as we have already seen, was placed into the first medallion because of their symbolic value, the depiction now concentrates on the creation of the animals living on land and in the forests. This logically follows the preparatory creation of meadows and woods the day before.

THE FIFTH DAY

> *Auch sprach got fürbrengen die wasser krichende tyr lebendiges geistes und gevogel uf der erden under dem firmament des himels. Und got schepfte grose walvische und alle lebendige sele und bewegliche die do fürbrachten die wasser in irr gestalt. Und alles gevogel noch seinem geslechte. Und got sach das es gut was und gesegent in und sprach. Wachset und meret euch und erfullet die wasser des meres und die vogel sullen sich meren uf der erden. Und wart gemacht abent und morgen der funfte tag.* (Cod. 2759, fol. 3r)⁹⁴

---

92 Franz Unterkircher, *König Wenzels Bibelbilder: Die Miniaturen zur Genesis aus der Wenzelsbibel* (Graz, 1983), at 40.
93 'And God said: Let there be lights made in the firmament of heaven, to divide the day and the night, (...) to give light upon the earth. And it was so done. And God made two great lights: (...) and the stars. And he set them in the firmament of heaven to shine upon the earth. (...) And God saw that it was good. And the evening and morning were the fourth day.' (Gen 1:14–19, quoted according to *The Holy Bible: Douay-Rheims Version*).
94 'God also said: Let the waters bring forth the creeping creature having life, and the fowl that may fly over the earth under the firmament of heaven. And God

With this representation, the *conceptor* once more smoothly took up the rhythm established by the Genesis text and showed the creation of those animals that live in the air and in the water.

THE SIXTH DAY

> *(...) und got sach das es gut was und sprach. Mache wir einen menschen noch unserm bilde und noch unserem gleichnisse das er vorwese den vischen des meres und den gevogeln des himels und den wilden der erden und aller erden und allen krichenden das sich ruret in der erden. Und got schepfte einen menschen czu seinem bilde czu gotes bilde schepfte er in man und wip schepfte er sie. Und got gesegent in und sprach. Wachset und meret euch und erfullet die erden (...)* (Cod. 2759, fol. 3r)[95]

In Ephrem's text, we read about angels again and about the meaning of the four elements: 'And the angels saw that when these four weak materials were placed in the palm of his right hand, that is, cold and heat and dryness and humidity, God formed Adam.' Ephrem continues: 'The crown of glory was placed on his [Adam's] head, there he was made king and priest and prophet, there God made him sit on his honorary throne, and there, God gave him dominion over all creatures and things.'[96] This passage, when compared to the Wenceslas Bible, suggests that the Prague *conceptor* actually knew Ephrem's *Cave of Treasures* or Pseudo-Methodius' *Revelationes*. He chose to accompany precisely this sixth medallion (showing the creation of the primordial couple Adam and Eve) with the figure of King Wenceslas, because the king was perceived as the successor of Adam, the first king by God's grace. In order to regain the

---

created the great whales, and every living and moving creature, which the waters brought forth, according to their kinds, and every winged fowl according to its kind. And God saw that it was good. And he blessed them, saying: Increase and multiply, and fill the waters of the sea: and let the birds be multiplied upon the earth. And the evening and morning were the fifth day.' (Gen 1:20–3, quoted according to *The Holy Bible: Douay-Rheims Version*).

95 '(...) And God saw that it was good. And he said: Let us make man to our image and likeness: and let him have dominion over the fishes of the sea, and the fowls of the air, and the beasts, and the whole earth, and every creeping creature that moveth upon the earth. And God created man to his own image: to the image of God he created him: male and female he created them. And God blessed them, saying: Increase and multiply, and fill the earth (...)' (Gen 1:25–8, quoted according to *The Holy Bible: Douay-Rheims Version*).

96 *The Cave of Treasures of St. Ephrem the Syrian*, trans. from the Syriac by E. A. Wallis Budge (London, 1927) <https://archive.org/details/stephrembookofthecaveoftreasure> [accessed 10 March 2023].

purity of Adam in Paradise, Wenceslas, like every Christian king, had to undergo a ritual (spiritual) bath before his coronation. The bath attendant has at least two meanings in this context, since emblems are by nature ambivalent and multilayered in their meanings: on the one hand, she is Adam's partner (her tuft of leaves resembles those of Adam and Eve at the expulsion from Paradise), and on the other hand, as the bath attendant, she is responsible for the royal bath.[97] After the ritual bath, the king, in the coronation sequence, took an oath to God and the crown: he married 'Lady Crown', as Laurentius of Březová put it.[98] Therefore, we see the king constrained by means of the crowned letter *e*, which symbolizes the *vinculum iugale* here. The letter *e* itself can be read as a complete Middle-High-German word – *Ehe* – and meant 'marriage', 'union'. The crown with cross, bow and mitre represents the crown of the Empire, even though it is not a realistic depiction of the original (and even though Wenceslas was never crowned Emperor by the pope). Above it, we see a torque as a symbol of union and a kingfisher that stands for eternal conjugal love, union, and rebirth – both belong to the king's emblematic repertoire.[99] The kingfisher embodies an allegory, which reaches back to the ancient story of Alcyone from Ovid's *Metamorphoses*.[100] Additionally, we may see here again the influence of St Ambrose's *Hexameron*. Ambrose, and after him also Isidor of Seville, Hrabanus Maurus and many others, celebrated this bird as one of the first animals created by the Lord; moreover, it is considered a symbol of robust fertility.[101] On the first page of the Genesis in King Wenceslas' Bible, the emblems are furthermore

---

97 Since Julius von Schlosser, 'Die Bilderhandschriften Königs Wenzel I.', countless attempts have been made to interpret the emblems of King Wenceslas IV. An overview of the history and the interpretations in circulation is provided by Maria Theisen, in Jenni and Theisen, *Mitteleuropäische Schulen IV*, 5–12. <https://e-book.fwf.ac.at/o:571 (text) [accessed 10 March 2023].
98 Karel Hruza, 'Audite Celi! Ein satirischer hussitischer Propagandatext gegen König Sigismund', in *Propaganda, Kommunikation und Öffentlichkeit*, Forschungen zur Geschichte des Mittelalters, 6 (Vienna, 2002), 129–51.
99 Maria Theisen, 'The Emblem of the Torque and its Use in the Willehalm Manuscript of King Wenceslas IV of Bohemia', *Journal of the British Archaeological Association* 171:1 (2018), 131–53.
100 Ovid, *Metamorphoses* XI, vv. 410–748; Ernst Carl Christian Bach, *P. Ovidi Nasonis Metamorphoseon Libri XV. Mit kritischen und erläuternden Anmerkungen, zweiter Band, VIII–XV* (Hannover, 1836), 220–45; Schlosser, 'Die Bilderhandschriften Königs Wenzel I.', 283; Edmund W. Braun, 'Ceyx und Alcyone', in *Reallexikon zur Deutschen Kunstgeschichte* 3 (Munich, 1954), coll. 403–5.
101 Cf. Hana Hlaváčková, 'Courtly Body in the Bible of Wenceslas IV', 371–82. Hlaváčková also sees an allegory of fertility in all other emblems of the king, and suggests interpretation of the 'e' as '*Erde*' [(mother) earth], the letter 'W' as '*Welt*' [world]; cf. Hlaváčková, 'K dataci a emblematice Bible Václava IV / On the Dating

associated with the imperial coat of arms. Opposite we see a Bavarian coat of arms painted over in white.[102] It stands for one of his wives (both were from the house of Wittelsbach in Bavaria). The Bohemian coat of arms and the royal insignia at the right margin form the third vertical row of illuminations on this page. All these elements clearly connect the king with God's Creation and the history of Salvation, as testified by the angels, Old Testament prophets and New Testament apostles within the architectural framework of this initial.

CONCLUSION

The above observations provide new insights into the conceptual work underlying the pictorial programme of the Wenceslas Bible. They highlight the role played by Latin paraphrases of the Vulgate to direct the craftsmen creating illuminations for a German text suspected of heresy. The Genesis initial in particular reveals more than any other the spiritual and scholarly hothouse atmosphere of Prague around 1400. With its pronounced exegetical function, it provides a link between the past as reflected in the texts of Holy Scripture, and the king's present. Its programme echoes the

---

and Emblematics of the King Wenceslaus IV's Bible', 46–8. See also the contribution by Gia Toussaint in this volume.

102 Ulrike Bodemann suggested that this painting-over took place under the reign of Emperor Sigismund or Emperor Frederick III: 'Bibeln. Handschrift Nr. 14.0.20', in *Katalog der deutschsprachigen illustrierten Handschriften des Mittelalters, begonnen von Hella Frühmorgen-Voss, fortgeführt von Norbert H. Ott zusammen mit Ulrike Bodemann*, vol. 2 (Munich, 1996), 170–4. It is remarkable, however, that the Bavarian coat of arms does not appear in any other Wenceslas manuscript. Therefore, the possibility must be considered that King Wenceslas IV decided to reorganize and focus the pictorial programme of the Bible more exclusively on Bohemia and the Empire; this probably occurred after the death of his first wife Johanna on New Year's Eve 1386 (the black torques in the first quires of the Willehalm trilogy, Vienna, ÖNB, Cod. Ser. n. 2643, may have been an expression of grief over her death). This assumption would support Hlaváčková's conviction that the queen depicted in the prologue is indeed Johanna, while Schmidt, 'Kunsthistorischer Kommentar', had declared himself in favour of Queen Sophia, who had married Wenceslas in 1389; regarding this problem cf. Jenni and Theisen, *Mitteleuropäische Schulen IV*, 210. Whether we can necessarily conclude from this that the Wenceslas Bible was commissioned ten years earlier than the Willehalm manuscript for King Wenceslas IV, dated 1387, as Hlaváčková argues ('K dataci a emblematice Bible Václava IV / On the Dating and Emblematics of the King Wenceslaus IV's Bible'), must be left open; cf. Hana Hlaváčková, 'Knižní malba v době krále Václava IV', in Jiří Kuthan and Jakub Šenovský (eds), *Římský a český král Václav IV. a počátky husitské revoluce* (Prague, 2019), 131–53. Both are possible from the art historian's point of view; further in-depth analysis of the text might bring more clarity.

thoughts of the most prominent theological circles at Prague University and their proto-reformatory ideas, as well as the input from the Prague Jewish community represented by their chief rabbi, Avigdor Kara. Close readings of the medallions of the Genesis initial revealed that their *conceptor* worked together with, or was himself, an expert theologian who had internalized not only the verses of the Bible but also texts written by authors such as Ambrose, Thomas Aquinas, John of Sacrobosco, and Peter Comestor. In addition, he was familiar with apocryphal texts such as Ephrem's *Cave of Treasures* and with rabbinic literature linked to ancient scientific and philosophical sources. The whole project was closely linked to the representation of Wenceslas IV as King of Bohemia and King of the Romans (and eventually-to-be-crowned Holy Roman Emperor) through an equally learned emblematic programme and heraldic devices. Didactically laid out for their royal patron, all recipients were to look, read and learn by interpreting these images, which had been beautifully painted in praise of God – and of Wenceslas, his worldly representative.[103]

---

103 The writing of this essay was supported by the Czech research grant project 'The Construction of the Other in Medieval Europe' of the Faculty of Philosophy, University of Ostrava (IRP 201820, Director: PhDr. Daniela Rywiková, PhD).
This project is dedicated to questions of social, religious and cultural interaction, cooperation, co-existence and demarcation in medieval and early modern Europe. I thank Sammie A. Cunningham (Cambridge) for her great help in translating my article into English. My thanks also go to Karl Kügle, Ingrid Ciulisová and Václav Žůrek for their continuous and invaluable support during the editing process.

CHAPTER 8

THE NAKED KING: REPRESENTING WENCESLAS IN HIS ILLUMINATED BIBLE

GIA TOUSSAINT

Pictorial portraits of rulers are characterized by insignia of power: splendid robes, sovereign poses and dynastic attributes are an indispensable part of ruler iconography. A stark-naked ruler seems unimaginable, even more so in a copy of the Bible – but this is precisely the case in the Wenceslas Bible (Vienna, Österreichische Nationalbibliothek, Cod. 2759–2764). King Wenceslas IV of Bohemia (1361–1419) is shown stark naked several times, and not alone. Bath maids, a trade of questionable reputation, are depicted next to him. It would be short-sighted to attribute a love affair in this milieu to Wenceslas. However, neither does dismissing these depictions as grotesques do justice to the matter. All this suggests that this anomaly is about more than an ostentatious display of nudity and hedonistic *joie de vivre* of the ruler.

King Wenceslas, who commissioned the manuscript as the patron, was evidently not displeased with the depiction of his nudity and the associated violation of norms. As the son of Emperor Charles IV, he inherited a difficult legacy. His father, one of the most influential and important rulers of the late Middle Ages in Europe, had continuously expanded and consolidated his rule with great political skill. In contrast, Wenceslas was not such a consummate politician.[1] Although he was prepared by his father from childhood for later ruling tasks, he did not possess sufficient personal skills to fulfil them comprehensively.[2] After the death of Charles IV (29 November 1378), Wenceslas became the plaything of political interests and intra-family power struggles, which he could do little to oppose. The year 1400 marked the low point of his reign: he was declared deposed by four of the seven electoral princes of the Holy Roman Empire.[3]

Wenceslas was also unlucky in his personal life. Already as a child, in 1370, he was wed to Johanna (Joan) of Bavaria-Straubing, who died in 1386. A few years later, in May 1389, he married again; his new wife, the Wittelsbach princess Sophia of Bavaria (1376–1425), was not crowned Queen of Bohemia until 1400, and survived her husband.[4] Both marriages remained childless, making the continuation of the dynasty extremely problematic. Childlessness was also commonly understood as bad luck, if not a sign of male incapacity.

As unfortunate as Wenceslas' political actions might have been, his cultural interests were all the more ambitious and fruitful. He mastered three languages – Czech, German, and Latin.[5] As in his father's time, book production flourished in Prague during his reign.[6] Wenceslas, as a bibliophile and owner of an extensive private library, is known to

---

1 See the concise characterization of King Wenceslas by Martin Kintzinger, 'Wenzel (1376–1400, † 1419)', in Bernd Schneidmüller and Stefan Weinfurter (eds), *Die deutschen Herrscher des Mittelalters: Historische Portraits von Heinrich I. bis Maximilian I. (919–1519)* (Munich, 2003), 433–45.
2 On Wenceslas as 'the most negatively rated' (p. 17) ruler of Central European history, see Ivan Hlaváček, 'Der Hof Wenzels IV. als führendes Kulturzentrum Mitteleuropas', in H. Heger et al. (eds), *Die Wenzelsbibel: Kommentar* (Graz, 1998), vol. 2, 9–36, at 17–19.
3 The relevant source states that 'we [consider] the aforementioned Lord Wenceslas as unreliable, incompetent and unworthy to hold the Holy Emperorship. It is from this same Holy Roman Emperorship that we wish to remove and dethrone him completely and once and for all at this very moment' ('wir den vorgeschriben hern Wenczelaw als eynen vorsumer, entgleder und unwirdigen des heiligen richs von demselben heiligen Romischen riche und alle der wirde darczu gehorig zu dißer zijt wollen genczlichen und zumale abethun und abeseczen'). See 'Absetzung König Wenzels, 1400. Aug. 20 (no. 135)', in Karl Zeumer (ed.), *Quellensammlung zur Geschichte der Deutschen Reichsverfassung in Mittelalter und Neuzeit* (Tübingen, 1907), 189–92, at 191. See further Helmut G. Walther, 'Der gelehrte Jurist als politischer Ratgeber: Die Kölner Universität und Absetzung König Wenzels 1400', in Albert Zimmermann (ed.), *Die Kölner Universität im Mittelalter: Geistige Wurzeln und soziale Wirklichkeit* (Berlin, 1989), 467–87.
4 Cf. Ulrike Jenni and Maria Theisen, *Mitteleuropäische Schulen. IV (ca. 1380–1400). Hofwerkstätten König Wenzels IV. und deren Umkreis. Textband* (Vienna, 2014), 3.
5 Hlaváček, 'Der Hof Wenzels', 24.
6 Hlaváček, 'Der Hof Wenzels', 25–6.

have commissioned numerous codices, including several magnificent manuscripts produced between 1385 and 1400.[7] These manuscripts were undoubtedly created for his personal use. The so-called Wenceslas Bible, an early German translation of the Bible, is one of the most magnificent of these manuscripts. The prologue shows that this bible was written for Wenceslas (Cod. 2759, fol. 2r).[8] Although intended as a full bible in several volumes, only an incomplete Old Testament was produced, which initially existed in unbound quires. These were bound into three volumes by the middle of the fifteenth century; a new binding in six volumes was produced in the eighteenth century.[9] It is still unclear today when work on the Wenceslas Bible began and when and why it was discontinued.[10] The most recent detailed description of the manuscript by Maria Theisen gives the date of origin as '1389 to 1400 (?)'.[11]

Opulent illustrations adorn the work. There are more than 600 miniatures – representing less than a third of the miniatures intended. If the manuscript had been completed, there would be around 2000 individual pictures.[12] Several master illuminators were involved in the production.[13] This was an extremely ambitious project that eclipsed all previous German-language bibles in magnificence and execution. The miniatures can be divided into three types: historiated initials, pictures inserted into

7   For a list of works made for the library of Wenceslas, see Hlaváček, 'Der Hof Wenzels', 28–32. A special list dedicated to luxury manuscripts can be found in Gerhard Schmidt, 'Kunsthistorischer Kommentar', in Hedwig Heger et al. (eds), *Die Wenzelsbibel: Kommentar*, vol. 2, 125–72, at 125–6.
8   See the description of the manuscript by Theisen in Jenni and Theisen, *Mitteleuropäische Schulen*, 158–212, at 159. The relevant passage reads: 'Der schol nu dancken dem vrumen / Von dem dicz gestift ist kumen / Dem hochgeborne(n) kunig wenczlab vein / Und der durchluchtigsten kuniginne sein' ('Let him [the reader] give thanks to the pious one, to the high-born King Wenceslas and his most noble queen, by whom this [work] was donated'). In this case it is clear that the donor actually owned the manuscript.
9   The original covers of the fifteenth-century binding are no longer extant. See Theisen in Jenni and Theisen, *Mitteleuropäische Schulen*, 159.
10   The problems associated with the dating are discussed by Theisen in Jenni and Theisen, *Mitteleuropäische Schulen*, 210–11. Theisen explains that it is not clear whether the queen depicted next to Wenceslas in the miniature of the prologue is to be identified as Johanna (Joan) of Bavaria-Straubing or as her successor Sophia of Bavaria-Munich. Johanna of Bavaria-Straubing died on New Year's Eve 1386. Sophia was married to King Wenceslas IV in May 1389. These two historically secure dates are, as it were, the cornerstones of today's discussions about the beginning of the production process of the manuscript – either around 1385 or around 1390. See also below, n. 19, and the contribution by Maria Theisen to this volume.
11   Theisen in Jenni and Theisen, *Mitteleuropäische Schulen*, 158.
12   Schmidt, 'Kunsthistorischer Kommentar', 132.
13   See the listing in Schmidt, 'Kunsthistorischer Kommentar', 130.

the text columns (mostly illustrations of biblical episodes), and foliate bar borders framing the columns. Other pictorial motifs, some of which are *drôleries*, are interwoven within these borders, including depictions of the naked king or the king trapped in a letter, accompanied by a bath maid. All pages are elaborately decorated in this way. It is not known who was responsible for the pictorial programme, but it can be concluded from the many preserved painting instructions 'that it was a well-read clergyman, in whose memory were stored not only the text of the Vulgate, but precisely also striking passages from the commentary literature'.[14] According to Maria Theisen, the complexity of the iconography in the Wenceslas Bible can be explained only on the basis of the assumption that the painters had been carefully instructed.[15] To anticipate what we are going to demonstrate in what follows: these instructions must also have related to the sexually explicit depictions such as the circumcision of Abraham, the coitus scenes, and the unmistakable phallic symbolism of the naked Wenceslas in the bath.

Apart from depictions of biblical themes, there are numerous personal elements in the illustrations, some of which are encoded and continue to puzzle researchers. For example, there has been much speculation about the meaning of the isolated letters *e* and *w* within individual miniatures, the symbolic meaning of the pictorial motif of the cloths intertwined into knots, and the depiction of the kingfisher that decorates many pages.[16] Even more puzzling, however, seems to be the portrayal of the king himself. He appears first as a ruler with the insignia of royal power, then dressed as a nobleman, crammed into certain letters as between the jaws of a vice, and, thirdly, as a naked man being cared for by scantily clad bath maids. At first glance, these three modes of representation seem to have nothing to do with each other. However, a look at the biography of the ruler and his personal situation, as well as the association of the individual depictions of Wenceslas with certain biblical texts, reveal a telling pattern. In the first book of the Bible, the Book of Genesis, no image of the king is designed at random; when read in conjunction with the associated biblical text, the illustrations point to a very personal problem of Wenceslas – his childlessness. The reason for Wenceslas' childlessness is unknown. What was known, however, was the problem itself. The depictions of Wenceslas,

---

14   Schmidt, 'Kunsthistorischer Kommentar', 139.
15   See also the discussion of this question in Maria Theisen's contribution to this volume.
16   The various interpretations of the letters and symbols associated with Wenceslas are listed in Schmidt, 'Kunsthistorischer Kommentar', 150–73. The 'knot' is also discussed in Maria Theisen, 'The Emblem of the Torque and its Use in the Willehalm Manuscript of King Wenceslas IV of Bohemia', *Journal of the British Archaeological Association* 171 (2018), 131–53.

naked and in the company of bath maids, consistently appear when the biblical narrative refers to the procreation of new life or the genealogical preservation of the clan or dynasty. This observation sheds new light on the illustrations of the Wenceslas Bible, and also offers a more coherent alternative to the interpretation suggested by Josef Krása.[17] At the same time, and seemingly contradicting this, the artists never depicted the king's body as weak; on the contrary, phallic symbolism and portrayals as a Wild Man make Wenceslas appear powerful and vigorous. The king's childlessness remained a problem which was neither directly addressed nor illustrated. The Wenceslas Bible wanted to convey the image of a potent ruler and yet, through the recurring theme of procreation and sexuality in combination with Wenceslas' nakedness, pointed precisely to the sore spot: would Wenceslas be able to preserve the dynasty through descendants and remedy his 'genealogical deficit'?[18] The answer was unknown at the time of the commission. The illustrations can therefore be read as expressing Wenceslas' hopes and self-reassurance that he would in due course be granted biblical-style blessings of numerous offspring.

The Wenceslas Bible, with its numerous different depictions of the king – as ruler, nobleman, and naked man – is about the physicality of the ruler; this is particularly evident in the display of Wenceslas' naked body. How the body of the king is staged as an official or political body, but above all as a natural, naked body, and how both intertwine in the context of the biblical text, will be explored below.

THE KING AS RULER: WENCESLAS SET IN THE COLUMNS

King Wenceslas as ruler is always shown in the classical style of royal images – enthroned as a crowned king with regalia. He is the King of Bohemia. This iconography of Wenceslas is almost exclusively found in the pictorial fillings of decorative initials, each marking the beginning of a biblical book. An exception is the prologue at the beginning of the

---

17 Josef Krása, *Die Handschriften König Wenzels IV.* (Vienna, 1971), associated the appearance of the bath maidens in the Wenceslas Bible with three phenomena: 1 – Old Testament couples and figures prefiguring Christ; 2 – Old Testament ritual: the Ark of the Covenant, scenes of purification, anointing, or sacrifice; 3 – mentions of the Promised Land.
18 On the genealogical awareness of medieval dynasties, see Julian Führer, 'Gegenwart der Vorgänger und genealogisches Bewusstsein bei den Kapetingern (987–1223)', in Hartwin Brandt, Katrin Köhler and Ulrike Siewert (eds), *Genealogisches Bewusstsein als Legitimation: Inter- und intragenerationelle Auseinandersetzungen sowie die Bedeutung von Verwandtschaft bei Amtswechseln* (Bamberg, 2009), 145–66, at 147.

manuscript which depicts God himself. In the inner field of the letter *O* arched over by a canopy (fol. 1r: 'O Got ...') we can see God the Father as the ruler of the world. Enthroned in a frontal view, he holds a book in his left hand, while his right hand is raised in a gesture of blessing. Thus, the illumination indicates that this manuscript was made in honour of God, and that as the Bible it is the book of God.

On the following leaf, fol. 2r, in the filling of the next initial letter, the capital letter *D*, Wenceslas is presented as the occupant of the throne ('Dises buches aufgangk ...'), as the king with the insignia of his reign – crown, orb and sword – accompanied by his spouse (Fig. 8.1).[19] The representational scheme is taken from the opening initial letter (God the Father, fol. 1r), except that now the ruler and his spouse share the throne bench. To the right and left of the couple, the coats of arms of Bohemia and of the Empire are displayed outside the initial. At this point the first puzzling element appears in the marginal illustrations: vegetable tendrils, which cover the entire left-hand side of the page, springing from a wooden bucket that figures prominently in the many bathing scenes that follow. In the context of a picture representing the power of rulership, its presence seems almost grotesque.[20]

The first book of the Bible, Genesis, which follows the prologue, does without a representation of a ruler in favour of a single-column splendid initial (fol. 2v). In the following book, Exodus, Wenceslas is again depicted at the beginning of a *D* initial ('Ditz sint die Namen ...') as the enthroned ruler. Although the artist changed, the layout remained the same, and Wenceslas is portrayed as a bearded king with a full head of brown hair. Here Wenceslas can be understood as representing or echoing Pharaoh, who plays an authoritative role in the Book of Exodus.[21]

Not surprisingly, in the miniatures accompanying the text of the four Books of Kings, Wenceslas often takes the form of the kings described there.[22] In the opening initials, Wenceslas is depicted enthroned, as seen

---

19 As mentioned earlier, the identity of the queen remains unclear, because after the death of his first wife, Wenceslas remarried; on what this means for the dating of the manuscript, see above, n. 10. Pointing out later over-paintings of coats of arms, a 1993 study suggested that the queen depicted must be Joan of Bavaria, Wenceslas' first wife. See Hana Hlaváčková, 'Courtly Body in the Bible of Wenceslas IV', in Thomas Gaethgens (ed.), *Künstlerischer Austausch – Artistic Exchange* (Berlin, 1993), vol. 2, 371–82.
20 A similar image is found on fol. 41v where tendril formations also spring from a water bucket; the bucket is marked with the letter *W* for Wenceslas.
21 *Wenzelsbibel: König Wenzels Prachthandschrift der deutschen Bibel, erläutert von Horst Appuhn* (Dortmund, 1990), vol. 1, 236.
22 Today, the Vulgate's and the Wenceslas Bible's four Books of Kings (*Regum*) are given different names: 1 Regum = 1 Samuel, 2 Regum = 2 Samuel, 3 Regum = 1 Kings, 4 Regum = 2 Kings.

Fig. 8.1. King and Queen enthroned in royal majesty, Vienna, ÖNB, Cod. 2759, fol. 2r.

at the beginning of Regum 1 (= 1 Samuel; Cod. 2760, fol. 33r) where, clad in an ermine coat and holding the ruler's insignia, he is depicted seated on a luxurious throne-like cushion. At the beginning of Regum 2 (= 2 Samuel; Cod. 2760, fol. 74r), Wenceslas is again portrayed enthroned, accompanied, in the picture field of the *E* initial, by the coats of arms of the Empire and Bohemia ('Es geschach aber ...'). In the opening initial *S* (Solomon) of the Book of Paralipomenon 2 (= 2 Chronicles; Cod. 2761, fol. 36r), Wenceslas appears enthroned as King Solomon, the wisest of all kings. The apocryphal prayer of King Manasseh, prefixed to the Book of Esdras (1 Ezra; Cod. 2761, fol. 81r), also shows an enthroned ruler intended to be identified as Wenceslas. The text of the following biblical books is missing or only fragmentary, and only partially illustrated, without a representational image. Nevertheless, the above list makes it clear that, from the beginning and throughout the entire text corpus, Wenceslas was repeatedly shown as the ruling king with the insignia of his power.

THE NAKED KING: WENCESLAS IN THE MARGINS

The portrayal of the ruling king is counteracted by images that would have been perceived as a violation of the norm: the depiction of Wenceslas as a naked male with nothing that indicates his royal status. Often, the nude Wenceslas is surrounded by lightly dressed bath maidens; he is also shown dressed as a nobleman in the company of Wild Men, or as a Wild Man himself. He appears accompanied by symbols such as the letters *w* and *e*, kingfishers, and artistically knotted scarves, as well as an enigmatic motto, *toho pzde toho*. None of these motifs can be located inside the biblical text. They are mostly found in the margins, but also occasionally in the opening initials of individual Old Testament books.[23] How might we explain the presence of such images in a bible? Their placement in the margins, especially in the *bas-de-page*, gave rise to the superficial assumption that they simply show a grotesque, sometimes crude counter-world.[24] In the late Middle Ages, the margins of manuscripts often served as a playground for the absurd, for a world turned upside-down. Is this also the case in the Wenceslas Bible, or is there more to these 'images

---

23 See 3 Reg (= 1 Kgs; Cod. 2760, fol. 108r), and Paralipomenon 1 (= 1 Chr; Cod. 2761, fol. 2v); Paralipomenon 1 has a picture of Wenceslas as a Wild Man at the very beginning.
24 See especially Jean Wirth, *Les marges à drôleries des manuscrits gothiques* (Geneva, 2008); Margot McIlwain Nishimura, *Images in the Margins* (Los Angeles, 2009); and the contributions in Katrin Kröll and Hugo Steger (eds), *Mein ganzer Körper ist Gesicht* (Freiburg im Breisgau, 1994).

Fig. 8.2a. The beginning of the Book of Genesis, Vienna, ÖNB, Cod. 2759, initial I, fol. 2v.

Fig. 8.2b The beginning of the Book of Genesis, Vienna, ÖNB, Cod. 2759, initial I, fol. 2v, detail.

on the edge'?[25] Might they be able to reveal some profound truths in a playful way?

A starting point to trace the meaning of these puzzling motifs is offered by the beginning of Genesis (Cod. 2759, fol. 2v). Its magnificent historiated initial *I* ('*In anegenge ...*') extends over the entire left-hand column of the page (Fig. 8.2a). With all its extensions framing the right-hand text column, it is the largest image in the entire bible, and the one with the richest repertory of motifs used. Within the shaft of the letter *I*, depictions of God's works of creation are set in seven medallions in descending chronological order.[26] On the sides, the medallions are accompanied by 14 unnamed figures, some of whom can be recognized by their attributes as Apostles; others seem to be Prophets who, arranged in two groups of four, enclose the body of the letter at the top and bottom. Outside the letter *I*, but directly accompanying it, are the unconventional elements mentioned above that are to accompany Wenceslas in the further course of the bible. The depiction of Wenceslas and a bath maiden is significant (Fig. 8.2b): facing each other, they frame the penultimate medallion, the creation of Eve from Adam's rib. Wenceslas himself is dressed in the clothes of a nobleman, but in a distorted position inside a letter, the minuscule *e*. The *e* itself is decorated with a relatively large crown at the top. On the

---

25 Michael Camille, *Image on the Edge: The Margins of Medieval Art* (London, 1992).
26 For a detailed analysis of this initial, see the essay by Maria Theisen in this volume.

opposite side of the medallion, a bath maiden with a wooden bucket and a green bath broom turns towards the scene of creation. Clearly, the figure of Wenceslas wedged into the letter *e*, the act of creation at the centre, and the bath maiden are related to each other. But what does this strange composition mean? One is only slowly made familiar with the symbolism and its context in the course of the following pages.

God creates Eve (fol. 4r)

In the entire biblical text, rectangular column pictures are placed inside the continuous text of the Genesis narrative. This also applies to the first illustration following the large creation initial, the creation of Eve from Adam's rib (fol. 4r; Fig. 8.3). The image pattern and iconography on fol. 4r resemble that of the sixth medallion of the large opening initial *I* (fol. 2v; Fig. 8.2): God the Father creates Eve from the rib of the sleeping Adam. A glance at the right-hand margin below the image reveals two symbols, at least one of which is aimed directly at Wenceslas: the letter *w*, which, scholars agree, stands for Wenceslas. Placed above the *w* is a ribbon artfully knotted into a round, which has been interpreted in literature as a 'love knot', a sign of conjugal love, but also as a professional sign of the guild of bathers.[27] Independently of this, the knotted ribbon can be read as a symbol for any kind of bond; in medieval understanding, the knot can also be magically charged.[28]

The text directly next to the knot motif and the *w* states what results from Eve's creation: Adam takes Eve as his wife, in the wording of Genesis 2:24–5: 'and [he] shall cleave to his wife, and they shall be two in one flesh. And they were both naked, Adam and his wife, and they were not ashamed' (fol. 4r: *Unt wirt anhangen seiner hausvrowen. Und werden tzwei sein in einem vleische. Sie waren aber beide nackent, Adam und sein hausfrawe und schamten sich nicht*). This passage is about the (innocent) prelapsarian union of Adam and Eve, which the knot sensibly accompanies as a bonding motif. The *w* for Wenceslas is right next to the lines 'und schamten sich nicht'. Wenceslas, nakedness, and freedom from shame appear for the first time in this context.

Expulsion from Paradise (fol. 5r)

The next illustration follows on fol. 5r – the expulsion from Paradise (Fig. 8.4). There, the themes of 'nakedness' and 'shame' are taken up again, and Wenceslas, too, appears once more in the marginal illustration. The Fall of

---

27 See the summary in Schmidt, 'Kunsthistorischer Kommentar', 160–2.
28 Cf. Wolfgang Aly, 'Knoten', in Hanns Bächthold-Stäubli (ed.), *Handwörterbuch des deutschen Aberglaubens* (repr., Augsburg, 2005), vol. 5, cols. 16–23.

Fig. 8.3. Creation of Eve, Vienna, ÖNB, Cod. 2759, fol. 4r, detail.

Man itself is not illustrated, only its consequences: an angel with a flaming sword shows Adam and Eve the way into the world. Both are naked and cover their sex with a tuft of leaves. Eve also grabs her left breast as she becomes aware of her sexuality. Below the miniature, a new chapter begins, Genesis 4: 'And Adam knew his wife Eve, and she conceived and bore Cain' (*Adam vor war erkante euam sein hausvrowe. die enpfieng vnd gebar cayn*). The image and the text that follows are associated with themes of sexuality and procreation. To illustrate this further, at the *bas-de-page* there is another couple: a bath maiden and Wenceslas. They are separated from each other and at the same time tied together by a vegetal knot, artfully twisted and intertwined. Clearly, Wenceslas and the young woman do not form a couple in the sexual sense; they appear rather as people with a different, not immediately determinable, relationship. Is there a connection between the two couples, Adam and Eve, and Wenceslas and the bath maiden? A small pictorial detail establishes a subtle connection: it is the tuft of leaves that the bath maiden holds in her hands – it is the same object that Adam and Eve hold in front of their sex. This unobtrusive detail, as well as the arrangement of all the figures on one page, creates a formal relationship between them. Could the theme of the upper picture – sexuality and procreation – also have a meaning for Wenceslas and the bath maiden?

Looking back at fol. 2v (Fig. 8.2a), it is striking to see that there, too, Wenceslas and the bath maiden are associated with an act of creation or procreation – the creation of Eve. The depiction of Wenceslas is similar: on fol. 2v as well as on 5r (Fig. 8.4), Wenceslas is wedged inside the letter *e* as if in a pillory and thus greatly reduced in his mobility.[29]

The Tower of Babel (fol. 10v)

We see that already on the first pages of the bible Wenceslas is conspicuously integrated via images and texts into the thematic field of creation, reproduction, nudity, the connection between man and woman,

---

29 To date, research has not been able to resolve unequivocally what the letter *e* stands for. The various proposals fail to convince in the end; see the list in Schmidt, 'Kunsthistorischer Kommentar', 165–9, and the more recent article of Diethelm Gresch, 'Das "e" in der Wenzelsbibel', *Kunstchronik* 57 (2004), 131–7. I would like to suggest that the *e* be understood as a title: *e* stands for *Excellentissimus* (Excellency) – a title that distinguished kings and emperors; only after the Middle Ages was it transferred to royal governors and princes. See the article 'Exzellenz', in *Meyers Konversations-Lexikon*, vol. 6 (fifth edition, Leipzig, 1894), 105–6. Alternatively, I suggest we consider *w* and *e* unspectacularly as the first letters of the name Wenceslas. In her contribution to this volume, Maria Theisen takes up the idea that the *e* might stand for 'Ehe', the German word for 'marriage'.

Fig. 8.4. Expulsion from Paradise, Vienna, ÖNB, Cod. 2759, fol. 5r.

Fig. 8.5a. Tower of Babel, Vienna, ÖNB, Cod. 2759, fol. 10v.

Fig. 8.5b. Tower of Babel, Vienna, ÖNB, Cod. 2759, fol. 10v, detail.

and sexuality. On fol. 10v follows the next miniature inserted into the text – the Tower of Babel – as well as, in the *bas-de-page*, another depiction of Wenceslas (Fig. 8.5a). Wenceslas is portrayed in two scenes, separated by two volutes (Fig. 8.5b). On the left-hand side, he can be seen in the already familiar motif of the nobleman clamped within an *e* armed with locks, and on the right-hand side, naked in the care of two bath maidens. The two maidens seem to dominate the naked man sitting at their feet, with gestures that would be unthinkable towards a ruler, but appropriate towards someone in need of care and attention. In the bathing scene, the king is reduced to his natural state as a mere human being. All signs of royalty are discarded; the caring nurturing of the body and its functions take centre stage.[30]

Even if it is ostensibly a matter of personal hygiene – the maiden on the right washes the naked man's hair while the one on the left-hand side carries a bucket of water – a few erotic allusions cannot be ignored.[31] The naked Wenceslas sits between the spread legs of the right-hand maid. Attractive to the male gaze, the maids present themselves with dresses that reveal more than they conceal: arms and legs are bare, delicate white fabric contours their female body shapes, the breasts are pleasingly plump. Wenceslas' gaze is unmistakably fixed on the bosom, openly displayed, of

---

30 On the functions of private and public bathing in the Middle Ages, see Diane Wolfthal, *In and Out of the Marital Bed: Seeing Sex in Renaissance Europe* (New Haven, 2010), 121–53.

31 The tasks of bathers in bathhouses included head and body washing, but also minor medical interventions; see Susanne Arnold, 'Baden und Badewesen im Mittelalter', *Denkmalpflege in Baden-Württemberg* NF 25 (1996), 23–9.

the maiden on the left. Meanwhile, she points downwards with the index finger of her left hand to something that Wenceslas holds upright between his legs, pointed at the bath attendant. The identity of this object is not clear because it remains largely hidden behind the wooden bucket that the maid holds in her right hand. Only the base of the object reveals that it must be the bundle of leafy twigs used as a bath broom by the maidens. Its upright position between the legs enables a visual ambiguity that permits the viewer to interpret the object as a phallus and fertility symbol.[32] A similarly erotically charged depiction is found at the beginning of the Book of Deuteronomy (Cod. 2759, fol. 174v; fig. 8.6) where the two maidens are about to wash Wenceslas' hair. Again, the bath broom is positioned between the legs of the naked man in such a way that, although the sex is hidden from view, the phallic symbolism is all the more obvious.

This type of representation returns even more explicitly in the marginal illustrations at the beginning of the Book of Joshua (Cod. 2759, fol. 214r; figs 8.7a and 8.7b) which, together with the opening initial letter of the book, highlight the royal theme. In the filling of the initial letter U ('Und es geschach …') we can see the two crowned heraldic animals – eagle and lion – that represent the Empire and the Kingdom of Bohemia. In the *bas-de-page*, Wenceslas appears sitting naked on a bench, the bath broom again clamped phallus-like between his legs. With outstretched arms he reaches for the maidens whose breasts he seems to touch while they massage his shoulders and upper arms.

But let us return to the Tower of Babel, the theme of fol. 10v (Fig. 8.5). Why are the text and images of the building of the tower complemented by an erotically connoted exchange between maids and naked ruler? The story of the Tower of Babel is not only about the building of the tower, but also, as a result, about the formation of a dynasty based on blood relations (Gen 11:10–32): 'These are the generations of Sem: Sem was a hundred years old when he begot Arphaxad, two years after the flood. And Sem lived after he begot Arphaxad, five hundred years, and begot sons and daughters. And Arphaxad lived thirty-five years, and begot Sale' (*'Ditz sint die geperungen sems. Sem was hundert iar alt do er geperte arphaxat tzwei iar noch der flute. Und sem lebte dornach vnd er geperte arphaxat funfhundert iar vnd geperte sune vnd tochter. Dornach arphaxat lebte funf und dreissig iar vnd geperte sale'*), and so it goes on. The biblical text emphasizes who begat whom. 'Begetting' is the main theme of fols 10v–11r conveyed through the text, namely the begetting and spreading

---

32 On erotically symbolic and sexually explicit illustrations in the Middle Ages, see Albrecht Classen, *Sex im Mittelalter: Die andere Seite einer idealisierten Vergangenheit* (Badenweiler, 2011), 22–33.

Fig. 8.6. Beginning of the Book of Deuteronomy, Vienna, ÖNB, Cod. 2759, fol. 174v, D initial, detail.

of a dynasty that spans hundreds of years from Shem to Abram, Nahor, and Haran.

The tower of the miniature accompanying the text of the Tower of Babel story may include a reference to Wenceslas' royal building activity. The picture field is enclosed by a wide frame that is primarily decorated with the repeated letter *w* and, at the foot of the frame, with the coats of arms of Bohemia and the Empire. It seems as if Wenceslas were the master of a great construction project, which, if we take the accompanying biblical text as a basis, can also be understood as a project to expand the dynasty of the Luxembourgs.

Fig. 8.7a. Beginning of the Book of Joshua, Vienna, ÖNB, Cod. 2759, fol. 214r.

Fig. 8.7b. Beginning of the Book of Joshua, Vienna, ÖNB, Cod. 2759, fol. 214r, detail: Wenceslas with a bath maid.

WENCESLAS, DYNASTY, AND CHILDLESSNESS

Only one thing stood in the way of the straightforward dynastic succession of the Luxembourgs: Wenceslas' childlessness and obvious infertility – both of his two marriages remained childless. Admitting infertility was like admitting weakness. Only a few medieval rulers dealt with the problem openly, such as Emperor Henry II and his wife Cunegonde, which led to the extinction of the Ottonians in the male line.[33] But even without public confession, the lack of offspring could not be hidden. While he had already been accused by contemporaries of being incapable of ruling, the lack of direct descendants was another weighty problem.[34] It called

---

33 Klaus van Eickels, 'Männliche Zeugungsunfähigkeit im mittelalterlichen Adel', *Medizin, Gesellschaft und Geschichte* 28 (2009), 73–95, at 82–3. Richard II of England, husband of Wenceslas' half-sister Anne of Bohemia, was also infertile (p. 87): Kristen L. Geaman, 'Anne of Bohemia and Her Struggle to Conceive', *Social History of Medicine* 29 (2014), 224–44. In many cases the problem was not openly expressed, but was nevertheless known; see the survey in van Eickels' paper, 84–7.
34 On suitability or unsuitability to rule, see Cristina Andenna and Gert Melville (eds), *Idoneität – Genealogie – Legitimation: Begründung und Akzeptanz von dynastischer Herrschaft im Mittelalter* (Cologne, 2015).

into question the continuity of the dynasty, weakened loyalty to the ruler, and led to disputes over the throne at an early stage.[35] In Wenceslas' case, it was his half-brother Sigismund and his cousin Jobst of Moravia who tried to usurp power early on through various family intrigues. In view of Wenceslas' personality, legitimate offspring would probably not have prevented this kind of conflict, but would have made it considerably more difficult to challenge him.

The consequences of male infertility in the dynastic sphere have, as Klaus van Eickels states, been little researched.[36] In his medical-history essay, Van Eickels shows that infertile rulers usually knew about their sterility. In many cases, bearing children out of wedlock was the norm in ruling houses, understood as confirming the ruler's fertility.[37] Making matters worse, in the Middle Ages, childlessness was regarded as divine punishment, while abundant offspring was considered as God's gift[38] because it implemented God's injunction to be fruitful and multiply (Gen 9:7), a passage taken to imply that a lack of fertility might stand in the way of God's plan.

Aside from all that, having offspring was simply considered a duty of rulers – a duty that could become a compulsion, especially if the longed-for offspring failed to appear. This sheds light on Wenceslas who, when not depicted as regent, always appeared as if caught or trapped inside a letter (fols 2v, 5r, 10v; figs 8.2a, 8.4, 8.5a).

---

35 With reference to the Valois, who also faced great problems due to a lack of descendants, Loughran and Davis state: 'Their inability to provide legitimate heirs at a time of civil strife not only caused a succession crisis, but also undermined their authority and the stability of the kingdom.' Loughran and Davis, 'Introduction: The Body Politic and the Infertile Body', in Tracey Loughran and Gayle Davis (eds), *The Palgrave Handbook of Infertility in History: Approaches, Contexts and Perspectives* (London, 2017), 143–50, at 145. On the Valois and their dynastic succession problem, see Penny Roberts, 'Sterility and Sovereignty: The Succession Crisis of the Late Valois Monarchy', 151–70 in the same *Palgrave Handbook*.
36 Van Eickels, 'Männliche Zeugungsunfähigkeit', 76. An essay by Karl Ubl also addresses this question, but is limited to the eleventh century; see Karl Ubl, 'Der kinderlose König: Ein Testfall für die Ausdifferenzierung des Politischen im 11. Jahrhundert', *Historische Zeitschrift* 292 (2011), 323–63. Further, Wilhelm Müller, *Über die Bedeutung der Infertilität des Mannes in der Medizingeschichte mit Beispielen aus der Weltgeschichte* (Würzburg, 1957), 57–84. A recent monograph on infertility in the Middle Ages surprisingly ignores the subject altogether; see Regina Töpfer, *Kinderlosigkeit: Ersehnte, verweigerte und bereute Elternschaft im Mittelalter* (Stuttgart, 2020).
37 Van Eickels, 'Männliche Zeugungsunfähigkeit', 77–8.
38 Van Eickels, 'Männliche Zeugungsunfähigkeit', 82 and 90.

Bath and bathing

In stark contrast to the figure of the constricted ruler, the bath maidens, often arranged as his counterpart, pursue their business free of care. Bath maidens, it must be said, did not enjoy the best reputation, as they seem to have been seen as sexually available.[39] The skimpily dressed bath maidens are quite obviously ready for other services as well, as the title page of the Golden Bull commissioned by King Wenceslas seems to reveal (Figs 8.8a and 8.8b).[40] There, as in the Wenceslas Bible, the robed Wenceslas is clamped within the letter *w*, which has various holes into which arms and legs can be put. In the Golden Bull (Cod. 338), too, the *w* is in the middle of two vegetal volutes in which bath attendants go about their business. Wenceslas' scowl turns to two maidens, the first of whom presents him with an expansive décolleté. Her hand moves towards Wenceslas' without touching. The second maiden, placed behind her, is naked, with only a blue knotted cloth covering her pubic area. She grasps her well-formed naked bosom with her left hand, ostentatiously displaying it, while wielding a duster with her right. This may be read as a sign of fertility – sexual services not excluded.

Significantly, the poem serving as a prologue to the Golden Bull in the Cod. 338 version takes up the theme of fertility and water in detail, creating a connection to the title-page illustration with the bath maidens and its implied theme of fertility (Fig. 8.8a):

> Sed potius virtute tui, quem diligis, huius
> Cesaris insignis Karoli, deus alme, ministra,
> Ut valeat ductore pio per amena virecta
> Florentum semper nemorum sedesque beatas
> Ad latices intrare pios, ubi semina vite
> Divinis animantur aquis a fonte superno
> Letificata seges spinis mundatur ademptis,
> Ut messis queat esse dei mercisque future

---

39   Gertrud Blaschitz, 'Das Freudenhaus im Mittelalter', in Albrecht Classen (ed.), *Sexuality in the Middle Ages and Early Modern Times: New Approaches to a Fundamental Cultural-Historical and Literary-Anthropological Theme* (Berlin, 2008), 715–50, at 737.
40   Vienna, ÖNB, Cod. 338. Within the vast literature on the Golden Bull, the facsimile edition of Cod. 338 is particularly relevant for present purposes: Armin Wolf, *Die Goldene Bulle König Wenzels: Handschrift. Codex Vindobonensis 338 der Österreichischen Nationalbibliothek, Faksimile und Kommentar* (Graz, 2002). Cod. 338 was made in 1400. It was the last copy of the Golden Bull prepared at the request of Wenceslas; see the note at fol. 46v. The king is portrayed in the same way as in the Wenceslas Bible only on the title page, fol. 1r; in the rest of the manuscript, bath maidens no longer figure in the illustrations.

Fig. 8.8a. Golden Bull, Prologue, Vienna, ÖNB, Cod. 338, fol. 1r.

Fig. 8.8b. Golden Bull, Prologue, Vienna, ÖNB, Cod. 338, fol. 1r, detail: King Wenceslas and bath maidens.

> Maxima centenum per horrea fructum.[41]
>
> Most kind God: let your people, led by Charles,
> the illustrious Emperor, whom you have loved
> from time immemorial 'enter the pleasant glades
> via sacred streams, a happy dwelling place
> with ever-flowering groves, where the seeds of life
> are nourished with divine water, and where the glad fields
> (minus thorns) are cleansed from a celestial fountain,
> so that God may have a harvest, and the first fruit of future reward
> may pile up one hundred-fold in huge barns.'[42]

Although the Golden Bull is the work of Charles IV, it was his son Wenceslas who created a precious setting for this weighty work in 1400. The self-portrayal of Wenceslas and the bath maidens in the *bas-de-page* surrounding him are not merely ornamental decoration, but meant as an individual statement. The words 'ubi semina vite divinis animantur aquis a fonte superno' ('where the seeds of life are nourished with divine water from a celestial fountain') are not coincidentally framing the miniature of the world ruler set in the text in the right-hand text column. In connection

---

41 Wolfgang D. Fritz, *Die Goldene Bulle Kaiser Karls IV. vom Jahre 1356. Text* (Weimar, 1972), 43.

42 This portion of the poem includes several lines quoted from an ancient Christian poem, the 'Paschal Song' by Sedulius; the poem's English translation given here is cited from Sedulius, *The Paschal Poem and Hymns*, transl. Carl P.E. Springer (Atlanta, GA, 2013), 5 (book 1:53–9).

with Wenceslas' (presumed) infertility, this poetic text takes on a personal significance, for Wenceslas is still without offspring. The reference to the germs of life that may bring forth a prosperous kingdom can also be related to Wenceslas, who has not yet been able to produce these 'semina vitae', and who implores God to grant him the gift of fertility. A look at the bath maidens may support this interpretation.

Were the bath maidens in fact prostitutes supposed to stimulate Wenceslas' sexual potency? The more than one hundred bath maidens scattered throughout the Wenceslas Bible have been puzzling researchers for many years. They have been interpreted as the king's mistresses,[43] personifications of Venus,[44] or associated with a bathing order,[45] to name but a few conjectures.[46] Was Wenceslas a regular brothel-goer? And if that was the case, would it have been repeatedly addressed in his Bible?

Karel Stejskal has compiled relevant sources that provide an insight into Prague's bathing culture at the turn of the fourteenth and fifteenth centuries.[47] Obviously, Wenceslas loved bathing, which, however, enjoyed a rather negative reputation and was associated with idleness. Indeed, Wenceslas was said to neglect his official duties to enjoy himself in the forest (hunting) and bathing instead. Antonius de Lemaco,[48] for example, wrote to King Wenceslas in October 1384, angry that he was not rushing to Italy's aid: 'Et tu per lucos et thermas inania consilia agitas, nil de ecclesia, nil de imperio, nil de Italia, nil de te ipso prorsus cogitans' ('in the woods and in the baths you pursue useless plans, while you care neither for the Church, nor for the Empire, nor for Italy, and certainly not for yourself').[49] In addition to private baths, Wenceslas could also use numerous public baths in Prague: 'From the middle of the 14th century until 1419, forty-seven independent bathhouse attendants were active in Prague, and in 1395 a "royal" bathhouse attendant ... as well as a *balneum regis* [royal bathhouse] next to the Altstätt bridge tower are also mentioned around the same time.'[50] The bathing scenes have been associated with a guild of

---

43 Julius von Schlosser, 'Die Bilderhandschriften König Wenzel I.', *Jahrbuch der Kunsthistorischen Sammlungen des Allerhöchsten Königshauses* 14 (1893), 214–317, at 278.
44 Josef Krása, 'Handschriften', 87–9.
45 Von Schlosser, 'Die Bilderhandschriften', 299–300.
46 Schmidt, 'Kunsthistorischer Kommentar', 164 and 168.
47 Karel Stejskal, 'Exkurs: Historische Realien zum Schmuck der Wenzelsbibel', in H. Heger et al. (eds), *Die Wenzelsbibel: Kommentar* (Graz, 1998), vol. 2, 173–5.
48 On Antonius de Lemaco, see Franz Palacký, *Geschichte von Böhmen größtentheils nach Urkunden und Handschriften* (Prague, 1845), vol. 3/1, 26–7.
49 Franz Palacký, *Über Formelbücher, zunächst in Bezug auf böhmische Geschichte* (Prague, 1847), vol. 2, 35.
50 Karel Stejskal, 'Exkurs', 173: 'Ab der Mitte des 14. Jahrhunderts bis 1419 waren in Prag 47 selbständige Bademeister tätig, und 1395 werden auch ein "königlicher"

bathing attendants founded by Wenceslas, but the guild's purpose remains unspecified in the sources, and the argument is not conclusive.[51]

There is in fact no clue as to the actual setting of the bathing scenes. Since the king is shown naked, a private setting is to be assumed, and we know that bathing rooms existed at courts.[52] An example of a private bath with courtly staff can be found in the Codex Manesse, copied in the first quarter of the fourteenth century in Zurich (Heidelberg University Library, Cod. Pal. germ. 848, fol. 46v). One page shows the minne poet Jakob of Warte naked in a large bathtub (Fig. 8.9).[53] The four young women who care for him are dressed demurely in courtly, high-collared long robes. Any overt display of sexual attributes is absent. The bather shows his naked upper body, but his balding head and grey hair identify him as an older man whose erotic charisma is just as restrained as that of the courtly-dressed girls.

Another medieval bathing scene from a private courtly milieu, illustrated in Bruges c. 1470 (London, British Library, Royal MS 17 F. IV, fol. 297r; fig. 8.10), presents itself quite differently. Bathing and dining together are part of the preparation for what is to happen afterwards: 'Lovers first bathe together, then dine together, and finally have sex together in bed.'[54] The couple enjoy themselves unclothed in the same bathtub, from which they can reach for the food and drink that is provided. Simultaneously, what happens afterwards is depicted: the couple have passed through the open door into the bedroom. While she covers her sex with her hand and seems altogether more restrained, her partner grabs her breasts and points unmistakably with his other hand to the bed as the place where he intends to lead her.

Contemporary texts also address the communal bath with clear sexual allusions. Oswald von Wolkenstein, later a diplomat at the court of Wenceslas' half-brother and successor Sigismund, speaks of the intimate pleasures of (marital) bathing culture in his song 'Wol auff, wol an':

Bademeister ... sowie um die gleiche Zeit ein *balneum regis* neben dem Altstätter Brückenturm erwähnt.'
51   Suggested by Krása, 'Handschriften', 78–97, this idea is often referred to, for instance by Wolf, 'Goldene Bulle', 41–2, and by Schmidt, 'Kunsthistorischer Kommentar', 163.
52   Arnold, 'Baden und Badewesen im Mittelalter', 24.
53   Even though the bathing scene is probably to be located on the meadow referred to in the adjacent song text, the staff is courtly and does not come from the milieu of public urban bathing. Walter Koschorreck and Wilfried Werner (eds), *Codex Manesse: Die große Heidelberger Liederhandschrift. Kommentar zum Faksimile* (Kassel, 1981), 122.
54   Wolfthal, 'In and out of the Marital Bed', 150.

Fig. 8.9. Codex Manesse, Jakob of Warte, Heidelberg University Library, Cod. Pal. germ. 848, fol. 46v.

Fig. 8.10. Lovers in the bath, British Library, London, Royal MS 17 F. IV, fol. 297r.

Pring den buttern,
lass uns kuttren
'wascha, maidli,
mir das schaidli!'
'reib mich, knäblin,
umb das näblin!
hilfst du mir,
leicht vach ich dir das rëtzli'.

Bring the bathtub,
let us have some fun:
'wash, my dear maid,
my head!'
'rub, my dear young man,
my tummy!
If you help me,
I might grab the little rat.'[55]

Bathing together, cleansing, eroticism, and finally sexual union seem to be closely interwoven in the courtly environment, but also in public bathhouses, to which the whiff of the brothel was attached. It would be difficult to imagine the queen herself taking on the role of bath maiden in the marginalia alongside Wenceslas. In order to depict the intimate process of sexual stimulation and pleasure without compromising the dignity of the queen, bath maidens might have been chosen to take on this role, as it were by proxy.[56]

Preservation of the dynasty

Unlike the miniature from Bruges (Fig. 8.10), the Wenceslas Bible leaves to the imagination what happens after the bath. Superficially, the images of the naked king with bath attendants are aimed at the process of bathing and cleansing. Only the references to the biblical text and the miniatures integrated into it provide further information about the potential meaning of the bathing scenes. In a deeper, non-explicit layer, the illustrations in the bible, set both in the text and in the margins, are about fertility and the preservation of the dynasty.

---

55 Quoted after Classen, 'The Cultural Significance of Sexuality in the Middle Ages, the Renaissance, and Beyond', in Albrecht Classen (ed.), *Sexuality in the Middle Ages and Early Modern Times: New Approaches to a Fundamental Cultural-Historical and Literary-Anthropological Theme* (Berlin, 2008), 45.
56 It was von Schlosser who suggested we understand the bath maidens as taking the role of the queen; see von Schlosser, 'Die Bilderhandschriften', 297.

Fig. 8.11. Circumcision of Abraham, Vienna, ÖNB, Cod. 2759, fol. 14v.

All of this is confirmed by other depictions in the bible which do not restrain themselves in representing sexuality, procreation, and genealogical succession with an emphasis on the bodily organs that serve this purpose. On fol. 14v (Cod. 2759; fig. 8.11), when Abraham's circumcision is depicted, the sexual organs are shown realistically. The scene is taken from Genesis 17: God commands Abraham and all the men of his household to be circumcised. Circumcision was meant to secure or enhance male fertility.[57] With this procedure, God made a covenant with Abraham, promising him he would be the progenitor of many nations. The theme of the progenitor

---

57 In the biblical period, 'circumcision was a marriage or fertility rite'; see Robert G. Hall, 'Circumcision', in *The Anchor Bible Dictionary*, 6 vols (New York, 1992), vol. 1, 1025–31, at 1026.

Fig. 8.12. Lot and his daughters, Vienna, ÖNB, Cod. 2759, fol. 17v.

is also dealt with in the next but one miniature inserted into the text (Cod. 2759, fol. 17v; fig. 8.12), which visualizes Lot sleeping with his daughters. Not wanting to remain childless, the daughters of Lot get their father drunk and have intercourse with him, from which children – the progenitors of new generations – are born (Genesis 19:37–8). The scene is observed outside the miniature on the left-hand edge of the folio by a kingfisher with a knotted ribbon fluttering around its neck. In its beak it carries Wenceslas' motto, 'toho pzde toho', which escapes interpretation to this day.[58] Certainly, the voyeuristic kingfisher is an item of drôlerie,

---

58 On the motto of Wenceslas, see Schmidt, 'Kunsthistorischer Kommentar', 152–4, 169–71, and Krása, 67–9. On the figure of the kingfisher, see Schmidt, 'Kunsthistorischer Kommentar', 159–60. On the function of the mottos of medieval

but one that alludes to the main theme of the page. The inscription band with the slogan of Wenceslas in the bird's beak refers to the king whose offspring, like Lot's, is in question. The sexual theme is highlighted by the long and pointed bird's beak which, in its extension, points directly to Lot's male organ.

A little later, on fol. 21r (Cod. 2759; fig. 8.13), we encounter a marginal medallion with Wenceslas enclosed in a *w* that doubles up as stocks. Next to it is another medallion with a bath maiden turning towards the 'prisoner'; both figures are connected by eye contact. While Wenceslas looks somewhat skeptical, the maid's gaze is open and friendly. With both hands, she presents to the motionless prisoner the already familiar water bucket and bath broom that seems to grow out of the bucket like a small leafy tree – perhaps also to be read as a sexual allusion. Vegetable power and motionlessness are juxtaposed without being able to meet. The corresponding biblical text tells of Abraham's servant Eliezer at the well who is to look for a suitable wife for Isaac, and finds her in Rebekah (Genesis 24). But the couple remained childless for 20 years – to then be blessed with great fertility: 'Isaac was forty years old when he took Rebekah to be his wife. … And Isaac prayed to the Lord for his wife because she was barren, and the Lord heard him, and made Rebekah to conceive. … Isaac was sixty years old when the children were born unto him' (Gen 25:20–6). Rebekah gave birth to twins: Esau and Jacob. If one associates the Rebekah narrative with the marginal illustrations, the question arises: did Wenceslas hope that, as in the case of the biblical couple, offspring would eventually be divinely granted?

The following marginal illustrations with Wenceslas caught in the letter seem to confirm this assumption (Cod. 2759, fol. 29r; fig. 8.14). The story in Genesis 29–30 tells of the complicated events surrounding the (in)fertility of Jacob's two wives, the sisters Rachel and Leah, and their maidservants, all of whom wanted to give Jacob as many sons as possible. Leah finally becomes pregnant with the help of an aphrodisiac, a mandrake, and after years of waiting she gives birth to a son. The whole episode, about fertility first denied and then restored by God, features only one goal: the production of sons. The horizontally divided rectangular miniature transposes the biblical narrative. While in the upper part Leah shows her sister Rachel the mandrake promising fertility, in the lower part

---

nobility, see Laurent Hablot, 'Le décor emblématique chez les princes de la fin du Moyen Âge: un outil pour construire et qualifier l'espace', in Société des Historiens Médiévistes de l'Enseignement Supérieur Publique (ed.), *Construction de l'espace au Moyen Age: pratiques et représentations. Actes des congrès de la Société des historiens médiévistes de l'enseignement supérieur public, 37ᵉ congrès, Mulhouse 2006* (Paris, 2007), 147–65.

Fig. 8.13. Rebekah at the well, Vienna, ÖNB, Cod. 2759, fol. 21r, detail: Wenceslas and a bath maiden.

the success becomes visible: Jacob and Leah perform the act from which a son is born.

The situation is quite different for the protagonists of the marginal illustration: Wenceslas and the bath maiden sit opposite each other in separate volutes, both wedged in letters doubling up as stocks: Wenceslas in an *e*, the maid, wielding bath broom and bucket, in a *W*. Both cannot find each other, they are stuck; a reinvigoration of Wenceslas with the help of an aphrodisiac, i.e., an erotic encounter with the bath maiden, seems impossible.

Again and again, bath maidens are closely associated with the theme of fertility. Thus, a bath maiden comments on a biblical scene which at

Fig. 8.14. Jacob, Rachel, and Leah; at bas-de-page: Wenceslas and bath maiden, Vienna, ÖNB, Cod. 2759, fol. 29r.

first glance does not seem to deal with fertility: the episode of Moses and Zipporah fleeing to Egypt (Exodus 4), fol. 57r. The miniature inserted in the text shows Moses leading the donkey with his wife and four children. Although Moses in the Bible has only two sons, Gershom and Eliezer, his wife is carrying a child in her arms, and three more peep out from the donkey's pannier. The illustrated blessing with children has no biblical basis. Added to the scene is a marginal commentary in the form of a bath maiden whose words 'w. e . thoho . mily . boze', a variation of the royal motto 'toho bzde toho', have been interpreted as 'Wenceslas' marriage [grant this] dear God.'[59] As elsewhere, the maiden carries a green bathing tassel upright in front of her like a fertility symbol, while a fantasy bird, placed on her head, points with its beak to the offspring; at the same time, the inscription, whose positioning is also not coincidental, emerges from the bird's beak. It accompanies the very words that speak of the circumcision of the eldest son to protect Zipporah's husband Moses against God's anger (Exodus 4:25). Since Moses apparently could not be circumcised as an adult, the son is circumcised by the mother and, as a substitute for circumcision, the child's blood is applied to Moses. Thus, Moses becomes the 'bloody spouse' as Zipporah dubs him – a legitimate, fertile husband. The importance of the application of blood to the 'breutigam des blutes' (fol. 57r) is shown by the bath maiden's tub (filled with blood?), placed exactly at the level of the line that mentions the bloody spouse. In this way, Wenceslas is associated with Moses, the fertile leader of Israel.

FERTILITY – WENCESLAS AND THE WILD MEN

The biblical narratives deal extensively with themes such as fertility and reproduction, but also their absence, as well as ways and means of solving the problem. The king's inability to procreate and his lack of offspring are not openly discussed, but indirectly alluded to by the association of biblical texts and illustrations with the marginal pictures. Nevertheless, Wenceslas does not appear impotent in the miniatures, on the contrary. The phallus-like bath broom clamped between his legs is meant to testify to his virility. The frequent accompaniment of Wenceslas by so-called Wild Men – and his identification with them – is also a sign of unbridled

---

59 I would like to thank Maria Theisen, who drew my attention to this episode. See Maria Theisen, 'Texte und Bilder einer Zeitenwende: Illuminierte deutschsprachige Handschriften aus dem Besitz des Königs Wenzel IV. von Böhmen', in Balázs Sára (ed.), *Quelle und Deutung I/1. EC-Beiträge zur Erforschung deutschsprachiger Handschriften des Mittelalters und der Frühen Neuzeit* (Budapest, 2014), 127–9 (Fig. 6).

Fig. 8.15. Birth of Esau and Jacob; at bas-de-page: Wild Men as heraldic supporters, Vienna, ÖNB, Cod. 2759, fol. 24r.

strength and 'legendary sexual prowess'.[60] These completely hairy, broad-shouldered men were regarded as wild, unpredictable natural beings; they 'embody strength, fertility and fortitude'.[61] These creatures have a strong presence in the Wenceslas Bible.

Already in Genesis (Gen 25), two Wild Men appear in a significant place at the *bas-de-page* as heraldic supporters;[62] the associated biblical text narrates and illustrates the birth of Esau and Jacob (fol. 24r; fig. 8.15). The Wild Men are set in similar side-by-side medallions as Wenceslas and the bath maidens elsewhere. While the Wild Man on the left-hand side shows the coat of arms of the Empire with the black eagle aligned frontally, his counterpart in the right medallion presents the coat of arms of Bohemia. A vulva-like fertility symbol is placed between the medallions. Prosperous fertility is also the theme of the biblical birth narrative and the miniature set in the text column: Rebekah has given birth to the twins Esau and Jacob. She sits upright and bare-breasted in her bed, holding one of the sons in her arms while the other is being cared for by a wet nurse. Twins were regarded as a sign of special fertility, a theme reinforced by the Wild Men at the bottom and associated with the Empire and Bohemia by means of the coat of arms.

Wenceslas shows himself as a Wild Man, too. In the opening initial of the Book of Paralipomenon 1 (today called 1 Chronicles; Cod. 2761, fol. 2v) he emphasizes his special strength as well as the stability and preservation of Bohemia (Fig. 8.16). His body is completely hairy. In his right hand he holds the banner of Bohemia, in his left hand a shield with Bohemia's coat of arms, while his head is adorned with a feathered helmet and the imperial crown. Thus, Wenceslas stands upright in knightly fashion in front of the *A* initial. Wenceslas' unusual appearance as a Wild Man is puzzling, but in harmony with the contents of the first Book of Paralipomenon. The letter *A* stands for the name Adam. At the beginning of this biblical book are genealogies that start with the forefathers Adam, Seth and Enos. Wenceslas, costumed as a Wild Man, stages himself as a progenitor whose virile potency will bring forth dynasties; he is the crowning glory of the

---

60 Timothy Husband, *The Wild Man: Medieval Myth and Symbolism* (New York, 1980), 74.
61 Vincent Mayr, 'Wilde Leute' in the section 'Charakter und Tätigkeit', in *RDK Labor* (2019), URL: https://www.rdklabor.de/wiki/Wilde_Leute [accessed 9 March 2023].
62 On the widespread depiction of Wild Men as heraldic supporters, see Grossmann, 'Wilde Leute im Wandel der Zeiten', in Peggy Große, G. Ulrich Grossmann and Johannes Pommeranz (eds), *Monster: Phantastische Bilderwelten zwischen Grauen und Komik* (Nürnberg, 2015), 205–19, at 211–14.

Fig. 8.16. Beginning of the Book of Paralipomenon, Vienna, ÖNB, Cod. 2761, fol. 2v, detail: Wenceslas as a Wild Man.

dynasty of the Luxembourgs, that, styling itself as *sacra stirps*, can trace itself back to Adam.[63]

---

63 Just how important genealogical descent was to the Luxembourgs is shown by the two fresco cycles at Prague Castle and Karlštejn Castle. They are now lost but survive in tracings; see Gia Toussaint, *Das Passional der Kunigunde von Böhmen: Bildrhetorik und Spiritualität* (Paderborn, 2003), 68, n. 107.

CONCLUSION: THE KING'S BODY

Generally speaking, nakedness denotes weakness. In the Bible, the Book of Job is quite clear on this. The very poor 'go about naked, without clothing' (Job 24:10). Job, once a rich man, has lost everything, including his health; considering his poverty, he melancholically states that 'naked I came from my mother's womb, and naked shall I return' (Job 1:21). A naked king would be one stripped of his clothes that were originally part of, and signifying, his royal power. A naked king, therefore, must be a weak king, someone reduced to his mere humanity.

This interpretation of nakedness does indeed apply to some of the illustrations included in the Wenceslas Bible. When the king is portrayed as being clamped in a *w*-shaped object, he is certainly represented as someone in a most problematic situation. As argued above, this situation includes that of childlessness due to infertility, impotence, or both. Owing to the king's lack of descendants, the continuity of the Luxembourg dynasty was in question. But not only the king's weak, helpless body is conspicuously displayed in the bible's miniatures; we also see – in addition to the images that show the king enthroned – a strong, self-assured, healthy, masculine body.[64]

A closer analysis of the relevant iconography and the associated biblical texts reveals two strategies that are used for solving the problem of the king's childlessness: a courtly, profane one, and a biblical, religious one. The courtly solution is seen in what we may call a bathing cure, complete with its erotic overtones indicated by the conspicuous presence of bath maidens. From a bathing cure, the king would expect an enhancement of his virility. Biblically, the problem of royal childlessness is associated with the Genesis patriarchs' problem of childlessness, and with its solution. In biblical times, the continuation of the people of God depended upon child-producing couples. The Book of Genesis tells of two patriarchs – Abraham and Isaac – whose marriages remain for some time without offspring. But in both cases, God eventually grants fertility (as it happens, to their wives). In fact, the Lord probably could not do otherwise, because he himself had once ordered humans 'to be fruitful and multiply' – a reason for the king to hope to be eventually granted the same blessing as that received by the biblical families. While the courtly solution to the king's problem might have involved a profane, active, almost medical intervention, religion supplied a complementary sacred atmosphere of passive, prayerful, and confident waiting.

---

64 As Hans-Joachim Schmidt, *Herrschaft durch Schrecken und Liebe: Vorstellungen und Begründungen im Mittelalter* (Göttingen, 2019), 466, explains, the *potentia* of a king rests on his health, *sanitas*: 'To support and preserve it must be the foremost of all royal tasks.'

And how about the 'Wild Man' image? Here a third, folk idea of natural fertility seems to come into play. Nature, with its woods and wonders, exudes a sense of fertility stronger and possibly superior to that of the human, civilized realm. The fact that Wenceslas is also associated with this unstructured realm and that realm's energy suggests that the king and his artists meant to draw upon all possible resources for overcoming the king's problem.

All the imagery and ideas associated with the naked king are enlisted to create an atmosphere in which one would expect the pregnancy of the queen to happen any time and thus to ensure the continuation of the Luxembourg dynasty and, along with it, the well-being of both Bohemia and the Empire. The scenes serve the king's masculine self-assurance, highlighting his virility; at the same time, they are addressed as a prayer to God: may he grant the king and queen the longed-for offspring.

CHAPTER 9

DEALING WITH THE LUXEMBOURG COURT: ELLWANGEN ABBEY AND THEIR IMPERIAL OVERLORD[1]

MARK WHELAN

In the Staatsarchiv Ludwigsburg in southern Germany there exists an unremarkable looking codex of some 90 folios recording the incomes and expenses between 1427 and 1435 of the imperial abbey of Ellwangen, a Benedictine monastery founded in Swabia in the eighth century.[2] Even a

---

1   The archival material upon which this article is principally based was stumbled across while conducting research in the Staatsarchiv Ludwigsburg (Baden-Württemberg) for the Leverhulme-funded project, 'Bees in the Medieval World: Economic, Environmental and Cultural Perspectives', led by Alexandra Sapoznik at King's College London [Leverhulme Trust RPG-2018-080]. I am grateful to Alex for her permission to expand this find into an article and for her consistent support. My thanks also to Corinna Knobloch (Staatsarchiv Ludwigsburg) for her helpful correspondence and for facilitating access to archival materials. The following references are not (and cannot be) exhaustive and only the most recent and relevant scholarship will be cited, and unless otherwise stated, all gulden referred to are Rhenish. When quoting directly from manuscripts I have expanded abbreviations, standardized capitalization, and inserted punctuation to make reading easier.
2   Staatsarchiv Ludwigsburg, B 383, V/9, 1428–1435 [hereafter StaL, V/9]. The codex is not foliated, so I have 'silently' foliated the manuscript, beginning with fol. 1r at the first written folio and stopping at the last folio to bear writing (91v).

brief perusal of the manuscript, drawn up under the supervision of Konrad Schreiber (*Conrad Schryber*), the secretary of the abbey's accounting office (*rechenampt*), can teach one much about the daily operations of an abbey, including the management of their fish weirs, the renting of the bathhouse to locals, and the purchase of sugared confectionary for their monks.[3] Scattered throughout the codex, however, are recurring references to 'the King', that is Sigismund of Luxembourg, their sovereign and overlord. Unpublished and hitherto unused by scholars, the abbey's accounts for the period between 1427 and 1435 offer a unique and compelling window into how a monastic community dealt with the series of diplomatic, economic, and logistical challenges inherent when treating with their usually distant king – from sending emissaries on dangerous diplomatic missions to Hungary, to disbursing the cash necessary to secure royal privileges, to even hosting Sigismund and his entourage in 1431. This article offers the first analysis of Ellwangen's unpublished financial accounts as they relate to contact with Sigismund and his court, situating them against a broader backdrop of epistolary and chronicle material produced by communities in the Holy Roman Empire that together draw attention to some of the challenges late medieval contemporaries faced in both locating and dealing with the itinerant Luxembourg court. Framed against this backdrop, a close study of the abbey's financial records sheds new light on the financial and personal costs that a small community bore when treating with itinerant Luxembourg royalty and offers fresh perspectives on how the dynasty's subjects in the Holy Roman Empire engaged with their enigmatic and peripatetic overlord.

A ruler of many lands, first as King of Hungary (from 1387), then King of the Romans (1410), King of Bohemia (1419), and Holy Roman Emperor (1433), Sigismund of Luxembourg's diplomatic contacts spanned across Christendom and beyond, including even the exchange of emissaries with a Tartar khan.[4] Research by Oliver Daldrup, Duncan Hardy, and Alexandra Kaar, among others, has brought renewed impetus to the study of Sigismund's handling of his political relationships with his subjects in the Holy Roman Empire. This, in turn, has stimulated reassessment of how the last Luxembourg scion to hold imperial office engaged with the panoply of aristocrats, knightly and noble societies and civic and

---

The account book is in a hand contemporary to the second quarter of the fifteenth century and on paper with a binding of parchment. I have been unable to identify the faint watermark visible on fol. 60r.

3   For examples, StaL, V/9, 1428–1435, fols 3v (for the income from weirs), 18r (for gloves from Nördlingen), 52v (for *zucker candit*, i.e., 'sugar candy').

4   On 'Korolock the Tartar', see Mark Whelan, 'Sigismund of Luxemburg and the Imperial Response to the Ottoman Turkish Threat, c. 1410–1437' (Unpublished PhD dissertation, Royal Holloway, University of London, 2014), 80–3.

ecclesiastical communities in the sprawling Central European region encompassed within the Holy Roman Empire, moving the focus beyond the traditional study of late medieval emperors and their relationships with imperial free cities and secular and ecclesiastical magnates.[5] Generally, modest ecclesiastical communities such as imperial abbeys infrequently leave the evidence required for a detailed exploration of their relationship with their overlord, with the survival of Ellwangen's detailed accounts perhaps unique for such a religious foundation in the later medieval period. Imperial abbeys therefore rarely feature in the analyses referred to above, with the richer source bases left by civic communities and, more occasionally, princely houses and bishoprics, understandably receiving more scholarly attention.[6]

Ellwangen's unpublished accounts are, therefore, of significant value, shedding light on more humble layers of diplomatic exchange that often escape the attention of historians. The detailed costings throughout Ellwangen's accounts, furthermore, provide a unique perspective on the financial outlay involved with remaining in contact with a distant king, in supporting his travels, and in helping fund political and military policies for which he was wholly or in part responsible. In a very literal sense, then, the costs of Luxembourg overlordship can be reckoned in hard currency, and compared with the abbey's concurrent management of their relationships with the papal curia, the episcopal court in Augsburg, and the comital court of Württemberg. After placing the abbey of Ellwangen in its geographical and political context, this study will use Konrad's

---

5   Oliver Daldrup, *Zwischen König und Reich: Träger, Formen und Funktionen von Gesandtschaften zur Zeit Sigmunds von Luxemburg (1410-1437)* (Münster, 2010); Duncan Hardy, *Associative Political Culture in the Holy Roman Empire: Upper Germany, 1346-1521* (Oxford, 2018), 198-214; Alexandra Kaar, *Wirtschaft, Krieg und Seelenheil: Papst Martin V., Kaiser Sigismund und das Handelsverbot gegen die Hussiten in Böhmen* (Cologne, 2020), 281-94. The work of Martin Kintzinger remains the standard on Sigismund's foreign politics: *Westbindungen im spätmittelalterlichen Europa: Auswärtige Politik zwischen dem Reich, Frankreich, Burgund und England in der Regierungszeit Kaiser Sigmunds* (Stuttgart, 2000).
6   For an example: Alexandra Kaar, '*Die stadt (…) viel privilegirt, aber wenig ergötzt*: Sigismunds Herrschaftspraxis und seine Urkunden für die "Katholischen" königlichen Städte Böhmens', in Karel Hruza and Alexandra Kaar (eds), *Kaiser Sigismund (1368-1437): Zur Herrschaftspraxis eines europäischen Monarchen* (Cologne, 2012), 267-300. For further examples of research focused on civic communities, see the bibliographic references in Martin Kintzinger, 'Luxemburger als Diplomaten – Diplomaten der Luxemburger', in Sabine Penth and Peter Thorau (eds), *Rom 1312: Die Kaiserkrönung Heinrichs VII. und die Folgen. Die Luxemburger als Herrscherdynastie von gesamteuroäpischer Bedeutung* (Cologne, 2016), 389-408 (on 406, nn. 34-5), and the contributions in Thomas Lau and Helge Wittmann (eds), *Kaiser, Reich und Reichsstadt in der Interaktion* (Petersburg, 2016).

accounts as a prism through which to examine the troubled attempts of the new abbot in the later 1420s to secure imperial confirmation of his new status, and the costs involved when one's royal court was usually based in another kingdom. I will then assess the political context informing Sigismund's visit to the abbey in February 1431, before considering how Ellwangen's financial records shed new light on the relationship between the Luxembourg dynasty and its subjects in the Holy Roman Empire more generally.

ELLWANGEN ABBEY IN THE LATER MEDIEVAL PERIOD

Ellwangen was an imperial abbey situated about 20 miles north-east of Stuttgart with a heritage stretching back into the eighth century.[7] The abbey enjoyed imperial immediacy ('Reichsunmittelbarkeit'). It was, therefore, subject to the King of the Romans/Holy Roman Emperor and needed to treat with him directly. In practice, however, the role of protector had been assumed by the Count of Württemberg since the 1370s.[8] As an imperial abbey it was nominally removed from episcopal oversight, but the foundation lay within the geographical boundary of the bishopric of Augsburg and the bishop – as Konrad's account book demonstrates – frequently involved himself in Ellwangen's affairs. Ellwangen commanded significant local resources, including legal rights to local offices and ownership of weirs, mills, vineyards, estates, and a bathing house, as well as flocks of cattle and sheep, besides other natural resources, but was probably not markedly different in status or wealth to the dozens of other imperial abbeys across the southern and eastern stretches of the Holy Roman Empire. The abbot throughout the period covered by Konrad's accounts, Johann von Holzingen (1427–52), was an unremarkable member of the local lower nobility and travelled to diplomatic meetings in the later 1420s and early 1430s – such as the Reichstags in Nuremberg – with

---

7   Background here is kept to a minimum. Readers requiring more information are pointed to Shami Ghosh, 'The Imperial Abbey of Ellwangen and its Tenants: A Study of the Polyptych of 1337', *Agricultural History Review* 62 (2014), 187–209 (esp. 189–92); Dieter Stievermann, 'Das geistliche Fürstentum Ellwangen im 15. und 16. Jahrhundert: Politische Selbstbehauptung im Schatten Württembergs', *Ellwanger Jahrbuch* 32 (1987/88), 35–47 (esp. 39–41).
8   Or, to follow the contemporary terminology of the abbot writing in March 1428, 'on [i.e., ohne] mittel undertenig'. See StaL, B 389, U 149. On the protectorship ('Schirmherrschaft') of the counts of Württemberg, see Stievermann, 'Das geistliche Fürstentum Ellwangen', 36.

an entourage of around 20 horse.[9] Of the 29 abbeys ordered to provide military forces at the Reichstag in 1431 for the anti-Hussite crusade that summer, all but one were to muster between one and five 'lances', with Ellwangen's contribution set at three.[10] Ellwangen, therefore, appears a 'middling' abbey, neither spectacularly wealthy or terribly poor, nor particularly noteworthy in leadership, resources, and stature. This is an important point to consider, for Ellwangen's experiences in dealing with their imperial overlord can shed light – if only tentatively – on how other imperial abbeys in the broader region may have engaged with the Luxembourg court, but whose experiences have been obliterated by the total or partial eradication of their archives.[11]

ELLWANGEN ABBEY AND THE CHALLENGES OF THE EARLY 1400S

Konrad's account book bears witness to the tense, complicated and often distressing political conditions that Ellwangen and its region endured in the later 1420s and early 1430s. For Ellwangen itself, the election of Holzingen after the death of Abbot Siegfried (1400–27) required the abbey to gain imperial confirmation of the new abbot's status, a process that proved expensive, convoluted, and fraught with unforeseen expense. Of more significance to the abbey, however, was the regional instability generated by the Hussite Wars, which had afflicted communities across the southern and eastern stretches of the Holy Roman Empire ever since the Hussite religious and political movement had removed the Kingdom of Bohemia from allegiance to pope and king in 1419–20.[12] The spurned King of Bohemia was Sigismund himself, who wasted no time marshalling the resources of his subjects in Hungary and in the remainder of the Holy Roman Empire in his efforts to extirpate Hussitism. In an initial effort

---

9   Karl Fink, 'Zur Geschichte der Leitung der Abtei Ellwangen', in Viktor Burr (ed.), *Ellwangen 764–1964: Beiträge und Untersuchungen zur Zwölfhundertjahrfeier* (Ellwangen, 1964), 107–53 (on 147).
10 Readers interested in Ellwangen's experience of the Hussite Wars are pointed to the following: Mark Whelan, 'Taxes, Wagenburgs, and a Nightingale: The Imperial Abbey of Ellwangen and the Hussite Wars, 1427–1435', *Journal of Ecclesiastical History* 72 (2021), 751–77.
11 For discussion of the archive left by Ellwangen, see Alois Seller, *Das Schriftgut von Kloster und Stift Ellwangen im Staatsarchiv Ludwigsburg: Eine Beständeübersicht* (Stuttgart, 1976), 3–4.
12 For a concise introduction to the Hussite Wars, see Pavel Soukup, 'Religion and Violence in the Hussite Wars', in Wolfgang Palaver, Harriet Rudolph and Dietmar Regensburger (eds), *The European Wars of Religion: An Interdisciplinary Reassessment of Sources, Interpretations, and Myths* (Farnham, 2016), 19–44.

to regain the Bohemian crown, Sigismund led an unsuccessful crusade into Bohemia in summer 1420.[13] It was inconceivable, however, that Bohemia, having been in Luxembourg hands since 1310, could be lost to the dynasty.[14] Not for nothing did one of Sigismund's heralds, who visited the abbey in December 1418, bear the official name of Karlstein (*Karelstein*) – almost certainly named after the fortress and reliquary built by Emperor Charles IV, Sigismund's father, on a promontory overlooking the south-western approaches to Prague – so important was the kingdom, its status, and its resources, to the dynasty's image.[15] Bohemia was therefore not to be abandoned lightly. Throughout the 1420s and early 1430s, the abbey of Ellwangen, its community, and its resources, were therefore drawn into a broader game of Luxembourg power play, with Konrad's accounts bearing witness to the abbey's contributions to Catholic campaigns aimed at crushing the Hussite movement and their raising of resources for local defence in the face of Hussite raids.[16] Even their hosting of Sigismund in 1431, touring the region to gain support for the fifth (and final) anti-Hussite crusade of that summer, should be seen through the prism of the Hussite Wars and the need for the Luxembourg dynast to oversee preparations then underway in Franconia, Bavaria, and Upper Swabia, aimed at reclaiming his inheritance.

13   For a summary of events, Kaar, *Wirtschaft*, 56–60.
14   On the Luxembourg seizure of Bohemia and its significance, see Robert Antonín, 'Der Weg nach Osten: Heinrich VII. und der Erwerb Böhmens für die Luxemburger', in Sabine Penth and Peter Thorau (eds), *Rom 1312: Die Kaiserkrönung Heinrichs VII. und die Folgen. Die Luxemburger als Herrscherdynastie von gesamteuroäpischer Bedeutung* (Cologne, 2016), 9–22.
15   The visit of Karlstein is recorded in an account book covering the abbey's finances between 1409 and 1421. See StaL, B 383 V/7, fol. 253v: *Item I guld des küngs herolt Karelstein uff Lucie* [1418]. For more information about Karlstein's service in Sigismund's court, see Nils Bock, 'Die drei (Wappen-)Könige des Kaisers: Die Heroldsämter der Luxemburger in europäischer Perspektive', in Martin Bauch, Julia Burkhardt, Tomáš Gaudek and Václav Žůrek (eds), *Heilige, Helden, Wüteriche: Herrschaftsstile der Luxemburger (1308-1437)* (Cologne, 2017), 63–82 (esp. 71–4); on the practice of heralds in imperial service taking names after important royal residences or lands, such as the heralds *Ungarland* (Hungary) and *Luxemburg* (Luxembourg) as well as Karlstein, see Nils Bock, *Die Herolde im römisch-deutschen Reich: Studien zur adligen Kommunikation im späten Mittelalter* (Ostfildern, 2015), 141–2, 149, 188–9.
16   On these raids, see Kaar, *Wirtschaft*, 60–1. The international reverberations of the Hussite Wars are discussed in Mark Whelan, 'The "Conciliar" Front of the Hundred Years' War: Scotland, France and England at the Council of Pavia-Siena, 1423–4', *Historical Research* 93 (2020), 420–42 (on 437–40).

FINDING THE LUXEMBOURG COURT

Amidst the instability brought to the region by the Hussite Wars, Ellwangen underwent a change in leadership in 1427, with the death of Prince-Abbot Siegfried heralding the election of Holzingen as their new leader, who then was obliged to confirm his abbey's privileges with its overlord. Konrad's account book records incomes and expenditure from 22 February 1428 through seven accounting years until 9 March 1435, but the travails Holzingen experienced in securing confirmation of his office and rights can be followed in their full extent because the first accounting year contains a range of entries stretching back into 1427. The election of a new abbot always came with expenses. For starters, Konrad needed to purchase wax and candles worth around 16 gulden for the late abbot's funeral services and find further cash to construct an appropriate tomb.[17] Konrad needed to find a further 20 gulden to pay a goldsmith in Ulm to make for Holzingen two new sealing matrices, a sealing ring, and a gilded vestment.[18] These costs paled in comparison to the hundreds of gulden needed to secure imperial confirmation of the abbot's new status, a process that required the dispatch of one of the abbey's trusted servants, a certain Hans von Wolmershausen, to Hungary to treat with Sigismund and secure the appropriate letters. As we shall see, hundreds more gulden needed to be found after Wolmershausen lost the imperial letters on his return journey when he was captured (and ransomed) by an anonymous gang of criminals, identified vaguely by Konrad's entries as 'the rascals' (*die büben*). With no letters and a now presumably shaken Wolmershausen, more money needed to be found to send him to Hungary again, this time by ship rather than overland, perhaps because riverine travel was safer. It was not until November 1429 that Holzingen had secured imperial confirmation of the abbey's regalian rights and had been formally enfeoffed at significant cost to the abbey.

Wolmershausen's experience illuminates an often overlooked facet of diplomacy and communication in the realms of the Luxembourg dynasty: the reality of diplomatic travel across multiple and diverse kingdoms and polities. Casual remarks regarding Charles IV's presence in an anonymous chronicle composed in Magdeburg in the later 1300s underline how the subjects of Luxembourg monarchs needed to travel far and wide and in all directions in search of an audience with their sovereign. In 1359, for example, the chronicle reports how the city dispatched an embassy to Mainz, some 400 miles to their south-west, in an attempt to gain an audience with Charles IV, who they heard was returning that way from a trip to Aachen. In 1368, the city's secretary was similarly dispatched

---

17 StaL, V/9, fols 4v, 19r.
18 StaL, V/9, fol. 5r.

roughly 350 kilometres south-east to Prague, to secure letters from the imperial chancery.[19] It was not always that simple, however, as there was no guarantee that Luxembourg rulers would be in residence in their traditional power bases in Central Europe, such as Prague and (later, for Sigismund) Buda and Bratislava. Subjects of the Luxembourgs therefore often travelled extensive distances in search of their peripatetic monarchs who regularly travelled the breadth of much of Christendom.[20] The embassy of the City of Strasbourg was relatively lucky when it tracked down a travelling Sigismund to Paris in February 1416, but the rulers of the Luxembourg dynasty could travel much more widely.[21] Sigismund's itinerary, for example, records stays in places as far apart as Constantinople in the south-east and Windsor in the north-west, while his grandfather, John, sojourned in Prussia and the Kingdom of Poland no less than three times.[22] Even if embassies succeeded in tracking down their frequently elusive monarchs, they could still be disappointed. Such was the case for Claus Redwitz, for example, a Knight of the Teutonic Order. After travelling perhaps over 1000 kilometres from Prussia to find Sigismund in Vienna in 1425, Redwitz asked the imperial chancellor for certain letters desired by his superior, the Grandmaster of the Teutonic Order. Sigismund's chancellor, as Redwitz wrote to his Grandmaster, gave a disappointing reply, claiming that he didn't have the letter with him

---

19   Karl Janicke (ed.), *Die Chroniken der deutschen Städte vom 14. bis in's 16. Jahrhundert. Die Chroniken der niedersächsischen Städte: Magdeburg, ester Band* (Leipzig, 1869), 227–9, 258. For a discussion of the audience in Mainz, see Klaus Graf, 'Die Magdeburger Schöppenchronik: Anregungen für die künftige Forschung', *Sachsen und Anhalt* 30 (2018), 131–72 (on 140–2).
20   Petr Elbel highlighted how the dynasty retained many aspects of the so-called 'travelling kingdoms' (*Reisekönigtum*) of the early and high medieval periods. For further discussion, see Petr Elbel, 'Prag und Ofen als Kaiserresidenzen: Die Verlagerung des Reichsschwerpunkts nach Osten unter den Luxemburgern und deren Folgen für das Reich', in Sabine Penth and Peter Thorau (eds), *Rom 1312: Die Kaiserkrönung Heinrichs VII. und die Folgen. Die Luxemburger als Herrscherdynastie von gesamteuroäpischer Bedeutung* (Cologne, 2016), 259–329 (at 259–60).
21   On Strasbourg's embassy, see Mark Whelan, 'Dances, Dragons and a Pagan Queen: Sigismund of Luxemburg and the Publicizing of the Ottoman Turkish Threat', in Norman Housley (ed.), *The Crusade in the Fifteenth Century: Converging and Competing Cultures* (Routledge, 2017), 49–63 (on 52–3).
22   On Sigismund's itinerary, Jörg K. Hoensch, *Itinerar König und Kaiser Sigismunds von Luxemburg 1368–1437* (Warendorf, 1995), 63 (for Constantinople) and 96 (for Windsor). On Sigismund's stay in England, see Len Scales, 'Court and Control: Sigismund in England, 1416', in Petr Elbel and Stanislav Bárta (eds), *Hof und Kanzlei Kaiser Sigismunds als politisches Zentrum und soziales System* (Cologne, forthcoming). On John's travels, Werner Paravicini, *Adlig leben im 14. Jahrhunderts. Weshalb sie fuhren: Die Preußenreisen des europäischen Adels. Teil 3* (Göttingen, 2020), 511–13.

in Vienna, but he thought that it could be in Buda, having been carted over from Bohemia with other documents that had originally been in Karlštejn.²³ Tracking down a king who regularly moved between three kingdoms could be difficult for contemporaries, but as the chancellor's comments highlight, the logistical and bureaucratic issues such itineracy raised for the Luxembourgs and their entourage could likewise pose problems for their administration as well as those of their subjects.²⁴

Kintzinger and Daldrup discussed in detail the technical and legal frameworks that – at least in the minds of contemporary jurists – regulated the exchange of emissaries and messengers during Sigismund's reign. Ellwangen's accounts – not to mention the examples above – serve as a helpful reminder that, in practice, things could be different.²⁵ In a similar vein, much discussion has been focused on the challenges that Luxembourg rulers faced in exercising rule over vast geographical expanses. However, the hindrances that their subjects faced in interacting with their often-distant ruler are awarded much less consideration.²⁶ The challenges and considerations that came with dealing with the multinational and multilingual Luxembourg court could surface in a variety of ways. These were given life even in the quotidian record-keeping of imperial subjects. Financial accounts compiled in The Hague in the later 1350s for Albert, Count of Holland and Duke of Bavaria, recorded the arrival of an embassy from 'the City of Glatau' ('der stat von Glatouwen', i.e., modern-day Klatovy, now in the Czech Republic), a city that Charles IV had granted the aristocrat as a wedding gift in 1353. The location of this perhaps obscure town, however, was unclear to the contemporaries that vetted the accounts, so the scribe added the gloss that the settlement in question 'stood in the land of Bohemia' ('int land van Beem state').²⁷ It is here where Ellwangen's experience of treating with Sigismund is so valuable,

---

23 Berlin, Geheimes Staatsarchiv Preußischer Kulturbesitz, XX, Ordensbriefarchiv [hereafter Berlin, OBA], 4378.
24 A detailed study of how the different administrative organs of the Luxembourg dynastic lands interacted and operated alongside each other is sorely needed, but for now see the following, focused on the first ten years of Sigismund's reign as King of Hungary and of the Romans: Márta Kondor, 'The Ginger Fox's Two Crowns: Central Administration and Government in Sigismund of Luxembourg's Realms, 1410–1419' (Unpublished PhD dissertation, Central European University, Budapest, 2017), 80–3.
25 Daldrup, *Zwischen König und Reich*, 61–5; Kintzinger, *Westbindungen*, 216–28.
26 On the first point, see Alexandra Kaar, 'Urkunden, Rituale und Herrschaftspraxis eines europäischen Monarchen', in Karel Hruza and Alexandra Kaar (eds), *Kaiser Sigismund (1368–1437): Zur Herrschaftspraxis eines europäischen Monarchen* (Cologne, 2012), 467–75 (on 474).
27 D.E.H. de Boer and J.W. Marsilje (eds), *De rekeningen van de grafelijkheid van Holland uit de Beierse periode. Serie I: De hofrekeningen en de dijkgraafsrekeningen van de Grote Waard. Deel: 1358–1361* (The Hague, 1997), 179.

for it sheds light on the realities of diplomatic travel for subjects of the Luxembourg dynasty and on the dangers faced by emissaries of lower status such as Wolmershausen, who was never made a *familiaris regis* in the Luxembourg court and presumably lacked the clout that came with representing an imperial free city or a powerful secular or ecclesiastical lordship.[28]

In a special section under the rubric 'So has Konrad given out for my lord's regalia [and] to ride to Hungary to the King [and for] expenses and letters etc' ('So hat Conrad dornach ußgeben umb meins herren regalia zeryten gen Ungarn zum küng zerung umb brieff etc') follow two entries here given in full:

> Item, one gave Hans von Wolmershausen 368 Rhenish gulden, with which he covered his expenses, conveyed fees and letters to the King, purchased horses, and with the rest [of it] was waylaid on the return journey. Item, one gave him [i.e., Hans] seventy-five Rhenish gulden once again for [travel] to Hungary for the regalia and letters, because on the first journey he was waylaid and lost the letters etc.[29]

Three issues are alluded to here, that will now be tackled in turn: the journey to Hungary to meet with Sigismund; the costs involved; and the disruption Hans experienced on his return home.

HANS VON WOLMERSHAUSEN'S JOURNEY TO HUNGARY

Wolmershausen probably began his first journey from the Holy Roman Empire to Sigismund's court in late 1427 or early 1428. Reaching Hungary's western border from Upper Swabia probably took at least a week, and contemporaries could find venturing that far daunting enough.[30] Sigismund, for example, in 1429 convened a Reichstag in Bratislava (Pressburg/Poszony), a city on the Kingdom of Hungary's western border with the Duchy of Austria. This was, however, met with opposition

---

28 On the *familia regis* see Kintzinger, *Westbindungen*, 165–70 (for discussion of the term) and 417–70 (for a list of visitors, including *familiares regis*, to Sigismund's court).
29 StaL, V/9, fol. 4v: 'Item iii^c lxviii Rÿnischer guldin gab man Hansen von Wolmerßhusen, dovon er zert dem küng gab und brieff ußbracht pferd aufft, und mit dem übrigen nÿderlag an der widerfart. Item lxxv Rinischer guld gab man im zum andern mal gen Ungarn umb die Regalia und brieff, als er an der ersten fart nÿdergelegen was, und die brieff etc verloren hett.'
30 On perceptions of Hungary in the Holy Roman Empire, see Len Scales, *The Shaping of German Identity: Authority and Crisis, 1245–1414* (Cambridge, 2012), 454.

throughout the Holy Roman Empire's German-speaking territories for it was, in the minds of contemporary critics, further east than Vienna, the furthest point that lords and their emissaries in the heartlands of the Reich generally wished to travel. Attendance at the assembly therefore proved disappointing, with only two of the electoral princes bothering to venture such a distance to attend in person.[31] But Holzingen had no choice but to send a representative to Hungary if he wanted to secure confirmation of his office. Wolmershausen's first journey to Hungary was probably made by horse, the costs of which were included in the 368 gulden referred to in the entry above. For Wolmershausen's second journey Konrad entered individual expenses that allow us to reconstruct his trip in more detail, including twelve and a half shillings (roughly half a gulden) to hire a vessel to travel the waters of the Danube downstream towards Hungary ('uff dem wasser gen Ungern') as well as a further gulden for supplies such as cheese 'and other things [required] on board the ship' ('und ander ding uff das schiff').[32] By land or by water, even once in western Hungary there was no guarantee that Sigismund's court would be in either of the two most accessible sites for visiting diplomats – Bratislava or Buda – located as they were towards the north-western edge of the kingdom and handily reached via ship directly from Danube ports upstream such as Regensburg and Passau.[33] Hungary was a vast kingdom with long borders, and Sigismund – along with much of his court and administrative machinery – might be hundreds of kilometres further east in Transylvania, or similar distances to the south (towards Serbia and Bosnia) or north-east (towards Poland and Moldavia). Even if Sigismund was relatively nearby in north-western Hungary, finding him could exercise even patient individuals. Arriving in Hungary, Peter Wacker, for example, an emissary attempting to track down Sigismund in summer 1424 on behalf of the electoral princes, spent the better part of a week going from village to village, eventually tracking his king to an isolated settlement where he was found hunting.[34] Upon arriving in western Hungary, Wolmershausen was no doubt disappointed to have discovered that Sigismund was at least several weeks travelling away, for in

---

31 Daldrup, *Zwischen König und Reich*, 297–9.
32 StaL, V/9, fol. 6v.
33 On some of Sigismund's sites of administration, see Márta Kondor, 'Hof, Residenz und Verwaltung: Ofen und Blindenberg in der Regierungszeit König Sigismunds – unter besonderer Berücksichtigung der Jahre 1410–1419', in Karel Hruza and Alexandra Kaar (eds), *Kaiser Sigismund (1368–1437): Zur Herrschaftspraxis eines europäischen Monarchen* (Cologne, 2012), 215–33.
34 Peter Wacker's embassy is discussed in detail in Whelan, 'Sigismund of Luxemburg', 42–5. Wacker's biographical details are listed in Daldrup, *Zwischen König und Reich*, 465.

the winter of 1427–8 the embattled king was hundreds of kilometres away in the vicinity of Belgrade, overseeing a military campaign against the Ottoman Turks.[35] This was not the only instance when Wolmershausen's luck would falter on his diplomatic mission.

That Wolmershausen probably arrived at Sigismund's court in late March or early April 1428 can be inferred from the evidence in the so-called 'Reichsregisterbücher' (the 'Imperial register books'), administrative registers recording some of the correspondence and paperwork passing through Sigismund's imperial chancery.[36] One codex contains three entries relating to the abbey of Ellwangen dated 13 April 1428 in Kovin (now in Serbia), a fortress settlement a few miles east of Belgrade ('datum in Kervyn anno domini mcccc° xxviii feria secunda proxima post dominicam quasimodogeniti'), which were presumably drawn up in response to Wolmershausen's requests made once he had arrived at court.[37] In tracking down his king, then, Wolmershausen had to leave the Holy Roman Empire and traverse the length of the Kingdom of Hungary southwards to the borders of Serbia. The first entry confirmed Holzingen in his regalian rights as Abbot of Ellwangen and saved him a lengthy journey, for he could render the oath due for receiving his regalia to Count Ludwig of Württemberg rather than Sigismund. The second entry confirmed the monastery in all its privileges, and the third made provision for Count Ludwig to act as protector of the religious house for as long as Holzingen was satisfied or until Sigismund or one of his successors saw fit to change this state of affairs.[38] The last provision merely confirmed what was already in motion: in a letter dated 18 March 1428, Holzingen continued in his predecessor's wake and confirmed Count Ludwig of Württemberg as the abbey's 'lord and protector' ('herren und schirmer').[39] These three imperial grants, of which only the summaries survive in the registers, would have been composed into formal letters bearing seals and entrusted to Wolmershausen, who would convey them to Holzingen, but they were not given for free.

---

35 On Sigismund's military campaigns in the later 1420s, see Whelan, 'Sigismund of Luxemburg', 45–55. On Sigismund's itinerary, Hoensch, *Itinerar*, 113–14.

36 On the registers, see Gerhard Seeliger, 'Die Registerführung am deutschen Königshof bis 1493', *Mitteilungen des Instituts für Österreichische Geschichtsforschung: Ergänzungsband* 4 (1893), 223–364. For the volumes now labelled E-M that cover the years roughly coterminous with Sigismund's reign as King of the Romans and Emperor, see ibid., 263–76.

37 Vienna, Haus, Hof, und Staatsarchiv, Reichsregisterbücher [hereafter Vienna, RRB], I, fol. 3v; calendared in Altmann, *Regesta Imperii*, no. 7037.

38 Vienna, RRB, I, fol. 3v; calendared in Altmann, *Regesta Imperii*, nos 7038–9.

39 StaL, B 389, U 149.

THE COSTS OF DEALING WITH THE LUXEMBOURG COURT

Travelling the thousand or so kilometres from Ellwangen to visit Sigismund in the vicinity of Belgrade would have been costly, but the major part of the 368 gulden given Wolmershausen by Konrad would have been intended to be spent on meeting expenses at the imperial court, and it is worth considering what these were. In a royal or aristocratic court, everything had a price, from trifling bribes to sweeten chamber attendants to the sometimes eye-watering sums necessary to have privileges confirmed in writing. When a delegation from Halberstadt arrived in Bratislava to visit Sigismund's court in January 1430 to pursue a legal case, they had to find two and a half Hungarian gulden for a treasury official, two and a half Rhenish gulden for a royal notary, and nine Hungarian gulden for a courtier to promote their cause, even before they could begin to go about their business proper.[40] The chancery charged much larger sums for producing privileges and grants in written form.[41] The attempts in the later 1420s of the Teutonic Order, for example, to secure confirmation of their ownership of the New Mark, an eastern strip of the margraviate of Brandenburg, illustrate the sums of money at stake and the negotiations that went on behind closed doors.[42] After several years of discussion, the officer in charge of the negotiations, Claus Redwitz, secured the 'great privilege from the chancery and also other necessary letters relating to the New Mark' at a cost of 800 Hungarian gulden in October 1429.[43] This was a large sum and he had to bargain hard to whittle down the price from the 1000 Hungarian gulden previously quoted by the Bishop of Zagreb, a member of Sigismund's chancery. Even then, Redwitz needed to borrow money from two men in Bratislava to secure the cash.[44] The Luxembourg court was, therefore, like any other in Christendom: the usual

---

40 G. Schmidt, 'Eine Reise von Halberstadt nach Pressburg und zurück: 1429 Dec. bis 1430 Febr.', in *Mitteilungen des Instituts für Österreichische Geschichtsforschung* 7 (1886), 647–52 (payments on p. 50).
41 An overview of this practice with illustrative examples (albeit from the reign of Frederick III) is offered in Eberhard Isenmann, 'Reichsfinanzen und Reichssteuern im 15. Jahrhundert', *Zeitschrift für Historische Forschung* 7 (1980), 1–76 (on 45–6).
42 On the political background, see Jürgen Sarnowsky, 'The Military Orders and Crusading in the Fifteenth Century: Perception and Influence', in Norman Housley (ed.), *Reconfiguring the Fifteenth-Century Crusade* (London, 2017), 123–60 (on p. 127).
43 Berlin, OBA, 5197: '… hab ich gegeben acht hundert gulden zü losung aus der kantzelleÿ der grossen privilegÿ und auch ander noturftiger brief die dartzu gehoren auff die newen margk.'
44 Berlin, OBA, 5245. For discussion of Redwitz and this document, see Mark Whelan, 'Between Papacy and Empire: Cardinal Henry Beaufort, the House of

gifts and payments in cash and kind were needed to grease the wheels of the bureaucratic machinery. Around 1418, an unidentified emissary at Sigismund's court wrote to the city council of Frankfurt am Main stressing the importance of giving gifts. After the author reeled off the various bribes and gifts he had distributed, he punned that 'schangck iz danck und grosze schangck is groszer danck' (roughly translated: 'gift equals thanks and bigger gift equals bigger thanks').[45] In 1437 another Frankfurter put it even more pithily, writing that in the chancery 'with money one can get what they want' ('man keyfit umb gelt waz man wil').[46] Wolmershausen's experience of the Luxembourg court would have been no different.

It is unfortunate that Konrad did not break down the costings behind the 368 gulden given Wolmershausen to travel to Hungary, purchase horses, and secure the needed privileges and letters from Sigismund's chancery, but a reasonable estimate of the cash the emissary had to disburse in the imperial court can be made. Later in the account book, Konrad paid a hundred gulden to Wolmershausen for the horses which the latter 'brought with him from Hungary' ('mit im von Ungern bracht') and a further ten gulden for their transport, suggesting that the 368 gulden were primarily used for travel and for securing the privileges, and that the horses ('meiden') were purchased using a different pot of money.[47] If we then subtract 75 gulden from this sum for travel expenses – 75 being the amount Konrad gave Wolmershausen to make his second trip to Hungary – it can be assumed that Wolmershausen disbursed around 300 gulden in bribes and payments to secure the letters his superior in Ellwangen required. Whereas under Sigismund's predecessor, King Rupert (1400–10), supplicants to the imperial court might have paid anywhere between 60 and 100 gulden to confirm their privileges, under the Luxembourg regime prices skyrocketed, with some imperial free cities paying tenfold compared to what they had before.[48] Konrad's account book offers a 'bottom-up' view of how the abbey of Ellwangen, an institution of relatively modest

---

Lancaster, and the Hussite Crusades', *English Historical Review* 133 (2018), 1–31 (on 25–6).

45 Johannes Janssen (ed.), *Frankfurts Reichscorrespondenz nebst andern verwandten Aktenstücken von 1376–1519* (Freiburg, 1863), I, no. 550, p. 319.

46 Ibid., I, no. 769, p. 412.

47 StaL, V/9, fols 6v (for transport costs) and 12v (for the purchase price).

48 Adolf Nuglisch, 'Das Finanzwesen des Deutschen Reiches unter Kaiser Sigmund', *Jahrbücher für Nationalökonomie und Statistik* 21 (1901), 145–67 (on 161–2). For a more recent discussion of this issue, see Jörg K. Hoensch, *Die Luxemburger: Eine spätmittelalterliche Dynastie gesamteuropäischer Bedeutung 1308–1437* (Stuttgart, 2000), 302–5.

resources, was similarly swept up in Sigismund's drive to engineer more income from any source possible.[49]

Sigismund's drives to squeeze ever greater profits out of his imperial chancery did not go unnoticed by his subjects in the Holy Roman Empire, and the Luxembourg court and its figurehead enjoyed a reputation for penury and money-grabbing. Walter of Schwarzenberg, a veteran diplomat who represented Frankfurt am Main throughout Sigismund's reign as King of the Romans and Emperor, reported from the imperial court in winter 1433 'that he [i.e., Sigismund] dearly wanted money' ('daz er gern gelt hette').[50] Such a state of affairs was a near-constant one for the monarch. The near-contemporary *Klingenberg Chronicle* had much to say about Sigismund's state of financial affairs, claiming that he 'had a rough time when it came to money and was always needy and poor'. The author went on to allege that Sigismund rarely had the coin necessary to pay the innkeeper when it came to settle his bill in the morning and would ennoble anyone he could in return for payment.[51] Ellwangen's accounts offer a unique insight into the costs of dealing with the Luxembourg court in comparative perspective, for the abbey had to treat with three more courts – the curia in Rome, the comital Württemberg court (usually in Urach or Waiblingen), and the Bishop of Augsburg and his administration – in order to ensure that Holzingen's installation as abbot was accepted by the principal figures who wielded influence in the abbey's political and diplomatic milieu. The fact that Konrad had to find the most coin for costs associated with the imperial court lends credence to the disgruntled contemporaries that found voice in the *Klingenberg Chronicle*, and points to the significant expense that came with Ellwangen's imperial immediacy and their concomitant need to treat with Sigismund directly.

When treating with the pontiff, Konrad spent 348 gulden 'on the matter in Rome' in order to secure 'his new lord's confirmation from the Pope and cardinals', as well as a further 50 gulden for advice from one of the

---

49 For overviews of Sigismund's efforts to raise income, see Karel Hruza, 'König Sigismund und seine jüdischen Kammerknechte, oder: wer bezahlte "des Königs neue Kleider"?', in Karel Hruza and Alexandra Kaar (eds), *Kaiser Sigismund (1368–1437): Zur Herrschaftspraxis eines europäischen Monarchen* (Cologne, 2012), 76–135 (esp. 81–3); Franz Irsigler, 'Konrad IX. von Weinsberg, Königin Barbara (von Cilli) und die ritterliche Gesellschaft zum Phönix', *Hémecht: Revue d'histoire luxembourgeoise* 68 (2016), 261–79 (esp. 262–5).
50 For further discussion, see Christopher Folkens, 'Städtische Gesandte als Akteure im Spannungsfeld zwischen Reichsstadt, Reich, und Königtum: Das Beispiel des Frankfurter Gesandten Walter von Schwarzenberg', in Thomas Lau and Helge Wittmann (eds), *Kaiser, Reich und Reichsstadt in der Interaktion* (Petersberg, 2016), 181–206 (on 197).
51 Eberhard Wüst, *Die sog. Klingenberger Chronik des Eberhard Wüst, Stadtschreiber von Rapperswil*, ed. Bernhard Stettler (Sankt Gallen, 2007), 201–2.

abbey's allies on how best to secure the desired papal confirmation.⁵² Securing the acquiescence of Peter von Schaumberg, Bishop of Augsburg (1424–69), to Holzingen's election proved less expensive, but probably involved more planning on the ground. Schaumberg was invited to Ellwangen to consecrate Holzingen as abbot, and in return received two vestments gilded in silver worth 25 gulden.⁵³ To judge from Konrad's accounts, Schaumberg arrived with most of his household in tow, all of whom needed some form of gift or special treatment. One of the bishop's administrative officers (*der official*) was accompanied to the consecration and then onwards to Schwäbisch Gmünd by a member of the abbey's community at a cost of almost three shillings, and other guests required similar escorts.⁵⁴ Wine, apples, herbs and candles needed to be purchased for the consecration as well as gifts in cash found for most of Schaumberg's entourage, including two gulden for the bishop's chaplain, two gulden for his chamberlain, one gulden and seven and a half shillings for his beadle, one gulden for his cook, and ten shillings for the cook's servant.⁵⁵ As we read earlier, Sigismund allowed Holzingen to offer his oath and receive his regalian rights directly from Count Ludwig of Württemberg, so the new abbot spent four days with an entourage of 18 horse rendering homage at Waiblingen in March 1429 at a cost of around 20 gulden.⁵⁶ Arrangements were then made for Holzingen formally to be enfeoffed by the count ('seine lehen zu empfahen'), and on 10 November the abbot travelled to Urach with his entourage, where 'he received his fief from my lord of Württemberg in place of the King' ('gen Urach als er seine lehen empfieng von miner herren von Wurttemberg an des kungs stat'), a trip that cost roughly 14 gulden.⁵⁷ At the same time ('eodem tempore'), a servant of the abbey was dispatched to Ulm at a cost of just over one gulden to fetch an item of jewellery 'to give as a present' ('von eins claÿnods wegen zuverschencken'), presumably to the count, although the cost of the jewellery is not recorded. In line with Hardy's recent work highlighting the dense associative networks connecting lordships and communities of Upper Germany, the expenses outlined above draw attention to the co-existence of local, regional and international networks of allegiance and affiliation alongside the abbey's relationship with the Emperor necessitated by its imperial immediacy.⁵⁸ They also reveal, furthermore, that the journey to and expenses incurred in the imperial court consumed

52 StaL, V/9, fol. 4v.
53 Ibid.
54 Ibid., fol. 5r.
55 Ibid., fol. 4v.
56 Ibid., fol. 5r.
57 Ibid., fol. 7r.
58 Hardy, *Associative Political Culture*, 4–11.

the most revenue when payments for privileges, advice and transport are considered together. The Luxembourg court may have been one of many that an abbey such as Ellwangen needed to treat with, but it continued – in financial terms at least – to loom the largest. As Wolmershausen would discover, however, the roughly 400 gulden he spent in journeying to the southern borders of Hungary and treating at his monarch's court would not prove sufficient in light of the unforeseen events afflicting his return.

HANS VON WOLMERSHAUSEN'S KIDNAP AND RANSOM

After leaving Sigismund in the vicinity of Belgrade, Wolmershausen at some point on his return journey experienced the misfortune of capture and detention at the hands of a criminal gang, losing his precious letters in the process. His imprisonment not only illustrates the dangers associated with diplomatic travel across the vast Luxembourg domains, but highlights how the status and sponsor of captured diplomats could influence the price of their ransom. It is difficult to tell where Wolmershausen was waylaid from the usually laconic entries in the accounts. That Konrad sent several servants of the abbey (including Wolmershausen's own *knecht*) and sums of money amounting to over 20 gulden to Munich 'on account of Wolmershausen' or 'towards Munich because he [i.e., Wolmershausen] was waylaid' suggests that he had been captured in Bavaria and that negotiations for his release were undertaken in that locale.[59] In an undated entry falling at some point in the accounting year between 22 February 1428 and 27 March 1429, Konrad entered the following: 'Item, one gave seventy-two gulden to the rascals [*den büben*] as ransom money because they imprisoned Hans von Wolmershausen.'[60]

Just who his captors were is unclear, and this may have been related to a feud, but the instability brought to the region by the Hussite Wars meant that capture by parties of armed men was not an uncommon occurrence.[61] On 2 February 1424, for example, one priest in the Upper

---

59 StaL, V/9, fols 5v–6r. To take three examples: 'Item x guldin schickt man Hansen von Wollmerßhusen gen München als er nidergelegen was penthecostis' (on fol. 5v); 'Item iii lb heller verzart Conrad Heffner gen München von Hansen von Wollmershusen wegen eodem tempore [i.e., dominica trinitatis]'; 'Item x guldin Hansen von Wollmershusen geschickt gen Munchen ze zerung sabato post Corporis Christi' (both on fol. 6r).
60 StaL, V/9, fol. 6v: 'Item lxxii guldin gab man den büben ze schatzgelt, als sie Hansen von Wollmershausen gefangen hetten.'
61 For examples, see Kaar, *Wirtschaft, Krieg und Seelenheil*, 97–8, 101, 117, 158–9, 203–4. On feuding and the imprisonment of individuals, see Hardy, *Associative Political Culture*, 56–68.

Palatinate complained in his parish book that very few people attended his religious service that day on account of the panic caused by the capture of a local nobleman by the Hussites.⁶² It is clear that emissaries and diplomatic travellers were targeted, too, for Ellwangen Abbey was not the only community to suffer their representative falling into the hands of criminals. Walter of Schwarzenberg was captured in 1436 on his return to Germany from Hungary via Prague, this time by a gang identifying themselves as the 'Maidens of Bohemia' ('Jungfrauen zu Böhmen').⁶³ Schwarzenberg was a member of Sigismund's court, so his capture became an imperial concern, with the latter interceding in person to secure his release.⁶⁴ That Frankfurt's city council gave 500 gulden in thanks to Sigismund suggests that the monarch probably had to distribute gulden in the hundreds to ensure Schwarzenberg's release. Wolmershausen's ransom amounted to 72 gulden, indicating both his lower status as an emissary and the more modest income of Ellwangen Abbey compared to a wealthy imperial free city such as Frankfurt.

Wolmershausen's travails bring a human element to some of the scholarly debates that surround Sigismund and his place in the kingdoms he ruled. Sigismund was termed the 'distant Emperor' ('Der ferne Kaiser') in the title of an Austrian research project that ran for several years from 2008. It explored his rule of Germany, Hungary, and Bohemia, and the role that 'the sheer spatial distance' ('die schiere räumliche Distanz') between ruler and subject played in conditioning Sigismund's ruling style proved an important theme in an influential collection of essays on the monarch that appeared in 2012.⁶⁵ This approach echoes the thesis of Peter Moraw, who posited that the late medieval Reich was increasingly divided into geographical zones that enjoyed proximity to their monarch (*königsnah*) and those that did not (*königsfern*).⁶⁶ Wolmershausen's travails reveal the financial cost and human hardship involved in maintaining connections with a king

---

62 Franz Fuchs, 'Dörflicher Alltag in der Hussitenzeit: Aus den Aufzeichnungen eines Oberpfälzer Landpfarrers', in Hans-Jürgen Becker (ed.), *Der Pfälzer Löwe in Bayern: Zur Geschichte der Oberpfalz in der kurpfälzischen Epoche* (Regensburg, 1997), 37–55 (on 53).
63 On Walter of Schwarzenberg, see Mark Whelan, 'Walter of Schwarzenberg and the Fifth Hussite Crusade Reconsidered (1431)', *Mitteilungen des Instituts für Österreichische Geschichtsforschung* 122 (2014), 322–35. On his capture and ransom, see Franz Kirchgässner, *Walter von Schwarzenberg: Ein Frankfurter Gesandter des 15. Jahrhunderts* (Marburg, 1910), 59–62.
64 On Schwarzenberg's status, see Kintzinger, *Westbindungen*, 202.
65 See Kaar, 'Urkunden, Rituale und Herrschaftspraxis', 474–5.
66 For a summary of Moraw's approach and critique, see Len Scales, 'The Illuminated Reich: Memory, Crisis and the Visibility of Monarchy in Late Medieval Germany', in Jason Philip Coy, Benjamin Marschke and David Warren Sabean (eds), *The Holy Roman Empire Reconsidered* (New York, 2010), 73–92 (on 73–5).

that was far away, but also highlight the continuing importance attached by contemporaries to their relationship with the imperial office. Konrad's accounts also complicate the picture further, for Ellwangen's Luxembourg overlord was not always so distant. Not long after Wolmershausen's return from Hungary, Sigismund would not just be in Upper Swabia, but before Holzingen himself, feasting on the abbot's wine and food and expecting generous gifts while doing so. It is to Sigismund's visit of Ellwangen Abbey that we now turn.

SIGISMUND'S VISIT TO ELLWANGEN ABBEY

Although Sigismund claimed in 1429 to be too unwell to lead the crusade against the Hussites in person, he was well enough to travel, and he toured the southern stretches of the Holy Roman Empire in the winter of 1430–1, enjoying the hospitality of cities and religious houses along the Bodensee and across Upper Swabia, Bavaria, and Franconia. This tour, accomplished with his entourage of Italians, Germans, Hungarians, Bohemians, and even Turks, Sigismund undertook much to the chagrin of the political leaders and emissaries assembled then in Nuremberg, who would have preferred that their king attend personally to the preparations for the upcoming military campaign against the Hussites. It was during this tour that Sigismund visited Ellwangen.

Konrad placed the expenses for Sigismund's visit in the accounting year running 16 April 1430 to 7 March 1431, beginning the section by stating that '100 gulden was gifted to our lord the King when he was here on [St] Blaise['s day]' ('Item c guld unsern herren dem küng geschenckt als er hie was uff Blasii'). Konrad's 'uff Blasii' can perhaps be interpreted loosely, indicating when he registered the expenses rather than the exact date of the royal visit, but Sigismund's itinerary would suggest a visit around late January or very early February.[67] Once in Ellwangen, Sigismund was treated to a warm welcome, with Konrad recording gifts in cash and kind and the liberal dispensing of alcohol and food. Sigismund received 68 gulden in cash and a gilded cup worth a further 32, as well as four *aymer* (a liquid measurement of a couple of hundred litres) and five quarts of Alsatian wine worth around ten Rhenish gulden.[68] More than 25 gulden was spent on wine from the Neckar region amounting in volume to twelve and a half *aymer* and four quarts, as well as 'other things', such as 'fish, meat, oats etc.' ('ander ding von visch, flaisch, habern etc.').[69] The fish and meat was probably meant for Sigismund and his companions,

---

67   Hoensch, *Itinerar*, 116. St Blaise's Day is celebrated on 3 February.
68   StaL, V/9, fol. 45v.
69   Ibid.

while the oats made good fodder for the horses. Konrad also recorded two cash gifts to members of Sigismund's entourage, including ten gulden for 'Kaspar Schlick, the King's chancellor' and two gulden for an individual named Quatterloch, who was probably a court fool or jester.[70] Even playing host briefly to the peripatetic entourage of the Luxembourg Emperor-elect was not cheap, costing around 150 gulden, with Konrad entering these expenses into a section of his accounts entitled 'hospitality expenses' (*schenckgelt*). This was a significant sum considering that in the years 1428–35 Konrad usually disbursed, on average, about 35 gulden per annum in 'hospitality expenses'.

Although generous in its context, the hospitality Ellwangen offered to Sigismund paled in comparison to that offered by nearby civic communities. That same year, for example, the citizens of Augsburg, a wealthy free imperial city, presented Sigismund with a cup worth 168 gulden with 1000 gulden in cash contained within.[71] In late 1433, the citizens of Basel showed similar generosity, gifting Sigismund a cup worth 55 gulden with 1000 gulden in cash inside it, as well as finding a further 1017 gulden to pay for the accommodation of his retinue for two months and – among many other expenses – an additional 13 shillings to pay for 'shoes and socks' for their imperial visitor.[72] The citizens of Augsburg and Basel seem stingy when compared with their peers in Nuremberg, for on top of gifts and hospitality worth thousands of gulden, by summer 1431 Sigismund had run up debts owed to the city council amounting to no less than 9000 gulden.[73] When the Grandmaster of the Teutonic Order heard rumour in January 1431 that Sigismund planned to visit him personally, he ordered his representative at the imperial court to discourage the king from this idea, fearing the exorbitant amount of money it would drain out of his

---

70 Ibid.: 'Item x guldin Caspar Sligk des küngs kantzler geschenckt'; 'Item ii guld dem Quatterloch auch also geschenckt.' On Quatterloch's status as a court fool, see Dietrich Huschenbett, *Hermann von Sachsenheim: Namen und Begriffe. Kommentar zum Verzeichnis aller Namen und ausgewählter Begriffe im Gesamtwerk* (Würzburg, 2007), 225–6. On the possible meaning of *Quatterloch*, perhaps akin to 'arsehole', see Stefan Hannes Greil and Martin Przybilski (eds), *Nürnberger Fastnachtspiele des 15. Jahrhunderts von Hans Folz und aus seinem Umkreis: Edition und Kommentar* (Berlin, 2020), 391.
71 Nuglisch, 'Das Finanzwesen', 150.
72 Gerrit Jasper Schenk, 'Von den Socken: Ein Beitrag zur Kulturgeschichte der Politik am Beispiel des Einzugs König Sigismunds zum Konzil in Basel 1433', in Karel Hruza and Alexandra Kaar (eds), *Kaiser Sigismund (1368–1437): Zur Herrschaftspraxis eines europäischen Monarchen* (Cologne, 2012), 386–409 (on 408–9).
73 Jörg K. Hoensch, *Kaiser Sigismund: Herrscher an der Schwelle zur Neuzeit, 1368–1437* (Munich, 1996), 366–7, 587 (n. 45).

treasury.[74] Kintzinger rightly remarked upon the impact that Sigismund's personal participation in political events could have in impressing people to action, but, as contemporaries such as the Grandmaster knew, it also came at significant financial cost to the institutions and communities that hosted him.[75] Small it may have been in relative terms, but Ellwangen's hospitality remains instructive, for it illustrates the role played by some of the more modest institutions in making possible the tours and perambulations of Luxembourg monarchs throughout the Holy Roman Empire. In the same manner as imperial free cities, smaller communities such as Ellwangen similarly needed to find the money and resources necessary to host their imperial overlord. Konrad's experience – preserved by chance in the abbey's meticulous accounts – was no doubt replicated many times throughout the fourteenth and fifteenth centuries across the network of ecclesiastical institutions along the southern stretches of the Holy Roman Empire: the road along which the Luxembourgs journeyed countless times from their eastern kingdoms into the heartlands of the Holy Roman Empire.

CONCLUSIONS

Konrad's accounts bring new perspectives to the complexities experienced by one community in Central Europe when managing their relationship with their overlord, shedding light more broadly on the challenges and issues contemporaries experienced in the Holy Roman Empire when engaging with the kind of peripatetic and travelling court that was such a salient feature of Luxembourg rule throughout the later medieval period. Hoensch characterized the Luxembourg domains comprising the Holy Roman Empire, Bohemia, and Hungary, as a 'Danube kingdom' ('ein Donaureich'), a term suggesting a certain freedom of movement for people, material, and ideas along the length of the river that runs from its source in the Black Forest to the shores of the Black Sea.[76] There is much to support this view in Konrad's accounts. Were it not for Sigismund holding the Hungarian crown, it is unlikely that Ellwangen would have played host to the younger Count of Cilli, scion of the influential Hungarian aristocratic family, and his pipers at some point in 1431 as they rode to

---

74 Friedrich Georg von Bunde et al. (eds), *Liv-, est- und kurländisches Urkundenbuch nebst Regesten: Abteilung I, Band 8 (Mai 1429–1435)* (Aalen, 1974), 230–1 (n. 395).
75 Kintzinger, 'Luxemburger als Diplomaten', 406.
76 Hoensch, *Die Luxemburger*, 309.

fight the Hussites.⁷⁷ The vivid entries detailing Wolmershausen's capture, however, also illustrate some of the obstacles associated with traversing the vast Luxembourg realms and the costs involved in treating with an often distant sovereign. When discussing Ellwangen's relationship with the Emperor in the fourteenth and fifteenth centuries, Stievermann posited that the Count of Württemberg's appointment as protector in 1370 represented the 'cutting off' ('Abschneidung') of the abbey from the Holy Roman Empire and its 'integration' ('Einbindung') into a nascent Württemberg territorial state.⁷⁸ This is certainly not the impression offered by Konrad's accounts, with the imperial abbey investing substantial personal and financial resources in securing imperial privileges, in hosting the monarch in person, and in prosecuting imperially-sponsored military campaigns against the Hussites that aimed to restore the allegiance of a critical possession to the Luxembourg dynasty.⁷⁹ In the final analysis, Konrad's accounts underline how the apparent geographic and political liminality of the itinerant Luxembourg court did not necessarily diminish its significance to contemporaries in the late medieval Holy Roman Empire.

---

77   StaL, V/9, fol. 57r. As an introduction to the Cilli family, see Peter Štih, *The Middle Ages between the Eastern Alps and the Northern Adriatic: Select Papers on Slovene Historiography and Medieval History* (Leiden, 2010), 338–79.
78   Stievermann, 'Das geistliche Fürstentum Ellwangen', 36–7. The general approach taken by Stievermann is critiqued in Hardy, *Associative Political Culture*, 6–7.
79   On the latter issue, see the detailed exploration in Whelan, 'Taxes, Wagenburgs, and a Nightingale'.

CHAPTER 10

ASSESSING THE LUXEMBOURGS: THE IMAGE OF WENCESLAS AND SIGISMUND IN THE CORRESPONDENCE OF ITALIAN AMBASSADORS[1]

ONDŘEJ SCHMIDT

The desire to investigate the personality of medieval rulers is a common aspiration in the study of political history. However, due to multiple methodological constraints, largely connected to the preservation and the nature of the available sources, this is a difficult, if not impossible, task. It may thus be useful to take advantage of two recent approaches that promise new perspectives and research possibilities. The first is the concept of a 'rulership style' (*Herrschaftsstil*), conceived 'as a variable set

---

1   This essay follows on from an earlier, as yet unpublished, paper of mine: 'Mantuan Envoys at the Court of Sigismund of Luxembourg and Their Dispatches', in Petr Elbel, Klara Hübner and Stanislav Bárta (eds), *Der Hof Kaiser Sigismunds als personelle Bühne und internationales Zentrum* (in press). The research for the present essay was supported by the international project GF19-29622L: 'Grey Eminences in Action: Personal Structures of Informal Decision-Making at Late Medieval Courts', financed by the Czech Science Foundation (GAČR) and the Austrian Science Fund (FWF) and carried out at the Faculty of Arts of Masaryk University. I would like to thank Karl Kügle for his comments.

of personally shaped modes of action and behaviour of a ruler, which is suitable to shape the image of the sovereign – both performatively and mediated by artistic representations – in the eyes of his subjects and, in the most favourable case, to have a legitimizing effect on his rule'. This concept, developed by a group of historians, has already been successfully applied with regard to the rulers of the Luxembourg dynasty.[2] Charles IV has become a particular focus of scholarly interest, given his exalted religiosity, predilection for sophisticated rituals, and passionate relic collecting.[3] Other scholars such as Duncan Hardy, using the concept of 'charisma', have suggested investigating a sovereign's multifaceted ability to inspire 'enchantment' in his subjects as a crucial factor in establishing his authority. In this regard Sigismund of Luxembourg demonstrated outstanding skill.[4] Thanks to these two partially overlapping concepts, it is possible to shed new light on the personality of a ruler and his reflection in culture, and also on the extent to which he was (or was not) accepted as a leader by his contemporaries.[5] Even so, many problems remain.

WENCESLAS VERSUS SIGISMUND

In this essay, which is partly inspired by the approaches outlined above, I will focus on Wenceslas (IV), King of the Romans (1378–1400) and of Bohemia (1378–1419), and his younger (half-)brother Sigismund, King of

---

2   Martin Bauch, Julia Burkhardt, Tomáš Gaudek and Václav Žůrek (eds), *Heilige, Helden, Wüteriche. Herrschaftsstile der Luxemburger (1308–1437)*, Forschungen zur Kaiser- und Papstgeschichte des Mittelalters – Beihefte zu J. F. Böhmer, Regesta Imperii, 41 (Cologne, Weimar, and Vienna, 2017). See, in particular, the introduction by Martin Bauch, Julia Burkhardt, Tomáš Gaudek, Paul Töbelmann and Václav Žůrek, 'Heilige, Helden, Wüteriche: Eine konzeptionelle Skizze zu "Herrschaftsstilen" im langen Jahrhundert der Luxemburger', 11–27, with the quoted definition at 27: 'Ein Herrschaftsstil ist dabei als ein variables Set personal geprägter Handlungs- und Verhaltensweisen eines Herrschers zu verstehen, das geeignet ist, das Image des Herrschers – sowohl performativ wie durch künstlerische Darstellungen vermittelt – in den Augen seiner Untertanen zu prägen und im günstigsten Fall herrschaftslegitimierend zu wirken.'
3   Cf. Václav Žůrek, *Karel IV. Portrét středověkého vládce* (Prague, 2018). See also the essay by Ingrid Ciulisová in this volume.
4   Duncan Hardy, 'The Emperorship of Sigismund of Luxemburg (1410–37): Charisma and Government in the Later Medieval Holy Roman Empire', in Brigitte Miriam Bedos-Rezak and Martha Dana Rust (eds), *Faces of Charisma: Image, Text, Object in Byzantium and the Medieval West*, Explorations in Medieval Culture, 9 (Leiden and Boston, 2018), 288–321.
5   With reference to this approach, see Veronika Proske, *Der Romzug Kaiser Sigismunds (1431–1433): Politische Kommunikation, Herrschaftsrepräsentation und -rezeption*, Forschungen zur Kaiser- und Papstgeschichte des Mittelalters – Beihefte zu J. F. Böhmer, Regesta Imperii, 44 (Vienna, Cologne, and Weimar, 2018).

Hungary (1387–1437), King of the Romans (1411–33) and King of Bohemia (1420–37), as well as Holy Roman Emperor (1433–7). My analysis will be based on diplomatic correspondence produced by various Italian ambassadors who were sent to the imperial court. On the basis of these sources, I shall analyse the personal rulership styles of the two sovereigns with regard to their behaviour, the conduct of their court, and their self-presentations through rituals, ceremonies, and festivities. Finally, in a comparison of the results, I shall outline the differences between the two Luxembourg kings.

Wenceslas is generally considered a troubled figure on the imperial throne.[6] His contemporaries and, consequently, also later historians maligned Wenceslas, accusing him of many failings and misdeeds including cruelty, sloth, godlessness, alcoholism, and oppression of the Church, which subsequently led to the king's two imprisonments and, eventually, his deposition from the Roman throne in 1400. Some of these allegations and the bizarre anecdotes illustrating them can be rejected as the product of the considerable amount of propaganda originating from the Rhenish electors and the mainstream Church milieu, while others are at least partly justified. By contrast, it has been demonstrated that the Bohemian Utraquist tradition saw Wenceslas rather positively, as a popular and just king who favoured their reform movement.[7] In 2017 a conference attempted to provide a new, less biased picture of Wenceslas'

---

6 Cf. František Michálek Bartoš, *České dějiny*, vol. 2/6, *Čechy v době Husově (1378–1415)* (Prague, 1947); Jiří Spěváček, *Václav IV. 1361–1419. K předpokladům husitské revoluce* (Prague, 1986).

7 For Wenceslas' reflection in contemporary and modern historiography, see Petr Čornej, *Tajemství českých kronik: Cesty ke kořenům husitské tradice*, second edition (Prague and Litomyšl, 2003), 67–115; Petra Roscheck, 'König Wenzel IV. – Opfer einer Schwarzen Legende und ihrer Strahlkraft', in Peter Thorau, Sabine Penth and Rüdiger Fuchs (eds), *Regionen Europas – Europa der Regionen. Festschrift für Kurt-Ulrich Jäschke zum 65. Geburtstag* (Cologne, Weimar, and Vienna, 2003), 207–29; Klara Hübner, 'Herrscher der Krise – die Krise des Herrschers: König Wenzel IV. als Projektionsfläche zeitgenössischer Propaganda', *Biuletyn Polskiej Misji Historycznej / Bulletin der Polnischen Historischen Mission* 11 (2016), 294–320; eadem, 'Am Anfang war Propaganda: Vom widerspenstigen Begriff zu den Umrissen einer politischen Kommunikationskultur in der Zeit Wenzels IV. Ein Erfahrungsbericht', in Petr Elbel, Alexandra Kaar, Jiří Němec and Martin Wihoda (eds), *Historiker zwischen den Zeiten: Festschrift für Karel Hruza zum 60. Geburtstag* (Vienna, Cologne, and Weimar, 2021), 163–79; Christian Oertel, 'Wenceslaus alter Nero: Die Darstellung Wenzels IV. in der Historiographie des späten 14. und 15. Jahrhunderts', *Deutsches Archiv für Erforschung des Mittelalters* 74:2 (2018), 673–702.

rulership practice but, at the same time, also succeeded in confirming some old stereotypes.[8]

In order to put Wenceslas' image as reflected in the correspondence of Italian ambassadors into proper context, it is necessary to briefly discuss his relations with the powers on the Apennine Peninsula. Although an analysis of the king's Italian policy is yet to be written, it is possible to outline its basic features.[9] Wenceslas' activity with regard to 'Italian affairs' turns out to be considerably more intensive than has commonly been thought. Especially during the 1380s the monarch exerted considerable effort to support the authority of the Roman Pope Urban VI and to prepare his own descent into Italy for the imperial coronation, which, however, never took place due to the unfavourable political situation.[10] The most powerful ruler on the Peninsula at the time was Giangaleazzo Visconti of Milan (1385–1402), whose relationship with the King of the Romans changed quite dynamically. Initially rather hostile relations turned into a pragmatic alliance during the 1390s, which benefited both sides: Visconti gained the ducal title in 1395 and became the main supporter of the Roman monarch in Italy even after his deposition in 1400.[11]

Similarly, Sigismund[12] was long regarded with a certain animosity in most of his former kingdoms, and for various reasons: in Bohemia, his role in the execution of Jan Hus (1415) and the subsequent crusades against the Hussites (1420–31) was a key factor, while the Hungarians could not forget his 'foreign' origin and the loss of Dalmatia to the Venetians. This view, which was marked by the narrow perspective

---

8 Klara Hübner and Christian Oertel (eds), *Wenzel IV. (1361–1419): Neue Wege zu einem verschütteten König* (in press).
9 See Marie-Luise Favreau-Lilie, 'König Wenzel und Reichsitalien: Beobachtungen zu Inhalt, Form und Organisation politischer Kommunikation zwischen dem Reich und Italien im ausgehenden Mittelalter', *Mitteilungen des Instituts für Österreichische Geschichtsforschung* 109 (2001), 315–45; Ondřej Schmidt, 'Politika, diplomacie, písemnosti: Komunikace mezi císařským dvorem a Mantovou v letech 1378–1437' (Unpublished PhD dissertation, Masaryk University, 2020). See also the essays by Maria Theisen and Gia Toussaint in this volume.
10 Cf. Johann Lechner, 'Zur Geschichte König Wenzels (bis 1387)', *Mitteilungen des Instituts für Österreichische Geschichtsforschung – Ergänzungsband* 6 (1901), 339–54, at 342–50.
11 Ivan Hlaváček, 'Wenzel (IV.) und Giangaleazzo Visconti', in Paul-Joachim Heinig, Sigrid Jahns, Hans-Joachim Schmidt et al. (eds), *Reich, Regionen und Europa im Mittelalter und Neuzeit: Festschrift für Peter Moraw*, Historische Forschungen, 67 (Berlin, 2000), 203–26; Ondřej Schmidt, 'Druhé zajetí Václava IV. z italské perspektivy', *Studia mediaevalia Bohemica* 9:2 (2017), 163–214.
12 Cf. Wilhelm Baum, *Kaiser Sigismund: Hus, Konstanz und Türkenkriege* (Graz, Vienna, and Cologne, 1993); Jörg K. Hoensch, *Kaiser Sigismund: Herrscher an der Schwelle zur Neuzeit 1368–1437* (Munich, 1996).

of nineteenth- and twentieth-century nationalist historiographies, has gradually been overcome. Recent studies on Sigismund stress his role as a key 'international' figure in European politics (perhaps under a certain retrospective influence of today's attempts at integration of the Continent). They also praise the enormous energy and perseverance with which he pursued his goals (with varying degrees of success), for example, the preparation of the ecclesiastical councils in Constance and Basel, the efforts to establish peace between France and England in the mid-1410s, the ending of the Papal Schism (1417), the incessant organization of the defence against the Turks, his imperial coronation in Rome (1433), and the eventual acquisition of the Bohemian crown (1436).[13]

Sigismund's Italian policy appears to be quite transparent compared to that of his predecessor.[14] The reign of the 'last Luxembourg' in the *Regnum Italiae* was long dominated by conflict with the Republic of Venice over territory in north-eastern Italy and Dalmatia. Sigismund's relationship with Duke Filippo Maria Visconti of Milan, which oscillated between hostility and alliance, also underwent many twists and turns.[15] Given the unreliability of the Milanese ruler, the Roman monarch often relied on smaller allied princes and *signori*, such as Count/Duke Amadeus VIII of Savoy or the Lord of Mantua, Gianfrancesco Gonzaga.[16] Unlike his elder (half-)brother, Sigismund undertook two trips to Italy in person (1412–14 and 1431–3). In particular, the second campaign, during which Sigismund succeeded in obtaining the imperial crown in Rome and settling relations with Venice, contributed to the creation of a rather positive image of the monarch by the Italian 'public'.[17]

---

13   For a detailed historiographical overview, see Petr Elbel, 'Der Hof Kaiser Sigismunds im Kontext der internationalen Hofforschung: Stand, Lücken und Fragen', in Elbel, Hübner and Bárta (eds), *Der Hof Kaiser Sigismunds* (in press).
14   Cf. Otto Schiff, *König Sigismunds italienische Politik bis zur Romfahrt (1410–1431)* (Frankfurt am Main, 1909).
15   Cf. Ernst Kagelmacher, *Filippo Maria Visconti und König Sigismund, 1413–1431* (Greifswald, 1885); Francesco Somaini, 'Les relations complexes entre Sigismond de Luxembourg et les Visconti, ducs de Milan', in Michel Pauly and François Reinert (eds), *Sigismund von Luxemburg: Ein Kaiser in Europa* (Mainz, 2006), 157–98.
16   Cf. Schmidt, 'Politika'; Péter E. Kovács, 'Zsigmond császár Mantovában', in Ildikó Horn, Éva Lauter, Gábor Várkonyi et al. (eds), *Művészet és mesterség: Tisztelgő kötet R. Várkonyi Ágnes emlékére*, vol. 2 (Budapest, 2016), 87–102.
17   Proske, *Der Romzug*; cf. Péter E. Kovács, *König Sigmund in Siena* (Budapest, 2018); idem, *Studien über die Zeit von Sigismund von Luxemburg* (Toruń, 2021); idem, *Die Krönung Kaiser Sigismunds in Rom* (Debrecen, 2022).

THE DIPLOMATIC CORRESPONDENCE

In order to compare the perceptions of Wenceslas and Sigismund, two (half-)brothers often in conflict with each other,[18] on the Italian peninsula, I shall use the perspective of the Italian ambassadors staying at the imperial court at the turn of the fifteenth century. The dispatches (*dispacci*) they sent, that is, the letters to their superiors giving an account of the course of the respective diplomatic missions and other events, constitute a very valuable but somewhat neglected source with regard to studies of the Luxembourg dynasty.[19] In accordance with the general developments of historiographical paradigms, the scholarly use of diplomatic correspondence has changed over time. Initially, it was mainly a source for a positivist reconstruction of events and relations between states. Nowadays historians strive for a more complex approach to such letters, focusing on the nature of the documents themselves, techniques of communication, ambassadorial networks, or the influence of humanism, to name but a few of the more recent methodologies.[20] For our research question, these sources are significant because they give us a vivid picture of the otherwise mostly 'hidden' political agendas at the court.

Numerous collections of ambassadors' correspondence have been preserved in the archives from as early as the Trecento. With regard to the following century, the number of surviving letters increased exponentially, undoubtedly due to the intensification of communication. However, the preservation of diplomatic correspondence is also contingent on the history of the respective archive; it therefore does not always reflect in

---

18 Cf. Ivan Hlaváček, 'Zu den Spannungen zwischen Sigismund von Luxemburg und Wenzel IV.', in Josef Macek, Ernő Marosi and Ferdinand Seibt (eds), *Sigismund von Luxemburg, Kaiser und König in Mitteleuropa 1387–1437. Beiträge zur Herrschaft Kaiser Sigismunds und der europäischen Geschichte um 1400*, Studien zu den Luxemburgern und ihrer Zeit, 5 (Warendorf, 1994), 45–52.

19 The studies on Frederick III, on the other hand, are inspiring: cf. Karl-Friedrich Krieger, 'Der Hof Kaiser Friedrichs III. – von außen gesehen', in Peter Moraw (ed.), *Deutscher Königshof: Hoftag und Reichstag im späteren Mittelalter*, Vorträge und Forschungen, 48 (Stuttgart, 2002), 163–90; Jörg Schwarz, 'Politische Kommunikation – Selbstzeugnisse – Rechtfertigungsstrategien: Städtische Gesandtenberichte vom kaiserlichen Hof in Wiener Neustadt aus der Mitte des 15. Jahrhunderts', in Franz Fuchs, Paul-Joachim Heinig and Martin Wagendorfer (eds), *König und Kanzlist, Kaiser und Papst: Friedrich III. und Enea Silvio Piccolomini in Wiener Neustadt*, Forschungen zur Kaiser- und Papstgeschichte des Mittelalters – Beihefte zu J. F. Böhmer, Regesta Imperii, 32 (Vienna, Cologne, and Weimar, 2013), 89–119.

20 See, in particular, the excellent synthesis of Italian diplomacy by Isabella Lazzarini, *Communication and Conflict. Italian Diplomacy in the Early Renaissance, 1350–1520* (Oxford, 2015).

full its original extent and importance.²¹ Thus, the once great collection of medieval dispatches by the envoys of the Republic of Venice was lost in one of the fires of the Palazzo Ducale in the sixteenth century. Even more devastating was the destruction of the Visconti archives in Milan amid the turmoil of the mid-fifteenth century. Luckily, however, previously unknown fragments of dispatches drawn up by a Visconti embassy at the court of Wenceslas in the years 1386–7 have survived, for reasons unknown, in the archives of the Farnese family in Parma.²² As for incoming diplomatic correspondence, the otherwise rich archives of the Republic of Florence seem to be rather deficient. Nevertheless, they do preserve several extensive letters from the 1420s, when Florentine representatives stayed with Sigismund in Hungary.²³

Surprisingly, the most valuable dispatches are preserved in the archives of some less powerful *signorie* and republics. Particularly colourful are the more than 40 letters written by the Gonzaga envoys – first and foremost, the skilful diplomat Simone da Crema, who visited the courts of both Wenceslas and Sigismund.²⁴ The representatives of the Tuscan republics Lucca and Siena also left behind some interesting testimonies with regard to Wenceslas and Sigismund.²⁵ On the other hand, there are no letters of

---

21   A useful survey, albeit with a focus on the second half of the Quattrocento, is provided by Vincent Ilardi, 'Fifteenth-Century Diplomatic Documents in Western European Archives and Libraries (1450–1494)', *Studies in the Renaissance* 9 (1962), 64–112; idem, 'The Ilardi Microfilm Collection of Renaissance Diplomatic Documents ca. 1450–ca. 1500', in David Abulafia (ed.), *The French Descent into Renaissance Italy 1494–95: Antecedents and Effects* (Aldershot, 1995), 405–83. In the following, by no means exhaustive, overview, I restrict myself to northern and central Italy, i.e., mostly those parts of the peninsula, with the exception of the Republic of Venice, belonging to the Holy Roman Empire.
22   Archivio di Stato di Parma (hereafter cited as ASPr), Carteggio farnesiano estero, Boemia, busta 4, fols 1r–42v. I intend to analyse these important, yet very damaged, manuscript copies more extensively in a separate publication.
23   The relevant Florentine sources have been collected by Gianluca Masi, 'Sigismondo di Lussemburgo e Firenze (testimoni manoscritti negli archivi fiorentini)', in Cristian Luca and Ionel Cândea (eds), *Studia varia in honorem Professoris Ștefan Ștefănescu Octogenarii* (Bucharest and Brăila, 2009), 227–70.
24   Cf. Alessandro Luzio, *L'Archivio Gonzaga di Mantova*, vol. 2, *La corrispondenza familiare, amministrativa e diplomatica dei Gonzaga* (Verona, 1922), and a new critical edition of the Mantuan correspondence from the court of Wenceslas and Sigismund: Ondřej Schmidt (ed.), *Briefe vom Kaiserhof: Die letzten Luxemburger in der diplomatischen Korrespondenz aus dem Archiv der Gonzaga von Mantua (1380–1436)* (Brno, 2022). For Simone da Crema, see Gabriele Nori, 'Crema, Simone da', in *Dizionario Biografico degli Italiani*, vol. 30 (Rome, 1984), 592–3; Schmidt, 'Politika', 220–2 and passim.
25   For Lucca, see Luigi Fumi (ed.), *Carteggio degli Anziani*, vol. 2, Archivio di Stato in Lucca, Regesti 2 (Lucca, 1903). As for the extensive *carteggio* of Siena, no detailed

any interest in the archives of the counts and (from 1416) dukes of Savoy in Turin, the Este dynasty in Modena, the Carrara lords in Padua, the patriarchs of Aquileia in Udine, the city of Bologna, or the prince-bishops of Trento.[26] Among the smaller communes, the registers of Belluno are worthy of attention, as they contain seven dispatches from Sigismund's court in Constance. In total, there are several dozen ambassadors' letters from the imperial court from around 1400, the majority of them relating to Sigismund. This disproportion can be primarily explained by two factors: the gradually increasing production of correspondence, which does not play in Wenceslas' favour, and Sigismund's closer (and personal) involvement in Italian politics, which also brought about more intensive communication with local powers.

Diplomatic correspondence evolved into a specific genre and became a sophisticated means of communication during the fourteenth and fifteenth centuries.[27] As a source type, the dispatches have the indisputable advantage that – unlike charters, administrative books, or chronicles – they provide an immediate and fresh insight into the mechanisms of politics, the behaviour of the monarch, and everyday life of the court. Moreover, since the dispatches were drawn up by professionals with access to a vast range of both official and unofficial sources, generally the information provided is as reliable as it can possibly be. However, there are also some serious limitations with regard to the interpretation of dispatches.

While the form of correspondence in general terms was subject to the basic rules of the genre, it was also conditioned by specifics such as, among other things, the education, cultural background, and personal style of each ambassador. Although the aim of a dispatch was usually to describe as faithfully as possible what the envoys had done, seen, and heard, each

---

inventory of individual letters is available at present, only an alphabetical index of senders in manuscript. More systematic research is yet to be carried out. For a general overview, see *Archivio di Stato di Siena. Archivio del Concistoro del Comune di Siena. Inventario*, Pubblicazioni degli Archivi di Stato, 10 (Rome, 1952).

26 For the information regarding Trento, I am grateful to Petr Elbel.

27 For an excellent analysis of diplomatic correspondence, see Francesco Senatore, '*Uno mundo de carta*': *Forme e strutture della diplomazia sforzesca* (Naples, 1998); idem, 'Ai confini del "mundo de carta": Origine e diffusione della lettera cancelleresca italiana (XIII–XVI secolo)', in Isabella Lazzarini (ed.), *I confini della lettera: Pratiche epistolari e reti di comunicazione nell'Italia tardomedievale*, Reti Medievali Rivista, 10 (Florence, 2009), 1–53; Isabella Lazzarini, 'Materiali per una didattica delle scritture pubbliche di cancelleria nell'Italia del Quattrocento', *Scrineum Rivista* 2 (2004), 1–85; eadem, 'Corrispondenze diplomatiche nei principati italiani del Quattrocento: Produzione, conservazione, definizione', in Andrea Giorgi and Katia Occhi (eds), *Carteggi fra basso medioevo ed età moderna: Pratiche di redazione, trasmissione e conservazione*, Annali dell'Istituto storico italo-germanico in Trento – Fonti, 13 (Bologna, 2018), 13–37.

did so in a slightly different way: some letters thus take the form of 'dry' reports focusing almost exclusively on the factual details of the negotiations that were taking place, while others elaborate in more detail on the life of the imperial court. As the diplomats were only human, it is clear that they could not write completely *sine ira et studio*. We must also bear in mind that the letters were written by envoys and therefore addressed not to the public but to the powers that sent them on a diplomatic mission, whether it was an autocratic *signoria* or a collectively administered republic.[28] Envoys understandably tried their utmost to give the impression of being loyal servants, bearing in mind only the interests of their masters without regard for their own. This attitude of self-justification is a classic feature of diplomatic correspondence and can severely distort the representation of ambassadors' activities.[29] Another problem is self-censorship: envoys were always aware that correspondence might fall into the wrong hands, and therefore, both out of caution and fear of possible scandal, might have written not entirely candidly about a foreign monarch and events at his court. The resulting picture may be further influenced by the political context, as we might expect representatives of friendly Italian powers to report more favourably on the Roman monarch than diplomats of his enemies (this was not always the case, though).

Furthermore, when reporting on the Transalpine environment, we must also take into account fifteenth-century Italians' conviction of their own cultural superiority, which not infrequently implied a certain disdain for 'barbarians'. This stylization is particularly evident in the case of humanistically educated diplomats who attempted to make their literary skills evident through their letters. On the other hand, in our material, the humanist influence is still rather negligible.[30] This is related to the gradual transformation of the genre of diplomatic correspondence in the direction of greater narrativity, which can seriously deform the image of the persons depicted and their behaviour. These are just a few of the many *topoi* of diplomatic correspondence that somewhat diminish the value of the information contained therein. Nevertheless, all in all, the Italian dispatches to be discussed in what follows constitute an excellent source for the study of Wenceslas' and Sigismund's rulership style and court, even though, as do any other historical documents, they also require an adequate sense of critical distance.

---

28 For the characteristics and various *topoi* of diplomatic correspondence, see Senatore, '*Uno mundo de carta*', esp. 218–49.
29 Cf. e.g., Schwarz, 'Politische Kommunikation'.
30 The letters by Uberto Decembrio from Wenceslas' court are an exception. See Daniela Pagliara, 'Uberto Decembrio: A Humanist in Prague at the End of the Fourteenth Century', *Acta Universitatis Carolinae – Historia Universitatis Carolinae Pragensis* 55:1 (2015), 123–30.

THE SOVEREIGN AND HIS REFLECTION

In the remainder of this essay, I shall address three mutually interconnected and overlapping topics. The first of them is the reflection of the sovereign himself, in terms of his personality and behaviour, in the ambassadorial dispatches. As for Wenceslas, the sources have very little to say in this regard. The well-known and most extensive dispatch by the Mantuan envoy, Bonifacio delle Coppe da Montefalco, from 1383 does not describe the king at all. It seems that delle Coppe spent very little time with Wenceslas directly during his audience. The sovereign heard his message and did not even give his answer personally, responding instead through an unknown counsellor. Given the ambassador's unusual reticence, it seems that Wenceslas made little or perhaps not a particularly favourable impression on his Italian interlocutor.[31] As will be seen, the authors of some other dispatches, such as the envoy of Lucca in 1381, were not even given the privilege of appearing before the king and had to make do with members of his council.

The correspondence of the Visconti ambassadors, Corrado Cavalli and Beltrando Rossi, from 1386–7 is slightly more helpful.[32] Again, there is no direct appraisal of the king, but as the diplomats visited him more often, they were able to report a curious event. When the Milanese appeared before Wenceslas to ask him for permission to leave the court and return home (a very important feature of diplomatic protocol),[33] the jovial part of the king's nature came to the fore. He granted them permission and asked them to convey to the Visconti his desire to obtain one or several specimens of their lord's dogs, as they had promised. Finally, 'out of his kindness, he had wine brought to drink with [the envoys] three times

---

31 Rudolf Knott (ed.), 'Ein mantuanischer Gesandtschaftsbericht aus Prag vom Jahre 1383', *Mittheilungen des Vereines für Geschichte der Deutschen in Böhmen* 37 (1898–9), 337–57, at 348–50; new edition in Schmidt (ed.), *Briefe*, 46–7, no. 5. Delle Coppe came from Umbria, was a doctor of law and briefly served the Gonzaga in the 1380s. At Wenceslas' court, he was to obtain privileges for the lord of Mantua. See Silvestro Nessi, 'Alle origini della famiglia de Cuppis', *Montefalco* 27 (2013), 1–16; Filippo Orsini, 'Todi e Montefalco: rapporti storico-genealogici intorno a Palazzo Tempestivi', *Bollettino della Deputazione di storia patria per l'Umbria* 111:1–2 (2014), 1–8; Favreau-Lilie, 'König Wenzel', 324–7; Schmidt, 'Politika', 215–16 and passim.
32 Rossi came from a noble family established in Parma, while Cavalli belonged to the Veronese nobility connected not only to the Visconti but also to Wenceslas' court. They were both counsellors to the lord of Milan. Cf. Marco Gentile, *Terra e poteri: Parma e il Parmense nel ducato visconteo all'inizio del Quattrocento* (Milan, 2001), 63, 144, 164; Luisa Miglio, 'Cavalli, Giorgio', in *Dizionario Biografico degli Italiani*, vol. 22 (Rome, 1979), 736–9.
33 Cf. Garrett Mattingly, *Renaissance Diplomacy* (Baltimore, 1955), 38.

with great insistence' and reminded them once again to have Giangaleazzo Visconti send him dogs.³⁴

Such a farewell was probably far from usual (and therefore worthy of record) and points to at least two characteristics that may be assigned to Wenceslas. The first is a pronounced tendency towards alcoholism, which has been documented in several sources. The most famous incident occurred in 1398, when Wenceslas visited the King of France in Reims and got so drunk that he was unable to attend the feast prepared in his honour.³⁵ Consuming alcohol, especially wine, was obviously an integral part of official events at medieval courts; however, in the case of Wenceslas, sources suggest that his predilection for drinking sometimes interfered seriously with his duties as a sovereign. On the other hand, the Milanese ambassadors may have mentioned the episode because they felt honoured by the king's cordial behaviour towards them. In fact, the general tone of their letter is rather positive.

The second, probably even better known, characteristic associated with Wenceslas is his love of dogs. He had a menagerie with hounds acquired all over Europe, which accompanied him on his hunting trips. In 1390, an Italian diplomat in Wenceslas' service, Cristoforo de Valle, advised Francesco Gonzaga of Mantua that in order to obtain the king's friendship, he should send him 'a big and beautiful dog, wild against people, as the Emperor delights in these'.³⁶ Moreover, in contemporary sources, there is plenty of evidence that indicates that Wenceslas' dogs sometimes attacked people, including his master of the court (*Hofmeister*),

---

34 ASPr, Carteggio farnesiano estero, Boemia, b. 4, fol. 39r: '... and then this King gave us his gracious permission, telling us that we should ask you [i.e., Visconti] in his name to send him dogs, and that we should also send [some] to him, and in the meantime, out of his kindness, he had wine brought to drink with us three times with great insistence [...] he reminded us that we should tell you about your dogs, and so we left him.' ('... et tunc ipse rex nobis suam graciosam concesit licenciam dicendo nobis quod rogare vos deberemus ex sui parte quod ei mitere deberetis de canibus et etiam nos sibi mitere deberemus et interim quo sui [*sic*] benignitate fecit portari vinum pro bibendo nobiscum bene ter cum magna instancia [...] recordavit, quod vobis dicere deberemus de vestris canibus et sic ab i[pso] recessimus.') The embassy negotiated with Wenceslas about the possibility of a marriage between the Luxembourgs and the Visconti.
35 For Wenceslas' visit to Charles VI, see Gerald Schwedler, *Herrschertreffen des Spätmittelalters: Formen – Rituale – Wirkungen* (Ostfildern, 2008), 370-1, 455-6. However, Schwedler also considers the possibility of chronicler's bias.
36 Ondřej Schmidt, 'Václav IV., Jošt a Prokop očima italského vyslance: K situaci v lucemburském rodě roku 1390', *Časopis Matice moravské* 137:1 (2018), 3–27, at 26, or idem (ed.), *Briefe*, 58, no. 9: '... unum canem magnum et pulcrum, ferocem contra personas, quia imperator maxime talium letatur ...'

Conrad of Kraig, in 1385.³⁷ According to some contemporaries, one of the king's dogs even caused the death of his first wife, Johanna of Bavaria-Straubing, in 1386. However, as has recently been demonstrated, these rumours were unfounded and the queen died of some febrile illness, probably tuberculosis.³⁸

Wenceslas' eager demand for a gift of dogs expressed towards the Visconti envoys can be extended to his attitude towards gifts in general. This somewhat 'childish' side of the king's personality is also reflected in the diplomatic correspondence. Bonifacio delle Coppe explicitly states that the first thing Wenceslas did upon learning of his arrival in Prague was to find out what gifts the lord of Mantua had sent him. When these 'small presents' (*munuschula*) were finally presented during the first audience, the king was apparently disappointed. The envoy came to the conclusion that had he brought weapons, the handling of his affairs would have been quicker.³⁹ Some years later, Cristoforo de Valle made a similar comment: 'The Lord Emperor delights more in a thing of small value and brought or sent from far away than he would in a castle.'⁴⁰ Although other examples could be cited, it may be deduced from those listed that Wenceslas' predilection for (especially exotic) gifts, aggressive dogs, and alcohol probably exceeded the common or expected standards and, in the perception of his contemporaries, necessarily influenced their views of his rulership style. Of course, for foreign envoys, playing into Wenceslas' 'vices' could also be a welcome means to achieve their goal.

Sigismund, on the other hand, appears in the ambassadors' correspondence in a different light, as can be seen from the recent analysis by Veronika Proske, who investigated the rich Italian sources (including

---

37   Conrad came from Carinthia and was active mostly in Austrian lands, but he also served Wenceslas. See Friedrich W. Leitner, 'Die Herren von Kraig: Eine genealogische Skizze zu den Erbtruchsessen in Kärnten', *Archiv für Diplomatik, Schriftgeschichte, Siegel- und Wappenkunde* 46 (2000), 225–75, at 239–45.
38   Ondřej Schmidt, 'Der Tod der Königin Johanna von Bayern (1386): Prolegomena zur Erforschung einer neu entdeckten italienischen Quelle', in Elbel, Kaar, Němec and Wihoda (eds), *Historiker zwischen den Zeiten*, 295–312.
39   Knott (ed.), 'Ein mantuanischer Gesandtschaftsbericht', 355, or Schmidt (ed.), *Briefe*, 52, no. 5: 'The gift was considered modest by everyone [...]. As soon as I arrived, the king asked some [people] what I had brought him, and whether I had brought him weapons; and if I had had weapons, I would certainly have been heard by him sooner.' ('Exenium fuit reputatum modicum ab omnibus [...]. Statim rex interogavit aliquos, dum fui hic, quid portassem sibi et si portasem sibi arma, et si habuisem arma, citius fuisem auditus ab eo pro certo.')
40   Schmidt, 'Václav IV.', 26, or idem (ed.), *Briefe*, 58, no. 9: 'Dominus imperator magis delectatur unius rei parvi valoris et ducte seu mis[se] a partibus longe distancie, quam non letaretur unius castri ...'

dispatches) related to the Luxembourg king's *Romzug* from 1431–3.[41] Diplomats frequently stressed the sovereign's kindness and pleasant manners. In 1433, Simone da Crema appeared before the Emperor, who 'willingly saw [him] and [...] asked as cordially as it can be expressed' about the conditions of the margrave of Mantua, his wife, and children, and talked with [the diplomat] all the way from Foligno to Santa Maria degli Angeli near Assisi'.[42] A few weeks later, the Sienese representatives had a similar experience: 'We were seen and received with great kindness and humanity, and seen as cheerfully as it can be said.'[43] In 1414, Corrado Boiani of Cividale del Friuli also praised Sigismund's polite behaviour during an audience in Constance.[44]

Sigismund made an excellent impression not only during diplomatic negotiations but also during public events. For instance, his visit to Lucca in 1432 was enthusiastically described by a direct witness, Bartolomeo Martini, in a letter to his brother Giovanni abroad (this testimony is worth quoting, despite the fact that the author was only a local bystander and not a diplomat).[45] He thought there could not be a 'more pleasant, gracious and familiar lord, as God really endowed him with those graces that belong to this office and dignity to which he is deputed'. Sigismund 'demonstrated great joy' at his welcome in the Tuscan city and immediately won the affection of the citizens, whom he treated 'with so much love that it seemed they were all his own children'. Martini also referred to the king's attractiveness ('although he is already old, he remembers good

---

41 Proske, *Der Romzug*, esp. 223–37 (the chapter 'Situatives Herrscherhandeln im Alltag'). Most of the examples from 1431–3, cited in the following, have also been used by Proske.
42 Schmidt (ed.), *Briefe*, 106, no. 34: '... me incontray ala presencia delo serenissimo inperatore, el quale de tuto volere me vide, et alo prefato cum hogni debita reverencia fato le re[chomen]dacione a me inposte per la prefata i[llustre] s[ignoria] v[ostra] tanto cordialemente me dimandò del bono stato de quela e dela illustre et excelssa m[adona] marchexana e de tuti li illustri et incliti filgioli de quela, più dire se posese, e poy tuta la via de lì a questo loco de Nostra Dona di Angeli soto Asixe senpre vene raxonando cum mi.'
43 Archivio di Stato di Siena (hereafter cited as ASSi), Concistoro, Carteggio, b. 1930, no. 87: '... fumo veduti et ricevuti con grandissima benignità et humanità et tanto allegramente veduti quanto più si potesse dire ...'
44 Copies in Museo Archeologico Nazionale di Cividale del Friuli (hereafter cited as MAN), Archivio Capitolare, Fondo Diplomatico, b. 16, no. 109, and Biblioteca Civica 'Vincenzo Joppi' di Udine (hereafter cited as BCU), Fondo Principale, b. 896/IV, no. 322: '... he graciously received us and heard us ...' ('... qui nos benigne suscepit et audivit ...').
45 Bartolomeo belonged to a local merchant family. See Salvatore Bongi (ed.), *Lettera di Bartolommeo Martini su la venuta in Lucca di Sigismondo re de' Romani (ann. MCCCCXXXII)* (Lucca, 1871), 6–9.

times and in this way, he flourishes through this joy'), and mentioned his courteous attitude to the local ladies, once again emphasizing the incomparable 'magnificence, pleasantness and *domestichezza* of this noble lord'.[46] The last of the aforementioned qualities, denoting the ability to act in an informal, familiar way, aptly sums up how Sigismund managed to win the hearts of the citizens of Lucca.

Envoys also remarked on Sigismund's wisdom.[47] With it came a kind of pragmatic mercifulness, which was observed in the years 1436-7, when he had finally made peace with the Hussites and was acknowledged as King of Bohemia. Cristoforo da Velate, a Milanese ambassador staying in Prague in the spring of 1437, wrote that 'the Emperor is very beloved and accepted by both princes and the folk of this kingdom because of his manners, not taking revenge against those who had been against him [...] and leaving and confirming them much of what they held from the property of the Crown and some churches'.[48] Sigismund's 'infinite humanity' ('infinita sua humanitade') towards the Hussites did not escape Simone da Crema, who described his *adventus* in Prague in 1436 and praised the compromise which the Emperor had reached with the former heretics (the Compacts of Basel).[49]

---

46 Ibid., 13–14: 'Nè mai credo che si vedesse il più piacevole e gratioso signore; chè veramente Dio l' ha ben dotato di quelle gratie che appartengano a tal offitio e degnità, alla quale lui è deputato. Et grande allegrezza ha dimostrato, vedendosi tanto allegramente esser ricevuto [...] con tanto amore che pareva che tutti fussero suoi propri figliuoli [...] Io ben credo, che ancora che sia antico, si arricordi del buon tempo & così gli giovi pigliarsi piacere ...' Ibid., 17: '... a vedere tanta magnificenza, piacevolezza e domestichezza di questo nobil signore & de' suoi signori & baroni.' For Sigismund's (publicly displayed) affection towards women in this and other sources, see Proske, *Der Romzug*, 223, 233–5.

47 Schmidt, 'Druhé zajetí', 213, no. 7, or idem (ed.), *Briefe*, 73, no. 19: 'I went to the said King of Hungary, with whom I hoped to settle my affairs at once, for he is wise in understanding.' ('... andai dal prefato serenisimo re de Hongaria, dal quale me credia subito eser fornito, perché le intendere è savio ...').

48 Gustav Beckmann (ed.), *Deutsche Reichstagsakten*, vol. 12, *Deutsche Reichstagsakten unter Kaiser Sigismund 1435–1437* (Gotha, 1901), 164, no. 102: '... imperator satis dilectus et commendatus est tam a principibus, quam a popularibus regni illius propter observatos modos in non vindicando contra illos, qui sibi contrarii fuerunt, ut non haberet regnum Bohemie, ac dimittendo et confirmando eis multa que tenent pertinencia corone et aliquibus ecclesiis.'

49 Ondřej Schmidt, 'Co si Italové mysleli o husitských Čechách: stereotypy a divergence', in Bronislav Chocholáč, Jiří Malíř, Lukáš Reitinger and Martin Wihoda (eds), *Pro pana profesora Libora Jana k životnímu jubileu* (Brno, 2020), 523–34. For the edition of two dispatches from Bohemia, see Schmidt (ed.), *Briefe*, 147–54, nos 51 and 52, and Péter E. Kovács, 'Der Bericht Simone da Cremas, des Botschafters von Mantua, über den Prager Einzug Sigismunds' (in press).

What probably contributed further to the acceptance and positive impression of Sigismund was his spontaneous behaviour that appeared authentic to the public.[50] When in Lucca, Sigismund used to touch the common people, let them kiss his hand, and gave and received flowers.[51] The Florentine envoy Piero Guicciardini, who visited the king in Hungary in 1427–8, reported that upon his leave, the king took him by the arm and said to him in a confidential manner: 'If I come to Italy, as I believe and as is my desire, I will act so that after my death all the Italians will have a reason to pray for my soul.'[52] Simone da Crema recorded a very tense moment from the year 1402, when Sigismund imprisoned his brother, King Wenceslas, and attempted to seize power in Bohemia. As the situation worsened, Sigismund needed to neutralize the leader of the growing opposition to him, namely, Margrave Prokop of Moravia, his cousin. Da Crema witnessed that, after a division in the king's council, against the advice of his entourage, at night and in heavy rain, the armed Sigismund mounted a horse and exclaimed: 'Who loves me, follow me! I want to find Margrave Prokop so I can fight him!', whereupon he left with 500 horsemen.[53] In various ways, in all these episodes Sigismund appeared not only as a monarch but also a man of flesh and blood. Judging by how he is reflected in the examined dispatches, he was mostly successful in creating this impression.

There has been much discussion in historiography on the use of publicly (and excessively) displayed emotions of monarchs. Whether we tend to think of them as calculated performances or spontaneous feelings (such a distinction can sometimes be hypothesized from the context, other times not), it is evident that Sigismund resorted to them quite often. His outbursts of 'royal anger' (*ira regis*) were famous and are also

---

50 For the 'unreflected behaviour', cf. Bauch et al., 'Heilige', 20–2.
51 Bongi (ed.), *Lettera di Bartolommeo Martini*, 13–14, 17; cf. Proske, *Der Romzug*, 233.
52 Archivio di Stato di Firenze (hereafter cited as ASFi), Signori, Dieci di Balìa, Otto di Pratica, Legazioni e Commissarie, Missive e Responsive, b. 75, fol. 10v [137v]: '… quando fu in sul'uscio, mi prese in sul braccio e disse: "Se io passo in Italia, chom'io credo e chome è il mio disiderio, io mi porterò in forma che dietro alla mia vita tucti Italiani arano chagione de preghare Iddio per la mia anima."' Partially quoted in G[iuseppe] Canestrini, 'Sopra alcune relazioni della Repubblica Fiorentina col Re d'Ungheria e con Filippo Scolari', *Archivio Storico Italiano* 4:1 (1843), 185–213, at 208; Proske, *Der Romzug*, 1.
53 Schmidt, 'Druhé zajetí', 207, no. 2, or idem (ed.), *Briefe*, 65, no. 14: '… e in concluxione se partì in dexachordo e cum homo desperado si montò a chavalo, armado, contra la volontade di soy amixi, dicendo luy: "Chi me ama, me segua! Io si volgio trovare el marchexe Prochopio per eser ale mane chum luy!" E partise eri dale 24 hore cum una gran pioza achonpagnato forse d(e) D^c chavali …'

reflected in the dispatches of the Italian ambassadors.[54] The episode that occurred in 1417 in Constance, where Sigismund publicly reprimanded his imperial vicar in Belluno and Feltre, Oldřich Skála of Luleč, and even threatened to have him beheaded, was described by the Bellunese envoys present at court.[55] When he came into conflict with Florence in 1432, he refused to receive the city's envoys and sent them back.[56] At the Council of Basel, the Emperor temporarily expelled the Milanese ambassadors.[57] By contrast, Sigismund was also capable of expressing extraordinary joy when accepting a gift from the margrave of Mantua. His representative at the imperial court reported: 'I certainly do not know whether it would be possible to express thanks with more love, with more praise and with more humanity than he did for this gift.'[58] The repertoire of the Luxembourg king's publicly expressed emotions included anger, joy, and even an extreme display of compassion and sorrow upon hearing about the damage wrought by Florentine troops in Lucchese territory.[59]

---

54 Joachim Schneider, 'Herrschererinnerung und symbolische Kommunikation am Hof König Sigismunds: Das Zeugnis der Chronik des Eberhard Windeck', in Karel Hruza and Alexandra Kaar (eds), *Kaiser Sigismund (1368-1437): Zur Herrschaftspraxis eines europäischen Monarchen*, Forschungen zur Kaiser- und Papstgeschichte des Mittelalters – Beihefte zu J. F. Böhmer, Regesta Imperii, 31 (Vienna, Cologne, and Weimar, 2012), 429-48, at 442-7; Annabell Engel, 'Herrschen mit Emotionen: Zorn als Herrschaftsinstrument Sigismunds von Luxemburg auf dem Konstanzer Konzil', in Bauch et al. (eds), *Heilige, Helden, Wüteriche*, 245-59; for a more general discussion of the phenomenon, see Gerd Althoff, 'Ira regis: Prolegomena to a History of Royal Anger', in Barbara H. Rosenwein (ed.), *Anger's Past: The Social Uses of an Emotion in the Middle Ages* (Ithaca and London, 1998), 59-74.
55 Harry Bresslau, 'Zur Geschichte Kaiser Sigismunds', *Forschungen zur deutschen Geschichte* 18 (1878), 385-91, at 388-9; cf. Ondřej Schmidt, 'Vikáři a hejtmani krále Zikmunda na severu Benátska (1411/12-1420)', *Studia mediaevalia Bohemica* 7:1 (2015), 81-113, at 103-4; Péter E. Kovács, 'Imperia im Imperium: Unterhaltung und Spektakel auf dem Konzil von Konstanz', in Attila Bárány and Balázs Antal Bacsa (eds), *Das Konzil von Konstanz und Ungarn* (Debrecen, 2016), 107-29, at 127. For more examples, see Schmidt, 'Mantuan Envoys'.
56 ASSi, Concistoro, Carteggio, b. 1926, no. 22; cf. Proske, *Der Romzug*, 228, n. 32.
57 Gustav Beckmann (ed.), *Deutsche Reichstagsakten*, vol. 11, *Deutsche Reichstagsakten unter Kaiser Sigismund 1433-1435* (Gotha, 1898), 82, no. 43.
58 Schmidt (ed.), *Briefe*, 107, no. 34: 'Certo non so, che cum più amore, cum più laude, se cum più humanitade posese referire gracia, quanto de questo dono fece.' Similarly, ibid., 118, no. 39; cf. idem, 'Mantuan Envoys'.
59 Bongi (ed.), *Lettera di Bartolommeo Martini*, 15-16: 'It is impossible to describe how this act struck the Emperor, who almost died – so great was the pain he felt because of it.' ('Non si può scrivere quest' atto di dare il guasto quanto annoiò l' Imperatore, che non haveva se non a morire, tanto fu grande il dolore che n' hebbe.') See also Proske, *Der Romzug*, 227-8.

Obviously, no one knows what Sigismund really felt in those moments; it is clear, however, that his emotional outbursts made a deep impression on his audiences.

On the basis of the evidence presented, and taking into account the limitations associated with its interpretation by virtue of its sheer paucity, it seems that Wenceslas did not make much of an impression on the Italian diplomats. Unlike his older (half-)brother Wenceslas, a coherent picture of whom, however, cannot be deduced from the dispatches, Sigismund, thanks to his charisma and generally pleasant but sometimes judiciously placed emotional behaviour, managed to win the affection of the public and the ambassadors visiting his court, who mostly spoke of him with admiration.[60] The different personal styles of the two Luxembourg kings had without doubt a profound impact on their rule and, as argued by Duncan Hardy, conditioned the ultimate 'failure' of Wenceslas as well as the relative success of Sigismund.[61]

Still, other factors must also be taken into account that may have influenced these marked differences in the perceptions of the two monarchs. The portrayal of both sovereigns may be distorted due to the disproportion in the extant (and the contemporaneous production of) correspondence, as well as, more importantly, due to the evolution of the genre itself. During the fifteenth century, diplomatic dispatches gradually moved away from their accustomed, austere, and formulaic language and became increasingly colourful.[62] In other words, the sources may as much indicate a change in the practice of reporting as reflect differences in the behaviour of the sovereign as such. Sigismund may appear more appealing than Wenceslas simply because of the fact that the ambassadors wrote about him more and in a rather different fashion.

THE COURT AND THE COURTIERS

The second area of investigation is the court and its functioning. The court can be understood not only as an institution, but also as a space where various political networks operated and where negotiations and decision-making took place. The perception of Wenceslas' court in historiography has been mostly negative, with an emphasis on general decline and corruption. This, to a certain extent biased, view is seemingly supported by the dispatch of Bonifacio delle Coppe from 1383. The

---

60 See also Proske, *Der Romzug*, passim, and the conclusion at 237: 'In any case, his habitual self-presentation was a complete success in Italy.' ('Seine habituelle Selbstdarstellung war in Italien jedoch in jedem Falle ein voller Erfolg.')
61 See Hardy, 'The Emperorship'.
62 See Lazzarini, *Communication*, 202–11, 220–5.

Mantuan diplomat very colourfully described his struggle to obtain an audience with the king, including his long wait for a final decision, the power, and greed of members of the royal council.[63] Although we must accept these grievances, insinuated carefully between the lines, we also need to put them into an appropriate context. In fact, there is no reason to believe that such practices were specific to Wenceslas; on the contrary, it is possible to observe them in any other late medieval princely court. Moreover, it should be noted that the often-cited mission of Bonifacio delle Coppe was a great success in the end: not only did he manage to obtain all privileges for his master, he himself was even appointed count palatine and king's counsellor.[64]

Nevertheless, the difficulties experienced by Bonifacio point to one characteristic feature of Wenceslas' style – his reluctance to receive foreign ambassadors, participate in negotiations, and engage in politics in person, all of which had to be delegated to his royal council.[65] This impression is also confirmed by Giovanni Vergiolesi from Lucca. In 1381, he reported from Prague that the king 'stays here only a little'; he 'is always out hunting and rarely resides here more than one night in a row'.[66] Political matters were dealt with by the counsellors: 'Whoever comes and has anything to do at the court of the King, he needs to turn to them or to some of them, and through them all matters are dealt with'; only 'in the case of disagreement, are the matters passed to the King, who then commits them to a part of [the council]'.[67] Unlike Delle Coppe and Vergiolesi, the

---

63 Knott (ed.), 'Ein mantuanischer Gesandtschaftsbericht'; Schmidt (ed.), *Briefe*, 42–54, no. 5. Cf. Bartoš, *České dějiny*, vol. 2/6, 55–8, and especially Spěváček, *Václav IV.*, 171–4, who spoke about 'new, dismal conditions at the royal court', where 'unbelievable corruption and sloppiness blossomed', 'the shameful behaviour of the King's favourites' and 'the quick decay of Wenceslas' royal power'.
64 Schmidt, 'Politika', 39–47; cf. also Favreau-Lilie, 'König Wenzel', 324–7; Nessi, 'Alle origini'; Orsini, 'Todi'.
65 Cf. Ivan Hlaváček, 'Wenzel IV., sein Hof und seine Königsherrschaft vornehmlich über Böhmen', in Reinhard Schneider (ed.), *Das spätmittelalterliche Königtum im europäischen Vergleich*, Vorträge und Forschungen, 32 (Sigmaringen, 1987), 201–32, at 218, who stressed 'the isolation of the sovereign from public life' and the importance of Wenceslas' favourites.
66 Salvatore Bongi (ed.), *Lettera di Giovanni de' Vergiolesi ambasciatore di Lucca presso Venceslao re dei Romani, MCCCLXXXI* (Lucca, 1869), 12: 'È vero che messer lo Re ci sta molto pogo. Sempre sta fuora alla caccia, & rade volte ci alberga più che una notte per volta.'
67 Ibid.: 'Ai quali consiglieri, chi capita di qua & abia a fare neiente nella Corte collo Re, conviene che capiti a loro, o vero a parte di loro, & per loro mezo si spacciano tutte le viciende; però ch' ellino danno a disentire allo Re li casi che intervengono, & elli commette a parte di loro; & per questo modo si dà spaccio a chi ci viene.' An envoy from Frankfurt had a similar experience in 1394. See Rudolf

Visconti ambassadors apparently had no problem obtaining an audience with the king in 1386–7; on the contrary, thanks to influential friends at the court, they visited him quite often. The one exception was their report of arriving at Karlštejn (Karlstein) Castle and learning that Wenceslas had gone hunting. After his arrival, late in the evening, he came down with a fever, so the ambassadors had to return to Prague without an audience.[68] We can assume that the reason for this better position of the Milanese embassy compared to their Italian colleagues was both the significantly greater power and importance of Giangaleazzo Visconti as well as better knowledge of Wenceslas' court.

The courtiers, as a social group, consisted of people of various status, position, and influence, and the court therefore was in a constant state of flux. The image of Wenceslas' court in both scholarly and popular literature was long dominated (and still is) by the overwhelming presence of courtly favourites from the ranks of the lower nobility and burghers, such as the well-known social climbers Sigismund Huler and Jíra of Roztoky, who were again seen as a manifestation of the decay of royal power. However, this perception is largely an unfounded myth, as has been demonstrated by Robert Novotný.[69] Nevertheless, like any other sovereign, Wenceslas had his preferred interlocutors and, through their preferential access to the ruler, they had a significant influence on the decision-making process and politics. These people often appear in the dispatches of the Italian diplomats who had to negotiate with them. In the 1380s, there were many such influential courtiers, including Margrave Jobst; the Silesian prince Přemek of Teschen; the Prince-Bishop of Bamberg, Lamprecht of Brunn; Těma of Koldice; and Henry of Dubá, as well as others. It is interesting that the respective envoys mostly single out different people, which could mean that the power structures of the court were changing quite

---

Helmke, *König Wenzel und seine böhmischen Günstlinge im Reiche* (Halle [Saale], 1913), 87.

68 ASPr, Carteggio farnesiano estero, Boemia, b. 4, fols 29v–30r.

69 Robert Novotný, 'Ráj milců? Nižší šlechta na dvoře Václava IV.', in Dana Dvořáčková-Malá and Jan Zelenka (eds), *Dvory a rezidence ve středověku*, vol. 2, *Skladba a kultura dvorské společnosti*, Mediaevalia Historica Bohemica, 11 – Supplementum, 2 (Prague, 2008), 215–29; idem, 'Der niedere Adel um Wenzel IV.: Ein Sonderfall?', in Bauch et al. (eds), *Heilige, Helden, Wüteriche*, 193–208; cf. Peter Moraw, 'König Wenzels (1378–1419) Hof, eine Günstlingswirtschaft?', in Jan Hirschbiegel and Werner Paravicini (eds), *Der Fall des Günstlings: Hofparteien in Europa vom 13. bis zum 17. Jahrhundert*, Residenzenforschung, 17 (Ostfildern, 2004), 163–75; for the general European context, see Dries Raeymaekers and Sebastiaan Derks (eds), *The Key to Power? The Culture of Access in Princely Courts, 1400–1750*, Rulers & Elites, 8 (Leiden and Boston, 2016).

dynamically; it could, however, also be due to a temporary absence of particular individuals from the court, or to a generational change.[70]

Finally, one cannot overlook the accusations of avarice levelled at some of the counsellors. Bonifacio delle Coppe famously claimed that at the Prague court 'everyone cares more about the state of the purse than trust and letters of credence'.[71] Milanese diplomats also reported that the three courtiers with whom they were interacting 'expect gifts and have their mouths open, although they seem to love [Giangaleazzo Visconti] very much'.[72] They even mentioned an episode when the king claimed to have learned about their (vehemently denied) attempt to bribe some courtiers in order to reach a favourable decision on matters of their concern. Wenceslas, however, merely told them that such efforts were futile without showing any sign of concern.[73]

---

70 Cf. Bongi (ed.), *Lettera di Giovanni de' Vergiolesi*, 11–13: Přemek of Teschen, Jobst of Moravia, Conrad of Craig, Lutz of Landau, Henry of Brzeg, *Lanchario* [?], Peter of Vartenberk, [Tĕma] of Koldice; Knott (ed.), 'Ein mantuanischer Gesandtschaftsbericht', 345, 355; Schmidt (ed.), *Briefe*, 43 and 52, no. 5: Tĕma of Koldice, Henry of Dubá, Peter of Vartenberk; ASPr, Carteggio farnesiano estero, Boemia, b. 4, passim: among others, Přemek of Teschen, Lamprecht of Brunn, Kraft of Hohenlohe.

71 Knott (ed.), 'Ein mantuanischer Gesandtschaftsbericht', 355, or Schmidt (ed.), *Briefe*, 52, no. 5: '… licet hic tractetur ab omnibus de salute bursie pocius quam de fide et credulitate literarum …'

72 ASPr, Carteggio farnesiano estero, Boemia, b. 4, fol. 26r: '… sed isti tres munera expectant et habent gulas apertas, tamen videntur vos multum diligere …'

73 Ibid., fol. 37r: 'This king told us that he knew for certain that we had offered some members of his council a large sum of money, namely 400,000 florins. To this we replied that we had certainly never promised anything to anyone, nor could anyone find out that we had promised anything to anyone, and that we were willing to insist on it in any inquiries that [the king] might wish to make about it. He replied that he had been told with certainty that we had promised this money, and that there was no need for us to promise or give money, because if we did we would waste it, for it is he alone who wants to contract the marriage, and who can confirm or refuse the marriage, and none of his council, however powerful, has the power or the will to do so, but he alone.' ('Etiam ipse rex nobis dixit quod certe sciebat nos obtulisse aliquibus de conscilio suo magnam quantitatem pecunie, videlicet florenum quadraginta milia vel circha. Cui respondidimus quod certe nu[m]quam aliquid alicui promiximus nec poterit per veritatem reperiri nos alicui aliquid promisisse, et parati eramus de hoc stare ad omnem experienciam, quam de hoc facere vellet. Qui nobis respondidit quod pro certo sibi dictum fuerat quod ipsam pecuniam promixeramus et quod non erat nobis necesse pecuniam promitere neque dare, quia si eam daremus ipsam abiyceremus, quia ipse solus erat ille qui volebat parentelam et qui parentelam poterat [a]ffirmare et denegare, nec aliquis de conscilio suo, quantum foret potens, potestatem habebat nec intendebat quod haberet nixi ipse solus afirmandumque denegandum parentelam.')

His younger (half-)brother Sigismund, conversely, demonstrated an exceptional passion for politics and direct, face-to-face negotiations throughout his life. From the examined diplomatic correspondence, it can be clearly seen that the 'last Luxembourg' preferred to deal with incoming ambassadors in person, when he could take full advantage of his rhetorical and persuasive skills. The envoys usually had little problem obtaining a timely audience before the sovereign.[74] Even in his old age, suffering from gout, Sigismund was reluctant to renounce this duty. Present at the Council of Basel in 1434, Simone da Crema reported that the Emperor 'cannot walk at all and has to be continually carried from place to place, nonetheless, he gives audiences every day, and deals with all the princes and lords, and all the matters are decided in the presence of His Majesty'. The ambassador remarked that Sigismund's engagement was 'a very great fatigue [for him] and everyone wonders about it'.[75] Some years earlier, the Florentines remarked on the king's eagerness to conduct negotiations and desire for news.[76]

Even with this frenetic activity, the negotiations and the decision-making process sometimes dragged on to an unbearable extent. This was apparently the case at the Council of Constance, where the king had to attend to the election of the future pope 'for which [he] had toiled so much and endured so many hardships and inconveniences'.[77] The ambassadors of Belluno had expected their mission would take around two months but, at the time of writing their letter to the city council, they had already been in Constance for six months.[78] In other dispatches, they cited 'an enormous number of matters of princes, prelates and knights' that bore down on the sovereign. When they urged Sigismund to attend to their request, he 'responded with a slightly raised voice: "You see well our affairs and that I cannot!"' The ambassadors added that it was 'his custom to give

---

74 Proske, *Der Romzug*, 229–30, came to the same conclusion.
75 Schmidt (ed.), *Briefe*, 119, no. 40: '... per la Dio gracia lo nostro s[erenissimo] imperatore è pur stato melgio dela infirmitade soa, benché però non pò niente andare, anzi convien' continuamente esser portato di loco a loco. Ma non sta però, che ogni zorno non daga audiencia e fa rasone a tuti li principi e signori e tute le questione fino diffinite ala presentia dela maiestade soa, che certo li è una grandissima fatiga e certo ziaschuno se ne maravelgia.' Similarly, ibid., 124, no. 42: 'Our Most Serene Emperor is constantly recovering from his illness [...] now dressed and entirely seated, he grants an audience to everyone.' ('... lo nostro serenissimo imperatore dela sua malatia continuamente procede de ben in meglio [...]. Hora vestito e sedendo interamente a ciaschuno dà audientia.')
76 ASFi, Signori, Dieci di Balia, Otto di Pratica, Legazioni e Commissarie, Missive e Responsive, b. 75, fol. 10v [137v].
77 Bresslau, 'Zur Geschichte', 389–90: '... pro quibus serenissimus dominus noster tociens insudavit, et tot et tantas lugubrationes et incommoda est perpessus ...'
78 Ibid., 386.

answers in this way'.⁷⁹ Other embassies, who had waited in vain for their mission to be accomplished, found themselves in an even worse situation, as some were forced to stay a year.⁸⁰ In the end, the Bellunese diplomats also spent a whole year in Constance without achieving anything at the royal court.⁸¹

Just like in the case of Wenceslas, Sigismund's politics were, of course, shaped by several key courtiers. This was especially true in Hungary in the period up until 1403, before the opposition of the Hungarian barons against Sigismund had finally been neutralized. In this period, the young Sigismund (b. 1368) seemed at least to some observers to be a helpless puppet in the hands of the nobility. In 1395, for example, the Mantuan envoy Paolo Armanini wrote from Buda that the king 'cannot be called his own master', having to 'follow the will of his princes and barons, as a man who does not, in a certain sense, have a firm position'.⁸² This state of affairs changed as the years went by, but even during Sigismund's rule in the Holy

---

79 Archivio Storico del Comune di Belluno, Libri iurium, libro B, fol. 105r: 'Adventum nostrum non citum moramini quia innumerosa copia agendorum principum, baronum, prelatorum et militum adeo prelibatum dominum nostrum opprimunt quod expediri presto quasi impossibile esset [...] dum nuperime, videlicet heri in mane, comparuissemus coram eo et peteremus ut amore Dei dignaretur expedire nos de Cividado, ipse respondit voce aliquantulum elevata: "Vos bene videtis facta nostra et quod non possumus." Et huiusmodi eius mos est etiam responsiones facere.'

80 Ibid., fol. 109r: 'We think that there are doubts about our delay, and not only ours, but also that of many others who are staying here – some for a year, some for six months, others for eight. But we are junior in rank, and hopefully will not have to stay longer than next month.' ('... credimus nascitur omnis suspicio dillacionis nostre, nec nostre tantum, sed plurimorum aliorum qui secuti hunc moram traxere – aliqui anno, aliqui mensibus sex, aliqui octo. Nos autem iuniores summus et utinam non egrediamur mensem futurum.')

81 Ondřej Schmidt, 'Il governo di re Sigismondo di Lussemburgo nel Veneto orientale (1411–1420)', *Archivio Storico Italiano* 177:4 (2019), 719–72, at 751–7.

82 Lajos Thallóczy, *Mantovai követjárás Budán 1395* (Budapest, 1905), 99–100, no. 5: '... he, who cannot be called his own master, must follow the will of his princes and barons, as a man who does not, in a certain sense, have a firm position because of the differences of opinion and the great hatred that prevails among them, for the Hungarian barons especially are not content to have him as their King, and he daily tries to please them in every way he can.' ('... ipsum, qui suus dominus dici non potest, sequi oportet voluntates suorum principum et baronum, tamquam homo non habens statum suum aliquatenus firmum propter varias opiniones et invidias magnas regnantes inter ipsos cum male contentanturmaxime barones Ungarie ipsum in suum regem habere, et ipse eis cotidie complacere conatur in omnibus, quibus potest.') Also quoted in Julia Burkhardt, 'Ein Königreich im Wandel: Ungarn um 1400', *Biuletyn Polskiej Misji Historycznej / Bulletin der Polnischen Historischen Mission* 11 (2016), 407–37, at 412, n. 10.

Roman Empire after 1411, a narrow circle of influential figures managed to establish singularly powerful positions of influence at Sigismund's court.

Judging by the ambassadors' correspondence, the most distinct of these 'powerbrokers'[83] to gain considerable influence were the imperial (vice-) chancellor Caspar Schlick and the Italian exile Brunoro della Scala. In the 1420s and 1430s, these political insiders, along with a few others, were the most important members of Sigismund's council and chancery and, as such, they maintained the closest of proximity to the sovereign, dealt with foreign embassies, and also acted as diplomats themselves.[84] Schlick's era also saw his notorious 'fiscalization of the [imperial] chancery',[85] a phenomenon that seems to have found an echo in the despatches of Italian envoys, when in 1437 Cristoforo da Velate from Milan spoke of a 'chancery full of avarice' ('cancellaria avaricie plena').[86] In Della Scala's case, the perspective of our sources may be slightly distorted, as the Italian ambassadors clearly used to turn to their compatriots at the imperial court, thus overstating their real position and influence, while overlooking that of others.[87]

Generally, the situation at Wenceslas' court is presented in a worse light than at Sigismund's. The Italian diplomats found it difficult to obtain an audience with Wenceslas, to negotiate in person with the sovereign, and to secure his assent. Wenceslas' reluctance to engage in politics directly

---

83 Cf. Robert Stein (ed.), *Powerbrokers in the Late Middle Ages: The Burgundian Low Countries in a European Context / Les courtiers du pouvoir au bas Moyen-Âge: Les Pays-Bas bourguignons dans un contexte européen*, Burgundica, 4 (Turnhout, 2001).
84 Petr Elbel and Andreas Zajic, 'Die zwei Körper des Kanzlers? Die "reale" und die "virtuelle" Karriere Kaspar Schlicks unter König und Kaiser Sigismund – Epilegomena zu einem alten Forschungsthema I–III', *Mediaevalia historica Bohemica* 15:2 (2012), 47–143; 16:1 (2013), 55–212; 16:2 (2013), 73–157; Ondřej Schmidt, 'Exile as a Means of Social Ascent? Brunoro della Scala at the Court of Emperor Sigismund' (in press); Proske, *Der Romzug*, 94–8 and 102–9; Schmidt, 'Mantuan Envoys'.
85 Paul-Joachim Heinig, 'War Kaspar Schlick ein Fälscher?', in *Fälschungen im Mittelalter*, vol. 3, *Diplomatische Fälschungen*, Monumenta Germaniae Historica – Schriften, 33/III (Hannover, 1988), 247–81, at 248–9.
86 Beckmann (ed.), *Deutsche Reichstagsakten*, vol. 12, 178–9, no. 111.
87 Schlick also claimed Italian ancestry, but its real basis remains uncertain. See Petr Elbel, 'Collaltovská stopa v Čechách 15. století, aneb pocházel Kašpar Šlik z hraběcího rodu Collalto? / Le tracce dei Collalto nella Boemia del XV secolo, ovvero proveniva Gaspare Šlik dalla famiglia comitale dei Collalto?', in idem, Ondřej Schmidt and Stanislav Bárta (eds), *Z Trevisa do Brtnice. Příběhy šlechtického rodu Collalto ukryté v českých archivech (katalog výstavy) / Da Treviso a Brtnice. Storie della famiglia nobile dei Collalto nascoste negli archivi cechi (catalogo della mostra)* (Brno, 2019), 73–92.

and in person with his counterparts[88] also meant necessarily delegating some of his power to his representatives. On the other hand, it can hardly be described as a 'decay' of royal power, as Wenceslas' administration and chancery functioned quite efficiently.[89] Nevertheless, given his much more personable style (energetic political activity), Sigismund was certainly better at dealing with foreign embassies (and other actors) than Wenceslas. Even in Sigismund's case, however, the outcome of any diplomatic mission depended heavily on its importance, the social status of the ambassadors, their personal connections to both the sovereign and his courtiers, and the circumstances that prevailed at the particular time. In a broader historical context, it should be noted that there were influential favourites and clientelistic networks at every princely court. In the case of Wenceslas, the presence of 'grey eminences' seems to have been more complex and fluid, while Sigismund was surrounded by a smaller coterie of insiders, who monopolized their prominent position for quite a long period of time.

RITUALS, CEREMONIES, AND FESTIVITIES

Rituals, ceremonies, and festivities constituted an indispensable element of courtly life. Through the performance of symbolic public acts with clearly understandable meaning, the sovereign demonstrated and legitimized his prominent status within the social hierarchy, while the holding of feasts, balls, and other entertainments added to the attractiveness of the court. In this sense, Wenceslas' court seemed far from attractive to the representatives of his foreign partners and subjects. Not one of the Italian diplomats writing in 1381, 1383, and 1386–7 remarked on any of the usual courtly activities, with the only exception being the oath of allegiance taken by young Margrave Frederick IV of Meissen at the Imperial Diet in Nuremberg in 1382.[90] In fact, Wenceslas' court – be it in Prague or at one of the surrounding localities – seems to have been a rather inhospitable

---

88 The same feature was also characteristic of Frederick III. See Krieger, 'Der Hof', 181: 'It was probably one of the peculiarities of Frederick III's rulership style to tend to avoid personal negotiations with supplicants and to meet requests for audiences with corresponding restraint.' ('Allerdings gehörte es wohl zu den Eigenheiten des Herrschaftsstiles Friedrichs III., persönliche Verhandlungen mit den Petenten eher zu vermeiden und Wünschen nach Audienzen entsprechend zurückhaltend zu begegnen.')
89 For an analysis of Wenceslas' chancery, see Ivan Hlaváček, *Das Urkunden- und Kanzleiwesen des böhmischen und römischen Königs Wenzel (IV.) 1376–1419: Ein Beitrag zur spätmittelalterlichen Diplomatik* (Stuttgart, 1970).
90 Fumi (ed.), *Carteggio degli Anziani*, vol. 2, 157–8, no. 955. The Milanese ambassador Bartolomeo Sorana, in his letter to the allied city of Lucca, stressed that 'all kneel' before the king ('omne genus sibi flectitur') and that 'this spontaneous

place: Bonifacio delle Coppe even reported that Wenceslas had houses under Křivoklát (Pürglitz) Castle burned down so that no one could stay there and disturb him during his hunting trips.[91]

The Mantuan ambassador personally experienced discomfort and inadequate hospitality from the royal counsellors during his stay.[92] Only Giovanni Vergiolesi briefly mentioned 'substantial preparations' being made for the journey and accompaniment of Princess Anne of Bohemia to England (1381), where she was to marry King Richard II.[93] The Visconti envoys reported that they encountered the king riding a horse one day on the streets of Prague so 'splendidly dressed and accompanied that [they] did not recognize him'.[94] This remark also reveals a certain degree of surprise on the part of the Milanese ambassadors, who were not used to seeing the king displayed in his royal finery. Finally, there are two letters, written in a humanist lofty fashion by another ambassador of Giangaleazzo Visconti, Uberto Decembrio, in 1394,[95] which served a rather different purpose than to inform about a diplomatic mission. Above all, they were meant to demonstrate the author's skill and knowledge of Classical Latin and literature. While the reader learns nothing about Wenceslas' court, he is presented with quite a curious description of the city of Prague, its exotic inhabitants, and their customs.[96]

---

oath of allegiance is considered a great thing here' ('istud juramentum spontaneum fidelitatis reputatur hic pro uno magno facto').
91 Knott (ed.), 'Ein mantuanischer Gesandtschaftsbericht', 345, or Schmidt (ed.), Briefe, 43, no. 5: 'I was told that the Lord King did not want to hear anyone there, and that he had some houses burned there because certain people had been accommodated in them; and it was true.' ('... dictum erat mihi, quod dominus rex ibi aliquem audire nolebat et quod fecerat conburi certas domos ibidem, quia certos ospitaverant, et verum erat.') Architectural historian František Záruba, 'The Castles of King Wenceslaus IV as Venues for Diplomatic Negotiations', Przegląd Historyczny 112:2 (2021), 247–59, also speaks of Wenceslas' 'difficult accessibility [...] outside Prague' but points out that the king 'made some attempts at dealing with this' (251).
92 Roscheck, 'König Wenzel IV', 227–8, n. 94, saw this lack of hospitality as a means of symbolic communication and a pressure strategy on the part of the royal council.
93 Bongi (ed.), Lettera di Giovanni de' Vergiolesi, 14: 'Along all the roads, great preparations are being made to do them great honour.' ('Per tutti li camini si fa grandissimo aparecchio per fare loro grande honore.')
94 ASPr, Carteggio farnesiano estero, Boemia, b. 4, fol. 26v: '... invenimus regem [...] splendide erat inductus et asociatus quod ipsum non cognovimus ...'
95 For the chronology of Decembrio's mission, see Francesco Novati, 'Aneddoti Viscontei', Archivio Storico Lombardo, Ser. 4, 35 (1908), 193–216, at 208–16.
96 Attilio Hortis, 'La città di Praga descritta da un umanista nel MCCCXCIX', Archeografo Triestino, NS, 7 (1880–1), 439–51; new critical edition in Angelo

Sigismund's court, on the other hand, was usually judged more favourably by the Italians. Nevertheless, there were quite radical differences of opinion among the various observers. In 1395, Paolo Armanini from Mantua famously claimed that the Buda court was impoverished to the point that it 'does not deserve to be called a court'.[97] In 1428, Piero Guicciardini from Florence pointed out the lack of noblemen at the Hungarian court.[98] Moreover, Cristoforo da Velate from Milan noted the 'extreme poverty' of the royal court in the Kingdom of Bohemia in 1437, as it even lacked adequate supplies of food and clothing despite its relatively small size in the aftermath of the war against the Hussites.[99] In contrast to these unflattering opinions, the Florentine Rinaldo Albizzi, for instance, praised the castle of Visegrád (Plintenburg), Filippo Scolari's (Pippo Spano's) chapel in Székesfehérvár (Stuhlweißenburg), and also his residence in Ozora, which he visited in 1426.[100] If it was referred to at all, the attractiveness of Sigismund's court, whether he was residing in German lands, Bohemia, or Italy, was signalled most implicitly by Simone da Crema's dispatches in the 1430s.

Like his father Charles and unlike his (half-)brother Wenceslas, Sigismund placed great emphasis on the performance of rituals and ceremonies. In the examined diplomatic correspondence, it is possible to find a number of examples that describe the court as a place of impressive public events. Many of them did not take place at Sigismund's residence, but on his numerous travels around Europe, that is to say, in

---

Piacentini (ed.), *L'epistolarum liber di Uberto Decembrio*, Medioevo milanese, 2 (Rome, 2020), 184–93, nos 5 and 6. See also Pagliara, 'Uberto Decembrio'.
97 Thallóczy, *Mantovai követjárás Budán*, 110, no. 8: 'Ad factum residentie mee hic nescio ad quid perditio hec multis rationibus, nam curia ista que nomen curie non meretur, tanta paupertate viget ...' Cf. Luzio, *L'Archivio Gonzaga*, vol. 2, 106.
98 ASFi, Signori, Dieci di Balia, Otto di Pratica, Legazioni e Commissarie, Missive e Responsive, b. 75, fol. 21r [148r]: 'In truth, His Majesty was very lonely in the number of barons, of whom only a few remained.' ('... nel vero, la maestà era molcto solo de' baroni che pochi n'erano rimasti colui ...')
99 Beckmann (ed.), *Deutsche Reichstagsakten*, vol. 12, p. 164, no. 102: 'The revenues of this crown are completely exhausted, the Emperor and his courtiers find themselves in extreme poverty even with regard to provisions and clothing, although his court is not very large.' ('... intrate illius corone totaliter extincte sunt, imperator cum illis de curia sua est in extrema paupertate etiam circa victum et vestitum, quamvis curia sua non multum sit ampla.')
100 Cesare Guasti (ed.), *Commissioni di Rinaldo degli Albizzi per il Comune di Firenze dal MCCCXCIX al MCCCCXXXIII*, Documenti di storia italiana pubblicati a cura della R. Deputazione sugli studi di storia patria per le provincie di Toscana, dell'Umbria e delle Marche, 1–3 (3 vols, Florence, 1867–73), vol. 2, 580, 588, 589.

rather improvised conditions.[101] Of particular importance were the rituals of feudal investiture, which symbolically highlighted the superiority of imperial status, from which all power was delegated.[102] His solemn entries into his subject cities, such as Constance in 1414, Lucca in 1432, and Prague in 1436, demonstrated the sovereign's takeover of power and its subsequent delegation to the local municipal government.[103]

In addition to rituals and ceremonies *stricto sensu*, Sigismund's visible participation in banquets, balls, tournaments, processions, and Masses did not escape the attention of the Italian diplomats. It was the great European events such as the Councils of Constance and Basel and the coronation journey to Rome, in particular, that were the perfect stage for Sigismund to display his majesty, power, and splendour.[104] Not even in moments of great tension did Sigismund underestimate the importance of symbolic communication. For example, during the siege of Golubac (Galambóc) in 1428, he knighted some of his warriors and conducted 'other ceremonies as it is appropriate in arms' in order to lift the spirits of the Hungarian army under attack from the Turks.[105]

In summary, it seems that Wenceslas did not dedicate enough attention to public rituals, ceremonies, and festivities and did not recognize the potential of such public acts for the representation of his royal majesty.[106] On the contrary, he evidently preferred more secluded forms

---

101 As is well known, unlike Sigismund, Wenceslas spent most of his time in Bohemia, especially in Prague. See Ivan Hlaváček, *K organizaci státního správního systému Václava IV. Dvě studie o jeho itineráři a radě* (Prague, 1991), 33–72. This difference also significantly shaped the rulership styles of both monarchs.
102 E.g., Schmidt (ed.), *Briefe*, 142–3, no. 49; for more details, see idem, 'Mantuan Envoys'. For the symbolic meaning of investiture, cf. Karl-Heinz Spiess, 'Kommunikationsformen im Hochadel und am Königshof im Spätmittelalter', in Gerd Althoff (ed.), *Formen und Funktionen öffentlicher Kommunikation im Mittelalter*, Vorträge und Forschungen, 51 (Stuttgart, 2001), 261–90, at 277–85.
103 MAN, Archivio Capitolare, Fondo Diplomatico, b. 16, no. 109, or BCU, Fondo Principale, b. 896/IV, no. 322; Bongi (ed.), *Lettera di Bartolommeo Martini*; Schmidt (ed.), *Briefe*, 151–4, no. 52. For the *adventus* in general, see Gerrit Jasper Schenk, *Zeremoniell und Politik: Herrschereinzüge im spätmittelalterlichen Reich* (Cologne, Weimar, and Vienna, 2003).
104 For the Council of Constance, see E. Kovács, 'Imperia'; for Sigismund's descent into Italy, see Proske, *Der Romzug*, 167–222.
105 ASFi, Signori, Dieci di Balia, Otto di Pratica, Legazioni e Commissarie, Missive e Responsive, b. 75, fol. 18r [145r]: '... e fece il re chavalieri e altre ceremonie chome si richiede in narme [sic] ...'
106 The same conclusion can be found in Ivan Hlaváček, 'Hof und Hofführung Wenzels IV. (1376–1419)', in Moraw (ed.), *Deutscher Königshof*, 105–36, at 116 ('One could even state – a little exaggeratedly – that he [Wenceslas] also in this respect purposefully aimed at the opposite, i.e. not to present himself as a ruler accordingly.' 'Man könnte gar – freilich ein wenig überspitzt – konstatieren, daß er auch in

of entertainment, especially the often-mentioned hunting. This feature of his rulership style also accords with what we know about the king's passion for beautiful illuminated manuscripts, in the sense that they were luxury items intended for a restricted audience only.[107] As Milena Bartlová and Dušan Buran conclude, 'Wenceslas seems to have used art in a rather personal and [...] local context whereas Sigismund developed much wider models for the employment of visual arts in his services, both in interpersonal and international respects.'[108] In the end, Wenceslas' inactivity with regard to his public representation, interpreted as neglect of his sovereign duties, might have been an important factor in his deposition in 1400. By contrast, Sigismund, as he appears in the correspondence of the Italian ambassadors, was the opposite of his older brother. Like his father, Charles, he took full advantage of the possibilities inherent in his imperial status and continuously and skilfully demonstrated it. This way, he often managed to counterbalance an effective lack of power and financial means.

CONCLUSION

When we compare Wenceslas and Sigismund, we see two sovereigns with substantially different 'rulership styles'. An episode from Bohemia in 1402, in which both Luxembourg brothers featured, may serve as an eloquent concluding illustration of this point. In the dispatches of Simone da Crema, Wenceslas, who at that time was the prisoner of his younger sibling, gives the impression of a childish puppet. While he is playing with his favourite goshawk, Sigismund is energetically engaging in political activity and expressing his determination to drag his (half-)brother to his coronation in Rome, even against his will. It is also quite telling that the envoy dedicates almost all his attention to Sigismund, King of Hungary, and not Wenceslas, (deposed, but in Italy still recognized as) King of the Romans and his effective sovereign.[109]

---

dieser Hinsicht zielbewußt das Gegenteil anstrebte, d. h. sich als Herrscher nicht entsprechend zu präsentieren'), 122–3.

107 For Wenceslas' manuscripts, see Hana Hlaváčková, 'Knižní malba v době krále Václava IV.', in Jiří Kuthan and Jakub Šenovský (eds), *Římský a český král Václav IV. a počátky husitské revoluce* (Prague, 2019), 131–53, and the papers by Maria Theisen and Gia Toussaint in this volume.

108 Milena Bartlová and Dušan Buran, 'Comparing the Incomparable? Wenceslas IV and Sigismund, Their Queens, and Their Images', in Jiří Fajt and Andrea Langer (eds), *Kunst als Herrschaftsinstrument: Böhmen und das Heilige Römische Reich unter den Luxemburgern im europäischen Kontext* (Berlin and Munich, 2009), 368–76, with the quotation at 374.

109 Schmidt, 'Druhé zajetí', 206–13, nos 1–7, or idem (ed.), *Briefe*, 64–74, nos 13–19.

Although it is a cliché, Sigismund certainly inherited and adopted more of Charles IV's style and 'charisma', while lacking other key traits, such as his father's extreme emphasis on public religiosity. Wenceslas appeared to the Italian envoys as not very active or attractive, his court as less accessible. Sigismund, on the other hand, was able to make full use of his 'human potential' and persuasive skills to achieve his aims, which was evident both in his personal dealings with foreign envoys and his engagement in symbolic public acts designed to underline his imperial majesty.[110] The presence of influential 'powerbrokers' can be seen at both courts; however, in Sigismund's milieu, these influential council and chancery members seem to have formed more stable structures than under Wenceslas, with the monarch retaining greater oversight over the day-to-day administrative agenda.

Many of the old stereotypes concerning the two brothers still seem to ring true, while others may be re-evaluated to a certain extent. However, we must take into account a number of methodological limitations, which again somewhat relativize the resulting picture. This is especially true with regard to the disproportion in the preservation of correspondence, and the structural transformation of diplomatic dispatches over the period investigated in this essay. Furthermore, it must be borne in mind that the view provided by the sources considered is by necessity very selective, and for a better understanding of Wenceslas' and Sigismund's 'personal aspects of rulership'[111] it would be necessary to supplement the dispatches examined here with as many other kinds of sources as possible that reflect the two rulers' personalities, including their representations in chronicles and works of art.[112] Finally, it might reasonably be argued that through the surviving texts and objects, we are, at least partly, influenced by the propaganda (or lack of it) of the courtly milieus of Sigismund and

---

110 I can only agree with the similar assessment by Karel Hruza, 'König Wenzel (1361–1419), der Ehre beraubt? Eine kommentierte Skizze seines Lebens', *MIR Texte* 6 (2017), online: https://www.oeaw.ac.at/fileadmin/Institute/imafo/pdf/forschung/MIR/timelab/MIR_Text_6.pdf [accessed 15 March 2023], 17: '… Wenceslas did not appear to be a charismatic king, even though he may have possessed a charming and eloquent side. This distinguishes him from his charismatic father and his half-brother Sigismund, who was said to be able to win people over. Compared to these two, Wenceslas probably appeared to his contemporaries as a king without glamour and shine.' ('… Wenzel allem Anschein nach nicht als ein charismatischer König auftrat, auch wenn er eine charmante und eloquente Seite besessen haben mag. Das unterscheidet ihn von seinem charismatischen Vater und seinem Halbbruder Sigismund, dem nachgesagt wurde, er könne die Menschen für sich gewinnen. Gegenüber diesen beiden erschien Wenzel seinen Zeitgenossen wohl als König ohne Glanz und Schein.')
111 Bauch et al., 'Heilige', 14.
112 Inspiringly in this sense, cf. Bartlová and Buran, 'Comparing the Incomparable?'.

Wenceslas. But this is precisely the point: if, in these sources, Sigismund appears in a better light, it means that he and his team of 'imagemakers' did a better job than Wenceslas.

PART IV

STUDYING THE LUXEMBOURGS: WHAT HAS BEEN NEGLECTED

CHAPTER 11

HEIRESSES, REGENTS, AND PATRONS: FEMALE RULERS IN THE AGE OF THE LUXEMBOURGS[1]

JULIA BURKHARDT

In 1387 the tears of a queen made Sigismund of Luxembourg King of Hungary. At least, this was the interpretation offered by the Hungarian chronicler John of Thurócz (János Thuróczy, c. 1435–90). In his *Chronicle of the Hungarians*, composed in the second half of the fifteenth century, John of Thurócz described the dynastic conflicts that broke out after the death of the last Anjou king Louis I in 1382. The Hungarian nobles had – in accordance with the deceased king's wishes – consented to the succession of Louis' daughter Mary to the Hungarian throne. Competing parties, however, also raised claims to the Hungarian crown, and years of struggles and war followed. Finally, Mary – the heiress and crowned queen – married her fiancé Sigismund of Luxembourg in order to secure her position, and Sigismund was crowned in Székesfehérvár.[2] Diverging to a certain extent

---

1 Special thanks to Karl Kügle for the kind translations of all Latin quotations into English unless otherwise stated.
2 Szilárd Süttő, 'Der Dynastiewechsel Anjou-Luxemburg in Ungarn', in M. Pauly and F. Reinert (eds), *Sigismund von Luxemburg: Ein Kaiser in Europa* (Mainz, 2006), 79–87; Dániel Bagi, 'Changer les règles: la succession angevine aux trônes hongrois et polonais', in F. Lachaud and M. Penman (eds), *Making and Breaking the Rules: Succession in Medieval Europe, c. 1000–c.1600 / Établir et abolir les normes: la succession dans l'Europe médiévale, vers 1000–vers 1600* (Turnhout, 2008), 89–95; J. Burkhardt, 'Ein Königreich im Wandel: Ungarn um 1400', *Biuletyn Polskiej Misji*

from the chronology, John of Thuròcz had the already dramatic events of those years culminate in an even more dramatic scenario. He reported that Queen Mary tried to convince the Hungarian nobles of her fiancé's suitability for the crown during a general assembly. Her appearance with 'her cheeks previously wet from streams of tears' seemed an emotional reflection of her political enthusiasm:[3] Queen Mary addressed the nobles in an ardent speech, diligently listing political and dynastic arguments in favour of Sigismund. 'Behold then', she concluded, 'I make a king of my betrothed; and to him I yield jurisdiction over the Kingdom together with the diadem. I do this chiefly because I am aware that you do not like the rule of a woman, and that such a rule is not strong enough to guide the reins of so violent a people, as events demonstrate.'[4] Certain elements of this episode seem to allude to Mary's inability to rule: her emotional state, her seemingly weak appearance, and her renouncing the crown. But Thuròcz's story can also be read against the grain. Sigismund's Hungarian

---

Historycznej/ Bulletin der Polnischen Historischen Mission 11 (2016), 407–37, https://apcz.umk.pl/BPMH/article/view/BPMH.2016.013/10356 [accessed 22 March 2023]. On Mary of Anjou and her relation to Sigismund, see Jaroslav Perniš, 'Posledná Anjouovská Kráľovná Mária Uhorská (1371–1395)', *Historický Časopis* 47 (1999), 3–17; Norbert C. Tóth, 'Királynőből királyné: Mária és Zsigmond viszonya a források tükrében', *Acta Historica* 132 (2011), 59–71; and Christopher Mielke, *The Archaeology and Material Culture of Queenship in Medieval Hungary, 1000–1395* (Cham, 2021), 225–63.

3 János Thuróczy, *Chronicle of the Hungarians*, translation by Frank Mantello, foreword and commentary by Pál Engel (Bloomington, 1991), ch. 198, 39. Johannes de Thurocz, *Chronica Hungarorum*. I: Textus, ed. Elisabeth Galántai and Julius Kristó (Budapest, 1985), 207: 'Ubi regina Maria cuncto in unum convocato nobilium cetu media stetit inter illos, ablutisque prius genis lachrymarum rivulis non gravibus sine suspiriis ad populum hanc vocem fecit [...]'. On the symbolic meaning (and intentional usages) of tears, see the contributions in E. Gertsman (ed.), *Crying in the Middle Ages: Tears of History* (New York, 2012).

4 Thuróczy, *Chronicle*, 40; Johannes de Thurocz, *Chronica*, 208: 'Ecce igitur de sponso regem efficio, iusque regni partior et diadema illi cedo, potissime cum nec femineum vos amare imperium, neque ad dirigendas tam impetuose gentis habenas factis testantibus illud sufficere animadvertam'. On female rulership in late medieval Hungary, see Marianne Sághy, 'Aspects of Female Rulership in Late Medieval Literature: The Queens' Reign in Angevin Hungary', *East Central Europe* 20–3:1 (1993–6), 69–86; János M. Bak, 'Queens as Scapegoats in Medieval Hungary', in Anne J. Duggan (ed.), *Queens and Queenship in Medieval Europe: Proceedings of a Conference held at King's College London, April 1995* (Woodbridge, 1997), 223–33; on earlier traditions, see Attila Zsoldos, *The Árpáds and Their Wives: Queenship in Early Medieval Hungary, 1000–1301* (Rome, 2019), and Christopher Mielke, 'Doubly Crowned: The Public and Private Image of Two Fourteenth-Century Hungarian Queens', in Walker Vadillo and Mónica Ann (eds), *Ambiguous Women in Medieval Art* (Budapest, 2019), 145–67, https://trivent-publishing.eu/history/ambiguouswomen/6.%20Christopher%20Mielke.pdf [accessed 22 March 2023].

kingship then fully depended on the authority and the dynastic rights of his wife: he is only accepted as king because Mary – deliberately playing with contemporary doubts about women's weakness – won the political community's support: she *made* the king.

Thurócz's episode – albeit brief and with a contentious reading – is an example for both the opportunities and the limitations of studies on female rulers in the Middle Ages: it underlines the importance of historical figures like Mary of Anjou as heiresses and rulers; and at the same time, through the silence or ambiguity of contemporary sources, it reveals the problem of overcoming (historical) gender stereotypes and deciphering the actual impact of female rulers. Against this background, this study proposes to look at 'the other side of the coin' by discussing the role, agency, and impact of female rulers in the 'long Luxembourg century' (fourteenth to mid-fifteenth century).[5] It is not my objective to claim or strive for a comprehensive approach. Instead, I would like to highlight key aspects of noble women's agency in the age of the Luxembourgs, thereby taking up recent debates in medieval studies.

For quite some time, studies on medieval rulers and their sociopolitical or cultural impact tended to focus on male representatives of monarchies and dynasties, thereby contributing to an incomplete and insufficient picture of medieval rulership, with no attention paid to females and their influence.[6] In recent decades, however, several studies on different European dynasties and realms have shed light on various institutionalized and informal expressions of female agency in politics, religion, and cultural patronage.[7] This meant a considerable enrichment

---

5   On the 'long Luxembourg century', see Martin Bauch, Julia Burkhardt, Tomáš Gaudek, Paul Töbelmann and Václav Žůrek, 'Heilige, Helden, Wüteriche: Eine konzeptionelle Skizze zu "Herrschaftsstilen" im langen Jahrhundert der Luxemburger', in Bauch et al. (eds), *Heilige, Helden, Wüteriche: Herrschaftsstile der Luxemburger (1308–1437)* (Köln/Weimar/Vienna, 2017), 11–27.
6   Christina Lutter, 'Herrschaft und Geschlecht: Relationale Kategorien zur Erforschung fürstlicher Handlungsspielräume', in Matthias Becher, Achim Fischelmanns and Katharina Gahbler (eds), *Vormoderne Macht und Herrschaft. Geschlechterdimensionen und Spannungsfelder* (Bonn, 2021), 201–31; Theresa Earenfight, 'Without the Persona of the Prince: Kings, Queens and the Idea of Monarchy in Late Medieval Europe', *Gender & History* 19 (2007), 1–21; Theresa Earenfight, 'Highly Visible, Often Obscured: The Difficulty of Seeing Queens and Noble Women', *Medieval Feminist Forum* 44 (2008), 86–90; Elena Woodacre and Cathleen Sarti, 'What is Royal Studies?', *Royal Studies Journal* 2 (2015), 13–20, http://www.rsj.winchester.ac.uk/index.php/rsj/article/view/42/70 [accessed 14 February 2022].
7   Though it is impossible to give a complete overview of recent publications, I would like to reference some particularly instructive studies: Lutter, 'Herrschaft und Geschlecht'; Nikolas Jaspert and Imke Just (eds), *Queens, Princesses and Mendicants:*

of former discussions, since research on the individual person of the male ruler and his environment of (male) counsellors was complemented by thorough analyses of the impact generated by princesses and noblewomen. Recent studies inspired by gender studies and their relational perspective have offered even more nuanced analyses: they successfully replace categories such as 'female' or 'male' power by careful assessments of individual behavioural motivations, the influence of multidimensional social relations, cultural traditions, and medieval representations of gender roles.[8]

Building on these recent achievements as well as on pioneering studies on individual representatives of the Luxembourg dynasty, this essay sounds out the political role and influence of female rulers in the age of

---

Close Relations in a European Perspective (Wien/Zürich/Münster, 2019); Elena Woodacre (ed.), *A Companion to Global Queenship* (Leeds, 2018); François Chausson and Sylvain Destephen (eds), *Augusta, Regina, Basilissa: la souveraine de l'Empire romain au Moyen Âge* (Paris, 2018); Claudia Zey (ed.), *Mächtige Frauen? Königinnen und Fürstinnen im europäischen Mittelalter (11.–14. Jahrhundert)* (Ostfildern, 2015); Murielle Gaude-Ferragu, *La Reine au Moyen Âge: Le pouvoir au féminin XIVe–XVe siècle* (Paris, 2014); Theresa Earenfight, *Queenship in Medieval Europe* (Basingstoke, 2013); Amalie Fößel, 'The Political Traditions of Female Rulership in Medieval Europe', in Judith Bennett and Ruth Karras (eds), *The Oxford Handbook of Women and Gender in Medieval Europe* (Oxford, 2013), 68–83; Edward William Monter, *The Rise of Female Kings in Europe, 1300–1800* (New Haven, 2012); Éric Bousmar, Jonathan Dumont, Alain Marchandisse and Bertrand Schnerb (eds), *Femmes de pouvoir, femmes politiques durant les derniers siècles du Moyen Âge et au cours de la première Renaissance* (Brussels, 2012); Amalie Fößel (ed.), *Die Kaiserinnen des Mittelalters* (Regensburg, 2011); Martina Hartmann, *Die Königin im frühen Mittelalter* (Stuttgart, 2009); Marcel Faure (ed.), *Reines et princesses au Moyen Âge: actes du cinquième colloque international de Montpellier, Université Paul-Valéry (24–27 novembre 1999)*, 2 vols (Montpellier, 2001); Amalie Fößel, *Die Königin im mittelalterlichen Reich: Herrschaftsausübung, Herrschaftsrechte, Handlungsspielräume* (Stuttgart, 2000).

8 See, for example, the contributions in Christina Lutter and Andre Gingrich (eds), *Kinship and Gender across Historical Asia and Europe: Comparative Reassessments between the 8th and 19th Centuries CE* (London, 2021); Christina Lutter, 'Zur Repräsentation von Geschlechterverhältnissen im höfischen Umfeld Maximilians I.', in Johannes Helmrath, Ursula Kocher and Andrea Sieber (eds), *Maximilians Welt. Kaiser Maximilian I. im Spannungsfeld zwischen Innovation und Tradition* (Göttingen, 2018), 41–60; Christina Antenhofer, 'Gonzaga Sisters Married into German Courts: Biographies, Correspondences, Material Culture and Spheres of Action', in Chiara Continisio and Raffaele Tamalio (eds), *Donne Gonzaga a corte: reti istituzionali, pratiche culturali e affari di governo* (Rome, 2018), 123–44; Nikolas Jaspert, 'Indirekte und direkte Macht iberischer Königinnen im Mittelalter: "Reginale" Herrschaft, Verwaltung und Frömmigkeit', in Zey (ed.), *Mächtige Frauen?*, 73–130.

the Luxembourgs in a comparative perspective.[9] The (albeit generalizing) collective term 'female rulers' includes women in different political positions (queens, duchesses, and princesses) as well as legal or social situations (wives/widows, heiresses, sisters, and daughters). In order to highlight common grounds and reveal regional differences, examples from Hungary, the Holy Roman Empire, Bohemia, Luxembourg, and England will be taken into consideration, thus encompassing both women in the home territories of their dynasties as well as representatives who married into other ruling families in Europe.

Methodologically, the present study is organized through a matrix combining three (possibly overlapping) 'types' of female rule (i.e., as heiresses, regents, patronesses) – each of them highlighting different forms of activities – supplemented by four criteria for closer analysis (social networks, political activities, dynastic representation, and *memoria*). This approach includes social elements such as women's personal milieux, their contact networks, or spatial conditions of their rule (e.g., preferred places of residence), but it also addresses political aspects like women's interactions with their husbands or other (male) members of the family, women's interventions in political affairs, and female-gendered patterns in deploying symbolic language. In order to determine the part played by these criteria in political and social decision-making, a broad range of sources, including administrative and narrative records, religious artefacts, and personal correspondences, will be evaluated. It needs to be underscored, however, that the limited survival rate of relevant sources marks a certain challenge: since normative and administrative sources (e.g., charters, privileges, last wills, or accounts books) are available only for a few female rulers or some periods of their reign, research on noblewomen significantly has to rely on narrative sources and is thus subject to contemporary stereotyping, as could be seen in the opening example of Mary of Anjou.[10]

---

9   In the subsequent notes, I will refer to relevant literature on selected Luxembourg women. For comprehensive and comparative approaches to dynastic and cultural questions, see Michel Margue, 'L'épouse au pouvoir: Le pouvoir de l'heritière entre dynasties et politique impériale à l'exemple de la maison de Luxembourg (XIIIe-XIVe s.)', in Bousmar et al. (eds), *Femmes de pouvoir*, 269–310; Amalie Fößel, 'Die Heiratspolitik der Luxemburger', in Sabine Penth and Peter Thorau (eds), *Rom 1312: Die Kaiserkrönung Heinrichs VII. und die Folgen. Die Luxemburger als Herrscherdynastie von gesamteuropäischer Bedeutung* (Köln/Weimar/Wien, 2016), 427–44; Amalie Fößel, 'Bücher, Bildung und Herrschaft von Fürstinnen im Umkreis des Prager Hofes der Luxemburger', in Wolfgang Haubrichs and Patricia Oster (eds), *Zwischen Herrschaft und Kunst: fürstliche und adlige Frauen im Zeitalter Elisabeths von Nassau-Saarbrücken (14-16. Jh.)* (Saarbrücken, 2013), 313–30.
10 Cf. for general observations Tracy Adams, 'Powerful Women and Misogynistic Subplots: Some Comments on the Necessity of Checking the Primary Sources', *Medieval Feminist Forum: A Journal of Gender and Sexuality* 51 (2016), 69–81, https://

HEIRESSES BETWEEN DYNASTY AND TERRITORY

Between 1300 and 1450 several heiresses either married into the Luxembourg dynasty or were the bearers of the family inheritance, testifying both to clever and circumspect marriage politics (in the first case)[11] and to a certain amount of historical contingency (in the second case).[12] Elizabeth of Bohemia (1292–1330), daughter/sister of the last Přemyslid kings and wife of John of Luxembourg,[13] the famous Tyrolian countess Margarete

---

scholarworks.wmich.edu/cgi/viewcontent.cgi?article=2038&context=mff [accessed 14 February 2022]; Katherine Louise French, 'Medieval Women's History: Sources and Issues', in Joel Rosenthal (ed.), *Understanding Medieval Primary Sources: Using Historical Sources to Discover Medieval Europe* (London, 2012), 196–209; Martina Hartmann, 'Sage – Klischee – Fiktion? Zum Bild der merowingischen Königinnen in den frühmittelalterlichen erzählenden Quellen', in Ewa Dewes and Sandra Duhem (eds), *Kulturelles Gedächtnis und interkulturelle Rezeption im europäischen Kontext* (Berlin, 2008), 23–32.

11 On Luxembourg marriage politics, see Fößel, 'Die Heiratspolitik'; Marek Suchý, 'England and Bohemia in the Time of Anne of Luxembourg: Dynastic Marriage as a Precondition for Cultural Contact in the Late Middle Ages', in Zoë Opačić (ed.), *Prague and Bohemia: Medieval Art, Architecture and Cultural Exchange in Central Europe* (Leeds, 2009), 8–21; Dieter Veldtrup, 'Ehen aus Staatsräson: Die Familien- und Heiratspolitik Johanns von Böhmen', in Michel Pauly (ed.), *Johann der Blinde, Graf von Luxemburg, König von Böhmen 1296–1346: Tagungsband der 9es Journées Lotharingiennes 22.-26. Oktober 1996, Centre Universitaire de Luxembourg* (Luxembourg, 1997), 483–543; Heinz-Dieter Heimann, 'Herrscherfamilie und Herrschaftspraxis: Sigismund, Barbara, Albrecht und die Gestalt der luxemburgisch-habsburgischen Erbverbrüderung', in Josef Macek, Ernő Marosi and Ferdinand Seibt (eds), *Sigismund von Luxemburg: Kaiser und König in Mitteleuropa 1387–1437. Beiträge zur Herrschaft Kaiser Sigismunds und der europäischen Geschichte um 1400. Vorträge der internationalen Tagung in Budapest vom 8.-11. Juli 1987 anläßlich der 600. Wiederkehr seiner Thronbesteigung in Ungarn und seines 550. Todestages* (Warendorf, 1994), 53–66; Dieter Veldtrup, *Zwischen Eherecht und Familienpolitik: Studien zu den dynastischen Heiratsprojekten Karls IV.* (Warendorf, 1988).

12 On contingency as a category of historical analysis, see the latest discussions in the following studies: Frank Becker, Benjamin Scheller and Ute Schneider (eds), *Die Ungewissheit des Zukünftigen: Kontingenz in der Geschichte* (Frankfurt, 2016); Frank Becker, Stefan Brakensiek and Benjamin Scheller (eds), *Ermöglichen und Verhindern: Vom Umgang mit Kontingenz* (Frankfurt, 2016); Cornelia Herberichs and Susanne Reichlin (eds), *Kein Zufall: Konzeptionen von Kontingenz in der mittelalterlichen Literatur* (Göttingen, 2009), and with a focus on dynastic change: Florian Hartmann, 'Thronfolgen im Mittelalter zwischen Erbe und Wahl, zwischen Legitimität und Usurpation, zwischen Kontingenz und (konstruierter) Kontinuität', in Matthias Becher (ed.), *Die mittelalterliche Thronfolge im europäischen Vergleich* (Ostfildern, 2017), 449–65.

13 For an excellent overview, see the contributions in Klára Benešovská (ed.), *A Royal Marriage: Elisabeth Přemyslid and John of Luxembourg 1310* (Prague, 2010); see also the titles given in the subsequent notes.

(1318–69), wife of John Henry of Luxembourg until their spectacular marriage dispute,[14] Duchess Joan (Jeanne) of Brabant (1322–1406), wife of Duke Wenceslas of Luxembourg,[15] and the aforementioned Mary of Anjou (c. 1371–95), wife of Sigismund of Luxembourg, all married male representatives of the Luxembourg dynasty. Elizabeth of Görlitz (1390–1451), daughter of John of Luxembourg, Duke of Görlitz,[16] and Elizabeth of Luxembourg (c. 1409–42), daughter of Sigismund of Luxembourg,[17] represented different family branches of the Luxembourg dynasty as their sole heirs.

As the last descendants of their respective families, heiresses were (in the absence of male heirs) the key to dynastic continuity.[18] As James C. Holt put it in his pioneering study on the phenomenon, 'this determined the woman's position as heir. If there were legitimate male heirs to her

---

14 See the contributions in Julia Hörmann-Thurn und Taxis (ed.), *Margarete "Maultasch": Zur Lebenswelt einer Landesfürstin und anderen Tiroler Frauen des Mittelalters. Vorträge der wissenschaftlichen Tagung im Südtiroler Landesmuseum für Kultur- und Landesgeschichte Schloss Tirol, Schloss Tirol, 3. bis 4. November 2006* (Innsbruck, 2007); and in Christoph Haidacher and Mark Mersiowsky (eds), *1363–2013: 650 Jahre Tirol mit Österreich* (Innsbruck, 2015).

15 Sergio Boffa, 'Les mariages de Jeanne de Brabant avec Guillaume de Hainaut et Wenceslas de Bohême (janvier 1331 et decembre 1351/mars 1352)', in Michel Pauly (ed.), *Die Erbtochter, der fremde Fürst und das Land: Die Ehe Johanns des Blinden und Elisabeths von Böhmen in vergleichender europäischer Perspektive / L'héritière, le prince étranger et le pays: Le mariage de Jean l'Aveugle et d'Elisabeth de Bohême dans une perspective comparative européenne* (Luxembourg, 2013), 181–207; Sergio Boffa, 'The Duchy of Brabant Between France, Burgundy and England: Geopolitics and Diplomacy During the Hundred Years War (1383–1430)', in L.J. Andrew Villalon and Donald J. Kagay (eds), *The Hundred Years War (Part III): Further Considerations* (Leiden/Boston, 2013), 475–97.

16 Gabriele Schmid and Wolfgang Schmid, 'Elisabeth von Görlitz († 1451): Letzte Lebensjahre, Nachlaßregelung und Grabdenkmal einer Herzogin von Luxemburg in Trier', in Michael Embach (ed.), *Kontinuität und Wandel: 750 Jahre Kirche des Bischöflichen Priesterseminars Trier. Eine Festschrift aus Anlaß der feierlichen Wiedereröffnung 1993* (Trier, 1994), 211–52; Zuzana Bolerazká, 'Poslední lucemburská princezna: Životní osudy Elišky Zhořelecké v letech 1390–1425 / The Last Princess of Luxembourg. The Life of Elizabeth of Görlitz in the Period between Years 1390–1425' (Diploma thesis, Charles University Prague, 2016), https://dspace.cuni.cz/handle/20.500.11956/79360 [accessed 22 March 2023]; see also the titles given in the subsequent notes.

17 Julia Burkhardt, 'Das Erbe der Frauen: Elisabeth von Luxemburg und Elisabeth von Habsburg', in Bauch et al. (eds), *Heilige, Helden, Wüteriche*, 261–84; see also the titles in the subsequent notes.

18 In this article, I will use the modern term 'heiress'. In the Middle Ages, the Latin term 'heres' was used for both men and women. On women ruling in their own right, see Roger Bartlett, *Blood Royal: Dynastic Politics in Medieval Europe* (Cambridge, 2020), 124–54.

father then she could not expect to succeed. If there were no male heirs then the inheritance was "hers" in the sense that it was no one else's, that the claim which she embodied was stronger than anyone else's. [...] She brought her lands to her husband and ultimately to her children.'[19]

Consequently, heiresses were closely related to their territories, being regarded as the embodiment of political heritage and thus as the bearers of claims to the throne. The support of the local nobility was of the utmost importance in order to have their rights – and of course those of their respective husbands – acknowledged and accepted. While this implies a prominent political role, Holt – though by no means denying the importance of the heiresses – also underlines their passive position: according to his observations on medieval England, heiresses were subordinate to their husbands and could 'only as a widow [...] hope to gain sole control'.[20]

A closer look at the heiresses from or attached to the Luxembourg dynasty seems, however, to reveal a slightly different picture – although it is sometimes difficult, as Michel Margue underlined in his pivotal work, to exactly determine the actual impact of heiresses.[21] Another aspect that comes into play is the relation between the respective heiresses and their husbands, who were regarded as 'alien' or 'foreigners' in the new territories. The political language of that time could thus be marked by strong references to own (only seemingly 'national') identities and aspects of 'foreignness' that were regarded as (or at least argumentatively marked as) unwelcome.[22]

---

19   James C. Holt, 'Feudal Society and the Family in Early Medieval England: IV. The Heiress and the Alien', *Transactions of the Royal Historical Society* 35 (1985), 1–28, at 3.
20   Ibid., at 4.
21   Michel Margue, 'Die Erbtochter, der fremde Fürst und die Stände: "Internationale" Heiraten als Mittel der Machtpolitik im Spannungsfeld zwischen Hausmacht und Land', in Pauly (ed.), *Die Erbtochter*, 27–45; idem, 'L'epouse au pouvoir'.
22   On foreignness as an argument in times of political change, see Julia Burkhardt, 'Argumentative Uses of "Otherness" and "Foreignness" in Pre-Modern Political Debates in Central Europe', *Historical Studies on Central Europe* 2:2 (2022), 22–42; Bartlett, *Blood Royal*, 397–428; Cathleen Sarti, 'Sigismund of Sweden as Foreigner in His Own Kingdom: How the King of Sweden Was Made an Alien', in Ana Maria Seabra de Almeida Rodrigues, Manuela Santos Silva and Jonathan Spangler (eds), *Dynastic Change: Legitimacy and Gender in Medieval and Early Modern Monarchy* (London, 2020), 86–102; Joanna Sobiesiak, 'Czechs and Germans: Nationals and Foreigners in the Work of Czech Chroniclers. From Cosmas of Prague (12th Century) to the Chronicle of the So-called Dalimil (14th Century)', in Andrzej Pleszczyński, Joanna Sobiesiak, Michał Tomaszek and Przemysław Tyszka (eds), *Imagined Communities: Constructing Collective Identities in Medieval Europe* (Leiden,

Probably the best example for these discursive mechanisms is the marriage between Elizabeth of Bohemia and John of Luxembourg. After the death of her father and brother, Wenceslas II and Wenceslas III in 1305 and 1306, Elizabeth and her older sister Anna (1290–1313) were the last remaining descendants of the Přemyslid dynasty. In 1306, Anna was married to Henry of Carinthia, who immediately raised claims to the Bohemian throne. Probably thanks to the initiative of his wife, Henry's claims were realized, although the new king was lacking support in Bohemia.[23] Meanwhile, another candidate – Rudolf of Habsburg, who had married the deceased king's widow – also tried to get hold of the Bohemian crown; years of conflict and negotiations about decisive factors in the succession question followed.[24] In these times of political uncertainty, polemic recourses to different forms of identity seemed to be of crucial importance: cultural or linguistic characteristics were used to semantically form groups of belonging and, consequently, to exclude opponents as 'foreigners'.[25]

2018), 322–34; Anna Aurast, *Fremde, Freunde, Feinde: Wahrnehmung und Bewertung von Fremden in den Chroniken des Gallus Anonymus und des Cosmas von Prag* (Bochum, 2019); Daniel Höffker and Gabriel Zeilinger (eds), *Fremde Herrscher: Elitentransfer und politische Integration im Ostseeraum (15.–18. Jahrhundert)* (Frankfurt, 2006).

23 See Dana Dvořáčková-Malá, 'Anne and Henry of Carinthia', in Benešovská (ed.), *A Royal Marriage*, 312–15; Kateřina Telnarová, '"Anna královna česká" nejstarší dcera Václava II. a její osudy', *Mediaevalia Historica Bohemica* 13:1 (2010), 77–110.

24 See Dana Dvořáčková-Malá, 'Elisabeth Richenza of Poland and Rudolph, Mocked as "King Porridge"', in Benešovská (ed.), *A Royal Marriage*, 316–21; Éloïse Adde, 'Les bourgeois de Bohême et l'impossible legitimation? La conjuration de Prague et de Kutná Hora de février 1309', in *Contester au Moyen Âge: de la désobéissance à la révolte: XLIXe Congrès de la SHMESP (Rennes, 24–27 mai 2018)* (Paris, 2019), 171–85; Robert Antonin, 'Probleme bei der Gründung einer neuen Dynastie', in Sławomir Moździoch and Przemysław Wiszweski (eds), *Consensus or Violence? Cohesive Forces in Early and High Medieval Societies (9th-14th c.)* (Wrocław, 2013), 189–201.

25 Éloïse Adde-Vomácka, *Les débuts de l'historiographie nationale tchèque en langue vulgaire au XIVe siècle* (Paris, 2016); Éloïse Adde, 'Die deutschsprachige Übersetzung der *Dalimil*-Chronik: Ein Versuch der politischen Legitimation der städtischen Eliten im Böhmen der Luxemburger?', in Amelie Bendheim and Heinz Sieburg (eds), *Prag in der Zeit der Luxemburger Dynastie: Literatur, Religion und Herrschaftskulturen zwischen Bereicherung und Behauptung* (Bielefeld, 2019), 119–40; Jana Fantysová Matějková, 'The Virtual Region of the Conglomerate State and Its *Communitas*: The Discourse of Cohesion of the Land. Communities in the Historiography of the 14th Century, especially in the Chronicle of Zbraslav', in Lenka Bobková and Jana Fantysová Matějková (eds), *Terra, Ducatus, Marchionatus. Regio: Die Bildung und Entwicklung der Regionen im Rahmen der Krone des Königreichs Böhmen* (Prague, 2013), 110–41.

This complex situation gave Henry VII, King in the Holy Roman Empire and soon-to-be Emperor, the opportunity of expanding his political influence eastwards: Henry and a delegation of Bohemian Cistercians negotiated a marriage between Elizabeth and Henry's son, John of Luxembourg.[26] One of the key accounts of these years, the so-called 'Zbraslav Chronicle', remarkably ascribes the key agency not to the men involved, but to princess Elizabeth: when she realized what harm the political conflicts and especially the reign of Henry of Carinthia had done to her country, she approached the abbot of the Cistercian Zbraslav (German: Königsaal; Latin: *Aula regia*) Monastery. The abbot then came to understand that the frictions in the kingdom were only to be resolved by a new dynastic marriage, offering the country the chance of peace. Although the narrative is full of stereotypes – Elizabeth appears weak, in despair, crying and sighing – it is she who understands her responsibility towards the realm and her dynasty.[27] Though her agency is seemingly based on weakness, it motivates the abbot to reflect about further options and to successfully negotiate the marriage to John of Luxembourg – Elizabeth's agency is thus of prime importance. Accordingly, Elizabeth is represented

---

26 I forego listing the extensive literature on the matter. For an overview, see Robert Antonin, 'Der Weg nach Osten: Heinrich VII. und der Erwerb Böhmens für die Luxemburger', in Penth and Thorau (eds), *Rom 1312*, 9–21, and the numerous contributions in Benešovská (ed.), *A Royal Marriage*; see also Lenka Bobková, 'Die Reise von Prinzessin Elisabeth von Böhmen zur Hochzeit mit Johann von Luxemburg', *Hémecht* 66 (2014), 135–54.

27 Joseph Emler (ed.), 'Petra Žitavského kronika zbraslavská', in *Fontes rerum Bohemicarum 4* (Prague, 1884), 1–337, chapter 89 ('Qualiter domicella Elizabeth dominum Conradum, abbatem primum Aule Regie, ad sui promocionem exhortata fuerit anno MCCCIX'), 123–4, at 123: 'orphana, inquit, ego sum utroque orbata parente; regnum patrum meorum et hereditas dissipatur et hic meus sororius, quem meum consolatorem et regni reformatorem speraveram, factus est quasi omni populo in derisum. Melius expedit michi mori, quam sic misere vivere et meam regnique desolacionem videre' ('I am an orphan, she said, having lost both of my parents; the kingdom of my fathers and [my] inheritance are being wasted, and my own sister's husband, who I had hoped would be my comfort and a reformer of the Kingdom, has become the laughing stock of virtually the entire population. It is better for me to die than to live in such misery and see the desolation of myself and the Kingdom'). For a German translation, see *Die Königsaaler Chronik. Aus dem Lateinischen von Josef Bujnoch † und Stefan Albrecht. Mit einer Einleitung von Peter Hilsch* (Frankfurt, 2014), 271. On the perception of Elizabeth in the 'Zbraslav Chronicle', see (with an explicit gender history approach) Věra Vejrychová, 'Role královny a jejich reflexe ve Zbraslavské kronice', *Studia Mediaevalia Bohemica* 7:1 (2015), 55–79, esp. 62–3, and Věra Vejrychová, 'Figures de reines dans les chroniques tchèques du XIVe siècle: idéal, pouvoir, transgressions', *Médiévales* 67 (2014), 31–48, esp. 34–8, http://journals.openedition.org/medievales/7377 [accessed 22 March 2023].

as the rightful and worthy heiress, not only because of her blood lineage, but also because of her sense of responsibility.[28]

Despite the diligent negotiations and preparations on all sides, the connection between Elizabeth and John alone would not calm the opposing political voices in Bohemia. In order to ensure that local rights and privileges would be acknowledged, John of Luxembourg was obliged to codify the nobles' rights in two inaugural charters: he promised to appoint only local people to local positions – again, the idea of different identities, a 'foreign' and a 'local' Bohemian or Moravian one, became relevant.[29] These codified privileges equipped the nobles with a means of exerting pressure, and the following years would show that they knew how to make use of it: continuous debates about the 'foreign' counsellors of King John and the king's long absences from Bohemia marked the years after the couple's coronation in 1311. Finally, the political and military influence of some opposing nobles around Henry of Lipá (1297–1329) grew considerably. They successfully challenged the position of the king's (mostly, but not exclusively) German – primarily Rhenish – representatives and deputies, among them Archbishop Peter von Aspelt of Mainz, who had been entrusted with governmental affairs in John's absence.[30] Even

---

28 It should, however, not be forgotten that the 'Zbraslav Chronicle' was composed in the early fourteenth century, thus in the time of King John and the early years of his son Charles IV, who – as the direct heir to Elizabeth and John – must have had a vivid interest in strengthening the argument of a female law of inheritance. See Běla Marani-Moravová, *Peter von Zittau: Abt, Diplomat und Chronist der Luxemburger* (Ostfildern, 2019), and the contributions in Stefan Albrecht (ed.), *Chronicon Aulae regiae: Die Königsaaler Chronik. Eine Bestandsaufnahme* (Frankfurt, 2013).
29 Lenka Bobková, 'From an Inexperienced Youth to a Knowledgeable King: The Essential Characteristics of the First Ten Years of the Reign of John of Luxembourg in Bohemia', in Benešovská (ed.), *A Royal Marriage*, 194–207; Lenka Bobková , 'Das Königspaar Johann und Elisabeth: Die Träume von der Herrlichkeit in den Wirren der Realität', in Pauly (ed.), *Die Erbtochter*, 47–74; Eloïse Adde, 'Les "Diplômes inauguraux": Le contrat politique entre Jean l'Aveugle et la communauté des Tchèques', *Die Warte / Perspectives (Luxemburger Wort)* 15 (November 2018), 10–11. These lines of conflict were reinforced by the increasing economic influence of a German-speaking urban elite and the concomitant feeling of eroding power among the Bohemian nobility. See Jana Fantysová Matějková, 'Boemi and the Others: Shaping the Regional Identity of Medieval Bohemia between the Twelfth and the Fourteenth Centuries', in Dick E.H. de Boer and Luís Adão da Fonseca (eds), *Historiography and the Shaping of Regional Identity in Europe: Regions in Clio's Looking Glass* (Turnhout, 2020), 69–89.
30 Dana Dvořáčková-Malá, 'Peter of Aspelt at the Prague Court', in Benešovská (ed.), *A Royal Marriage*, 402–9; David Kirt, *Peter von Aspelt (1240/45–1320): Ein spätmittelalterlicher Kirchenfürst zwischen Luxemburg, Böhmen und dem Reich* (Luxembourg, 2013). On the argument about the Rhenish counsellors, see also Johannes Abdullahi, 'Johann der Blinde und seine "Rheinischen Hansel": Geld und

the birth of the long-awaited heir Wenceslas (the later Charles IV) in 1316 could not smooth things over. When in 1317 Archbishop Peter returned to his home territory and King John consented to release his German counsellors the year after, political responsibilities fell on Queen Elizabeth's shoulders, since King John remained absent from Bohemia. Elizabeth, however, did not succeed in uniting the competing parties in Bohemia (which is remarkable, if we consider the praise of Elizabeth as the source of political legitimacy in the chronicles). On the contrary: while the community of nobles and their own political assemblies became more powerful, Elizabeth seemed to have fallen out with her husband and withdrew (or fled?) with her children to Loket (German: Elbogen) Castle in western Bohemia.[31] Some time and several military conflicts later, Elizabeth and John reconciled, and from then on, in what were to be the last years of her life, Elizabeth seems to have focused on the support of religious institutions. In this context, her awareness of dynastic bonds became even more visible – for example, when she made endowments to the Dominican nuns of Prague in 1320.[32]

This fourteenth-century Bohemian case study reveals the complexity of political structures and the various layers of communication: while dynastic tradition and respective arguments such as continuity, suitability, and family ties were pivotal aspects in the debates of the time, the participation of the political community with its right to elect or at least formulate participative conditions grew in importance as well. This again underlines the ambivalent position of the heiress between territory and family: as the last descendant of the previous dynasty, Elizabeth represented the legitimacy of rule and the legal traditions of the land as

---

Hof im zeitgenössischen Diskurs', in Eva Schlotheuber and Hubertus Seibert (eds), *Soziale Bindungen und gesellschaftliche Strukturen im späten Mittelalter (14.–16. Jahrhundert)* (Göttingen, 2013), 261–79.

31 Eloïse Adde-Vomáčka, 'Idéologie nobiliaire et espace public dans les pays de la couronne de Bohême au XIVe siècle', *Hémecht* 67 (2015), 401–20.

32 Josef Emler (ed.), *Regesta diplomatica nec non epistolaria Bohemiae et Moraviae* (Prague, 1890), no. 603 at 255 (endowment dating 15 August 1320): '[…] *vt in nostro parentumque nostrorum felicis recordacionis domini Wenczelai, magnifici quondam Boemie et Polonie regis, et domine Gute, consortis eius, nec non domini Wenczelai junioris regis, fratris nostri, et domine Anne, olim ducisse Karinthie sororis, nostrorum predictorum anniuersariis misse defunctorum cantentur* […]'; see also idem, no. 633 at 267 (another endowment for the Dominican nuns, dating 19 November 1320). On Elizabeth's endowments in favour of churches and monasteries, see Božena Kopičková, *Eliška Přemyslovna: královna česká 1292–1330* (Prague, 2008), esp. 91–119; Zdeněk Vašek, 'Die Stiftungen Johanns von Luxemburg und seiner Verwandtschaft zugunsten der böhmischen Kirche', *Hémecht* 66 (2014), 5–24.

codified by her ancestors.[33] John, on the other hand, received the polemic label of the newcomer king, or as his son Charles IV would later phrase it in his autobiography: 'But you are a foreigner' ('vos autem estis advena').[34]

Almost a century later, astonishingly similar discourses were applied when another heiress, now representing the Luxembourg family, ascended the Hungarian throne together with her 'foreign' husband: Elizabeth of Luxembourg, daughter of Sigismund of Luxembourg, Holy Roman Emperor as well as King of the Romans, King of Bohemia, and King of

---

33   For comparative findings for Joan of Brabant, see Margue, 'L'épouse au pouvoir', 302–7.

34   Vita Caroli Quarti. *Die Autobiographie Karls IV: Einführung, Übersetzung und Kommentar von Eugen Hillebrand* (Stuttgart, 1979), ch. 8, 114–29, at 120–2: 'Domine, provideatis vobis, filius vester habet in regno multa castra et magnam sequelam ex parte vestri; unde si diu ita prevalebit, expellet vos, quando voluerit; nam et ipse heres regni et de stirpe regum Boemie est, et multum diligitur a Boemis, vos autem estis advena' ('My lord, watch out for yourself, your son has many strongholds in the Kingdom and a large following among your entourage: therefore, if he persists in this manner for a long time, he will expel you whenever he wants to; for he himself is both the heir to the Kingdom and a descendant of the royal house of Bohemia, and is much liked by the Bohemians, but you are a foreigner'). See also Eva Schlotheuber, 'Die "größtmögliche Veränderung" (*maxima mutacio*) des Königreiches Böhmen: Peter von Zittau und die politische Wende Johanns von Luxemburg', in Magdaléna Nespěšná Hamsíková, Jana Peroutková and Stefan Scholz (eds), *Ecclesia docta: Společenství ducha a umění. K životnímu jubileu profesora Jiřího Kuthana* (Prague, 2016), 105–29, the recent study by Pierre Monnet, *Karl IV.: Der europäische Kaiser* (Darmstadt, 2021), and Christa Birkel, 'Vos autem estis advena: John of Luxembourg and the Political Argument of Foreignness in Fourteenth-Century Bohemia', *Historical Studies on Central Europe* 2:2 (2022), 5–21. The distinction between Bohemian-born and 'foreign' kings is also attested by the following entry to the *Annales Bohemiae brevissimi*, ed. G.H. Pertz (MGH Scriptores 17), (Hannover, 1861), 719–21, at 721: 'Reges Boemie naturales et regine ipsorum: Rex Przemyssl Ottokarus Boemie; regina Constancia uxor sua. Rex Wenceslaus Boemie; regina Cunegundis uxor sua. Rex Ottokarus Boemie; regina Cunegundis uxor sua. Rex Wenceslaus Boemie; regina Guta uxor sua. Rex Wenceslaus Boemie; regina Phiolta uxor sua. Alienigene: Rudolphus dux Austrie; regina Elizabeth uxor sua. Henricus dux Carinthie; regina Anna uxor sua. Iohannes comes de Luczlburg; regina Elizabeth uxor sua. Iohannis filius Wenceslaus, qui post Karolus quartus imperator nominatus' ('The native-born Kings of Bohemia and their queens: King Przemyssl Ottokar of Bohemia; Queen Constance his wife. King Wenceslas of Bohemia; Queen Cunegundis his wife. King Ottokar of Bohemia; Queen Cunegundis his wife. King Wenceslas of Bohemia; Queen Guta his wife. King Wenceslas of Bohemia; Queen Phiolta his wife. Foreign-born: Rudolph Duke of Austria; Queen Elizabeth his wife. Henry Duke of Carinthia; Queen Anne his wife. John Count of Luxembourg; Queen Elizabeth his wife. John's son Wenceslas who later was called Charles IV, Emperor'). On the *Annales*, see Michael Müller, *Die Annalen und Chroniken im Herzogtum Bayern 1250–1314* (München, 1983), 164–7.

Hungary, and her husband Albert of Habsburg. Elizabeth, who was born around 1409, was the only child of Sigismund and his wife Barbara of Cilli (c. 1390/95–1451).[35] At the age of two, Elizabeth was betrothed to Albert of Habsburg on the initiative of Sigismund, who thereby built on earlier (fourteenth-century) dynastic agreements between the Luxembourgs and the Habsburgs. In 1421, a formal marriage contract and complementary inheritance agreements reinforced the earlier settlements, and their legal terms once more exposed Sigismund as a player with foresight: Elizabeth should succeed her father in Bohemia, Moravia, and Hungary only if Sigismund fathered no more sons. Accordingly, Elizabeth was addressed as Sigismund's 'rightful heir and successor in all of our [i.e., Sigismund's] kingdoms, principalities and dominions'.[36]

In 1437 this exact situation arose when Sigismund died without having left any other children: Elizabeth and Albert, who had married amidst the Hussite Wars in 1421, were now accepted as king and queen by the Hungarian nobles and crowned in January 1438; a similar process followed in Bohemia, where Albert received the crown in summer 1438. What sounds straightforward at first was actually the result of a tough negotiation process: in the run-up to their Hungarian coronation, the couple had to endure significant conflicts with the Hungarian nobility and town representatives, and twice were forced to consent to certain conditions in exchange for their elevation to the throne.[37] It is noteworthy that the first document was issued in the couple's name: in a charter dating from December 1437 (so before the Hungarian coronation), Albert and Elizabeth promised to respect and maintain the ancient laws and privileges

---

35 On Barbara, see Daniela Dvořaková, *Barbara von Cilli: Die schwarze Königin (1392–1451). Die Lebens-geschichte einer ungarischen, römisch-deutschen und böhmischen Königin* (Frankfurt, 2017), and the recent English translation, *Barbara of Cilli (1392–1451): A Hungarian, Holy Roman, and Bohemian queen* (Leiden/Boston, 2021); see also the subsequent footnotes.

36 '… und wann die vorgenannte Elizabeth noch aller unserr kunigreich, furstentume und herschefte rechte geerbe und nachfolgerynne ist …' (inheritance agreement of 28 September 1421, no. 6, in Petr Elbel, Stanislav Bárta and Wolfram Ziegler, 'Die Heirat zwischen Elisabeth von Luxemburg und Herzog Albrecht V. von Österreich: Rechtliche, finanzielle und machtpolitische Zusammenhänge (mit einem Quellenanhang)', in Paweł Kras and Martin Nodl (eds), *Manželství v pozdním středověku: Rituály a obyčeje* (Prague, 2014), 79–152, at 145–7, quote at 146. In case Sigismund would father further daughters, Elizabeth would either be allocated one of the kingdoms or she might select herself. See also Heimann, 'Herrscherfamilie und Herrschaftspraxis'.

37 On the Hungarian succession conflicts, see the new findings by Daniela Dvořaková, 'Smrť Žigmunda Luxemburského a nástup Albrechta Habsburského na uhorský trón', *Historický časopis* 69 (2021), 27–47. See also her recent study on Elizabeth's reign: Daniela Dvořáková, *Pod vládou ženy* (Budmerice, 2021).

of the kingdom and the nobility. Elizabeth and Albert called themselves *rex electus* and *regina electa*, thereby underlining that the nobles' consent to their succession weighed heavier than their dynastic claims. Two other commitments draw attention to argumentative mechanisms that (in a similar manner) are known to us already from the fourteenth-century Bohemian example: Elizabeth and Albert promised to appoint only Hungarian-born individuals to offices and not to marry off their daughters without prior consultation of the nobles and the inhabitants of the realm.[38] Two years later, Albert was forced to repeat these promises, because his long absence from Hungary and a riot in Buda (German: Ofen) culminating in the king's imprisonment had caused severe discontent among the nobles. Among the articles already mentioned, one passage particularly refers to Queen Elizabeth, obliging her as the heiress to also do without foreigners in her court: 'Then, that provision for the most serene princess lady Queen Elizabeth and for the preservation of the honour of her station, whence she is the heir of this kingdom, should be made wherever she wishes in the kingdom; with this exception, that the lady queen should not have the power of conferring her own honours and offices on strangers and foreigners, but only on inhabitants of this kingdom, whomever she prefers, and of removing these from them according to her own will.'[39]

---

38 Document from 17/31 December 1437, no. 8a, in János M. Bak, *Königtum und Stände in Ungarn im 14.–16. Jahrhundert* (Wiesbaden, 1973), 136–8, quote at 137: 'Item alienigenis et forensibus hominibus cuiuscumque nationis et linguagie officia in ipso regno non committemus, ne castra, fortalitia, metas[,] possessiones, honores, prelaturas, baronias absque consolio consiliariorum nostrorum Hungarie conferemus … Item supra maritatione filiarum nostrarum agemus secundum consilia nostrorum consanguiueorum [*sic*], nostrorum consiliariorum et aliarum terrigenarum nostrarum' ('Also we shall not commit offices to foreign-born people or foreigners from whatever genealogical or language-related background in this [same] Kingdom, or confer castles, fortifications, borderlands, estates, honours, prelateships or baronies on them without consulting our counsellors from Hungary … Also concerning the marriages of our daughters, we shall act according to the council of our own blood relatives, our counsellors and of the other women born in this land').
39 See János M. Bak, *Online Decreta Regni Mediaevalis Hungariae. The Laws of the Medieval Kingdom of Hungary* (Logan, Utah, 2019). Online: https://digitalcommons.usu.edu/lib_mono/4 [accessed 22 March 2023], Law of King Albert of 29 May 1439, 497–517, here art. 12 at 500 (English translation by the editors at 509): 'Item quod dispositio pro serenissima principe domina Elizabeth regina et eius status honoris conservatione ex quo est heres huius regni, fiat ubicunque vult in regno, sic tamen, quod ipsa domina regina honores et officiolatus suos non extraneis et alienigenis, sed incolis huius regni, quibuscunque maluerit, conferendi et collatos, dum sibi placuerit, ab eis secundum suum arbitrium habeat facultatem auferendi.' On the political background of the 1439 crisis, see Bak, *Königtum und Stände*, 39–41; Martyn Rady, 'Government of Medieval Buda', in Balázs Nagy, Martyn Rady, Katalin Szende and András Vadás (eds), *Medieval Buda in Context* (Leiden, 2016), 303–21, esp.

Comparable to the semantics applied in Bohemia, the Hungarian document distinguished between 'foreigners' (*alienigenae, forenses, extranei*) as defined by origin and language on the one hand and native inhabitants of the Hungarian realm (*incolae regni, terrigenae*) on the other hand.[40] On various levels, then, Elizabeth's political claims based on dynastic arguments somehow seem to have merged with the nobles' rights: together, they advanced to be the decisive political voice, guaranteeing the realm's welfare and safeguarding its important dynastic currency (the couple's children).

REPRESENTING FAMILY, REALM, AND CROWN: FEMALE REGENTS

Elizabeth as the heiress of the Hungarian realm remained a pivotal figure in the political developments and debates of the following years. According to some (albeit highly provocative) narrative sources of the time, the queen was more accepted in Hungary than her husband. In his *De viris illustribus*, Enea Silvio Piccolomini (1405–64) gave a rather polemical explanation:

> Hungari enim eam honorabant, quia et linguam sciebat, et haeres regni fuerat, Albertum autem propterea susceperant, quia vir eius esset, nec amabant Teutonicum, praesertim Vngari sermonis nescium. Illa insuper mulier callida fuit et astuta, et in corpore femineo virilem gestabat animum, maritumque suum, quo volebat, trahebat.[41]

> [The Hungarians kept her in high esteem, because she was proficient in their language and because she was the heiress of the realm. Albert, however, was only accepted because he was her husband. They did not like him because of his German origin, and especially because he did not know the Hungarian

---

313–14; and on the context of Albert's reign, Julia Burkhardt, 'Albert II of Habsburg's Composite Monarchy (1437–1439) and its Significance for Central Europe', in Paul Srodecki, Norbert Kersken and Rimvydas Petrauskas (eds), *Unions and Divisions: New Forms of Rule in Medieval and Renaissance Europe* (Abingdon, 2023), 224–36.
40 See Burkhardt, 'Argumentative Uses'; for instructive methodological suggestions on the use of language in times of political conflict, see Jan Dumolyn and Jelle Haemers, '"A Bad Chicken Was Brooding": Subversive Speech in Late Medieval Flanders', *Past and Present* 214 (2012), 45–86.
41 *Enee Silvii Piccolomini postea Pii PP II De viris illustribus*, ed. Adrianus van Heck (Vatican City, 1991), at 58. On Piccolomini's points of view about Hungarian kings, see Enikő Csukovits, *Hungary and the Hungarians: Western Europe's View in the Middle Ages* (Rome, 2018), esp. 99–105.

language. Moreover, she was a clever and astute woman, and in
the body of a woman carried the spirit of a man, and usually
brought her husband to do what she wanted.]

Again, dynastic background and cultural identity come into play to shape forms of belonging and hence generate a greater extent of political acceptance.

Probably even more astonishing is the reversal of gendered models: while Albert appears to be weak and passive, Elizabeth is praised for her origin as well as her agency and assertiveness. Several factors might have contributed to this picture. In the years after their coronation, Elizabeth was almost continuously present in Hungary, while her husband spent a lot of time in Austria, more or less commuting from Vienna to either Bohemia or (to a lesser extent) Hungary. In these years, the couple shared political responsibilities in the region. Elizabeth – though of course the legitimate crowned queen herself – acted as regent for her husband in Hungary: together with the royal council, she took care of governmental affairs.[42] Several charters issued in the name of the queen testify to her crucial role as an arbitrator in legal disputes, to her authority in dispensing waivers for tax liabilities, or to her central role in the enlargement of the realm's fortifications.[43] Her power base consisted of a variety of towns and fortresses situated mainly in the northern part of Hungary.[44]

---

42 Elemér Mályusz, 'Az első Habsburg a magyar trónon. Albert király 1438–1439', *Aetas* (1994), 120–50; Daniela Dvořaková, 'Alžbeta Luxemburská, Žigmundova dcéra, v rokoch 1438–1442', *Historie – Otázky – Problémy* 3 (2011), 143–59.
43 In 1439, for example, Elizabeth took on the role of arbitrator after the Archbishop of Esztergom, the original arbitrator in the case, had died. She justified her decision with the legal traditions of her father and predecessor Sigismund and deduced from that her exclusive right to decide the dispute: 'Vnde cum iuxta quod nostrae declaratum est maiestati, vigore litterarum eiusdem quondam Domini Imperatoris, quarum serie discussioni [*sic*] personali suae praesentiae praefata causa deducta extiterat, nullus alter, quam Maiestas nostra deinceps se de iucidio et tractationi huiusmodi causae intromittere poterit, aut quomodolibet iudicialiter discutere de eadem […] Nos enim vna cum praedictis Baronibus nostris tandem maturius deliberare intendimus […]' ('Therefore, since – besides what is stated by force of a letter by the same deceased Lord Emperor in the aforementioned matter which had been resolved by him personally in a series of discussions – none other except our Majesty will be able to intervene in the judgement and treatment of a matter of this kind, or discuss it from a juridical point of view in whichever way […] Therefore we alone together with our aforementioned Barons intend eventually to discuss this matter at greater length […]'). *Codex diplomaticus Hungariae ecclesiasticus ac civilis, Vol. XI Ab anno 1438–1440*, ed. Georgius Fejér (Buda, 1844), no. CLXVIII, 330–1. For further examples, see Burkhardt, 'Erbe der Frauen'.
44 Renáta Skorka and Boglárka Weisz, 'The Town and the Widow: The Journey of Elisabeth of Luxembourg to Pozsony', *Mesto a dejiny* 8 (2019), 6–21, <https://www.

This model was by no means new: whenever a king was absent, minor in years, or in bad health, female rulers – the king's mother or the king's wife for example – could act as regents, sometimes just in an informal, pragmatical way, at other times as official appointees entrusted with full political authority.[45] During the reign of Sigismund of Luxembourg, there had been different phases of female regency: when Sigismund was absent from the Kingdom of Hungary between 1412 and 1419 due to obligations in the Holy Roman Empire and elsewhere in Europe, his wife Barbara of Cilli governed the realm together with the royal council.[46] When his brother Wenceslas IV of Bohemia (1361–1419) died, Sigismund made his sister-in-law Sophia of Wittelsbach regent of the Kingdom of Bohemia.[47]

Elizabeth's case was, however, different: with her, of course, being the legitimate crowned queen, she reigned not only as regent for her husband while he still lived (*vivente rege*), but also continued to do so for her yet-to-be-born son when Albert quite suddenly died from dysentery in October 1439 on his journey back home from the Serbian front against the Ottomans.[48] Albert left two daughters (Anna and Elizabeth) and his

---

upjs.sk/public/media/22368/MaD_2019_2_Skorka-Weisz.pdf> [accessed 22 March 2023].

45 Cf. Julia Burkhardt, 'Selbstverständnis und Herrschaftspraxis schlesischer Regentinnen im 13. Jahrhundert', in Gabriela Signori and Claudia Zey (eds), *Regentinnen und andere Stellvertreterfiguren: Vom 10. bis zum 15. Jahrhundert* (Berlin, 2023), 157–76; Bettina Elpers, *Regieren, erziehen, bewahren: Mütterliche Regentschaften im Hochmittelalter* (Frankfurt, 2003). See also the contributions in Franca Varallo (ed.), *In assenza del re: le reggenti dal XIV al XVII secolo (Piemonte ed Europa)* (Florence, 2008). For examples from late medieval France, see Tracy Adams, 'Christine de Pizan, Isabeau of Bavaria, and Female Regency', *French Historical Studies* 32 (2009), 1–32; Earl Jeffrey Richards, 'Political Thought as Improvisation: Female Regency and Mariology in Late Medieval French Thought', in Jacqueline Broad (ed.), *Virtue, Liberty, and Toleration: Political Ideas of European Women, 1400–1800* (Dordrecht, 2007), 1–22; and with an instructive iconographical approach to Byzantine examples, Branislav Cvetković, 'Iconography of Female Regency: An Issue of Methodology', *Niš & Byzantium* 10 (2012), 405–14.

46 Márta Kondor, 'Absente rege: Luxemburgi Zsigmond magyarországi vikáriusai (1414–1419)', in Tamás Fedeles, Márta Font and Gergely Kiss (eds), *Kor-szak-határ: A Kárpát-medence és a szomszédos birodalmak (900–1800)* (Pécs, 2013), 119–38; Norbert C. Tóth, 'A király helyettesítése a konstanzi zsinat idején: Az ország ügyeinek intézői 1413–1419 között', in Attila Bárány and László Pósán (eds), *Causa unionis, causa fidei, causa reformationis in capite et membris: Tanulmányok a konstanzi zsinat 600. évfordulója alkalmából* (Debrecen, 2014), 289–313; see also Fößel, 'Barbara von Cilli', 104–9.

47 Daniela Dvořáková, 'Žofia Bavorská a Žigmund Luxemburský: K bratislavskému pobytu českej kráľovnej', *Studia Medievalia Bohemica* 1 (2010), 3–42.

48 On Albert's reign, see Burkhardt, 'Albert II of Habsburg's Composite Monarchy'; on his death and contemporary reactions to it, see Rudolf J. Meyer, *Königs- und*

pregnant wife. In this rather dramatic situation, Queen Elizabeth once more demonstrated her talent for pragmatic politics: either convinced that she would give birth to a son, or willfully calculating with the political risk, she refused to marry the young King of Poland as suggested by some nobles. Instead, she had her maid Helene Kottanner (c. 1400–52) steal the Holy Crown of Hungary and fled with her children and the crown to Frederick of Habsburg (since 1440 King of the Romans), who was responsible for the children as guardian.[49] Understandably, this episode received broad attention in both historical and literary studies, not least because Helene Kottanner herself authored an account of the events in German (*Die Denkwürdigkeiten der Helene Kottannerin*) and depicted motives, doubts, and agency of both women in astonishing detail.[50] In

---

Kaiserbegräbnisse im Spätmittelalter: Von Rudolf von Habsburg bis zu Friedrich III. (Köln, Weimar, Wien, 2000), 159–74; Christian Jörg, 'Trauerfeierlichkeiten für Kaiser Sigismund und König Albrecht II.: Gedanken zu den Leistungen städtischer Führungsgremien und Gemeinschaften für den verstorbenen Herrscher während des Spätmittelalters', in Frank Hirschmann and Gerd Mentgen (eds), *'Campana pulsante convocati': Festschrift anläßlich der Emeritierung von Prof. Dr. Alfred Haverkamp* (Trier, 2005), 249–80; Wilhelm Hauser, 'Der Trauerzug beim Begräbnis des deutschen Königs Albrecht II. († 1439)', *Adler: Zeitschrift für Genealogie und Heraldik* 7 (1965), 191–5.

49 On Helene Kottanner, see Julia Burkhardt and Christina Lutter, *Ich, Helene Kottannerin: Die Kammerfrau, die Ungarns Krone stahl* (Darmstadt, 2023); Maya C. Bijvoet, 'Helene Kottanner: The Austrian Chambermaid', in Katharina M. Wilson (ed.), *Women Writers of the Renaissance and Reformation* (Athens, GA and London, 1987), 327–49; Albrecht Classen, *The Power of a Woman's Voice in Medieval and Early Modern Literatures: New Approaches to German and European Women Writers and to Violence Against Women in Premodern Times* (Berlin and New York, 2007), ch. 9, 309–37. On the historical background, see Andreas Rüther, 'Königsmacher und Kammerfrau im weiblichen Blick: Der Kampf um die ungarische Krone (1439/40) in der Wahrnehmung von Helene Kottanner', in Jörg Rogge (ed.), *Fürstin und Fürst: Familienbeziehungen und Handlungsmöglichkeiten von hochadeligen Frauen im Mittelalter* (Stuttgart, 2004), 225–46; Dorothee Rippmann, 'Königsschicksal in Frauenhand: Der "Kronraub" von Visegrád im Brennpunkt von Frauenpolitik und ungarischer Reichspolitik', in Jens Flemmig et al. (eds), *Lesarten der Geschichte: Ländliche Ordnungen und Geschlechterverhältnisse. Festschrift für Heide Wunder zum 65. Geburtstag* (Kassel, 2004), 377–401; James Ross Sweeney, 'The Tricky Queen and Her Clever Lady-in-Waiting: Stealing the Crown to Secure Succession, Visegrád 1440', *East Central Europe* 20–3 (1993–6), 87–100.

50 For a translation into modern German and an interpretation of the text, see Burkhardt and Lutter, *Ich, Helene*; a new critical edition of the text (including a commentary) is in preparation by the same authors. See also the previous critical edition, Karl Mollay (ed.), *Die Denkwürdigkeiten der Helene Kottannerin (1439–1440)* (Vienna, 1971), and the English translation, Maya Bijvoet-Williamson, *The Memoirs of Helene Kottanner (1439–1440)* (Cambridge, 1998). On the text, see Elisabeth Gruber, Christina Lutter and Oliver Jens Schmitt (eds), *Kulturgeschichte*

February 1440, Elizabeth gave birth to the long-awaited son and heir, and had him christened 'Ladislas' (commonly identified by his cognomen Postumus). Strategically, this was clever in two respects: St Ladislas (c. 1042/6–95) was not only one of the Hungarian saints particularly admired by her own father Sigismund; he was also one of the most important saints of the Hungarian Árpád dynasty.[51] Young Ladislas' name therefore was a self-confident statement of dynastic continuity in Hungary. A few months later, Elizabeth had her son crowned with the Holy Crown at Székesfehérvár (German: Stuhlweißenburg), the traditional Hungarian place of coronation.[52]

Still, Elizabeth's opponents who favoured a union with Poland in order to have a king capable of facing the Ottoman advance would not lag behind: a delegation went to Cracow, elected the Polish king Władysław III (1424–40), and accompanied him to Hungary, where he was crowned

---

der Überlieferung im Mittelalter: Quellen und Methoden zur Geschichte Mittel- und Südosteuropas (Vienna, 2017), 427–34; Horst Wenzel, 'Zwei Frauen rauben eine Krone: Die denkwürdigen Erfahrungen der Helene Kottannerin (1439–1440) am Hof der Königin Elisabeth von Ungarn (1409–1442)', in Regina Schulte (ed.), Der Körper der Königin: Geschlecht und Herrschaft in der höfischen Welt (Frankfurt, 2002), 27–48; English version: 'How Two Ladies Steal a Crown: The Memoirs of Helene Kottannerin (1439–40) at the Court of Queen Elisabeth of Hungary (1409–42)', in Regina Schulte (ed.), The Body of the Queen: Gender and Rule in the Courtly World, 1500–2000 (New York and Oxford, 2006), 19–42; Heike Sahm, 'Lizenz zum Stehlen: Helene Kottanners Denkwürdigkeiten (um 1450)', Euphorion 104 (2010), 295–316; Barbara Schmid, 'Raumkonzepte und Inszenierung von Räumen in Helene Kottanners Bericht von der Geburt und Krönung des Königs Ladislaus Postumus (1440–1457)', in Ursula Kundert and Ralf Eger (eds), Ausmessen – darstellen – inszenieren: Raumkonzepte und die Wiedergabe von Räumen in Mittelalter und früher Neuzeit (Zürich, 2007), 113–38.

51 See above all the magisterial study by Gábor Klaniczay, Holy Rulers and Blessed Princesses: Dynastic Cults in Medieval Central Europe (Cambridge, 2002), esp. 173–94. See also Illés Horváth, 'Szent László kultusza Luxemburgi Zsigmond uralkodói reprezentációjában', Aetas 32 (2017), 128–44; Doina Elena Crăciun, 'From "Adoption" to "Appropriation": The Chronological Process of Accommodating the Holy Hungarian Kings in the Noble Milieus of Late Medieval Hungary', in Thomas F. Head and Gábor Klaniczay (eds), Cuius Patrocinio Tota Gaudet Regio: Saints' Cults and the Dynamics of Regional Cohesion (Zagreb, 2014), 313–34; Ernő Marosi, 'Der heilige Ladislaus als ungarischer Nationalheiliger: Bemerkungen zu seiner Ikonographie im 14.-15. Jh.', Acta Historiae Artium Hungaricae 33 (1987), 211–56.

52 Cf. Gyula Siklósi, 'Székesfehérvár', in Julianna Altmann et al. (eds), Medium regni: Medieval Hungarian Royal Seats (Budapest, 1996), 43–88. On the coronation rite, see Dušan Zupka, Ritual and Symbolic Communication in Medieval Hungary under the Árpád Dynasty (1000–1301) (Leiden, 2016), 35–69; see also János M. Bak and Géza Pálffy, Crown and Coronation in Hungary 1000–1916 A.D. (Budapest, 2020).

in July 1440.⁵³ While it was easy to celebrate this coronation as well, the Holy Crown was missing. The nobles therefore issued a decree declaring that the power of the crown rested in the 'will of the people of the realm' and could therefore be transferred to another material crown.⁵⁴ With this coronation, Hungary had two kings with legitimate claims: on Ladislas' side dynastic claims from a Luxembourg-Habsburg lineage, combined with a coronation with the right crown at the right place, and on Władysław's side claims based on an election by the Hungarian nobles as well as a coronation justified, however, with a legal construct about the crown and the right place.

The widowed queen, however, obviously had no intention of giving in. While her three children were in Austria in their guardian's care, Elizabeth remained in Hungary, fighting for her son's rights: she pledged not only the Holy Crown, but also her own properties to raise funds (just as her father had done), hired mercenaries such as Jan Jiskra (c. 1400–69/70) to strengthen her position in the north of the realm, and tolerated Jiskra's policy of confiscating incomes. In 1441, military confrontations began. According to contemporary reports, Elizabeth fiercely defended her hereditary rights, 'terrifying almost the entire realm' with her demeanour and policy.⁵⁵ Still, similarly to her father

---

53 Ádám Novák and Balázs Antal Bacsa, 'Polish and Hungarian Lords in the Entourage of Władysław, King of Poland and Hungary 1440–1442', *Studia z Dziejów Średniowiecza* 23 (2019), 183–98; Ádám Novák, 'Additions to the Itinerary and Seals of King Władysław I of Hungary in the Light of Recent Hungarica Research', in Attila Bárány and Balázs Antal Bacsa (eds), *The Jagiellonians in Europe: Dynastic Diplomacy and Foreign Relations* (Debrecen, 2016), 41–55.
54 Coronation patent of King Wladislas [sic] I of Hungary, 20 July 1440, in Bak, *Online Decreta*, 532–41. See also János M. Bak, 'Ein – gescheiterter – Versuch Ungarn zum Ständestaat zu verwandeln', in Paweł Kras and Agnieszka Januszek (eds), *Ecclesia, cultura, potestas: Studia z dziejów kultury i społeczeństwa. Księga ofiarowana Siostrze Profesor Urszuli Borkowskiej OSU* (Cracow, 2006), 451–64; Julia Burkhardt, 'Frictions and Fictions of Community: Structures and Representations of Power in Central Europe, c. 1350–1500', *The Medieval History Journal* 19 (2016), 191–228.
55 These at least were the words of István Rozgonyi (died c. 1440), court officer (*ispán/comes*) of Preßburg county (Latin: *Comitatus Posoniensis*), in a letter to the city of Preßburg, dated April 1440, in Ernst Birk, 'Beiträge zur Geschichte der Königin Elisabeth von Ungarn und ihres Sohnes König Ladislaus MCCCCXL-MCCCCLVII', *Quellen und Forschungen zur vaterländischen Geschichte, Literatur und Kunst* 1 (1849), 209–58, at 214, n. 2: 'Licet tamen ipsa domina regina eius maligni fecerit id consilio certo ipsius, sue S. signanterque filio suo et domino nostro magnum intulit odprobrium, quis enim nostrum tali sub cautela deinceps ausus est accedere ad suam Serenitatem, quoniam perterreri fecit quasi totum regnum sue S. facto in eodem' ('Although said Lady, the Queen, committed this evil by her own resolute council, she committed a grave injustice against her own Serene Highness and her son, our Lord, for who of us, when faced which such jeopardy, dared

Sigismund, she also had a good sense of the political realities of her time: after about two years of war and thanks to the initiative of a papal ambassador, Elizabeth and her opponent, the Polish-Hungarian king Władysław, met in person and came to a rather pragmatic agreement: Władysław's reign over Hungary was acknowledged, while Elizabeth maintained her own son's claims to the throne for the future.[56] Only a few days later (19 December 1442), Elizabeth died unexpectedly. She left her son Ladislas a highly meaningful inheritance: when King Władysław died during one of the most famous military campaigns against the Ottomans at the battlefield of Varna in 1444,[57] regnal rule over Hungary in the Luxembourg-Habsburg line of succession was an option again. Building on the claims that his mother had so passionately defended, Ladislas Postumus returned to Hungary and ruled the country as king from 1453 until his early death in 1457.[58]

COMMUNICATING THROUGH ART, LITERATURE, AND RELIGION: LUXEMBOURG WOMEN AS CULTURAL PATRONS

Elizabeth's case is revealing as to the political and legal conditions of regnal rule. With her constant references to the person of her father, her family, or their religious preferences, Elizabeth publicly demonstrated and communicated her understanding of dynastic continuity.

This draws attention to symbolic and representative elements of female rule, and invites us to identify possible patterns in deploying symbolic language as well as options for decoding their significance. In

---

afterwards to approach her Serene Highness, given that she caused almost the entire Kingdom to be terrified to death by what her Serene Highness had done here').
56   Novák and Bacsa, 'Polish and Hungarian Lords', 194; Dvořaková, 'Alžbeta Luxemburská', 153–9.
57   Krystyna Łukasiewicz, 'Deceptive Practices in Fifteenth Century Europe: The Case of Władysław III Jagiellon (Varnensis)', *The Polish Review* 57 (2012), 3–20; Paul Srodecki, 'Władysław III and the Polish-Hungarian Bulwark Topoi Against the Background of the Ottoman Tin the 15th Century', in Dániel Bagi et al. (eds), *Hungaro-Polonica: Young Scholars on Medieval Polish-Hungarian Relations* (Pécs, 2016), 327–56.
58   On the political background, see Julia Burkhardt, 'Ostmitteleuropa als politische Region: Österreich, Ungarn und Böhmen im 15. Jahrhundert', in Bernd Schneidmüller (ed.), *König Rudolf I. und der Aufstieg des Hauses Habsburg im Mittelalter* (Darmstadt, 2019), 393–410; on Ladislas' education in Austria, see David Papajík, 'O výchově a vzdělávání krále Ladislava Pohrobka', *Kultúrne dejiny* 1 (2015), 46–64; on his reign, David Papajík, *Ladislav Pohrobek: (1440–1457): Uherský a český král* (České Budějovice, 2016).

order to discuss ways and mechanisms of communicating through the sponsorship of art, literature, and religion, I use the rather general term 'cultural patronage'. The concept of patronage has been controversial in both medieval history and art history, especially since attempts to exactly attribute works of art to the specific initiative of a single person often reveal themselves as inconclusive.[59] The following section therefore attempts to outline the contexts and resources that allowed female rulers in the age of the Luxembourgs to act as cultural patrons. Their activities could range from providing financial or material support in favour of religious communities or craftsmen to equipping them with personal networks, commissioning the craftsmen's works, or putting them into a new symbolic context.

Key requirements for such activities were a specific interest in the cultural developments of the time and, of course, the necessary education to understand them. Medieval contemporaries expected female rulers not only to have exemplary individual dispositions of character, such as exhibiting fidelity, piety, modesty, and beauty, but also to be educated in a suitable habitus of cultural sponsorship that would enable them to perform their duties. Intriguing insight into contemporary ideas on gender relations and social norms is provided in the *Book about the Game of Chess* (*Knížky o hře šachové*) by the Bohemian lay theologian Thomas of Štítné (c. 1330–1409).[60] Building on the example of the game of chess, Thomas described the social importance of king and queen in society. According to him, the queen had to be a shining example for all women in the realm: 'It is proper for the Queen and her maids to read good books that can give advice and warning, so that they carry the Lord and noble-

---

59 See the contributions in Colum Hourihane (ed.), *Patronage, Power, and Agency in Medieval Art* (Princeton, 2013), and in Heather J. Tanner, Laura L. Gathagan and Lois Lyn Huneycutt (eds), *Medieval Elite Women and the Exercise of Power, 1100–1400: Moving Beyond the Exceptionalist Debate* (Cham, 2019). See also Elizabeth Carson Pastan, 'Patronage: A Useful Category of Art Historical Analysis?', in Colum Hourihane (ed.), *Routledge Companion to Medieval Iconography* (London, 2017), 340–55. See also Barbara J. Harris, *English Aristocratic Women and the Fabric of Piety, 1450–1550* (Amsterdam, 2018).

60 On the author, see Pavlína Rychterová, 'Pursuing the Truth: The Czech Lay Theologian Thomas of Štítné (*c.* 1330 – *c.* 1400) and His Delight in Doing Miscellanies', in Sabrina Corbellini, Giovanna Murano and Giacomo Signore (eds), *Collecting, Organizing and Transmitting Knowledge: Miscellanies in Late Medieval Europe* (Turnhout, 2018), 115-30; see also Winfried Baumann, *Die Literatur des Mittelalters in Böhmen: deutsch-lateinisch-tschechische Literatur vom 10. bis zum 15. Jahrhundert* (München, 1978), 217–22.

mindedness in their hearts; the books should also enlighten their minds about what is necessary, rebuke evil, and praise things that are good.'[61]

Several examples from representatives of the Luxembourg dynasty – both male and female – testify to this awareness that a good education, including languages and learned knowledge, was integral for good rule and dynastic representation: they collected books, established libraries, commissioned authors or artists to produce new works, or had scholars and religious people advise them on moral or religious matters, often enough in vernacular languages. It can be assumed with justification that both Luxembourg princes and princesses were educated in several languages and (though not always to the same degree) also in reading and writing; the close relationship of the Luxembourgs to the French royal court had a noticeable impact here.[62] Still, specific information about the education of women is scarce and can often only be reconstructed through tracing the women's personal networks, analyzing their book inventories, and reading their correspondence.

Fortunately, exceptions may sometimes prove the rule, and this applies in the present case, too. Sophia of Wittelsbach (1376–1428), the daughter of Duke John II of Bavaria and Catherine of Görz, had married King Wenceslas IV of Bohemia in 1389.[63] After Wenceslas' first marriage to Johanna of Bavaria (d. 1388), his second marriage – as Milena Bartlová rightfully underlined – again 'constituted one detail in the long run of

---

61 'Knížky o hře šachové', in Tomáš Štítný ze Štítného, *Knížky o hře šachové a jiné*, ed. František Šimek (Prague, 1959), 351–405, at 331: 'Slušie také králové i paniem velikým po múdrosti státi. A téť jest bázen Božie počátek, bez téť právě žádný múdr nenie. Slušie také králové i paniem velikým v dobrých knihách čísti, ješto učie a napomínají, aby Bóh byl v srdci a šlechetnost, a rozum v potřebném osvěcují, zlé hyzdie a dobré chválé.' See also Dvořáková, 'Barbara von Cilli', at 294–5, n. 47, and 41; and Robert Antonín, *The Ideal Ruler in Medieval Bohemia* (Leiden, 2017), 42–5.
62 Eva Schlotheuber, 'Die Bedeutung von Sprachen und gelehrter Bildung für die Luxemburgerherrscher', in Penth and Thorau (eds), *Rom 1312*, 353–71; Gerrit Deutschländer, 'Höfische Erziehung und dynastisches Denken: Das Beispiel der Luxemburger', in Robert Šimůnek and Uwe Tresp (eds), *Wege zur Bildung: Erziehung und Wissensvermittlung in Mitteleuropa im 13.-16. Jahrhundert* (Göttingen, 2016), 61–80.
63 On her life, see Božena Kopičková, *Česká královna Žofie: Ve znamení kalicha a kříže* (Vyšehrad, 2018); John M. Klassen, *Warring Maidens, Captive Wives, and Hussite Queens: Women and Men at War and at Peace in Fifteenth-Century Bohemia* (New York, 1999), 226–36; Thomas Krzenck, 'Sophie von Wittelsbach – eine Böhmenkönigin im Spätmittelalter', in Gerald Beyreuther, Barbara Pätzold and Erika Uitz (eds), *Fürstinnen und Städterinnen: Frauen im Mittelalter* (Freiburg, 1993), 65–87; Rudolf Urbánek, 'Královny Johana a Žofie', in *Královny, kněžny a velké ženy české* (Prague, 1941), 143–58.

political marriages between the Luxembourgs and the Wittelsbachs'.[64] Although Sophia lived in Bohemia, she never cut her relationship to her Bavarian family. On the contrary: she kept in touch with her brothers, dukes Ernest and William III of Bavaria, through writing letters, as an entire collection with correspondences testifies. The collection's contents document that, between 1422 and 1428, Sophia and her brothers exchanged almost 40 letters on various political and personal issues. As Daniela Dvořáková showed in her thorough documentation and critical analysis of the letters, emotional remarks by the queen about her financial situation have led to misinterpretations of Sigismund's policy in earlier research.[65] Still, the correspondence reveals Sophia not only as a woman who could read and write, but also as a well-connected, politically active figure who knew how to use her personal networks very convincingly and effectively.[66]

Sophia died in November 1428, and only a few days later her brothers sent a delegation to Bohemia in order to document her belongings and have them sent to Munich.[67] The process of compiling the necessary data required several days and was performed with the approval of Sigismund of Luxembourg, who obviously regarded himself responsible for the execution of Sophia's last will. The inventory contained 161 entries, diligently listing different objects that were found in Sophia's estate. Among them were precious objects made of gold and silver, religious items, cloth, and clothing. Some of these objects can be attributed to Sophia's patronage.[68] According to the inventory, Queen Sophia also owned more than a dozen books of unknown provenance, the majority of them written in vernacular

---

64 Milena Bartlová, 'Was Queen Sophia of Bavaria an Art Patron?', in Markéta Jarošová, Jiří Kuthan and Stefan Scholz (eds), *Prag und die großen Kulturzentren Europas in der Zeit der Luxemburger (1310-1437) / Prague and great cultural centres of Europe in the Luxembourgeois era (1310-1437)* (Prague, 2008), 623-34.
65 See the list of the letters (and references to earlier inventories) in Daniela Dvořáková, 'Regesta Sophiana (Príspevok k problematike stredovekej epistolografie)', *Studia Historica Tyrnaviensia* 11-12 (2011), 81-104, and Dvořáková, 'Žofia Bavorská', 29-41; see also Toni Aigner, Sophia von Bayern - Königin von Böhmen: Jan Hus und die Wenzelsbibel (Lindenberg i. Allgäu, 2021).
66 See also the example of Anne of Bohemia, who exchanged autograph letters with her brother, King Wenceslas IV of Bohemia. In a letter probably dating from 1384/5, she wrote about political developments in Hungary and Bohemia as well as England, where she was at the time; see Kristen L. Geaman, 'A Personal Letter Written by Anne of Bohemia', *English Historical Review* 128, no. 534 (2013), 1086-94, with an edition of the letter at 1094.
67 Letter of 25 November 1428, in Dvořáková, 'Regesta Sophiana', 99.
68 The inventory is edited in Jakub Vítovský, 'Lampa z postostalosti kráľovnej Žofie Bavorskej v Mestskom múzeu v Bratislave', *Ars* (1991), 45-58, edition at 54-8. On the objects attributed to Sophia's patronage, including a chandelier, see Bartlová, 'Was Queen Sophia', 624-5.

languages (Czech, German) and dealing with religious topics.[69] Amalie Fößel convincingly argued that ownership of these books does not say much about their usage: we do not know whether Sophia actually read the books, or was read to from them, nor what she thought of them – not least because the books listed in the inventory cannot be located today. Still, some general conclusions might be drawn: both the languages and the probable contents of the books seem to suggest Sophia was interested in the current debates about church reform, dominated by the Hussites.[70]

In regard to both possession and content of the books, Sophia of Wittelsbach has been compared to her sister-in-law Anne of Bohemia (1366–94), the sister of King Wenceslas IV, who married King Richard II of England in 1381.[71] Anne of Bohemia is well-known not only for her role as a humble and pious intercessor before her 'tyrannic' husband – contemporary and modern descriptions are noticeably full of (gendered) stereotypes.[72] Beyond that, Anne is said to have been a supporter of the

---

[69] See the pivotal study by Amalie Fößel, 'Bücher, Bildung und Herrschaft von Fürstinnen im Umkreis des Prager Hofes der Luxemburger', in Wolfgang Haubrichs and Patricia Oster (eds), *Zwischen Herrschaft und Kunst: Fürstliche und adlige Frauen im Zeitalter Elisabeths von Nassau-Saarbrücken (14.–16. Jh.)* (Saarbrücken, 2013), 313–30, esp. 322–5.

[70] Milena Bartlová and Buran Dušan, 'Comparing the Incomparable? Wenceslas IV and Sigismund, Their Queens, and Their Images', in Jiří Fajt and Andrea Langer (eds), *Kunst als Herrschaftsinstrument: Böhmen und das Heilige Römische Reich unter den Luxemburgern im europäischen Kontext* (Berlin, 2009), 368–76; Alfred Thomas, '"Die Wyclifsche": Frauen in der Hussitenbewegung', in Fritz Peter Knapp, Jürgen Miethke and Manuela Niesner (eds), *Schriften im Umkreis mitteleuropäischer Universitäten um 1400: Lateinische und volkssprachige Texte aus Prag, Wien und Heidelberg. Unterschiede, Gemeinsamkeiten, Wechselbeziehungen* (Leiden, 2004), 251–67; see also Klassen, *Warring Maidens*, 231–6.

[71] Suchý, 'England and Bohemia'. See also Kristen L. Geaman, *Anne of Bohemia* (London, 2021); Alfred Thomas, *The Court of Richard II and Bohemian Culture: Literature and Art in the Age of Chaucer and the Gawain Poet* (Cambridge, 2020); Lynn Staley, 'Anne of Bohemia and the Objects of Ricardian Kingship', in Jenny Adams and Nancy Mason Bradbury (eds), *Medieval Women and Their Objects* (Ann Arbor, 2017), 97–122; William M. Ormrod, 'Knights of Venus', *Medium Aevum* 73 (2004), 290–305.

[72] Kristen L. Geaman, 'Beyond Good Queen Anne: Anne of Bohemia, Patronage, and Politics', in Tanner, Gathagan and Huneycutt (eds), *Medieval Elite Women*, 67–89; Alfred Thomas, *Reading Women in Late Medieval Europe: Anne of Bohemia and Chaucer's Female Audience* (New York, 2015); Michael van Dussen, 'Three Verse Eulogies of Anne of Bohemia', *Medium Ævum* 78 (2009), 231–60; Elizabeth M. Biebel-Stanley, 'Sovereignty through the Lady: "The Wife of Bath's Tale" and the Queenship of Anne of Bohemia', in S. Elizabeth Passmore and Susan Carter (eds), *The English 'Loathly Lady' Tales: Boundaries, Traditions, Motifs* (Kalamazoo, 2007), 73–82.

English Reformer John Wyclif (1330–84), providing another link to Sophia of Wittelsbach.⁷³ Both women's interest in religious topics of their time (independent of reform trends) mirrors contemporary developments: since the time of Emperor Charles IV, religious writing had played an important part in the libraries and collections of the Luxembourgs (with a noticeable shift to vernacular and reform-oriented writings at the end of the fourteenth century). Several beautiful Books of Hours that were owned or commissioned by male or female Luxembourg rulers confirm these observations.⁷⁴

As mentioned earlier, the mere possession of books is a rather thin proof for hypotheses on possible usages; still, sources such as inventory lists or testaments inform us about these women's possessions and can at least convey to us a certain idea of their interests. Testaments typically reflect individual forms of commitment or support and thereby throw a particularly striking light on female agency.⁷⁵ As the last will of Elizabeth of Görlitz, Duchess of Luxembourg, shows, they were not necessarily also reflections of dynastic consciousness: her last will, dating from 28 July 1451 (hence six days before her death), lists several donations and endowments for churches and monasteries in Trier, where Elizabeth had spent the last years of her life; additional amounts of money were

---

73 Katherine Walsh, 'Lollardisch-hussitische Reformbewegungen in Umkreis und Gefolgschaft der Luxemburgerin Anna, Königin von England (1382–1394)', in Elisabeth Müller-Luckner and František Šmahel (eds), *Häresie und vorzeitige Reformation im Spätmittelalter* (Munich, 1998), 77–108; Anne Hudson, 'From Oxford to Bohemia: Reflections on the Transmission of Wycliffite Texts', *Studia Mediaevalia Bohemica* 2 (2010), 25–37; Anne Hudson, *Studies in the Transmission of Wyclif's Writings* (Aldershot, 2008).
74 Fößel, 'Bücher, Bildung und Herrschaft', 330; Lynn Elisabeth Claude, 'Die Frauen der luxemburgischen Dynastie und ihre Stundenbücher' (Diploma thesis, University of Vienna, 2015), http://othes.univie.ac.at/38599/ [accessed 22 March 2023]. See also Hans-Walter Stork, 'Frömmigkeit einer Fürstin: Das Gebetbuch der Elisabeth von Görlitz', in Embach (ed.), *Kontinuität und Wandel*, 253–81; John Harthan, *Stundenbücher und ihre Eigentümer: Die kostbar illustrierten Gebet- und Andachtbücher von Königen und Fürsten des späten Mittelalters, vorgestellt in 34 der berühmtesten Exemplare und gewürdigt in ihrer künstlerischen und religiösen Bedeutung* (Freiburg im Breisgau/Basel/Wien, 1989).
75 Maria Clara Rossi (ed.), *Margini di libertà: Testamenti femminili nel Medioevo. Atti del convegno internazionale (Verona, 23-25 ottobre 2008)* (Verona, 2010); Amalie Fößel, 'Testamente römischer Königinnen im mittelalterlichen Deutschen Reich', in Brigitte Kasten (ed.), *Herrscher- und Fürstentestamente im westeuropäischen Mittelalter* (Cologne, 2008), 393–414; Markwart Herzog and Cecilie Hollberg (eds), *Seelenheil und irdischer Besitz: Testamente als Quellen für den Umgang mit den 'letzten Dingen'* (Konstanz, 2007); Barbara Harris, *English Aristocratic Women, 1450–1550: Marriage and Family, Property and Careers* (Oxford, 2002).

named in favour of Elizabeth's household servants.⁷⁶ Instead of casting an image of an influential heiress and ruler, this testament tells us of a devout woman wishing to settle her affairs – an impression that matches the contemporary remarks on Elizabeth as an impoverished widow. As Schmid and Schmid have cogently argued, this makes it likely that her epitaph in Trier was not commissioned by the duchess herself but rather by some representative of her family. Yet the ornamental design with several coats of arms, as well as the inscription, attest to Elizabeth's political importance and dynastic ties: while one heraldic shield refers to her second husband (John of Bavaria), another combines the coats of arms of several territories, including Luxembourg, Brandenburg, and Bohemia. An inscribed banner commemorates her as 'Elizabeth of Görlitz, Duchess of Bavaria and Luxembourg, Countess of Chiny, daughter of the excellent lord John, Duke of Görlitz and Margrave of Brandenburg whose brother was Sigismund, Emperor of the Romans, King of Hungary and Bohemia etc.'⁷⁷ The focus, hence, is not on the humble Elizabeth as mirrored by her last will, nor on her marriages. Instead, the epitaph reminds viewers of Elizabeth's role as the heiress and ruler to the Duchy of Luxembourg and as a representative of the Luxembourg dynasty.

***

This article discussed roles, forms of agency, and impact of female rulers in the age of the Luxembourgs in a geographically and diachronically comparative perspective. In order to highlight different forms of activities, I analyzed women in different legal and social conditions: as heiresses between dynasty and country; as regents representing family, realm, and crown; and as patrons communicating through art, literature, and religion. A special focus was put on the social networks, political activities, dynastic representation, and *memoria* of the respective women. Case studies from

---

76 Franz-Xaver Würtz-Paquet (ed.), *Table chronologique des chartes & diplomes relatifs à l'histoire de l'ancien pays de Luxembourg*, vol. II, Publications de la Section historique de l'Institut grand-ducal de Luxembourg 29 (1874), 1–108, here no. 272, pp. 102–4. See also Schmid and Schmid, 'Elisabeth von Görlitz', 215–18.

77 Translation by this author of a part of the transcription provided in Schmid and Schmid, 'Elisabeth von Görlitz', 224: 'Hic pausat illustrissima d[omi]na Elisab[eta] de Gorlitcz Bavarie [et] lucze[n]b[ur]ge[n]s[is] ducissa comit[issa] / de thryni [Chiny] filia p[re]clarissimi d[omi]ni Joh[annis] duc[is] de gorlicz ac marchio[n]is bra[n]d[en]b[ur]g[en]s[is] Glo[r]iosissi[m]i / p[ri]ncipis Sigismu[n]di Ro[ma]no[rum] Imp[er]ator[is] ungarie ac bohomie *(sic)* r[e]g[is] [et] c[etera] utriusq[ue] p[are]nt[is] / germa[n]i q[uae] obiit A[nn]o d[omin]i M CCCC L primo t[er]cio nonas Augusti Cui[us] a[n]i[m]a req[ui]escat in pace a[m]en'; see also ibid., 218–49, for a closer analysis of the epitaph.

Bohemia and Hungary exposed the ambivalent position of the heiress between territory and family and revealed the complexity of political structures as well as the various layers of communication heiresses had to deal with during succession crises: while dynastic lineage and related elements such as continuity, suitability, and family ties remained significant, communities of nobles with their rights to elect or at least to formulate conditions for a succession also could not be ignored. The kingdoms of Bohemia and Hungary with their traditions of an influential nobility regarding themselves as the representatives of the realm might represent a particular case in this context. Nevertheless, the comparative approach taken in this study was able to highlight regional differences as well as common grounds, especially with regard to the forms and the impact of female patronage. Luxembourg women were revealed as exceptionally important protagonists of dynastic presence, giving physical embodiment to family networks and dynastic lineages across medieval Europe. Both the institutionalized and the informal expressions of their agency in politics, religion, and cultural patronage complemented the activities of their husbands and male relatives significantly.

CHAPTER 12

IMAGE-MAKING, IMAGE-BREAKING, AND THE LUXEMBOURG MONARCHY

LEN SCALES

On 10 August 1420, a force of Hussites led by the priest Václav Koranda attacked the Cistercian monastery of Aula regia (Königsaal / Zbraslav), a few hours' march to the south of Prague. Founded by the Přemyslid king Wenceslas II (r. 1278–1305), the house enjoyed close ties to the Bohemian royal family. In the abbey church, several sources agree, they opened the grave of the Luxembourg king Wenceslas IV, interred there just a year previously, and desecrated his corpse.[1] On one account, the king's decomposing body was placed on an altar, bedecked with a straw crown, and doused with beer.[2] After setting fire to the monastic

---

1 Frederick G. Heymann, *John Žižka and the Hussite Revolution* (Princeton, 1955, repr. New York, 1969), 167–8; Rudolf J. Meyer, *Königs- und Kaiserbegräbnisse im Spätmittelalter: Von Rudolf von Habsburg bis zu Friedrich III.* (Cologne, Weimar, and Vienna, 2000), 139–40.
2 Miloslav Kaňák and František Šimek (eds), *Staré letopisy: z rukopisu křižovnického* (Prague, 1959), 25, 51–2. Other accounts of Wenceslas' post-mortem mistreatment, with different details, are V. Novotný (ed.), *Kronika velmi pěkná o Janovi Žižkovi čeledínu krále Vácslava* (Prague, 1923), 16; Wilhelm Altmann (ed.), *Eberhart Windeckes Denkwürdigkeiten zur Geschichte des Zeitalters Kaiser Sigmunds* (Berlin, 1893), 133; J. Loserth (ed.), *Der Tractatus de Longevo Schismate des Abtes Ludolf von Sagan* (Vienna, 1880), 478–9. For a discussion of the significance of these acts (and scepticism about whether some of them occurred at all), see František

buildings, the rebels returned in triumph to Prague, some wearing in their hats fragments of dismembered religious images.[3]

It would be rash to place too much weight on the events in the abbey church at Aula regia, whatever may have been their precise course. Whether what appears as a blasphemous parody of the Eucharist (if it occurred at all) was connected in the perpetrators' minds with Wenceslas' descent from a monarch who, as we shall see, repeatedly paralleled his own royal body with Christ's is impossible to tell.[4] The iconoclasm of the Hussites is well enough known, after all.[5] So, too, is their targeting of rich monastic foundations, which reached a highpoint of destructive fervour in the summer of 1420.[6] In some instances, as here, the rebels' inhibitions were doubtless loosened by access to well-stocked monastic cellars. Nor need the targeting of a recently deceased member of the ruling Luxembourg dynasty appear surprising. The Hussites' main military opponent at the time was Sigismund, King of Hungary and of the Romans and claimant to the Bohemian crown, who was not only a son of the emperor Charles IV (r. 1346/7–78) but half-brother to Wenceslas.[7] Sigismund was also widely

---

Šmahel, 'Blasfemie rituálu? Tři pohřby krále Václava IV.', in Ladislav Soukup (ed.), *Pocta Karlu Malému k 65. narozeninám* (Prague, 1995), 133–43. While over-interpretation is unwise, it might be noted in passing that the Empire's late medieval rulers were raised up on an altar at the time of their election in Frankfurt: Michail A. Bojcov, 'Warum pflegten deutsche Könige auf Altären zu sitzen?', in Michail A. Bojcov and Otto Gerhard Oexle (eds), *Bilder der Macht in Mittelalter und Neuzeit: Byzanz, Okzident, Rußland* (Göttingen, 2007), 243–314.

3   *Vavřince z Březové kronika Husitská*, in Josef Emler (ed.), *Fontes rerum Bohemicarum*, 5 (Prague, 1893), 399. For the fluid boundary between iconoclasm and looting and general destructiveness, from a much more recent, better documented case, see Mary Vincent, 'The "Martyrdom of Things": Iconoclasm and its Meanings in the Spanish Civil War', *Transactions of the Royal Historical Society*, 6th series, 30 (2020), 141–63, esp. 144–5.

4   Also noteworthy here is Charles' strongly Eucharistic piety, which finds repeated emphasis in his autobiography: Balázs Nagy and Frank Schaer (eds), *Autobiography of Emperor Charles IV and his Legend of St. Wenceslas* (Budapest and New York, 2001), chs 1, 4, 5, pp. 2–10, 36–7, 46–9.

5   For Hussite 'iconoclasm' and its complexities and difficulties, see Kateřina Horníčková and Michal Šroněk (eds), *Umění české reformace (1380–1620)* (Prague, 2010), esp. chs 3, 4; Milena Bartlová, 'Understanding Hussite Iconoclasm', in Zdeněk David and David R. Holeton (eds), *Bohemian Reformation and Religious Practice*, vol. 7 (Prague, 2010), 115–26.

6   A list of monasteries attacked is provided by the chronicler Laurence of Březova: Emler (ed.), *Vavřince z Březové kronika Husitská*, 409; and see Wácslaw Wladiwoj Tomek, *Dějepis města Prahy*, vol. 4 (Prague, 1879), 94–5.

7   For the course of events in the summer of 1420, see František Šmahel, *Die hussitische Revolution*, vol. 2, trans. Alexander Patchovsky (Hannover, 2002), 1088–99.

blamed for the execution of Jan Hus, while under the king's protection at the Council of Constance in 1415. And the reputation of Wenceslas himself at the time of his death hardly stood higher among the Bohemian reformers than among their adversaries.[8]

Yet the post-mortem dishonouring of King Wenceslas, whatever may have been its specific occasion, does not stand alone. While it is hard to discern, and no doubt misguided to seek, a political pattern in the general picture of Hussite attacks on religious foundations and their contents, scattered references in the sources remain suggestive. Other Luxembourg tombs appear to have been singled out.[9] The Austrian chronicler Thomas Ebendorfer tells of a visit to Prague in 1433 during which he viewed the tomb of Charles IV in St Vitus Cathedral, observing that the monument had been damaged in three places by the 'fury' of certain persons.[10] It is impossible to know whether Charles' mausoleum – about the design of which little is recorded – was deliberately targeted or a mere accidental victim of the recent disorders.[11] What is certain, however, is that no burial site articulated more powerfully the ideological claims of the Luxembourgs in Bohemia.

That Charles had been laid to rest in his Bohemian metropolis was itself a radical break with family tradition, which would have suggested burial in the western dynastic lands, at Clairefontaine or, like his father John, in Luxembourg minster.[12] Although perhaps the most ideologically imperialist of fourteenth-century emperors, he had likewise shunned burial

---

8   For Wenceslas' bad reputation, see Klaus Schreiner, '"Correctio principis": Gedankliche Begründung und geschichtliche Praxis spätmittelalterlicher Herrscherkritik', in František Graus (ed.), *Mentalitäten im Mittelalter* (Vorträge und Forschungen 35, Sigmaringen, 1987), 203–56, at 224–30.
9   The tomb of Charles' son John of Görlitz in St Vitus appears to have been destroyed during the Hussite era and his remains scattered: Lenka Bobková, 'Corona regni Bohemiae und ihre visuelle Repräsentation unter Karl IV.', in Jiří Fajt and Andrea Langer (eds), *Kunst als Herrschaftsinstrument: Böhmen und das Heilige Römische Reich unter den Luxemburgern im europäischen Kontext* (Berlin and Munich, 2009), 120–35, at 132, n. 99.
10 Thomas Ebendorfer, *Chronica regum Romanorum*, ed. Harald Zimmermann, 2 vols (*MGH Scriptores rerum Germanicarum, Nova series*, 18, Hannover, 2003), I.545–6.
11 For the little that is known about Charles' tomb, see Michael Viktor Schwarz, 'Felix Bohemia Sedes Imperii: Der Prager Veitsdom als Grabkirche Kaiser Karls IV.', in Michael Viktor Schwarz, *Grabmäler der Luxemburger: Image und Memoria eines Kaiserhauses* (Luxembourg, 1997), 123–53, at 129; Meyer, *Königs- und Kaiserbegräbnisse*, 117–18.
12 Olaf B. Rader, 'Aufgeräumte Herkunft: Zur Konstruktion dynastischer Ursprünge an königlichen Begräbnisstätten', in Ulrike Hohensee et al. (eds), *Die Goldene Bulle: Politik – Wahrnehmung – Rezeption*, 2 vols (Berlin, 2009), I.403–30 (here 412).

in the mausoleum of his forebears in the Reich, at Speyer on the Rhine.[13] The location of his tomb, within the new gothic choir of St Vitus, placed him instead at the centre of a potent matrix of Bohemian sacral-regnal symbolism which he himself had been centrally involved in devising.[14] Ranged around him in the choir were the remains of Bohemia's patrons, Saints Vitus, Adalbert, and – the object of Charles' special devotion, patronage, and imitation – Wenceslas. Close by was also the shrine to the sixth-century Burgundian martyr-king Sigismund, whose relics Charles had brought to Prague, whose cult he had promoted, and whose name was borne by the heir to the kingdom, the Hussites' adversary.[15] Surrounding Charles in the recently completed choir apses, beneath magnificent, paired effigies from the Parler workshop which emphasized both their sacral and monarchical qualities, lay his maternal ancestors, the Přemyslid kings.[16] To attack and deface Charles' tomb would therefore have been symbolically to strike at the heart of the Luxembourgs' titles to Bohemia and visibly to negate the consequences of their rule there.

Whether any such programmatic assault upon the dynasty through political iconoclasm was ever intended or implemented is impossible to establish with certainty, and this chapter's aims are more modest, though also broader. It is argued in what follows that the extensive programmes of dynastic and monarchical image-making sponsored particularly by Charles IV and his circle elicited a more complex range of responses than the positive ones which modern scholarship has identified and (more often) assumed. Among these reactions were hostility towards the monarch both despite and through engagement with the visible symbols of his rule, but also more nebulous forms of disfavour and unease. Attested instances of image-breaking form only a small part of the picture. This, however, lies in the nature of the subject-matter itself: there are good reasons both why the history of medieval political iconoclasm in general

---

13 For Speyer as burial site, see Caspar Ehlers, *Metropolis Germaniae: Studien zur Bedeutung Speyers für das Königtum (751–1250)* (Göttingen, 1996).
14 Paul Crossley and Zoë Opačić, 'Prague as a new capital', in Barbara Drake Boehm and Jiří Fajt (eds), *Prague: The Crown of Bohemia 1347–1437* (New Haven and London, 2005), 59–73, at 68; Paul Crossley, 'The Politics of Presentation: The Architecture of Charles IV of Bohemia', in Sarah Rees Jones et al. (eds), *Courts and Regions in Medieval Europe* (York, 2000), 99–172, at 162.
15 For Sigismund's cult, see Franz Machilek, 'Sigismund', in Stefan Samerski (ed.), *Die Landespatrone der böhmischen Länder: Geschichte – Verehrung – Gegenwart* (Paderborn, 2009), 223–30.
16 For the Přemyslid tombs, see Alfred Schädler, 'Peter Parler und die Skulptur des Schönen Stils', in Anton Legner (ed.), *Die Parler und der Schöne Stil 1350–1400*, 3 vols (Cologne, 1978), I.17–25.

is largely still to be written, and why so little is known about its course in the Luxembourg territories.

FRAGMENTS: THE PROBLEM OF POLITICAL ICONOCLASM

The nature of medieval visual culture ensured that it is now usually impossible to form a full picture of what once existed, what has been lost, and how any losses came about. In most cases, centuries of restoration, post-medieval remodelling, or outright obliteration have silently obscured any traces of earlier damage or disfigurement. Where, on the other hand, such damage is still to be seen – as, for example, on some of the bust effigies of members of the Luxembourg dynasty and court in the St Vitus triforium[17] – it is usually impossible to tell whether this attests to deliberate acts, or the wear and tear of centuries. We usually only know about acts of political iconoclasm at all where they left traces in the written record. Even outright destruction often leaves us grasping for clues. Why all but a tiny handful of the sumptuous painted manuscripts commissioned by Wenceslas were destroyed during the Hussite era lacks a certain answer.[18] All we have are hints such as those provided by Hus himself, who lamented that the painters of his day had abandoned portraying 'the martyrdom of holy virgins'.[19] Instead, they chose to depict 'the frolicking of foolish maidens and unchaste nudes' (the king's bathhouse attendants?) and 'figures of strange and unnatural constitution' (the rustic Wild Men who guard the Bohemian coat of arms in Wenceslas' de-luxe bible and Golden-Bull manuscript?).[20]

---

17 Johanna von Herzogenberg, 'Die Bildnisse Kaiser Karls IV', in Ferdinand Seibt (ed.), *Kaiser Karl IV.: Staatsmann und Mäzen* (Munich, 1978), 324–34, at 325–6. The breaking-off of the nose (a mutilation associated with the shaming of malefactors) of John of Luxembourg, the first member of the dynasty to wear the Bohemian crown, and the damage sustained by symbols of power such as Charles IV's crown, seem to suggest more than mere accident. These iconoclastic acts, if that is what they were, may however have been the work of seventeenth-century Calvinists rather than Hussites.
18 Josef Krása, *Die Handschriften König Wenzels IV.* (Prague, 1971), 17–19 with nn. 35–41 for further literature. On manuscript destruction, see Emler (ed.), *Vavřinec z Březové kronika Husitská*, 372, 404; *Staří letopisové česstí*, in František Palacký (ed.), *Scriptores rerum Bohemicarum*, 3 (Prague, 1829), 49. I am grateful to Maria Theisen for guidance on the fate of Wenceslas' manuscripts.
19 Jan Royt, 'Kirchenreform und Hussiten', in Jiří Fajt et al. (eds), *Karl IV. Kaiser von Gottes Gnaden: Kunst und Repräsentation des Hauses Luxemburg 1310–1437* (Munich and Berlin, 2006), 555–61, at 557–8.
20 On this matter, see also the essay by Gia Toussaint in this volume.

Political, as against religious, iconography was, moreover, at least in its more monumental forms, for most of the Middle Ages less ubiquitous than it had been in Antiquity or than it would become in post-medieval Europe.[21] It is, of course, quite misleading to draw any sharp distinction between medieval 'religious' and 'political' images. This, indeed, is demonstrated in exemplary fashion by the visual culture of the Luxembourg era: when what appear as purely devotional images and artefacts were broken and disfigured, we can never rule out that such acts were also directed against the dynasty, whose rulers have been celebrated by modern art historians as the patrons of such 'trademark' visual styles.[22] Nevertheless, it remains the case that throughout the medieval period, albeit less exclusively towards its close, the most costly, elaborate, and visually arresting artefacts were overwhelmingly made for cult purposes and sacred spaces.[23]

In societies where power was mediated principally through ritualized face-to-face encounters, the ruler's most important *imago* was his own person. Notwithstanding the role played by architecture and art objects, the principal media for the self-projection of the Luxembourg kings and emperors were ritual and performance, through which key groups among their subjects encountered them face-to-face. It is not without reason that the public staging of late medieval monarchy has been such a major focus of recent scholarship.[24] Iconoclasm was not therefore the generally natural first recourse of those seeking publicly to shame the monarch: other, more immediately arresting symbolic strategies were available. When Charles IV entered Cologne in February 1357, for example, the townspeople, probably unhappy at the implications for their liberties of the recently

---

21 Norbert Schnitzler, *Ikonoklasmus – Bildersturm: Theologischer Bilderstreit und ikonoklastisches Handeln während des 15. und 16. Jahrhunderts* (Munich, 1996), esp. 95–100.

22 See the examples of such disfigured devotional images in Horst Bredekamp, *Kunst als Medium sozialer Konflikte: Bilderkämpfe von der Spätantike bis zur Hussitenrevolution* (Frankfurt am Main, 1975), 298–9. For the fluid relationship between religious and political motives in iconoclastic acts, see Guy P. Marchal, 'Bildersturm im Mittelalter: Eine offene Frage', *Historisches Jahrbuch* 113 (1993), 255–82, esp. 258, 273–6.

23 For the importance of (to earlier ages, idolatrous) three-dimensional religious sculpture as characteristic of the later Middle Ages, see Jeffrey F. Hamburger, *The Visual and the Visionary: Art and Female Spirituality in Late Medieval Germany* (New York, 1998), 112.

24 For the Luxembourg era, see Gerrit Jasper Schenk, *Zeremoniell und Politik: Herrschereinzüge im spätmittelalterlichen Reich* (Cologne, Weimar, and Vienna, 2003); Bernd Schneidmüller, 'Inszenierungen und Rituale des spätmittelalterlichen Reichs: Die Goldene Bulle von 1356 in westeuropäischen Vergleichen', in Hohensee et al. (eds), *Die Goldene Bulle*, vol. 1, 261–97.

issued Golden Bull, received him in stony silence, withholding the joyful clamour that was expected to attend a royal entry.²⁵

Such images as *were* made, precisely on account of their sacral connotations, often enjoyed the protection of both strong stone walls and powerful taboos. While this might lend a special symbolic force to such iconoclastic acts as *did* occur (the destruction of dynastic tombs, for example),²⁶ it also helped ensure that such occurrences were infrequent. It is not hard to imagine how the rich furnishings of Karlštejn, with its multiple images of Charles IV, his queens, and his ancestors, would have fared at the hands of the Taborite armies; but inaccessibility and strong fortifications preserved the inner sanctum of Caroline sacral monarchy inviolate, throughout protracted siege.

There is no doubt that the later Middle Ages brought a rapid proliferation, particularly in public spaces in the towns, of mostly small-scale images of a clearly political kind, in the form of heraldic and para-heraldic devices.²⁷ In fourteenth-century Central Europe, the accession of new properties to the Luxembourg patrimony was signalled by the intrusion of the double-tailed Bohemian lion, with accompanying inscriptions, into town seals, and by its application to urban fortifications and façades.²⁸ The very ubiquity of heraldic signs must often have quickly obscured the effects of any assaults upon them: arms were readily put up, taken down, cleaned, repaired, or transformed with the flick of a painter's brush into other signs altogether.²⁹ They literally rose and fell along with the fortunes of their bearers and adherents.³⁰ A hostile poet recounts how the rebellious burghers of the episcopal town of Würzburg in 1400 had sought to place themselves directly under the lordship of the Reich.³¹ An

---

25 *Cölner Jahrbücher des 14. und 15. Jahrhunderts*, ed. H. Cardauns (*Die Chroniken der deutschen Städte vom 14. bis ins 16. Jahrhundert* 13, Leipzig, 1876), 37.

26 For the desecration of the Salian dynastic graves on the Harzburg by the rebellious Saxon peasantry in 1074, see W. Wattenbach (ed.), *Brunonis de Bello Saxonico Liber, Editio Altera* (*MGH Scriptores rerum Germanicarum* 15, Hannover, 1880), 23.

27 Marcus Meer, 'Cities, Citizens, and Their Signs: Heraldic Communication and Urban Visual Culture in Late Medieval England and Germany' (unpublished PhD thesis, Durham University, 2019).

28 Examples in Len Scales, 'Wenceslas Looks Out: Monarchy, Locality, and the Symbolism of Power in Fourteenth-Century Bavaria', *Central European History* 52 (2019), 179–210.

29 Ibid., 208.

30 For examples, see Claudius Sieber-Lehmann, *Spätmittelalterlicher Nationalismus: Die Burgunderkriege am Oberrhein und in der Eidgenossenschaft* (Göttingen, 1995), 50, 380.

31 For what follows, see R. von Liliencron (ed.), *Die historischen Volkslieder der Deutschen vom 13. bis 16. Jahrhundert*, vol. I (Leipzig, 1865, repr. Hildesheim, 1966),

envoy was dispatched to King Wenceslas, who showed himself supportive. The imperial eagle thus 'took flight' from Prague to Würzburg, where it was raised to a new perch on the *Rathaus* façade, to the piping of the town's musicians. Its stay was short-lived, however, and with the burghers' defeat and Wenceslas' deposition from the Empire, the poet imagines the eagle preparing to return to its, in his view, rightful masters, the Bavarian Wittelsbachs. Such heraldic comings and goings no doubt often occurred unrecorded. Yet the role of arms in encoding the honour of their dynastic or regnal subjects, and the centrality which they soon attained to parallel visual codes of *dis*honour, did make them particularly inviting media for expressing antipathy and disfavour.[32]

When Charles IV came to Passau in 1348, the imperial arms (*signa imperialia aquilarum*) set up to mark his lodgings were smeared with filth by partisans of the Wittelsbachs, with whom the king was in dispute.[33] In the towns of northern Italy, where the Empire had long been a source of bitter partisanship and factionalism, the eagle formed an obvious target for mistreatment in effigy.[34] Where surviving written records are more abundant than is usually the case in the northern territories of the Reich, we can attain a more detailed picture of the prevalence of heraldic iconoclasm. Yet even here it often remains a frustratingly incomplete one. In January 1382, at the time of King Richard II of England's marriage to Anne, Charles IV's daughter and sister to the reigning King Wenceslas, one Gottschalk of Westphalia was apprehended in the nocturnal act of defacing with a knife heraldic shields of the king and queen set up around the Conduit in London.[35] This followed an earlier attack on the same arms by an unknown perpetrator. Nothing, however, is recorded of Gottschalk's motives, of whether he harboured a particular animus against Anne's dynasty, whether his anger was directed more against the English king or some other object, or whether he was the mere agent of others.

---

pp. 175–7, vv. 760–4, 769–812, 871–962.

32   See generally Marcus Meer, 'Reversed, Defaced, Replaced: Late Medieval London and the Heraldic Communication of Discontent and Protest', *Journal of Medieval History* 45 (2019), 618–45.

33   Adolf Hofmeister (ed.), *Die Chronik des Mathias von Neuenburg* (*MGH Scriptores rerum Germanicarum, Nova series*, 4, Berlin, 1924), 260.

34   Lieselotte E. Saurma-Jeltsch, 'Zeichen des Reiches im 14. und frühen 15. Jahrhundert', in Matthias Puhle and Claus-Peter Hasse (eds), *Heiliges Römisches Reich Deutscher Nation 962 bis 1806: Von Otto dem Großen bis zum Ausgang des Mittelalters. Essays* (Dresden, 2006), 337–47, at 340.

35   Meer, 'Reversed, Defaced, Replaced', 635–7. For night and disfigurement, see Valentin Groebner, *Defaced: The Visual Culture of Violence in the Late Middle Ages* (New York, 2004), ch. 2.

The motives of late medieval political iconoclasts often remain the most elusive aspect of their activities.

LEAVING AN IMPRESSION: RESPONDING TO CAROLINE VISUAL CULTURE

The dissemination of a symbolic visual language of political power was a common trend across western Europe in the late Middle Ages. When at its most intense, the process was inherently competitive and contentious – a 'war' of jostling signs asserting often irreconcilable titles to power and status.[36] But to set up public symbols of power was everywhere to stake a claim, to issue a challenge. The northern territories of the Reich, including the Bohemian lands, were drawn into political image-making comparatively late, when visual cultures of monarchical and other forms of elite power were already well developed in neighbouring regions, notably France and Italy.[37] Visual representations of the Reich and its rulers grew in number, particularly in the imperial towns of western Germany, during the thirteenth and early fourteenth centuries.[38] In Bohemia, French gothic influences gained importance, particularly in Prague, under the first of the Luxembourg kings, John (r. 1310–46).[39] Both in his Bohemian dynastic lands and in the Empire north of the Alps, therefore, the sponsorship of architecture and the visual arts by Charles IV and his court built upon already-established traditions and currents of development. Influences from the French court and papal Avignon, from western Germany and the towns of northern and central Italy, as well as native Bohemian elements, all played a part, without any

---

36 For a specific example, see Simona Slanička, *Krieg der Zeichen: Die visuelle Politik Johanns ohne Furcht und der armagnakisch-burgundische Bürgerkrieg* (Göttingen, 2002).
37 Claire Richter Sherman, *The Portraits of Charles V of France (1338–1380)* (New York, 1969); Stephen Perkinson, *The Likeness of the King: A Prehistory of Portraiture in Late Medieval France* (Chicago and London, 2009); Nicolai Rubinstein, 'Political Ideas in Sienese Art: The Frescoes of Ambrogio Lorenzetti and Taddeo Bartolo in the Palazzo Pubblico', *Journal of the Warburg and Courtauld Institutes* 21 (1958), 179–207.
38 Lieselotte E. Saurma-Jeltsch, 'Das mittelalterliche Reich in der Reichsstadt', in Bernd Schneidmüller and Stefan Weinfurter (eds), *Heilig – Römisch – Deutsch: Das Reich im mittelalterlichen Europa* (Dresden, 2006), 399–439.
39 Bernd Carqué, 'Aporien des Kulturtransfers: Bau- und bildkünstlerische Zeichen von Herrschersakralität in Prag und Paris', in Eva Schlotheuber and Hubertus Seibert (eds), *Böhmen und das Deutsche Reich: Ideen- und Kulturtransfer im Vergleich (13.-16. Jahrhundert)* (Munich, 2009), 35–62.

one current gaining predominance.[40] The importance of Caroline visual culture lay in its transformative scale, as well as its character, media, and points of focus.[41] It possessed a monumentality and a breadth of vision and ambition which set it apart not only from what had gone before but also from the patronage of Charles' sons and successors Wenceslas and Sigismund. This goes far to explain the unmistakable impression which it made upon contemporaries.

'In the whole world there is no other castle and chapel so sumptuously decorated', wrote the court chronicler Beneš Krabice of the Holy Cross Chapel at Karlštejn, dedicated in 1365.[42] Beneš, a predictable enthusiast, is often cited as a witness for Caroline cultural projects. But the more ambivalent responses of other contemporary and later observers merit more attention than they have mostly received. Above all, the transformation of Prague (which, one chronicler noted, Charles had doubled in size),[43] as well as the heightened importance of Bohemia within the Empire were widely noticed. The south-German chronicler Heinrich von Diessenhofen remarked that the seat of imperial rule itself, once in Rome, then in Constantinople, was now in Prague.[44] But not all judged favourably the priorities which they perceived in this shift. The Strasbourg chronicler Matthias of Neuenburg complained that, instead of leaving the imperial regalia, with their Passion relics, at such traditional sites as Frankfurt or Nuremberg, Charles took them to Prague, to the boundless joy of the Bohemians.[45] Jakob Twinger, writing in Strasbourg in the generation after the Emperor's death, emphasized his eager acquisition of lands and riches, and remarked that everything which he acquired he diverted to the benefit of Bohemia, not the Reich.[46] The favour which Charles had shown to his dynastic realm at the Empire's expense became embedded as a *topos* in German writings.[47] Precisely the fact that the shift in power and rule had attained such monumentally *visible* forms helped to anchor it in the minds of some, but as a regrettable development.

40 Jiří Fajt, 'Was ist karolinisch an der Hofkunst Karls IV.?', in Hohensee et al. (eds.), *Die Goldene Bulle*, vol. 1, 349–68, with references to further literature.
41 See generally Jaromír Homolka, 'Zu den ikonographischen Programm Karls IV', in Legner (ed.), *Die Parler*, vol. 2, 607–18.
42 Josef Emler (ed.), *Kronika Beneše z Weitmile*, in *Fontes rerum Bohemicarum* 4 (Prague, 1884), 533.
43 Hofmeister (ed.), *Die Chronik des Mathias von Neuenburg*, 442.
44 A. Huber (ed.), *Heinrich Dapifer de Diessenhoven 1316–1361*, in *Fontes rerum Germanicarum: Geschichtsquellen Deutschlands*, vol. 4 (Stuttgart, 1868), 116.
45 Hofmeister (ed.), *Die Chronik des Mathias von Neuenburg*, 444.
46 C. Hegel (ed.), *Chronik des Jacob Twinger von Königshofen*, in *Die Chroniken der deutschen Städte vom 14. bis ins 16. Jahrhundert*, vol. 8 (Leipzig, 1870), 491.
47 See generally Beat Frey, *Pater Bohemiae – Vitricus Imperii; Böhmens Vater, Stiefvater des Reichs: Kaiser Karl IV. in der Geschichtsschreibung* (Bern, 1978).

Also widespread, in an age in which the Empire's rulers were most often mocked for the meagreness of their resources, was the view that Charles had become unprecedentedly rich. More than one writer claimed that he exceeded in wealth both his contemporaries and his predecessors.[48] Not everyone thought this achievement admirable. For an embittered chronicler in Augsburg, one of the imperial towns that bore the brunt of fiscal exactions in the troubled closing years of his reign, the devout Charles was a 'despiser of Christendom'.[49] The otherwise rarely outspoken author of the *Cologne World Chronicle* meant the Emperor no compliment in identifying him as a 'most voracious accumulator' of 'infinite riches'.[50] For some, Charles' cultural patronage may have served above all to highlight the heaped up treasure of a fiscally oppressive ruler.

It is in the light of contemporary perceptions of his unparalleled wealth, with its, for some, unmistakably negative implications, that some references to Charles' building projects must be read. The *Cologne World Chronicle* recorded that he 'adorned' Bohemia 'with many edifices, castles and fortifications, churches and monasteries, at great expense'.[51] There can be no doubt that Charles' ambitious sponsorship of a visual culture of monarchy attracted the attention of contemporaries, just as modern scholars have argued was his intent. Abbot Ludolf of Sagan, himself a subject of the Bohemian crown, remarked the 'sumptuous chapel, of marvellous decoration and workmanship', made for the king 'in castro Karlstein', and that of St Wenceslas in his new cathedral in Prague, its walls gilded and clad with precious stones.[52] Report of the 'royal chapel' constructed at 'a certain new castle' (i.e., Karlštejn) even reached far-off Cologne; but it was, predictably, the 'infinite cost' of its workmanship, in marble, gold, and gems, that seemed most remarkable.[53] Contemporaries' awareness of Charles' activity as a patron of artefacts and images did not guarantee favourable opinions. Johannes von Guben, town scribe of Zittau in Lusatia and another subject of Charles as Bohemian king, described the iconography of a Bohemian silver heller with an attentiveness that leaves no doubt as to the communicative power of Caroline image-making.[54]

---

48 Thus, e.g., Loserth (ed.), *Der Tractatus de Longevo Schismate*, 409.
49 F. Frensdorff (ed.), *Chronik von 1368 bis 1406 mit Fortsetzung bis 1447*, in *Die Chroniken der deutschen Städte vom 14. bis ins 16. Jahrhundert*, vol. 4 (Leipzig, 1865), 42.
50 Rolf Sprandel (ed.), *Die Kölner Weltchronik 1273/88–1376* (*MGH Scriptores rerum Germanicarum*, Nova series, 15, Munich, 1991), 111.
51 Ibid., 109.
52 Loserth (ed.), *Tractatus de Longevo Schismate*, 408.
53 Sprandel (ed.), *Die Kölner Weltchronik 1273/88–1376*, 109.
54 Ernst Friedrich Haupt (ed.), *Jahrbücher des zittauischen Stadtschreibers Johannes von Guben* (*Scriptores rerum Lusaticarum* I, Görlitz, 1837), 16.

Johannes knew that the king's heavy financial exactions had gone in part to pay for 'di schyf, dy man machte czu Prage' ('the church that was constructed at Prague'), i.e., the new metropolitan cathedral. But none of this prevented him from denouncing the king as an 'oppressive lord' ('eynen swerren herren') to his town.[55] That an observer like Johannes could simultaneously record with a keen eye the visible signs of Bohemian royal majesty *and* view with cold distance their contemporary bearer and embodiment ought to caution against unqualified judgements on Caroline visual 'propaganda' and its successes. The persuasive efforts of the Luxembourg king did not everywhere bear fruit, despite his magnificent public image. Some Caroline projects – the castle of Lauf to the east of Nuremberg, for example, with its armorial chamber lined with the incised devices mainly of Bohemian nobles – have been explicitly understood as attempts to win the magnates of the kingdom to the Luxembourgs' side.[56] But if that was the intention, it was in vain, as relations with the native nobility remained as difficult as they had been under Charles' father.[57] Lavish self-projection, moreover, did not prevent contemporaries from presenting a picture of a monarch with a full share of failures and public humiliations to his name.[58]

Charles' piety was widely acknowledged, and his devotion to the cult of saints and eagerness in acquiring and exalting their mortal remains well known. A fundamental study by Martin Bauch documents the massive scale of his acquisition of relics, many of which found a home in his Bohemian capital.[59] While emphasizing the inevitable limitations of the available data, Bauch charts a rise from the 77 identifiable relics present in Prague at the start of Charles' reign to 605 in and around the city by 1378. He proposes – while again stressing the high degree of uncertainty in such a calculation – that the king may have commissioned some 400 new reliquaries, conceivably costing in total around 40,000 gulden.[60] Even for a monarch of Charles' resources, this would have represented a very considerable outlay on silver, gold, and precious stones. Some of these sacred treasures were on public display during the annual showing

---

55 Ibid., 23.
56 Richard Němec, 'Herrscher – Kunst – Metapher: Das ikonografische Programm der Residenzburg Lauf an der Pegnitz als eine Quelle der Herrschaftsstrategie Karls IV', in Hohensee et al. (eds), *Die Goldene Bulle*, vol. 1, 369–402, esp. 378–9, 386.
57 See Ferdinand Seibt, 'Die Zeit der Luxemburger und der hussitischen Revolution', in Karl Bosl (ed.), *Handbuch der Geschichte der böhmischen Länder*, vol. 1 (Stuttgart, 1967), 349–568 (here esp. 397–9).
58 Examples in Scales, 'Wenceslas Looks Out', 189 with nn. 52, 53.
59 For what follows, see Bauch, *Divina favente clemencia*, esp. 311, 317. My debt to Dr Bauch's work in what follows will be clear.
60 Ibid., 311–12.

in Prague of the imperial Passion relics, which attracted large numbers of pilgrims to the city following its instigation as a feast of the Church in 1354.[61] Other Caroline reliquaries, distinguished with the Bohemian and imperial coats of arms, would have been visible in St Vitus and in other churches.

Contemporary and later commentators make clear the impression left by the king's sponsorship of saints' cults and his expenditure on acquiring and adorning their relics. This may, indeed, have been a principal contributor to the view of Charles' fabled riches. It is evident, however, that not all deemed the king's wealth to have been wisely spent. In a treatise written early in his reign, the Dominican Johannes von Dambach, a master at the new Prague *studium generale*, recounted the evils arising from the papal interdict imposed under Charles' predecessor in the Empire, Louis IV (r. 1314–47), and called on him to seek its revocation.[62] He urged the king to concentrate upon ensuring that his subjects might become fitting receptacles for the Eucharist – by which he meant the celebration of Mass, free of the taint of excommunication – before sponsoring costly receptacles for the bones of St Wenceslas. The state of the Church as a body, not merely the construction of rich church buildings, should be Charles' first concern. The devotional currents that would eventually ripen into the outright iconoclasm of the Hussite radicals were already stirring during Charles' lifetime, among figures well acquainted with his court's rich patronage of sacred objects.[63] There are good grounds for tracing a direct causal link. The Nuremberg chronicler Sigmund Meisterlin, writing towards the close of the fifteenth century, thought so: it was, he wrote, Charles' rich reliquaries that had (with the Hussites' sacking of churches) driven the Bohemians to covetousness.[64]

THE IMAGE OF THE EMPEROR

It was not without significance that Charles had borne since 5 April 1355 the title of ever-august Emperor of the Romans.[65] Before that date he was

---

61 Ibid., 371–2.
62 For what follows, see Albert Auer, 'Eine verschollene Denkschrift über das große Interdikt des 14. Jahrhunderts', *Historisches Jahrbuch* 46 (1926), 532–49 (here esp. 541, 543).
63 Bauch, *Divina favente clemencia*, 450–4.
64 Dietrich Kerler (ed.), *Sigmund Meisterlin's Chronik der Reichsstadt Nürnberg, 1488* (*Die Chroniken der deutschen Städte: Die Chroniken der fränkischen Städte*, vol. 3, Leipzig, 1864), 156.
65 For the development of imperial titles, see Jörg Schwarz, *Herrscher- und Reichstitel bei Kaisertum und Papsttum im 12. und 13. Jahrhundert* (Cologne, Weimar, and Vienna, 2003).

already, in consequence of his election by the German princes, King of the Romans, a title which his sons Wenceslas and Sigismund would also bear. Sigismund, too, would eventually be crowned Emperor in Rome, as Charles' paternal grandfather, Henry VII (r. 1308–13), had been before him. The Luxembourg age in Bohemia was an imperial age. And for Roman kings and emperors to engage in image-making by the fourteenth century carried particular significance.

If monarchs were, in the figure of the Babylonian king Ninus, the archetypal illicit image-makers, Roman emperors were for medieval people archetypal monarchs, with their own troubling associations with images.[66] Bad Roman emperors, in medieval tradition, as proud tyrants had wished to be worshipped in effigy. Illustrated manuscripts of the widely read thirteenth-century historical encyclopaedia of Vincent of Beauvais, for example, show the people kneeling before the sculpted image of the emperor on a pedestal, or show the emperor commanding forms of idolatrous behaviour.[67] Both an awareness of Roman imperial idolatry and a judgement on the behaviour proper to a pious emperor find expression in a story set down in the German-vernacular world chronicle of Heinrich von München, which may have been compiled during Charles IV's reign.[68] According to this text, Caesar Augustus, upon learning of the birth of Christ, had at once commanded that all images of *him* be destroyed, and that the emperor no longer be worshipped as a god in effigy. The good emperor, in this view, was no image-maker.

More recent history seemed to point to a similar moral. Before Charles IV, the medieval western emperor who had been most magnificently represented in effigy, although mainly south of the Alps, was the Hohenstaufen Frederick II (r. 1212–50). Frederick was distinguished by the monumental character of his self-representation – most strikingly in the Capua Gate, the neo-Roman portal, adorned with busts and inscriptions celebrating royal power and justice, which he constructed, facing onto papal territory at the northern extremity of his dynastic kingdom of Sicily.[69] Frederick was the first medieval emperor to be repeatedly portrayed in quasi-naturalistic three-dimensional sculpture (including a

---

66 For Ninus, see Michael Camille, *The Gothic Idol: Ideology and Image-Making in Medieval Art* (Cambridge, 1989), 50.
67 Ibid., 54–5, 64.
68 Frank Shaw et al. (eds), *Die Weltchronik Heinrichs von München: Neue Ee* (*Deutsche Texte des Mittelalters* 88, Berlin, 2008), 10, vv. 175–94; Norbert H. Ott, 'Heinrich von München', in Kurt Ruh (ed.), *Die deutsche Literatur des Mittelalters: Verfasserlexikon*, second edition, vol. 3 (Berlin and New York, 1982), coll. 827–37.
69 Jill Meredith, 'The Revival of the Augustan Age in the Court Art of Emperor Frederick II', in David Castriota (ed.), *Artistic Strategy and the Rhetoric of Power: Political Uses of Art from Antiquity to the Present* (Carbondale, 1986), 39–56.

classicizing bust effigy on the Capua Gate itself) – a medium in which Charles, too, would be repeatedly represented.[70] Frederick also, however, had the distinction of being deposed from office in 1245 by a general council of the Church under the pope, on charges which included heresy. That the Empire's rulers in the half-century after his death devoted so few resources to their own visual representation may have had to do with more than just their fabled penury.[71]

The imperial office, with its bearer's claim to a general responsibility, alongside the pope, for the well-being of Christendom, had a particular ideological character, with potential implications for image-making projects. The most celebrated charge of idolatry to arise during the years preceding the Luxembourg era had been levelled not against an emperor but against that most imperial of popes, Boniface VIII (r. 1294–1303). In contrast to Frederick II, the accusations of heresy brought by the agents of Boniface's adversary, King Philip IV of France, included explicit reference to illicit image-making. The pope, it was alleged, had commanded his own veneration through silver statues on church altars.[72] Having his own body placed, in effigy, upon an altar (we might recall here the unfortunate Wenceslas) would have represented a particularly clear case of idolatry. A subsequent, expanded version of the accusations, however, claimed that Boniface had also set up images of himself on church exteriors and, in Orvieto and elsewhere, on city gates, 'where long ago idols used to be kept'.[73]

Boniface's image in three-dimensional sculpted form was indeed to be found on the gate at Orvieto, as well as on cathedral façades in Florence and Anagni, though there is no reason to think that this was done at the pope's instigation. Nevertheless, the sensitivity of some contemporaries especially to this form of representation, and awareness of its precursors in pagan (and Roman-imperial) antiquity, is thought-provoking when we consider the prominence of monumental sculpted representations of the Luxembourg monarchs. Charles IV's image, too, appeared above urban gateways – most famously, though not only, on the Old Town Bridge Tower in Prague, accompanied by his heir Wenceslas.[74] He also

---

70 Guido Kaschnitz von Weinberg, 'Bildnisse Kaiser Friedrichs II. von Hohenstaufen', *Mitteilungen des Deutschen Archaeologischen Instituts, Römische Abteilung* 60/61 (1953/4), 1–21, and 62 (1955), 1–51.
71 Robert Suckale, 'Die Hofkunst im 14. Jahrhundert', in Puhle and Hasse (eds), *Heiliges Römisches Reich: Essays*, 323–35, at 323–4.
72 Tilmann Schmidt, 'Papst Bonifaz VIII. und die Idolatrie', *Quellen und Forschungen aus italienischen Archiven und Bibliotheken* 66 (1986), 75–107.
73 Camille, *The Gothic Idol*, 278–9; Perkinson, *Likeness of the King*, 114–16.
74 Marco Bogade, *Kaiser Karl IV.: Ikonographie und Ikonologie* (Stuttgart, 2005), 65–6; Iva Rosario, *Art and Propaganda: Charles IV of Bohemia, 1346–1378*

appeared, sometimes along with other members of his family and court, in monumental form on church exteriors. Here too, it seems that only in some instances did the images originate with the court's sponsorship.[75] But, at least in their number and magnificence, they were a new phenomenon, both in Bohemia and in other northern territories of the Reich in Charles' day. Although firm evidence is lacking, there are circumstantial reasons for thinking that their associations for contemporary observers may at times have been more troubling than modern scholarship has generally acknowledged.

The contentious nature of late medieval emperorship might itself invite iconoclasm. There are some signs that Charles' divisive predecessor on the imperial throne, the Wittelsbach Louis IV, whose reign was marked by bitter conflict with the Avignon papacy, was the subject of visual *damnatio memoriae*. Two known depictions of Louis in manuscripts, including one in a copy of his Upper Bavarian law-code (*Landrecht*), appear to have been defaced.[76] Robert Suckale has suggested that the fewness of surviving images and artefacts associated with Louis' court reflects systematic destruction, in which his successor, Charles, probably had a hand.[77] The pre-eminent fourteenth-century imperial image-maker, on this (admittedly uncertain) view, was himself an image-breaker. Portraying the Emperor was never a neutral act.

As well as an unprecedented number of depictions of Luxembourg kings and emperors themselves, in large- and small-scale media, Charles was the subject of images which inserted his stylized features into portrayals

---

(Woodbridge, 2000), 78–81; and for the Bridge Tower as a 'triumphal arch', ibid., 85. For invocation of Charles in the Charlemagne-statue set up on the Galgentor, one of the city gates of Frankfurt am Main, see Saurma-Jeltsch, 'Das mittelalterliche Reich in der Reichsstadt', 409; Legner (ed.), *Die Parler*, vol. 1, 238–9.

75 Thus, e.g., the church of St Mary at Mühlhausen, where the figures on the south portal, probably representing Charles IV, his queen, and courtiers, are thought to reflect local burgher patronage. See Hans Peter Hilger, 'Die Skulpturen an der südlichen Querhausfassade von St. Marien zu Mühlhausen in Thüringen', *Wallraf-Richartz-Jahrbuch* 22 (1960), 159–64; Hartmut Boockmann, 'Der Deutsche Orden in Mühlhausen', *Sachsen und Anhalt* 21 (1998), 9–35.

76 Matthias Puhle and Claus-Peter Hasse (eds), *Heiliges Römisches Reich Deutscher Nation 962 bis 1806: Von Otto dem Großen bis zum Ausgang des Mittelalters. Katalog* (Dresden, 2006), no. V10, pp. 379–81. On Louis' *damnatio memoriae*, see Gerald Schwedler, '"dampnate memorie Ludovici de Bavaria" – Erinnerungsvernichtung als metaphorische Waffe im Konflikt zwischen der Kurie und Kaiser Ludwig dem Bayern (mit Edition)', in Claudia Garnier and Johannes Schnocks (eds), *Sterben über den Tod hinaus: Politische, soziale und religiöse Ausgrenzung in vormodernen Gesellschaften* (Würzburg, 2012), 165–201. I am grateful to Gerald Schwedler for advice on this matter.

77 Robert Suckale, *Die Hofkunst Kaiser Ludwigs des Bayern* (Munich, 1993), 46–7.

of an array of sacral and imperial figures.[78] In scale at least, this was a quite new development. He is thus encountered in the guise of Solomon, David, Melchizedek, and as one of the three Magi, but also as ancient and medieval Christian emperors: notably, Constantine and Charlemagne.[79] The first of these identifications is, for this chapter's concerns, particularly important. Charles' association with the first Christian Roman emperor is implicit wherever he is shown in relation to the imagery of the cross. It is made explicit in the Karlštejn tympanum mural, where he appears together with a queen, perhaps Anna of Schweidnitz (as crypto-Helena), elevating a great reliquary cross in what has been interpreted as an act not merely of adoration but Constantinian exaltation and triumph.[80]

Charles had a well-documented interest in and identification with Constantine. This is made explicit in a letter of 1354 concerning his removal from Trier Cathedral treasury, with his own hands, of wood of the True Cross which it was believed St Helena had donated to Trier. Charles transferred the relic, in familiar fashion, to Prague.[81] Funeral orations to the Emperor repeatedly identified him as a second Constantine.[82] The same identification was implicit in the well-attended public ceremony when the imperial Passion relics – including the Lance, with its Constantinian associations – were shown annually to large crowds in the Bohemian capital.

Whether such performances directly influenced the perceptions of the reformers in Prague is impossible to say with certainty. What we know is that they came to view Constantine particularly in a strongly negative light, as a corrupter of the early purity of the Church. Significantly, Constantine was remembered in medieval tradition as an image-maker.[83] For the

---

78 Bogade, *Kaiser Karl IV.*, ch. 6; Robert Suckale, 'Die Porträts Kaiser Karls IV. als Bedeutungsträger', in Martin Büchsel and Peter Schmidt (eds), *Das Porträt vor der Erfindung des Porträts* (Mainz, 2003), 191–204.
79 For Charles and his Frankish namesake, see Jiří Fajt, 'Karl IV. – Herrscher zwischen Prag und Aachen', in Mario Kramp (ed.), *Krönungen: Könige in Aachen – Geschichte und Mythos*, 2 vols (Mainz, 1999), vol. 2, 489–500.
80 Rosario, *Art and Propaganda*, 40–5; Bogade, *Kaiser Karl IV.*, 192–6. The queen's identification is uncertain: Bogade argues against the widespread identification with Anna for Charles' Přemyslid mother, Elizabeth. See also Rudolf Chadraba, 'Der "zweite Konstantin": Zum Verhältnis von Staat und Kirche in der karolinischen Kunst Böhmens', *Umění* 26 (1978), 505–20.
81 Hans Horstmann, 'Ein Brief Kaiser Karls IV. über seinen Besuch in Trier 1354', *Trierer Zeitschrift* 22 (1953), 167–75; Wolfgang Schmid, 'Vom Rheinland nach Böhmen: Studien zur Reliquienpolitik Kaiser Karls IV', in Hohensee et al. (eds), *Die Goldene Bulle*, vol. 1, 431–64 (here 434–7).
82 Josef Emler (ed.), *Fontes rerum Bohemicarum*, vol. 3 (Prague, 1882), 429 (Archbishop Jan Očko of Vlašim), 436–7 (Adalbert Ranconis).
83 Camille, *The Gothic Idol*, 287.

reformer Petr Chelčicky, writing in the fifteenth century, it was under Constantine that 'idolatrous images' began to multiply in churches.[84] In Hussite Bohemia, as elsewhere in Latin Christian Europe, the historic role of emperors within the Church was a controversial matter. But in Bohemia, the Christian emperor as image-maker may have become a particular concern.

CHRIST, ANTICHRIST, AND THE MONARCH

Charles' image-making did not only invoke contestable imperial pasts but inserted his person into the course of Christian history and into its eschatological future – where emperors were likewise ascribed a central but controversial and contested role.[85] Charles did little to discourage such perceptions, appearing in public at the annual Prague relic-showings with, and probably touching with his own hands, the insignia that it was believed the triumphal Last Emperor would surrender on Golgotha, thereby initiating the End Times. A surviving lead pilgrim badge shows Charles, identified by his stylized facial features, clutching the (Constantinian) Holy Lance, in company with a saint-pope.[86] It has been proposed that both the St Wenceslas Chapel in St Vitus and the Holy Cross Chapel at Karlštejn, their walls adorned with gold and clad with semi-precious stones, were conceived as visible anticipations of the heavenly Jerusalem which would descend to earth at the Apocalypse.[87] Charles had inaugurated the practice of the Emperor reading, in the Christmas Eve Mass, the passage from St Luke's Gospel recounting the decree issued by Caesar Augustus.[88] When he appeared in this role, with the crown of Charlemagne on his head and Charlemagne's sword held before him, he articulated not only a richly complex vision of the Christian-Imperial past, but also a promise for the future.

Caroline image-culture and performance, as Paul Crossley and Zoë Opačić have powerfully shown, were all about dissolving and transgressing

---

84 In his *Net of True Faith* (*Siet' viery pravé*, c. 1443): see Bredekamp, *Kunst als Medium sozialer Konflikte*, 279–80. For the negative image of Constantine, particularly on account of his 'Donation' to the Church, in early Bohemian reforming texts and imagery, see also Thomas A. Fudge, 'Art and Propaganda in Hussite Bohemia', *Religio* 1 (1993), 135–53, at 137–8.
85 For emperors and eschatology, see generally Hannes Möhring, *Der Weltkaiser der Endzeit: Entstehung, Wandel und Wirkung einer tausendjährigen Weissagung* (Stuttgart, 2000).
86 Drake Boehm and Fajt (eds), *Prague: The Crown of Bohemia*, no. 70, p. 205.
87 Crossley, 'Politics of Presentation', 146–57.
88 Hermann Heimpel, 'Königlicher Weihnachtsdienst im späteren Mittelalter', *Deutsches Archiv für Erforschung des Mittelalters* 39 (1983), 131–206.

boundaries: between past, present, and future, between imperial and dynastic-regnal monarchy and memory[89] – but also between kingship and priesthood, and between sacred things and the legitimating trappings of monarchical power. They represented, fleetingly – in effect, though almost certainly not in Charles' conscious intention – an obliteration of the legacy of Canossa. In part, Charles was here continuing a trend which probably originated with his grandfather, Henry VII, as Roman king and emperor, and which further developed under Louis IV, towards the visual exaltation of the monarch's person.[90] This had accompanied Henry's revival of emperorship after more than half a century of mere German kings, and reflected the intellectual and cultural stimuli arising from the renewal of imperial expeditions into Italy. As a result, imperial dress took on an increasingly quasi-clerical aspect, while the crown came to incorporate a mitre, which appears to have increased in size over time. A Lübeck chronicler was thus able to remark, when Charles visited the town in 1375, that the Emperor resembled a bishop.[91]

But Charles' own actions went further, as Bauch has demonstrated. We have already encountered him handling the wood of the True Cross in Trier. In fact, he not only avidly accumulated relics but repeatedly touched them with his own hands, although canon law prohibited this to laypeople and earlier emperors had usually acted more circumspectly.[92] He secured papal grants of indulgence for those attending Masses where he was present. Most striking, however, is the direct assimilation of his own person to divine figures. The insertion of his stylized features into portrayals of holy kings and emperors has been encountered already. Perhaps especially significant, however, is Charles' visual identification with St Wenceslas, as seen on the Old Town Bridge Tower and elsewhere in his territories, as well as on the Prague University seal.[93] St Wenceslas, whose *Life* Charles had (re-)written and whose cult he massively promoted, is here significant

---

89 Crossley and Opačić, 'Prague as a New Capital', in Drake Boehm and Fajt (eds), *Prague: The Crown of Bohemia*, 71; and see generally Crossley, 'Politics of Presentation'.

90 Robert Suckale, 'Zur Ikonografie der deutschen Herrscher des 14. Jahrhunderts: Rudolf I. – Ludwig IV. – Karl IV.', in Hohensee et al. (eds), *Die Goldene Bulle*, vol. 1, 327–48, at 338–42.

91 Wilhelm Mantels, 'Kaiser Karls IV. Hoflager in Lübeck vom 20.-30. October 1375', *Hansische Geschichtsblätter* 3 (1873), 109–40, at 134: 'do toch he an ... syn keyserlike wede also en byschop'; Bauch, *Divina favente clemencia*, 122, n. 322.

92 For earlier emperors, saints, and relics, see Jürgen Petersohn, 'Kaisertum und Kultakt in der Stauferzeit', in Jürgen Petersohn (ed.), *Politik und Heiligenverehrung im Hochmittelalter* (Vorträge und Forschungen 42, Sigmaringen, 1994), 101–46.

93 Rosario, *Art and Propaganda*, 78, 80; for the seal, Bogade, *Kaiser Karl IV.*, 59–60, 112–13. For possible reference to Charles in a 'provincial' St Wenceslas sculpture (at Sulzbach in the Bavarian Oberpfalz), see Scales, 'Wenceslas Looks Out', 203.

not only as Bohemia's patron (and Charles' own maternal ancestor) but as a Christ-type.[94]

The Luxembourg Emperor's visible association with Christ took various forms. Beneš Krabice tells of how Charles would sit before the gates of Prague Castle in Holy Week and Easter Week, hearing in person 'the cases of paupers, orphans, and widows, and rendering judgement and justice'.[95] Charles and his queens were positioned in visual proximity to Christ and the Virgin, as, for example, on a monumental relief sculpture for the Carmelite church of Our Lady of the Snows in Prague (where in July 1419 the Hussite priest Jan Želivský would preach to large crowds against images).[96] Not only did his relic-collecting concentrate especially upon objects relating to Christ and his mother; he had copies made of miraculous images of Christ's face, the Vera Ikon, which he had seen in Rome, and the *Volto Santo* of Lucca, and brought these to Prague.[97] He was also repeatedly portrayed as king and emperor under Christ as apocalyptic judge. This took monumental and highly public form in the great mosaic set up on the south façade of St Vitus in the 1370s, where Charles and his last queen, Elizabeth of Pomerania, appear, accompanied by supplicatory Bohemian saints, beneath the majestic Christ of the Last Judgement.[98] The theme was not confined to the Bohemian capital, however, nor to works clearly deriving from the monarch's own patronage or that of his court: the same symbolism is found in sculpted form on the south portal of the church of St Mary in the imperial town of Mühlhausen in Thuringia.[99]

Christ as majestic judge and the Emperor-judge as Christ-imitator were starting to merge. An illustration in a manuscript made for Charles' chancellor, Johann von Neumarkt, shows an enthroned Christ wearing

---

94 Crossley and Opačić, 'Prague as a New Capital', in Drake Boehm and Fajt (eds), *Prague: The Crown of Bohemia*, 62; Nagy and Schaer (eds), *Autobiography of Emperor Charles IV*, esp. 194–9.
95 Emler (ed.), *Kronika Beneše z Weitmile*, 543.
96 For the sculpture, see Jiří Fajt, 'Charles IV: Toward a New Imperial Style', in Drake Boehm and Fajt (eds), *Prague: The Crown of Bohemia*, 3–21, at 9; for Želivský's preaching, Bredekamp, *Kunst als Medium sozialer Konflikte*, 260–1.
97 Bauch, *Divina favente clemencia*, 338–42.
98 Von Herzogenberg, 'Die Bildnisse', 324.
99 Andreas Puth '"Christus Dominus de hoc Seculo": Charles IV, Advent and Epiphany on the South Transept Façade of St Mary's in Mühlhausen', in Fajt and Langer (eds), *Kunst als Herrschaftsinstrument*, 515–33, esp. 520; Legner (ed.), *Die Parler*, vol. 2, 560–2. For a comparable scheme on the façade of the chapel of the Virgin in Nuremberg, see Thomas H. von der Dunk, *Das Deutsche Denkmal: Eine Geschichte in Bronze und Stein vom Hochmittelalter bis zum Barock* (Cologne, Weimar, and Vienna, 1999), 38.

contemporary imperial regalia.[100] It should be emphasized that none of the forms of identification discussed here was unorthodox or, taken on its own, necessarily controversial. But in an age of uncertain signs – both of divine presence and of monarchical legitimacy – the cumulative effect for some may have been unsettling.[101] The potential dangers of identification with Christ are indicated by the Velislav Bible, which dates from early in Charles' reign and which may have been commissioned by an important member of the Bohemian royal chancery.[102] It is unusual in including a pictorial cycle of the life and deeds of Antichrist. Also unusual, however, is the close assimilation of the figure of Antichrist to Christ himself, not only through his imitative acts but in his physical appearance.[103] Distinguishing pious *imitatio* from blasphemous counterfeit was no longer a simple matter.

Thought-provoking in a different though related way is another Antichrist cycle, in painted glass, in the church of St Mary in Frankfurt an der Oder which, as one of the principal towns of the Mark Brandenburg, passed from Wittelsbach into Luxembourg hands in 1373.[104] Important here is that the cycle includes a scene showing a monarch, identified as an emperor, honouring Antichrist and receiving his mark. Whether a contemporary political reference was intended and, if so, which monarch it sought to vilify, is impossible to discover. It is not known whether the glass was installed shortly before or soon after the Luxembourg takeover in the Mark, nor who were the patrons and the workshop responsible. As the Brandenburg glass makes clear, however, monarchs might be

---

100 Bauch, *Divina favente clemencia*, 85, with illustration at 721.
101 The Luxembourgs of the generation after Charles IV were patrons of the popular but controversial 'bleeding host' shrine at Wilsnack in the Mark Brandenburg, which reformers, including Hus, condemned as a deception: Jan Hrdina, 'Wilsnack, Hus und die Luxemburger', in Felix Escher and Hartmut Kühne (eds), *Die Wilsnackfahrt: Ein Wallfahrts- und Kommunikationszentrum Nord- und Mitteleuropas im Spätmittelalter* (Frankfurt am Main, 2006), 41–63.
102 This is the widespread view. For uncertainties, however, see Anna Kernbach and Lenka Panušková, 'Studying the Velislav Bible', in Lenka Panušková (ed.), *The Velislav Bible, the Finest Picture Bible of the Late Middle Ages* – Biblia depicta as Devotional, Mnemonic and Study Tool (Amsterdam, 2018), 15–33.
103 Pavlína Cermanová, 'The Life of Antichrist in the Velislav Bible', in ibid., 141–61. For the 'Christ-like' Antichrist, see Antonín Matějček, *Velislavova Bible a její místo ve vývoji knižní ilustrace gotické* (Prague, 1926), plates, fol. 135, 135v.
104 For what follows, see Maria Deiters, 'Glasmalerei zur Zeit Karls IV. in der Mark Brandenburg: Eine Spurensuche', in Jan Richter et al. (eds), *Karl IV.: Ein Kaiser in Brandenburg* (Berlin, 2016), 148–57, at 155–7; Joachim Seeger, 'Die Antichristlegende im Chorfenster der Marienkirche zu Frankfurt an der Oder', *Städel-Jahrbuch, Neue Folge* 6 (1977), 265–89. The entire Antichrist cycle can be viewed online: https://wgue.smugmug.com/Orte/Brandenburg/Frankfurt-Oder-Glasfenster/ [viewed 31 March 2023].

encountered in effigy in the Luxembourg lands not only imitating Christ but in company with his wicked emulator.

There are numerous indications that Charles IV's contemporaries were engaged by the figure of Antichrist and by his possibly imminent advent, and that such concerns were current in and around the Bohemian capital, as well as in the territories of the Reich more broadly.[105] Louis IV's protracted conflict with the Church, the resulting interdict on Germany, and the related question of who should be recognized as the Empire's legitimate ruler, had all stirred anxieties which persisted into Charles' reign.[106] Manuscript survivals attest to a lively interest in texts about Antichrist and his coming.[107] The positive eschatological role which the Caroline court and the writings of Luxembourg partisans seemed to ascribe to the Emperor might easily be reinterpreted by less sympathetic observers. Added to all this was now a visual culture of monarchy of unprecedented magnificence and startlingly rapid growth, which linked the monarch to contestable imperial pasts and futures while elevating his person into the sacral sphere.

It is reported of the reform preacher Jan Milíč of Kroměříž (d. 1374) that he once publicly pointed out Charles IV and named him as 'the great Antichrist'.[108] Milíč was a former canon of St Vitus and member of the royal chancery, who had resigned his offices for a life of poverty and preaching. He had founded in Prague a community of devout women in a former brothel which he named Jerusalem, a venture in which he had received support from the Emperor himself.[109] While Milíč had a well-established preoccupation with identifying the impending Antichrist,

---

105 For eschatological speculation in Charles' circle, see Sabine Schmolinsky, 'Prophetisch-endzeitliches Denken im Umkreis Karls IV', in Joachim Heinzle, L. Peter Johnson and Gisela Vollmann-Profe (eds), *Literatur im Umkreis des Prager Hofs der Luxemburger: Schweinfurter Kolloquium 1992* (Wolfram-Studien 13, Berlin, 1994), 92–105. A Swiss Antichrist-play from the 1350s identifies Charles as an adherent of Antichrist: ibid., 101, n. 23. A Mainz chronicler under the year 1357 juxtaposes (though without causally linking) Charles' presence in Mainz with rumours in the region that Antichrist had been born: C. Hegel (ed.), *Chronicon Moguntinum* (*Die Chroniken der deutschen Städte vom 14. bis ins 16. Jahrhundert*, vol. 18, Leipzig, 1882), 160.
106 For the figure of Antichrist in Louis' struggle with the papacy, see Suckale, *Hofkunst*, 44.
107 Cermanová, 'The Life of Antichrist', 147–8.
108 *Fontes rerum Austriacarum: Oesterreichische Geschichts-Quellen, Scriptores*, vol. 6: *Geschichtschreiber [sic] der husitischen [sic] Bewegung in Böhmen*, Theil II., ed. K. Höfler (Vienna, 1865), 42.
109 David C. Mengel, 'From Venice to Jerusalem and Beyond: Milíč of Kroměříž and the Topography of Prostitution in Fourteenth-Century Prague', *Speculum* 79 (2004), 407–42.

Charles therefore appears a surprising figure for him to have singled out. The sole source for the story is Milíč's disciple Matthias of Janov (d. 1393/4), another Prague canon, a Paris master, and an outspoken critic of images, who wrote in the generation after Milíč's – and Charles IV's – death. Matthias had strong motives for making his master's views conform to his own, more radical, ones, for which he had suffered ecclesiastical punishment, and the story may well be his own invention.[110]

But if so, this would only add to the anecdote's interest. In Milíč's day, Caroline Prague was still a building site, whereas Matthias lived long enough both to reflect with hindsight on Charles' reign and to see its great architectural and iconographic projects, such as the choir of St Vitus and the stone bridge with its monumental, decorated gate-tower, attain fruition. Like Milíč, he had spent time at the centre of institutional power and wealth in the capital before choosing a life propagating religious reform and material simplicity. Why – if the story does indeed originate with him – Matthias would have wished to see Charles designated as Antichrist is uncertain. But that the most outspoken critic of images among the early reformers should have targeted in this way Prague's richest and most prolific image-maker suggests more than coincidence.

By the time of Matthias' death, other Prague reformers had already counterposed the magnificent Christian-ecclesiastical culture of the rebuilt city with a very different visual vocabulary of devotion, in the form of the Bethlehem Chapel. Founded in 1391, within sight of the new choir of St Vitus on the hill across the river, the stark preaching house must have appeared to some as a visible rebuff also to St Vitus' royal patron – the first cathedral-building emperor since the Ottonians and Salians – whose features, in graven and painted form, remained visible across the city. Its interior decoration, moreover, explicitly denounced a visible Church not only papal but imperial: corrupted by the gifts of Charles' forebear and exemplar, Constantine the Great.[111]

---

110 A case convincingly argued by Eleanor Janega, 'Jan Milíč of Kroměříž and Emperor Charles IV: Preaching, Power, and the Church of Prague' (unpublished PhD thesis, University College London, 2015), 48–61.
111 Thomas A. Fudge, *The Magnificent Ride: The First Reformation in Hussite Bohemia* (Aldershot, 1998), 228. Charles' meeting with Urban V in Rome in 1368 was staged as an explicitly Constantinian act of protection/submission on Charles' part: Bauch, *Divina favente clemencia*, 154–62.

CONCLUSIONS

Since the late twentieth century the Luxembourg era, and particularly the reign of Charles IV, has recurrently been made the subject of major exhibitions, celebrating its achievements in the field of visual culture. The same period has witnessed a re-evaluation of the reputations of the Luxembourg monarchs, above all that of Charles, now judged to have been one of the most significant and successful rulers in fourteenth-century Central Europe. The exhibitions and the positive reassessment are clearly connected: an intense focus on the art, architecture, and material artefacts associated with his reign has underpinned a growing conviction that these represented cultural resources of state-building, powerful elements in a coordinated royal 'propaganda'. Charles' contemporaries, surely, can have been no less impressed than are twenty-first-century art historians and museum visitors.

But if we are to take seriously the communicative power of monarchical images, we must also allow for their capacity to stimulate negative responses. This chapter has argued that Charles' heavy expenditure on settings and materials for the presentation of his monarchy did indeed make a strong impression on observers at the time. But that impression was complex. In the German lands of the Reich, not everyone welcomed the shift in the monarchy's concerns that the massive development of Prague seemed to signal. Conspicuous sacral display reminded some of a high-taxing ruler, while others questioned the religious priorities which it appeared to reflect. In Bohemia, the Emperor's cultural programme did little to win over a sceptical nobility while, particularly in Prague, with the passage of time it probably nurtured responses that he had neither intended nor wished.

Charles and his son Wenceslas ruled in a time of shifting religious sensibilities. Charles himself embodied and reflected the tensions of his day, which his own patronage seemed further to heighten: between the shining apocalyptic Jerusalem of bejewelled interiors and the ascetic Jerusalem of poor women, to which he also for a time lent his support. In this new climate, both traditional ideas about emperorship and Charles' own self-presentation as a monarch deeply immersed in the sacral sphere had the capacity to stimulate uncertainty and, with time, more extreme reactions. The challenge which the Luxembourg monarchy offered to emerging currents of reforming spirituality was the more potent because it took such highly developed visual forms. Images of monarchy of many kinds and diverse media, three-dimensional figure sculptures with their potentially troubling echoes of idol-making,[112] and in Prague an entire

---

112 For the late medieval 'escape' of three-dimensional figure sculpture from the church into other public spaces, see Von der Dunk, *Das deutsche Denkmal*, 52.

sacral cityscape all came into being with bewildering speed. Such startling transformations may have contributed to one German chronicler's view, that Charles was proficient in the black arts.[113]

The role of the monarch and his court in the visual transformations of his reign should not be overstated. Often, the precise contribution of the Caroline court to specific projects is impossible to establish. In the sphere of secular power as in religious life, it was an image-making age. That it was also, politically, an image-breaking age is often harder to demonstrate directly, but there is no lack of circumstantial evidence. Political image-making expanded massively in Central Europe under the early Luxembourg monarchs, even if direct commissions from the court were only one element in this expansion. Targets for the iconoclast were now all around, and we know that some duly took aim. Whether those who exhumed King Wenceslas and broke the tomb of his image-making father should be numbered in this group must remain uncertain. But if so, their insensate victims had surely, in their day, done much to help forge the conceptual weapons in their hands.

---

113 C. Hegel (ed.), *Chronik des Jacob Twinger von Königshofen*, 484.

CHAPTER 13

THE ABSENT PRESENT: LUXEMBOURG COURTS, THEIR SONIC CULTURES, AND MUSIC HISTOR(IOGRAPH)Y

KARL KÜGLE

Unlike other prominent ruling families of the fourteenth and fifteenth centuries, the Luxembourgs are conspicuous by their relative absence in late-medieval music history. There are some exceptions, of course: the association of John of Luxembourg, King of Bohemia, with the Francophone poet-musician Guillaume de Machaut (d. 1377) as well as the presumed role of John of Luxembourg's daughter Bonne (1315–49) in the poet-composer's creative output received a great deal of attention from both literary and music scholars. The same is true of the role of Oswald von Wolkenstein (1376 or 1377–1445) at the court of Sigismund of Luxembourg. In the last years of Sigismund's reign, the singer and composer Johannes Brassart (c. 1400–55) entered Luxembourg service; he was the first master of the imperial chapel to whom mensurally notated polyphonic compositions can be ascribed.

There are some unanswered questions, too: Charles of Luxembourg (1316–78), John's eldest son and Bonne's younger brother, was educated at the court of France during the rule of King Charles IV (r. 1322–8) and the early years of Philip VI (r. 1328–50), and therefore was familiar with Francophone court culture. Charles ostensibly had a first-hand opportunity to secure Machaut's services and use them to his own political advantage after his father's death at Crécy in 1346. Why did Charles not continue or even expand the Luxembourg association with Guillaume de Machaut? Could 'sidelining' Machaut, and by extension abrogating Francophile musical and literary tastes, be a deliberate, political act on Charles' side?

Another puzzle is the cultural profile of Charles' half-brother Wenceslas (1337–83), Duke of Brabant and Luxembourg (r. 1354/5–83). Unlike Charles, Wenceslas was deeply involved in Francophone court culture as a patron of Jean Froissart (the entirety of Wenceslas' poetic oeuvre survives within Froissart's narrative *dits*), and two polyphonic songs have been associated with Wenceslas' court, with the text of one of them attributed to Wenceslas personally. But it is much less known that Wenceslas also supported Germanophone poets working in the vernacular antecedents of Dutch and German. He seems not to have sought any contact with Machaut. About the relationship to music of Charles IV's son and successor as King of the Romans, Wenceslas of Bohemia, hardly anything is known at all.

Among the musical repertories of the fourteenth and early fifteenth centuries, complex mensural polyphony has long been the focus of musicological research. Over and over again, musicologists have represented mensural polyphony both as the central evolutionary strand of European music and as a cultural practice conveying unrivalled prestige. If this is true, why did polyphony not play a more significant role in Luxembourg court culture, especially in Bohemia? All the more so as, from an art-historical and architectural perspective, Luxembourg achievements in the territories east of the Rhine stand tall; and exchanges between the Luxembourg domains and France as well as Avignon and Italy are both richly layered and amply documented? Is it conceivable that the Luxembourg acquisition of cultural capital in the areas of literary and musical patronage was focused elsewhere – at least in some of their courts? If so, which ones, and why?

In what follows, I offer a few preliminary considerations that might help account for what appears at first glance to be a curious cultural misalignment. The misalignment, I submit, is imaginary only, for it is the result of a historiographical distortion owed, in large part, to discipline formations developed in the nineteenth and twentieth centuries. These were designed to establish and reinforce national(ist) identities, and therefore focused on 'centres' typically associated with political and/or perceived cultural capitals of the respective nation states, such as Paris or Florence. A second historiographic force obfuscating Luxembourg cultural policies with regard to music is the traditional preference for complex polyphony in the established narration of the late-medieval history of European music – a narration shaped by nineteenth- and twentieth-century ideas of linear progress from 'simple' or even 'primitive' music to a cultural apex around 1800 by way of intermediate stages of increasing complexity found in the west and south of Europe. Both biases work against the Luxembourgs.

They inevitably impede our insight; they do so especially if the cultural landscapes of at least some of the Luxembourg courts were predicated on alternative patterns of creating and accumulating cultural capital than the ones following a model pioneered by the royal court of France and, later, the ducal court of Burgundy, and their cultural and political satellites. Some structural adjustments to our reading of the available evidence might therefore be needed to enable us to understand the positions occupied by members and associates of the house of Luxembourg more fully and on their own terms, allowing us to do justice to their places in the evolution and history of late-medieval cultures and their music.

Before we move into the discussion proper, a few words on terminology and methodology are in order, not least because words and music are so intimately connected in late-medieval cultural practice.[1] While the antecedents of modern Dutch and modern German are distinctly different, a lot of Middle Dutch poetry exhibits considerable linguistic influence from High German, the ancestor of modern German. The phenomenon is particularly acute at the courts of the Luxembourgs, whose territories not only straddled the dividing line between Romance and Germanic languages but also between High and Low German or Middle High German and Middle Dutch. I shall therefore designate texts in either Germanic language as well as hybridized forms as 'Germanophone'. Similarly, texts in Old French will be designated 'Francophone'; this does not necessarily imply that they originated in the Kingdom of France or within the confines of modern France. Finally, I deliberately blur the traditional division between 'poetry' or 'literature', and 'music' – in our established disciplinary structures, words and music still fall into distinct domains,[2] and are further dissociated by the various 'national' languages and styles. But these are precisely the obstructions that historically have impeded our understanding of the intrinsically multilingual and multicultural nature of the late medieval Luxembourg courts.

---

1 For two recent discussions of this nexus, see Helen Deeming, 'Music and the Book: The Textualisation of Music and the Musicalisation of Text', in Delia da Sousa Correa (ed.), *The Edinburgh companion to literature and music* (Edinburgh, 2020), 48–62; Elizabeth Eva Leach, 'Performing Manuscripts', in Ardis Butterfield, Henry Hope and Pauline Souleau (eds), *Performing medieval text* (Cambridge, 2017), 11–19.
2 For the fluidity of these categories in the late medieval period, see, for example, Sylvia Huot, 'Voices and Instruments in Medieval French Secular Music: On the Use of Literary Texts as Evidence for Performance Practice', *Musica Disciplina* 43 (1989), 63–113; and, more recently, Uri Smilansky, 'The Polyphonies of Function: Guillaume de Machaut and the Performance of Text and Music', in Jonathan Fruoco (ed.), *Polyphony and the Modern* (New York, 2021), 15–36 (= https://tandfbis.s3-us-west-2.amazonaws.com/rt-files/docs/Open+Access+Chapters/9781003129837_oachapter1.pdf, accessed 29 April 2023).

In what follows, I shall attempt to provide an overview of what can be said at present about the sonic cultures at the courts of four generations of Luxembourg rulers, from Count Henry of Luxembourg (= Emperor Henry VII) and (to some extent) his brother Balduin, Prince-Elector and Archbishop of Trier, to John of Bohemia, to John's children Bonne, Charles, and Wenceslas, and Charles' sons Wenceslas and Sigismund. In the process, the multifaceted and politically malleable nature of Luxembourg patronage will become visible, as will the political etiologies of what seem to me deliberate repertorial choices. As a result, the soundscapes of Luxembourg courts emerge as the dynamic products of Luxembourg cultural politics (and, if you will, Luxembourg political gyrations), asking us to recalibrate our musicological sensorium.

REMEMBERING HENRY: LUXEMBOURG REFLECTIONS IN THE EARLY FOURTEENTH CENTURY

The election of Henry of Luxembourg (c. 1279–1313)[3] to the imperial dignity, his coronation in Rome in 1312 and his unexpected death in 1313 significantly changed the political landscape of Europe. Unsurprisingly, Henry's sudden rise to the emperorship found reflection in a variety of cultural utterances across both the Empire and France. A closer look at a few of them will help us gain some insight into the cultural practices

---

3   Henry of Luxembourg was born in the Hainaut city of Valenciennes and educated in Paris. He was the son of Count Henry VI of Luxembourg and Béatrice of Avesnes. His succession to the comital dignity was triggered unexpectedly by his father's death in the Battle of Worringen (1288). He married Margaret of Brabant (1276–1311) in 1292; the couple had three children, about whom more below. Elected King of the Romans in 1308 and crowned Holy Roman Emperor in Rome in 1312, Henry died suddenly in Buonconvento near Siena on 24 August 1313, giving rise to rumours of murder by a Dominican who allegedly gave the Emperor a poisoned host. See Peter Thorau, 'Heinrich VII', in Bernd Schneidmüller and Stefan Weinfurter (eds), *Die deutschen Herrscher des Mittelalters: Historische Portraits von Heinrich I. bis Maximilian I. (919–1519)* (Munich, 2003), 381–92; Jörg K. Hoensch, *Die Luxemburger: Eine spätmittelalterliche Dynastie gesamteuropäischer Bedeutung* (Stuttgart, 2000), 25–50; Ellen Widder and Wolfgang Kraut (eds), *Vom luxemburgischen Grafen zum europäischen Herrscher: Neue Forschungen zu Heinrich VII.* (Luxembourg, 2008); Sabine Penth and Peter Thorau (eds), *Rom 1312: Die Kaiserkrönung Heinrichs VII. und die Folgen: Die Luxemburger als Herrscherdynastie von gesamteuropäischer Bedeutung* (Cologne, 2016). The only full-fledged biography remains Friedrich Schneider, *Kaiser Heinrich VII.* (Greiz and Leipzig, 1924–8). See also the contributions by Jana Fantysová Matějkova and Uri Smilansky in this volume.

that connected the Luxembourgs and their courts to the aristocracies of both France and the Empire.

Henry VII's death is referenced in an anonymous, three-voice polytextual motet, *Scariotis geniture / Jure quod in opere / Superne matris*. The composition – an invective against the Dominicans – is transmitted as a unicum in Book 1 of the interpolated version of the *Roman de Fauvel* in the manuscript Paris, Bibliothèque nationale de France, fr. 146 (fol. 2r). Codex fr. 146 was created in Paris around 1320, and sponsored by French royal court circles around Charles of Valois (1270–1325), the ambitious younger brother of the recently deceased King Philip IV the Fair (r. 1285–1314). From a political point of view, the motet takes a decidedly pro-Luxembourg position: Henry is identified in the motet by his name and rank ('Henricum imperatorem'), and praised as the leader of the world ('rector mundi') and the 'marvellous flower of flowers' (of the world) ('mirum florum florem').[4] What are the reasons for this favourable portrayal?

The two princes – Charles of Valois and Henry of Luxembourg (= Henry VII) – were multiply connected dynastically and politically: both formed part of a network of nobles that conjoined the extended French royal family to a small cluster of high-placed families enfeoffed with territories at the western and north-western borders of the Holy Roman Empire. These included the rulers of the counties of Hainaut (in personal union with Holland and Zealand) and of Bar, and the duchies of Brabant and Lorraine. To give an example of the degree of miscegenation: Henry of Luxembourg (= Henry VII), through his mother Beatrice of Avesnes, was related to the rulers of Hainaut – he was a cousin of the ruling count, William I of Avesnes (c. 1286–1337, r. 1304–37) – while William I of Avesnes' mother Philippa was a Luxembourg and hence Henry of Luxembourg's aunt. William I of Avesnes in turn had married Charles of Valois' daughter Joan (c. 1294–1342) in 1305, thereby indirectly connecting the Valois and the Luxembourgs. Moreover, one of William's siblings, Mary of Avesnes (1280–1354), in 1310 married Count Louis of Clermont (1279–1341, from 1327 the first Duke of Bourbon), one of Charles of Valois' cousins and one of his staunchest allies within the French court (they both were grandsons of King Louis IX); to musicologists, Louis of Clermont is known as the first patron of the administrator, poet and composer Philippe de Vitry.[5]

---

4   For an edition of the motet, see Leo Schrade (ed.), *The Roman de Fauvel. The works of Philippe de Vitry. French cycles of the Ordinarium Missae*, Polyphonic Music of the Fourteenth Century 1, 8–9; online facsimile: https://gallica.bnf.fr/ark:/12148/btv1b8454675g/f15.item (accessed 29 April 2023).

5   Philippe de Vitry (1291–1361) in turn is believed to have been heavily involved with the creation of the Fauvel manuscript (Bibliothèque nationale de France, fr. 146) as the music editor, and perhaps more. On the manuscript and its relation

A daughter from this Avesnes-Bourbon marriage, Beatrix of Bourbon (1320–1383), later became the second wife of Henry VII's son, John of Luxembourg (1296–1346), in 1334. The Valois, Bourbon, Avesnes, and Luxembourg gene pools therefore were closely intertwined, as were their political interests. It is hardly surprising that they might also have shared a cultural language.

If there is one hallmark of the Lotharingian courts, however, that distinguished them from the French royal court and its genetic offshoots, it is that they were, to varying degrees, multilingual and, by extension, multicultural. This circumstance came about because the ruling families typically governed and exerted influence over territories using both Romance and Germanic vernaculars. The father of Henry VII's wife Margaret of Brabant (1276–1311), for example, Duke John I of Brabant (1252/3–94), was an acknowledged Minnesänger. His texts were included in one of the most significant collections of Middle High German poetry, the Manesse codex. However, Duke John I also patronized Francophone trouvères such as Adenet le Roi, and took pride in the high quality of his minstrels.[6]

---

to Henry VII, see above. On Vitry's long-standing link to the house of Clermont (later: Bourbon), see Andrew Wathey, 'European Culture and Musical Politics at the Court of Cyprus', in Ursula Günther and Ludwig Finscher (eds), *The Cypriot-French Repertory of the Manuscript Torino J.II.9* (Neuhausen-Stuttgart, 1995), 33–54. On Vitry and his biography more generally, see Andrew Wathey, 'The Marriage of Edward III and the Transmission of French Motets to England', *Journal of the American Musicological Society* 45 (1992), 1–29; Andrew Wathey, 'The Motets of Philippe de Vitry and the Fourteenth-Century Renaissance', *Early Music History* 12 (1993), 119–50; Andrew Wathey, 'Philippe de Vitry, Bishop of Meaux', *Early Music History* 38 (2019), 215–68. See also the contributions by David Catalunya, Karen Desmond, Karl Kügle and Anna Zayaruznaya in the special Vitry issue curated by Karen Desmond and Anna Zayaruznaya, *Early Music* 46 (2018), 373–438.

6 On this subject, see, most recently, Remco Sleiderink, 'From Francophile to Francophobe: The Changing Attitude of Medieval Dutch Authors towards French Literature', in Christopher Kleinhenz and Keith Busby (eds), *Medieval Multilingualism: The Francophone World and Its Neighbours* (Turnhout, 2010), 127–43 (specifically on John I of Brabant: 129). Also Remco Sleiderink, '"Une si belle histoire de nos propres seigneurs": la noblesse brabançonne et la littérature en néerlandais (premiere moitié du XIVe siècle)', *Le Moyen Âge* 113 (2007), 549–67; Remco Sleiderink, *De stem van de meester: de hertogen van Brabant en hun rol in het literaire leven (1106–1430)* (Amsterdam, 2003), in particular 57–122; Frank Willaert, 'Lyriklandschaft Lotharingien', in Bernd Bastert, Helmut Tervooren and Frank Willaert (eds), *Dialog mit den Nachbarn: Mittelniederländische Literatur zwischen dem 12. und 16. Jahrhundert*, Zeitschrift für deutsche Philologie, Sonderheft zum Band 130 (2011), 37–49; Frank Willaert, 'Entre trouvères et Minnesänger: la poésie de Jean Ier, duc de Brabant', in Keith Busby and Erik S. Kooper (eds), *Courtly Literature – Culture and Context: Selected Papers from the 5th Triennial Congress of*

Henry of Luxembourg's and Margaret of Brabant's household(s) clearly formed part of a string of courtly establishments along the western fringes of the Empire where both French and various forms of Dutch and German were familiar means of expression.[7] Significant examples of narrative poetry in French reflecting the events of the early 1300s and produced at or for the Lotharingian courts along the Meuse valley include the *Voeux du paon* and the *Voeux de l'épervier*, while in Dutch the romance *Goedevaart metten baerde* may be associated directly with Henry's and his wife's patronage.[8]

No specific evidence is available at present about the role of musicians and poets within Henry's household itself.[9] With regard to Henry's chapel, the *Gesta Treverorum*, the 'official' chronicle of the Archbishopric of Trier, offers the following statement:

> Capellae quoque suae ornamenta, missalia magni ornatus ac pretiosa, ad quaecumque perrexerat loca, adhuc comes existens, suis cum sommariis secum vehere faciebat, et omni die coram se et collateralia sua, quando aderat, per suos cantores electos *canticis cum musicalibus*, missas et horas canonicas, impedimento non interveniente; set impedimento urgente, vesperas saltem et completorium, et hoc nulla die praetermittendo, celebrare solemniter faciebat. In missis vero audiendis, horisque canonicis cum die dicendis, maxime devotione pollebat; ita quod suis sacerdotibus capellanis maximam devotionem dicitur praestitisse.[10]

> (Already when he was a count, he [Henry] always made sure that the vessels and the highly embellished and expensive missals of his chapel were moving around with him along with his own necessities, no matter where he had gone, and every day [he ensured] that Mass and the Canonical Hours

---

the *International Courtly Literature Society, Dalfsen, The Netherlands, 9–16 August, 1986* (Amsterdam, 1990), 585–94.

7 See Sleiderink, *De stem van de meester*, 110–12.
8 These associations are based on the internal evidence of the respective texts; see the discussions in Elizabeth Eva Leach, 'The Provenance, Date, and Patron of Oxford, Bodleian Library, MS Douce 308', *Speculum* 97 (2022), 283–321, and Sleiderink, *De stem van de meester*, 110.
9 But see the rich indirect reflection of Henry's activities in poetic, narrative, and visual sources from the Meuse-Moselle region discussed in Michel Margue, 'Die Kaiserkrönung Heinrich VII. in den maas-moselländischen Quellen', in Penth and Thorau (eds), *Rom 1312: Die Kaiserkrönung Heinrichs VII.*, 113–30.
10 See Johannes Hugo Wyttenbach and Michael Franz Joseph Müller (eds), *Gesta Trevirorum integra lectionis varietate et animadversionibus illustrata*, vol. 2 (Trier, 1838), 204. Italics added.

were celebrated in his and his retinue's presence by his own select singers *with musical adornments* unless there was some impediment; but in case there was some impediment, he made sure that at least Vespers and Compline – which he omitted not a single day – were celebrated with solemnity. When hearing Mass and the Canonical Hours that were required for the day, he showed the utmost devotion; so much so that he is said to have been supremely devoted to his own priests and chaplains.)

The report may be overly enthusiastic, given that it was written under the aegis of Henry's younger brother Balduin of Luxembourg, the powerful archbishop-elector of Trier (born c. 1285, r. 1307–54). Like Henry, Balduin culturally straddled Francophone and Germanophone traditions. He studied at the University of Paris in the early 1300s. As Elector and Prince-Archbishop of Trier from 1307 onward, he played an important role in imperial politics throughout his long life, beginning with the election of his brother to the imperial dignity in 1308 (and later that of his great-nephew Charles in 1346).[11] Despite these caveats, the report is suggestive and invites further study. It is clear that plainchant played a highly significant role in the soundscape of Henry's court, but what are we to make of the 'cantores electos' who performed the liturgy 'canticis cum musicalibus'? It is tempting to think that they might have mastered the tradition of Parisian organum and of motets such as the ones documented in the final (eighth) fascicle of the Montpellier codex (Bibliothèque interuniversitaire, Bibliothèque universitaire de médecine, H.196), given Henry's strong connection at the time with the court of France.[12]

---

11 On Balduin of Luxembourg, see, among others, the essays in Reiner Nolden (ed.), *Balduin von Luxemburg: Erzbischof und Kurfürst von Trier (1308–1354)* (Trier, 2010), and Valentin Wagner and Bernhard Schmitt (eds), *Balduin aus dem Hause Luxemburg: Erzbischof und Kurfürst von Trier 1284–1354* (Luxembourg, 2009); Friedhelm Burgard, 'Balduin von Luxemburg (um 1285–1354): Kurfürst, Bischof und Landesherr', in Franz J. Felten (ed.), *Mainzer (Erz-)Bischöfe in ihrer Zeit* (Stuttgart, 2008), 35–58. On Balduin's education, see the *Gesta Trevirorum*, 194–5.

12 For information on music at the French court and in circles close to it around 1300, see the pertinent sections in Mark Everist and Thomas Forrest Kelly (eds), *The Cambridge History of Medieval Music* (Cambridge, 2018). Also Catherine A. Bradley and Karen Desmond (eds), *The Montpellier codex, the final fascicle: contents, context, chronologies* (Woodbridge, 2018); M. Cecilia Gaposchkin, *The making of Saint Louis: kingship, sanctity, and crusade in the later Middle Ages* (Ithaca, NY, 2008); and the essays in Margaret Bent and Andrew Wathey (eds), *Fauvel Studies: allegory, chronicle, music, and image in Paris, Bibliothèque nationale de France, MS français 146* (Oxford, 1997).

Alternatively or, perhaps better, additionally they were probably proficient in non-mensural techniques of performing plainchant polyphonically.[13]

It is worth noting a certain cultural shift in Henry's entourage after his election as King of the Romans. At this point in time, Henry added several new members to his court that gave it a distinctly Germanic flavour. The Prince-Bishop of Eichstätt, Philipp von Rathsamhausen, a Paris-trained Cistercian from Alsace, was appointed as adviser and tutor of Henry's son and expected successor, John of Luxembourg.[14] The archbishop-elector of Mainz, Peter von Aspelt (c. 1245–1320), had been a key ally in engineering Henry's election. He was also a significant patron of Minnesang; toward the end of his life, he was responsible for bringing the highly reputed Heinrich von Meißen (also known as Frauenlob, d. 1318) to Mainz, where Frauenlob was buried in the cathedral.[15] Frauenlob previously spent time at the court of King Wenceslas II of Bohemia, another prince of the Empire whose poetry appears in the Codex Manesse. From the moment of his election, then, Henry seems to have enhanced his inner circle with individuals steeped at least as much in the cultural patterns and expectations of the Germanophone regions as with the Francophone parts of Europe. Arguably, these shifts are in the first instance the product of necessity, having to deal with a new range of subjects and political agents. But they also suggest at least a wish, but more likely the compelling political need, to conform to cultural expectations associated with performing the role of emperor.

---

13   See the important discussion of this phenomenon by Reinhard Strohm, 'Klösterliche Mehrstimmigkeit: Arten und Kontexte', in *Musikleben des Spätmittelalters in der Region Österreich*, <https://musical-life.net/essays/kloesterliche-mehrstimmigkeit-arten-und-kontexte> (2019, accessed 29 April 2023). As Strohm points out, these techniques were not confined to monastic communities, his title notwithstanding, nor to the geographic region which is the primary focus of Strohm's article (modern-day Austria). They would have been readily accessible to Henry's singers.

14   For a biographical study, see, most recently, Alfred Wendehorst, 'Philipp von Rathsamhausen', in *Germania Sacra: Das Bistum Eichstätt. 1, Die Bischofsreihe bis 1535* (Berlin, 2006), 134–50. Also Médard Barth, 'Philipp von Rathsamhausen, Abt des Klosters Pairis O. Cist. (1301–1306) und Bischof von Eichstätt (1306–1322)', *Archives de l'église d'Alsace* 38 [= nouvelle série 22] (1975), 79–129.

15   On Peter von Aspelt, see, most recently, David Kirt, *Peter von Aspelt (1240/45–1320): Ein spätmittelalterlicher Kirchenfürst zwischen Luxemburg, Böhmen und dem Reich* (Luxembourg, 2013). See also Dana Dvořáčková-Malá, 'Petr z Aspeltu mezi Přemyslovci a Lucemburky', in Luděk Březina, Jana Konvična and Jan Zdichynec (eds), *Ve znamení zemí Koruny české: Sborník k 60. narozeninám prof. Ph.Dr. Lenky Bobkové, CSc* (Prague, 2006), 27–34; Tilmann Schmidt, 'Drogen für den Erzbischof: Peter von Aspelt (gest. 1320) und der Arzt Johann von Göttingen', *Archiv für mittelrheinische Kirchengeschichte* 58 (2006), 109–30.

Besides patronizing Germanophone poets such as the author of the aforementioned *Goedevaart metten baerde*, protocol also seems to have required a prince to maintain a significant standing contingent of minstrels as part of their courtly entourage. This is documented for Henry's younger brother Balduin in English court records dating from 1338.[16] As one of the most influential princes of the Empire, Balduin's social pedigree and his education might at first glance have positioned him excellently to participate in the rich music culture of the Francophone area of his time – of which the motet *Scariotis geniture / Jure quod in opera / Superne matris gaudia* is but one example. However, there is no tangible evidence of this. Balduin's activities as a cultural patron, as far as they have been surveyed, instead suggest a distinct focus on and deliberate conformity with the traditions of his – predominantly Germanophone – territories in the Moselle region.[17]

If Paris and the Luxembourg/Trier region, together with Brabant and Hainaut, mark the south-western and north-eastern geographical fixed points of the traditional Luxembourg sphere of influence, manuscript Oxford, Bodleian Library, Douce 308, another witness commemorating the events of Henry VII's emperorship, is emblematic of its south-eastern fringe. Douce 308 can be placed securely in the city of Metz in the 1310s, and its genesis, like the Latin-texted Parisian motet discussed earlier, appears related to the aftermath of Henry VII's election, his expedition to Italy and subsequent death, and the impact of these events on the Lotharingian aristocracy. Douce 308 includes not only a copy of the aforementioned *Voeux de l'épervier* which specifically commemorates the events triggered by Henry VII's election and premature death via the

---

16 As cited in Friedhelm Burgard, *Familia Archiepiscopi: Studien zu den geistlichen Funktionsträgern Erzbischof Balduins von Luxemburg (1307–1354)* (Trier, 1991), 241, n. 354 (payment to six minstrels in the service of Balduin for performing for King Edward III of England). See also Mary Lyon, Bryce Lyon, Henry S. Lucas and Jean de Sturler (eds), *The Wardrobe Book of William de Norwell, 12 July 1338 to 27 May 1340* (Brussels, 1983), 243: 'Henrico van Valbik et 5 sociis suis menestrallis domini archiepiscopi Treverensis facientibus menestraciam suam'; at the same occasion payments were made by English court officials to 'magistro Ithell et decem sociis suis menestrallis … imperatoris facientibus menestraciam suam' and 'decem aliis menestrallis diversorum aliorum magnatum Allemannie'; and Reinhold Pauli, 'Die Beziehungen König Eduards III. von England zu Kaiser Ludwig IV. in den Jahren 1338 und 1339', *Quellen und Erörterungen zur bayerischen und deutschen Geschichte*, Alte Folge 7 (1858; reprint 1969), 411–40, at 434.

17 See, most recently, Verena Keller, *Balduin von Trier (1285–1354): Kunst, Herrschaft und Spiritualität im Mittelalter* (Trier, 2012); also Franz J. Ronig, 'Kunst unter Balduin von Luxemburg', in Franz-Josef Heyen and Johannes Mötsch (eds), *Balduin von Luxemburg: Erzbischof von Trier – Kurfürst des Reiches, 1285–1354. Festschrift aus Anlass des 70. Geburtsjahres* (Mainz, 1985), 489–558.

medium of a courtly romance,[18] but also transmits detailed testimony of a very rich participatory musical culture among Lotharingian aristocrats, including high-placed women at court, in the preceding generation of Henry VII's parents in the account of the *Tournament of Chauvency* by Jacques Bretel.[19] One of the two surviving versions of the *Tournament* is contained in the third fascicle of manuscript Oxford, Bodleian Library, Douce 308; the fascicle complements the tournament narrative with a supplement of (unnotated) Francophone song and motet texts, all of which document an extremely varied musico-poetic culture in upper Lotharingia that the Luxembourgs seem to have been at ease with. The narrative by Jacques Bretel was completed in 1285 and looks back at an event that took place outside Chauvency-le-Château (present-day Département Meuse) in 1284. In the narrative, Henry VII's mother, Beatrice of Avesnes (styled as 'Countess of Luxembourg'), is the highest-ranking lady in attendance, and she takes a leading role as a performer in the musical entertainments surrounding the tournament.[20]

THE LUXEMBOURGS DECENTRED: JOHN, BONNE, AND THE EARLY CAREER OF GUILLAUME DE MACHAUT (c. 1330–50)

Bohemian nobles approached Henry VII in 1309 in order to negotiate the marriage of Henry's only son, John, to the last unwed princess in that

---

18   On this text, see the discussion in Leach, 'The Provenance, Date, and Patron of Oxford, Bodleian Library, MS Douce 308'; also Michel Margue, '*Voeux du paon* et *Voeux de l'épervier*: L'empereur et ses "meilleurs chevaliers" dans la culture courtoise entre Metz, Bar et Luxembourg (début XIVe siècle)', in Mireille Chazan and Nancy Freeman Regalado (eds), *Lettres, musique et société en Lorraine médiévale: Autour du 'Tournoi de Chauvency' (Ms. Oxford Bodleian Douce 308)* (Geneva, 2012), 105–36; idem, 'L'histoire impériale au service de la bourgeoisie: Les Chroniques de Jacques d'Esch et la maison impériale de Luxembourg', in Mireille Chazan and Gérard Nauroy (eds), *Écrire l'histoire à Metz au Moyen Âge: Actes du colloque organisé par l'Université Paul-Verlaine de Metz, 23–25 avril 2009* (Bern, 2011), 281–311; and idem, 'Les vœux sur les oiseaux: fortune littéraire d'un rite de cour – usages politiques d'un motif littéraire', in Catherine Gaullier-Bougassas (ed.), *Les Vœux du Paon de Jacques de Longuyon: originalité et rayonnement* (Paris, 2011), 255–89.
19   Jacques Bretel, *Le Tournoi de Chauvency*, ed. Maurice Delbouille (Liège, 1932). The manuscript as well as the *Tournament* narrative have recently been studied extensively; see Leach, 'The Provenance, Date, and Patron of Oxford, Bodleian Library, MS Douce 308'.
20   Leach, 'The Provenance, Date, and Patron of Oxford, Bodleian Library, MS Douce 308', 310. For a related Francophone song collection from Metz, see Elizabeth Eva Leach, Joseph W. Mason and Matthew P. Thomson (eds), *A Medieval Songbook: Trouvère MS C* (Woodbridge, 2022).

generation of the Přemyslid dynasty, Elizabeth of Bohemia. This marriage led to the acquisition of the crown of Bohemia (1310) for the house of Luxembourg and the subsequent coronation of John as King of Bohemia in Prague in 1311.[21]

After the death of his father in 1313, John undertook a bid to succeed him as King of the Romans but remained unsuccessful. He and his supporters conceded to Louis of Bavaria from the house of Wittelsbach in a contested election where Frederick of Habsburg emerged as the opposing candidate. John remained Louis' ally against the Habsburgs for almost ten years, until Louis' decisive victory in the Battle of Mühldorf (28 September 1322).[22] Nothing specific is known at present about John's cultural interests in those years.[23] Recognizing that his prospects in the Empire were going to be limited after Mühldorf for the foreseeable future, John from 1322 aligned himself and his politics ever more closely with the interests of the French royal family.[24] A first step in this direction was taken in the form of the marriage of his sister Marie to King Charles IV of France (1322). This was followed by the transfer of the King of Bohemia's firstborn son, Wenceslas (who in 1323, in France, adopted the name Charles), to the court of France in 1323 when the young prince was also betrothed to Blanche of Valois (1317–48), the youngest daughter of Charles of Valois and a cousin of the reigning king, Charles IV. Around the same time, in the early 1320s, Guillaume de Machaut and, possibly, his brother Jean entered the administration of the western (traditionally Luxembourg) part of John's realm.[25] The Luxembourg alliance with the Valois grew even stronger when Charles IV (d. 1 February 1328) was succeeded by Charles of Valois' eldest son, who became King Philip VI of France on 1 April 1328. In May 1329, Charles/Wenceslas and Blanche were formally married. In a

---

21 For the most recent biographical study, see Lenka Bobková, *Jan Lucemburský: Otec slavného syna* (Prague, 2018). For a recent study of the cultural aspects of John's reign, see Johannes Abdullahi, *Der Kaisersohn und das Geld: Freigebigkeit und Prachtentfaltung König Johanns von Böhmen (1296–1346)* (Luxembourg, 2019).
22 See Michel Pauly, 'Der Traum von der Kaiserkrone: Die vergeblichen Bemühungen König Johanns von Böhmen um die Kaiserwürde', *Zeitschrift für historische Forschung* 35 (2008), 549–79, at 550–4.
23 Aside from a life-long predilection for tournaments; see Abdullahi, *Der Kaisersohn und das Geld*, 48–130, in particular 78–93. For the musical components of such gatherings in the Meuse area, see Leach, 'The Provenance, Date, and Patron of Oxford, Bodleian Library, MS Douce 308'.
24 See Pauly, 'Traum von der Kaiserkrone', for a more detailed discussion of this move as part of John's strategy to recover the imperial crown.
25 Both Machauts' roles in John's administration – including Guillaume's single foray into Central Europe and Prussia – are discussed in detail by Jana Fantysová Matějková in this volume. Concerning Machaut's brother Jean, the first document substantiating his association with King John is dated 1333.

complementary move, John's daughter Bonne married John of Normandy, the eldest son of the first Valois king of France, Philip VI, in Melun near Paris on 28 July 1332. The apogee of John of Luxembourg's political alliance with the French royal house – suitably reinforced by strategic marital arrangements – was reached when John, in a second marriage, wed Beatrix of Bourbon (c. 1314–83) in 1334.[26]

While John kept pursuing his claims in Bohemia, Silesia, Poland, Prussia, Tyrol, and northern Italy throughout the 1320s and 1330s, and was therefore frequently absent, his pronounced political interests in Luxembourg and France required continuous and regular contact of a group of John's retainers with the high and mighty of France and Lotharingia.[27] This group included Guillaume and Jean de Machaut, but not in the leading positions. Maintaining John's network in the west created many opportunities for his clerks to interact (whether directly or indirectly) with top-ranked aristocrats such as Beatrix of Bourbon (c. 1314–83; later, John's second wife), Joan of Évreux (1310–71, the third wife and widow of Charles IV of France), Joan of Navarre (1312–49, the only daughter of Louis X and, from 1328, Queen of Navarre), Joan of Valois (c. 1294–1342, the Countess of Hainaut), or Joan of Burgundy (c. 1293–1349, Queen of France to King Philip VI), thereby opening up the possibility of them projecting John's standing as the most noble of the French king's vassals and an *exemplum* of contemporary chivalry through cultural activities of their own (poetry and music). In a similar manner, they must have interacted with male aristocrats such as Mathieu de Trie III (d. 1344, Marshal of France 1318–44 and a key member of the Valois-Luxembourg coterie).[28] This might have stimulated much of the French-texted (and the occasional Latin-texted) works created by Guillaume de Machaut during this period and collected in Paris, Bibliothèque nationale de France, fr.

---

26 On the political and military background of these marriages, see Jana Fantysová-Matějková, *Wenceslas de Bohême: Un prince au carrefour de l'Europe* (Paris, 2013), 17–27. Also Dieter Veldtrup, 'Ehen aus Staatsräson: Die Familien- und Heiratspolitik Johanns von Böhmen', in Michel Pauly (ed.), *Johann der Blinde: Graf von Luxemburg, König von Böhmen 1296–1346. Tagungsband der 9es Journées Lotharingiennes, 22.-26. Oktober, Centre Universitaire de Luxembourg* (Luxembourg, 1997), 483–543.
27 See the essay by Jana Fantysová Matějková in this volume for further details.
28 Mathieu's younger brother Guillaume de Trie (d. 1334) was Archbishop of Reims from 1324 to 1334 and as such, together with Mathieu, was instrumental in the coronation of Philip VI in Reims in 1328 and thus the establishment of the Valois on the throne of France to the detriment of the other potential candidates, notably Edward III of England and Joan of Navarre. Machaut wrote a motet in honour of Guillaume de Trie; on this composition, see, most recently, Karen Desmond, 'Traces of revision in Machaut's motet *Bone pastor*', in Lawrence Earp and Jared Hartt (eds), *Poetry, Art, and Music in Guillaume de Machaut's Earliest Manuscript (BnF fr. 1586)* (Turnhout, 2021), 397–432.

1586 (Machaut C). Arguably, these poetic and musical creations would have been perceived (and received) by their recipients as direct emanations of the 'soft power' which John was strategically projecting through the activities of his retainers (in Machaut's case, specifically in the fields of courtly poetry and song), even more so when his dependency on them increased from the late 1330s onward due to his blindness. As suggested by Uri Smilansky in this volume, John's daughter Bonne (1315–49, the Duchess of Normandy) may have been a relatively junior participant in a complex social network of aristocrats and clerics that underpinned and continuously stimulated such cultural exploits. If correct, this scenario would not only highlight the importance of the Franco-Lotharingian environment for enabling and sustaining Machaut's artistic development, but also underscore the importance of high-placed females for the creation and reception of courtly poetry and song, now increasingly delegated (and, hence, professionalized) to talented retainers like Machaut.[29] This stands in no contradiction to Machaut's almost reverential relationship to King John, whose protection and patronage, indeed, enabled all this for him, and to whom he felt – probably correctly – that he owed everything. Further studies of these French and Franco-Lotharingian aristocrats' lives and their activities as patron(esse)s of the arts will be needed to provide additional clarity about their influence on court culture in France, and the Francophone parts of the Empire, not least specifically in the area of song production, but it is clear that they overlap with the formative decades of the Ars Nova and of Machaut's personal lyrical and musical style in the 1330s and 1340s.

There is at this stage no indication of any proactive interest on the part of John in Germanophone poetry and song, although he spent significant amounts of time with nobles from the Rhineland whose native language was Dutch or German,[30] and so far was traced in four Germanophone

---

29 For additional materials supporting this line of thought, researched and published independently from work on this essay, see Andrew Wathey, 'Guillaume de Machaut and Yolande of Flanders', and Benjamin L. Albritton, '*Ex historia Guillelmi di Mascandio*: Machaut in the *Annales Hannoniae* of Jacques de Guise', both in Jared C. Hartt, Tamsyn Mahoney-Steel and Benjamin Albritton (eds), *Manuscripts, Music, Machaut: Essays in Honor of Lawrence Earp* (Turnhout, 2022), 111–26 and 127–50. Also Kevin Brownlee, 'Machaut as Poet Figure in the *Prise d'Alexandre*', in Hartt, Mahoney-Steel and Albritton (eds), *Manuscripts, Music, Machaut*, 207–17.

30 See Abdullahi, *Der Kaisersohn und das Geld*, in particular Chapter 3 ('Kostspielige Feste und Turniere') and Chapter 4 ('Umfangreiche Zuwendungen für rheinische "Hansel"'), 48–177. See also the insightful essay by Peter Moraw on the 'multicultural' composition of John's entourage; Moraw points out that at Crécy John was accompanied by two knights from the Upper Rhine region; see his 'Über den Hof Johanns von Luxemburg und Böhmen', in Michel Pauly (ed.), *Johann der Blinde*, 93–120, at 106. For a contrasting view emphasizing John's 'French-ness', see Philippe

texts.³¹ The records left by John's courts were also never studied systematically for evidence of contact with minstrels up to now. There may, therefore, be evidence lurking in the archives. By the same token, John's cultural and political proximity to Francophone court culture, combined with his uncertain status in the arena of imperial politics, may simply have pre-empted any need for serious cultural engagement with the Germanophone tradition – an assessment supported by art-historical research.³² The situation was certainly not helped by John's fraught relationship with his Přemyslid wife and his two sons, most importantly his eldest, Wenceslas/Charles.³³

DEFINING LUXEMBOURG EMPERORSHIP: CHARLES AND THE PŘEMYSLID TRADITION

Luxembourg (or Luxembourg-related) cultural output in the west in the 1330s and 1340s not only squares fully with Francophone cultural patterns

---

Contamine, 'Politique, culture et sentiment dans l'Occident de la fin du Moyen Âge: Jean l'Aveugle et la royauté française', in Pauly (ed.), *Johann der Blinde*, 343–61.

31 See Kurt Matthaei (ed.), *Minne und Gesellschaft: Mittelhochdeutsche Minnereden, vol. 1: Die Heidelberger Handschriften 344, 358, 376 und 393* (Berlin, 1913), Nr. 6, 65–71 ('Diz ist ein krig ob minnen beßer sie oder gesellschaft'); Jaap Tigelaar (ed.), '"Dese es van Behem coninck Jan": Een onbekende ererede over Jan de Blinde, graaf van Luxemburg, koning van Bohemen (1296–1346)', *Queeste: Tijdschrift over middeleeuwse letterkunde* 10 (2003), 146–61. See also the discussions of these texts – which may in their majority be posthumous to John himself – in Abdullahi, *Der Kaisersohn*, in particular 125–6.

32 See the contributions by Danielle Gaborit-Chopin, 'Les arts précieux à Paris (ivoires et orfèvrerie) au temps de Jean de Luxembourg', and Karel Otavský, 'Die Dynastie der Luxemburger und die Pariser Kunst unter den letzten Kapetingern', in Klára Benešovská (ed.), *King John of Luxembourg (1296–1346) and the Art of his Era* (Prague, 1998), 53–61 and 62–8.

33 But see the activities in both Luxembourg and Bohemia concerning his *memoria* toward the end of his life discussed in Michel Margue, '"Regum de stirpe" – Le prince et son image: Donations, fondations et sépultures des Luxembourg dans leur terres d'origine (première moitié du XIVe siècle)', in Klára Benešovská (ed.), *King John of Luxembourg (1296–1346) and the Art of his Era* (Prague, 1998), 100–16, and the discussion of the Prague residence by Klára Benešovská, 'Les residences du roi Jean de Bohème: leur function de représentation', in *King John of Luxembourg and Art*, 117–31, at 125–31. Attempts by John to introduce Francophone cultural habits to Bohemia were, however, met with resistance; see, for example, Abdullahi, *Der Kaisersohn und das Geld*, 78–81, but also Eva Schlotheuber, 'Die "größtmögliche Veränderung" (maxima mutatio) des Königreichs Böhmen: Peter von Zittau und die politische Wende Johanns von Luxemburg', in Magdaléna Nespěšná Hamsiková, Jana Peroutková and Stefan Scholz (eds), *Ecclesia docta: Spolčenství ducha a umění* (Prague, 2016), 105–29.

but indeed became constitutive in shaping our perception of these patterns.[34] The same cannot be said of John's first-born son, Wenceslas or, from 1323, by his adopted name: Charles. Charles participated in the administration of the eastern part of the Luxembourg possessions, the Kingdom of Bohemia, from the mid-1330s onward. Unlike his father John, who never gained full social acceptance with the Bohemian powers-that-be due to his non-Bohemian ancestry (although his legitimacy was never questioned), Charles enjoyed significant local sympathy and emotional support; this was without doubt owed substantially to the pedigree he inherited from his mother Elizabeth, the last Přemyslid princess, and by extension probably also to Charles' standing as the grandson of the great Wenceslas II. Charles consciously embraced this Přemyslid heritage, which he could use as a tool to distance himself – if and when strategically expedient – from his father and thereby solidify his and his family's hold on the Kingdom of Bohemia.[35]

Having been educated at the court of Paris in the 1320s, and mentored by Pierre Roger (later Pope Clement VI, 1342–52) in the years 1328–30, Charles was betrothed to Charles of Valois' youngest daughter, Marguerite (later renamed Blanche) at the age of seven, in 1323. The couple started residing in the Bohemian capital from 1334. In 1336, they were temporarily joined in Prague by Blanche's mother-in-law, Beatrix of Bourbon, John's second wife. However, Beatrix returned to Luxembourg in 1337, soon after the birth of her son Wenceslas, while Charles and Blanche remained in Bohemia. In the years that followed, the couple – then bearing the titles of Margrave and Margravess of Moravia – engaged in a wide range of cultural activities. Most conspicuous among these were the building activities they initiated which profoundly reshaped the Bohemian capital. First was the reconstruction of Prague Castle, including the establishment of a chapter of canons for the Chapel of All Saints there (1339). In 1344, the couple endowed a college of 24 resident canons (*mansionarii*) at St Vitus Cathedral in Prague (in addition to the long-established sitting chapter); their tasks were dedicated exclusively to the worship of the Virgin. In 1344, concomitant with the elevation of the see of Prague to an

---

34 Extremely so in the case of music history, where the Machaut manuscripts in relation to the paucity of other sources from the region have involuntarily been obstructing our perspective on Francophone music culture in the mid to late fourteenth and early fifteenth centuries.

35 On the complicated and highly charged relationship between John and Charles, see Heinz Thomas, 'Vater und Sohn: König Johann und Karl IV', in Michel Pauly (ed.), *Johann der Blinde*, 445–82. It is likely that Charles' turn toward Bohemia was spurred further by his father's second marriage to Beatrix of Bourbon and the birth of his half-brother Wenceslas (1337). According to his father's plans, Wenceslas was to inherit the Luxembourg possessions in western Europe, at Charles' expense.

archbishopric, the reconstruction of St Vitus Cathedral was begun. This was done in collaboration with King John, who may have taken the lead in this project; it was initially guided by a French architect brought in from Avignon, Matthias of Arras (c. 1290–1352), later by the famous Peter Parler. The next project followed in 1348 – two years after John's death at Crécy – and consisted of the foundation of the New Town of Prague and the establishment of Prague University. By that time, Charles had formally succeeded his father as King of Bohemia (he was crowned in 1347) and also, as it were, bested him as King of the Romans (first elected in 1346, confirmed in 1349). Charles was well on his way to his coronation as Holy Roman Emperor (1355).

The reconstruction of Prague Castle, the endowment of a chapter of canons at the castle chapel of All Saints, the enlargement of the capital city, and the foundation of a university all drew strong – albeit not exclusive – inspiration from Paris; indeed, the development of Paris under the Capetians seems to have served as a blueprint for Charles' cultural activities in Prague at least up to the confirmation of his election as King of the Romans in 1349. In the late 1330s and 1340s, Charles was preparing himself for his succession to the throne as King of Bohemia. From that vantage point, it made good political sense for him to take his cues from the highly successful cultural practices of kingship developed in the late thirteenth and early fourteenth centuries by the Capetians. These cultural-political strategies secured their kingdom a prominent place in Europe, which Charles had ample opportunity to observe during his early years in France. Applying this matrix not only to investments in architecture and in ecclesiastical foundations or educational institutions, but to all matters where religion, culture, and politics intertwined, for example with regard to the cultivation of ancestral saints, was an eminently sensible move to cement the Luxembourg position as kings of Bohemia. From the moment of Charles' election as King of the Romans, however, this French-inspired pattern began to be transformed. With the imperial crown within reach, the ultimate objective for Charles became no longer to emulate, but to transcend, Paris. Accustoming himself to his new, transnational role of Holy Roman Emperor required him to conspicuously distance himself from French models in order to demonstrate the singular quality assigned the emperorship within the geo-political framework of Latin Christian Europe. He did so at first by intensifying, then by surpassing, the French models he inherited, and at last by giving them entirely new meaning as components of his very own, Caroline performance of emperorship. As a descendant of the tenth-century Duke of Bohemia and martyr, St Wenceslas, for example, his saintly pedigree arguably matched, perhaps surpassed, that of the Capetians which rested on the relatively recently canonized Louis IX (1297).[36] To give this inheritance the fullest expression possible and merge it with his dynastic claims to the throne of Bohemia, Charles massively intensified the cult of Bohemian saints by creating the exquisite Chapel of St Wenceslas inside Prague Cathedral, augmented with chapels dedicated to saints Vitus and Adalbert; taking this strategy to the next level, the introduction of the relics of Sigismund, a saint originally associated with the Kingdom of Arles, into Prague Cathedral further supported Charles' claim to universal imperial power, while also giving expression to the dynastic aspirations of the Luxembourgs towards continued election to the emperorship in the generations that were to follow. The tombs designated for himself and his family were carefully arranged inside the choir, evoking but at the same time transcending the French royal necropolis at St Denis in sanctity due to a hitherto unheard-of accumulation of holiness within a single space.[37] All in all, he ensured that Prague, by the 1350s, began to outshine Paris, especially in terms of religious authority: its see, unlike that of Paris, was raised to an archbishopric in 1344, and its three towns not only harboured a systematically built-up array of relics which were regularly shown to the public, but also became the site of a diverse range of saints' cults, accompanied by newly founded chapters and monastic sites designed to mirror Prague's intended role as the physical and spiritual centre of a renewed Empire claiming truly universal authority.

Charles further bolstered this strategy of (self-)sanctification by instrumentalizing the cult of Charlemagne – again appropriated just a few years earlier by the late Capetians, with Philip IV claiming Capetian descendancy from the first Holy Roman Emperor. Charles had adopted Charlemagne early on in Paris as his (second) patron saint by taking on Charlemagne's name in addition to – and *de facto* as a replacement of –

---

36 Nevertheless, or perhaps precisely because of this, Charles' first queen, Blanche, between 1346 and 1348 ensured that an altar for St Louis was included in the new choir of the *mansionarii* at St Vitus Cathedral that was to serve both as an outsized Lady Chapel and, in due course, as the royal necropolis within the rebuilt cathedral. On the cult of St Louis, see M. Cecilia Gaposchkin, *The Making of Saint Louis*; eadem, *Blessed Louis, the Most Glorious of Kings: Texts Relating to the Cult of Saint Louis of France* (Notre Dame, IN, 2012).

37 On this subject, see the recent study by Petr Uličný, 'The Choirs of St Vitus's Cathedral in Prague: A Marriage of Liturgy, Coronation, Royal Necropolis and Piety', *Journal of The British Archaeological Association* 168 (2015), 186–233, and the essays collected in Jiří Kuthan and Jan Royt (eds), *The Cathedral of St. Vitus at Prague Castle* (Prague, 2011). Also, David C. Mengel, 'A Holy and Faithful Fellowship: Royal Saints in Fourteenth-Century Prague', in Eva Doležalová, Robert Novotný and Pavel Soukup (eds), *Evropa a Čechy na konci středověku: Sborník příspěvků věnovaných Františku Šmahelu* (Prague, 2004), 145–58.

his baptismal name Wenceslas.³⁸ He eventually repurposed the cult of Charlemagne for his emperorship by founding a monastery dedicated to that cult in Prague's New Town, as well as placing himself within a genealogy of patriarchs and rulers that reached from Alexander the Great via the emperors of Rome and Byzantium to Charlemagne in the decoration of the Great Hall of Prague Castle, and from Noah to Charlemagne at Karlštejn.³⁹ In addition, a comprehensive series of foundations both in his capital city of Prague and across the Empire, along with carefully placed public appearances, from the late 1340s onward ensured the projection of Charles' quasi-sacerdotal brand of imperial majesty through both visual and performative displays.⁴⁰ Ultimately, Charles' strategy was to turn Prague into a holy city rivalling, perhaps even surpassing, Rome or Constantinople in spiritual power, and turning the city into an image of

---

38 See the nuanced discussion of the political and ideological background of this name change in Reinhard Schneider, 'Karolus, qui et Wenceslaus'. Also important to bear in mind in this context is that Charles considered Charlemagne one of his direct ancestors (through the dukes of Brabant); see Schneider, 'Karolus, qui et Wenceslaus', 385–6.
39 On the importance of these genealogies, see Marie Bláhová, 'Herrschergenealogie als Modell der Dauer des "politischen Körpers" des Herrschers im mittelalterlichen Böhmen', in Andreas Speer and David Wirmer (eds), *Das Sein der Dauer* (Berlin, 2008), 380–97, and Václav Žůrek, 'L'usage comparé des motifs historiques dans la légitimation monarchique entre les royaumes de France et de Bohême à la fin du Moyen Âge' (PhD thesis, École des Hautes Études en Sciences Sociales, 2014). On the architecture, decoration, and symbolism of Karlštejn more generally, see the pertinent essays in Jiří Fajt (ed.), *Magister Theodoricus, Court Painter to Emperor Charles IV: The Pictorial Decoration of the Shrines at Karlštejn Castle* (Prague, 1998); Jiří Fajt (ed.), *Court Chapels of the High and Late Middle Ages and Their Artistic Decoration / Dvorské kaple vrcholného a pozdního středověku a jejich umělecká výzdoba* (Prague, 2003).
40 For discussions of this network of sacred sites and performances of emperorship, see Zoë Opačić, 'Carolus Magnus and Carolus Quartus: Imperial Role Models in Ingelheim, Aachen and Prague', in Ute Engel and Alexandra Gajewski (eds), *Mainz and the Middle Rhine Valley: Medieval Art, Architecture and Archaeology* (Leeds, 2007), 221–46; Václav Bok, 'Die niederrheinische Wenzelslegende *Der selige Wentzelao*', in Heinz Sieburg and Amelie Bendheim (eds), *Prag in der Zeit der Luxemburger Dynastie: Literatur, Religion und Herrschaftskulturen zwischen Bereicherung und Behauptung* (Bielefeld, 2018), 153–70. Also, Martin Bauch, 'Hegemoniales Königtum jenseits von Politik- und Verfassungsgeschichte: Zur sakralen Herrschaftspraxis Karls IV. ', in Christine Reinle (ed.), *Stand und Perspektiven der Sozial- und Verfassungsgeschichte zum römisch-deutschen Reich: Der Forschungseinfluss Peter Moraws auf die deutsche Mediävistik* (Affalterbach, 2016), 97–110.

the Heavenly Jerusalem as well as a symbolic representation of the Holy Roman Empire itself.[41]

Charles' passion for relics is legendary.[42] His efforts to accumulate in particular relics of the Passion of Christ were inspired by the French model, too. The creation of Karlštejn (initiated, like so many others of his projects, in 1348) as a castle outside the capital was to serve both as a quasi-monastic retreat (in contrast to the customary hunting lodges favoured by Charles' royal competitors) and as a reliquary for the holiest of Charles' relics as well as the imperial insignia. This took the French model of the Sainte-Chapelle significantly further – not only evoking, through its location and the choice of materials such as precious stone from Bohemia, the imperial architecture of Byzantium and Rome but also transforming the Capetian model into a new and distinctively Caroline, contemporary reinterpretation of emperorship.[43] Examples of further extensions of this personalizing cult of emperorship are the Frauenkirche in Nuremberg, and Charles' foundations supporting the cult of Wenceslas in the Rhineland.[44] Caroline emperorship, in the final consequence,

---

41 See Paul Crossley, 'The Politics of Presentation: The Architecture of Charles IV of Bohemia', in Sarah Rees Jones, Richard Marks and A.J. Minnis (eds), *Courts and Regions in Medieval Europe* (York, 2000), 99–172; Kateřina Kubínová, *Imitatio Romae: Karel IV. a Řím* (Prague, 2006); Zoë Opačić, 'The Sacred Topography of Medieval Prague', in Sæbjørg Walaker Nordeide and Stefan Brink (eds), *Sacred Sites and Holy Places: Exploring the Sacralization of Landscape Through Time and Space* (Turnhout, 2013), 253–81. Martin Bauch, *'Divina favente clemencia': Auserwählung, Frömmigkeit und Heilsvermittlung in der Herrschaftspraxis Kaiser Karls IV.* (Cologne, 2015), 383–4, proposed an interpretation of the sacred topography of Prague's New Town as a symbolic representation of the Empire itself.

42 For a comprehensive recent assessment of this phenomenon and its contexts, see Martin Bauch, *'Divina favente clemencia'*, passim.

43 For further discussion of Karlštejn as a reliquary and treasury, see Kateřina Horníčková, 'In Heaven and on Earth: Church Treasure in Late Medieval Bohemia' (PhD dissertation, Central European University, 2009), in particular chapters 4 and 5. For the depictions of musical instruments at Karlštejn, see Alexander Buchner, 'Musikinstrumente auf der Freske der Karlsteiner Apokalypse (Beitrag zur Geschichte der mittelalterlichen Musikinstrumente)', in Gustaf Hillestrőm (ed.), *Studia instrumentorum musicae popularis. III: Festschrift to Ernst Emsheimer on the occasion of his 70th birthday, January 15th 1974*, Musikhistoriska Museets skrifter, no. 5 (Stockholm, 1974), 32–41 and 259–61; Alexander Buchner, 'Hudoucí andělé na Karlštejně', *Sborník Národního Muzea v Praze. A: Historičký/Acta Musei Nationalis Pragae. A: Historia* 21 (1967), 1–72.

44 Further on the network of sacred places spanning the entire Empire, see, for example, Bok, 'Die niederrheinische Wenzelslegende'; Opačić, 'Carolus Magnus and Carolus Quartus'. For the dangers lurking underneath these policies, see the essay by Len Scales in this volume. For a nicely nuanced view of Charles' role in the interaction between the imperial city of Nuremberg and the Emperor and his

meant transforming Bohemia and the Holy Roman Empire into a new kind of Holy Land.

The Caroline conception of imperial rulership outlined above, then, can be described as a highly original fusion of cultural practices inherited, on the one hand, from the Přemyslid kings of Bohemia, and, on the other, the performances of sacred kingship observed in late Capetian France, and the histories, privileges and precedents associated with Charles' imperial predecessors, and his personal lineage.[45] They are reflective of a renewed imperial identity that is both decidedly retrospective and, through its unique readaptation and recombination of individual ingredients, singularly modern, responding to the needs and possibilities of Charles' times and personal circumstances. Taking this as our point of departure, what kind of music would have befitted such a cultural and political programme? Before answering that question, let us first take a look at Charles' approach to textual production in the various languages pertinent to his domains.[46]

Late-medieval Bohemia, and even more so the Holy Roman Empire, just like the Luxembourg possessions in Lotharingia, was a multilingual region. Besides Latin as the language of the Church, the prevailing vernaculars in Bohemia were Czech and German, with Czech playing the role of an ancestral language that distinguished the indigenous Slavic population and their dynasty from the immigrant Germanophone population concentrated in the towns and cities.[47] German in turn was the language connecting Bohemia with the neighbouring regions of the Empire. It also carried a certain social prestige since Charles' thirteenth-century Přemyslid ancestors actively supported Germanophone Minnesänger; notably, Charles' grandfather Wenceslas II (r. 1278–1305) wrote his own poetry, some of which, like that of Charles' great-grandfather John I of Brabant, made it into the Codex Manesse, testifying to its reception within the wider Germanophone communication space. Wenceslas II was also responsible for commissioning a reworking of the Tristan narrative

---

court, see Filip Srovnal, 'Der Triumphbogen für den kommenden Herrscher: Zur Ikonographie, Symbolik und Bedeutung der Skulpturenausstattung der Nürnberger Frauenkirche', *Umění* 67 (2019), 378–95.

45 Further enhanced by his Brabant ancestry through his grandmother: the Brabant family claimed direct ancestry from Charlemagne and disputed the competing Capetian/Valois claims. See Schneider, 'Karolus, qui et Wenceslaus', 385–6.

46 On this subject, see also the essays by Jaluška and Žůrek in this volume.

47 There was also a significant Jewish community writing in Hebrew and Yiddish. For a recent overview, see Lenka Jiroušková, 'Prague', in David Wallace (ed.), *Europe: A Literary History, 1348–1418* (Oxford, 2016), 617–51. Also, Sofia Lodén and Vanessa Obry (eds), *L'expérience des frontières et les littératures de l'Europe médiévale* (Paris, 2019).

(c. 1290) by Heinrich von Freiberg, and was the dedicatee of Ulrich von Etzenbach's (or Eschenbach's, c. 1250–c. 1300) *Alexandreis*, which in turn inspired an Old Czech version created shortly thereafter (c. 1300). Heinrich von Meißen (Frauenlob), whom we encountered earlier in our discussion of Henry VII's courtly entourage and who was far from forgotten in the mid-fourteenth century, is thought to have created his famous *Marienleich* at Wenceslas' court. Ulrich von Etzenbach's *Wilhelm von Wenden* (c. 1292) offers a portrait of an ideal ruler of Slavic origin which in turn provided potential models for both the portraits of John of Bohemia as the ideal knight by Guillaume de Machaut, and the sacred rulership embraced by Charles.[48]

If John of Luxembourg's absence from Prague contributed to a temporary decline of this tradition, significantly Charles, already during his time as John's lieutenant in the 1330s and early 1340s, revived it by attracting the services of Heinrich von Mügeln (c. 1320–after 1371) as part of his programme of cultural politics. Roughly coinciding with Charles' coronation in Rome (1355), Heinrich created the allegorical poem *Der meide kranz* celebrating Charles' rulership and reflecting the intensely intellectual, theologically tinged atmosphere prevailing at Charles' court.[49]

---

48 See Milan Tvrdík, 'Vom Minnesang am Hofe der letzten Přemysliden zur prähumanistischen Prosa der Stadtschreiber unter den Luxemburgern (1290–1420): Die neuen Wege tschechischer und deutschböhmischer Dichtung im Goldenen Zeitalter Karls IV', in Sieburg and Bendheim (eds), *Prag in der Zeit der Luxemburger Dynastie*, 73–84; Dana Dvořáčková-Malá, 'Wilhelm von Wenden und die Marienlegende des Heinrich Clûsenêre: Die höfische Literatur des Prager Hofes vom Ende des 13. Jahrhunderts im Lichte neuer Erkenntnisse', in Dana Dvořáčková-Malá, Kristýna Solomon and Michel Margue (eds), *Über den Hof und am Hofe: Literatur und Geschichtsschreibung im Mittelalter. Sammelband zur internationalen Konferenz des Projekts Forschungszentrum Höfe und Residenzen am Historischen Institut der Prager Akademie der Wissenschaften, Historischen Institut der Universität Luxemburg und Lehrstuhl für Germanistik der Philosophischen Fakultät der Palacký-Universität Olmütz, Prag, 29. Januar 2019* (Dresden, 2021), 29–44.

49 On Heinrich von Mügeln, see, most recently, Dániel Bagi, 'Zur Entstehungszeit und den Entstehungsumständen der zu Ungarns Geschichte verfassten Werke Heinrichs von Mügeln', *Zeitschrift für deutsches Altertum und deutsche Literatur* 150 (2021), 53–83; Alexandra Urban, *Poetik der Meisterschaft in 'Der meide kranz': Heinrich von Mügeln auf den Schultern des Alanus ab Insulis* (Berlin, 2021); Beate Kellner, 'Heinrich von Mügeln', in Dorothea Klein, Jens Haustein and Horst Brunner (eds), *Sangspruch / Spruchsang: Ein Handbuch* (Berlin, 2019), 430–9. For an edition of the melodies ascribed to Heinrich, see Horst Brunner and Karl-Günther Hartmann (eds), *Spruchsang: Die Melodien der Sangspruchdichter des 12. bis 15. Jahrhunderts*, Monumenta Monodica Medii Aevi 6 (Kassel, 2010), 134–47. For general context, see Hana Vlhová-Wörner, 'Die Spruchsang-Melodien im Kontext des spätmittelalterlichen einstimmigen Komponierens in Zentraleuropa', in Gert Hübner and Dorothea Klein (eds), *Sangspruchdichtung um 1300: Akten der Tagung in*

Heinrich's presence in Charles' entourage helps explain why Charles' interest in retaining the Francophone Machaut was perforce limited; there would have been little room or purpose for Francophone poetry in a courtly space with long-established, strong traditions in the two vernaculars of the kingdom, Old Czech and Middle High German, and a claim to a universal emperorship on a par to only one other authority, that of the pope.[50] From Charles' perspective, this made the French vernacular – while present within the Holy Roman Empire – not only irrelevant, but inimical to his political strategy. In the same vein, Charles' several forays into Italy did not furnish any productive exchange with practitioners of Trecento poetry or music; the one piece that can be associated confidently with Charles, the two-voice madrigal *Sovran uccello* by Donato da Firenze, is decidedly sceptical in its views about the Emperor and was almost certainly produced in Florence, an entrenched Guelph stronghold.[51]

Aspirations towards universality also help explain why, in addition to his patronage of the two dominant vernaculars spoken in his kingdom (and the influential role played by textual production in Prague in the development of the German language),[52] Charles from the late 1340s onwards made a decisive move towards Latin as the language of first choice as far as direct imperial sponsorship was concerned. Once again,

---

Basel vom 7. bis 9. November 2013 (Hildesheim, 2015), 275–92. See also the pertinent essays in Jens Haustein and Ralf-Henning Steinmetz (eds), *Studien zu Frauenlob und Heinrich von Mügeln: Festschrift für Karl Stackmann zum 80. Geburtstag* (Freiburg/Schweiz, 2002); Karl Stackmann, *Frauenlob, Heinrich von Mügeln und ihre Nachfolger* (Göttingen, 2002).

50 For further details on Charles' role in the development of Czech, see once more the essays by Jaluška and Žůrek in this volume.

51 For a full discussion, including other texts in Italian related to Charles, see Elena Abramov-van Rijk, 'The Italian Experience of the Holy Roman Emperor Charles IV: Musical and Literary Aspects', *Early Music History* 37 (2018), 1–44. Abramov-van Rijk argues against the traditional association of Jacopo da Bologna's madrigal *Aquil'altera/Creatura gentil/Uccel di Dio* with the coronation of Charles IV in Milan on 6 January 1355 and instead situates it in the intellectual milieu around Giovanni Visconti (1290–1354), Archbishop of Milan (1342–54) and a friend of Petrarch. The eagle then is to be read as a symbol not of the imperial dignity but, among other potential meanings, as the emblem of John the Evangelist, Giovanni Visconti's patron saint.

52 See the overview by Hans-Joachim Solms, 'Deutsch in Prag zur Mitte des 14. Jahrhunderts', in Sieburg and Bendheim (eds), *Prag in der Zeit der Luxemburger Dynastie*, 37–52. A similar case, *mutatis mutandis*, can be made for Czech (see the discussion in Jiroušková, 'Prague', 629–35) and even, by extension, for English, through the patronage of English as a new courtly language next to French at Richard II's court stimulated by Richard's queen, Anne of Bohemia (1382–94), one of the Charles' daughters. For the latter point, see Alfred Thomas, *The Court of Richard II and Bohemian Culture* (Cambridge, 2020).

he set down his claim towards universality – here embodied through the use of a transnational idiom sanctified by its ancestral and sacerdotal qualities. By becoming an author in his own right, producing various texts in Latin himself in addition to sponsoring a number of historiographic projects in Latin, he and his courtiers directly participated in a discourse conducted in the language universally recognized in western Christendom as the linguistic medium of supreme authority – a move truly befitting an emperor and recalling illustrious predecessors such as Frederick II or Marcus Aurelius, at the same time connecting Prague with the humanist movement.[53] Petrarch himself was in direct communication with the Emperor and his inner circle in the 1350s and early 1360s, and even visited the Bohemian capital in person. Several of Charles' most important courtiers – notably the Archbishop of Prague, Arnošt of Pardubice, and the Bishop of Olomouc, John of Středa/Johann von Neumarkt (Jan ze Střede) – remained in sustained contact with Petrarch and became protagonists of early humanism in Bohemia.[54]

In parallel to the notion of the sage-king – and the adoption of Latin as Charles' medium of choice for his imperial pronouncements – stands the idea of a sacred rulership, with its archetype King Solomon. Solomon was traditionally considered the author of several books of the Old Testament, notably the Song of Songs, thereby providing a biblical role model for Charles. Solomon as the builder of the Temple of Jerusalem is reflected in the many architectural projects initiated by Charles in Prague and throughout his realm, with further layers of inspiration provided by Jerusalem, Rome and Paris.[55] Charles' ideological (re-)turn to an

---

53 See Balázs Nagy and Frank Schaer (eds), *Karoli IV Imperatoris Romanorum vita ab eo ipso conscripta; et, Hystoria nova de Sancto Wenceslao Martyre = Autobiography of Emperor Charles IV; and, His Legend of St. Wenceslas* (Budapest, 2001). For further details on the role of chronicle-writing in Charles' cultural programme, see the essay by Žůrek in this volume.

54 On Petrarch, see Jiroušková, 'Prague', 621; Jiří Špička, 'Francesco Petrarca travelling and writing to Prague's court', *Verbum: Analecta Neolatina* 12 (2010), 27–40 (DOI: 10.1556/Verb.12.2010.1.2, accessed 12 October 2022). For an edition of the relevant correspondance, see Ugo Dotti (ed.), *Francesco Petrarca: Lettere all'Imperatore. Carteggio con la Corte di Praga* (Reggio Emilia, 2007). For biographical studies of the two (arch-)bishops, see Zdeňka Hledíková, *Arnošt z Pardubic: arcibiskup, zakladatel, rádce* (Prague, 2008); Joseph Klapper, *Johann von Neumarkt, Bischof und Hofkanzler: Religiöse Frührenaissance in Böhmen zur Zeit Karls IV.* (Leipzig, 1964). See also Paul Piur (ed.), *Briefe Johanns von Neumarkt* (Berlin, 1937).

55 For the figure of King Solomon as a programmatic aspect of Charles' emperorship from the start, see Hans Patze, '"Salomon sedebit super solium meum": Die Konsistorialrede Papst Clemens' VI. anlässlich der Wahl Karl IV.', in Hans Patze (ed.), *Kaiser Karl IV. 1316–1378: Forschungen über Kaiser und Reich* ([Göttingen],

emperorship based on Hohenstaufen, Carolingian and Roman models therefore invited, if not preconditioned, a (re-)turn to the most ancient and sacred forms of musical utterance available to him – plainchant. This perforce resulted in a traditionalist musical culture at his court that was fed from ecclesiastic models and traditions in the first instance. In addition, it offered the advantage that its performance could rely on the infrastructure provided by the Church. Moreover, it was understood across linguistic and political boundaries. Conversely, any other linguistic choice would have run the risk of alienating some of Charles' imperial subjects, or come with political strings attached.[56]

Charles' political investment in chant found its congenial implementation in the large number of ecclesiastical foundations that he and his queens or, later, empresses endowed: selected examples are the aforementioned new chapter for the Chapel of All Saints at Prague Castle (1339) and the college of *mansionarii* at St Vitus Cathedral in Prague (1343), as well as the chapter administering the Chapel of the Holy Cross at Karlštejn (1357), to name but three of the most conspicuous. All the holders of these new posts were by definition engaged in performing the liturgy, i.e., daily singing of a multitude of chants. Similarly, Charles' investments in the cults of royal and Bohemian saints, e.g., the enlargement of the

---

1978), 1–37. This sermon pronounced by Clement VI (= Charles' former tutor and mentor) at the moment of Charles' 1346 election confirms that the Solomon trope was present in the Emperor's mind from 1346 onward at the latest, but Charles' autobiography suggests that both men earlier exchanged thoughts about their respective roles and role models for the offices of pope and emperor. For an exhaustive treatment of the Solomon topic, including further contextualization, see Václav Žůrek, 'Der Weise auf dem Thron: Zu einem wichtigen Aspekt des Herrschaftsstils Karls IV', in Martin Bauch, Julia Burkhardt, Tomáš Gaudek and Václav Žůrek (eds), *Heilige, Helden, Wüteriche: Herrschaftsstile der Luxemburger (1308–1437)* (Cologne, 2017), 325–39.

56 On the deliberate embrace of Roman – hence, universalizing – models, see also the essay by Ingrid Ciulisová in this volume. For additional information and further details, see David Eben, 'Karl IV. und die Musik', in Jiří Fajt and Markus Hörsch (eds), *Kaiser Karl IV.: 1316–2016—Erste Bayerisch-Tschechische Landesausstellung: Ausstellungskatalog—Nationalgalerie in Prag, Wallenstein-Reitschule, 15. Mai–25. September 2016; Karls-Universität in Prag, Carolinum, Kreuzgang, 14. Mai–31. August 2016; Germanisches Nationalmuseum Nürnberg, 20. Oktober 2016–5. März 2017* (Prague, 2016), 174–81; the pertinent publications by Hana Vlhová(-Wörner), such as 'Hudba v době Karla IV', in Lenka Bobková and Mlada Holá (eds), *Lesk královského majestátu ve středoveku* (Prague, 2005); and, for the wider context, most recently, Jan Ciglbauer, 'Cantiones Bohemicae – Komposition und Tradition' (PhD dissertation, Charles University Prague, 2017); idem, 'From Tolerated Addition to Keepers of Tradition: The Authority of the "Past" in Latin Song in Central Europe in the Fourteenth and Fifteenth Centuries', in Karl Kügle (ed.), *Sounding the Past: Music as History and Memory* (Turnhout, 2020), 121–40.

Chapel of St Wenceslas at Prague Cathedral or the foundation of the monastery of Augustinian canons in Prague's New Town dedicated to his adopted patron saint, Charlemagne (1350), implied an intensification of the liturgy, i.e., of chanting the Offices of the saints concerned, often directly linked to his conspicuous architectural projects. The same can be said with regard to the foundation of the monastery of St Jerome (= Emmaus) using the Old Slavonic rite (1347), and the institution of new liturgical feasts, most prominently the Feast of the Lance and Nails of the Lord (1355), which was centred – but not limited in its performance – on the main chapel at Karlštejn. The list of Charles' and his associates' foundations both in his capital city of Prague – which he intended to be both a new Rome and a new Jerusalem – and in important spots within his realm is comprehensive; taken together, they created a network of holy places and associated liturgical practices extending across the entire realm. All these endowments included daily psalmody and singing during the performance of the respective liturgies; together they turned Charles' realm into a sonic approximation, indeed a simulacrum, of the perpetual adoration of the angels.

Charles' musical choices were no doubt reinforced by the theological underpinnings of his conception of rulership, expressed, for example, by his preference to personally perform, i.e., sing a section of, the Christmas liturgy.[57] Performing the first Lesson of the third nocturn of Matins on the vigil of Christmas Day on the night of 24 to 25 December was a special privilege allegedly reserved for the Holy Roman Emperors but in fact invented by Charles in collusion with his mentor Pierre Roger (Pope Clement VI). It singularly highlighted their notions of the sacrosanct quality of the imperial office as they understood and shaped it. Through personally participating as an officiant in the liturgy, and through enabling a multiplication of liturgical singing radiating outward from the new holy city of Prague throughout his realm and, indeed, the universe of Christendom, Charles reclaimed the liturgical aspects of the office of Holy Roman Emperor. It further allowed him to stake a new claim to a tradition of saintly rulers unmatched by any other European monarchs, reaching

---

57 For example, at Metz Cathedral at Christmas 1356 and in Cambrai Cathedral at Christmas 1377; see Michel Margue and Michel Pauly, 'Luxemburg, Metz und das Reich: Die Reichsstadt Metz im Gesichtsfeld Karls IV.', in Ulrike Hohensee, Matthias Lawo, Michael Lindner, Michael Menzel and Olaf B. Rader (eds), *Die Goldene Bulle: Politik, Wahrnehmung, Rezeption* (Berlin, 2009), 869–916, at 913. See also František Šmahel, *The Parisian Summit, 1377-78: Emperor Charles IV and King Charles V of France* (Prague, 2014), 77 and 182–3, for further references and background to the ceremony, that Charles actually invented himself and first carried out in Basel in 1347. See also Hermann Heimpel, 'Königlicher Weihnachtsdienst im späteren Mittelalter', *Deutsches Archiv für Erforschung des Mittelalters* 39 (1983), 131–206.

back to Charlemagne and Constantine, and reinforced in Charles' case by his personal connection to the saintly bloodline of Wenceslas, martyr and spiritual founder of the Bohemian monarchy.

When Charles took over, the chequered history of the Empire since the death of Frederick II meant that Charles had to reinvent the office of Emperor whether he wanted to or not: its existence needed justifying and its institutions needed remodelling. It is therefore not surprising to find that Charles sought to rely on the renewed authority attributed to the past in late medieval Europe.[58] Men in Charles' orbit, unsurprisingly, seem to have espoused similar tastes: we have already mentioned Heinrich von Mügeln, whose *Sangspruchdichtung* and poetic works vernacularized Charles' agenda in the medium of Middle High German. Active under both Charles and his successor Wenceslas, the slightly younger Jan of Jenštejn, Archbishop of Prague 1379–96 (b. 1347/8, d. Rome 1400), and the first Bohemian cardinal (under the Roman obedience), composed chant, Latin-texted monophonic song (*cantio*) and poetry, but did not show any interest in mensural polyphony.[59] The one place where polyphony did gain a foothold in Prague was not the court, but the university; there, knowledge of Ars Nova notation is documented by 1369/70.[60]

The presence of minstrels at the court is poorly researched at present and therefore remains something of an enigma. It would be extraordinary if they had not had a significant presence in courtly life, Charles' sacerdotal cultural politics notwithstanding. Perhaps the focus should shift here from Charles himself to the households of Charles' queens and empresses.[61]

---

58 For a more detailed discussion of this trend, see the pertinent essays in Karl Kügle (ed.), *Sounding the Past: Music as History and Memory* (Turnhout, 2020).
59 See, most recently, Rhianydd Hallas, 'Two Rhymed Offices Composed for the Feast of the Visitation of the Blessed Virgin Mary: Comparative Study and Critical Edition' (PhD dissertation, University of Bangor, 2021), for a comparative study of a rhymed Office composed by Jan of Jenštejn and further background. For general biographical information, see Ruben Ernest Weltsch, *Archbishop John of Jenstein (1348–1400): Papalism, Humanism and Reform in Pre-Hussite Prague* (The Hague, 1968).
60 See Alexander Rausch, 'Mensuraltraktate des Spätmittelalters in österreichischen Bibliotheken', in Michael Bernhard (ed.), *Quellen und Studien zur Musiktheorie des Mittelalters* 3 (Munich, 2001), 273–303, with an edition of the Prague Anonymous at 284–92. The treatise is versified in hexameters, and dated 1369 at or for Prague in two of the five manuscripts (274–5). Also R. Federhofer-Königs, 'Ein anonymer Musiktraktat aus der 2. Hälfte des 14. Jahrhunderts in der Stiftsbibliothek Michaelbeuern/Salzburg', *Kirchenmusikalisches Jahrbuch* 46 (1962), 43–60.
61 For an overview of what is known at present, see Eben, 'Karl IV. und die Musik', in Fajt and Hörsch (eds), *Kaiser Karl IV.: 1316–2016*, 174–81, at 174–6. Aside from the inevitable trumpeters, there is mention of a court fiddler ('figellator'). Hans Patze provides a reference to a piper ('fistulator') in the service of Sophia

While we are no doubt dealing with a literary topos at least in part, it may not be just a coincidence or a rhetorical flourish that one of the two lists of instruments given by Machaut in his oeuvre is part of the description of the court of Charles IV in the *Prise d'Alexandre*.[62] Future research may shed more light on this question. There seems to have been a tradition of the Emperor honouring the minstrels of other princes by conveying on them the title 'King of the Minstrels'. This is documented for one of the ducal minstrels of Brabant, Coninc Middach, who was named king of the minstrels in both the Holy Roman Empire and France by Charles IV.[63] Similarly, Charles crowned the jester Dolcibene de' Tori, employed at the court of the Visconti, 'King of Buffoons' during his stay in Milan in 1354–

---

of Bavaria, the second wife of Charles' successor Wenceslas, dated 1402; see Hans Patze, 'Die Hofgesellschaft Karls IV. in Prag', in Patze (ed.), *Kaiser Karl IV. 1316–1378: Forschungen über Kaiser und Reich* ([Göttingen], 1978), 733–73, at 754. For the presence of pipers and trumpeters at Sophia's coronation, see Uličný, 'The Choirs of St Vitus's Cathedral in Prague', 196 and 227 (n. 56).

62 See R. Barton Palmer (ed. and transl.), *Guillaume de Machaut: La Prise d'Alixandre – The Taking of Alexandria* (New York, 2002), 80–93. For the list of instruments kept in Charles' palace in Prague, see 88–9. The instrument listed first is the organ as the 'king of all instruments' ('de tous instrumens le roy', v. 1145) – possibly an innuendo relating to Charles' saintly reputation ('li secons salemons' = 'the second Solomon', v. 992), along with remarks about Charles' humility (vv. 1008–14), modest clothing style (vv. 1017–19), peace-making skills (vv. 1032–45), and rich ecclesiastical endowments (vv. 1003–6). Machaut's description of courtly life, and in particular the entertainments at Prague, seems to remain generic, however: 'lonc temps ores festie / dance . joustie . tournie' ('they ... made merry, danced, jousted and tourneyed for a long time', vv. 1259–60). For additional recent discussion of Machaut's knowledge of the Empire under Charles, and Charles' half-brother Wenceslas of Brabant as a potential source of information, see Uri Smilansky, 'Machaut and Prague: A rare new sighting?', *Early Music* 46 (2018), 211–23. For an isolated reference in French court records to one Johannes Convin, *menestrellus Regis Romanorum* (i.e., in the service of Charles as King of the Romans) who in June 1349 delivered a letter from Charles to Philip VI informing the King of France of Charles' second marriage to Anne of Bavaria, see Jules Viard (ed.), *Les journaux du trésor de Philippe VI de Valois, suivis de l'Ordinarium thesauri de 1338–1339* (Paris, 1899), 274; cited earlier in Nigel Wilkins, 'A Pattern of Patronage: Machaut, Froissart and the Houses of Luxembourg and Bohemia in the Fourteenth Century', *French Studies* 37 (1983), 257–84, at 262 and 280, and reprinted in Nigel Wilkins, *Words and Music in Medieval Europe* (Farnham, 2011), as item XII. Charles' second marriage ended in 1353 with Anne's premature death.

63 See Remco Sleiderink, 'Pykini's Parrot: Music at the Court of Brabant', in Barbara Haggh, Frank Daelemans and André Vanrie (eds), *Musicology and Archival Research / Musicologie et recherches en archives / Musicologie en archiefonderzoek* (Brussels, 1994), 358–91, at 378.

5.[64] Finally, a minstrel named Colignet Cassamus, a native of Metz, claims to have been in the service of the Emperor according to an inscription on his grave in Metz Cathedral, but given Colignet's whereabouts, this may have been more of an honorary title than an indication of formal employment at Charles' court in Prague.[65]

A CONTRASTING FOCUS IN THE WEST: WENCESLAS OF BRABANT

As a daughter of Louis of Bourbon and Marie of Avesnes, Beatrix of Bourbon belonged to the innermost circles of both the Valois monarchy and the Lotharingian aristocracy. Her marriage to Charles' father therefore cemented John's ever closer integration into the French cultural and political orbit, where he remained until his death in the Battle of Crécy (1346), and indirectly the possible alienation between Charles' own cultural identity and that of his stepmother; Beatrix' one-year (and only) sojourn in Prague may be emblematic of this conflict. Unsurprisingly, the relationship between Charles and Wenceslas (and probably Charles and Beatrix), like that of Charles to their father, John, was complicated: for a few years after John's death, Charles remained hesitant to carry out the stipulations of his father's testament which stated that the County of Luxembourg and associated possessions in western Europe should fall to Wenceslas.[66] However, Charles' attitude changed in the early 1350s (possibly triggered by Wenceslas' coming of legal age in 1351, and the conclusion of a marriage contract between Wenceslas and Joan of Brabant in May of the same year). Consequently, a balance of power and mutual interests was established where the two (half-)brothers were able to complement each other politically. All the more striking are the differences in the cultural profile of the two Luxembourg princes: Wenceslas of Brabant as well as his mother and his wife Joan of Brabant (1322–1406), who married Wenceslas

---

64 See Abramov-van Rijk, 'The Italian Experience', 24–5. See also Ezio Levi, 'Ultimo Re dei Giullari', *Studi Medievali* 6 (1928), 173–80, at 173–4, and Abramov-van Rijk's more general discussions of the music at Charles' coronation ceremonies in Milan and Rome, 'The Italian Experience', 20–6.
65 Michel Margue and Michel Pauly, 'Luxemburg, Metz und das Reich: Die Reichsstadt Metz im Gesichtsfeld Karls IV.', in Ulrike Hohensee, Matthias Lawo, Michael Lindner, Michael Menzel and Olaf B. Rader (eds), *Die Goldene Bulle: Politik, Wahrnehmung, Rezeption* (Berlin, 2009), 869–916, at 911 (n. 193).
66 See Michel Pauly, 'Karl IV. und sein Halbbruder Wenzel: Das Herzogtum Luxemburg und Karls Politik im Westen des Reiches', in Sieburg and Bendheim (eds), *Prag in der Zeit der Luxemburger Dynastie*, 13–35; on Wenceslas in general, Fantysová-Matějková, *Wenceslas de Bohême*.

as her second husband, were deeply invested in the Francophone cultural practices of the western European courts.

Two polyphonic chansons have been associated with Wenceslas' court: Nicolas de Picquigny, a chaplain at the Brussels court of Brabant 1364–89, canon of St Gudula 1374, may be the composer of the virelai *Plaisanche, or tost*.[67] Wenceslas himself may have been a keen singer, as suggested by Sleiderink's analysis of the text of the virelai. It is generally assumed that he wrote the corpus of poetry in the poetic *formes fixes* associated with Francophone courtly practice of the later fourteenth century that is transmitted in Jean Froissart's *Meliador*. His poem *Fuiés de moy* exists in a widely disseminated musical setting which was copied into sources from the court of Paris, the Rhineland, Austria, and Italy, suggesting dissemination both into Francophone and Germanophone areas as well as further afield into Italy, with the Paris source by far the earliest witness, and the other sources datable between c. 1400 and the second quarter of the fifteenth century.[68] Characteristically, the Italian sources tend to retain a (limited) interest in the French text, whereas the sources from the Germanophone regions either provide a Latin contrafactum text (*Quam pulchra es*) or transmit textless versions. Oswald von Wolkenstein adopted the setting in the early fifteenth century and provided it with a German text of his own (*Wolauff gesell wer jagen*). It remains to be seen whether Wolkenstein's interest was primarily in the musical setting, the author of which is unknown, or whether he and the other compilers were also aware of the connection with Wenceslas of Brabant.[69]

Wenceslas' and Joanna's court was also open to Germanophone poets as well as minstrels. The herald Peter Suchenwirt (d. after 1395), in the service of the Habsburg dukes of Austria, praised both Charles IV and

---

67 See the recent discussion of this setting in Elizabeth Eva Leach, 'Vernacular Song III: Polyphony', in Mark Everist and Thomas Forrest Kelly (eds), *The Cambridge History of Medieval Music* (Cambridge, 2018), 937–73, at 956–9. See also Sleiderink, *De stem van de meester*, 134–6; idem, 'Pykini's Parrot', passim.
68 For a list of concordances, see Michael Scott Cuthbert, 'Trecento Fragments and Polyphony Beyond the Codex' (PhD dissertation, Harvard University, 2006), 240; also David Fallows, *A Catalogue of Polyphonic Songs, 1415–1480* (Oxford, 1999), 168.
69 One of the Italian sources discussed in Cuthbert, 'Trecento Fragments', 240, attributes the setting to 'Alanus'. 'Alanus' may tentatively be identified with an English singer named W. Aleyn active around 1400; see Margaret Bent, s.v. 'Aleyn', in *Oxford Music Online* (https://www-oxfordmusiconline-com.ezproxy-prd.bodleian.ox.ac.uk/grovemusic/display/10.1093/gmo/9781561592630.001.0001/omo-9781561592630-e-0000000546?rskey=asFLOf&result=1, accessed 29 April 2023). Given the many connections between the Luxembourg courts in Brussels and Prague, and the English court in the period c. 1400, the lead provided by this ascription is suggestive and deserves closer investigation.

Wenceslas of Brabant for the splendour of their courts.[70] Among poets from the Low Countries, Augustijnken is the most prominent, together with the herald-poet, Godekijn van Tricht (= Maastricht). The Brussels poet Jan Knibbe wrote a memorial poem for Wenceslas, *Die claghe vanden Hertoghe Wenselijn van Brabant*. Augustijnken, moreover, provides a connection to the Wittelsbach court of Holland, Zealand and Hainaut via Jean II de Blois (c. 1342–81), a nobleman of French descent who inherited fiefs in southern Holland dependent on the counts of Holland and who maintained a satellite court in Schoonhoven to the Wittelsbach-Holland court in The Hague.[71] Another Dutchman in the orbit of the Duke and Duchess of Brabant is Pieter van Leiden, canon of St Gudula in Brussels from 1357. The ducal minstrels included Coninc Middach, named king of the minstrels in both the Empire and France by Charles IV.[72]

The pattern exhibited by this late fourteenth-century Luxembourg court in the Low Countries shows striking similarities with the musical as well as cultural multilingualism exhibited further north at the Wittelsbach court of Holland, Zealand and Hainaut in The Hague. There, a similar culturally hybrid court culture existed in the decades around 1400 which combined Dutch texts with the most sophisticated 'Ars subtilior' forms of French-derived polyphony alongside adaptations as well as appropriations of earlier Germanophone registers. Given the dynastic proximity of the Holland branch of the Wittelsbachs to the Valois dukes of Burgundy and to their cousin Isabeau of Bavaria (c. 1370–1435), Queen of France from 1389 to 1422, the continued process of hybridization instigated by the Brabant and Luxembourg courts in the Low Countries in the decades

---

70   See Sleiderink, *De stem van de meester*, 125 and, for much of what follows, 123–40, as well as Remco Sleiderink, 'Dichters aan het Brabantse hof (1356–1406)', *De nieuwe taalgids* 86 (1993), 1–16. Further on Suchenwirt and his cultural context, see, recently, Ulrich Müller, 'Sangvers-Lyrik und Sangvers-Epik in deutscher Sprache: Überlegungen zum musikalischen Repertoire im habsburgischen Zentraleuropa im späten 14. Jahrhundert und in der ersten Hälfte des 15. Jahrhunderts. Mit einem Ausblick auf moderne Aufführungen mittelalterlicher (einstimmiger) Musik', in Alexander Rausch and Björn R. Tammen (eds), *Musikalische Repertoires in Zentraleuropa (1420–1450): Prozesse & Praktiken* (Vienna, 2014), 253–70, at 257–8. Also Claudia Brinker-von der Heyde, *Von manigen helden gute tat: Geschichte als Exempel bei Peter Suchenwirt* (Frankfurt am Main, 1987); Stephanie Cain Van D'Elden, *Peter Suchenwirt and Heraldric Poetry* (Vienna, 1976).
71   For a detailed discussion of the musico-poetic culture of Holland-Zealand-Hainaut in the late fourteenth century, see Eliane Fankhauser, 'Recycling Reversed: Studies in the History of Polyphony in the Northern Low Countries Around 1400' (PhD dissertation, Utrecht University, 2018); also Rob Wegman, 'New Light on Secular Polyphony at the Court of Holland in the Early Fifteenth Century: The Amsterdam Fragments', *Journal of the Royal Musical Association* 117 (1992), 181–207.
72   Sleiderink, 'Pykini's Parrot', 378.

around 1400 must be considered as still inadequately explored; it certainly provides fascinating material for further study. The political constellations of the latter decades of the fourteenth century facilitated multiple connections not just between the Low Countries (Flanders-Burgundy, Holland-Zealand-Hainaut, and Brabant-Luxembourg) and Paris but also between the lands across the Channel and Prague. These are embodied in the marriage of one of Charles' daughters, Anne of Bohemia (1366–94), to Richard II of England in 1382.[73]

DIVERGENCE AND EMERGENCE: WENCESLAS, SIGISMUND, OSWALD AND THE IMPERIAL CHAPEL

Anne's marriage brings us to the reigns of Charles' sons Wenceslas (1361–1419, r. 1378–1419) and Sigismund (1368–1437, r. Hungary 1387– 1437, King of the Romans and later Holy Roman Emperor 1410–37, ruler of Bohemia 1419–37). In Wenceslas' time, the rise of the circle around Jan Hus would not have been possible without the toleration, indeed the active encouragement, of the court. While the so-called Wenceslas Bible is the most spectacular but by far not the only witness to a continued trend towards disseminating Scripture in the vernaculars,[74] the religious beliefs of Hus and his followers encouraged participation by the lay community in all aspects of piety, including singing, therefore favouring styles that were easily accessible to all. The long-standing tradition of monophonic sacred song (*cantio*) cultivated in the region encompassing modern-day Austria, Bavaria, and Bohemia, including a group of monophonic songs that were traditionally sung by the congregation on high feast days, lent itself for the purposes of the reformers. Hus and his followers built on that by enriching the repertory with further songs and hymns with Czech texts.[75]

At the same time, the cultivation of mensural polyphony first documented in university circles around 1370 intensified, and eventually gave rise to a Central European tradition of composed polyphony in its own right which flourished in Bohemia, present-day Germany and Austria within a network of educated ecclesiastics linked to each other through their ties

---

73 See the note above concerning the singer 'Alanus'. On the cultural climate at the court of Richard II and Anne of Bohemia, see Thomas, *The Court of Richard II*.
74 See the essays by Theisen, Toussaint, and Žůrek in this volume.
75 See the discussion of Hus' musical profile by David Holeton and Hana Vlhová-Wörner, 'The Second Life of Jan Hus: Liturgy, Commemoration, and Music', in František Šmahel and Ota Pavlíček (eds), *A Companion to Jan Hus* (Leiden, 2013), 289–324, at 291–301.

with the universities of Central Europe.⁷⁶ The courts of Central Europe were not at the epicentres of this activity, or – if so – only in a selective fashion, as can be seen in the corpus ascribed to the 'Mönch von Salzburg' created at the court of Archbishop Pilgrim von Puchheim (r. 1365–96) during the late fourteenth century. This corpus shows distinct evidence of knowledge of the western mensural polyphony; nevertheless, monophonic song remained the community's preferred medium of expression.⁷⁷

Under the rule of Sigismund, established patterns continued. Oswald von Wolkenstein (1376/7–1445) was intermittently in the service of Sigismund between 1415 and 1432, and life at court repeatedly influenced Oswald's creative output, but as an aristocrat in his own right Oswald's musico-poetic activities were not constitutive to any of the court appointments he held.⁷⁸ Musical life at Sigismund's court certainly involved the regular

---

76 See Jan Ciglbauer (ed.), *Septem Dies: Music at Prague University = Hudba na pražské univerzitě 1360–1460* (Prague, 2021); idem, 'K dějinám hudby na kolejích pražské univerzity v jejím nejstarším období', *Studia mediaevalia Bohemica* 9 (2017), 7–19. For discussions concerning the University of Vienna and its interaction with the Habsburg court, local and regional ecclesiastical institutions, and the city, see Susana Zapke, 'Universität und Musik: Musikbücher im universitären Umfeld', in *Musikleben des Spätmittelalters in der Region Österreich* <https://musical-life.net/essays/universitat-und-musik-musikbucher-im-universitaren-umfeld> (2016, accessed 29 April 2023); Marc Lewon, 'Das Phänomen "Neidhart"', in *Musikleben des Spätmittelalters in der Region Österreich* <https://musical-life.net/essays/das-phanomen-neidhart> (2017, accessed 29 April 2023); Reinhard Strohm, 'Überlieferung der Wiener Kirchenmusik des 15. Jahrhunderts', in *Musikleben des Spätmittelalters in der Region Österreich* <https://musical-life.net/essays/uberlieferung-der-wiener-kirchenmusik-des-15-jahrhunderts> (2018, accessed 29 April 2023). For material from Rostock, see Eva M. Maschke, 'Entfernte Einbandfragmente aus Altzelle und *Ars nova*-Fragmente auf Papier und Pergament: Neue Entdeckungen in der Universitätsbibliothek Leipzig', in Martin Kirnbauer (ed.), *Beredte Musik: Konversationen zum 80. Geburtstag von Wulf Arlt* (Basel, 2019), 261–75, at 269–74.
77 For recent work on the 'Monk', see David Murray, 'Controlling Voices in Fourteenth-Century Salzburg: Singing and Identity in the "Mönch von Salzburg Songs"', *Music & Letters* 104 (2023), 177–96, OA at https://doi.org/10.1093/ml/gcac062 (accessed 29 April 2023); idem, 'Ein "volles Lied": Übertragung und Klang am Beispiel der geistlichen Lieder des Mönchs von Salzburg', in Andreas Kraß and Matthias Standke (eds), *Geistliche Liederdichter zwischen Volkssprache und Liturgie: Übertragungen, Bearbeitungen, Neuschöpfungen in Mittelalter und Früher Neuzeit* (Berlin, 2020), 63–89; idem, '"Ju, ich jag": A Three-Part Song in the Mönch von Salzburg Corpus in Translingual Perspective', *Oxford German Studies* 49 (2020), 1–26.
78 The long-standing, if somewhat loose, association of Oswald von Wolkenstein with Sigismund is well-documented and researched; for initial information see Anton Schwob (ed.), *Die Lebenszeugnisse Oswalds von Wolkenstein: Edition und Kommentar*, 5 vols (Vienna, 1999–2013), and the essays in Ulrich Müller and

performance of plainchant. Sigismund also seems to have taken delight in minstrel performances. Literary patronage by Sigismund seems poorly explored so far, aside from his association with the humanist Pier Paolo Vergerio the Elder (1370–1444/5), who served as Sigismund's secretary from 1417 onward.[79] Sigismund was familiar with the sophisticated polyphony cultivated in western and southern Europe through his presence at the councils of Constance and Basel as well as occasional travel to France and Italy, but seems not to have been motivated to adopt this cultural practice for his own court establishment for a long time.[80]

Sigismund's position may have changed around a moment of particular importance, reflected across the centuries in the sonic splendour of Du Fay's motet *Supremum est mortalibus bonum*. The composition was created and sung by the papal chapel on Whit Sunday (21 May) 1431 especially for the purpose of giving acoustic lustre to the moment when Pope Eugenius IV received Sigismund on the steps of St Peter's at the very beginning of the coronation ritual that was, at long last, to transform Sigismund into the next Holy Roman Emperor.[81] The use of complex mensurally notated polyphony at the imperial court is plausible at least for festive occasions following the arrival of Johannes Brassart (c. 1405–55) and may have been facilitated by Sigismund as a cultural-political statement

---

Margarete Springeth (eds), *Oswald von Wolkenstein: Leben, Werk, Rezeption* (Berlin, 2011). Wolkenstein officially entered Sigismund's service in 1415 (Schwob, *Lebenszeugnisse*, vol. 1, no. 70). In 1431, he is mentioned as a member of Sigismund's Order of the Dragon (Schwob, *Lebenszeugnisse*, vol. 3, no. 222).

79 For a very brief synopsis of cultural matters, see Jörg K. Hoensch, *Kaiser Sigismund: Herrscher an der Schwelle zur Neuzeit 1368–1437* (Darmstadt, 1997), 478–81. For an informative overview focusing on the visual arts but including a few references to literary patronage, see Ernő Marosi, 'Sigismund, the last Luxembourg', in Barbara Drake Boehm and Jiří Fajt (eds), *The Crown of Bohemia, 1347–1437* (New York, 2005), 120–30.

80 For music and its cultural and political contexts at the councils of Constance and Basel, see the pertinent essays in, most recently, Stefan Morent, Silke Leopold and Joachim Steinheuer (eds), *Europäische Musikkultur im Kontext des Konstanzer Konzils* (Ostfildern, 2017); Gabriela Signori and Birgit Studt (eds), *Das Konstanzer Konzil als europäisches Ereignis: Begegnungen, Medien und Rituale* (Ostfildern, 2014); and Matteo Nanni (ed.), *Music and Culture in the Age of the Council of Basel* (Turnhout, 2013). For a different approach that might be explored fruitfully by musicologists in future research, see Chris L. Nighman, 'Citations of "Noster" John Pecham in Richard Fleming's Sermon for Trinity Sunday: Evidence for the Political Use of Liturgical Music at the Council of Constance', *Medieval Sermon Studies* 52 (2008), 31–41.

81 For a reconstruction of the ceremonial, see Laurenz Lütteken, *Guillaume Dufay und die isorhythmische Motette* (Hamburg, 1993), 320–4. On the remarkable musical features of the motet, see, most recently, Alejandro Enrique Planchart, *Guillaume Du Fay: The Life and Works* (Cambridge, 2018), 365–7.

after his coronation to Emperor. The political point would have been to match the soundscape that surrounded the pope, thereby distinguishing the imperial chapel from the music of the other princes of the Empire. This would have been in continuity with the musical politics of his father Charles, whose emphasis on plainchant matched the specific, highly 'conservative' sonic qualities of the papal ceremonial of mid fourteenth-century Avignon; a similar continuity may be observed in Sigismund's reading the Gospel in full regalia at Constance, again following the example set by his father.[82] Brassart is documented as a singer in the papal chapel of Eugenius IV in 1431, at the Cathedral of St Lambert in Liège in 1432, and as a member of the chapel of the Council of Basel in 1433, whence he entered imperial service in 1434; the fact that he was a member of the papal chapel might have made him particularly attractive to Sigismund, reflecting his new identity as crowned Emperor. Brassart stayed in this post after Sigismund's death in 1437, serving his successors Albert II (1438–9) and Frederick III (1440–93).[83]

REFLECTIONS: THE LUXEMBOURGS AS A CULTURALLY MULTILINGUAL DYNASTY

The cultural profiles of the Luxembourg courts of the long fourteenth century emerge from the above discussion as highly dynamic. They respond, in the first instance, to patterns and frameworks set by their predecessors or by local traditions. But they also remain susceptible to changes which move in tandem with the major political shifts undergone by the dynasty. This could be observed, for example, in the addition of Germanophone advisers to Henry VII's entourage in the wake of his election as King of the Romans, and the swerve back to a predominantly Francophone cultural profile under John of Luxembourg from the 1320s onward, with corresponding neglect of the (Czech and Germanophone) traditions of courtly patronage in Bohemia. Under John's successor

---

82 Discussed in Therese Bruggisser-Lanker, 'Music goes public: Das Konstanzer Konzil und die Europäisierung der Musikkultur', in Signori and Studt, *Konstanzer Konzil*, 349–78, at 351 and 371, but without referencing the precedent set by Charles IV. For the soundscape of the Avignon popes, see Andrew Tomasello, *Music and Ritual in Papal Avignon 1309–1403* (Ann Arbor, MI, 1983); on the use of polyphony almost exclusively for the Mass Ordinary and on occasions that were of lesser liturgical rank and hence 'less rigidly controlled by ancient and solemn liturgical tradition', see 116 and 189, at n. 116.

83 On Brassart and Sigismund see, most recently, Carlo Bosi, 'Johannes Brassart und Kaiser Sigismund: Versuch nach einer historischen Kontextualisierung anhand der Introiten', in Nanni (ed.), *Council of Basel*, 269–84.

Charles, on the other hand, cultural policies in Bohemia, at least as far as language-related art forms are concerned, seem almost aggressively anti-French (while at the same time adopting a wide range of rulership models taken from France, but taking them to a new level). On the other hand, the court of Wenceslas of Brabant stayed fully immersed in Francophone developments, but unlike the Valois courts in France also retained the bilingual culture which it inherited from the Brabant tradition. This allowed Brabant to play a special role in enabling cultural transfer between England, France, the Dutch- and German-speaking regions of the Holy Roman Empire, and Bohemia.

These dynamics are as much linked to linguistic and musical parameters as to political strategies. In other words, the deployment of mensurally notated, complex polyphony should not be seen as 'progress' which arrived late to Central Europe, but as a tool in the creation of social and political identities. Its adoption, or rejection, is a mark of difference of one community in relation to another (even when allowing mixing). In the case of the court of Charles IV in Bohemia, the central institutions of government promoted an identity associated with liturgical and paraliturgical monophony, leaving the 'space' of mensural polyphony to individuals wanting either to create an alternative community, or to mark out their individuality, for example at the university. In France and Italy, on the other hand, the institutions of power performed their (sonic) identity to a significant degree through the cultivation of complex polyphony, 'pushing' those interested in alternative forms of musical expression towards monophony or 'simple' forms of polyphony – be that 'popular' carolling, communal singing as in the music of confraternities and *laudesi*, or the sophisticated monophonic melodies captured in stroke notation in the Gruuthuse manuscript (The Hague, Koninklijke Bibliotheek, 79 K 10), compiled in Burgundian-ruled Bruges around 1400. Such differences are tags of social and cultural identity, regardless of the mixing and overlapping realities of musical practice.

The modern narrative of European music history for the long Luxembourg century has been focused on the development of complex mensural polyphony, thereby inevitably privileging the regions in the west and south of Europe where these repertoires were developed, cultivated, and left tangible traces in the form of manuscript sources. Studying the Luxembourg courts in Lotharingia and Bohemia in the depth they require will necessitate a shift in these inherited historiographic premises. By giving appropriate attention to the development of chant and of Germanophone (Dutch- and German-texted) musical and poetic repertoires as well as the still largely unexplored role of instrumentalists (minstrels and heralds) in courtly life, it will become possible to understand Luxembourg soundscapes and their cultural physiognomies on their own terms, and inscribe them into a revised history of the late medieval soundscapes of Europe.[84]

---

84 My thanks to the co-editors of this volume, Ingrid Ciulisová and Václav Žůrek, to Uri Smilansky and Grantley McDonald of the MALMECC team, and to Jana Fantysová Matjěková of the Department of Medieval History, Institute of History of the Czech Academy of Sciences in Prague for their many helpful comments and suggestions during the preparation of this text.

SELECT BIBLIOGRAPHY

MANUSCRIPT SOURCES
Albenga, Biblioteca capitolare, MS 6
Augsburg, Staats- und Stadtbibliothek, MS 2° 3
Belluno, Archivio Storico del Comune, Libri iurium, libro B
Cividale del Friuli, Museo Archeologico Nazionale, Archivio Capitolare, Fondo Diplomatico, b. 16, no. 109
Florence, Archivio di Stato, Signori, Dieci di Balia, Otto di Pratica, Legazioni e Commissarie, Missive e Responsive, b. 75
Heidelberg, Universitätsbibliothek, MS Cod. Pal. germ. 848
Karlsruhe, Staatliche Kunsthalle, inv. no. 243 1a-b
Krakow, Muzeum Narodowe, Biblioteka książąt Czartoryskich, MS 414
Litoměřice, Státní oblastní archiv, MS A 2
Litoměřice, Státní oblastní archiv, BIF 3/1
Litoměřice, Státní oblastní archiv, BIF 3/2
London, British Library, Royal MS 17 F. IV
London, British Library, Yates Thompson MS 1
Ludwigsburg, Staatsarchiv Ludwigsburg, B 383, V/9, 1428-1435
Lunel, Bibliothèque Municipale, MS 8
Madrid, Biblioteca Nacional de España, MS Res. 28
Mantua, Archivio di Stato, AG, b. 439
Mantua, Archivio di Stato, AG, b. 723
Mantua, Archivio di Stato, AG, b. 2391
Montpellier, Bibliothèque interuniversitaire, Section médecine, MS H.196
New York, The Morgan Library & Museum, MS Glazier 52
Olomouc, Státní vědecká knihovna, MS M III 1
Oxford, Bodleian Library, MS Douce 308
Paris, Bibliothèque nationale de France, f. fr. 146
Paris, Bibliothèque nationale de France, f. fr. 1586
Parma, Archivio di Stato di Parma, Carteggio farnesiano estero, Boemia, busta 4

Prague, Archiv Národní galerie v Praze, Varia, AA 2015
Prague, Archiv Pražského hradu, no. 405.480/02
Prague, Archiv Pražského hradu, no. 405.611/02
Prague, Archiv Pražského hradu, Knihovna Metropolitní kapituly, ms A CXXXI
Prague, Archiv Pražského hradu, Knihovna Metropolitní kapituly, ms B XXVIII
Prague, Knihovna Národního muzea, ms XIII A 12
Prague, Národní knihovna České republiky, ms I C 14
Prague, Národní knihovna České republiky, ms VIII G 27
Prague, Národní knihovna České republiky, ms VIII G 30
Prague, Národní knihovna České republiky, ms XI E 9
Prague, Národní knihovna České republiky, ms XIII G 18
Prague, Národní knihovna České republiky, ms XIV A 17
Prague, Národní knihovna České republiky, ms XV E 4
Prague, Národní knihovna České republiky, ms XVII D 8
Prague, Národní knihovna České republiky, ms XIX B 5
Prague, Národní knihovna České republiky, ms XIX B 26
Prague, Národní knihovna České republiky, ms XXIII C 124
Prague, Národní knihovna České republiky, ms Teplá b 10
Reims, Archives départementales de la Marne, ms 56 H 74, pièce A
Salzburg, Universitätsbibliothek, ms M III 20
Siena, Archivio di Stato, Concistoro, Carteggio, b. 1926
Siena, Archivio di Stato, Concistoro, Carteggio, b. 1930, no. 87
Stuttgart, Württembergische Landesbibliothek, ms HB II 7
The Hague, Koninklijke Bibliotheek, ms 79 K 10
Třeboň, Státní oblastní archiv, ms A 2
Třeboň, Státní oblastní archiv, ms A 16
Udine, Biblioteca Civica 'Vincenzo Joppi', Fondo Principale, b. 896/IV, no. 322
Vienna, Österreichische Nationalbibliothek, Cod. 338
Vienna, Österreichische Nationalbibliothek, Cod. 275
Vienna, Österreichische Nationalbibliothek, Cod. 556
Vienna, Österreichische Nationalbibliothek, Cod. 2352
Vienna, Österreichische Nationalbibliothek, Cod. 2378
Vienna, Österreichische Nationalbibliothek, Cod. 2759
Vienna, Österreichische Nationalbibliothek, Cod. 2760
Vienna, Österreichische Nationalbibliothek, Cod. 2761
Vienna, Österreichische Nationalbibliothek, Cod. 2762
Vienna, Österreichische Nationalbibliothek, Cod. 2763
Vienna, Österreichische Nationalbibliothek, Cod. 2764
Vienna, Österreichische Nationalbibliothek, Cod. Series nova 44
Vienna, Österreichische Nationalbibliothek, Cod. Series nova 2643

Vienna, Österreichisches Staatsarchiv, Abteilung Haus-, Hof-, und Staatsarchiv, Reichsregisterbücher, I
Wrocław, Biblioteka Uniwersytecka, MS R 199

PRINTED PRIMARY SOURCES

Albrecht, Stefan (ed.), *Chronicon Aulae regiae: die Königsaaler Chronik. Eine Bestandsaufnahme* (Frankfurt, 2013).
Böhmer, Johann F.; Alfons Huber (eds), *Regesta Imperii. Die Regesten des Kaiserreichs unter Kaiser Karl IV. (1346-1378)* (Innsbruck, 1877).
Dotti, Ugo (ed.), *Francesco Petrarca: Lettere all'Imperatore. Carteggio con la Corte di Praga* (Reggio Emilia, 2007).
Emler, Josef (ed.), 'Laurentii de Brzezowa Historia hussitica', in *Fontes rerum Bohemicarum*, vol. V (Prague, 1893), 327–534.
Emler, Josef (ed.), *Spisové císaře Karla IV.* (Prague, 1878).
Emler, Josef; Jan Gebauer (eds), 'Przibiconis de Radenin dicti Pulkavae Chronicon Bohemiae', in *Fontes rerum Bohemicarum*, vol. V (Prague, 1893), 1–326.
Flajšhans, Václav (ed.), *Klaret a jeho družina*, vol. I, II (Prague, 1926).
Hledíková, Zdeňka (ed.), *Monumenta Vaticana res gestas Bohemicas illustrantia. Tomus prodromus: Acta Clementis V. Johannis XXII. et Benedicti XII. 1305-1342* (Prague, 2003).
Hoepffner, Ernst (ed.), *Œuvres de Guillaume de Machaut*, 3 vols (Paris, 1908-11).
Klapper, Joseph (ed.), *Buch der Liebkosung*, Vom Mittelalter zur Reformation. Forschungen zur Geschichte der deutschen Bildung, 6/1, Schriften Johanns von Neumarkt, 1 (Berlin, 1930).
Klapper, Joseph (ed.), *Hieronymus. Die unechten Briefe des Eusebius, Augustin. Cyrill zum Lobe des Heiligen*, Vom Mittelalter zur Reformation, 6, Schriften Johanns von Neumarkt, 2 (Berlin, 1932).
Klicman, Ladislav (ed.), *Monumenta Vaticana res gestas bohemicas illustrantia: t. I Acta Clementis VI. Pontificis Romani: 1342-1352* (Prague, 1903).
Leach, Elizabeth Eva; Joseph W. Mason; Matthew P. Thomson (eds), *A Medieval Songbook: Trouvère MS C* (Woodbridge, 2022).
Matthaei, Kurt (ed.), *Minne und Gesellschaft: Mittelhochdeutsche Minnereden*, vol. 1: *Die Heidelberger Handschriftenschriften 344, 358, 376 und 393* (Berlin, 1913).
Mollay, Karl (ed.), *Die Denkwürdigkeiten der Helene Kottannerin (1439-1440)* (Vienna, 1971).
Palmer, R. Barton (ed. and transl.), *Guillaume de Machaut: La Prise d'Alixandre – The Taking of Alexandria* (New York, 2002).

Palmer, R. Barton (text ed. and transl.); Domenic Leo (art ed.); Uri Smilansky (music ed.), *The Debate Poems: Le Jugement dou Roy de Behaigne, Le Jugement dou Roy de Navarre, Le Lay de Plour*, in R. Barton Palmer and Yolanda Plumley (eds), *Guillaume de Machaut: The Complete Poetry & Music*, vol. 1 (Michigan, 2016).

Palmer, R. Barton (text ed. and transl.); Domenic Leo (art ed.); Uri Smilansky (music ed.), *The Boethian Poems*, in R. Barton Palmer and Yolanda Plumley (eds), *Guillaume de Machaut: The Complete Poetry & Music*, vol. 2 (Michigan, 2019).

Piur, Paul (ed.), *Briefe Johanns von Neumarkt. Sammlung mit einem Anhang: Ausgewählte Briefe an Johann von Neumarkt, urkundliche und briefliche Zeugnisse zu seinem Leben*, Vom Mittelalter zur Reformation 8 (Berlin, 1937).

Pumprová, Anna; Libor Jan; Robert Antonín; Demeter Malaťák; Lukáš Švanda; Zdeněk Žalud (eds), *Cronica Aule regie. Die Königsaaler Chronik*, Monumenta Germaniae Historica, Scriptores, 40 (Wiesbaden, 2022).

Schrade, Leo (ed.), *The Roman de Fauvel. The Works of Philippe de Vitry. French Cycles of the Ordinarium Missae*, Polyphonic Music of the Fourteenth Century, 1 (Monaco, 1956).

Thuróczy, János, *Chronicle of the Hungarians*. Translation by Frank Mantello, foreword and commentary by Pál Engel, Indiana University Uralic and Altaic Series, 155 (Bloomington, 1991).

Volfing, Annette (ed.), *Heinrich von Mügeln, 'Der meide kranz'. A Commentary* (Tübingen, 1997).

Wimsatt, James I.; William W. Kibler (text eds) with Rebecca A. Baltzer (music ed.), *Guillaume de Machaut: 'Le Jugement dou roy de Behaigne' and 'Remede de Fortune'* (Atlanta, GA, 1988).

Zachová, Jana (ed.), *Fontes rerum Bohemicarum, Series nova, Vol. I.: Chronicon Francisci Pragensis* (Prague, 1998).

SECONDARY SOURCES

Abdullahi, Johannes, *Der Kaisersohn und das Geld: Freigebigkeit und Prachtentfaltung König Johanns von Böhmen (1296–1346)* (Luxembourg, 2019).

Abramov-van Rijk, Elena, 'The Italian Experience of the Holy Roman Emperor Charles IV: Musical and Literary Aspects', *Early Music History* 37 (2018), 1–44.

Adde-Vomáčka, Éloïse, *La Chronique de Dalimil. Les débuts de l'historiographie nationale tchèque en langue vulgaire au xive siècle* (Paris, 2016).

Aigner, Toni, *Sophia von Bayern – Königin von Böhmen: Jan Hus und die Wenzelsbibel* (Lindenberg i. Allgäu, 2021).

Andenna, Cristina; Gert Melville (eds), *Idoneität – Genealogie – Legitimation: Begründung und Akzeptanz von dynastischer Herrschaft im Mittelalter* (Cologne, 2015).

Antonín, Robert, *The Ideal Ruler in Medieval Bohemia* (Leiden, Boston, 2017).

Arlt, Wulf, 'Machaut in Context', in Jacqueline Cerquiglini-Toulet and Nigel Wilkins (eds), *Guillaume de Machaut 1300–2000* (Paris, 2002), 99–114.

Bak, János M., 'Queens as Scapegoats in Medieval Hungary', in Anne J. Duggan (ed.), *Queens and Queenship in Medieval Europe. Proceedings of a Conference held at King's College London, April 1995* (Woodbridge, 1997), 223–33.

Bak, János M., *Königtum und Stände in Ungarn im 14.–16. Jahrhundert* (Wiesbaden, 1973).

Bartlová, Milena, 'Was Queen Sophia of Bavaria an Art Patron?', in Markéta Jarošová, Jiří Kuthan and Stefan Scholz (eds), *Prag und die großen Kulturzentren Europas in der Zeit der Luxemburger (1310–1437). Prague and great cultural centres of Europe in the Luxembourgeois era (1310–1437)* (Prague, 2008), 623–34.

Bartlová, Milena; Dušan Buran, 'Comparing the Incomparable? Wenceslas IV and Sigismund, Their Queens, and Their Images', in Jiří Fajt and Andrea Langer (eds), *Kunst als Herrschaftsinstrument. Böhmen und das Heilige Römische Reich unter der Luxemburgern im europäischen Kontext* (Berlin, Munich, 2009), 368–76.

Bauch, Martin, '"Et hec scripsi manu mea propria" – Known and Unknown: Autographs of Charles IV as Testimonies of Intellectual Profiles, Royal Literacy, and Cultural Transfer', in Sébastien Barret, Dominique Stutzmann and Georg Vogeler (eds), *Ruling the Script in the Middle Ages: Formal Aspects of Written Communication (Books, Charters, and Inscriptions)* (Turnhout, 2016), 25–47.

Bauch, Martin, *'Divina favente clemencia': Auserwählung, Frömmigkeit und Heilsvermittlung in der Herrschaftspraxis Kaiser Karls IV.* (Cologne, 2015).

Bauch, Martin; Julia Burkhardt; Tomáš Gaudek; Václav Žůrek (eds), *Heilige, Helden, Wüteriche. Herrschaftsstile der Luxemburger (1308–1437)*, Forschungen zur Kaiser- und Papstgeschichte des Mittelalters—Beihefte zu J. F. Böhmer, Regesta Imperii, 41 (Cologne, Weimar, Vienna, 2017).

Baum, Wilhelm, *Kaiser Sigismund. Hus, Konstanz und Türkenkriege* (Graz, Vienna, Cologne, 1993).

Baumann, Winfried, *Die Literatur des Mittelalters in Böhmen: Deutsch-lateinisch-tschechische Literatur vom 10. bis zum 15. Jahrhundert* (Munich, 1978).

Bayley, Charles C., 'Petrarch, Charles IV, and the "Renovatio Imperii"', *Speculum* 17 (1942), 323-41.
Bažant, Ján, 'Medusa, Ancient Gems, and the Holy Roman Emperor Charles IV', *Anodos: Studies of the Ancient World* 13 (2013), 35-50.
Behr, Hans-Joachim, *Literatur als Machtlegitimation. Studien zur Funktion der deutschsprachigen Dichtung am böhmischen Königshof im 13. Jahrhundert* (Munich, 1989).
Bell, Susan Groag, 'Medieval Women Book Owners: Arbiters of Lay Piety and Ambassadors of Culture', *Signs* 7 (1982), 742-68.
Bendheim, Amelie; Heinz Sieburg (eds), *Prag in der Zeit der Luxemburger Dynastie: Literatur, Religion und Herrschaftskulturen zwischen Bereicherung und Behauptung* (Bielefeld, 2018).
Benešovská, Klára (ed.), *A Royal Marriage: Elisabeth Přemyslid and John of Luxembourg* (Prague, 2011).
Benešovská, Klára (ed.), *King John of Luxembourg (1296-1346) and the Art of his Era* (Prague, 1998).
Benešovská, Klára, 'The House at the Stone Bell: Royal Representation in Early-Fourteenth-Century Prague', in Zoë Opačić (ed.), *Prague and Bohemia: Medieval Art, Architecture and Cultural Exchange in Central Europe* (Leeds, 2006), 48-53.
Berens, Aloysia R., *Maître de Vyšší Brod et de Guillaume de Machaut, peintre et enlumineur au XIVe siècle: étude sur Jean de Bondol et son rapport avec l'art en Bohême* (Luxembourg, 2018).
Biebel-Stanley, Elizabeth M., 'Sovereignty through the Lady. "The Wife of Bath's Tale" and the Queenship of Anne of Bohemia', in S. Elizabeth Passmore and Susan Carter (eds), *The English "Loathly Lady" Tales. Boundaries, Traditions, Motifs* (Kalamazoo, 2007), 73-82.
Bijvoet-Williamson, Maya, *The Memoirs of Helene Kottanner (1439-1440)* (Cambridge, 1998).
Birkel, Christa, 'Vos autem estis advena: John of Luxembourg and the Political Argument of Foreignness in Fourteenth-Century Bohemia', *Historical Studies on Central Europe* 2 (2022), 5-21.
Bláhová, Marie, 'The Genealogy of the Czech Luxembourgs in Contemporary Historiography and Political Propaganda', in E. Kooper and S. Levelt (eds), *The Medieval Chronicle IX* (Amsterdam, New York, 2014), 1-32.
Bláhová, Marie, 'Translations of Historiographical Writings Composed and Read in the Czech Lands up to the Hussite Revolution and Their Audience', *Prague Papers on the History of International Relations* (2018), 44-57.
Bláhová, Marie, 'Vernacular Historiography in Medieval Czech Lands', *Medievalia* 19 (2016), 33-65.
Blaschka, Anton, *Die St. Wenzelslegende Kaiser Karls IV.* (Prague, 1934).

Bock, Nils, *Die Herolde im römisch-deutschen Reich: Studien zur adligen Kommunikation im späten Mittelalter* (Ostfildern, 2015).
Boehm, Barbara Drake; Jiří Fajt (eds), *Prague: The Crown of Bohemia, 1347–1437* (New York, 2005).
Bowers, Roger, 'Guillaume de Machaut and His Canonry of Reims, 1338–1377', *Early Music History* 23 (2004), 1–48.
Brom, Vlastimil, 'The Rhymed German Translation of the Chronicle of the So-Called Dalimil and its Strategies of Identification', in Pavlína Rychterová and David Kalhous (eds), *Historiography and Identity VI: Competing Narratives of the Past in Central and Eastern Europe, c. 1200–c. 1600* (Turnhout, 2021), 257–80.
Brown, Peter; Jan Čermák (eds), *England and Bohemia in the Age of Chaucer* (Cambridge, 2023).
Burgard, Friedhelm, *Familia Archiepiscopi: Studien zu den geistlichen Funktionsträgern Erzbischofs Balduins von Luxemburg (1307–54)* (Trier, 1991).
Burkhardt, Julia, 'Albert II of Habsburg's Composite Monarchy (1437–1439) and its Significance for Central Europe', in Paul Srodecki, Norbert Kersken and Rimvydas Petrauskas (eds), *Unions and Divisions: New Forms of Rule in Medieval and Renaissance Europe* (Abingdon, 2023), 224–36.
Burkhardt, Julia, 'Argumentative Uses of "Otherness" and "Foreignness" in Pre-Modern Political Debates in Central Europe', *Historical Studies on Central Europe* 2 (2022), 22–42.
Burkhardt, Julia, 'Frictions and Fictions of Community. Structures and Representations of Power in Central Europe, c. 1350–1500', *The Medieval History Journal* 19 (2016), 191–228.
Burkhardt, Julia; Christina Lutter, *Ich, Helene Kottannerin: Die Kammerfrau, die Ungarns Krone stahl* (Darmstadt, 2023).
Cazelles, Raymond, *Jean l'Aveugle: comte de Luxembourg, roi de Bohème* (Paris, 1947).
Chailley, Jacques; Paul Imbs; Daniel Poirion (eds), *Guillaume de Machaut, poète et compositeur: Colloque–table ronde organisé par l'Université de Reims (Reims, 19–22 avril 1978)* (Paris, 1982).
Chlench-Priber, Kathrin, *Das Korpus der Gebete Johanns von Neumarkt und die deutschsprachige Gebetbuchkultur des Spätmittelalters* (Wiesbaden, 2020).
Ciglbauer, Jan (ed.), *Septem Dies: Music at Prague University = Hudba na pražské univerzitě 1360–1460* (Prague, 2021).
Ciglbauer, Jan, 'From Tolerated Addition to Keepers of Tradition: The Authority of the "Past" in Latin Song in Central Europe in the Fourteenth and Fifteenth Centuries', in Karl Kügle (ed.), *Sounding the Past: Music as History and Memory* (Turnhout, 2020), 121–40.

Ciulisová, Ingrid, 'The Power of Marvellous Objects: Charles IV of Luxembourg, Charles V of Valois and their Gemstones', *Journal of the History of Collections* 33 (2021), 1–13.

Crăciun, Doina Elena, 'From "Adoption" to "Appropriation": The Chronological Process of Accommodating the Holy Hungarian Kings in the Noble Milieus of Late Medieval Hungary', in Thomas F. Head and Gábor Klaniczay (eds), *Cuius Patrocinio Tota Gaudet Regio. Saints' Cults and the Dynamics of Regional Cohesion* (Zagreb, 2014), 313–34.

Crossley, Paul, 'The Politics of Presentation: The Architecture of Charles IV of Bohemia', in Sarah Rees Jones, Richard Marks and A.J. Minnis (eds), *Courts and Regions in Medieval Europe* (York, 2000), 99–172.

Černá, Soňa, 'The Letters of St Jerome of the Prague Chancellor and Notary John of Neumarkt: A Transmission History', in Pavlína Rychterová (ed.), *Pursuing a New Order. Vol. I. Religious Education in Late Medieval Central and Eastern Central Europe* (Turnhout, 2019), 47–74.

Daldrup, Oliver, *Zwischen König und Reich: Träger, Formen und Funktionen von Gesandtschaften zur Zeit Sigmunds von Luxemburg (1410–1437)* (Münster, 2010).

De Looze, Laurence, *Pseudo-Autobiography in the Fourteenth Century: Juan Ruiz, Guillaume de Machaut, Jean Froissart, and Geoffrey Chaucer* (Gainesville, 1997).

Desmond, Karen, *Music and the Moderni, 1300–1350: The Ars nova in Theory and Practice* (Cambridge, 2018).

Dietmar, Carl D., *Die Beziehungen des Hauses Luxemburg zu Frankreich in den Jahren 1247–1356* (Cologne, 1983).

Dillon, Emma, *Medieval Music Making and the Roman de Fauvel* (Cambridge, 2002).

Dussen, Michael van, 'Three Verse Eulogies of Anne of Bohemia', *Medium Ævum* 78 (2009), 231–60.

Dussen, Michael van, *From England to Bohemia: Heresy and Communication in the Later Middle Ages* (Cambridge, 2012).

Dvořáčková-Malá, Dana; Kristýna Solomon; Michel Margue (eds), *Über den Hof und am Hofe: Literatur und Geschichtsschreibung im Mittelalter* (Dresden, 2021).

Dvořaková, Daniela, *Barbara of Cilli (1392–1451): A Hungarian, Holy Roman, and Bohemian Queen* (Leiden, Boston, 2021).

Earp, Lawrence Marshburn, *Guillaume de Machaut: A Guide to Research* (New York, London, 1995).

Earp, Lawrence; Jared C. Hartt (eds), *Poetry, Art, and Music in Guillaume de Machaut's Earliest Manuscript (BnF fr. 1586)* (Turnhout, 2021).

Fajt, Jiří (ed.), *Court Chapels of the High and Late Middle Ages and Their Artistic Decoration / Dvorské kaple vrcholného a pozdního středověku a jejich umělecká výzdoba* (Prague, 2003).

Fajt, Jiří (ed.), *Magister Theodoricus, Court Painter to Emperor Charles IV: The Pictorial Decoration of the Shrines at Karlštejn Castle* (Prague, 1998).

Fajt, Jiří, *Nürnberg als Kunstzentrum des Heiligen Römischen Reiches: Höfische und städtische Malerei in der Zeit Karls IV. 1346–1378* (Berlin, 2019).

Fantysová-Matějková, Jana, *Wenceslas de Bohême: Un prince au carrefour de l'Europe* (Paris, 2013).

Fantysová Matějková, Jana, 'Boemi and the Others. Shaping the Regional Identity of Medieval Bohemia between the Twelfth and the Fourteenth Centuries', in Dick E.H. De Boer and Luís Adão da Fonseca (eds), *Historiography and the Shaping of Regional Identity in Europe. Regions in Clio's Looking Glass* (Turnhout, 2020).

Fillitz, Hermann, *Die Insignien und Kleinodien des Heiligen Römischen Reiches* (Vienna, 1954).

Fößel, Amalie, 'The Political Traditions of Female Rulership in Medieval Europe', in Judith Bennett and Ruth Karras (eds), *The Oxford Handbook of Women and Gender in Medieval Europe* (Oxford, 2013), 68–83.

Fößel, Amalie, *Die Königin im mittelalterlichen Reich. Herrschaftsausübung, Herrschaftsrechte, Handlungsspielräume* (Stuttgart, 2000).

Fritz, Wolfgang D. (ed.), *Die Goldene Bulle Kaiser Karls IV. vom Jahre 1356. Text* (Weimar, 1972).

Gaude-Ferragu, Murielle (transl. Angela Krieger), *Queenship in Medieval France, 1300–1500* (London, 2016).

Geaman, Kristen L., 'A Personal Letter Written by Anne of Bohemia', *English Historical Review* 128 (2013), 1086–94.

Geaman, Kristen L., 'Beyond Good Queen Anne: Anne of Bohemia, Patronage, and Politics', in Heather J. Tanner, Laura L. Gathagan and Lois Lyn Huneycutt (eds), *Medieval Elite Women and the Exercise of Power, 1100–1400: Moving beyond the Exceptionalist Debate* (Cham, 2019), 67–89.

Geaman, Kristen L., *Anne of Bohemia* (London, 2021).

Ghosh, Shami, 'The Imperial Abbey of Ellwangen and Its Tenants: A Study of the Polyptych of 1337', *Agricultural History Review* 62 (2014), 87–209.

Groot, Bouko de, 'The Battle of Worringen: The Charge of Six Thousand to Decide the Fate of Limbourg', *Medieval Warfare* 2 (2012), 42–6.

Gruber, Elisabeth; Christina Lutter; Oliver Jens Schmitt (eds), *Kulturgeschichte der Überlieferung im Mittelalter. Quellen und Methoden zur Geschichte Mittel- und Südosteuropas* (Vienna, 2017).

Hand, Joni M., *Women, Manuscripts and Identity in Northern Europe, 1350–1550* (Farnham, 2013).

Hardy, Duncan, 'The Emperorship of Sigismund of Luxemburg (1410–37): Charisma and Government in the Later Medieval Holy Roman Empire', in Brigitte Miriam Bedos-Rezak and Martha Dana Rust (eds), *Faces of Charisma: Image, Text, Object in Byzantium and the Medieval West* (Leiden, Boston, 2018), 288–321.

Hardy, Duncan, *Associative Political Culture in the Holy Roman Empire: Upper Germany, 1346–1521* (Oxford, 2018).

Hergemöller, Bernd-Ulrich, *Cogor adversum te. Drei Studien zum literarisch-theologischen Profil Karls IV. und seiner Kanzlei* (Wahrendorf, 1999).

Hlaváček, Ivan, *Das Urkunden- und Kanzleiwesen des böhmischen und römischen Königs Wenzel (IV.) 1376–1419. Ein Beitrag zur spätmittelalterlichen Diplomatik* (Stuttgart, 1970).

Hlaváčková, Hana, 'Courtly Body in the Bible of Wenceslas IV', in Thomas W. Gaethgens (ed.), *Künstlerischer Austausch. Akten des 28. internationalen Kongresses für Kunstgeschichte* (Berlin, 1993), 371–82.

Hlaváčková, Hana, 'Old Testament Scenes in the Bible of King Wenceslas IV', in Jan Heller, Shemaryahu Talmon, Hana Hlaváčková and Martin Prudký (eds), *The Old Testament as Inspiration in Culture. International Academic Symposium Prague, September 1995* (Třebenice, 2001), 132–9.

Hoensch, Jörg K., *Itinerar König und Kaiser Sigismunds von Luxemburg 1368–1437* (Warendorf, 1995).

Hoensch, Jörg K., *Die Luxemburger: Eine spätmittelalterliche Dynastie gesamteuropäischer Bedeutung 1308–1437* (Stuttgart, 2000).

Holladay, Joan A., 'Fourteenth-Century French Queens as Collectors and Readers of Books: Jeanne d'Evreux and Her Contemporaries', *Journal of Medieval History* 32 (2006), 69–100.

Horníčková, Kateřina; Michal Šroněk (eds), *From Hus to Luther. Visual Culture in the Bohemian Reformation (1380–1620)* (Turnhout, 2016).

Hourihane, Colum (ed.), *Patronage, Power, and Agency in Medieval Art* (Princeton, 2013).

Hruza, Karel; Alexandra Kaar (eds), *Kaiser Sigismund (1368–1437). Zur Herrschaftspraxis eines europäischen Monarchen* (Cologne, 2012).

Hudson, Anne, 'From Oxford to Bohemia: Reflections on the Transmission of Wycliffite Texts', *Studia Mediaevalia Bohemica* 2 (2010), 25–37.

Huot, Sylvia, *From Song to Book: The Poetics of Writing in Old French Lyric and Lyrical Narrative Poetry* (Ithaca, 1987).

Husband, Timothy, *The Wild Man: Medieval Myth and Symbolism* (New York, 1980).

Jaspert, Nikolas; Imke Just (eds), *Queens, Princesses and Mendicants: Close Relations in a European Perspective* (Vienna, Zurich, Münster, 2019).

Jenni, Ulrike; Maria Theisen (eds), *Mitteleuropäische Schulen IV (ca. 1380–1400). Hofwerkstätten König Wenzels IV. und deren Umkreis* (Vienna, 2014).

Jindra, Petr, 'The Iconography of Christ in the Resurrection Panel of the So-Called Hohenfurth Cycle in an Exegetic View', *Bulletin of the National Gallery in Prague* 25 (2015), 6–37.

Jiroušková, Lenka, 'Prague', in David Wallace (ed.), *Europe. A Literary History. 1348–1418* (Oxford, 2016), 617–51.
Kavka, František, *Am Hofe Karls IV.* (Leipzig, 1989).
Keller, Verena, *Balduin von Trier (1285–1354): Kunst, Herrschaft und Spiritualität im Mittelalter* (Trier, 2012).
Kelly, Douglas, *Machaut and the Medieval Apprenticeship Tradition: Truth, Fiction and Poetic Craft* (Cambridge, 2014).
Kintzinger, Martin, *Westbindungen im spätmittelalterlichen Europa: Auswärtige Politik zwischen dem Reich, Frankreich, Burgund und England in der Regierungszeit Kaiser Sigmunds* (Stuttgart, 2000).
Klaniczay, Gábor, *Holy Rulers and Blessed Princesses: Dynastic Cults in Medieval Central Europe* (Cambridge, 2002).
Klapper, Joseph, *Johann von Neumarkt, Bischof und Hofkanzler. Religiöse Frührenaissance in Böhmen zur Zeit Kaiser Karls IV.* (Leipzig, 1964).
Klassen, John M., *Warring Maidens, Captive Wives, and Hussite Queens: Women and Men at War and Peace in Fifteenth-Century Bohemia* (Boulder, CO, New York, 1999).
Klípa, Jan, 'The Enthroned Madonna from Dijon: A Recently Discovered Painting from the Workshop of the Master of the Vyšší Brod Altarpiece', *Umění* 67 (2019), 215–25.
Knowles, Christine, 'Caxton and His Two French Sources: The "Game and Playe of the Chesse" and the Composite Manuscripts of the Two French Translations of the "Ludus Scaccorum"', *The Modern Language Review* 49 (1954), 417–23.
Kovács, Péter E., *Studien über die Zeit von Sigismund von Luxemburg* (Toruń, 2021).
Krása, Josef, *Die Handschriften König Wenzels IV.* (Vienna, 1971).
Kügle, Karl (ed.), *Sounding the Past: Music as History and Memory* (Turnhout, 2020).
Kügle, Karl (ed.), *The Networked Court: New Methodologies, New Perspectives*, Proceedings of the British Academy (Oxford, forthcoming).
Kuthan, Jiří; Jan Royt (eds), *The Cathedral of St. Vitus at Prague Castle* (Prague, 2011).
Land, William G., *The Prayer Book of Bonne of Luxembourg: A Personal Document* (Washington, 1984).
Lazzarini, Isabella, *Communication and Conflict. Italian Diplomacy in the Early Renaissance, 1350–1520* (Oxford, 2015).
Leach, Elizabeth Eva, 'Guillaume de Machaut, Royal Almoner: *Honte, paour* (B25) and *Donnez, signeurs* (B26) in Context', *Early Music* 38 (2010), 21–42.
Leach, Elizabeth Eva, 'Ripping Romance to Ribbons: The French of a German Knight in *The Tournament at Chauvency*', *Medium Ævum* 89 (2020), 327–49.

Leach, Elizabeth Eva, 'The Provenance, Date, and Patron of Oxford, Bodleian Library, MS Douce 308', *Speculum* 97 (2022), 283–321.

Leach, Elizabeth Eva, 'Vernacular Song III: Polyphony', in Mark Everist and Thomas Forrest Kelly (eds), *The Cambridge History of Medieval Music* (Cambridge, 2018), 937–73.

Leach, Elizabeth Eva, *Guillaume de Machaut: Secretary, Poet, Musician* (Ithaca, Leuven, 2011).

Leo, Domenic, '"The Beginning is the End": Guillaume de Machaut's Illuminated Prologue', in Yolanda Plumley, Giuliano Di Bacco and Stefano Jossa (eds), *Citation, Intertextuality and Memory in the Middle Ages and Renaissance* (Exeter, 2011), 96–112.

Livingston, Michael; Kelly DeVries (eds), *The Battle of Crécy: A Casebook* (Liverpool, 2015).

Lowden, John, 'Beauty or Truth? Making a *Bible Moralisée* in Paris around 1400', in Godfried Croenen and Peter Ainsworth (eds), *Patrons, Authors and Workshops: Books and Book Production in Paris around 1400* (Leuven, 2006), 197–222.

Lowden, John, 'The Royal / Imperial Book and the Image and Self-Image of the Medieval Ruler', in Anne J. Duggan (ed.), *Kings and Kingship in Medieval Europe* (London, 1993), 213–40.

Macek, Josef; Ernő Marosi; Ferdinand Seibt (eds), *Sigismund von Luxemburg: Kaiser und König in Mitteleuropa 1387–1437. Beiträge zur Herrschaft Kaiser Sigismunds und der europäischen Geschichte um 1400. Vorträge der internationalen Tagung in Budapest vom 8.–11. Juli 1987 anläßlich der 600. Wiederkehr seiner Thronbesteigung in Ungarn und seines 550. Todestages* (Warendorf, 1994).

Malfatto, Irene, 'John of Marignolli and the Historiographical Project of Charles IV', *Acta Universitatis Carolinae: Historia Universitatis Carolinae Pragensis* 55 (2015), 131–40.

Marani-Moravová, Běla, *Peter von Zittau. Abt, Diplomat und Chronist der Luxemburger* (Ostfildern, 2019).

Margue, Michel; et al., *Un itinéraire européen: Jean l'Aveugle, comte de Luxembourg et roi de Bohême, 1296–1346* (Luxembourg, 1998).

Marin, Olivier, *L'archevêque, le maître et le dévot. Genèses du mouvement réformateur pragois (années 1360–1419)* (Paris, 2005).

Masařík, Zdeněk, *Die mittelalterliche deutsche Kanzleisprache in Süd- und Mittelmähren* (Brno, 1966).

Maxwell, Kate, 'A Multimodal Reading of MS C: Order, Decoration, Mutation', in Lawrence Earp and Jared C. Hartt (eds), *Poetry, Art, and Music in Guillaume de Machaut's Earliest Manuscript (BnF fr. 1586)* (Turnhout, 2021), 133–53.

Mengel, David C., 'Bohemia's Treasury of Saints: Relics and Indulgences in Emperor Charles IV's Prague', in Marie-Madeleine de Cevins and

Olivier Marin (eds), *Les saints et leur culte en Europe centrale au Moyen Age (XIe-début du XVIe siècle)* (Turnhout, 2017), 57-76.

Měřínský, Zdeněk; Jaroslav Mezník, 'The Making of the Czech State: Bohemia and Moravia from the Tenth to the Fourteenth Centuries', in Mikuláš Teich (ed.), *Bohemia in History* (Cambridge, 1998), 39-58.

Meyer, Rudolf J., *Königs- und Kaiserbegräbnisse im Spätmittelalter. Von Rudolf von Habsburg bis zu Friedrich III.* (Köln, Weimar, Wien, 2000).

Monnet, Pierre, *Karl IV.: Der europäische Kaiser* (Darmstadt, 2021).

Morand, Kathleen, *Jean Pucelle* (Oxford, 1962).

Müller, Ulrich; Margarete Springeth (eds), *Oswald von Wolkenstein: Leben, Werk, Rezeption* (Berlin, 2011).

Murray, David, *Poetry in Motion: Languages and Lyrics in the European Middle Ages* (Turnhout, 2019).

Nagy, Balász, 'Memories of the Self. The Autobiography of Charles IV in Search of Medieval Memories', in Rafał Wójcik (ed.), *Culture of Memory in East Central Europe in the Late Middle Ages and the Early Modern Period* (Poznań, 2008), 161-6.

Nagy, Balázs; Frank Schaer (eds), *Karoli IV Imperatoris Romanorum vita ab eo ipso conscripta; et, Hystoria nova de Sancto Wenceslao Martyre = Autobiography of Emperor Charles IV; and, His Legend of St. Wenceslas* (Budapest, 2001).

Nechutová, Jana, *Die lateinische Literatur des Mittelalters in Böhmen* (Cologne, 2007).

Nejedlý, Martin, 'La Bohême et ses habitants vus par quatre auteurs français du Moyen Age (Guillaume de Machaut, Eustache Deschamps, Jean Froissart, Jean d'Arras)', *Listy filologické / Folia philologica* 128 (2005), 21-34.

Nolden, Reiner (ed.), *Balduin von Luxemburg: Erzbischof und Kurfürst von Trier (1308-1354)* (Trier, 2010).

Oetjens, Lena, 'Charles IV and Learned Order: The Discourse on Knowledge in "Der meide kranz"', *Acta Universitatis Carolinae: Historia Universitatis Carolinas Pragensis* 55 (2015), 141-52.

Opačić, Zoë (ed.), *Prague and Bohemia. Medieval Art, Architecture and Cultural Exchange in Central Europe* (Leeds, 2009).

Opačić, Zoë, 'Karolus Magnus and Karolus Quartus: Imperial Role Models in Ingelheim, Aachen and Prague', in Ute Engel and Alexandrea Gajewski (eds), *Mainz and the Middle Rhine Valley: Medieval Art, Architecture and Archaeology* (Leeds, 2007), 221-46.

Opačić, Zoë, 'The Sacred Topography of Medieval Prague', in Sæbjørg Walaker Nordeide and Stefan Brink (eds), *Sacred Sites and Holy Places: Exploring the Sacralization of Landscape Through Time and Space* (Turnhout, 2013), 253-81.

Penth, Sabine; Peter Thorau (eds), *Rom 1312: Die Kaiserkrönung Heinrichs VII. und die Folgen. Die Luxemburger als Herrscherdynastie von gesamteuropäischer Bedeutung* (Cologne, 2016).
Péporté, Pit, 'When "Jan Lucemburský" Meets "Jean l'Aveugle": A Comparison of King John of Bohemia's Representation in the Czech Lands and Luxembourg', *Husitský Tábor* 17 (2012), 29–49.
Pešina, Jaroslav, *The Master of the Hohenfurth Altarpiece* (Prague, 1989).
Plumley, Yolanda, 'Guillaume de Machaut and the Advent of a New School of Lyric c.1350: The Prestige of the Past', in Lawrence Earp and Jared C. Hartt (eds), *Poetry, Art, and Music in Guillaume de Machaut's Earliest Manuscript (BnF fr. 1586)* (Turnhout, 2021), 315–40.
Plumley, Yolanda, *The Art of Grafted Song: Citation and Allusion in the Age of Machaut* (Oxford, 2013).
Poirion, Daniel, *Le Poète et le prince: L'évolution du lyrisme courtois de Guillaume de Machaut à Charles d'Orléans* (Paris, 1965).
Prioult, Albert, 'Un poète voyageur: Guillaume de Machaut et la "Reise" de Jean l'Aveugle, roi de Boheme, en 1328-1329', *Lettres Romanes* 4 (1950), 3–29.
Proske, Veronika, *Der Romzug Kaiser Sigismunds (1431–1433). Politische Kommunikation, Herrschaftsrepräsentation und -rezeption* (Vienna, Cologne, Weimar, 2018).
Pyun, Kyunghee, 'The Master of the *Remede de Fortune* and Parisian Ateliers c.1350', in Lawrence Earp and Jared C. Hartt (eds), *Poetry, Art, and Music in Guillaume de Machaut's Earliest Manuscript (BnF fr. 1586)* (Turnhout, 2021), 195–216.
Pyun, Kyunghee; Anna D. Russakoff (eds), *Jean Pucelle: Innovation and Collaboration in Manuscript Painting* (London, 2013).
Rady, Martyn, 'Government of Medieval Buda', in Balázs Nagy, Martyn Rady, Katalin Szende and András Vadás (eds), *Medieval Buda in Context* (Leiden, 2016).
Raeymaekers, Dries; Sebastiaan Derks (eds), *The Key to Power? The Culture of Access in Princely Courts, 1400–1750* (Leiden, Boston, 2016).
Robertson, Anne Walters, *Guillaume de Machaut and Reims: Context and Meaning in his Musical Works* (Cambridge, 2002).
Rychterová, Pavlína, 'Pursuing the Truth. The Czech Lay Theologian Thomas of Štítné (c. 1330–c. 1400) and His Delight in Doing Miscellanies', in Sabrina Corbellini, Giovanna Murano and Giacomo Signore (eds), *Collecting, Organizing and Transmitting Knowledge: Miscellanies in Late Medieval Europe* (Turnhout, 2018), 115–30.
Rychterová, Pavlína, 'The Chronicle of So-Called Dalimil and Its Concept of Czech Identity', in Pavlína Rychterová and David Kalhous (eds), *Historiography and Identity VI. Competing Narratives of the Past in Central and Eastern Europe, c. 1200–c. 1600* (Turnhout, 2021), 171–206.

Sághy, Marianne, 'Aspects of Female Rulership in Late Medieval Literature: The Queens' Reign in Angevin Hungary', *East Central Europe* 20–3 (1993–6), 69–86.

Scales, Len, 'The Illuminated Reich: Memory, Crisis and the Visibility of Monarchy in Late Medieval Germany', in Jason Philip Coy, Benjamin Marschke and David Warren Sabean (eds), *The Holy Roman Empire Reconsidered* (New York, 2010), 73–92.

Scales, Len, *The Shaping of German Identity: Authority and Crisis, 1245–1414* (Cambridge, 2012).

Scheller, Robert W., *Exemplum: Model-Book Drawings and the Practice of Artistic Transmission in the Middle Ages (ca. 900 – ca. 1470)* (Amsterdam, 1995).

Schenk, Gerrit Jasper, *Zeremoniell und Politik. Herrschereinzüge im spätmittelalterlichen Reich* (Cologne, Weimar, Vienna, 2003).

Schiff, Otto, *König Sigismunds italienische Politik bis zur Romfahrt (1410–1431)* (Frankfurt am Main, 1909).

Schmidt, Hans-Joachim, 'Power Through Poverty: Mendicant Friars at the Imperial Courts in the 14th Century', in Gert Melville and James D. Mixson (eds), *Virtuosos of Faith. Monks, Nuns, Canons, and Friars as Elites of Medieval Culture* (Münster, 2020), 189–208.

Schmidt, Hans-Joachim, *Herrschaft durch Schrecken und Liebe: Vorstellungen und Begründungen im Mittelalter* (Göttingen, 2019).

Schmidt, Ondřej, *Die Briefe vom Kaiserhof. Wenzel IV. und Sigismund von Luxemburg im Lichte der diplomatischen Korrespondenz aus dem Archiv der Gonzaga von Mantua (1380–1436)* (Brno, 2022).

Schwedler, Gerald, *Herrschertreffen des Spätmittelalters. Formen—Rituale—Wirkungen* (Ostfildern, 2008).

Seibt, Ferdinand (ed.), *Karl IV. und sein Kreis* (Munich, 1982).

Sichálek, Jakub, 'European Background: Czech Translations', in Elizabeth Solopova (ed.), *The Wycliffite Bible: Origin, History and Interpretation* (Leiden, 2017), 66–84.

Skorka, Renáta, 'De Luxembourg à Oradea: Histoire de la reine Béatrice de Hongrie', *Mélanges de l'École française de Rome – Moyen Âge* 129 (2017), <http://journals.openedition.org/mefrm/3663> [accessed 16 March 2023].

Skorka, Renáta; Boglárka Weisz, 'The Town and the Widow: The Journey of Elisabeth of Luxembourg to Pozsony', *Mesto a dejiny* 8 (2019), 6–21.

Slavický, Tomáš, 'Czech Rorate Chants, Missa Rorate, and Charles IV's Foundation of Votive Officium in Prague Cathedral: The Testament of Choral Melodies to the Long-Term Retention of Repertoire', *Hudební věda* 55 (2018), 239–64.

Sleiderink, Remco, 'From Francophile to Francophobe: The Changing Attitude of Medieval Dutch Authors towards French Literature', in

Christopher Kleinhenz and Keith Busby (eds), *Medieval Multilingualism: The Francophone World and Its Neighbours* (Turnhout, 2010), 127–43.

Sleiderink, Remco, 'Pykini's Parrot: Music at the Court of Brabant', in Barbara Haggh, Frank Daelemans and André Vanrie (eds), *Musicology and Archival Research / Musicologie et recherches en archives / Musicologie en archiefonderzoek* (Brussels, 1994), 358–91.

Smilansky, Uri, 'Creating MS C: Author, Workshop, Court', *Early Music History* 39 (2020), 253–304.

Smilansky, Uri, 'Machaut and Prague: A Rare New Sighting?', *Early Music* 46 (2018), 211–23.

Smilansky, Uri, 'Texts on the Move: Book Presentation as Performative Space', in Karl Kügle (ed.), *The Networked Court: New Methodologies, New Perspectives* (Oxford, forthcoming).

Smilansky, Uri, 'The *Ars Subtilior* as an International Style', in Stefan Morent, Silke Leopold and Joachim Steinheuer (eds), *Europäische Musikkultur im Kontext des Konstanzer Konzils* (Ostfildern, 2017), 225–49.

Smilansky, Uri, 'The Polyphonies of Function: Guillaume de Machaut and the Performance of Text and Music', in Jonathan Fruoco (ed.), *Polyphony and the Modern* (New York, 2021), 15–36.

Sobiesiak, Joanna, 'Czechs and Germans: Nationals and Foreigners in the Work of Czech Chroniclers: From Cosmas of Prague (12th Century) to the Chronicle of the So-Called Dalimil (14th Century)', in Andrzej Pleszczyński, Joanna Sobiesiak, Michał Tomaszek and Przemysław Tyszka (eds), *Imagined Communities. Constructing Collective Identities in Medieval Europe* (Leiden, 2018), 322–34.

Soukup, Pavel, 'Religion and Violence in the Hussite Wars', in Wolfgang Palaver, Harriet Rudolph and Dietmar Regensburger (eds), *The European Wars of Religion: An Interdisciplinary Reassessment of Sources, Interpretations, and Myths* (Farnham, 2016), 19–44.

Stackmann, Karl, *Frauenlob, Heinrich von Mügeln und ihre Nachfolger* (Göttingen, 2002).

Staley, Lynn, 'Anne of Bohemia and the Objects of Ricardian Kingship', in Jenny Adams and Nancy Mason Bradbury (eds), *Medieval Women and Their Objects* (Ann Arbor, 2017), 97–122.

Stein, Robert (ed.), *Powerbrokers in the Late Middle Ages: The Burgundian Low Countries in a European Context / Les courtiers du pouvoir au bas Moyen-Âge: Les Pays-Bas bourguignons dans un contexte européen* (Turnhout, 2001).

Stejskal, Karel, *European Art in the Fourteenth Century* (Prague, 1978).

Sterling, Charles, *La peinture médiévale à Paris 1300–1500* (Paris, 1987).

Stokes, Jordan, 'In Search of Machaut's Poetics: Music and Rhetoric in *Le Remede de Fortune*', *The Journal of Musicology* 31 (2014), 395–430.

Stollberg-Rilinger, Barbara, *Holy Roman Empire: A Short History* (Princeton, 2018).
Studničková, Milada; Maria Theisen (eds), *Art in an Unsettled Time. Bohemian Book Illumination before Gutenberg* (Prague, 2018).
Šmahel, František, *Die hussitische Revolution* (Hannover, 2002).
Šmahel, František, *Charles University in the Middle Ages: Selected Studies* (Leiden, Boston, 2007).
Šmahel, František, *The Parisian Summit, 1377–78. Emperor Charles IV and King Charles V of France* (Prague, 2015).
Šorm, Martin, 'Reading About Men and For Men. Daughters Against Fathers, Violence and Wisdom in One Medieval Manuscript', in Daniela Rywiková and Michaela Antonín Malaníková (eds), *Premodern History Through the Prism of Gender* (Lanham, 2021), 161–95.
Špička, Jiří, 'Francesco Petrarca Travelling and Writing to Prague's Court', *Verbum: Analecta Neolatina* 12 (2010), 27–40.
Štih, Peter, *The Middle Ages between the Eastern Alps and the Northern Adriatic: Select Papers on Slovene Historiography and Medieval History* (Leiden, 2010).
Tanner, Heather J. (ed.), *Medieval Elite Women and the Exercise of Power, 1100–1400: Moving beyond the Exceptionalist Debate* (London, 2019).
Theisen, Maria, 'Picturing Frana', in Zoë Opačić and Achim Timmermann (eds), *Image, Memory and Devotion. Studies in Gothic Art* (London, 2010), 103–12.
Theisen, Maria, 'The Emblem of the Torque and its Use in the Willehalm Manuscript of King Wenceslas IV of Bohemia', *Journal of the British Archaeological Association* 171 (2018), 131–53.
Thomas, Alfred, *Anne's Bohemia: Czech Literature and Society, 1310–1420* (Minneapolis, 1998).
Thomas, Alfred, *Reading Women in Late Medieval Europe: Anne of Bohemia and Chaucer's Female Audience* (New York, 2015).
Thomas, Alfred, *The Court of Richard II and Bohemian Culture. Literature and Art in the Age of Chaucer and the Gawain Poet* (Cambridge, 2020).
Thomas, Heinz, *Zwischen Regnum und Imperium: Die Fürstentümer Bar und Lothringen zur Zeit Kaiser Karls IV.* (Bonn, 1973).
Thomson, S. Harrison, 'Learning at the Court of Charles IV', *Speculum* 25 (1950), 1–20.
Tomasello, Andrew, *Music and Ritual in Papal Avignon 1309–1403* (Ann Arbor, 1983).
Torunsky, Vera, *Worringen 1288: Ursachen und Folgen einer Schlacht* (Cologne, 1988).
Toussaint, Gia, *Das Passional der Kunigunde von Böhmen: Bildrhetorik und Spiritualität* (Paderborn, 2003).

Uličný, Petr, 'The Choirs of St Vitus's Cathedral in Prague: A Marriage of Liturgy, Coronation, Royal Necropolis and Piety', *Journal of the British Archaeological Association* 168 (2015), 186–233.

Unterkircher, Franz, *König Wenzels Bibelbilder. Die Miniaturen zur Genesis aus der Wenzelsbibel* (Graz, 1983).

Urban, Alexandra, *Poetik der Meisterschaft in 'Der meide kranz': Heinrich von Mügeln auf den Schultern des Alanus ab Insulis* (Berlin, 2021).

Vale, Malcolm, 'The World of the Courts: Content and Context of the Fauvel Manuscript', in Margaret Bent and Andrew Wathey (eds), *Fauvel Studies: Allegory, Chronicle, Music, and Image in Paris, Bibliothèque Nationale de France, MS Français 146* (Oxford, 1998), 591–8.

Veldtrup, Dieter, *Zwischen Eherecht und Familienpolitik. Studien zu den dynastischen Heiratsprojekten Karls IV.* (Warendorf, 1988).

Verkholantsev, Julia, 'St. Jerome as a Slavic Apostle in Luxemburg Bohemia', *Viator* 44 (2013), 251–86.

Verkholantsev, Julia, *The Slavic Letters of St. Jerome. The History of the Legend and Its Legacy, or, How the Translator of the Vulgate Became an Apostle of the Slavs* (DeKalb, 2014).

Wagner, Valentin; Bernhard Schmitt (eds), *Balduin aus dem Hause Luxemburg: Erzbischof und Kurfürst von Trier 1284–1354* (Luxembourg, 2009).

Ward, Benedicta, *Miracles and Medieval Mind. Theory, Record and Event, 1000–1215* (Aldershot, 1987).

Wathey, Andrew, 'European Culture and Musical Politics at the Court of Cyprus', in Ursula Günther and Ludwig Finscher (eds), *The Cypriot-French Repertory of the Manuscript Torino J.II.9* (Neuhausen-Stuttgart, 1995), 33–54.

Wathey, Andrew, 'Gervès du Bus, the Roman de Fauvel, and the Politics of the Later Capetian Court', in Margaret Bent and Andrew Wathey (eds), *Fauvel Studies: Allegory, Chronicle, Music and Image in Paris, Bibliothèque Nationale MS Français 146* (Oxford, 1998), 599–613.

Wathey, Andrew, 'Guillaume de Machaut and Yolande of Flanders', in Jared C. Hartt, Tamsyn Mahoney-Steel and Benjamin Albritton (eds), *Manuscripts, Music, Machaut: Essays in Honor of Lawrence Earp* (Turnhout, 2022), 111–26.

Wathey, Andrew, 'The Marriage of Edward III and the Transmission of French Motets to England', *Journal of the American Musicological Society* 45 (1992), 1–29.

Wathey, Andrew, 'The Motets of Philippe de Vitry and the Fourteenth-Century Renaissance', *Early Music History* 12 (1993), 119–50.

Wegman, Rob, 'New Light on Secular Polyphony at the Court of Holland in the Early Fifteenth Century: The Amsterdam Fragments', *Journal of the Royal Musical Association* 117 (1992), 181–207.

Weiss, Roberto, 'Petrarch the Antiquarian', in Charles Henderson (ed.), *Classical, Medieval and Renaissance Studies in Honor of Berthold Louis Ullman* (Rome, 1964), 199–209.

Weitzmann, Kurt; Herbert L. Kessler, *The Cotton Genesis: British Library, Codex Cotton Otho B VI* (Princeton, 1986).

Weltsch, Ruben Ernest, *Archbishop John of Jenstein (1348–1400): Papalism, Humanism and Reform in Pre-Hussite Prague* (The Hague, 1968).

Wenzel, Horst. 'How Two Ladies Steal a Crown: The Memoirs of Helene Kottannerin (1439–40) at the Court of Queen Elisabeth of Hungary (1409–42)', in Regina Schulte (ed.), *The Body of the Queen. Gender and Rule in the Courtly World, 1500–2000* (New York, Oxford, 2006), 19–42.

Whelan, Mark, 'Between Papacy and Empire: Cardinal Henry Beaufort, the House of Lancaster, and the Hussite Crusades', *The English Historical Review* 133 (2018), 1–31.

Whelan, Mark, 'Dances, Dragons and a Pagan Queen: Sigismund of Luxemburg and the Publicizing of the Ottoman Turkish Threat', in Norman Housley (ed.), *The Crusade in the Fifteenth Century: Converging and Competing Cultures* (Routledge, 2017), 49–63.

Whelan, Mark, 'Taxes, Wagenburgs, and a Nightingale: The Imperial Abbey of Ellwangen and the Hussite Wars, 1427–1435', *Journal of Ecclesiastical History* 72 (2021), 751–77.

Whelan, Mark, 'The "Conciliar" Front of the Hundred Years' War: Scotland, France and England at the Council of Pavia-Siena, 1423–4', *Historical Research* 93 (2020), 420–42.

Whelan, Mark, 'Walter of Schwarzenberg and the Fifth Hussite Crusade Reconsidered (1431)', *Mitteilungen des Instituts für Österreichische Geschichtsforschung* 122 (2014), 322–35.

Widder, Ellen; Wolfgang Kraut (eds), *Vom luxemburgischen Grafen zum europäischen Herrscher: Neue Forschungen zu Heinrich VII.* (Luxembourg, 2008).

Wilkins, Nigel, 'A Pattern of Patronage: Machaut, Froissart and the Houses of Luxembourg and Bohemia in the Fourteenth Century', *French Studies* 37 (1983), 257–84.

Wilkins, Nigel, *Words and Music in Medieval Europe* (Farnham, 2011).

Wolf, Armin, *Die Goldene Bulle: König Wenzels Handschrift. Codex Vindobonensis 338 der Österreichischen Nationalbibliothek, Faksimile und Kommentar* (Graz, 2002).

Wolfthal, Diane, *In and Out of the Marital Bed: Seeing Sex in Renaissance Europe* (New Haven, 2010).

Wolverton, Lisa, *Cosmas of Prague. Narrative, Classicism, Politics* (Washington, 2015).

Woodacre, Elena (ed.), *A Companion to Global Queenship* (Leeds, 2018).

Woodacre, Elena; Cathleen Sarti, 'What is Royal Studies?', *Royal Studies Journal* 2 (2015), 13–20.

Záruba, František, 'The Castles of King Wenceslaus IV as Venues for Diplomatic Negotiations', *Przegląd Historyczny* 112 (2021), 247–59.

Zayaruznaya, Anna, 'Old, New, and Newer Still in Book 7 of the *Speculum musice*', *Journal of the American Musicological Society* 73 (2020), 95–148.

Zey, Claudia (ed.), *Mächtige Frauen? Königinnen und Fürstinnen im europäischen Mittelalter (11.–14. Jahrhundert)* (Ostfildern, 2015).

Zsoldos, Attila, *The Árpáds and Their Wives: Queenship in Early Medieval Hungary, 1000–1301* (Rome, 2019).

Zupka, Dušan, 'Medieval Dynasties in Medieval Studies: A Historiographic Contribution', *Forum Historiae* 13 (2019), 89–101.

Zupka, Dušan, *Ritual and Symbolic Communication in Medieval Hungary under the Árpád Dynasty (1000–1301)* (Leiden, 2016), 35–69.

Žůrek, Václav, 'Godfrey of Viterbo and his Readers at the Court of Emperor Charles IV', in Thomas Foerster (ed.), *Godfrey of Viterbo and his Readers: Imperial Tradition and Universal History in Late Medieval Europe* (Farnham, 2015), 87–102.

Žůrek, Václav, *Charles IV. A Portrait of a Medieval Ruler* (Prague, 2023).

Žůrek, Václav; Pavlína Rychterová, 'Slavonic and Czech Identity in the *Chronicon Bohemiae* by Přibík Pulkava of Radenín', in Pavlína Rychterová and David Kalhous (eds), *Historiography and Identity VI. Competing Narratives of the Past in Central and Eastern Europe, c. 1200–c. 1600* (Turnhout, 2021), 225–56.

INDEX

Aachen   139–143, 168–170, 327
   Palatine Chapel   141
Abenragel, Abu l-Hasan (d. c. 1040)   271–272
Abraham, Abram (biblical figure)   285, 299, 310, 312, 319
Adam (biblical figure)   247, 273, 275, 278–279, 291–292, 294, 317–318
Adenet le Roi (fl. 1270s–1280s; trouvère)   434
Adolph de La Marck (Prince-Bishop of Liège 1313–1344)   79, 91
Adoration of the Magi   107, 110, 117
Albert (Albrecht) of Habsburg (1397–1439; King of the Romans 1438–1439)   4, 388–392, 463
Albert (Albrecht) I of Wittelsbach (1336–1404; Duke of Bavaria-Straubing 1353–1404, Count of Holland 1388–1404)   329
Albertus Magnus (1200–1280)   156–157, 272
Alexandreis (Ulrich von Etzenbach)   187, 206, 450
Alexandria   141, 160, 170
Alkabitius, al-Qabīṣī (d. 967)   271
Amadeus VIII of Savoy (1383–1451; Count, later Duke of Savoy 1391–1440)   347
Amiens   84–85, 97
Anagni   418
Angevin   56
Anjou   2, 40, 150–151, 375–377, 379, 381

Anne (Anna) of Bohemia (1290–1313; Queen of Bohemia 1306–1310)   383, 387
Anne of Bohemia (1366–1394; Queen of England 1382–1394)   2, 6, 132, 174–175, 301, 367, 399–400, 411, 451, 460
Anne (Anna) of Habsburg (daughter of Albert of Habsburg)   392
Anne (Anna) of Luxembourg (youngest daughter of John of Luxembourg)   90
Anne (Anna) of Schweidnitz, Świdnica (1339–1362; Queen of Bohemia 1353–1362, Holy Roman Empress 1355–1362)   167, 420
Antichrist   421, 424–426
Antonia Minor   159–161, 170
Antonius de Lemaco   306
Aquileia   350
Aragon   38
Aristotle   267–268, 271–272
Ark of the Covenant   117, 286
Arles (Kingdom of)   81, 44
Arphaxad (biblical figure)   298
Arras   42, 59, 85, 93, 445
Ars Nova   442, 455
Ars Subtilior   459
Augsburg   323–324, 335–336, 340, 414
Augustijnken (fl. 1358–1363; poet)   459
Augustus (63 BCE–14 CE; Roman emperor)   141–142, 417, 421
Aula Regia *see* Zbraslav

INDEX

Austria 4–5, 8–9, 67, 69, 95, 244, 264, 275, 330, 354, 387, 391, 395–396, 437, 458, 460
Austrian Bible Translator 244
Auxerre 93
Averroës, Abū l-Walīd (d. 1198; philosopher) 271
Avigdor Kara ben Isaac (d. 1439; chief rabbi of Prague's Jewish community) 247, 275, 281
Avignon 5, 76–77, 91–96, 99–100, 104, 113, 127, 131, 171, 412, 419, 430, 445, 463
Avranches 75–76, 93, 99
Aymeries 80, 85
Azzo(ne) Visconti (1302–1339; Lord of Milan 1329–1339) 216

Balduin (Baldwin) of Luxembourg (c. 1285–1354; Archbishop-Elector of Trier 1307–1354) 2, 82, 95–96, 432, 436, 438
Bar (County, later Duchy of) 30, 32, 38, 45, 51, 82, 88–89, 101–102, 433
Barbara of Cilli (Celje, c. 1390/95–1451; Queen of Hungary 1405–1437, of the Romans 1411–1437, of Bohemia 1419–1437, Holy Roman Empress 1433–1437) 388, 392
Bartolomeo Martini 355
Bartolus of Sassoferrato (1313–1357; jurist) 177
Basel 340, 454
Basil (bishop of Caesarea) 267
Battle
  of Crécy (1346) 31, 83, 97, 99, 430, 442, 445, 457
  of the Milvian Bridge (312) 139
  of Mühldorf am Inn (1322) 62, 82, 440
  of Poitiers (1356) 101
  of San Felice, near Modena (1332) 160
  of Worringen (1288) 28, 432
Bautzen 79, 182
Bavaria 33, 67, 69, 80, 91, 96, 127, 155, 168, 170, 249, 280, 283–284, 287, 326, 329, 337, 354, 398–399, 402, 411, 419, 422, 440, 455–456, 459–460

Beatrice of Avesnes and Beaumont (c. 1260–1321; Countess of Luxembourg) 28, 85, 87, 432–433, 439
Beatrice of Bourbon (c. 1314–1383; Queen of Bohemia 1334–1346) 30–32, 35, 43, 73, 80, 83, 87, 89–90, 92, 132
Beatrice of Luxembourg (1305–1319; Queen of Hungary 1318–1319) 2, 33
Beaumont (Count of) 28, 80, 83, 85, 87, 89, 98, 432–433, 439
Beghard movement 195
Beguine movement 195
Běla (mythical figure) 234
Belgium 3–5
Belgrade 332–333, 337
Belluno 350, 358, 363
Beltrando Rossi 352
Benedetto Caetani *see* Boniface VIII
Benedict XII (Jacques Fournier, 1285–1342; Pope 1334–1342) 75, 78, 104, 155
Beneš Krabice of Weitmil (chronicler) 180, 413, 423
Bernardus de Montepulciano 92
Bethlehem 215
Bethlehem Chapel *see* Prague
Binche 80, 86
Black Forest (Germany) 341
Black Sea 341
Blanche of Burgundy (1296–1326; Queen of France 1322) 81
Blanche (Marguerite) of Valois (1317–1348; Queen of Bohemia 1346–1348, of the Romans 1347–1348) 13, 15, 30–31, 87–88, 90, 113, 151, 188, 440, 444, 446
Blois 80, 459
Bodensee *see* Lake Constance
Boemund of Saarbrücken (archdeacon) 95
Bohemia 1–11, 13–15, 29–31, 34–36, 51, 54–55, 58–65, 67–76,

79–84, 86–91, 93, 95–97, 99,
    103–105, 112–114, 124, 126–127,
    129–133, 137, 143, 146, 149,
    152, 155, 164–165, 167–168,
    170, 174–177, 179, 181–184,
    186–187, 191, 195–197, 199, 201,
    204–206, 209, 211, 219–220,
    222, 224–225, 227, 229–230,
    233, 235–240, 243, 249–251,
    258, 267–270, 280–283,
    286–287, 289, 298–299,
    301, 317, 320, 322, 325–329,
    329, 338–339, 341, 344–347,
    356–357, 367–370, 379–380,
    383–392, 397–400, 402–408,
    410, 412–417, 419–421, 423–425,
    427, 429–430, 432, 437,
    439–441, 443–446, 448–450,
    452–453, 455, 460, 462–464
Boleslaw (Boleslas, Boleslav) III
    (1291–1352; Duke of Legnica
    and Brzeg)   62–64, 72
Bonaventura (1221–1274)   273
Boniface VIII (Benedetto Caetani,
    1235–1303; Pope 1294–1303)
    78, 418
Bonifacio delle Coppe da Montefalco
    352, 354, 359–360, 362, 367
Bonn   170
Bonne (= Guta, Jutta) of Luxembourg
    (1315–1349) (Duchess of
    Normandy; first wife of King
    John II of France)   2, 30–32,
    34, 36–43, 49–55, 57, 82–83,
    87, 89–91, 99, 105, 132, 151–152,
    429, 432, 441–442
Book about the Game of Chess (*Knížky o
    hře šachové*) (Thomas of Štítné)
    397
Book of Hours   401
Bosnia   331
Botticelli *see* Sandro Botticelli
Bourges   35
Bouvines   96
Brabant (Duchy of)   3, 28–29, 55, 86, 91,
    132, 197, 381, 387, 430, 432–435,
    438, 447, 449, 456–460, 464
Brandenburg (Margravate of)   2, 168,
    179, 182, 231, 333, 402, 424

Bratislava (Pressburg/Pozsony)   328,
    330–331, 333, 395
Brescia   73, 95
Breslau *see* Wrocław
Brie   95
Brno   67, 94–95, 121, 193
Bruges   307, 309, 464
Brunoro della Scala   365
Brussels   132, 458–459
    St Gudula (church)   458–459
Buch der Liebkosung   191
Buda (Ofen)   328–329, 331, 364, 368,
    389
Budweis *see* České Budějovice
Buironfosse   97
Buonconvento   432
Burgundy   2–3, 34, 37, 41–43, 46,
    51–55, 81, 151, 431, 441,
    459–460
    (French) Duchy of   2–3, 41–42, 151,
    431, 459
    (Imperial) County of   41–42
Byzantium   138, 164, 447–448

Cain (biblical figure)   294
Cambrai   88, 454
Cambrésis   98, 103
Canossa   422
cantio   455, 460
Capetian dynasty   5, 21, 25, 53, 148,
    445–446, 448–449
Capua (Gate)   165, 417–418
Carrara   350
Casimir III the Great (1310–1370; King
    of Poland 1333–1370)   63
Cassel   83
Catherine of Görz   398
Cave of Treasures (Ephrem the Syrian)
    269–270, 273, 277–278, 281
Centre Luxembourgeois de
    Documentation et d'Études
    Médiévales   8
České Budějovice   69
Chaillou de Pesstain   86
Champagne   84–85
chanson   458
Chapel of All Saints (Prague) *see* Prague
Chapel of the Instruments of Christ's
    Passion *see* Karlštejn

INDEX 489

Charlemagne (Holy Roman Emperor;
 r. 800–814) 88, 141, 156–157,
 159, 168–170, 197, 419–421,
 446–447, 449, 454–455
Charles I of Hungary (Charles Robert)
 (1288–1342; King of Hungary
 1308–1342) 33–34
Charles IV (originally: Wenceslas) of
 Luxembourg (1316–1378; King
 of the Romans 1346–1378,
 of Bohemia 1347–1378, Holy
 Roman Emperor 1355–1378)
 1, 5–6, 8–9, 13–16, 30–31, 38,
 41, 60, 65, 70, 77, 83, 87–88,
 90. 97, 99–102, 104, 113, 116,
 126, 129–132, 137–139, 141–143,
 146–153, 155–157, 159–160,
 164–168, 170–209, 211–220,
 229–231, 233, 236–239, 243,
 246, 251, 258, 261, 270,
 282–283, 305, 326–327, 329,
 344, 368, 370–371, 385–388,
 401, 405–430, 432, 436, 440,
 443–460, 463–464
Charles IV (le Bel) of France (1294–
 1328; King of France 1322–
 1328) 1–2, 28, 30, 37–38, 41,
 43, 79–82, 88, 91, 102, 429,
 440–441
Charles of Évreux, of Navarre
 (1332–1387; Count of Évreux
 1343–1378, King of Navarre
 1349–1387) 101–102
Charles of Valois (1270–1325; Count
 of Valois 1285–1325, Latin
 Emperor of Constantinople
 1301–1307) 28, 80, 82, 86, 88,
 186, 433, 440, 444
Charles University, Prague *see* Prague
Charles V of Valois (the Wise, *le Sage*)
 (1338–1380; regent of France
 1356–1360, King of France
 1364–1380) 1–2, 13, 48, 53,
 83, 99, 101–102, 111, 130, 132,
 150–152, 188
Charles VI of Valois (1368–1422; King
 of France 1380–1422) 1–2,
 85, 353

Charles VIII of Valois (1470–1498; King
 of France 1483–1498) 150
Château Gaillard 81
Chauvency-le-Château 439
Cher (department) 35, 83
childlessness 283, 285–286, 301–302,
 319
Chiny 91, 402
Christian of Limburg 95–96
Christian of Prachatice (d. 1439;
 mathematician) 271
Christmas 88, 421, 454
Chronica Bo(h)emorum (Cosmas) 205,
 224
Chronicon Aulae regiae (*Zbraslav
 Chronicle*) (Otto of Thuringia
 and Peter of Zittau) 61, 65,
 383–385
Chronicon Bohemiae (Přibík Pulkava of
 Radenín) 181, 204, 207–209,
 228–230, 234–235
Chronicon imperatorum et pontificum
 (Martin of Troppau) 209
Cilli (Cilje), Counts of 341–342
Clairefontaine 406
Claretus (1320–1370; writer) 199–200
Claudius (Roman emperor) 159
Claudius Ptolemy (Alexandrian
 mathematician) 271
Claus Redwitz (knight) 328, 333
Clement VI (Pierre Roger, 1291–1352;
 Pope 1342–1352) 5, 77, 83,
 100, 171, 444, 453–454
Cola di Rienzo (Nicola di Lorenzo,
 1313–1354) 191
Colignet Cassamus (minstrel) 457
Cologne 120, 170, 409
Cologne World Chronicle 414
Compacts of Basel 356
Condé-sur-l'Escaut 89–90
Condren 83
Confessiones (Augustine) 273
Comfort d'Ami (1357) (Guillaume de
 Machaut) 103
Coninc Middach (minstrel) 456, 459
Conrad of Craig (Konrad von Kraigk,
 Konrád Krajíř z Krajku)
 (Carinthian noble) 354, 362

Conrad of Halberstadt the Younger (chronicler) 177, 180
Conrad of Vechta (c. 1370–1431; Archbishop of Prague 1413–1425) 271
Constance (Queen of Bohemia, Ottokar I Přemysl's wife) 387
Constance (city) 350, 355, 358, 363–364, 369, 463
Constantine the Great (c. 280–337; Roman emperor 306–337) 138–139, 152–153, 164–165, 420–421, 426, 455
Constantinople 138, 328, 413, 447
Emperor's Forum 152
Coronation Cross of Bohemia 14–15, 143–149, 152, 157, 159, 161–164, 166–168, 170–173
Corrado Boiani of Cividale del Friuli (diplomat) 355
Corrado Cavalli (diplomat of the house of Visconti) 352
Cosmas, canon of Prague (c. 1045–1125) 205, 224, 226, 235
Cotentin 75
Cotton Genesis (manuscript) 263
Councils
of Basel (1433–1449) 5, 209, 347, 358, 363, 369, 462–463
of Constance (1414–1417) 4, 5, 347, 363, 369, 406, 462
Fourth Lateran (1215) 268
Third Lateran (1179) 78
Coutances 75–76, 93, 96
Cracow see Krakow
Crécy 31, 83, 97, 99, 430, 442, 445, 457
Creil-sur-Oise 80, 87
Cremona 73, 95
Cristoforo da Velate (Milanese jurist, diplomat) 356, 365, 368
Cristoforo de Valle (diplomat) 353–354
Croatia 5, 9, 225, 233
Croatian (language) 6
Crown
of St Stephen see Hungary, Holy Crown of
of Thorns 149–150, 152
Crucifixion 108, 110, 117, 120, 126–128, 150, 159

crusade 62, 65, 70, 84, 89, 95, 325–326, 339, 346
crux gemmata 139, 148, 172
Cunegonde (Cunigunde, Kunigunde) (Queen of the Romans 1002–1024, Holy Roman Empress 1014–1024) 301
Curia (papal) 76, 95, 100, 104, 113, 127, 176, 323, 335
Czech
Bible 196, 198, 244, 246
Collegium 245
language 5–15, 31, 129, 174–175, 177–178, 184, 186–188, 194–202, 204–206, 211, 220, 225, 227, 229–230, 232, 235, 239, 244, 246, 261, 268–269, 283, 400, 449–451, 460, 463
Passional 196

Dalimil Chronicle (1312–1314) 14–15, 205–207, 209, 220–222, 224–227, 229–231, 233–236, 239
Dalmatia 346–347
Damvillers 87
Danube 69, 331, 341
David (biblical figure) 257, 262, 420
De doctrina christiana (Augustine of Hippo) 213
De l'Ipocrisie des Jacobins (Jehan de Condé) 92
De magistro (Augustine of Hippo) 207
De mineralibus (*Book of Minerals*) (c. 1248–1252) (Albertus Magnus) 156
De viris illustribus (Enea Silvio Piccolomini) 390
Denmark 68
Der Meide Kranz (Heinrich von Mügeln) 189, 450
Decembrio, Uberto see Uberto Decembrio
Die claghe vanden Hertoghe Wenseslijn van Brabant (Jan Knibbe) 459
Die Denkwürdigkeiten der Helene Kottannerin (Helene Kottanner) 393
Dietmar Maul of Schlotheim (of Meckbach) (1310–1378; notary of Charles IV 1342–1359) 95

INDEX 491

Dit dou Lyon (Guillaume de Machaut) 37, 100
Dolcibene de' Tori (jester, nicknamed King of Buffoons) 456
Domenico Ghirlandaio (painter) 171
Donato da Firenze (composer) (fl. 1350-1370) 451
Durbuy 60, 86, 100
Dutch (language) 6-7, 10-11, 430-431, 435, 442, 459, 464

Échecs d'amours (c. 1380) 24
Echternach 76
Edward III (1312-1377; King of England 1327-1377) 97, 438, 441
Egidius (IV) of Rodemack (c. 1320-1381; noble from Luxembourg) 82
Egypt 141, 315
Eichstätt 76, 115, 437
Eliezer (Abraham's servant) 312
Eliezer (Moses' son) 315
Elisabeth of Oettingen (c. 1360-1406) 193-194
Elizabeth of Luxembourg (c. 1409-1442; Queen of Hungary 1437-1439, of the Romans 1438-1439) 2, 4, 381, 387-396
Elizabeth (1436-1505; Queen of Poland 1454-1492) 2, 392
Elizabeth of Bohemia, Elizabeth Přemysl (1292-1330; Queen of Bohemia 1310-1330) 2, 8, 29-31, 34, 36, 73, 79, 87, 90, 93, 126, 181, 188, 230, 380, 383-386, 420, 440, 443-444
Elizabeth of Görlitz (1390-1451; Duchess of Luxembourg 1415-1443) 381, 401-402
Elizabeth of Pomerania (c. 1347-1393; Queen of Bohemia 1363-1378, of the Romans 1363-1378, Holy Roman Empress 1365-1378) 423
Ellwangen Abbey 16, 321-327, 329, 332-342
Elucidarium (Honorius Augustodunensis) 268
Empedocles 266
Emperor's Forum *see* Constantinople

Enea Silvio Piccolomini *see* Pius II
England 2, 4-5, 12, 29, 42, 89, 132, 174-175, 301, 328, 347, 367, 379, 381-382, 399-400, 411, 438, 441, 460, 464
English (language) 3-4, 6-8, 10-11, 24, 28, 56, 154, 174-175, 185, 190, 206, 222, 226, 254, 269, 305, 388-389, 393-394, 451
Enguerrand de Marigny (1260-1315; chamberlain of Philip IV 1302-1314) 87
Enos 317
Ephrem the Syrian (c. 306-373; theologian and hymnographer) 269, 273-274, 278, 281
Epistola de cautela a venenis ad Johannem, regem Bohemie 155
Ernest of Bavaria (Duke) 399
Ernest (Arnošt) of Pardubice (1297-1364; Bishop of Prague 1343-1344, Archbishop of Prague 1344-1364) 4, 121, 127, 195, 200, 258, 261, 452
Esau (biblical figure) 312, 316-317
Escaudoeuvres 98, 104
Eschez amoureux moralises (Evrard de Conty) 24
Esslingen 73
Este 350
Eugenius IV (Gabriele Condulmer, c. 1383-1447; Pope 1431-1447) 462-463
Eve (biblical figure) 275, 279, 291-294
Evodos (Greek engraver) 157
Evrard de Conty (d. 1405) 24

Faillouël 83
Farnese (family) 349
Farnese cup (Tazza Farnese) 171
Fauvain 86
Fauvel 53, 86, 433
Feast of the Lance and Nails of the Lord 454
Fécamp Bible 272
Feltre 358
Filippo Lippi (c. 1406-1469; painter) 171

Filippo Maria Visconti (1392–1447; Duke of Milan 1412–1447)   347
Filippo Scolari (Pippo Spano) (1369–1426; Florentine strategist)   368
Flanders   11, 38, 68, 81, 94, 460
Florence   160, 349, 357–358, 363, 368, 418, 430, 451
    Museo dell'Opera del Duomo   150–151
    Santa Maria Novella   171
formes fixes   41, 458
Frana (illuminator)   257, 276
France   2–5, 12, 14, 22, 29, 34–35, 38–40, 42–43, 45–46, 51, 68, 74, 79–80, 83–85, 88, 93, 95, 97, 99, 101–103, 113, 120–121, 131–132, 148, 171–172, 188, 211, 258, 347, 353, 392, 412, 429–433, 436, 440–442, 445, 449, 456, 459, 462, 464
Francesco I Gonzaga (1366–1407; Lord of Mantua 1382–1407)   353
Francesco Petrarca *see* Petrarch
Francis of Prague (d. 1362; chronicler)   70–71, 180
Franconia   326, 339
Frankfurt am Main   334–335, 338, 360, 405, 413, 419
Frankfurt an der Oder
    St Mary's church   424
Frauenkirche *see* Nuremberg
Frauenlob (d. 1318) *see* Heinrich von Meißen
Frederick II of Hohenstaufen (1194–1250; Holy Roman Emperor 1220–1250)   4, 159–160, 163–164, 417–418, 455
Frederick III of Habsburg (1415–1493; King of the Romans 1440–1493, Holy Roman Emperor 1452–1493)   249, 280, 333, 348, 366, 393, 463
Frederick IV, Margrave of Meissen (c. 1384–1440)   366
French (language)   6–7, 10–11, 22, 29, 32, 35, 39, 103, 130, 154, 175, 177–178, 186, 188, 205, 229, 269, 431, 435, 441, 451, 458, 464

Froissart, Jean *see* Jean Froissart
Fuiés de moy   458

Gascony   83
Gaucher de Châtillon-Porcien (1249–1329; Constable of France 1302–1329)   82
Geoffrey Chaucer (c. 1340s–1400; poet)   3, 52
German (language)   3–13, 15, 35, 68, 80, 129, 174–175, 177–179, 182, 184, 186–189, 191–196, 202, 204–205, 227, 229–230, 243–246, 248–249, 256–257, 269, 279–280, 283–284, 294, 331, 385, 393, 400, 413, 417, 430–431, 434–438, 442–443, 449, 451, 455, 458–459, 463–464
Germany   2–5, 8, 11, 16, 68, 93, 95, 127, 196, 275, 321, 336, 338, 368, 412, 425, 427, 460
Gershom   315
Gervais du Bus (French writer) (fl. 1310–1314)   86
Gervasius (Gervase) of Tilbury (c. 1150–c. 1235) (English cleric and writer)   154
Gesta Treverorum   435
Ghent
    St Nicolas church   95
Ghirlandaio *see* Domenico Ghirlandaio
Giangaleazzo Visconti (1351–1402; Lord of Milan 1385–1395, Duke of Milan 1395–1402)   346, 353–354, 361–362, 367
Giovanni d'Andrea (writer)   193
Giovanni de' (John of) Marignolli (clergyman and chronicler)   177, 180, 184
Giovanni Vergiolesi (diplomat)   360, 367
Giovanni Visconti (1290–1354; Archbishop of Milan 1342–1354)   451, 456
Glagolithic script   194, 269
Glazier, William Simon   23, 46
Głogów   95
Glossarius (Claretus)   200

Gobelinus de Catheneyn (cleric)   95–96
Godefroi of Juliers (Jülich; Prince of Juliers)   89
Godekijn van Tricht (Maastricht) (herald-poet)   459
Goedevaart metten baerde (anonymous)   435, 438
Golden Bull (1356)   4–5, 178, 209, 303–305, 408, 410
Golden Legend (Jacobus de Voragine) see *Legenda Aurea*
Golgotha   421
Gonzaga   347, 349, 352
Görlitz (Upper Lusatia)   79
Gottschalk of Westphalia   411
Grand Camée de France   171
Grandes Chroniques de France   132, 188
Great Schism (1378–1417)   4–5, 164, 243, 250, 347
Gruuthuse manuscript   464
Guelph   451
Gui de Boulogne (1313–1373; Cardinal of Santa Cecilia 1342–1373)   100
Guillaume *see also* William
Guillaume de Landstein (d. 1356; Bohemian noble)   168
Guillaume de Machaut (1305–1377; canon of Reims 1337–1377, writer, poet, musician)   3, 11–12, 22–24, 30–31, 35–41, 43–45, 48, 50–55, 57–82, 84–87, 89, 91–98, 100–104, 111, 130, 186, 429–430, 440–442, 444, 450–451, 456
Guillaume de Trie (d. 1334; Archbishop of Reims 1324–1334)   53, 97, 441
Guillaume Du Fay (d. 1474) (singer-composer)   462
Guillaume of Avesnes, Count of Hainaut (c. 1286–1337) *see* William of Avesnes
Guillaume of Juliers (c. 1299–1361; Count of Juliers 1328–1356, Duke of Juliers 1356–1361)   89
Guillaume Pinchon (d. 1363; canon of Verdun 1326–1363, chancellor of John of Luxembourg's Francophone fiefs 1331–1342)   75–76, 93–97, 99–103
Guillaume Roger III de Beaufort (1332–1395; Count of Beaufort)   83
Guta of Habsburg (1271–1297; Queen of Bohemia 1285–1297)   52, 387
Guy de Châtillon (d. 1342)   80
Guy I, Count of Blois (1307–1342; Marguerite of Valois' husband)   80

Habsburg dynasty   2–4, 8–9, 114, 230, 388, 395–396, 440, 458, 461
Hainaut   35, 59–60, 80, 83, 85–87, 89–90, 92, 95, 103, 432, 438, 459–460
Halberstadt   333
Hanina (Chanina) ben Dosa (rabbi)   274
Hans von Wolmershausen (Ellwangen Abbey's envoy)   327, 330–334, 337–339, 342
Haran (biblical figure)   299
Harcourt   40
Heinrich Schatz of Nuremberg (cleric; John of Luxembourg's notary)   67, 93, 96
Heinrich von Diessenhofen (chronicler)   413
Heinrich von Freiberg (fl. c. 1290; poet)   450
Heinrich von Meißen (also known as Frauenlob, d. 1318; poet)   437, 450
Heinrich von Mügeln (c. 1320–after 1371; poet, writer)   4, 11, 177, 189–190, 202, 450, 455
Heinrich von München (chronicler)   417
Helene Kottanner, Kottannerin, von Kottanner (c. 1400–1452; writer, maid of Elizabeth of Luxembourg)   393–394
Helfenburk (castle)   143
Hellenism   267
Henry Haille, Halle (cleric, familiar of John of Luxembourg)   76, 86, 91, 95

Henry I the Fowler (c. 876–936; Duke of Saxony 912–936, King of East Francia 919–936) 185
Henry II (973–1024; Holy Roman Emperor 1014–1024) 139, 301
Henry (IV) of Bar (1315–1344; Count of Bar 1336–1344) 32, 101
Henry of Brzeg (1343/45–1399; Duke of Brzeg 1361–1399) 362
Henry of Carinthia (c. 1265–1335; Duke of Carinthia, Landgrave of Carniola, Count of Tyrol 1295–1335, King of Bohemia 1306–1310) 383–384, 387
Henry of Dubá (fl. 1381–1390s; Bohemian noble and courtier) 361–362
Henry of Habsburg (1299–1327; Duke of Austria) 62
Henry of Jodoigne (1300–1352; diplomat and legal councillor) 90–91
Henry of Lipá (d. 1329; Bohemian noble) 237, 385
Henry (XIV) of Lower Bavaria (1305–1339; Duke of Lower Bavaria 1310–1339) 69
Henry V of Luxembourg (1216–1281; Count of Luxembourg 1247–1281) 29, 87
Henry VI of Luxembourg (c. 1240–1288; Count of Luxembourg 1281–1288) 28, 432
Henry VI of Silesia (1294–1335; Duke of Wrocław 1311–1335) 63–65
Henry VII of Luxembourg (1273–1313; Count of Luxembourg 1288–1313, King of the Romans 1308–1313, Holy Roman Emperor 1312–1313) 1–2, 8, 28–30, 33, 80, 82, 92, 138, 256, 384, 417, 422, 432–439, 450, 463
Herman of Prague (fl. 1330s; cleric, envoy at the papal court) 96
Hermann Menhardt (d. 1963; philologist) 247–248
Hexameron (Ambrosius) 267, 279

Hippocrates (c. 460 BCE–c. 370 BCE; Greek scientist, physician) 266, 272
Histoire de Fauvain (Raoul le Petit) 86
Hohenzollern 9
Holland 433, 459–460
Holy Cross 115, 148, 150, 153, 164
Holy Cross Chapel *see* Karlštejn
Holy Lance 148, 150, 420–421, 454
Holy Land 449
Holy Week 423
Honorius Augustodunensis (c. 1080–1150, Benedictine monk, writer) 268–269
Hôtel de Bohême (residence in Paris) 88
Houdain 59, 75, 78, 85
Hradčany 244, 271
Hue le Large (fl. 1340s; alderman of Reims) 61, 98
Hungarian (language) 6–7, 390
Hungary 1–2, 4–5, 9, 67–68, 322, 325–327, 330–332, 334, 337–339, 341, 349, 357, 364, 375–376, 379, 388–396, 399, 403
 Holy Crown of 393–394
Hussite Wars 325–327, 337, 388
Hussites 338–339, 342, 346, 356, 368, 400, 404–405, 407–408, 416, 460
hymn 117, 121, 460

iconoclasm 405, 407–412, 416, 419, 428
illumination 16, 23, 25, 36, 39, 47–48, 50, 103, 111, 126, 130, 133, 246–249, 262, 267, 269, 280, 287
Imperial Cross 148
Imperial Crown 80, 129, 156, 249, 317, 347, 440, 445
infertility 301–302, 306, 319
Inquisition 195–196
Isaac (biblical figure) 312, 319
Isaac Kara (d. 1389; victim of the Easter pogrom) 275
Isabeau of Bavaria (c. 1370–1435; Queen of France 1389–1422) 459

INDEX 495

Isidore of Seville (c. 560–636; theologian, cleric) 216
Israel (people of) 257–258, 315
István Rozgonyi (d. c. 1440; Hungarian noble) 395
Italian (language) 5–6

Jacob (biblical figure) 312, 316–317
Jacob ben Moses Moellin (c. 1360–1427) 275
Jacobus de Cessolis (c. 1250–c. 1322; writer) 24
Jacobus de Voragine (d. 1298; Dominican writer, theologian, Archbishop of Genoa 1292–1298) 153, 196
Jacques Bretel (fl. 1285; poet) 439
Jacques la Barbe (clerk) 83
Jakob of Warte (before 1274 – after 1331; poet) 307–308
Jakob Twinger von Königshofen (1346–1420; cleric, chronicler) 413
Jan Hus (c. 1370–1415; theologian, religious reformer, heretic) 195, 243–245, 250, 271, 275, 346, 406, 408, 424, 460
Jan IV of Dražice (d. 1343; Bishop of Prague 1301–1343) 70, 127
Jan Jiskra (c. 1400–1469/70; mercenary leader) 395
Jan Knibbe (poet) 459
Jan Milíč of Kroměříž (d. 1374; reform preacher, canon of the Metropolitan Chapter, Prague) 425–426
Jan Očko of Vlašim (d. 1380; Archbishop of Prague 1364–1378, Cardinal 1378–1380) 143, 168, 420
Jan of Jenštejn (Jenstein) (1347/8–1400; Archbishop of Prague 1379–96) 178, 209, 250, 455
Jan Šindel (d. 1455/1458; mathematician, astronomer) 264–265, 271
Jan Volek (d. 1351; Provost of Vyšehrad Chapter, John of Luxembourg's chancellor 1315–1334, illegitimate brother of Queen Elizabeth of Bohemia) 93

Jan Želivský (d. 1422; radical Hussite priest, preacher at the church of Our Lady of the Snows, Prague 1419–1422) 423
Jan ze Středy see John of Neumarkt
Jean see also Johann(es), John
Jean Bondol (artist) 129–130
Jean d'Ivoix (minstrel) 92
Jean de Châtillon (d. 1344; Count of Saint-Pol 1317–1344) 82
Jean de Machaut (fl. 1330s–1340s; cleric) 76, 78, 82, 84–85, 94, 101–102, 440–441
Jean de Raing (Charles VI's secretary 1381, Wenceslas of Luxembourg's *châtelain* and *receveur* of Aymeries and Raismes) 85
Jean de Sy see Master of the Bible of Jean de Sy (illuminator)
Jean de Vienne (d. 1351; Archbishop of Reims 1340–1351) 60, 97
Jean de Vignay (fl. 1330s–1340s; writer, translator) 24, 37, 41, 43, 45–52
Jean Froissart (c. 1337–c. 1405; poet, historiographer) 3, 11, 45, 89, 132, 430, 458
Jean Pucelle (illuminator) 127
Jean II de Blois (c. 1342–1381; Count of Blois and Dunois 1372–1381) 459
Jeanne see also Joan, Joanna
Jeanne de Châtillon (c. 1320–1385; sister of Hugues, canon of Reims, wife of Egidius of Rodemack) 82
Jeanne (Joan) of Brabant (1322–1406; Wenceslas of Luxembourg's wife, heiress to the Duchy of Brabant) 86, 132, 381, 387, 457, 459
Jeanne of Valois (c. 1294–1342; Countess of Hainaut) 80, 86, 89–90, 433, 441
Jehan (Jean) du Vivier (fl. 1377; goldsmith) 152
Jehan d'Ynteville (counsellor of Charles V) 97

Jehan de Condé (poet) 92
Jehan de le Mote (fl. 1330s–1340s; writer) 43, 86
Jerusalem
    city in the Holy Land 138, 258, 264, 274
    community of devout women in Prague 425, 427
    heavenly city 154, 157, 421, 427, 448, 454
Jesus 116–117, 121, 152, 199, 211, 215, 258, 261, 264
Jesus Sirach (Ben Sirach) 258
Jeu des Eschés moralisé 24
Jíra of Roztoky (d. 1413; Bohemian noble, Wenceslas IV's courtier) 361
Joan, Joanna *see also* Jeanne
Joan of Bavaria-Straubing (d. 1386; Queen of Bohemia 1376–1386) 283–284, 287
Joan of Burgundy (1291–1330; Queen of France 1316–1322, Countess of Imperial Burgundy 1303–1330, of Artois 1329–1330) 34, 41–42
Joan of Burgundy (1293–1349; Queen of France 1328–1349) 34, 37, 40–47, 51–55, 441
Joan of Évreux (1310–1371; Queen of France 1326–1328) 37, 53, 88, 441
Joan of France (1308–1347; Duchess consort of French Burgundy 1318–1347, Countess of Artois and Imperial Burgundy 1330–1347) 34, 41–42, 51
Joan of France (1343–1373; Queen of Navarre 1360–1373) 2
Joan of Navarre (1312–1349; Queen of Navarre 1328–1349) 441
Joan of Wittelsbach *see* Joan of Bavaria-Straubing
Joanna of Rethel (d. 1328; Countess of Rethel) 81
Jobst of Moravia (d. 1411; Margrave of Moravia 1375–1411, King of the Romans 1410–1411) 1, 302, 361–362

Jochanan (d. c. 80; rabbi) 274
Joffrid of Leiningen (cleric, envoy) 95–96
Joffrid of Rodemack (cleric) 88
Johann von Göttingen *see* Johannes Hake
Johann von Holzingen (d. 1452; Abbot of Ellwangen Monastery 1427–52) 324–325, 327, 331–332, 335–336, 339
Johann von Neumarkt *see* John of Neumarkt
Johannes (cleric and secretary, son of Egidius, arbalester of Luxembourg) 60, 96, 100, 103
Johannes Brassart (c. 1400–1455; singer and composer) 3, 429, 462–463
Johannes Gal[l]icus (Prague painter) 129
Johannes de Sacrobosco (1195–1256; mathematician, astronomer) 269, 281
Johannes Hake, Johann von Göttingen (c. 1280–1349; John of Luxembourg's physician) 155
Johannes of Arlon (cleric) 77, 96
Johannes of Nassau (John of Luxembourg's secretary and relative) 76
Johannes of Pistoia (d. 1371; John of Luxembourg's notary, Prince-Bishop of Trent 1348–1349, Bishop of Spoleto 1349–1371) 75, 77, 93, 95–96, 100–101
Johannes von Dambach (Dominican master at Prague University) 416
Johannes von Guben (town scribe of Zittau) 414–415
John *see also* Jan, Jean, Johann(es)
John of Beaumont (1288–1356; Lord of Beaumont, Count consort of Soissons) 80, 83, 87, 89, 98
John I of Brabant (1252/3–1294; Duke of Brabant 1267–1294, Duke of Limburg 1288–1294, Minnesänger) 28–29, 434, 449

INDEX 497

John of Hainaut *see* John of Beaumont
John II of Wittelsbach (d. 1397; Duke
    of Bavaria-Munich 1375–1397)
    398
John II of France, John the Good
    (1319–1364; Duke of Normandy
    1332–1355, King of France
    1350–64) 1–2, 30–32, 34,
    36–43, 45–48, 50, 53–55, 90,
    98–99, 101–102, 130, 151–152,
    441
John Henry of Luxembourg (1322–1375;
    Count of Tyrol 1335–1341,
    Margrave of Moravia 1349–
    1375) 193
John of Bavaria (1374–1425; Duke of
    Bavaria-Straubing 1418–1425,
    Count of Holland and Hainaut
    1418–1425, Elizabeth of Görlitz's
    second husband) 402
John of Berry, of France (1340–1416;
    Duke of Berry 1360–1416) 2,
    13, 36, 38, 101
John of Jenštejn (Jenstein) see Jan of
    Jenštejn (Jenstein)
John of Luxembourg, John of Bohemia
    (1296–1346, later 'the Blind';
    King of Bohemia 1310–1346,
    Count of Luxembourg
    1313–1346) 1–2, 8–9, 12, 14–15,
    29–38, 42–45, 51–54, 57–105,
    113, 126–127, 132, 137, 155, 181,
    186, 205, 217–219, 225–226,
    230, 237, 328, 380, 383–387,
    406, 408, 412, 429, 432, 434,
    437, 439–445, 450, 457, 463
John of Luxembourg (1370–1396;
    Duke of Görlitz, Margrave of
    Brandenburg) 381, 402, 406
John of Marignolli (chronicler) *see*
    Giovanni de' Marignolli
John of Nepomuk (d. 1393; Vicar
    General of the Archbishop of
    Prague) 250
John of Neumarkt (c. 1310–1380; scholar,
    writer, Bishop of Litomyšl
    1353–1364, of Olomouc 1364–
    1380, Charles IV's chancellor
    1353–1374) 4, 175, 190–194,
    197–198, 200, 202, 251, 452
John of Procida (writer) 208
John of Středa *see* John of Neumarkt
John of Thurócz, János Thuróczy,
    Johannes de Thurocz (c. 1435–
    1490; chronicler) 375–376
John of Victring (Viktring) (d. 1347;
    chronicler, Abbot of Viktring
    Monastery 1312–1347) 89
John Scotus (c. 815–877; scholar) 268
John the Evangelist (biblical figure)
    212, 214, 258, 261, 265, 451
John V Paleologos (1332–1391; Byzantine
    emperor 1341–1391) 164
John Wyclif (c. 1330–1384; scholar,
    theologian, religious reformer)
    174, 244, 401
John XXII (Jacques Duèze, 1249–1334;
    Pope 1316–1334) 78, 80, 96
Josephus Flavius (37/38–100; Jewish
    scholar, historian) 231
Josquin Desprez (composer) 12
Judaism 258, 267–268
Judas Thaddeus (biblical figure) 261
Judith, Jutta von Habsburg *see* Guta von
    Habsburg
Jugement dou Roy de Navarre
    (Guillaume de Machaut) 100
Julia (daughter of Emperor Titus)
    157–158
Juliers (Jülich), County/Duchy of 89
Jupiter (Roman god) 197
Jutta of Luxembourg (1315–1349)
    see Bonne of Luxembourg
    (1315–1349)

Karlstein, Karelstein (Sigismund of
    Luxembourg's herald) 326
Karlštejn, Karlstein (castle) 112,
    130–132, 143, 167, 197, 326, 329,
    361, 410, 420, 448
    Chapel of the Instruments of Christ's
    Passion 160, 167
    Holy Cross Chapel 413–414, 421,
    453–454
    Genealogical Cycle 111, 129–130,
    132–133, 197, 318, 447

Kaspar (Caspar, Gaspare, Kašpar) Schlick, Šlik (d. 1449; Bohemian burgher and noble, Sigismund of Luxembourg's chancellor)   340, 365
Kladruby (abbey)   250
Klatovy (town)   329
Klingenberg Chronicle   335
Königsaal *see* Zbraslav
Konrad Schreiber, Conrad Schryber (clerk in Ellwangen Abbey) 322–327, 330–331, 333–337, 339–342
Kottanner, Kottannerin, von Kottanner Helene *see* Helene Kottanner
Kovin (city)   332
Krakow   62–63, 68, 394
Křišťan z Prachatic see Christian of Prachatice
Křivoklát (castle)   62, 238–239, 367
Kunigunde *see* Cunegonde

La Roche (town)   60, 86
Laa (town)   67, 69, 95
Ladder to Heaven   251
Ladislas the Short (1260–1333; King of Poland 1320–1333)   63
Ladislaus (c. 1042/46–1095; King of Hungary 1077–1095)   394
Ladislaus, Ladislas, Ladislav Postumus, Pohrobek (1440–1457; King of Hungary 1440–1457, of Bohemia 1453–1457)   394–396
Lake Constance (= Bodensee)   339
Lamprecht of Brunn (d. 1399; Charles IV's and Wenceslas' advisor, Prince-Bishop of Bamberg 1374–1399)   361–362
Landau an der Isar   67, 69
Languedoc   97
Last Judgement   264, 423
Latin (language)   1, 3, 5–6, 12, 15, 24, 35, 46, 49, 51, 95, 129–130, 155, 160, 162, 165, 174–180, 184, 186–187, 189, 191–194, 196–197, 199–202, 204–205, 208–209, 211, 215, 222, 224–225, 227, 229–230, 232–233, 235, 246, 249, 256–258, 264, 268, 271, 280, 283, 367, 381, 421, 438, 441, 445, 449, 451–452, 455, 458
laudesi   464
Lauf (castle)   415
Laurentius of Březová (chronicler)   279
Lauretanian Litany   258, 261
Leah (biblical figure)   312–314
Legend of Saint Wenceslas (Charles IV) 185, 196–197, 230
Legenda Aurea (Jacobus de Voragine) 153, 160, 196
Letters of St Jerome   193
Leuze-en-Hainaut   85
Libellus de moribus hominum et officiis nobilium ac popularium super ludo scachorum (Jacobus de Cessolis)   24
Liber de sphaera (or *De sphaera mundi*) (Johannes de Sacrobosco) 269
Liber philosophorum moralium antiquorum (John of Procida) 208
Liber viaticus (John of Neumarkt)   197, 251
Libretto of Louis of Anjou (reliquary) 150
Libuš (castle)   234
Libuše (Bohemian legendary figure, Princess of Bohemia)   8, 226, 234–235, 237
Liège   76, 93, 97
  St Lambert Cathedral   463
Life of Saint Arnulfus   197
Litoměřice-Třeboň Bible   244
Litomyšl   191–192, 251
Livre de la moralité des nobles hommes et des gens du peuple sus le gieu des ésches (Jean de Vignay) 24
Loket (castle)   386
Lombardy   68, 73, 177–178, 229
London   6, 152, 411
Lorraine (Duchy of)   101, 433
Lot (biblical figure)   311
Lothair Cross   140–142
Lothar II (c. 835–869; King of Lotharingia 855–869)   141

Lotharingia
    region 10, 93, 101, 434–435,
        438–439, 441–442, 449, 457,
        464
    Kingdom of 141
Louis *see also* Ludwig
Louis I of Anjou (1326–1382; King of
    Hungary 1342–1382) 375
Louis I of Anjou (1339–1384; Duke of
    Anjou 1360–1384) 2, 150–151
Louis I of Flanders (d. 1346; Count of
    Flanders, Nevers and Rethel)
    81
Louis II of Flanders (1330–1384; Count
    of Flanders, Nevers and
    Rethel) 81
Louis IV of Bavaria, of Wittelsbach (d.
    1347; Duke of Bavaria, King of
    the Romans 1314–1347, Holy
    Roman Emperor 1328–1347)
    67, 69, 80, 91, 96, 127, 155, 168,
    170, 416, 419, 422, 425, 440
Louis IX (1214–1270; King of France
    1226–1270) 29, 148, 172, 433,
    446
Louis X (1289–1316; King of Navarre
    1305–1316, of France 1314–1316)
    441
Louis of Brandenburg (1316–1361) 168
Louis of Clermont, of Bourbon
    (1279–1341; Count of Clermont
    1317–1341, Duke of Bourbon
    1327–1341) 433, 457
Louis of Loos and Chiny (d. 1336;
    Count of Loos and Chiny) 91
Low Countries 11, 14, 32, 132, 195,
    459–460
Lübeck 422
Lucca 73, 195, 349, 352, 355–357, 360,
    366, 369, 423
Lucifer 175, 275
Ludolf of Sagan (d. 1422; Abbot of the
    Augustinian Monastery in
    Sagan) 414
Ludwig *see also* Louis
Ludwig (1297–1311; heir to the Duchy of
    Bavaria) 33
Ludwig IV (Wittelsbach) *see* Louis IV of
    Bavaria

Ludwig of Württemberg (d. 1450; Count
    of Württemberg, Lord and
    Protector of Ellwangen Abbey)
    332, 336
Luke (evangelist) 421
Lusatia
    Upper Lusatia 79
    Lower Lusatia 187
    region 182, 187, 414
Luther *see* Martin Luther
Luxembourg (Grand Duchy of) 3, 8–9

madrigal 451
Magdeburg 327
Mahaut of Artois (1268–1329) 42
Maimonides, Rabbi Moshe (1138–1204,
    rabbi from Cordoba) 272
Maine (County of) 40
Mainz
    city 100, 327–328, 425, 437
    Prince-Archbishopric and Electorate
        385, 437
Manasseh (biblical king) 289
Manesse codex 307–308, 434, 437, 449
Mantua
    city 166, 368
    Lordship of 349, 352–355, 358, 360,
        364, 367
Marco Battagli (chronicler) 180
Marcus Aurelius (121–180; Roman
    emperor) 452
Margaret of Brabant (1276–1311; Queen
    of the Romans 1309–1311) 29,
    432, 434–435
Margaret of France (1254–1271; Duchess
    of Brabant 1270–1271) 28
Margaret of Bohemia, of Luxembourg
    (1335–1349; Queen of Hungary
    1342–1349) 2
Margarete 'Maultasch' (1318–1369;
    Countess of Tyrol 1335–1363)
    380–381
Marguerite of Flanders (1350–1405;
    Countess of Artois, Auvergne,
    Boulogne and Flanders
    1384–1405) 81
Marguerite of Luxembourg (1281–1337;
    Prioress of Marienthal Abbey,
    Luxembourg) 90

Marguerite of Valois (1295–1342; Countess of Blois) 80
Marie *see also* Mary
Marie of Avesnes (1280–1354; Countess of Clermont, Duchess of Bourbon) 87, 433, 457
Marie of Luxembourg (c. 1305–1324; Queen of France and Navarre 1323–1324) 2, 30, 33–34, 41, 82, 87–88, 91, 440
Marienleich (Heinrich von Meißen) 450
Marienthal (abbey in the County of Luxembourg) 32–33, 90
m'arrat gazzê ('Ephrem the Syrian') *see* Cave of Treasures
Marsilius de Rubeis (d. c. 1343; scholar) 217–218
Marsy 87
Martin Luther 6
Martin of Troppau (d. 1279; Dominican monk, papal chaplain, chronicler) 209
Martin Rotloew, Rotlev, *Mertein Rotleb* (d. 1392; Prague patrician, royal mint master 1379–1392, commissioner of the Wenceslas Bible) 195, 245
Mary *see also* Marie
Mary of Brabant (1254/6–1321/2; Queen of France 1274–1285) 28
Mary Magdalene (biblical figure) 152
Mary of Anjou (c. 1371–1395; Queen and heiress of Hungary) 375–377, 379, 381
Masovia 68
Master of the Bible of Jean de Sy (illuminator) 129–131
Mathieu de Trie III (d. 1344; Marshal of France) 97, 441
Matthew (evangelist) 211, 213, 265
Matthias of Arras (c. 1290–1352; architect) 445
Matthias of Janov (d. 1393/4; theologian, religious reformer) 426
Matthias of Neuenburg (Strasbourg chronicler) 413
Maubuisson-lès-Pontoise 97
Maxentius (d. 312; Roman emperor) 139, 153

Meaux 94
Medici 171
Meditationes vitae Christi (pseudo-Bonaventure) 198
Mehun-sur-Yèvre (castle) 35, 80, 82–83, 87, 92, 99
Meissen
  city 437, 450
  Duchy of 182
Melchizedek (biblical figure) 420
Meliador (Jean Froissart) 132, 458
Melun 441
mendicants 176, 191, 207
mensural notation 429, 462, 464
mensural polyphony 12, 17, 430, 455, 460–462, 464
Merovingian family 197
Metamorphoses (Ovid) 279
Metz 95, 438–439, 454, 457
Meuse valley 435, 439–440
Michael (archangel) 159, 275
Milan
  city 267, 349, 368, 451, 456–457
  Duchy of 346–347, 356, 358, 365
  Lordship of 346, 352–353, 361–362, 366–367
Minnesang 437
Minnesänger, Minnesinger 3, 187, 434, 449
minstrel 92, 434, 438, 443, 455–459, 462, 464
Modena
  city 73, 160
  Lordship of 217, 350
Moldavia 331
Mönch von Salzburg 461
monophony 12, 455, 460–461, 464
Montpellier codex 436
Montreuil 94
Moralitates Caroli quarti imperatoris (1370s) 204
Moravia
  region 67, 89, 181–182, 385
  Margravate of 99, 187, 388, 444
Moselle (region) 435, 438
Moses (biblical figure) 315
motet 92, 95, 433, 436, 438–439, 441, 462
Mühldorf am Inn 62, 82, 440

INDEX 501

Mühlhausen (Thuringia)
    St Mary's Church 419, 423
Munich 168, 269, 337, 399
musicology 4, 7, 12, 53, 430, 432–433, 462

Narcissus 212
Navarre (Kingdom) 2
Neplach (1322–1371; Abbot of Opatovice Abbey 1348–1371, chronicler) 180
New Testament 117, 244, 248, 258, 261–262, 265, 280
Nicasius de Wavrechain (d. 1349; John of Luxembourg's chaplain) 85, 91
Nicholas (canon of St Vitus in Prague, theologian, astronomer) 271
Nicholas of Lyra (theologian, scholar) 231–232, 276
Nicholas Wurmser (Strasbourg burgher, painter, master of the Luxembourg Genealogy) 130–131
Nicolas de Picquigny (fl. 1364–1389; canon of St Gudula, chaplain at the Brussels court) 458
Nicolas Efficax of Luxembourg (fl. 1320s–1340s; cleric, John of Luxembourg's notary, Cardinal Gui de Boulogne's *familiaris*) 75, 93, 95–96, 100
Nicolas Mensdorf of Luxembourg (fl. 1330s; cleric, university master, John of Luxembourg's envoy) 77, 96
Nicolas of Fulda (Henry VII's physician, university master) 92
Nicolas of Ybbs (d. 1340; Bishop of Regensburg 1313–1340) 76
Nicolas Pinchon 75, 102
Nicole de Margival 86
Ninus 417
Noah (biblical figure) 197, 203, 447
Normandy
    region 98
    Duchy of 43–44, 48
North Sea 132
Noyon 86, 91, 94, 103–104

Nuremberg, Nürnberg 2, 16, 67, 93, 96, 115, 131, 324, 339–340, 366, 413, 415–416, 423, 448
    Frauenkirche 16, 448

Odo IV of Burgundy (1295–1349; Duke of Burgundy 1315–1349) 42–43
Office (liturgy) 185, 454–455
Old Czech (language) 15, 194, 196, 198, 205, 220, 222, 230, 235, 239, 269, 450–451
Old Testament 219, 244, 258, 280, 284, 286, 289, 452
    Book of Deuteronomy 298–299
    Book of Esdras 289
    Book of Genesis 285, 290–291, 319
    Book of Job 319
    Book of Joshua 298, 300–301
    Book of Kings 287
    Book of Proverbs 258
    Book of Wisdom 266
    Books of Paralipomenon (Chronicles) 289, 317–318
Oldřich Skála of Luleč (Bohemian noble) 358
Olomouc (Bishopric of) 191, 452
Olomouc Bible 244
Orange (dynasty) 9
Ordo ad benedicendum reginam 165, 209
Ordo ad coronandum regem Bohemorum 165, 209, 239
Orvieto 418
Oswald von Wolkenstein (c. 1376/1377–1445; South Tyrolean noble and poet-musician) 3, 307, 429–430, 458, 461–462
Otia Imperialia (Gervasius of Tilbury) 154
Otto III (980–1002; Holy Roman Emperor 996–1002) 141
Otto IV of Brunswick (1175–1218; Holy Roman Emperor 1209–1218) 154
Otto of Habsburg (1301–1339; Duke of Austria) 69, 96
Otto of Thuringia (d. 1314; Cistercian monk, Abbot of Zbraslav Monastery, chronicler) 61

Ottokar I Přemysl (d. 1230; King of Bohemia 1198–1230)   164, 225, 387
Ottoman Empire   394
Ottoman Turks   332, 392, 396
Ottonians   141, 301, 426
Ourscamp   91, 104
Ovid   279
Ozora   368

Padua (Lordship of)   350
Paolo Armanini (fl. 1390s; Mantuan envoy, writer)   364, 368
Paris   25, 30, 38, 41, 50, 59–60, 74–75, 85, 87–88, 90–91, 93–95, 99, 103, 111–113, 127, 129–132, 138, 151, 158, 165, 186, 188, 279, 328, 430, 432–433, 436–438, 441, 444–446, 452, 458, 460
   Cathedral School   268
   Jardin du Luxembourg   3
   Palais du Luxembourg   3
   Sainte-Chapelle   88, 150, 171, 448
   Saint-Hilaire   269
   University   155, 179, 269, 272, 426, 436
Parler *see* Peter Parler
Parma   73, 217, 349, 352
Passau   331, 411
Paudy   87
Paul (apostle)   261, 265
Pavia   156, 207, 218–219
Penede (castle)   160
Pentecost   88, 103, 117, 269
Peter (apostle)   261, 265, 462
Peter Abelard (1079–1142; theologian, scholar)   269
Peter Comestor (c. 1100–1178; chronicler, scholar)   268, 274–275, 277, 281
Peter I of Lusignan (1328–1369; King of Cyprus and Jerusalem 1358–1369)   44
Peter Lambeck (d. 1680; court librarian)   247
Peter Lombard (1095–1160; scholar)   268
Peter of Brno   94
Peter of Dusburg   74
Peter of Louny   95
Peter of Aspelt (d. 1320; Archbishop-Elector of Mainz 1306–1320)   385–386, 437
Peter of Vartenberk   362
Peter of Waben (cleric, John of Luxembourg's *familiaris*)   86, 93–96
Peter of Zittau (d. 1339; Cistercian monk, chronicler)   34, 51, 61–73, 84, 90, 92, 103, 188
Peter Parler (1330–1399; architect of St Vitus Cathedral, Prague)   445
Peter Suchenwirt (d. after 1395; herald and poet)   458
Peter von Schaumberg (1388–1469; Bishop of Augsburg 1424–1469)   336
Peter Wacker (fl. 1420s)   331
Peter Zmrzlík ze Svojšína, von Schweißing (d. 1421; Bohemian noble, royal mint master, commissioner of the Litoměřice-Třeboň Bible)   244
Petr Chelčický (d. c. 1460; religious reformer)   421
Petr I of Rožmberk, Rosenberg (d. 1347; Lord Chamberlain of Bohemia)   113–114, 118
Petrarch   4, 166, 176, 191, 451–452
Petrus de Castro Reginaldi (Dominican monk)   92
Philip (apostle)   261
Philip ('the Bold', 1342–1404; Duke of Burgundy 1363–1404)   2, 151
Philip III (1245–1285; King of France 1270–1285)   28
Philip IV ('the Fair', 1268–1314; King of France 1285–1314)   28, 45, 418, 433, 446
Philip of Rathsamhausen (1240/1245–1322; Bishop of Eichstätt 1306–1322)   76, 437
Philip V (c. 1291–1322; King of France 1316–1322)   34, 42, 79
Philip VI of Valois (1293–1350; King of France 1328–1350)   30, 34–35, 37, 41–48, 52–54, 80, 82–83, 88, 90–91, 97–99, 103–104, 151, 171, 429, 440–441, 456

Philippa of Hainaut (c. 1314–1369; Queen of England 1327–1369)   89–90
Philippa of Luxembourg (1252–1311)   87, 433
Philippe de Vitry (1291–1361)   41, 53–54, 433
Picquigny *see* Nicholas de Picquigny
Pier Paolo Vergerio the Elder (1370–1444; humanist)   462
Piero Guicciardini (Florentine envoy)   357, 368
Pierre de Mortemart (Bishop of Auxerre, Cardinal-Priest of St Stephen in Coelio Monte, John of Luxembourg's chancellor 1334–1335)   93
Pierre Roger *see* Clement VI
Pieter van Leiden (canon of St Gudula, Brussels)   459
Pietrasanta   73
Pilgrim von Puchheim (c. 1330–1396; Prince-Archbishop of Salzburg 1365–1396)   461
Pinchon family *see* Guillaume, Nicolas, Radulphus, Thomas de Pinchon
Pippo Spano *see* Filippo Scolari
Pius II (Enea Silvio Piccolomini, 1405–1464; Pope 1458–1464)   390
Pistoia   77
plainchant   12, 436–437, 453, 462–463
Plaisanche, or tost (Nicolas de Picquigny?)   458
Plato   266–267, 269, 271–272
Poland   1–2, 4–5, 9, 62–64, 66, 68, 328, 331, 394, 441
Polish (language)   6–7, 227
polyphony   430, 455, 459–460, 462–464
Pont-sur-Sambre   80
Postillae Perpetuae (Nicholas of Lyra)   231
Poznań   67, 95, 98
Pozsony *see* Bratislava
Prague   1, 4, 6, 8, 13, 15, 31–34, 43, 72, 84, 87–90, 104–106, 112–113, 120–121, 124–127, 129–131, 133, 143, 149, 160, 168, 174–177, 184–189, 191–192, 194–195, 200–201, 204–205, 208–209, 224, 230–231, 233, 236, 239, 244–245, 247, 262–264, 266, 269–271, 275–276, 278, 280–281, 283, 306, 326, 328, 338, 354, 356, 360–362, 366–367, 369, 386, 404–407, 411–413, 415–416, 420–421, 423, 425–427, 440, 443–448, 450–452, 454–458, 460
   Bethlehem Chapel   426
   Castle   113–114, 126, 131, 146, 199–200, 243, 318, 423, 444–445, 447, 456
   Chapel of All Saints   444–445, 453
   Chapel of St Wenceslas (in St Vitus Cathedral)   421, 446, 454
   Charles University   176, 179, 190–191, 201, 243, 245, 247, 268–271, 281, 416, 422, 445, 453
   Church of Our Lady of the Snows   423
   Collegiate Church of St Giles   230
   New Town   131, 160, 195, 445, 447–448, 454
   Old Town   126, 165, 181, 199
   Old Town Bridge Tower   165, 306, 418–419, 422
   Old Town Hall   264, 271
   St Vitus Cathedral   113–114, 118, 143, 171, 261, 271, 406–408, 414–416, 421, 423, 425–426, 444–446, 453–454
   St Vitus Chapter (Metropolitan Chapter)   156, 200, 267
   Slavonic Monastery of St Jerome (Emmaus Monastery)   131, 194–195, 269, 454
   St George Convent   32, 126, 199
   University *see* Charles University
   Vyšehrad Castle   235
   Vyšehrad Chapter   93
Přemek of Teschen (1365–1433)   361–362
Přemysl Ottokar I *see* Ottokar I Přemysl
Přemysl the Ploughman (mythical Duke of Bohemia)   8, 181, 209, 226–227, 234–238

Přemyslids 2, 8, 14, 29, 31–32, 63, 73, 181, 187, 205, 211, 225, 230, 236, 239, 270, 380, 383, 404, 407, 420, 440, 443–444, 449
Pressburg *see* Bratislava
Přibík Pulkava of Radenín (d. before 1380) 180–184, 196–197, 204, 207–208, 227–229, 238
Prise d'Alexandre (c. 1370) (Guillaume de Machaut) 44, 59, 61, 74, 456
Prokop of Moravia (c. 1358–1405; Margrave of Moravia 1375–1405) 35
Provins 82
Prussia 9, 62, 64–65, 68, 70, 84, 89, 103, 328, 440–441
Psalms 244, 265, 262, 265, 276, 454
Pseudo-Methodius (7th-century author) 247, 270, 278
Pürglitz *see* Křivoklát

Quesnoy, Le (town) 89

Radulphus Pinchon (member of John of Luxembourg's court) 75, 102
Raismes 80, 85
Raoul le Petit (author) 86
Rebekah (biblical figure) 312–313, 317
Regensburg 331
Reggio 217
Reims 23, 38, 59–61, 75, 78, 81–85, 88, 93–94, 97–98, 101–104, 353, 441
  Saint-Nicaise 78
  Saint-Rémy 75, 78, 82
Reginald (Reinald) of Guelders (1255–1326; Count of Guelders 1271–1326) 28
Reginald II (Reinald, Renaud) of Guelders (c. 1295–1343; Count, later Duke of Guelders 1326–1343) 91
Remede de Fortune (Guillaume de Machaut) 23–24, 37, 39, 41–42, 44–45, 49–52, 54
Rethel (County of) 81
Rhine (river) 12, 68, 71, 407, 430
Rhineland 120, 127, 179, 442, 448, 458
Richard II of England (1367–1400; King of England 1377–1399) 6, 132, 174, 301, 367, 400, 411, 451, 460

Rinaldo Albizzi (Florentine envoy) 368
Robert du Palais (Robertus de Palatio; King John of Luxembourg's secretary) 85, 94
Robert III of Artois (1287–1342; nobleman) 35, 42
Roman de Fauvel (Gervais du Bus and Chaillou de Pesstain) 86, 92, 186, 433
Romania 4–5
Romanian (language) 6
Rome 5, 15, 29, 69, 81, 83, 124, 129, 138–139, 141, 160, 165–166, 168, 170, 176, 190–191, 197, 209, 249–250, 335, 346–347, 369–370, 413, 417–418, 420, 423, 426, 432, 447–448, 450, 452, 453–455, 457
Roudnice nad Labem (monastery) 195, 244, 250
Rouen 76, 91, 93
Rožmberk family 15, 113–114, 118
Rudolf of Habsburg (1282–1307; King of Bohemia 1306–1307) 383
Rudolf II of Habsburg (1552–1612; Holy Roman Emperor 1576–1612) 8
Rupert of the Palatinate (1352–1410; Elector Palatine 1398–1410, King of the Romans 1400–1410) 334
Russia 68
Ruth Master (illuminator) 257
Rzip (Říp) (mountain) 233

Saints
  Adalbert (956–997; Bishop of Prague 982–997) 407, 446
  Ambrose, Ambrosius (Bishop of Milan, 339–397) 66, 247, 267, 279, 281
  Arnulfus 197
  Augustine of Hippo (354–430) 192, 207–208, 213, 237, 267–268, 272–273
  Catherine (of Alexandria) 65, 160, 167–168, 170
  Hedwig 198
  Helena 152, 420
  Jerome 193–194
  Ludmila 196

INDEX 505

Procopius 196
Sigismund 407, 446
Vitus 185, 407, 446
Saint-Denis (abbey) 150–151, 158–159, 446
Saint-Laurent (abbey) 76
Saint-Martin-des-Champs (priory) 75
Saint-Quentin (collegiate church) 59, 83, 85, 91–92, 97, 104
Salerno 263
Samar (biblical location) 224, 226
Sandro Botticelli (1444–1510; painter) 171
Sangspruch 455
Sanso de Calvemonte 96
Saturn 197
Savoy 68, 347, 350
Scariotis geniture / Jure quod in opere / Superne matris 92, 433, 438
Schlick, Caspar (Kaspar) *see* Kaspar Schlick
Schoonhoven 459
Schwäbisch Gmünd 336
Sedulius 305
Sem (biblical figure) 298
Sennar (biblical location) 231
Serbia 331–332, 392
Seth (biblical figure) 317
Shakespeare 6
Shem (biblical figure) 299
Siege
 of Cambrai (1339) 97
 of Golubac (Galambóc) (1428) 369
 of Poznań (1331) 67
 of Tournai (1340) 95, 97
Siegfried (Abbot of Ellwangen, 1400–1427) 325, 327
Siena 120, 349, 432
Sigismund Huler (member of Wenceslas IV's court) 361
Sigismund of Luxembourg (1368–1437; King of Hungary 1387–1437, of the Romans 1411–1433, of Bohemia 1420–1437, Holy Roman Emperor 1433–1437) 1, 4–5, 15–16, 166, 280, 302, 307, 322–341, 343–344, 346–351, 354–359, 363–366, 368–372, 375–376, 381, 387–388, 391–392, 394–396, 399, 402, 405, 407, 413, 417, 429, 432, 460–463
Sigismund Albicus of Uničov (c. 1359–1427; physician, astrologer) 271
Sigmund Meisterlin (chronicler) 416
Silesia 2, 9, 62–66, 72, 79, 121, 187, 361
Simon Zelotes (biblical figure) 261
Simone da Crema (Mantuan envoy) 349, 355, 356–357, 363, 368, 370
Simone Martini (painter) 113
Simson Master (illuminator) 257
Slavonic (language) 5, 178, 194–195, 232–233, 269, 454
Slovakia 5, 9
Slovenia 5, 9
Slovenian (language) 6
Soliloquium anime ad deum (Pseudo-Augustinus) 191
Sol (Roman deity) 264
Solomon (biblical figure) 258, 289, 420, 452–453, 456
Solomon Ibn Gebirol 272
Song of Songs (Bible) 452
Sophia of Bavaria, of Wittelsbach (1376–1428; Queen of Bohemia 1389–1419) 249, 280, 283–284, 392, 398–401, 455–456
soundscape 432, 436, 463, 464–465
Sovran uccello (Donato da Firenze) 451
Speyer 407–408
Stadice (village) 236–239
Stephan (Stephen) Langton (Archbishop of Canterbury 1207–1228) 268
Story of Saint John the Baptist (Ghirlandaio) 171
Strasbourg 130–131, 328, 413
Straubing 69
Supremum est mortalibus bonum (Guillaume Du Fay) 462
Suzanne (place) 94
Swabia 73, 321
Székesfehérvár (Stuhlweißenburg) 368, 375, 394

Tanakh 275
Tancarville 40

Těma of Koldice 361–362
Temple of Solomon (biblical location) 452
Tent of Revelation 251–252
Teutonic Order 328, 333, 340
Thiérache 97
Thomas Aquinas 247, 273, 281
Thomas Ebendorfer (chronicler) 406
Thomas of Štítné (c. 1330–1409; writer) 397
Thomas Pinchon (Vicomte of Avranches) 75, 102
Thun-l'Évêque 98
Thüringen 73, 419
Timaios (Plato) 266–267, 269
Tobias (biblical figure) 254, 256
Torah 258
tournament 86–90, 251, 369, 439–440
  Condé-sur-l'Escaut (1327) 89–90
  's-Gravenzande (1328) 89
Tournament of Chauvency (1285) (Jacques Bretel) 439
Tower of Babel 224, 231–232, 296–299
Transylvania 331
Trenčín 95
Trento 100, 350
Trier 2, 93, 95, 103, 401–402, 420, 422, 435, 438
Tristan 449
triumphal arch 139, 419
Troja 197
True Cross 153, 420, 422
Turin 350
Tyrol 3, 211, 380, 441

Uberto Decembrio (ambassador of Giangaleazzo Visconti) 351, 367
Udine 350
Ulm 327, 336
Ulrich von Etzenbach (or Eschenbach, c. 1250–c. 1300; poet) 450
Umbria 352
Upper Palatinate 337–338
Upper Swabia 326, 330, 339
Urach 335–336
Urban V (Guillaume de Grimoard, 1310–1370; Pope 1362–1370) 246, 346, 426

Urban VI (Bartolomeo Prignano, 1318–1389; Pope 1378–1389) 346
Ústí nad Labem 236
Utraquism 345

Václav Koranda (Hussite priest) 404
Valenciennes 89, 91, 95, 432
Varna 396
Velislav Bible 263, 424
Venice 346–347, 349
  San Marco (mosaic) 263
Venus 306
Vera Icon 423
Verdun 30, 59, 77–78, 87, 93, 96, 101
  Saint Mary Magdalen (church) 60, 100
Vermandois 84–85, 92, 97
Verona 217
Vespers 436
Vienna 8, 208–209, 271, 328–329, 331, 391, 461
Vienne 81
Vincennes 41, 47, 54, 60, 83, 97, 99
Vincent of Beauvais (c. 1190–1264; Dominican scholar) 417
virelai 458
Virgin Mary 110, 116–117, 215, 258, 261
Visegrád (Plintenburg) 95, 368
Vita Caroli (*Karoli*) or *De vita sua* (c. 1350) 90, 177, 184, 204, 207–208, 210–215, 219, 223, 229–230, 233
Vita Karoli Magni (Einhard) 209
Vladislas II Jagiellon (1456–1516; King of Bohemia 1471–1516, of Hungary 1490–1516) 168
Vlasta (mythical figure) 226–227, 234–236
Vocabularius (Claretus) 200
Voeux de l'épervier (anonymous) 435, 439
Voeux du paon (anonymous) 435
Vok I of Rožmberk 114
Vratislav of Bohemia (c. 1032–1092; Duke, later King of Bohemia 1061–1092) 225
Vyšehrad *see* Prague
Vyšší Brod
  abbey 113–114

cycle (paintings)   13, 15, 105, 111–121, 125–126, 129
Master   111, 119, 133

Walerand of Juliers (Jülich) (1299–1361; Count, later Duke of Juliers 1328–1361)   89
Walerand of Luxembourg-Ligny (Lord of Ligny 1303–1354)   89
Walter of Schwarzenberg (diplomat)   335, 338
War
   of the (Bohemian) Maidens (mythical event)   226, 233–235
   of the Limburg Succession (1283–1289)   28
Wartburg   32
Welislas of Sedlčany (member of Charles IV's chancery)   75, 77, 93–95
Wenceslas of Luxembourg (1337–1383; Count, later Duke of Luxembourg 1353–1383, Duke of Brabant and Limburg 1355–1383)   3, 32, 73, 83, 85, 87, 92, 132, 381, 430, 432, 444, 456–457, 459, 464
Wenceslas Bible   13, 16, 243, 245–247, 249, 251, 263–264, 266–267, 272, 276, 278–280, 282, 284–287, 289, 303, 306, 309, 317, 319, 460
Wenceslas of Bohemia (c. 907–935; Duke of Bohemia)   8–9, 142, 165, 170, 185, 407, 414, 416, 421–422, 445, 448, 455–446
Wenceslas I of Přemysl (1205–1253; King of Bohemia 1230–1253)   238, 387
Wenceslas II of Přemysl (1271–1305; King of Bohemia 1278–1305, of Poland 1300–1305)   383, 387, 404, 437, 444, 449–445
Wenceslas III of Přemysl (King of Hungary as Ladislas V 1301–1306, of Bohemia 1305–1306, of Poland 1305–1306)   225, 383, 387

Wenceslas IV of Bohemia (1361–1419; King of the Romans 1378–1400, of Bohemia 1378–1419)   1, 13, 15–16, 195–196, 209, 245–247, 249–252, 261–262, 264, 267, 269–271, 275–276, 278–287, 289, 291–292, 294, 297–299, 301–303, 305–307, 309, 311–315, 317–318, 320, 344–346, 348–354, 357, 359–362, 364–372, 392, 398–400, 404–406, 408, 411, 413, 417–418, 427–428, 430, 432, 455–456, 460
Wilhelm von Wenden (c. 1292) (Ulrich von Etzenbach)   450
William *see also* Guillaume
William of Avesnes (c. 1286–1337; Count of Hainaut, Holland, and Zealand 1304–1337)   59–60, 80, 83, 85, 87, 90–91, 94, 102, 433
William of Avesnes (1307–1345; Count of Hainaut 1337–1345)   98
William III of Bavaria (1375–1435; Duke of Bavaria 1392–1435)   399
Windsor   328
Wittelsbach (dynasty)   2–3, 249, 280, 283, 399, 411, 419, 424, 440, 459
Władysław III (1424–1444; King of Poland 1434–1444)   394–396
Wolauff gesell wer jagen (Oswald von Wolkenstein)   458
Wrocław (Breslau)   62–65, 84, 95, 103
   Saint John the Baptist (cathedral)   64
Württemberg   323–325, 332, 335–336, 342
Würzburg   410–411

Yiddish (language)   6, 449
Yolanda of Bar (Violant de Bar, 1365–1431; Queen of Aragon 1380–1395)   38
Yolanda of Flanders (1326–1395; Countess of Bar)   38, 45, 101–102

Zbraslav (Aula Regia, Königsaal; Cistercian monastery) 32–33, 61, 121, 125, 384, 404–405
Zbraslav Chronicle see *Chronicon Aulae regiae*
Zealand (Zeeland) 433, 459–460
Zedekiah (biblical king) 219
Zenon of Ela (philosopher) 266
Zipporah (biblical figure) 315
Zittau 414
Život Krista Pána (anonymous) 198
Znojmo 67

www.ingramcontent.com/pod-product-compliance
Lightning Source LLC
Chambersburg PA
CBHW042117300426
44117CB00021B/2972